The Frontiers of Development Studies

The Frontiers of Development Studies

PAUL STREETEN

First edition 1972
Reprinted 1979

Published by
THE MACMILLAN PRESS LTD
London and Basingstoke
Associated companies in Delhi
Dublin Hong Kong Johannesburg Lagos
Melbourne New York Singapore Tokyo

British Library Cataloguing in Publication Data

Streeten, Paul
    The frontiers of development studies
    1. Economic development
    I. Title
    330.9   HD82

ISBN 978-0-333-27553-5   ISBN 978-1-349-05017-8 (eBook)
                              DOI 10.1007/978-1-349-05017-8

To ANN

Contents

List of Tables and Figures

TABLES

FIGURES

Preface

THE book is a collection of essays on the problems of development in a world in which rich and poor countries coexist and where the presence and the policies of the rich crucially affect the development efforts and prospects of the poor. Most, but not all, essays have been published previously. Those previously published were slightly revised for this collection.

The title of this book may suggest the existence of a boundary within which the light of established knowledge shines and beyond which the darkness of ignorance, prejudice and error reigns. In fact, however, the fight for knowledge is not a series of frontier battles but a guerilla war. The advancement of knowledge does not proceed only by pushing out boundaries and consolidating conquered territory, but also by demolishing pockets of error within the citadels of established beliefs. No stretch of conquered territory can remain safe. Knowledge advances by the removal of erroneous, though established, orthodoxies, and what seemed like knowledge yesterday has to be abandoned today. Within the citadels of orthodoxy there are certain fastnesses whose strength I attempt to probe in this book; not in order to demolish them, but in order to see how sound they are.

The book consists of four parts. The first part contains papers concerned mainly with method. The unifying theme is the limitations of the application of concepts, modes of thought and approaches developed in Western industrial societies, to the less developed societies of Asia, Africa and Latin America. It has been said that the study of history is not a way to help us understand the present, but our knowledge of the present helps us understand history. In studying societies at different stages of development the reverse is true: self-knowledge is not a way to understand societies with different attitudes and institutions, but the study of their structures helps us to understand ourselves. The theme is illustrated by a critique of such concepts as 'capital/output ratio', 'employment', 'underemployment' and 'returns to investment in human capital'.

In the second part there are discussions of the movement of capital, money and goods across national boundaries. Again, as with our ideas and theories, a crucial difference is made by the international scene in which the poor countries find themselves and by the partial nature of some of these movements (e.g. professional man-power but not unskilled). The essays are concerned mainly with private foreign investment and government aid. Their contribution to development is examined and challenges to the institutional imagination are presented.

The third part deals with policy issues such as methods of project appraisal, policies in the face of conflicts between employment and output, how analysis of the problems of the environment can be applied to developing countries and how technology can most effectively be generated and transferred. The final part is concerned with the future of the Commonwealth and in particular our relations with India.

My greatest intellectual debts are to Thomas Balogh and Gunnar Myrdal. I am grateful for editorial help and critical comments to Miss Diane Elson and Mr Michael Sharpston, and for secretarial assistance to Mrs Muriel Payne.

I am indebted to the following for permission to reprint material used previously. Penguin Books (Chapters 1 and 3 appeared in *Development in a Divided World*, edited by Dudley Seers and Leonard Joy); *Banca Nazionale del Lavoro Quarterly Review* (Chapter 4 appeared in no. 69, June 1964); Frank Cass and Co. Ltd (Chapter 5 appeared in *The Teaching of Development Economics*, edited by K. Martin and J. Knapp; Chapter 18 in *The Journal of Development Studies*, vol. 5, July 1969; Chapter 24 in a book edited by myself and Hugh Corbet, entitled *Commonwealth Policy in a Global Context*; material used in Chapters 1 and 2 in *The Journal of Development Studies*, vol. 4, October 1967, and Chapter 16 in *Foreign Resources and Economic Development*, edited by T. Byres); The Twentieth Century Fund, New York (Chapter 6 appeared as part of Appendix 3 in Gunnar Myrdal, *Asian Drama: An Inquiry into the Poverty of Nations*, vol. 3); *Archives Européennes de Sociologie* (Chapter 7 appeared in vol. XI, no. 1, 1970); Ernst Klett Verlag and the Institut für Bildungsforschung in der Max-Planck-Gesellschaft (Chapter 8 appeared in *Bildungsökonomie – eine Zwischenbilanz*, edited by Klaus Hüfner and Jens Naumann); *Revue européenne des sciences sociales* and the United Nations Division of Human Rights (Chapter 9 appeared in *Revue européenne des sciences sociales*, vol. X, no. 26, and was initially commissioned by the United Nations, whose views must not necessarily be identified with mine); the Università degli Studi, Bari (Chapter 10 appeared as a contribution to a volume of essays in honour of Antonio de Viti de Marco); the Royal Institute of International Affairs (Chapter 13 appeared in *International Affairs*, vol. 46, no. 1, January 1970, and Chapter 25 in *The Crisis of Indian Planning*, edited by myself and Michael Lipton and published by the

Oxford University Press); the *International Currency Review* (Chapter 14 appeared in vol. 2, no. 6, January–February 1971); the *Revue de la Société d'Études et d'Expansion à Liège, Venture* and *Ceres* (material used in Chapter 11 appeared in the *Revue de la Société d'Études et d'Expansion à Liège*, no. 238, November–December 1969, *Venture*, vol. 22, no. 1, January 1970, and *Ceres*, vol. 2, no. 2, March–April 1969, and Chapter 27 appeared in vol. 5, no. 2, March–April 1972); *The New Society* (Chapter 23 appeared on 3 July 1969 and Chapter 17 on 1 February 1968); the Oxford University Press (Chapter 19 appeared in *Oxford Economic Papers*, July 1969); Blackwell's (Chapter 20 appeared in the *Bulletin of the Oxford University Institute of Economics and Statistics*, February 1972, and Chapter 21 in a book edited by J. L. Ford and Charles Carter entitled *Uncertainty and Expectations in Economics*, Essays in Honour of G. L. S. Shackle); George Allen and Unwin Ltd (Chapter 12 appeared in a volume edited by John Dunning, entitled *The Multinational Enterprise*); *The Scottish Journal of Political Economy* (Chapter 22 appeared in November 1973 issue); and Gerald Duckworth & Co. Ltd (Chapter 15 appeared in *The Labour Government's Economic Record 1964–1970*, edited by Wilfred Beckerman).

P. P. S.

Part One

Development Theory and Policy

1 Development in an International Setting

I. TRADE AND DEVELOPMENT

POVERTY and stagnation in some areas coexist today with abundance and rapid progress in others. This coexistence has many implications, some of which are explored in this chapter. Amongst them are the opportunities afforded by international trade. Economic theory has looked upon international trade as the instrument for a more efficient allocation of resources through international specialisation. The theory of comparative advantage as formulated first by David Ricardo in the early nineteenth century represents an important and distinct intellectual achievement and to point to some of its limitations does not detract from its enormous value. It assumes that all productive resources are fully employed and that they can be devoted either to domestic use directly or to producing exports, which can be exchanged for imports. Trade is beneficial when resources devoted to producing goods for export yield more in imports obtained in exchange than they would by direct production of the imported goods. This implies the re-allocation of national resources in response to changing international exchange opportunities and to new technological possibilities. The analytical and political conclusions of this theory are by no means obvious and are still often ignored.

But in many poor countries certain productive resources – particularly land and labour – can be shifted only at *very* high costs or only after a *very* long time, into alternative lines, either for export or for domestic use. The function of international trade in such a situation is not to promote a more efficient allocation through the international division of labour than would have been possible under autarky: it is rather to provide the demand for the output of the resources which would otherwise lie idle. In such a situation more exports do not reduce domestic production.

The existence of idle resources implies either or both of two conditions: lack of responsiveness of domestic demand for the exportable product, so that even quite large price reductions of, say, coffee or sugar or rubber would not increase domestic purchases; and specificity of resources producing it, so that the land and the labour could not be shifted to alternatives which would be demanded at home. Such conditions prevail in the indigenous smallholder sector for the production of many primary products, such as rubber, tea, cocoa, coffee, sugar, bananas, and coconuts.

The existence of actual or potential surplus capacity in land and labour for the production of certain primary products can work either to the advantage or to the disadvantage of the trading country. If a country is fortunate and there is a large and expanding foreign demand for its exports, the exporting sector might stimulate further economic development. In conjunction with appropriate human attitudes, social institutions and public policies, it can provide, at low or zero costs in terms of forgone domestic opportunities, a source of rising domestic incomes, foreign exchange, savings, fiscal revenue and perhaps the basis for industrialisation such as raw-material-based processing. It can thereby contribute to the creation of those flexibilities and mobilities whose absence caused the initial imbalance. Such was the case in the nineteenth century with dairy exports in Denmark, timber exports in Sweden,[1] and coffee exports in Brazil. Today some oil producing (Iraq, Venezuela) and mining countries (Chile) enjoy similar forms of export-led development, though clearly only some resources employed in the production of these primary commodities would otherwise have been unemployed.

But this type of development depends on the existence of market outlets and a state of international demand such that extra exports will increase the exporter's foreign exchange earnings. An increase in the total volume of the exports of a primary commodity may, however, lower its price to such an extent that it leads to a fall in the total value of exports. Thus, although in such a situation a newly exporting country may add to its foreign exchange earnings, it does so only at the expense of established exporters.

This is typically the situation in the world primary commodity markets. It places severe limits on poor countries' abilities to increase the value of their exports – and to give profitable employment to otherwise unprofitably occupied resources – by increasing the volume of their exported production. There may be gain, however, from entering new lines of export: including also, perhaps, spreading the risks of the price of any particular commodity collapsing.

Yet the exploration of market opportunities may not proceed readily. In a rich, more developed economy, there exists an equilibrating mechanism of flexible prices to which producers and consumers

---

[1] For an illuminating account see A. J. Youngson, *Possibilities of Economic Progress* (Cambridge University Press, 1959).

respond. If there is a surplus of a commodity, its price falls. This encourages, in the short run, demand, and discourages, in the longer run, supply. Capital, management and labour will move out of the production of this commodity and will seek higher rewards elsewhere. There will also be a wide spectrum of substitutable techniques and goods to choose from, combining factors in different proportions according to price signals and profit incentives. This market mechanism is often weak in poor countries and it may be especially insensitive to international opportunities. The complex system of signals, incentives, mobility and substitution is not, as simple theoretical models sometimes assume, the *cause* of international trade: it is rather its *result*. Only in a developed, complex economy does it become a cause. Lack of flexibility, itself a symptom of poverty, in the face of receding, or slowly growing, international demand and advancing foreign technology, explains the paradoxical coexistence of surplus productive capacity with low incomes in poor countries, which perpetuates poverty.

II. STAGES OF GROWTH

Deeply embedded in current thought on development is the view that each country passes, at different times, through a series of comparable stages of development; that there are basic similarities in this process; and that we can therefore learn from the pre-industrial phase of now industrialised societies lessons which are applicable to underdeveloped societies today.

I wish to question this belief on the ground that at any rate some of the conditions crucial to development at any particular stage depend on the stages which other societies have reached at the same time. Since the co-existence of a number of different societies, each at a different stage of development, crucially determines the development prospects of the least-developed ones, an essentially historical feature must form part of any valid analysis and prognosis. The fact that advanced industrial societies already exist when countries embark on development, makes a number of important differences to the development prospects of underdeveloped societies.

Some of these differences, and perhaps the most obvious ones, clearly benefit underdeveloped countries. A growing stock of scientific, technical and organisational knowledge has been accumulated, on which the underdeveloped countries can draw. They do not have to go through the laborious process of acquiring this knowledge for themselves and can therefore avoid a number of errors and false starts. The higher level of income in advanced industrial countries and its steady and continuing growth create a demand for the products of the underdeveloped countries and enable them to benefit from wider international specialisation than was possible for the pioneers. Private investment, financial aid and technical assistance contribute to the transfer of resources and skills from the rich countries to the poor and thus enable these to draw on a bigger pool of resources. These benefits were not available, or available only to a smaller extent, when the now industrialised countries embarked on their development.

Some authors derive much hope from the economic forces that tend to diffuse technical progress from the advanced countries to the poor. If only the level of demand and employment is kept high and growing, so that the rich economies are forced to search outside their own boundaries for low-cost sources of raw materials and minerals and for manufactured products requiring much labour, if restrictions on the movement of goods, capital and men are removed and if technical assistance and aid are provided on an adequate scale, the progress achieved in the centre, according to this view, will automatically spread to the periphery and the benefits will be widely distributed.[1]

On the other hand, the coexistence of rich and poor countries and the policies pursued by rich countries have a number of drawbacks for the underdeveloped countries. Some of these result from the relationships between countries at different stages of development, others from the fact that rich countries exist.

1. The most important difference is that the advanced state of medical knowledge makes it now possible to reduce deaths cheaply and rapidly, without having, at least until recently, contributed to an equally cheap and readily acceptable reduction in births. This has upset the population equilibrium and has caused the large and accelerating rates of population growth, which present the underdeveloped countries with much more difficult obstacles than those the now advanced countries faced in their pre-industrial phase, when the rate of population growth was considerably less and was partly the *result* of successful development and rising levels of living.

2. Although a stock of scientific and technical knowledge is available on which underdeveloped countries can draw, the modern technology is ill-adapted to the conditions and the factor endowments

---

[1] The existence of a powerful economic mechanism of diffusion, frustrated by wrong-headed policies, has been strongly argued in H. G. Johnson, *Economic Policies Toward Less Developed Countries* (Allen & Unwin, 1967), especially pp. 48–52. See also D. Keesing, 'Outward-looking Policies and Economic Development', *Economic Journal*, LXXVII 306 (June 1967) 303–20. But some of the differences between Professor Johnson's arguments and those put forward below depend upon what one considers established and what removable features of the current scene and also on what one wishes to call economic and political forces.

of the underdeveloped countries. Modern technology was evolved in conditions of labour scarcity and its purpose is therefore to save labour in relation to capital. The transfer of these sometimes inappropriate methods, which is encouraged by attitudes towards modernisation and by the prestige of Western technology, tends to aggravate the gross under-utilisation of labour from which the underdeveloped countries are suffering. When inappropriate technology is transferred and when the labour force grows rapidly, obstacles are created which are fundamentally different from those which the now industrial societies had to overcome in their preindustrial phase.

3. Not only most available techniques of production, but also existing models of organisations and institutions are ill-adapted to the needs of the underdeveloped world. Modern trade union structure and attitudes, like technology, have evolved in different social conditions and can therefore be damaging if transferred to conditions in which labour is not fully utilised. The demand for the adoption of social welfare services, which have no or negative impact on development and which were introduced in advanced industrial welfare states at a late stage, has often proved an impediment to development and, far from contributing to greater social justice, has strengthened vested interests and pockets of privilege. Large public expenditure on curative medicine, higher education and on indiscriminate subsidies to consumption has absorbed scarce resources and reinforced attitudes and practices hostile to development. Even political institutions, such as parliamentary democracy, are not always adapted to the needs of developing countries and, under the guise of constitutional legitimacy, reinforce the reluctance to touch vested interests and to use compulsion for development.

4. For a number of reasons capital and skilled men, including those of the underdeveloped countries, are attracted to the richest industrial societies. Capital flight is substantial, attracted by higher rates of return and greater political security. Skilled men and professionals, on whose education and training large public funds have been spent, have greater opportunities for emigration, are better and more rapidly informed about them and have stronger incentives to seize them. As a result some of the scarcest, most valuable and most expensive factors of production are drained away from the poor periphery to the rich centre.

5. But the mobility of factors is partial and biased. Whereas in the pre-industrial phase of now-industrialised societies (with the exception of Japan) areas rich in natural resources were still unsettled and were able to receive immigrants, the world has now been parcelled up and immigration of unskilled men and women, particularly if they

are coloured, is severely restricted. This, together with population growth, growing under-utilisation of labour and the loss of the scarcest and most expensive resources, greatly increases the obstacles to development.

6. As Dudley Seers has shown,[1] high levels of remuneration for professional skills in advanced countries raise obstacles to development in underdeveloped countries which go beyond the losses through emigration. By the creation of an international market in these skills, not only are internal inequalities without functional justification increased in underdeveloped countries, but obstacles are put into the path of development. International inequality has an impact on internal income distribution in underdeveloped countries which, like the impact of modern technology and modern institutions, impedes development.

7. Systematic scientific research and institutionally built-in innovation, which are reflected in the annual growth of productivity which is characteristic of rich economies, have not only been heavily biased towards products which are not suited for production in underdeveloped countries but they have, in some cases, also led to a reduction in the demand for the traditional primary exports of underdeveloped countries. Technical progress has reduced the need for the imports of the staple products of developing countries

    (*a*) because synthetics have been substituted for natural products,
    (*b*) because there has been increasing economy in the use of raw materials, and
    (*c*) because demand has shifted towards services and products with low primary import content.

For such reasons, as well as because of protectionist policies, and in particular cascading tariffs, rising with the stage of processing, the trade opportunities for primary products of underdeveloped countries have been reduced and their ability to diversify and industrialise has been hampered, though their incentive to do so has been increased. These obstacles go beyond the often bewailed, but not fully confirmed, trend in the terms of trade. They are themselves the expression of a desire to insulate a rich and comfortable society from the disturbance of change, even at the cost of some reduction in the benefits derived from international specialisation. (See also below point 9.) In any cost/benefit calculus of the impact of research in industrial societies, the disturbances caused to poor growers of primary products are not

---

[1] *The Transmission of Inequality*, unpublished paper read at the Haile Selassie I Prize Trust Conference in Addis Ababa, October 1966. See also D. Seers, 'Graduate Migration as an Obstacle to Equality', in *Unfashionable Economics*, Essays in Honour of Lord Balogh, ed. Paul Streeten (Weidenfeld & Nicolson, 1970).

counted. Recent technical progress in methods of birth control, of producing staple food crops and cheap protein, of transport, desalination and even, on a small scale, of more appropriate industrial technology, has begun to compensate for the earlier bias in research, but it is as yet early to say how effective these compensations will prove.

8. While it is true that foreign private enterprise can help to transfer material resources and human skills from rich to poor countries, it also creates greater difficulties than did borrowing from abroad by industralised societies in their pre-industrial phase. Then money was borrowed at fixed interest rates of between 5 and 6 per cent and default was not uncommon. Now almost all long-term private capital takes the form of equity at 15–25 per cent pre-local tax and 10–15 per cent post-local tax, which is higher even allowing for inflation; moreover, default on loans, whether private or official, is hardly ever allowed to occur. Remitting profits, interest and dividends creates or aggravates the balance of payments problems of underdeveloped countries, partly because of their height compared with the lower interest rates in the nineteenth century, and partly because of inadequate reinvestment.

9. Advance has meant national progress and national consolidation in the industrial countries. The benefits of the welfare state are largely confined to its citizens. National consolidation in rich countries has encouraged nationalism in underdeveloped countries and the attempts of the former to integrate the nation by protectionist and welfare policies have tended to lead to international disintegration.[1] Attempts to maintain full employment, and to insulate the national economy from outside influences have strengthened the forces of protection in the welfare states and reduced the opportunities for trade and migration. Export of capital and scarce skills, and immigration that threatens to upset industrial peace, are restricted by the advanced countries.

In the early enthusiasm with full employment and welfare policies after the last war, it was thought that the achievement and maintenance of full employment would reduce the need for protectionist policies and would restore the era of free international trade and international solidarity. In the event, full employment has created its own strong motivation for restrictions on trade, payments and immigration. First, full employment tended to cause inflationary pressures and balance of payments difficulties to those who inflated faster than others; these led to restrictions. Second, full employment tended to be interpreted as applying to all regions and occupations, and structural unemployment, which some low-cost imports would

[1] G. Myrdal, *An International Economy* (Routledge & Kegan Paul, 1956).

have entailed, was disliked. Third, full employment was accompanied by the desire to make the fullest use of resources and brought the terms-of-trade argument for tariff restrictions to the fore; in particular, it became important to keep the prices of imported food and raw materials as low as possible. Fourth, the desire to maintain and raise wages constituted a powerful argument against immigration of workers who would weaken the bargaining power of trade unions. Fifth, the need to mobilise savings for domestic objectives set limits to the outflow of aid and private capital. For these and similar reasons, the national welfare state has turned out to be a not very good neighbour to other countries which depended on trade, migration and capital.

10. We have suggested that technical and organisational knowledge are ill-adapted and that their transfer can be harmful to the underdeveloped countries. In addition, Western economic concepts and theories, and policies based on these, are often inappropriate and misleading when applied to current development problems. Economic analysis and policy have tended to focus on investment (whether in fixed capital assets or in 'human capital' called 'education') to the neglect of essential reforms of human attitudes and social institutions; and they have tended to formulate categories of aggregates which obscure the relevant distinctions and neglect the actual behaviour on which the concepts, models and policies are based.[1]

11. Some people have argued that government aid has obstructed progress towards development by supporting and upholding feudal or conservative regimes which are unwilling to carry out the social and political reforms necessary for progress. Aid policies directed at investments and neglecting social reforms are encouraged, intellectually, by the escape mechanism provided by Western economic theorising and, politically, by powerful vested interests on both the donors' and the recipients' side.

12. While for these reasons the opportunities to develop have been reduced, the sense of urgency among the ruling élites and the still small middle classes overseas has greatly increased. Seeing opulence and rapid growth abroad means feeling the pain of their absence all the more acutely. It is true not only that what you *don't know doesn't hurt you*, which must have made things easier for the now industrialised societies in their pre-industrial stage, but also that what you *do know does hurt*. This clearly reduces the patience with which the development process is viewed by the ruling élites in the underdeveloped world.

[1] P. Streeten, 'The Use and Abuse of Models in Development Planning', in K. Martin and J. Knapp (eds.), *The Teaching of Development Economics* (Frank Cass, 1967) pp. 57–83, and Chapter 5 in this volume.

It is this coexistence of rich and poor, rather than the intentional or unintentional colonial or neo-colonial exploitation, or even neglect, which can have detrimental effects on development efforts. And it is this coexistence which sets limits to the ready transfer of the lessons of one historical setting to an entirely different one. No analysis can be valid which does not allow for this change in the world setting in which development occurs.[1]

These considerations also bear on the frequently deplored widening gap between the living standards of the rich and poor countries. On the face of it, it might seem that much more important than the gap is the rate at which the lot of the mass of the people in the poor countries is improving. Should we not all prefer a growth rate of 6 per cent per year in the poor countries combined with one of 8 per cent in the rich to one of 3 per cent in the poor combined with 2 per cent in the rich, even although the former combination would widen, while the latter would narrow this gap? Maybe so. But the rate of progress in the rich countries affects the development prospects and strategies of the poor and it is not obvious that, on balance, faster growth of the rich world is always beneficial to the poor. Many of the difficulties raised for developing countries under the above headings 1–12 grow when international differentials increase, and it may therefore be sensible, and not just the result of a dog-in-the-manger attitude, to aim at reducing growing international income differentials, even if this means some slowing down of income growth.

Finally, it follows that development strategies must differ not only, as is now generally recognised, in space, from country to country and region to region, but also in time, from stage to stage. Each stage must be related to the stages reached by other countries. The need to take full account not only of the position in space, but also of the relative position in time, in forging a development strategy greatly complicates the process of planning and reduces the value of lessons from the past and of universal prescriptions. A country, particularly if it is small, must pay attention not only to its own peculiar history, resource endowment and institutions, but also to the events and activities in the countries ahead of it (as well as in

[1] Special problems are created also by the coexistence of poor and poor. The treatment of the Third World as if it were a homogeneous group and the interests of each member in harmony with those of the others is misleading. Competition in exports of a narrow range of primary and manufactured goods, competition for a limited amount of capital and skilled services, competitive nationalism and the refusal to sacrifice sovereignty for gains in production, beggar-my-neighbour tax concessions, tariffs and other import restrictions have led to the mutual impoverishment of a group of countries which should set an example in mutual help.

those behind it) and must weigh the benefits and drawbacks of outward-looking strategies against those of shielding its frontiers and turning inwards.[1]

[1] See D. Seers, 'The Other Road', *International Development Review*, IX 4 (Dec 1967) 2-4.

2 Single Barrier Theories of Development

THERE is no scarcity of economic theories which attempt to explain the absence of development or its difficulties. Many of them share certain presuppositions. The reasoning commonly takes the following form. It is assumed that all men prefer higher incomes and therefore higher production to lower incomes. Since the knowledge of advanced methods of production is available and need only be transferred from the industrialised countries of the West, there is a presumption that these methods would be adopted everywhere. Since in fact we observe many countries which have not adopted these methods and therefore do not enjoy high incomes, there must be obstacles to development. Many of these theories then single out one obstacle.

Marxian versions see in colonialism and imperialistic exploitation the chief barrier. It is the vested interests of powerful monopolies which prevent the transfer of modern technology and the rise in incomes. But it is not difficult to point to countries and periods where development did not occur, although they were not dominated by colonial powers.

Non-Marxian theories have stressed a number of economic barriers. According to one group of writers, lack of savings keeps down investment, which in turn confines production to primitive techniques, which result in low productivity, low incomes and inability to save. The vicious circle of poverty can be broken only by somehow raising the savings ratio to the point of 'take-off'. Yet, in many of these societies distribution is very unequal and there should be no difficulty, if we ignore political factors, in extracting savings from the richest groups. There is also evidence that even the poorest set aside a part of their income for non-essential purposes, spending it on gold, jewellery, festivities, etc. Very poor countries are known to have been able to save quite considerable proportions for defence or war, for building cathedrals, temples, pagodas or pyramids. All this suggests that in few societies are levels of income so low that all income must be devoted to current expenditure on essentials.

A refinement of this argument says that it was easier for the

Egyptians to build pyramids and for medieval princes and kings to build cathedrals because they did not have to keep up with any rich Joneses whose consumption levels made their mouths water and weakened the sinews of saving. It is the so-called international Demonstration Effect – the evidence of high living in rich countries – which presents a barrier to higher savings in poor countries. In particular, the élites in the less developed countries, it is argued, take their bearings from the high consumption societies of the West, emulating them on the beaches in the South of France or in Miami, on yachts, or in cadillacs in Paris or Rome. But this theory leaves unexplained why the élites seek to imitate luxury living but not habits of scientific research, experiment, hard work, rational management and entrepreneurial initiative. Savings, as well as consumption, are higher in advanced countries and the demonstration effect could apply to either.

Another theory sees the main obstacle to development in the lack of incentives to invest in productive plant and equipment. According to this theory, savings are, or would be, available, but they are wasted on non-productive investment, such as the acquisition of land, the maintenance of a large number of useless retainers, on palaces and luxury housing, or they are tucked away safely abroad. The incentive to invest, according to this theory, is weak because productive equipment must be put up with a minimum capacity to be efficient, but markets are too small to justify this minimum capacity. Once again, there is a vicious circle: low incomes cause small markets and small markets prevent the installation of capacity which would raise productivity and incomes and which would widen the market.

But first, it is possible to find many countries in which domestic markets could quite easily be created by cutting off imports. Second, there are numerous manufacturing activities which can be carried out economically in quite small-scale enterprises. Third, many of these countries pride themselves on having development plans. They could co-ordinate the investment decisions and ensure that markets are provided for large-scale investment projects, by their being undertaken jointly.

Another theory attributes the blockage to the difficulty of constructing overhead capital. Roads, railways, harbours, power stations, require large lumps of capital. Poor countries cannot afford these. But without them, development cannot proceed. Although such projects can be very useful in promoting development, they can often be constructed with labour-intensive methods and, initially, on a relatively small scale and piecemeal. Where large-scale projects have been carried out with foreign aid, they have often turned out to be badly managed and underutilised.

A more recent group of writers, impressed by the inadequacy of explanations that concentrate on physical capital as the main condition for accelerating development, has stressed 'inadequate investment in human resources', or, more simply, lack of education and skills. Yet, it is evident that many underdeveloped countries spend too much on the wrong kind of education and, failing to take other necessary measures, have produced a class of educated unemployed who provide a fertile ground for reactionary rather than economic activity.

Others again have attributed considerable responsibility to deteriorating terms of trade and trading opportunities generally. Yet, countries which enjoy large oil revenues or have a plentiful supply of foreign exchange for other reasons have not been more successful in accelerating development.

The argument so far has been that, although many of these theories point to important obstacles, and although some may be true for certain regions at certain times, they certainly do not show that the removal of these barriers is a sufficient condition for development. In addition, it is possible to point to successful development which occurred in spite of the presence of many of these barriers. Development has taken place even though trading opportunities were unfavourable, even though no foreign loans were available, where the population had not been educated, etc. Even although rising savings and investment ratios have normally accompanied development, it is as plausible to argue that they were the *result* of development as it is to say that they were its *cause*.

Such considerations suggest scepticism towards any single-barrier explanation. Obstacles are numerous and interrelated, though clearly some are more important at certain times and in certain places than others.

It is helpful to look at the situation in underdeveloped countries as a social system. In this system a large number of 'conditions' are causally interrelated, in the sense that a change in any one condition will cause changes in some or all the others. It is possible to group these conditions into the following six broad categories:[1]

1. Output and Incomes.
2. Conditions of production.
3. Levels of living (including nutrition and housing and facilities for health, education and training).
4. Attitudes to work and life.
5. Institutions.
6. Policies.

[1] See Gunnar Myrdal, *Asian Drama*, and Chapter 6 of this book.

The first three categories comprise what are usually called 'economic' conditions, while categories 4 and 5 would normally be called 'non-economic', psychological, social, and cultural conditions. Category 6 is a mixture and is regarded as 'economic' if policies aim at changing categories 1, 2 and 3, but not if they aim at changes in human attitudes and social institutions. Sometimes only categories 1 and 2 are considered proper topics of 'economic' analysis.

This particular ordering is arbitrary. Since conditions are interdependent, there can be no 'primary' and 'secondary' conditions, no categories that are more fundamental than others. For certain purposes entirely different categories may be appropriate.

When we speak of an 'underdeveloped society', we imply that the conditions 1 to 6 are undesirable, judged from the point of view of the ideal of development.

This is not the place to discuss the manner of interaction of these conditions. A change in any one condition can change others either in the same or in the opposite direction and a very great variety of different outcomes are possible. Some of these give rise to a stable equilibrium, others to an unstable equilibrium (a cumulative process upwards or downwards). The types of questions which one would wish to discuss include the following:–

I. Is this particular classification the most convenient? Does it cover the ground or does it omit any important category? In particular, is it convenient to include facilities for health, education, and training in 'levels of living'?

II. Is it possible to use quantitative indexes for these categories and will it be possible to assign coefficients of interdependence to the relationships?

III. Can these relationships be studied independently of the direction of change, the previous history of the system and the simultaneous conditions in other social systems which have reached higher stages of development?

IV. Is the distinction between 'economic' and 'non-economic' conditions tenable? If not, does this distinction contain a systematic bias which is liable to be reflected in biased policy recommendations?

One important advantage of presenting the conditions of development in this way is to reduce the emphasis laid a decade ago on the accumulation of physical capital. But, from another point of view, it is possible to widen the concept 'capital' so as to include anything that yields a stream of production and income over time.[1] A general-

---

[1] See pp. 119–21.

ised approach to capital accumulation may help to correct both biases. It may help to approach different investment complexes (the components of which are complementary) as substitutes in a strategy for development. The returns of such complexes or packages could, in principle, be compared. But it would amount to the evaluation of different large strategic decisions, not of marginal or infinitesimal moves.

The role of agriculture

The system may be illustrated by asking what are the prerequisites for the breakthrough in agriculture discussed on pp. 33–5.[1]

1. Agricultural output and incomes both determine and depend upon:
2. Conditions of production:
   assuming an adequate infrastructure of roads, irrigation, etc., it is necessary to increase inputs such as chemical fertilisers, insecticides and farm tools; and to improve the skills of farmers by training.
3. Levels of living:
   it is necessary for the farmer to have a minimum level and the right kind of education, health and nutrition.
4. Attitudes to work and life:
   it is necessary to increase availability of incentive goods, i.e. things which the farmer and his family would work harder to get; the resistance to work in the country on the part of urban youth and technicians must be broken down.
5. Institutions:
   there must be a system of land tenure which permits the farmer to reap the benefits of his efforts; credit must be available at low rates of interest to make him change the composition of his crops and raise productivity; the marketing organisation should prevent middle-men from creaming off so much as to leave the farmer inadequate incentive to switch from export crops to domestic food production; diversification often depends on more efficient marketing.
6. Policies:
   the farmer must be assured of a steady and remunerative price; technical assistance relevant to his soil, weather conditions and change in technology must be made available *on the spot*.

It can be seen that these conditions interact. Better education, of the right kind, makes farmers more receptive to technical assistance and ready to use irrigation, better seeds, fertilisers and tools. The

[1] See Chapter 3.

result of their improved efforts must be marketable at a stable and remunerative price, which reinforces confidence in further improvements and strengthens inducements to undergo the right kind of training.

It has become part of the current orthodoxy to say that agricultural reform must be given the highest priority. It is, however, not always made clear why precisely this breakthrough in agriculture is considered to be crucial, nor how advance on this front is related to advances on other fronts. In addition, much talk of agricultural reform seems to be a rationalisation of an urban, industrial bias, which insists that surpluses of workers, food and savings be squeezed out of the rural sector to advance the industrial sector.

A widespread view, therefore, is that agricultural progress is necessary in order to supply, firstly, *a surplus of labour* for industry, secondly, *a marketable surplus* of food for industrial workers and, thirdly, an *investible surplus* of savings for urban industry.

The doctrine of the need for a *labour surplus* is no longer tenable. The problem in the foreseeable future is not labour shortage but shortage of jobs. The need to provide employment opportunities in agriculture and in rural industry calls for technological research, because the available technology is adapted to a shrinking, not an expanding, rural labour force. It also calls for land reform, extension services, irrigation and drainage, improved seeds, fertilisers and pesticides, improved storage, transport, credit and marketing facilities and more reliable prices for the produce sold. It would be quite illusory to believe that urban industry can wholly absorb the growing labour force. If we assume that the rate of population growth is the same in agriculture as in industry, say 3 per cent, that the labour force grows at the same rate as population and that 80 per cent of the labour force are in the rural sector and 20 per cent in urban industry, urban industry's demand for labour would have to grow at 15 per cent in order to absorb the whole growth of the labour force. The high growth of the labour force will continue for the next thirty years, however effective birth control were to become now. The need for the creation of employment opportunities in the rural sector is aggravated by the facts: (*a*) that population grows more rapidly in the rural sector than in the urban sector, (*b*) that there is already substantial rural underutilisation of labour, and (*c*) that the technology used in the urban sector saves labour in relation to capital. It follows that the emphasis on agricultural and rural employment opportunities, far from presenting a case against industrialisation, shows the importance of agricultural advance as a necessary condition for industrialisation. Rural underutilisation of labour damages in a number of ways the prospect of successful industrialisation.

The doctrine of the need for a *marketable surplus*, to feed and supply with raw materials the rapidly, and indeed increasingly rapidly, growing proportion of the labour force in industry, unlike the doctrine of the labour surplus, has not been seriously questioned.

There can be no doubt that it is essential to improve the diet and to raise levels of living, both because these are objectives worth pursuing for their own sake and because this would improve the quality of the labour force by reducing apathy and increasing health, strength and vigour. In particular, there is a crying need to improve the diet and level of living of the *rural* population in under-developed countries who, while ministering to the basic needs of life, suffer from the most depressed levels of consumption. It is they – the landless labourers, the small tenant farmers, the share-croppers and the peasants with tiny plots of land – who form the proletariat of the world today. Compared with them, the employed industrial workers in the underdeveloped countries are an aristocracy. Rural reform would therefore, in addition to breaking the main development bottleneck, contribute to a reduction of the most glaring social inequality.

But the application of the doctrine of the marketable surplus may make the fate of the small subsistence farmer, the share-cropper and the landless labourer worse rather than better. The stimulation of urban market opportunities, though clearly desirable, if pursued ruthlessly, benefits the big farmer rather than the small man, may increase rural inequalities and may worsen rural malnutrition. Many of the recent agricultural success stories do not survive the test of rural welfare, reduced inequality and advance on a wide front.

Finally, the doctrine of the need to squeeze an *investible surplus* out of agriculture, in order to finance urban industrial investment, ignores the potentially higher returns to some forms of investment in agriculture. Typically, 20 per cent of investment is allocated to the rural sector, comprising 70 per cent of the population. While it is now generally accepted that higher investment is not a sufficient condition for agricultural growth and while some glaringly bad agricultural investment projects stare one in the eye, it is equally clear that the absorptive capacity for capital in agriculture can be substantially raised. The division into agriculture and industry is probably too aggregative and crude to provide sound investment criteria. One agro-industrial investment complex may show high returns, while other projects, both in agriculture and industry, may yield low returns. Calculations of sectoral capital–output ratios are no substitute for careful project selection. But none of this can be used as an argument to squeeze savings out of agriculture into urban industry. The need to secure agricultural savings is clear. But the place to reinvest these may well be within the agricultural sector. Big farmers must be taxed, not in order to finance industry, but in order to secure a wider spread of agricultural progress.

The endowment per worker of capital, calories and protein is lower in the villages than in the towns. Increases in any of these will yield more extra output. Equality, growth and development in this area do not conflict; they reinforce one another. Not only justice, but also economic progress require that savings and food surpluses should be kept in the rural areas.

Agricultural reform can be used in some cases to reduce balance-of-payments strains. This can be done by raising the supply of exports, either directly by producing domestic food and raw materials for those engaged in exporting manufactured goods, or by substituting domestic food and raw materials for imports.

The ability of the rural sector to supply food and raw materials to industry, through the maximisation of this surplus, implies that the rural sector provides a market for industrial products. The higher the productivity of the rural sector, the higher will be its demand for industrial products. If industry adopts methods of mass production and exploits economies of scale, a prosperous rural sector, by providing an ever-widening market, is a condition for progress in industry. But the need for greater emphasis on agriculture and rural development has been used to reinforce policies which discriminate against the rural poor and the rural tillers of the land.

3 How Poor are the Poor Countries and Why?

COUNTRIES are neither poor nor rich. It is *individuals* that are well-fed or hungry, sick or healthy, literate or illiterate, happy or miserable. This is so obvious as to be hardly worth saying, were it not for the fact that we often speak, write and act as if we had forgotten it. The ultimate purpose of production, trade, migration, foreign investment and aid is to improve the lot of individuals. When we speak of poor countries we are using shorthand, and we must not be misled by our metaphor.

By a poor country we therefore mean one in which the people are poor. The simplest and commonly used way of expressing this is to divide the total national income by the number of people in the country and to arrive at a figure showing income per head of the population. Most underdeveloped countries turn out, by this criterion, to be low income-per-head countries, though there are some exceptions, like Kuwait with GNP per head of $3,540 in 1968, the highest after the USA.

TABLE 3.1

Population (mid-1968) and Average Annual Growth Rate (1961–68)

Countries with populations of 1 million or more

Country	Population (thousands)	Growth Rate (percent)	Country	Population (thousands)	Growth Rate (percent)
China (Mainland)	730,000	1·5	United Kingdom	55,283	0·7
			Italy	52,750	0·8
India	523,893	2·5	France	49,920	1·1
USSR	237,798	1·3	Mexico	47,627	3·5
United States	201,152	1·4	Philippines	35,883	3·4
Pakistan	123,163	2·6	Thailand	33,693	3·1
Indonesia	112,825	2·4	Turkey	33,550	2·5
Japan	101,090	1·0	Spain	32,621	0·9
Brazil	88,209	3·0	Poland	32,305	1·1
Nigeria	62,650	2·4	United Arab Republic	31,693	2·5
Germany, Fed. Rep. of	60,165	1·0			

TABLE 3.1 (*continued*)

Country	Population (*thousands*)	Growth Rate (*percent*)	Country	Population (*thousands*)	Growth Rate (*percent*)
Korea, Republic of	30,470	2·7	Upper Volta	5,175	2·2
Iran	27,150	3·0	Southern Rhodesia	4,940	3·2
Burma	26,353	2·1	Denmark	4,870	0·8
Ethiopia	24,212	2·0	Guatemala	4,864	3·1
Argentina	23,617	1·6	Mali	4,787	2·1
Canada	20,772	1·9	Finland	4,689	0·7
Vietnam (*North*)	20,700	3·2	Bolivia	4,680	2·6
Yugoslavia	20,154	1·1	Haiti	4,671	2·0
Colombia	20,043	3·2	Tunisia	4,660	2·3
South Africa	19,781	2·3	Malawi	4,270	2·6
Romania	19,721	0·9	Ivory Coast	4,100	2·8
Vietnam, Rep. of	17,414	2·7	Zambia	4,065	3·0
Germany (*Eastn.*)	17,084	− 0·1	Dominican Rep.	4,029	3·6
Congo, Dem. Rep. of	16,730	2·1	Hong Kong	3,927	3·1
Afghanistan	16,113	2·0	Norway	3,819	0·8
Sudan	14,770	2·9	Niger	3,806	3·6
Morocco	14,580	2·9	Guinea	3,795	2·7
Czechoslovakia	14,362	0·6	Senegal	3,685	2·1
China, Rep. of	13,466	3·0	Chad	3,460	1·5
Korea (*North*)	13,000	2·6	Burundi	3,406	2·0
Algeria	12,943	2·3	Rwanda	3,405	3·1
Peru	12,772	3·1	El Salvador	3,267	3·6
Netherlands	12,725	1·3	Ireland	2,910	0·3
Tanzania	12,508	2·5	New Zealand	2,828	2·2
Australia	12,031	2·0	Laos	2,825	2·4
Ceylon	11,970	2·4	Uruguay	2,818	1·3
Nepal	10,652	1·8	Somalia	2,747	4·0
Malaysia	10,386	3·1	Israel	2,745	3·3
Hungary	10,255	0·3	Puerto Rico	2,723	1·8
Kenya	10,209	2·9	Lebanon	2,580	2·6
Venezuela	9,686	3·5	Dahomey	2,571	2·9
Belgium	9,619	0·6	Sierra Leone	2,475	1·3
Portugal	9,465	0·9	Honduras	2,413	3·4
Chile	9,351	2·5	Papua and New Guinea	2,300	2·4
Greece	8,803	0·7	Paraguay	2,231	3·1
Iraq	8,634	2·8	Jordan	2,103	2·7
Ghana	8,376	2·7	Albania	2,019	2·9
Bulgaria	8,370	0·8	Singapore	1,988	2·5
Cuba	8,270	2·4	Jamaica	1,908	2·0
Uganda	8,133	2·5	Nicaragua	1,848	3·4
Sweden	7,918	0·7	Libya	1,803	3·7
Austria	7,350	0·5	Togo	1,769	2·6
Mozambique	7,274	1·3	Costa Rica	1,650	3·5
Saudi Arabia	7,112	1·7	Central African Republic	1,488	2·4
Cambodia	7,087	3·4	Panama	1,372	3·3
Malagasy Rep.	6,500	2·4	Mongolia	1,210	3·0
Switzerland	6,147	1·7	Southern Yemen	1,195	2·3
Syria	5,701	2·8	Liberia	1,130	1·7
Ecuador	5,695	3·4	Mauritania	1,120	1·8
Cameroon	5,590	2·2	Trinidad and Tobago	1,021	2·6
Yemen	5,440	2·1			
Angola	5,362	1·3			

TABLE 3.2

Gross National Product Per Head (1968) and its Average Annual Growth Rate (1961–68)

Countries with populations of 1 million or more

Note: In view of the usual errors inherent in this type of data and to avoid a misleading impression of accuracy, the figures for GNP per capita have been rounded to the nearest $10.

Country	GNP per capita (US dollars)	Growth Rate (percent)	Country	GNP per capita (US dollars)	Growth Rate (percent)
United States	3,980	3·4	Mexico	530	3·4
Sweden	2,620	3·2	Uruguay	520	– 1·4
Switzerland	2,490	2·4	Yugoslavia	510	4·2
Canada	2,460	2·8	Chile	480	1·8
France	2,130	3·7	Jamaica	460	0·8
Australia	2,070	2·4	Portugal	460	5·0
Denmark	2,070	3·3	Costa Rica	450	2·1
New Zealand	2,000	1·7	Mongolia[b]	430	0·8
Norway	2,000	4·1	Albania[b]	400	4·9
Germany, Fed. Rep. of	1,970	3·4	Peru	380	3·5
			Nicaragua	370	3·8
Belgium	1,810	3·2	Saudi Arabia	360	7·2
United Kingdom	1,790	2·0	Malaysia	330	4·3
Finland	1,720	3·2	Guatemala	320	1·7
Netherlands	1,620	3·0	Colombia	310	1·4
Germany (Eastern)[b]	1,430	4·0	Cuba[b]	310	– 2·0
			Iran	310	5·0
Israel	1,360	4·7	Turkey	310	3·2
Puerto Rico	1,340	5·9	Dominican Republic	290	0·5
Austria	1,320	3·6			
Czechoslovakia[b]	1,240	3·7	El Salvador	280	2·1
Italy	1,230	4·6	China, Rep. of	270	6·5
Japan	1,190	9·9			
USSR[b]	1,110	5·8	Honduras	260	1·2
Libya	1,020	19·4	Iraq	260	2·9
Hungary[b]	980	5·2	Ivory Coast	260	4·8
Ireland	980	3·1	Jordan	260	4·8
Venezuela	950	1·4	Brazil	250	1·6
Poland[b]	880	5·5	Korea (North)[b]	250	5·9
Trinidad and Tobago	870	4·4	Paraguay	230	1·3
Argentina	820	1·0	Algeria	220	– 3·5
Romania[b]	780	7·8	Ecuador	220	1·2
Bulgaria[b]	770	6·7	Southern Rhodesia	220	– 0·1
Greece	740	5·9			
Spain	730	6·5	Tunisia	220	2·7
Hong Kong	710	8·1	Zambia	220	3·6
Singapore	700	3·8	Liberia	210	0·7
South Africa	650	3·7	Papua and New Guinea	210	2·5
Panama	580	4·6			
Lebanon	560	2·4	Syria	210	3·5

TABLE 3.2 (*continued*)

Country	GNP per capita (US dollars)	Growth Rate (percent)	Country	GNP per capita (US dollars)	Growth Rate (percent)
Mozambique	200	3·6	Pakistan	100	3·1
Angola	190	2·1	Sudan	100	− 0·4
Morocco	190	0·4	Togo	100	0·5
Ceylon	180	2·3	China	90	0·3
Korea, Rep. of	180	5·6	(*Mainland*)[b]		
Mauritania	180	11·3	Congo,	90	− 0·3
Philippines	180	0·8	Dem. Rep. of		
Ghana	170	− 0·7	Guinea	90	2·7
Senegal	170	− 1·4	Mali	90	1·3
United Arab	170	1·5	Vietnam (*North*)[b]	90	3·3
Rep.			Afghanistan	80	− 0·3
Bolivia	150	1·8	Dahomey	80	1·1
Sierra Leone	150	1·5	Nepal	80	0·3
Thailand	150	4·6	Tanzania	80	1·2
Cameroon	140	1·1	Burma	70	1·6
Kenya	130	1·4	Ethiopia	70	2·6
Vietnam, Rep. of	130	1·9	Haiti	70	− 3·3
Cambodia	120	0·6	Niger	70	− 1·6
Central African	120	− 0·6	Nigeria	70	− 0·3
Republic			Rwanda[a]	70	1·5
Southern	120	− 4·9	Yemen[a]	70	2·0
Yemen[a]			Chad	60	− 1·5
Uganda	110	1·1	Somalia[a]	60	0·2
India	100	1·0	Burundi	50	0·0
Indonesia	100	0·8	Malawi	50	2·2
Laos[a]	100	0·2	Upper	50	0·1
Malagasy Rep.	100	− 0·2	Volta		

[a] Estimates of GNP per head and its growth rate are tentative.

[b] Estimates of GNP per head and its growth rate have a wide margin of error mainly because of the problems in deriving the GNP at factor cost from net material product and in converting the GNP estimate into US dollars.

Source: *World Bank Atlas*, IBRD, 1970.

I. PROBLEMS OF MEASURING POVERTY AND INCOME

But the procedure of diving total income by the number of heads may be misleading unless there is a fair amount of equality and not very great deviations from the average. One would not wish to call a community rich in which one man had all the money while all the others had nothing.

Perhaps the reason why we feel that it is all right to speak about *countries* as being rich or poor, as shown by their income per head, is that we tacitly assume that countries set up institutions and pursue policies which aim at correcting extremes of inequality, through taxation, subsidies, social services, etc. Such institutions do not exist to even out inequalities between nations. Thus if we had two entirely separate and sovereign nations with the same population, one with income per head of £100 and the other with income per head of £1,000, it would not be meaningful to say that the average income of the two is £550.

Yet something like this is true within many underdeveloped countries. They are deeply divided societies. Even brief and superficial visits to these countries show the existence of extreme inequalities in many spheres: air-conditioned cadillacs or jet planes next to bullock carts; luxury skyscrapers towering over shanty towns. There is inequality not only in income and wealth, but also in technology and productivity, in education and health. A distinguished international civil servant used to say that you could tell the poverty of a country by the size and luxury of the limousines in which its delegates would arrive.

The split between the few rich and the many poor is reinforced by differences between urban and rural levels of living, between large foreign companies operating in mines, oil, or plantations and small-scale indigenous activities, between modern industrial enterprises and primitive crafts, between luxurious residential universities and rural illiteracy, between the most modern hospitals and village traditional healers. The dualism is often further reinforced by a division along racial, ethnic or religious lines, so that the small enclave of the privileged oligarchy is largely or entirely recruited from one community. While some of these divisions reinforce one another, some of them run across social groups, so that those who are deprived in one respect may be privileged in another. Where the status and position of women is low, even the women of rich families suffer from discrimination. The same is true of racial or religious minorities who are confined to certain activities and barred from others. Though the rural sector is poorer on average than the urban, the misery of the unemployed inhabitants of the shanty towns matches that of the sharecroppers.

Such social and economic divisions greatly increase the difficulties of using low average income per head as an index of poverty or its rise as an index of development. For the question 'Who benefits?' can no longer be put aside, as it sometimes can in a country like Britain or America. It goes to the heart of the matter. This is not to say that development is advanced only when everyone, or the poorest, or the majority, benefit now. For when profits accrue to a small minority who save and reinvest them, the process may lead to greater benefits for a larger group later. The difficulty created by a dualistic society is not simply the prevalence of inequality, but the absence of interaction, at any rate positive, mutually beneficial interaction, between what are sometimes described as two sectors but what may often be two distinct societies, built on different institutions and regulated by different rules – though particular individuals may participate, permanently or temporarily, in both and although some transactions take place between the two sectors. It is the absence of spill-over from the modern, often export-orientated but sometimes import-replacing, industrial enclave into the stagnating, indigenous, partly subsistence economy which makes aggregation of income and division by heads illegitimate. Income per head may grow as a result of a rise in world prices of the metal mined and exported by the modern enclave, which results in higher profits and perhaps also higher wages and tax receipts. Even so-called development projects can remain confined to a narrow area. We should not speak of development as having taken place in circumstances where poverty has not, either directly or indirectly, been relieved.

A better guide than average income per head would be the median income if reliable figures were available. If we arrange all family incomes in ascending order from the smallest to the largest, the median is the value halfway up this order. Or the mode, which is the income earned by most families in the community, could be used as an index.

In addition to income per head, one may wish to measure the rate of encroachment of the money economy on the traditional sector. The reason for this is not that there is anything particularly wonderful about cash, but that it provides a rough index of increasing differentiation, specialisation and, given certain assumptions, of rising levels. What we are after is an index of the lot of the mass of the people, their level of living, their poverty or prosperity. That part of income which contributes to current consumption is one component of this level, but it contains others, such as the amount, unpleasantness and conditions of work, life expectancy, availability of medical services, the certainty of employment or threat of unemployment, and others. Different societies set aside different proportions of their income for such purposes as defence, which adds neither to current nor to future consumption, and to investment in capital, which, if wisely selected, directed and used, raises future consumption. One of the important differences between advanced and underdeveloped societies is that many consumption expenditures which do not raise production in rich countries, do so in poor ones. More and better food for an under- and ill-nourished labour force reduces apathy and raises ability to work; so does better health, sanitation, education and housing. Much of private and social consumption can therefore be productive, while the mere erection of structures, even though labelled 'investment', need not raise future consumption.

Apart from the difficulties already discussed, a new set of difficulties arises when income indexes are required for the purpose of international comparisons of consumption or income per head. Conversion of national income at exchange rates, the method used by the United Nations (see Table 3.1) is unsatisfactory, for these do not reflect purchasing power equivalents. They lead to such incredible results as that the average Ethiopian has an income of only eleven cents a day and yet manages to survive. To avoid this anomaly one would wish to compare incomes, using a common set of prices. But this method can give widely varying results according to which country's prices we use; for the things which are plentiful and cheap in America are scarce and dear in Ethiopia, while some of those which are cheap in Ethiopia are dear in America. This is the result partly of different factor endowments, so that products requiring much capital and skill are relatively cheap in America, and partly of different preferences, so that the Ethiopians enjoy local products which would be dear in America.

Quite apart from pricing problems, however, the available statistics provide only a very frail basis on which to build our comparisons. We depend largely on guesswork for transactions in the large traditional sector of the economy. Good agricultural statistics are not only expensive to collect, but accurate information is difficult to extract from an illiterate and suspicious peasantry, hostile to central authority. Figures for the rest of the economy are somewhat easier to get and less unreliable, which tends to reinforce our general bias in favour of the enclave. Foreign trade figures are often the best.

People have tried to get round this difficulty by using non-monetary indicators such as the stock of telephones, energy consumption, steel consumption, cement consumption, the number of vehicles, the stock of doctors and dentists, daily newspaper circulation, post-primary school enrolment ratio, quality of diet, meat consumed, letters posted, stock of cinemas, etc. Professor Wilfred Beckerman has recently correlated many of these non-monetary indicators with real income and consumption for a large number of countries for which reliable data were available and suggested ways of 'predicting' the latter from the former, where they are not.

The main reason for experimenting with this method is the relatively much greater availability of data for non-monetary indicators than for national income or consumption (see Table 3.3).[1]

[1] W. Beckerman, *International Comparisons of Real Income* (Development Centre, OECD, Paris, 1966) p. 28. See also W. Beckerman and R. Bacon, 'International Comparisons of Income Levels: A Suggested New Measure', *Economic Journal*, LXXVI 303 (Sep 1966) 519–36.

TABLE 3.3

Some Economic and Social Data about Groups of Countries with
Different Annual Incomes per Head (1955–60)

	Group					
	I	*II*	*III*	*IV*	*V*	*VI*
Annual income in $ per head	1,000 *and above*	576– 1,000	351– 575	201– 350	100– 200	100
Total population in millions	275	340	165	320	270	1,390
% of the national income from agriculture	11	11	15	30	33	41
Expectation of life at birth	71	68	65	57	50	45
Inhabitants per doctor	885	944	1,724	3,132	5,185	13,450
Infant deaths in first year per thousand live births	24	34	68	75	100	150
% of illiterates	2	6	19	30	49	71
Consumption of energy per head (1,000 kilogrammes of coal equivalent)	4	2·8	1·9	0·7	0·4	0·2
School attendance (%)	90	83	75	60	43	37
Caloric consumption per head (in 1,000 units)	3·2	2·8	2·8	2·5	2·2	2
Carbohydrate content of food (%)	44	52	60	72	68	82
Annual domestic letters sent per head	186·8	110·1	47·3	46·6	13·6	4·8
Stock of road vehicles per head	0·2091	0·0720	0·0306	0·0157	0·0073	0·0021

Source: Jan Tinbergen, *Development Planning* (Weidenfeld & Nicolson, 1967) and Wilfred Beckerman, *International Comparisons of Real Income* (Development Centre of the OECD, Paris, 1966).

Although Professor Beckerman's observations do not contain as many low-income countries as high-income countries and would be improved by the addition of further very low-income countries, he achieves strikingly high correlations between private consumption and some non-monetary indicators. With all its limitations, the method suggested by Beckerman of using the number of letters sent per head, steel consumed per head and the stock of telephones per head provides a cheap way of getting at international income or consumption comparisons.

But these comparisons themselves suffer from certain faults. Thus, although urban workers enjoy a multiple of the income of peasants and sharecroppers, a part of this should not be counted as income but as an expense necessary to earn income. Housing and transport costs are necessary expenses in urban employments, while they are lower in the country without an equivalent loss of welfare. So are shoes and clothing. The price of food in towns is higher than in the country, not necessarily because the quality is better, but because the price must cover costs of transport, storage, packaging and retail distribution. The urban worker must therefore earn a higher income in order to buy the same food (although it is less fresh) as the peasant who grows it in his plot.

In addition to consumption per head, there are other indexes of social welfare, such as rates of infant mortality, life expectancy, literacy rates, unemployment rates, etc. Again, many of these variables are correlated with one another and with income per head, although no simple uni-causal explanations can be derived from these correlations. There is, normally, mutual causation, higher literacy rates or longer life expectancy causing higher incomes, which in turn raise literacy and life expectancy. The expectation of life of a newly born baby boy in the advanced North is between sixty and seventy years, while in the underdeveloped world it is between twenty-five and forty-five. Only poor countries have infant mortality rates greater than 6 per cent, while in developed countries they are less than 3 per cent. Illiteracy rates vary from 2 per cent in advanced countries to 70 per cent or more in the least developed countries.

Any index of poverty and development is bound to contain, implicitly or explicitly, value judgements, for development means change towards a social state judged desirable. It is important to make the value judgements explicit by showing *who* enjoys the incomes.

Not only the aggregation of heads but also the aggregation of a bundle of commodities and services into a composite 'income' presents difficulties. In countries where land is not plentiful and food production cannot easily be increased, a further disaggregation is necessary. Not only do we have to distinguish between what happens to income per head in the sophisticated money economy and what happens in the traditional sector, but we must also distinguish between the growth of food per head, which is essential to the mass of the people, and other goods and services. Even this may constitute too much aggregation if there are serious transport difficulties, storage problems or political obstacles to the distribution of food surpluses to areas where food is deficient. A 10 per cent rise in the production of bicycles, accompanied by a 2 per cent fall in food may show up as an increase of income, but it will, in conditions of extreme poverty, mean a rise in poverty.

In using income per head as an index of poverty, and its growth over time as an index of the rate of development, we must, then, beware of two logical traps. First, in a society rent into at least two separate components, one traditional, rural and stagnant, the other specialised, modern and often export-orientated (though it can also be import-replacing), the crucial question is: income and development for whom? Second, gross inequalities of income would not matter if we were looking at the production *potential* of the economy. Thus it might make good sense to ask: how much would there be per head if incomes were equally distributed? In attempting to answer this question we convert different goods and services to a common measure by using their prices. But this procedure assumes either that all goods and services are potentially consumed by all people, or, if different income groups demand different things, that the factors of production could be switched from producing, say, luxury flats for the rich to producing food for the poor. These assumptions are warranted in a rich country but not in most poor ones. For the factors of production used for luxury building, four-lane highways and personal services could not be switched to the production of more food, though foreign exchange could. To equate one block of luxury flats with so many tons of wheat is therefore economically meaningless. We must examine separately what is happening to food production and what to construction and industrial production, even if we are concerned only with the *production potential* and entirely ignore actual distribution.

II. THE RELATION BETWEEN INCOME AND DEVELOPMENT

We have seen that low income per head cannot be used as an entirely satisfactory index of poverty, nor its rate of growth over time as an index of the rate of development, because of the dual structure of underdeveloped economies and because of the different products and factors necessary to meet the needs of the people in the two parts of the economy. Even if we had a satisfactory index of real incomes to measure the change in the extent of poverty, its use as a measure of development would still miss a great deal that is conveyed by that term.

Development is both more and less than rising real incomes. It has become a platitude to say that development means modernisation and modernisation means the transformation of human beings. Development as an objective and development as a process both embrace a change in fundamental attitudes to life and work and in social, cultural and political institutions. The difference between economic *growth* in advanced countries, which, of course, is reflected in faster 'development' as measured by growth of income per head, and *development* in so-called 'developing' countries is that in the former attitudes and institutions are, by and large, adapted to change, and society has innovation and progress built into its system, while in the latter attitudes and institutions and even policies are stubborn obstacles to development.

But the transformation of a tradition- or authority-bound society into a modern, innovating, experimenting, progressing one *may* be successfully achieved without registering for a considerable time any growth in income or income per head. Institutional and human reforms, like building an educational system; land reform; recruiting and training an efficient and honest administrative service; nursing an entrepreneurial class interested in saving, working, risk-taking and large-scale producing; laying the foundations for national, political unity; these and other measures take time and may not be accompanied initially by increasing production. The most important measure is often an effective population policy which aims at raising incomes per head by reducing the number of heads over which future income has to be spread. But, although some economic benefits of population control are noticeable very soon, the full benefits accrue only after one or two generations and rapid development can occur without a substantial rise in current income per head. Just as there can be economic growth without development, there can be development without economic growth.

We may conclude therefore that development is certainly not synonymous with rising income or income per head and care must be exercised if these concepts are to be used as rough measures or indicators of development. An ideal measure would need to account for such factors as the rate of encroachment of the modern sector on traditional ways of life and work, and embrace so-called non-economic factors such as human attitudes and social institutions. Pseudo-precision, expressed in single indexes of income per head and growth rates, often reflecting habits of thought acquired in the advanced industrial North, can be misleading if used in isolation. Above all, it is important to remember that such measures cannot but imply value judgements about the aims of development about which there will be no universal agreement.

III. CHARACTERISTICS OF POOR COUNTRIES

While poor countries differ from one another in many respects – some are densely, others sparsely populated; some are humid, others dry; some have been independent for long, others have emerged only recently; some are small, others large; some have been populated by Europeans, others not, etc. – they have a number of common characteristics.[1]

[1] A long list of characteristics of underdeveloped areas is found in H. Leibenstein, *Economic Backwardness and Economic Growth* (New York: John Wiley, 1963), pp. 40–1.

It is easier to enumerate these than to say whether they are causes or effects of poverty or both, whether they are caused by a third factor or whether they are just coincidences.

Perhaps the most striking fact is that most underdeveloped countries lie in the tropical and semi-tropical zones, between the Tropic of Cancer and Tropic of Capricorn. Recent writers have too easily glossed over this fact and considered it largely fortuitous. This reveals the deepseated optimistic bias with which we approach problems of development and the reluctance to admit the vast differences in initial conditions with which today's poor countries are faced compared with the pre-industrial phase of more advanced countries. But a hot and humid climate reduces the efficiency of men, cattle and land. Work generates body heat and is clearly more difficult in a hot climate. In addition, land erosion of the top soil, through wind and rain, is much more serious in tropical countries. So is leaching (the washing downwards by the action of water of essential ingredients in the soil) which is particularly serious in tropical areas with high rainfall and is one cause of rapid loss of fertility. In other areas inadequate or uncertain rainfall is often severely limiting. Moreover, high rates of evaporation mean that irrigation aimed at overcoming water scarcity can lead to soil salination unless extra care, and investment, is provided for meticulous control of water applications, or unless drainage is installed to carry away surplus water. It is, of course, true that the growth of science and technology has created a prospect of prodigious technological advance with respect to such matters as the control of tropical diseases and pests affecting cattle and plants, the scientific introduction of improved strains of crops and livestock and the improvement of methods of production, storage and distribution. But much scientific research has been applied to solving medical and agricultural problems in temperate zones and much of the knowledge gained cannot be directly applied to the different conditions of the tropics. Many of the problems of tropical agriculture and of tropical diseases have had to be tackled afresh and much remains yet to be done.

Yet a feature common to all the poor countries is the large proportion of the domestic product that is generated in agriculture, even when compared with such 'agricultural' countries as Australia and Canada (see Table 3.4). In India, for example, the proportion contributed by agriculture and mining is 52 per cent. Moreover, unlike the advanced countries which display a rough correspondence between output and numbers employed (in Britain the 5 per cent of the work force in agriculture contribute 5 per cent of the gross domestic product and the 44 per cent in manufacturing contribute

TABLE 3.4

Industrial Origin of Gross Domestic Product at Factor Cost

Approximate Percentage Distribution

Country	*Manufacturing and construction*[a]	*Ag and mining*[b] *(Also electricity, power and water)*	*Services*[c]
Uganda (1967)	10	62	28
Peru (1966)	20	28	52
India (1967)	17	54	29
United States (1967)	33	7	60
France (1961)	44	13	43
United Kingdom (1967)	41	8	51
Japan (1967)	36	12	52
Thailand (1967)	19	34	47
Jordan (1967)	13	25	62
Denmark (1967)	39	10	51

[a] International Standard Industrial Classification 2, 3, 4 (Old Classification).
[b] ISIC 0, 1, 5 (Old Classification).
[c] ISIC 5–8 (Old Classification).

Source: *UN Yearbook of National Account Statistics* 1968, vol. II: International Tables. N.B.—Source gives percentage distribution for ISIC 1–3, 5: for ISIC 0: for ISIC 2–3: and for ISIC 4. Column one of this table is derived as (ISIC 2–3) + (ISIC 4); column two as (ISIC 0) + (ISIC 1–3, 5) – (ISIC 2–3); column three as 100–column one–column two.

TABLE 3.5

Structure of the Economically Active Population

Percentages

Country	Year	*Manufacturing and construction*	*Agriculture and mining*	*Services*
United Kingdom	1966	42·6	5·4	52·0
France	1968	37·0	16·6	46·4
United States	1960	32·7	7·5	59·8
	1969(est.)	32·1	5·1	62·8
Canada	1961	30·1	14·0	55·9
	1970(est.)	27·1	9·1	63·8
New Zealand	1966	35·9	13·7	30·4
Australia	1966	35·7	10·6	53·7
Argentina	1960	30·8	18·3	50·9
Brazil	1960	12·4	54·1	33·5
Mexico	1960	17·3	55·4	27·3
India	1961	10·6	73·4	16·0
UAR (Egypt)	1960	11·0	56·9	32·1
Niger	1960	0·6	96·9	2·5
Sierra Leone	1963	6·1	79·9	14·0

N.B.—Services is a residual category, and may be subject to rounding errors.
Source: *ILO Yearbook*, 1970.

41 per cent), the poor countries display a marked disparity (see Table 3.4). Thus India's agricultural and mining contribution of 52 per cent is produced by 73 per cent of the work force, while the 17 per cent contribution of manufacturing is generated by 11 per cent of the workers. Hence the disparity in personal income between agricultural and industrial workers is much greater in a poor country than in a rich one.

So far, only a few of the many characteristics of poor countries have been touched on. We have, however, set down a list of a number of these characteristics as they relate especially to the backward indigenous sector of a poor country.[1] The items selected may to some extent be disputable or at least in need of qualification; their grouping is to some extent arbitrary for the economic and social system is a complex and interrelated whole. No moral or other judgements are implied by this presentation.

1. *Economic index*

   low output/worker
   low income/population

'Economic' forces operating on output per worker and income per head

2. *Conditions of production*

   small industrial sector
   absence of economies of scale
   primitive and crude techniques
   absence of specialisation
   little capital per worker
   scarcity of products requiring much capital
   small savings per head of the bulk of the population
   little enterprise
   inadequate physical and social infrastructure
   low output per acre, particularly of protein foods
   concentration of exports on a few primary products
   low volume of international trade per head
   low labour utilisation:
       low participation
       short duration
       low efficiency

[1] The classifications, though not the items enumerated, follow generally those in G. Myrdal, *Asian Drama* (Penguin, 1968), Appendix 2, section 5, pp. 1,859–64. See also Chapters 2 and 5 of this book.

3. *Levels of living*

    large proportion of expenditure on food and necessities
    under-nutrition
    malnutrition
    high mortality rates
    bad housing and overcrowding
    bad hygiene, public health and sanitation
    inadequate medical attention
    inadequate cultural facilities

4. *Aptitudes*

    absence of training facilities
    inadequate education
    illiteracy
    ignorance, false beliefs and useless or harmful knowledge

'Non-economic' forces operating on output per worker and income per head

5. *Attitudes to work and life*

    poor discipline
    no punctuality
    caste, religious or racial prejudice
    superstition
    lack of foresight
    lack of ambition
    weak acquisitive motivation
    apathy
    lack of adaptability
    unwillingness to bear risks, venture, innovate
    inability to cooperate outside the family or tribe
    contempt for manual work
    submissiveness
    low standards of hygiene
    work-spreading attitudes
    absence of birth control and high fertility rates

6. *Institutions*

    land tenure hostile to improvements
    uneconomic division of plots
    poor markets for labour, credit, capital

poor marketing facilities for products
poor information
weak government (national and local)
political uncertainty
corrupt, inefficient and inadequate administration
rigid class, caste system
inequality
absence of opportunities
arbitrary legal administration
non-enforcement of contracts
prevalence of child labour
inferiority of women's status
weak or absent middle class

7. *Policies*

soft state: unwillingness to enforce law and to legislate for development
concentration on 'economic' action to escape painful institutional reforms
ineffective taxation

TABLE 3.6

Table Illustrating Some Forms of Circular Causation Within and Between the Six Categories of Conditions

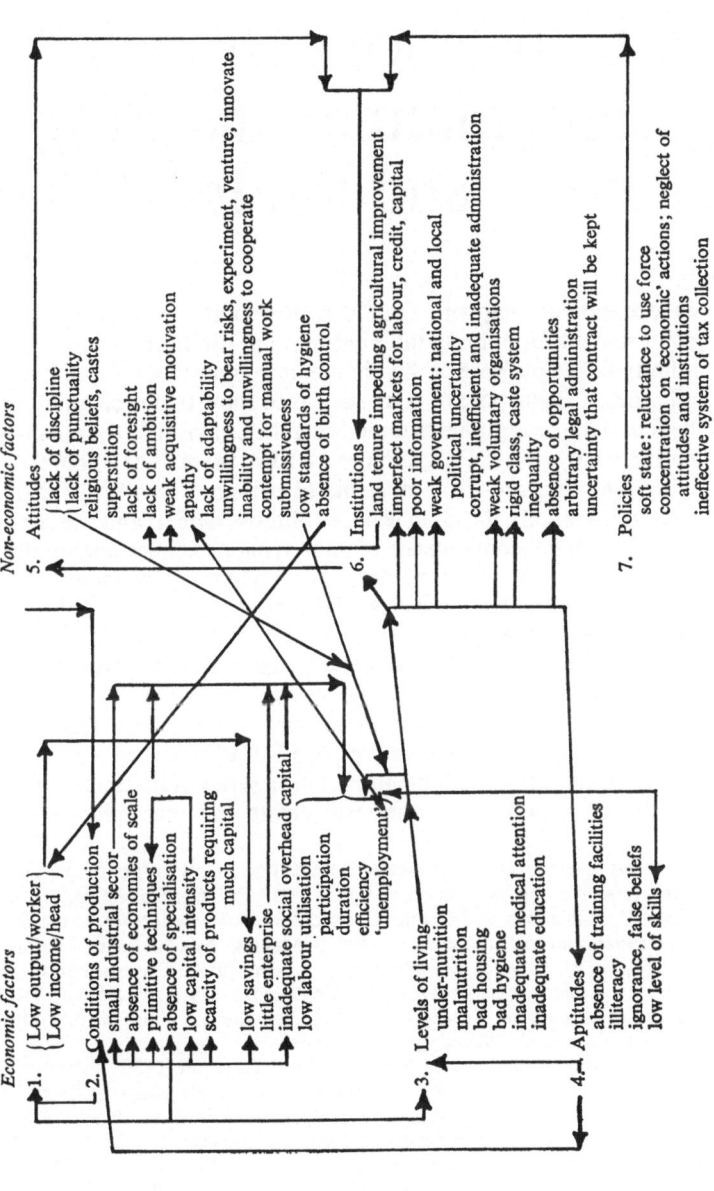

Economic factors

1. {Low output/worker / Low income/head}

2. Conditions of production
small industrial sector
absence of economies of scale
primitive techniques
absence of specialisation
low capital intensity
scarcity of products requiring much capital
low savings
little enterprise
inadequate social overhead capital
low labour utilisation
participation
duration
efficiency
'unemployment'

3. Levels of living
under-nutrition
malnutrition
bad housing
bad hygiene
inadequate medical attention
inadequate education

4. Aptitudes
absence of training facilities
illiteracy
ignorance, false beliefs
low level of skills

Non-economic factors

5. Attitudes
lack of discipline
lack of punctuality
religious beliefs, castes
superstition
lack of foresight
lack of ambition
weak acquisitive motivation
apathy
lack of adaptability
unwillingness to bear risks, experiment, venture, innovate
inability and unwillingness to cooperate
contempt for manual work
submissiveness
low standards of hygiene
absence of birth control

6. Institutions
land tenure impeding agricultural improvement
imperfect markets for labour, credit, capital
poor information
weak government: national and local
political uncertainty
corrupt, inefficient and inadequate administration
weak voluntary organisations
rigid class, caste system
inequality
absence of opportunities
arbitrary legal administration
uncertainty that contract will be kept

7. Policies
soft state: reluctance to use force
concentration on 'economic' actions; neglect of attitudes and institutions
ineffective system of tax collection

4 Unbalanced Growth, Programmes and Prognoses and the Ideal Plan[1]

IT occasionally happens that ideas formulated in entirely different contexts and for entirely different reasons, are found to have certain affinities. The purpose of this chapter is to show that such affinities can affinities. The purpose of this article is to show that such affinities can be found in the arguments underlying the criticism of the means-ends model in my essay 'Programmes and Prognoses'[2] and those underlying the criticism of the doctrine of balanced growth.[3] I shall first summarise briefly the main features of those models and the criticism, then discuss the convergence of underlying principles and finally link this up with some current notions of planning in underdeveloped countries, in which the notions of balanced growth and of the means-ends model converge.

The *doctrine of balanced growth* states that investment, to be successful, must be applied to the production of a variety of products in accordance with income elasticities of demand. 'The case for "balanced growth" rests on the need for a "balanced diet".'[4] Since human wants are complementary, only a series of investment projects which cater for one another will create the mutually supporting

---

[1] Views similar to those presented here can be found in 'Economic Development, Research and Development, Policy Making: Some Converging Views', by Albert O. Hirschman and Charles E. Lindblom, *Behavioral Science*, vol. 7, no. 2 (Apr 1962), and in 'Tinbergen on Policy Making' by Charles E. Lindblom in *The Journal of Political Economy*, LXVI, 6 (Dec 1958). The inspiration to the approach in this article comes from T. Balogh and G. Myrdal who have, repeatedly but with little success, pleaded for a rationality which is aware of the limitations of mechanistic model thinking in economics.

[2] In Gunnar Myrdal, *Value in Social Theory* (London, 1958), Introduction.

[3] Albert O. Hirschman, *The Strategy of Economic Development* (New Haven, 1958); Paul Streeten, 'Unbalanced Growth', *Oxford Economic Papers* (June 1959 and Mar 1963); 'Balanced versus Unbalanced Growth', *The Economic Weekly* (20 Apr 1963), and *Economic Integration*, 2nd ed. (Sythoff), chapters 6 and 7.

[4] Ragnar Nurkse, *Problems of Capital Formation in Underdeveloped Countries* (1953) p. 11.

markets which will justify each project. Various qualifications were introduced as the debate continued, such as the restriction of the doctrine to final goods (the exclusion of intermediate goods), the limitation of the principle to that of an ultimate objective (to the exclusion of the process of achieving this objective), etc. But the main idea remains: the emphasis on the complementarity of markets, requiring an investment 'package'.

The *means-ends model* is the accepted form of thinking about economic policy. It appears in the Social Welfare Function as the basis of modern welfare economics and in Professor Tinbergen's distinction between target variables and instrument variables in his elegant formulation of the theory of economic policy.[1]

We are confronted with a given set of ends and we have knowledge of the structural relations of the economy. Turning the causes and effects of economic analysis into the means and ends of economic policy, we are able to construct, with sufficient knowledge, a system of interdependent relationships. If the ends can be rendered commensurable, so that we can indicate how much sacrifice of one is worth more of some other, we can reduce the problem to that of the maximisation of an end index. In order to separate the sphere of values from the sphere of facts successfully, we would have to assume:

(1) that people attach to means no independent value but only instrumental value;
(2) that people attach to ends independent value only, and never consider them as means to other ends;
(3) no other effects of means than the 'given' ends have independent value.

Both the balanced growth model and the means-ends model contain a sharp separation of two spheres: in the Social Welfare Function the ends of economic policy, assumed to be given, are separated from the means, which can be deployed in different ways. In the doctrine of Balanced Growth (BG) the projects dictated by income elasticities of demand are separated from the investment/income ratio, while incentives, human attitudes to work and life, and social and political institutions are assumed to be constant and fully adapted to economic requirements. In both cases one type of pattern, suited for the understanding of certain conditions, is elevated to the model of rational behaviour *par excellence*. The following criticism is intended not to reject this type of model, but to show some of its limitations.

[1] Cf. J. Tinbergen, *On the Theory of Economic Policy* (1952) and *Economic Policy: Principles and Design* (1956). See also, e.g., R. A. Mundell, 'On the Selection of a Program of Economic Policy . . .', *Banca Nazionale del Lavoro Quarterly Review* (Sep 1963).

The presentation often begins with statements which appear innocuous, indeed platitudinous, such as: we should specify clearly our ends before embarking on policies; we should choose between the available means those best adapted to achieve our specified ends; policies should be mutually consistent and should be framed only after full consideration of all alternatives and their implications; they should be scrutinised for their side-effects and attention should be paid to interactions, etc. Yet, if formulated precisely and extended to economic policy in general, these apparently self-evident admonitions are misleading. It is peculiar to both Unbalanced Growth (UG) and Programmes and Prognoses (P & P) that they probe 'into the hidden rationality of practices that are perpetually at odds with established doctrine'.[1]

Bottlenecks and imbalances appear to be signs of bungling and blundering. The lack of a clear separation of ends from means seems to be a symptom of muddle-headedness. In fact, they sometimes point to the limitation of the conventional notions of rationality. Unbalance can be the inevitable result or even a necessary condition of progress. The re-alignment and creation, rather than the acceptance, of ends may be the objective of planning.

The converging criticisms can be summarised briefly.

The separation of given ends from alternative neutral means is not always appropriate. More ultimate ends are frequently clarified, emerge or disappear in the process of attempting to achieve inter-mediate ends; means acquire and lose the characteristics of ends. Similarly in UG: the desire to seize profit opportunities is neither given and constant nor created by the existence of profit oppor-tunities, but has itself to be planted and nursed. In other words, the task is not simply to promote given ends, but to create the desire for new ends: e.g. to transform a society governed by tradition into one susceptible to experiment and innovation; to remove end-character-istics from certain activities (stigma or dignity attached to certain jobs and professions) and to endow others with end-characteristics (business success; experimentation; novelty; enrichment). Indeed, from this point of view the whole process of economic development from a tradition-bound to an advanced society can be described as: let there be means where there were ends![2] The introduction of the

[1] Albert O. Hirschman (ed.), *Latin American Issues* (1961), p. 41, n. 4.
[2] The reclamation from an all-pervasive morass of end-valuations of the dry land of rational planning, and thus human liberation, is well illustrated by the ultimate ambition of Faust, in his extreme old age:

> 'Below the hills a marshy plain
> Infects what I so long have been retrieving;
> This stagnant pool likewise to drain
> Were now my latest and my best achieving.

cash nexus where previously incommensurable duties and rights prevailed, and the substitution of contract for status, widen the area of instrumental values which replace independent values. In many underdeveloped societies the payment and receipt of interest on loans above a certain limit is immoral and illegal. The removal of the moral, stigma and of the legal restriction paves the way for a rational use of scarce capital. Similarly, the notion of a *justum pretium* endows with moral value prices which, in a more advanced society, have purely instrumental value.[1] The process of UG can be interpreted as the creation and the destruction of human attitudes and valuations in order to initiate and accelerate development. BG, on the other hand, assumes these to be given and constant.

Those who find the means-ends model and the BG model useful, look upon problems of economic policy and development as if they were, in principle, like puzzles. Granted consistent premises, there is always a 'correct' solution. There is always an unambiguous 'scientific' test of whether we have solved the puzzle. No doubt, many problems of economic policy are of this type. Some people, perhaps the technocrats, believe that all problems are. It is certainly tempting to assimilate all problems to this type and to say that a problem has been solved when certain ideal rules are obeyed.[2] But the question, e.g., whether a certain rise of income per head per year should be a primary objective of development policy is altogether different. We might consider this rise simply as a means to some other

> To many millions let me furnish soil,
> Though not secure, yet free to active toil;
>
>   . . .
>
> And such a throng I fain would see,
> Stand on free soil among a people free!'
>
> *Act V, Scene vi*

[1] It is worth noting that at a later stage of development independent (political) value tends to be once again attached to certain prices. In welfare societies such prices as wage rates, house rents, interest rates, foreign exchange rates, etc. acquire again something of the quality of the *justum pretium* and are removed from the *purely instrumental* sphere. Sometimes independent value is attached to a specific price – such as the pre-war value of sterling in 1925, sometimes merely to stability of price, whatever its value happens to be. In the U.S. independent negative value is attached to a budget deficit. It may also be that variables are valued as instruments only within a range, but independently outside that range. Small exchange rate variations or small budget deficits are permitted, but large ones not. Expressions such as 'defending the price of bonds' or 'defending the exchange rate' indicate the independent value attached to certain prices.

[2] Professor J. C. Maxwell told me that a critic of B. L. Joseph's book on *Elizabethan Acting* (Oxford, 1964), which maintains that the techniques were extremely formal, notes that one of his arguments is drawn from the practice of wagers on actors' skill in declaiming set-pieces. Joseph infers from this that they must have had a 'generally accepted body of rules as to what was a fault'.

end – say, preventing revolution. But neither economic development nor a rise in income per head is simply a means to some other end or only an end in itself. Although we cannot apply simple and definite tests and present a 'scientific' solution, the answer to the question as to whether development has proceeded is not arbitrary. Although value judgements enter into our judgement of the situation, they are not like the 'ends' in the puzzle-solving model. The test of successful development is not found in confronting certain facts with a set of value judgements. Analysis and prognosis are skills which cannot always be subjected to the rules of the means-ends game. Although they involve judgements which have some of the characteristics of valuations, they are not for that reason 'subjective', arbitrary or mere matters of taste.

The conventional models of efficient resource allocation assume that there is normally a wide choice of means to promote the given ends. In the means-ends model this presupposes a wide sphere of non-valued activities; in the BG model this assumes mobility, flexibility and transferability of resources. In underdeveloped economies these assumptions are notoriously unwarranted. Available means may be so limited that there is little or no choice. This may be either because means are also valued independently, or because resources are not flexible. The situation is like that of the drunk who has lost his key and looks for it not where he dropped it but under the street lamp – because this is where the light is. If there were alternative options, such behaviour would be irrational. But it may become rational if action is hemmed in by obstacles. These obstacles may be either valuations or physical restraints. To those whose thinking is confined to the conventional model, it looks as if means were dictating conduct. But the range of choice presupposed by this way of thinking does not exist. It therefore looks as if the means dictated the end, as if what should be done depended on what can be done.

The purpose of using means is not only to promote given ends but also to explore new ends. When we travel in new countries, taste new dishes, meet new people, read new books, educate ourselves, etc., we are not trying to satisfy given tastes, for we do not know what these satisfactions will be like: we are exploring new experiences in order to discover new ends. Similarly, in the process of UG new objectives are explored and discovered whose existence is presupposed in the doctrine of BG. What I have described as the anabolism of wants[1] consists in the pressure exerted by the satisfaction of existing wants upon the creation (or discovery) of new wants. Similarly for investment incentives and developmental decisions generally. A railway, a road, a dam may meet existing needs, but they

[1] *Economic Integration*, 2nd ed. (A. W. Sythoff, Leiden, 1964), pp. 115ff.

also lead to the discovery or the creation of a cluster of new aspirations and development opportunities. The erection of factories generates opportunities and fosters attitudes to seize profits, which previously lay dormant or did not exist. Again, the conventionally postulated process is reversed: means are not used to achieve given ends but are used to explore, awaken, create new ends.

Whether we describe the process as one of the discovery of latent ends or of the creation of new ends does not matter. The point is that ends previously not part of the observed value pattern emerge as a result of the use of certain means. One set of wants is often generated in the process by which another set of wants is satisfied, or by the mere fact that new means become available.

In particular, imbalance can create and build up wants as in the case of the Hi-Fi enthusiast who always improves the weakest link in the chain of tuner, amplifier, player and speaker, where the elimination of one source of trouble shows up new weaknesses, raising the standards of the performance he requires all the time.[1] Similarly, in the UG process, disequilibrium calls into existence remedial forces and this process pulls along the economy, which would not have been activated had it not been for the series of disequilibria. The crossword puzzle, picked up in the dentist's waiting room, can lead to crossword puzzle addiction. The well-chosen disequilibrium can spark off the process of development. Sometimes not only are the specific ends not planned, but the process of emergence of new ends itself is unplanned, as in the story of the sons who were told to dig for treasure in the vineyeard: they found no treasure but improved the soil. Important results of our actions are indirect and incidental. The ends follow the means.[2]

Another common feature of the two convergent criticisms is that both point out that a system is never complete and finished. The Social Welfare Function, the notion of the Ideal Plan (in which a set of social objectives is contrasted with a set of policies to achieve these), the doctrine of BG, all presuppose finished systems. The appropriate investment policies spring, like Pallas Athene, fully armed from the head of Zeus. P & P and UG, on the other hand, postulate permanently unfinished systems. Yesterday's ends turn into today's means, and yesterday's means motivate or create today's ends. What

---

[1] Ibid., p. 116. There are numerous other illustrations from common experience how new ends are generated in the process of satisfying quite different ones, and how ends are adjusted to means subservient to other ends. A course of planned reading corresponds to the means-ends pattern, but books picked up at random lead to the discovery of new tastes. Forced to prepare a lecture or to write an article on a subject outside one's sphere of interest, one discovers or creates a new range of interests.

[2] Paul Streeten, *Economic Integration*, pp. 107–8.

looks like the fulfilment of one sequence opens up another sequence. The system moves because it is continually out of gear, and what looks like grit in the engine, in the eyes of BG, becomes the engine of growth in the eyes of UG.

UG and P & P stress the limitations of knowledge and the absence of clearly defined, generally agreed upon ends. Policies therefore must not only promote 'given' ends, but must also improve knowledge, clarify and illuminate ends and promote agreement. They must be directed at changing what are viewed as parameters in the conventional models. Unbalanced advance has certain merits in improving knowledge compared with balanced advance. Ignorance, uncertainty and conflict can be reduced by actions which, were it not for ignorance, uncertainty and conflict, would appear wasteful and irrational.

Thus the concentration on one sector, or one region, or one project, in defiance of the requirements of balance, may have the following merits.

1. It may clarify ends which were previously confused. Such would be the effect of a model village or a model farm in demonstrating methods of cultivation.
2. It may promote agreement between previously conflicting groups. Thus the emphasis on raising the level of living of the lowest 20 per cent to a certain minimum can, given certain assumptions about income distribution, remove or reduce conflicts as to how to raise total GNP.
3. It may improve knowledge about likely bottlenecks and reduce uncertainty about the required consequential actions.
4. It may remove or reduce obstacles in the form of human valuations. The availability of ancillary work for women following the location of a large factory in an underdeveloped region may weaken the opposition to the employment of women. Attitudes and valuations often adjust to facts rather than the other way round.
5. It may remove or reduce the inhibitions of the planners. Successful resistance to the claims of a number of different regions will strengthen the hand of planners in resisting other pressure groups.
6. It may remove obstacles presented by rigidities of responses and immobility of resources. A railway will enable and encourage people to move. A bus service to a village or a cinema will create new wants, incentives and responses.

These forces can interact. Improved knowledge will change valuations. Successful co-operation convinces high-caste Hindus that contact with lower castes is not degrading. Dietary habits, and with them health, are improved as religious taboos are weakened. Professional, occupational and regional mobility are increased as caste notions of trades and occupations are shed.

The doctrines of BG and the means-ends model converge in the notion of the *Ideal Plan*. It is behind much of the theory of planning and model-building: given the objectives of policy it is the task of the Plan to specify a set of measures which would promote the consistent objectives maximally. Where inconsistency arises, the Social Welfare Function tells us how much of one objective can be sacrificed for a given gain in a rival objective while the level of Social Welfare is constant. Thus inconsistencies are resolved and a one-dimensional end-index can be constructed.

The set of objectives or targets is then contrasted with a set of means or instruments which must normally not contain fewer variables than the number of objectives. On the assumption that we have complete knowledge of all relevant conditions and their causal connections, we must then estimate their initial magnitudes and their coefficients of change. These coefficients would normally vary according to the direction, size and speed of the change, according to whether the instruments are applied autonomously or in response to other changes, and according to whether the instruments are applied in isolation or in several possible combinations. Although many objectives will have not only independent value but will also be of instrumental value, very few instruments will have instrumental value only. Thus few instruments can be viewed as merely means for the Plan targets. The independent value attached to the means, again, will normally vary with the direction, size and speed of the change and according to what accompanying measures are taken.

Quite apart from the practical impossibility of acquiring even a fraction of the required knowledge, and apart from the difficulty of selecting the relevant objectives and clarifying their independent and instrumental values, there are logical difficulties in formulating such a Plan. The picture presented by the model not only fails to correspond to any conceivable practical Plan, but is also seriously misleading as an abstract guide for planners, though it may have useful limited applications.

First, the causal relations and the coefficients will change as a result of development. The Plan itself and its execution will alter the material which it assumes to be given. Obstacles to development put up by inertia, resistance and hostility, which present initial limitations, will normally be weakened or removed, though some may be strengthened.

Second, inhibitions of the planners themselves, when it comes to executing reforms which weaken the power and prestige of the classes to which they belong, constitute another form of initial limitation. Again, it is part of the purpose of the Plan to weaken and overcome these. This means that these obstacles and inhibitions can be treated neither as physical limitations, defining means nor as ends.

Third, the objectives chosen must not be arbitrary but must themselves reflect the objectives of the society to which they are applied, for otherwise the Plan can never be implemented. Unless the objectives express actual valuations, relevant to the developing economy, the Plan remains an idle dream. The relevant valuations are therefore rooted in the social conditions which the model attempts to separate from them.

But although an effective Plan is based upon actual social valuations, it also attempts to alter them; although it may disregard actual social valuations by setting up ends *in abstracto*, it is bound to remain a mere academic exercise if it does only this.

The (workable) Plan is not a complete blueprint. It is an unfolding vision with a built-in tendency for change. It neither accepts all political obstacles as ultimate constraints nor ignores them as 'non-economic' factors. Its function is to turn means into ends and ends into means where the development process requires this, and to improve on itself by so doing. To postulate a sharp means-ends or targets-instruments dichotomy is to ignore this process of transformation, and thus the political reality of a development Plan.

Albert O. Hirschman interprets the publications and activities of the Economic Commission for Latin America not as the blueprint of planners, but as protests against 'certain inveterate traits such as the propensity to improvise, the lack of foresight, the failure ever to see the handwriting on the wall'. ECLA's programme springs from the 'desire to stamp out those traditional traits which are felt to be hindrances and handicaps on the road to economic progress'.[1] From this point of view the function of the planners is to reform the national framework of planning itself: the point of the programme is to change the dismal prognosis which the acceptance of existing obstacles, including institutions, valuations and attitudes, would involve.

Similarly, a plan for the acceptance of certain minimum living standards after 15 years for the poorest 20 per cent of the people was proposed by the Perspective Planning Division of the Indian Planning Commission in 1962 not only as an obviously desirable objective, but also as a rallying point of divergent political interests and as a means

---

[1] A. O. Hirschman (ed.), *Latin American Issues* (1961), pp. 22–3.

of achieving agreement on certain consequential policies. The aim is to achieve a convergence of ends and agreement to act.[1]

One of the tasks of planning is thus to create and improve the process of planning itself. There is no confrontation of a sphere of social ends with a sphere of available neutral means, but a continual interaction of necessarily incomplete programmes and prognoses, both containing political and social, as well as physical limitations.

We therefore conclude that the notion of an ideal or optimum plan is misleading if it assumes: (1) that objectives are given *a priori*; (2) that we can draw upon a full causal analysis of instruments and their coefficients, which would differ if applied singly and in various combinations, once-for-all and sustained, and that we know co-efficients which will differ according to the direction, size and speed of the change; (3) that there is no interdependence between the spheres of given objectives and known instruments. In fact, the Plan should be regarded as a steadily forward-moving pattern of policies, which have to be modified continually in the light of newly emerging events, changing causal connections and modified valuations. The programmes of the planners and the prognoses of social researchers are not two independent areas, but the programmes affect and alter the prognoses, and the prognoses in turn alter and modify the programmes. The Plan is not a static two-tier structure but an evolving process. Planning aims not at an *optimum* but at *improvements*. It is guided by a vision, but the vision is open-ended and flexible, not closed and rigid. It contains a rough perception of the connections between conditions prevailing over a period of time and the possibilities of moving, through rationally co-ordinated policies, towards changing objectives.

The transformation of ends into means can be illustrated by the literal and metaphorical desanctification of sacred cows in India. Some slaughtering would improve the quality of the surviving stock and raise the level of human consumption. Similarly, the choice of a profession by Hindus will, as a result of implementing the Plan, lose end-characteristics and acquire means-characteristics. For a Brahmin's son in India to cultivate the land is as scandalous as for a canon's son in our society to become a pimp. But the change in

---

[1] 'Another function of the perspective plan is to educate public opinion on issues of development and to promote the kind of open discussion that is likely to secure a common consensus of political parties. This is perhaps easier in a poor society in which all can agree without controversy on at least one objective: the abolition of poverty. When the purpose is nothing less than to transform society, planning ceases to be an esoteric subject or a mathematical exercise. It must be imbued with deep social purpose and revolutionary zeal.' Pitambar Pant, 'The Development of India', *Scientific American* (Sep 1963), p. 196, reprinted in *Technology and Economic Development*, a Pelican Book, 1965, p. 172.

valuations, which deprives certain activities of their stigma, increases the flexibility of resources. As workers can be switched from tending machines to sweeping floors because caste attitudes have been shed, 'labour' acquires a significance which it does not have if trades are reserved for specific castes. In this way changes in valuations reduce obstacles to economic development. This in turn strengthens the positive values attached to development and eases the way for introducing further measures to reduce these obstacles. But it would be quite misguided to begin planning with a notion of homogeneous 'labour' which bears no relation to actual social institutions, attitudes and values.

Similarly, 'underemployment' and 'unemployment' acquire significance only in relation to a standard working week, discipline and punctuality, which do not exist in rural peasant societies. Leisure and work are not substitutes and the question of a comparative evaluation does not arise. Only the introduction of wage-labour and organised production changes the valuations, clears an area of 'means' (viz. working hours supplied) and can then be fitted into the Plan. To begin planning with the notion of 'unemployment' in such a society is doubly misleading: it begs the policy issue as to what specific measures are necessary to mobilise human resources and it tacitly assumes the valuation of an urban industrial society with respect to the standard working week and attitudes to work. Yet, in the process of successful planning, as independent valuations of each trade are shed and as work and co-operation are organised, 'underemployment' and 'unemployment' and their underlying value judgements acquire significance and become meaningful and measurable.

The conventional models assume that a harmony of interests must precede policy formulation, otherwise a consistent system of ends cannot be given, and that differences about means can be removed by scientific analysis. The UG and P & P models, on the other hand, award a positive role to certain types of conflict. In the emergence of ends, conflicts are necessary if it is impossible to institute an authority above all interest conflicts which is both willing and able to act in accordance with 'the social interest'. The 'communistic fiction'[1] inherent in much liberal thought, that the State is such an authority, is either sociologically false or logically empty. False if it is postulated that the State is the seat of such authority. Empty if 'general welfare' or the 'public interest' is postulated as the proper end of state activity. The objectives emerge as a resultant of the conflicting actions of different groups, including public bodies, and conflict is both inevitable and, up to a point, desirable. In UG, conflict assumes an

[1] Cf. Gunnar Myrdal, *The Political Element in the Development of Economic Theory* (London, 1953).

activating role. The pressure of industrial development on public authorities to provide social overhead capital, or the competing claims of different sectors, contribute to the formulation of the Plan as a moving design.

A particular illustration is the much-discussed problem whether the Indians should disperse new industries widely so as to meet the claims of the different states and regions and to spread the benefits of development, or whether they should concentrate on a few growth poles so as to reap economies of scale and external economies. Much of this discussion ignores the political aspects of these decisions. If the forging of political unity and the prevention of fragmentation is one of the objectives of planning, compromise and concessions must be made. If the Plan is to be a political reality and more than an academic exercise, these political forces must be part of its framework, like the facts of geography, climate and technology. But they must not be taken as given once-for-all. On the contrary, an important purpose of the Plan will be to mould the political pressures and to harness them for accelerated growth. A simple confrontation of political ends and economic means will not serve. It is the interaction of (changing) programmes and (hypothetical) prognoses which forms the pattern of advance.

This is not just criticising a theoretical model for not 'paying attention to political possibilities'. For the costs of overcoming obstacles to the achievement of objectives must surely be part of a full theoretical model. If resistance to end E_1 can be overcome by incurring costs C_1 imposed by a unit pursuing end E_2 which conflicts with E_1 and if the pursuer of E_1 in turn can impose a levy C_2 on the pursuer of E_2, the necessary sacrifices C_1 or C_2 are an essential element in appraising the pursuit of ends E_1 and E_2.

Furthermore, variety of valuations and divergence of political pressures is not only a practical necessity, to which planners have to pay attention, but it is also a desideratum of democratic life. Full uniformity of values and the resulting conformity, which is implied by the conventional model, is rejected by the ethos of a vigorous democratic society.

The dominance of the conventional approach can itself be explained by the triumph of means over ends, or the 'law of the instrument' according to which a small boy, given a hammer, will find everything worth pounding. Separation of ends underlies the methods of computers, operations research, linear programming and other powerful mathematical techniques. Their success induces us to assimilate all problems to those amenable to the successful technique. Indeed, it has become almost tantamount to a definition of rationality. It would be absurd to deny that these techniques have wide areas of useful application. But it would also be wrong to ignore the fact that economic planning in underdeveloped countries is not itself amenable to such techniques. To postulate a clear separation of given ends from alternative neutral means, to postulate balanced growth and to incorporate both in the Ideal Plan in which 'objectives of policy' or 'targets' are confronted with 'instruments of policy'[1] is misleading because it assumes away such problems as the planned transformation of ends and means, the role of conflict, and the open-endedness of effective planning, and because it interprets rationality too narrowly.

The distinction between target variables and instrument variables provides a powerful technique for decision-making in certain restricted circumstances. But it does not illuminate the process of planning in underdeveloped countries and can be highly misleading if the technique is permitted to dominate and obscure the political process.

It may be thought that the criticisms can be formally expressed by saying that the Social Welfare Function, instead of being independently given, is itself a function of (a) the structural relations in the economy and (b) the policies employed to maximise it. If the Social Welfare Function, though dependent on structural relations, is independent of the policies to maximise it, one type of economy may generate a Social Welfare Function SWF_1, which can then be maximised by one set of measures. Another type of economy may generate SWF_2 which can be maximised by another set of measures. The two sets of policies are incomparable, unless a Super Welfare Function provides criteria of choice between SWF_1 and SWF_2. But since there is no society to generate SWF_3, no such criteria exist. Otherwise, whichever society happens to exist will, *ex ante*, seem superior, though a change of structure will, *ex post*, turn out to be justified.

If SWF is a function not only of the structure but also of the specific policies necessary to maximise it, the implementation of SWF_1 transforms it into SWF_2, for which a different set of policies is appropriate, which in turn transforms it into either SWF_3 or back into SWF_1, etc. This interdependence may be cyclical or subject to a trend, or both. The situation may be further complicated by an inability to distinguish between errors in optimising constant aims and failure to optimise changing aims. Regrets over past mistakes may be indistinguishable from hankering after abandoned ideals.

But such a formal interpretation of the criticism would miss the important point that Social Welfare Functions are not appropriate

[1] Cf. J. Tinbergen, *On the Theory of Economic Policy* (Amsterdam, 1952) and *Economic Policy: Principles and Design* (New York, 1956).

abstractions, even as variables dependent on either economic structure or economic policy. Social objectives lack the logical coherence and completeness postulated. What unity they possess is the unity of personality: it is psychological, not logical: to be understood, not to be deduced.

5 The Use and Abuse of Models in Development Planning[1]

THE following criticism is not intended as a rejection of all models in the analysis of underdevelopment and in planning for development. All thought presupposes implicit or explicit model building and model using. Rigorous abstraction, simplification and quantification are necessary conditions of analysis and policy. But models must be realistic, relevant and useful. The trouble with many current models is that they are shapely and elegant, but lack the vital organs.

I. SYSTEMATIC BIASES

Model thinking shows four systematic biases, which are related to each other and overlap, and which can be called:

1. Adapted *ceteris paribus* or automatic *mutatis mutandis*.
2. One-factor analysis.
3. Misplaced aggregation.
4. Illegitimate isolation.

1. Adapted 'ceteris paribus' or automatic 'mutatis mutandis'

It is interesting to note that the conclusions of orthodox liberal and of Marxian economics, though derived from very different premisses, converge in this respect. The separation of parameters from variables in Western orthodox models is partly determined by what is appropriate for advanced industrial nations, partly by ideology and vested interests, and partly by convenience of analysis. Thus psychological attitudes and valuations and social institutions are normally assumed

[1] I am indebted to Miss P. Ady, R. Portes, M. FG. Scott and D. Whitehead for helpful comments. The paper owes much to collaboration with Gunnar Myrdal and M. Lipton.

to be given and adapted. We assume that there is a legal framework, that contracts are enforced, that an efficient Civil Service carries out government orders and an honest judiciary adjudicates; that people are able and willing to work if opportunities arise, that they are literate, skilled and able to co-operate with discipline, appearing on time and carrying out orders, that money spent is efficiently spent and not diverted into the pockets of corrupt officials, that alternatives are considered largely on their pecuniary merits, etc. It follows that none of these matters is considered a suitable area for planning.

In the Marxian scheme (though not always in Marx's own writings), what are parameters become dependent variables. Cultural, political and social institutions are the superstructure, which is determined by the methods of production. It reflects these conditions and gives rise to tensions and contradictions in due course. These tensions between the degree of development of the forces of production and the prevailing relations of production (the institutions and attitudes) in turn give rise to revolution. After the revolution the attitudes and institutions reflect the new conditions of production. Hence social, cultural and political attitudes and institutions, the so-called 'relations of production', though dependent variables, are, after a time-lag, adjusted to the extent required by the dynamic productive forces. Once again, though for fundamentally different reasons, planning the superstructure is not in question. It would be futile before the revolution and unnecessary after it. It was indeed for their attempts to speculate on how social attitudes and institutions could and should be reformed that Marx and Engels ridiculed the 'Utopian' thinkers. Yet, in many ways the early Utopian socialists were more akin to modern planners, including the planners in Soviet Russia, than many of the cruder versions of Marxian thought.

Thus the conservative judgement that a reform of attitudes and institutions is undesirable, and the Marxian judgement that it is either impossible or inevitable, lead to the same conclusion, distracting attention from conscious policy directed at a radical reform of the so-called 'non-economic' factors in economic development. It is, of course, true that textbooks, articles and plans pay lip service to the need to reform the social framework before economic planning can begin. But these declarations are usually forgotten later when the discussion turns to the conventional concepts of income, employment, savings, investment, etc. At that stage either the assumption of *ceteris paribus* is tacitly reintroduced, so that the conventional economic variables can be considered in isolation, or the assumption of automatic *mutatis mutandis* is made, implying that where other things cannot be assumed constant, they will without special policies be adapted to the required extent as a result of economic transformation.

The intellectual framework, which reflects this bias, is supported by value judgements and by vested interests. As we shall see, reforms of institutions and human attitudes violate entrenched interests and are therefore more painful to implement than financial expenditure programmes.

In a bias-free model, the distinction between parameters and variables would be determined, not by ideological preconceptions, but by the situation to which the model is intended to apply and by the questions asked about this situation. To be useful, models will have to be, at least initially, much more specific to individual cases and much less general and 'theoretical'. In particular, the distinction between parameters and variables should not run along the line drawn between 'economic' and 'non-economic' factors operating in a situation. Thus social and political reform should neither 'precede' nor 'follow' economic development: social reform must accompany development, reinforce it, create the conditions necessary for it, but is itself promoted and determined by development. The process is one of continual mutual causation.

2. One-factor analysis

Although economists ought to be particularly trained to discern interdependence and particularly immune to uni-causal explanations, it is a fact that frequently one factor is selected as the strategic factor in development, although the choice of this factor is subject to fashion and ideology. If the Physiocrats stressed *Land* as the source of all wealth and the classical economists *Labour*, *Capital* has recently played the strategic role. Keynes's emphasis on the income-creating aspect of capital was combined with Marx's emphasis on its output-creating aspect in the Harrod-Domar model which has strongly influenced planners. The relationship which equates the rate of growth of income to the savings ratio divided by the capital/output ratio has been one of the chief vehicles by which Western economic thought has been carried into the plans and discussions of the plans of underdeveloped countries. Capital is sometimes regarded as a necessary and sufficient condition of growth, sometimes as the strategic variable. It soon became obvious, however, that numerous other conditions both account for past growth in advanced countries and are required for development in underdeveloped countries. But instead of embarking on a careful analysis of the necessary direction and co-ordination of policies in particular cases, a new one-factor analysis has tended to replace the old one. *Education* has, for a while, been identified as the source of residual growth and we are told of the high returns that 'investment in human beings' yields. There is often little thought as to education of whom, for what, how long, in conjunction with what other measures. It is interesting to speculate what other factors will be singled out as discussion progresses. 'Research and Development' are already popular, and perhaps we shall soon study the returns from appropriate child-training, which produces experimental innovating personalities, or from expenditure on child prevention.

3. Misplaced aggregation

Almost all concepts formed by aggregation suitable for analysing Western economies must be carefully reconsidered before they can be applied to underdeveloped economies. 'Capital', 'income', 'employment', 'unemployment', 'price level', 'savings', 'investment', presuppose conditions which are absent in many underdeveloped countries. 'Employment' presupposes a fairly homogeneous, mobile labour force, willing and able to work and responsive to incentives. In a society of isolated communities, some of them apathetic or with religious prejudices against certain kinds of work, illiterate and unused to co-operation, the notion 'Labour Force' does not make sense. Similarly 'underemployment' or 'disguised unemployment' presupposes that if only demand and machines were available, men and women would be able and willing to work. In fact, much more would be required: a breakdown of caste prejudices, of apathy, of lack of interest in money rewards, of resistance to co-operation, discipline and punctuality, etc. Any attempt to calculate 'disguised unemployment' also presupposes a value judgement as to the length of the appropriate working day and working week.[1]

If economies are divided into sectors between which there is little or no substitution, either in consumption in response to changes in relative prices, or in production in response to changes in relative factor rewards, aggregation of incomes or prices is inappropriate. Even though the indigenous sector may sell its surplus in the market, and even though some of its members may occasionally participate in the transactions of the money sector, if the indigenous sector neither depends upon nor interacts with the capitalist sector, aggregation can be meaningless. The income of an industrial enclave may grow, while real income per head of the indigenous population stagnates or declines. In what sense is 'average income' rising? The problem is not merely how to get at the facts in the indigenous sector and how to appraise them properly. More fundamental is the problem what weights to attach to a small decline of essentials and to a large

[1] For a more detailed discussion see Chapters 6 and 7.

increase of non-essentials. Paasche and Laspeyres indices may give contradictory results. Habits of thought induce us to use concepts which are applicable to one set of conditions, because substitution is possible, responses exist, and value judgements are appropriate, in an entirely different context, where these presuppositions of legitimate aggregation are absent. The statistical manifestation of this would be contradictory results according to which of several equally plausible sets of weights were applied to the same change. Using base period weights, we should register a rise in income per head, and therefore conclude that development is proceeding, while we have begged the political question 'development for whom?'[1]

The distinction between consumption and investment can have various justifications. In the context of development, it is based upon the assumption that investment enables us to produce more later than we would otherwise have done, while consumption is current enjoyment. But if more food and better health now reduce apathy and raise ability to work, they share in the characteristics of investment: consumption, too, is productive of more output.[2] If different investment projects require different sums to bribe corrupt officials, what guide is their cost to the resources used up? To abstract from the differences in such cases is to pour out the baby with the bath water.

It is correct to say that a man is male, a woman female, but it does not make sense to ask: 'Is your family male or female?' One can discuss the differences between the British and the French Constitutions, and also the connections between the Cabinet, Parliament and the Church of England, but it does not make sense to ask 'What transactions go on between the House of Commons and the British Constitution?'[3] Similarly, it is what philosophers call a 'category mistake' to ask what is the capital, income, employment, price level, etc., of a society sharply divided into non-communicating sectors. Just as words can be spelt, but letters of the alphabet cannot be spelt, not because it is very difficult but because it is an improper request,[4] so asking questions about certain aggregates commonly used in advanced industrial countries in the context of underdeveloped

---

[1] I am aware that I shut my eyes to these problems in the 'Sketch of a Model of Development' (see pp. 63 ff. below).

[2] 'It has been estimated that the combined effect of malnutrition and ill-health in Ecuador, for example, reduces the average worker's production to 48 per cent of his potential capacity, as opposed to 93 per cent in the United States (see Hector Correa, *The Economics of Human Resources* (Den Haag: Drukkerij Pasmans, 1962) p. 44).' – Anthony Bottomley, *Economic Journal* (Mar 1964) n. 2 p. 233.

[3] Gilbert Ryle, *The Concept of Mind* (London, 1949), pp. 17 and 168.

[4] Op. cit., p. 206.

countries, is improper. The solution of a jigsaw puzzle consists in putting each piece where it belongs, not in lumping them together arbitrarily.

4. Illegitimate isolation

The converse of misplaced aggregation, but related to one-factor analysis, which is a particular manifestation of it, is the bias of illegitimate isolation. It consists in assigning the role of sufficient condition to what may or may not be one of several necessary conditions of development. If a component is illegitimately isolated from its necessary complements, and then aggregated with others similarly isolated, we get a combination of misplaced aggregation and illegitimate isolation. The case can be illustrated by successive missions going to a country. The first says entrepreneurial *incentives* are inadequate, and if we nurse these by *low taxes*, resources will soon become available. The next goes and says *resources* are the bottleneck and decisions will soon come forth if we set free resources by *high taxation* to generate a large budget surplus. But the correct policy would be high taxation of certain incomes and property, perhaps land, combined with generous investment allowances and incentives where these yield results. The division should not be resources *versus* incentives, but certain incentives combined with certain resources.

Education, which is now often advocated as a panacea, may simply result in a group of educated unemployed and unemployables, as in India. Equipment may lie unused and unmaintained. Irrigation water flows unused and reservoirs are silting, because 'investment' has not been co-ordinated with the right kind of education, land reform and civil service reform. The price we pay for misplaced aggregation and illegitimate isolation is wasted resources and possibly hardened resistance to and growing cynicism about the process of development.

The problem is illustrated in Table 5.1. The horizontal groupings indicate the conventional Western categories of thought and, if applied to underdeveloped countries, misplaced aggregation; the vertical groupings indicate 'packages' relevant to development and, if torn from their vertical links, illegitimate isolation. Expenditure on birth control, like expenditure on health and teachers' salaries, is normally classified as consumption. But in conjunction with the construction of clinics and schools and the reform of the administrative system, it is in many societies the most important single *per caput* income-raising force. Much of the potential benefit of irrigation schemes is wasted because schistosomiasis is spread and reduces human efficiency, or because land ownership systems deprive peasants

TABLE 5.1
Aggregation and Isolation 1

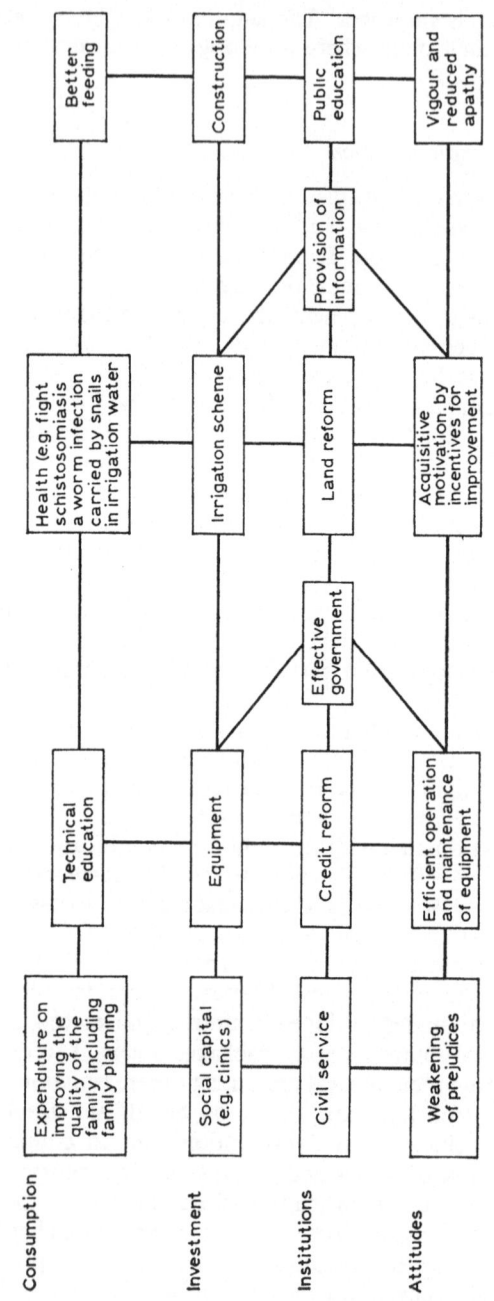

of both incentives and opportunities to make use of the water even if they wanted to raise yield. The vertical groupings represent blocks of sufficient conditions for accelerated development, whilst the horizontal groupings apply the false Western categories according to which institutions and attitudes are given (Liberalism) or adjusted to the required extent (Marxism), consumption is current enjoyment which does not contribute to higher production later, and investment is the strategic instrument to raise output and income.

Table 5.2 illustrates the misplaced aggregation of all forms of education and the illegitimate isolation of certain forms (agronomy, engineering) from the necessary equipment which is required to embody the knowledge and apply the training.

TABLE 5.2

Aggregation and Isolation 2

Education in				Investment in human beings
Sanscrit	Law·	Agronomy	Engineering	

Investment in				Investment in physical assets
Palaces	Embassies	Agricultural implements	Industrial equipment	

An illustration of a shift from a horizontal to a vertical alignment can be found in the recently popular notion of technical knowledge embodied in new equipment. In the old framework, 'the state of the arts' or technical and managerial knowledge were separated from physical equipment. In the new models, knowledge is infused through equipment and the productivity of the total stock of equipment is a function of its age composition.

II. SOCIOLOGY OF KNOWLEDGE

It is not enough to point to biases, particularly if they are so plain. The interesting question is, how is it that they have such a strong grip on thought, in spite of their obvious faults? This is a question in the sociology of knowledge, or rather the sociology of ignorance or of false belief. It is a strange fact that social scientists, whose special interest is social reality, are exceedingly naïve when it comes to examining the social origins of their own theories and models. We investigate workers, priests, prostitutes, entrepreneurs, soldiers, politicians, and analyse the social roots of their behaviour. But rarely do we examine the social determination of our own thought. It is as if a physician were able and ready to cure others but unwilling or incapable of healing himself.

There are perhaps six reasons, not of equal importance, why these models have such a strong hold on our thought and are even more deep-rooted in the discussion in underdeveloped countries.

1. Western economics has a high prestige value. With its 'Effects', 'Processes' and 'Mechanisms', it is admired in underdeveloped countries, and the highest honours in the profession go to those who work on the most esoteric mathematical problems. Economists from underdeveloped countries write about the problems that arise when all wants will be satisfied, and turnpikes, to them, often do not mean roads but von Neumann–Dorfman–Solow–Samuelson growth paths.

2. Perhaps the above is a caricature, but the employment prospects of economists depend upon their rating by the standards evolved by Western economics, and to forge into unorthodox explorations can be too risky for a young man who has to make his career. As a result, the rumbles of discontent with established categories of thought do not come from the underdeveloped countries which often are *'plus royaliste que le roi'*, but from economists in the West. Dudley Seers has mapped out a cycle of economic theories:[1] classical consolidation maintains a powerful grip in spite of accumulating evidence against it. Thus economists refused to permit underemployment equilibrium into their analysis in spite of the plain facts around them. An underworld of Hobson, Gesell, Major Douglas pointed out the obvious, but were dismissed as cranks. Although their instincts were right, they did not formulate them in an alternative rigorous model. Then Keynes replaced the old orthodoxy by a new one, articulating clearly the feelings of the underworld, which now became respectable, because the inadequacies of one model were shown up by a different model. It may be that underdeveloped economics is now, as Dudley Seers suggests, in its Hobson–Gesell phase, the underworld worthily represented by Myrdal, Prebisch, Singer and Co. Will there, or can there, be a Keynes to articulate the instincts which, as yet, have not found coherent expression?

3. A third reason is that attitudes and institutions can, as we have

---

[1] 'The Limitations of the Special Case', *Bulletin of the Oxford University Institute of Statistics* (May 1963), reprinted in *The Teaching of Development Economics*, ed. K. Martin and J. Knapp (London, 1967).

seen, legitimately be separated in advanced Western countries. These habits are transferred to underdeveloped countries. Developed markets, the dissemination of information, an educated labour force, transport and power facilities, flexibility of resources, an honest and efficient Civil Service, effective tax legislation and tax collection, all make it legitimate to assume a hinterland adapted to the conduct of economic activities and suited for conceptual aggregation.

4. Fourthly, 'economic facts' are *rightly* considered more accessible to investigation and quantification than 'non-economic facts'. It is easier to calculate how much different irrigation works will cost than to calculate how effectively peasants will use and maintain them. It is easier to specify the costs of a pump or a steel mill than to predict how effectively it will be used, how long it will take to build, and what people will learn from using it. It is easier to say how much contraceptives cost than to say how human beings can be changed to wish to use them.

5. Fifthly, 'economic quantities' are *wrongly* thought to be more objective than non-economic considerations. The economic calculus is often contrasted with moral and political choices. It is now well known that this view is false and that all economic choices presuppose moral and political valuations. The weighting system by which a heterogeneous collection of goods and services is made homogeneous and comparable with other collections, and on which 'economic' choices are based, expresses social valuations of the relative social significance of different goods and services. If these comparisons pretend to be 'objective', the underlying valuations are tacit (such as the acceptance of a given income distribution implied in freely determined market prices as guides to income distribution) and therefore *less* objective than choices based on explicit valuations.

The difficulty is acknowledged but not overcome by the employment of concepts such as 'accounting prices' or 'shadow prices'. Jan Tinbergen defines these as the 'intrinsic values that would prevail if (i) the investment pattern under discussion were actually carried out, and (ii) equilibrium existed on the markets . . .'.[1] Although the concept is useful in bringing out the arbitrary nature of actual market prices as a basis for planning, it is misleading because it begs a number of questions and re-creates a spurious impression of objectivity. In particular, it begs the question of equilibrium in other markets and the question of the length of the time period over which equilibrium is assumed: is it before the investment projects are carried out, while they are under construction or after they have been finished? It also fails to distinguish sufficiently clearly between the use of prices as the basis for taking decisions as to the allocation of scarce resources and

[1] Jan Tinbergen, *The Design of Development* (Baltimore, 1958) p. 39.

their use as incentives and deterrents. And finally it fails to bring out the need to postulate an income distribution and social objectives *before* the appropriate equilibrium prices can be determined.

Though logically fallacious, this type of reasoning, which attempts to substitute 'objective' criteria for political choices, provides an intellectual escape mechanism from difficult or unpleasant political decisions.

6. The intellectual escape mechanism is powerfully supported by a moral and political escape mechanism. Strong obstacles amongst those whose activities are planned, and serious inhibitions in the minds and hearts of the planners, who are themselves part and parcel of the society which they intend to reform, stand in the way of economic development. Land reform may be opposed and may hurt one's cousins and friends. To sack corrupt officials may be disloyal and may incur wrath. To change one's own mind and heart may involve a more radical conversion than is humanly possible. In view of these difficulties, an easy escape is offered. Concentrate on financial expenditure, select variables that hurt least and side-step the crucial decisions! Soft handling, reluctance to use force, can then be rationalised as the democratic process, reinforced by disparaging allusions to colonial oppression and Soviet labour camps. Thus economic models support the forces of resistance to change. Much easier to say money spent on investment or on education yields high returns than to carry out a land reform, impose an effective tax system or clean up public administration.

We have already seen how Marxism, with its diametrically opposed premisses, leads to very similar conclusions. Although attitudes and institutions here are not parameters but dependent variables, they adjust to the required extent. Planning and social engineering are futile or unnecessary. Marxists have often been very naïve about the problem of planning. Marxist theory has, ironically, a strong *laissez-faire* streak. But Soviet practice diverges substantially from this theory. Soviet Plans did not just stress the accumulation of capital. The savings *squeeze* (inferred from a model of capital accumulation) was reinforced by a consumption *twist*. It was clearly seen in practice, though not in theory, that the promotion of certain forms of consumption, in particular better feeding of workers, improving their health and literacy, but keeping down house building, can accelerate development.

Again, Japanese and German development in the nineteenth century started with a thorough reform of attitudes and institutions. One wonders what would have happened if Japan and Germany had then had the benefit of the advice of modern economists. But perhaps we are too presumptuous in our claims for the influence of economics. Economics is possibly just a modern theology. Perhaps only a small part of the iceberg – the planning ideology – is visible above the water, while the larger part of the actual practice of planning is carried on sensibly, paying attention to the right combination, co-ordination and timing of policies, without heeding distinctions between 'economic' and 'non-economic' variables. This conclusion, though pessimistic from the point of view of the significance of economics, would be optimistic from the point of view of development. But one cannot help expressing a faith, perhaps irrationally, in the value of rationality and the contribution that an economic theory which is realistic, relevant and applicable could and should make to effective planning for development.

A sketch of a model of development

The following sketch outlines a possibly fruitful approach to the analysis of underdevelopment and to the policy of planning for development. The model is essentially that used by Mr Kaldor to analyse the trade cycle[1] and by Professor Trevor Swan to illustrate mutual causation between White prejudices against Negroes and Negro standards of living. This note follows closely Professor Swan's article.[2] Cumulative processes have been analysed by Wicksell and have been emphasised in various contexts by Myrdal.

In Fig. 5.1 we trace on the horizontal axis an index of the level of economic development and on the vertical axis an index of the forces that raise the level of development. A good index of economic development has not yet been designed and we have therefore recourse to income per head as a rough-and-ready index. There are, as we have indicated, numerous difficulties both in giving precise meaning to *per caput* income and in using this as an index of development. The average may conceal wide dispersions; a rise in income per head may be due to improved terms of trade, the benefit of which accrues to a small enclave, etc. But it will do for the moment, if we bear in mind its limitations.

The index of the income-raising forces is even more difficult to devise. Investment, education, market size, economies of scale, human attitudes to growth and change and, above all, family limitation, may all contribute to development if applied in conjunction with the appropriate measures. We shall specify some of these forces later. We require an independent measure for each of these forces separately and we can then combine them, weighting each by their respective

[1] *Economic Journal* (1940).
[2] *Economic Record* (1962). See also H. Leibenstein, *Economic Backwardness and Economic Growth* (New York, 1957), chapters 3 and 8.

contributions to output and income. The situation would be exactly like that of different inputs and their contribution to increases in output. Ideally, one would want not a combined index but separate relations, connecting each of the forces both to its effects on income and to other forces. In order to simplify such *n*-dimensional functions and illustrate them on a two-dimensional diagram, we assume the possibility of such an index. The problem is further complicated by the fact that there are income-*depressing* forces, above all a high rate of population growth, but also various resistances to development: inertia, prejudice, etc. Ideally, the index should be an index of the excess of raisihg over depressing forces, i.e. it should be *net*. There would then be a zero point, below which the income-depressing forces would prevail. But this raises a further difficulty. The index of the forces should be related not to the level of income, but to the (positive or negative) *rate of growth* of income, while it is the *level* of income which determines the forces. The model would be exactly parallel to the accelerator-multiplier model.[1] But for our purposes we regard the income level determined by the income-raising forces as an average over the planning period.

It may well be that these difficulties are fatal and that no such index can be constructed. But let us assume that it is possible to devise an index of the net forces raising income per head which does not use shares of income generation as weights.

[1] The path taken by income if the Forces $F = f(Y)$ and $\frac{dY}{dt} = \phi(F)$ can be illustrated on the following diagram. Income at time t_0 is at A_0; this income determines the level of Forces at B_0 which in turn determine the increase in income in the next period at C_0. OD_0 is added to A_0 after a period at t_1 (so that $A_1E = D_0O$) and the same process is repeated from A_1.

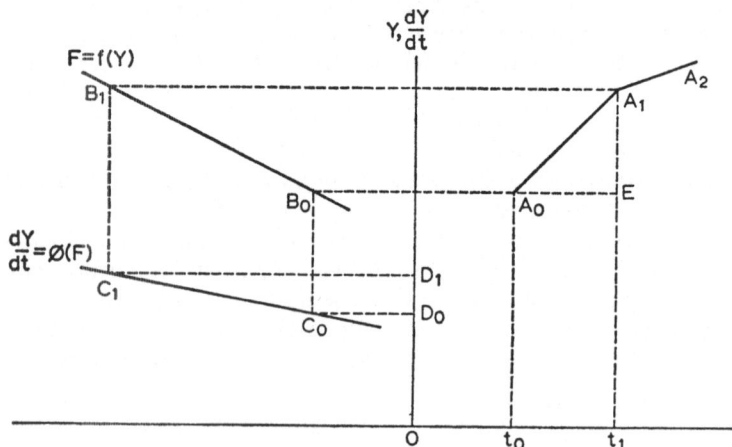

We next note that the Income-Raising Forces and Income per Head interact: there is a feedback. The higher is Income per Head (Y), the stronger will tend to be the Income-per-Head-Raising Forces (F), and the higher the Forces, the higher will tend to be Income per Head. The former relation may be due to the ability to extract a larger savings and investment ratio, the existence of a larger market with economies of scale, a weakening of tradition, improved education, etc. Obviously, the higher the level of F the higher will be Y.

The fact that there is interaction (mutual causation, feedback) between F and Y is not sufficient to produce instability, although, in certain conditions, it can have snowball effects (cumulative processes). If the coefficients are as illustrated in Fig. 5.1, this will be the case. At any point to the left of the line F→Y (showing the level of Income as a function of the Forces) Income will be less than that generated by the Forces, and the Forces will tend to raise Income. At any point to the right, Income will be larger than that which is generated by the Forces and they will tend to lower Income.

At any point above the line Y→F (showing the Forces as a function

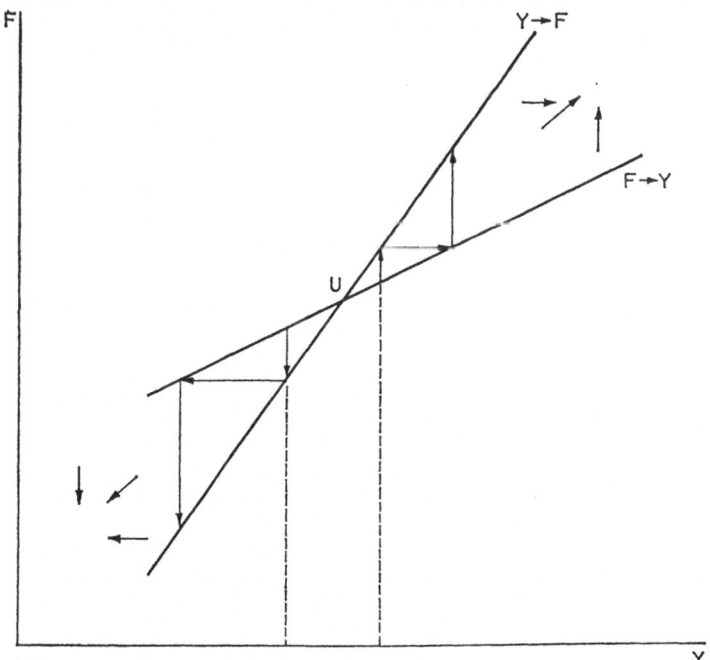

Fig. 5.1
Linear interdependence: cumulative movements

of Income) the Forces are greater than is warranted by the Income level and will therefore contract. At any point below, the Forces will expand. These causal relations are clearly subject to time-lags. The lines show the long-run static relationships towards which the values will tend to move. The point of intersection U in Fig. 5.1 is a point of unstable equilibrium. The smallest deviation sparks off a vicious or a virtuous circle.

In Fig. 5.2 we have reduced the response coefficients of both functions so as to produce a stable equilibrium at S, in spite of mutual causation. The Forces are less responsive to Income and Income is less responsive to the Forces and a disturbance will not cause a permanent alteration. In order to make interaction yield cumulation, the response coefficients must be above certain critical values. This explains why, in spite of the ubiquity of interdependence in social life, development (or decay) is a rare phenomenon. While this is a pessimistic conclusion for those who hope for cumulative processes wherever there is interdependence, it opens a wider range of policies to planners.

There are important differences between a situation as depicted

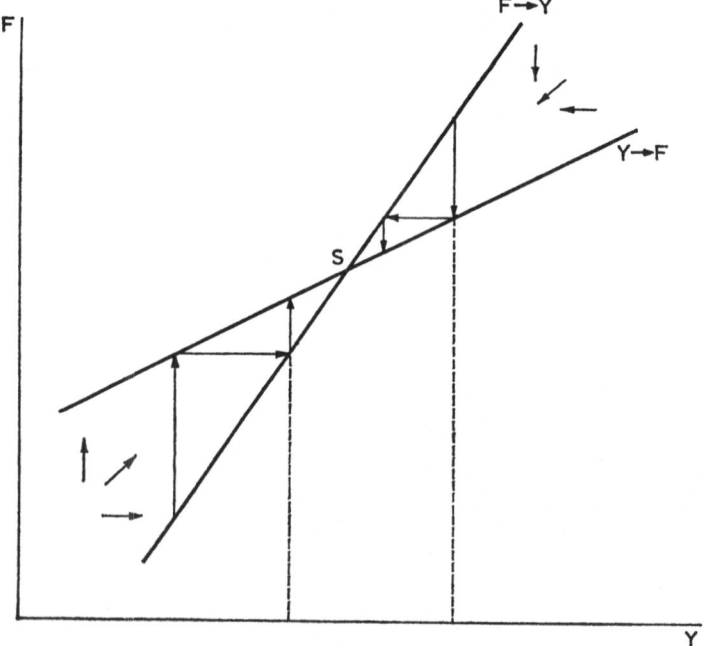

Fig. 5.2
Linear interdependence: stability

in Fig. 5.1 and Fig. 5.2 according to whether we apply a once-for-all push (say a single injection of foreign aid) or a sustained development effort (say an annually recurrent sum of aid). In unstable equilibrium (Fig. 5.1) there is no difference between these two policies. Either will induce development. But in stable equilibrium (Fig. 5.2) a once-for-all push will not alter the final position of the system, whereas a sustained effort of a given size will be exactly like the multiplier process: the process will converge towards a higher new equilibrium position which will be a multiple of the size of the sustained effort.

We know from the most casual observations that neither the stability of Fig. 5.2 nor the instability of Fig. 5.1 corresponds to reality and, like the archetypal model of Kaldor and Swan, we must postulate non-linearity and multiple equilibria as in Fig. 5.3. S_1 and S_2 are points of stable, U of unstable equilibrium. It is not difficult to think of reasons why the sensitivity of both functions should be low for both low and high values, and high for intermediate values. At low levels Y will not have much effect on F because tradition has a strong hold, the forces of resistance are strong, it will be difficult to squeeze out even a moderate investment ratio, the market will be small, ignorance and imperfections will prevail, etc. F in turn will have small effects on Y because population growth will wipe out a large part of any increase in income per head. Similarly, one may speculate that, at high values, people get tired of the effort required by growth, the third generation has less vigour, opposition and destructive criticisms grow. One could build a philosophy of history upon the values of these functions. For intermediate values responsiveness will be high, both because the obstacles to development will

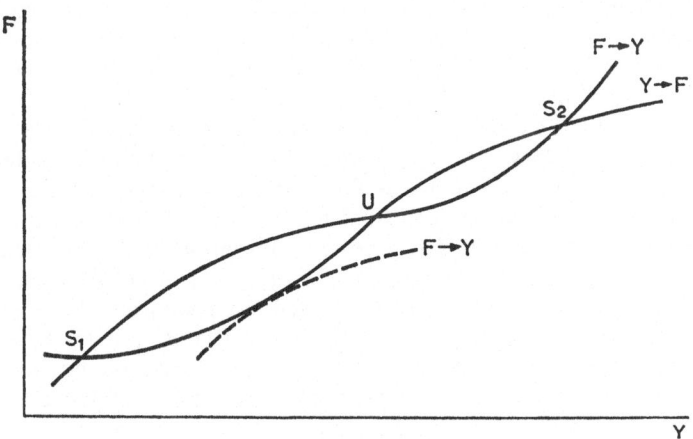

Fig. 5.3
Non-linear interdependence

have been overcome successfully, particularly population pressure, and because the higher income level makes it much easier to do all kinds of things conducive to faster development.

Planners now have a choice between three types of policy.

(a) They may go for the 'Big Push', or the 'Critical Minimum Effort', or rev up to 'Take-Off Speed'. This means accepting the response coefficients and raising the system from S_1 to just above U. Beyond that they can rely on automatic development.

(b) They may attempt to shift the curves to tangency. They can either lower the $F \rightarrow Y$ curve (so that for any given level of the Forces the resulting income will be higher) or raise the $Y \rightarrow F$ curve (so that for any given level of Income the resulting Forces will be higher).

(c) Finally they may attempt to change the relative slopes of the curves, thus turning S_1 into an unstable equilibrium, though they must also take care to avoid a downward slide.

An illustration of (a) would be a large and long industrialisation programme, combined with improvements in health and education, as Russia experienced under Stalin. An illustration of (b) would be fairly simple measures such as an effective land reform or the establishment of an effective tax system, which, in Argentina or Chile, might be quite sufficient to induce growth. Illustrations of (c) are more difficult to think of, although the Argentine case might do, where Peron may have changed the slopes of the curve so as to produce decay.

As for historical explanation, the length of the distance between S_1 and U explains why the same events have different consequences in different historical contexts. At certain times, in certain places, quite small events spark off revolutionary sequences. At other times and places, the same events are swallowed up by the big waves of history. It explains why, sometimes, small causes have large effects, while at other times large causes are required to produce these same effects: why history sometimes seems like a thick syrup and at others like a plaything of accidents. A Polish inventor invented machinery for weaving cloth in the twelfth century and was hanged for threatening the established order. The same invention in the eighteenth century triggered off the Industrial Revolution. Hero of Alexandria, and before him Ctesibius, had invented the piston and the steam engine and other sophisticated mechanical devices. But these were used to enable the priesthood of Alexandria to impose on the simple-minded. Hydraulic bellows operated by the doors of the temple sounded a fanfare of trumpets whenever a worshipper entered. Another device, fixed below the altar, operated levers which led to the holy shrine. The altar stone was heated during sacrificial burning, the air below expanded, pressed on the lever and opened the door, revealing the image of God. This could be carefully timed according to the amount of heat generated on the altar. The knowledge of electricity and steam power was used, not to move the wheels of industry, but the minds of men, in a direction inimical to development.[1] S_1 and U in those constellations were far apart. In eighteenth-century England they were close together.

The task begins when we attempt to specify and to construct an independent index for the income-raising and income-depressing forces and to analyse their interaction. The list in Chapter 3, pp. 33–5, contains a possible way of classifying these forces, although no attempt is made to indicate the numerous possible links between them. A few positive and negative feedbacks can be indicated by way of illustration.

Positive feedback

1. Higher income – higher savings/income ratio – higher investment/income ratio – higher income.
2. Higher income – better health – greater vigour and ability to sustain work – higher income.
3. Higher income – greater economies of scale – higher production – higher productivity – higher income.
4. Higher income – stable government – increased political and business confidence – greater national solidarity – higher income.
5. Higher income – reduced caste prejudice – less corruption – better administration – higher income.

Negative feedback

1. Higher income – faster population growth through reduced death rates – reduced income per head.
2. Higher income – more change – stronger resistance to change – reduced income.
3. Higher income – faster population growth – employment of more labour-intensive techniques with low learning content – reduced rate of growth of income per head.
4. Higher income – faster population growth – work-spreading habits and attitudes both among employers and employees:

[1] The story of a premature innovator in ancient Rome, confronted with an Emperor reluctant to apply these innovations and aware of some of the obstacles, is told by William Golding in his story 'Envoy Extraordinary'.

premium on preserving low productivity ways lest someone loses his job: obstacles to innovation – reduced growth rate.

5. Higher income – higher unemployment – introduction of capital-intensive production methods – greater social prestige attached to better off not doing manual work but leaving it to the poor – reinforcement of attitudes that despise manual work and attach low social prestige to it – reduced growth.

It might be useful to end this chapter by specifying in what respects we should particularly beware of possible traps in established doctrines and in what ways these can be either improved or replaced. In addition to the already discussed problems of misplaced aggregation and illegitimate isolation, one might consider the following points.

1. Be on guard against assuming continuous and smooth functions. Discontinuities and kinks may occur in relationships such as capital coefficients, supply of effort, production functions, foreign trade, etc. Consider Indivisibilities and Complementarities.

2. Be not content with less than at least two sectors where inter-sectoral relations are crucial to a problem. Clearly, the marginal returns from disaggregation decline and may become negative, but Keynesian aggregation too is often misleading.

3. Consider the implications of unstable equilibria, whether static or dynamic. Cumulative processes and polarisation are not as exceptional as the concentration on stable equilibrium suggests.

4. Include, where necessary, variables which are exogenous in advanced countries, as dependent variables. Examples are administration, political stability, acquisitive motivation, population growth, technical progress.

5. Keep in mind the specific limitations of the free market system as a guide to certain important decisions. Distinguish clearly between the free market system and price policies. The latter are an instrument of planning.

6. Beware of abstracting from time: the phasing of projects, the time-flow of consumption, the effects on learning are crucial.

7. Be content to provide (at least initially) *sufficient* conditions for certain sequences rather than full *explanations*. Discard these sufficient conditions only if they are contradicted by observations.

6 A Critique of the 'Capital/Output Ratio' and its Application to Development Planning[1]

Introduction

THERE is one type of model that dominates the literature and the plans. This is the Harrod-Domar model and its numerous variations. In this, the strategic variables that are selected are aggregates such as employment, investment and output. But instead of the neo-classical assumption of perfect substitutability of capital for labour, the starting point is the assumption of fixed technical or behavioural coefficients, so that aggregate output is related to the stock of capital by the capital/output ratio, otherwise known as the capital coefficient. This is the salient feature added by the Harrod-Domar model to the Keynesian short-period theory of employment. The crucial role, in economic theory and planning, of the 'capital/output ratio' is well brought out in an article by an Indian writer:

> If there is one concept that has dominated recent discussions on growth theory and development planning, it is that of the capital-output ratio, or the capital-coefficient as it is sometimes called. It has been extensively used in various growth models, e.g., those of Harrod, Domar, Kaldor, and Mahalanobis, and it has also helped the formulation of our First and Second Five Year Plans.[2]

---

[1] O. Braun, W. Eltis, K. Griffin, G. Mathur, S. R. Merrett, J. M. Montias, G. Ohlin, L. Pasinetti and A. K. Sen contributed very helpful comments to earlier drafts of this paper.

[2] Pankaj Kumar Sen, 'Use of the Capital-Output Ratio in Economic Planning', *The Indian Economic Review*, v 1 (Feb 1960) 23. See also the report of a group of experts: 'After estimating the current rate of savings, the *crucial* question will be what amount of net national output can be expected from the investment to be made on the basis of the estimated savings. A number of studies have been made

Another approach, less pertinent to problems of economic planning in South Asia, uses a Cobb-Douglas production function of the form $Y = aK^\beta L^\alpha$ where K and L are the quantities of capital and labour, respectively, and a, α, β are assumed constants, where $(\alpha + \beta)$ may equal, exceed, or be less than 1, according to whether constant, increasing or decreasing returns to scale are assumed. In this kind of approach there are also certain difficulties, such as how to treat changes in the *quality* of capital and labour, how to incorporate *changes* in knowledge and the passage of *time*, and how to determine the magnitude of the *constants*. The capital/output ratio in this formulation is not a determining variable, but a resultant of the changes in K and L as well as in α and β. While one can therefore easily deduce average and marginal capital/output ratios from the production function, these are endogenous variables, not determinants as they are in the Harrod-Domar analysis.[1] Since the plans are concerned primarily with the capital/output ratio as a strategic relationship in determining the rate of growth, we can in our discussion largely

---

on the amount of capital required to increase output by one unit per annum in each sector of economy and for a national economy as a whole. This amount is called the "capital-output ratio", or "capital coefficient".' United Nations, *Programming Techniques for Economic Development: With special reference to Asia and the Far East*, Report by a group of experts (Bangkok, 1960, pp. 10–11).

And: 'The rate of economic growth may be analytically considered as being a function of two factors, (a) the rate of capital formation and (b) the capital/output ratio: accordingly development policies may be described as aiming to increase the former, reduce the latter, or do both.' UN, ECAFE, 'Economic Development and Planning in Asia and the Far East', *Economic Bulletin for Asia and the Far East*, VI 3 (Nov 1955) (Bangkok, 1955) 25–6.

Lewis's book *The Theory of Economic Growth*, especially the chapter on capital, illustrates the central position of this concept together with that of the savings ratio: 'The central problem in the theory of economic growth is to understand the process by which a community is converted from being a 5 per cent to a 12 per cent saver – with all the changes in attitudes, in institutions and in techniques which accompany this conversion.' W. Arthur Lewis, *The Theory of Economic Growth* (London: Allen & Unwin, 1955) pp. 225–6. This is based on a required growth rate for national income of approximately 3 per cent and a capital/output ratio of approximately 4.

[1] In an article entitled 'The Production Function in Allocation and Growth: A Synthesis', *American Economic Review*, LII 5 (Dec 1962) 995–1022, Marvin Frankel shows how, mathematically, a micro-economic Cobb-Douglas function for each individual firm can be combined with a macro-economic Harrod-Domar function. Production in the enterprise is governed by a function of the form $P_i = aHK^\beta_i L^\alpha_i$ where H is called the 'development modifier', a parameter for the enterprise but a dependent variable if all enterprises expand together. If $H = (K/L)^\gamma$ the aggregate production function is $P = a(K/L)^\gamma K^\beta L^\alpha$; and if $\gamma = \alpha$ and $(\alpha + \beta) = 1$, it reduces to $P = aK$, the Harrod-Domar relation. In terms of our Fig. 6.2 (below, Section 5), each individual enterprise believes it moves along a diminishing returns curve, but if all grow together they move up the straight line.

ignore the Cobb-Douglas production function. Some of the criticisms would, however, apply to any of the traditional notions of a 'production function'.[1]

A critical analysis of the capital/output ratio would examine:

(a) its meaning and measurement;
(b) its use in planning or in providing explanations, prognoses, or predictions of development;
(c) the meaning and validity of its use as a criterion for the allocation of capital, as exemplified by the phrases: 'minimize the capital/output ratio', 'maximise the reciprocal of the *social* marginal capital/output ratio', or 'allow for the fact that the capital/output and the savings ratios are interdependent'.

Our discussion is concerned with (a) and (b), but has implications for (c). Criticism of the ratio may be *transcendental* or *immanent*; that is, the assumptions on which it rests may be examined in terms of the logic of their adequacy to reality; or we may accept the assumptions, and consider particular ambiguities, inconsistencies and difficulties within this framework. A transcendental critique shows that the ratio displays four systematic biases: adapted *ceteris paribus* or automatic *mutatis mutandis*, one factor analysis, misplaced aggregation and illegitimate isolation.[2]

Misplaced aggregation and illegitimate isolation go hand in hand when differentiated items are aggregated and the components are separated from their supplementary and complementary conditions. In the capital/output model all forms of capital are aggregated and each piece of construction and equipment is isolated from (a) its specific relation to other pieces of construction and equipment; (b) other influences, such as levels of living (including facilities for acquiring skills), human attitudes, and social institutions; and (c) policies directed at other conditions. Yet all three factors crucially affect the contribution to output of the particular piece of investment.

Illegitimate isolation is a specific manifestation of the assumption that all other conditions remain constant and adapted to development. For if conditions are assumed to be constant whose change is either necessary to the required results or makes an important difference in their direction, speed and size, there has been illegitimate abstraction.

---

[1] After a brief discussion of the use of this type of production function in *forecasting* (not planning) growth in *advanced countries* (not in underdeveloped countries, where statistics are vastly inferior), Otto Eckstein concludes: 'Since aggregate production functions so far have not yielded reliable estimates of the relationship between investment and growth, one must try other methods.' ('Capital Theory and Some Theoretical Problems in Development Planning', *American Economic Review, Papers and Proceedings*, LI 2 (May 1961) p. 98.)

[2] See Chapter 5.

If automatic *mutatis mutandis* is relied on, so that it is assumed that these other conditions will change but in such a way that they will always be automatically adapted, there is no isolation. But, as we have seen, this assumption must be questioned on both empirical and logical grounds. Empirically we know that in underdeveloped countries conditions are not automatically adapted in the required fashion. Logically, the specific contribution of the variables under consideration remains indeterminate if we always keep in the pack a joker that can take all tricks. If we have an unspecified combination of the two assumptions, both illegitimate isolation and indeterminacy are present. It is the purpose of both the *ceteris paribus* and the *mutatis mutandis* assumptions to isolate the study of the causal relationship between capital input and aggregate output. This approach introduces the bias that capital is the only, or the main, source of development in underdeveloped countries. The separation of capital from certain components in the level of living that affect labour input and labour efficiency, and from attitudes and institutions crucial for effective capital use, is one of the main forms of illegitimate isolation.

The effects of plant and equipment on output depend not only on where and how the investment occurs but also on what other policies that affect levels of living, attitudes and institutions are pursued. In the underdeveloped countries the two last-named conditions cannot be regarded either as already adapted to development or as automatically adaptable through investment. The effects of a development plan with a given amount of investment will differ greatly according to what policies with regard to attitudes and institutions are pursued in conjunction with the investment.

Moreover, illegitimate isolation is implicit in aggregation if the complementarities between the components of the aggregate are ignored. The output effects of one investment project depend on other investment projects that are embarked on either simultaneously or in sequence as phases of a co-ordinated programme. In an economy where each project is infinitesimally small and can profit from adapted attitudes and institutions, aggregation irrespective of composition may be legitimate. But in underdeveloped countries investment projects are large, in relation to both the existing stock of that type of capital and annual additions to it. The resulting output varies sharply according to the availability of complementary supplies, such as appropriate construction elsewhere and other pieces of equipment, and the existence of appropriate demand. It is then entirely misleading to treat 'capital' as a homogeneous quantity. It is a heterogeneous collection of specific bits and pieces that have to be fitted together.

Much investment, particularly public investment – in highways, power stations, ports, railways, workers' houses – provides opportunities and possibly incentives for consequential output-generating investment. This, indeed, is one of the reasons for carrying out public investment, which often seems unlikely to recover its costs by profits. But many forms of private investment are also of this nature. The short-term and sectoral capital/output ratio of a given project may be high, but the long-term ratio may be much lower, if it can be calculated at all. It will depend on fuller utilisation of the project's own capacity and the capacities of other already existing enterprises and also on the seizure of consequential investment opportunities and the output generation to which these give rise.[1] If, on the other hand, it turns out that operating, maintenance and supervision costs are unexpectedly high or that the expected complementary investment is not forthcoming, the long-term ratio, which includes external effects on other projects, will be high or may rise. Certain projects, such as improvements in cultivation methods, may themselves require little capital, but may require complementary investment in transport, power, storage and other facilities. In either case, it is certainly misleading to pay attention only to the initial investment and its direc effects.

If a series of investment projects are interrelated, either sectorally or temporally, each depending on the others for its success, the very notion of a capital/output ratio for any one of them in isolation becomes as meaningless as the question, What is the contribution of the first violin to the Ninth Symphony?[2] It is the composition and the relationship of the parts that matter in appraising the result. Misplaced aggregation and illegitimate isolation conceal this. The problem is like that of putting the pieces of a jigsaw puzzle together. It is the placement of the pieces in relation to each other that matters, not the display of any single piece (illegitimate isolation), nor the counting of the total number of pieces thrown together at random (misplaced aggregation).

If changes in attitudes and institutions are taken into account in appraising capital projects, some projects are seen to be more productive than others not only, and often not primarily, because of their physical effectiveness but also because of their impact on decision-taking, incentives to entrepreneurial or political action,

[1] Changes in utilisation are discussed in Section 9 below. The creation of investment opportunities falls outside the scope of the normal assumptions and embraces variables normally assumed constant and adapted or adaptable.

[2] Except in a situation of general equilibrium, in which a capital/output ratio can be attributed to each industry on the assumption that the required adjustments are made in all other industries.

attitudes towards work and venture, and the formation, reforms or destruction of habits, traditions, customs and aspirations of workers and entrepreneurs. The application of improved techniques is in many ways related to investment. Improving levels of living, particularly levels of nutrition, health and education, will raise output. The conclusion is that unless supplementary and consequential actions are taken on a wide front, an investment project may misfire; and in spite of a positive direct flow of production from it, the ratio – including effects on other projects and enterprises and, often, private and public actions – may rise to infinity or become negative for capital increases.[1] The success and effectiveness of investment in contributing to the growth of output depend not only on its being an addition to an aggregate 'stock of capital' but on its direction (neglected by aggregation), its composition, and the present and future complementary policies with which it is packaged (neglected by isolation).

An appendix at the end of this chapter compares briefly the different ways in which the concept is used in the plans of the countries of South Asia and its estimated values. The uselessness of this concept is confirmed by the large differences between anticipated and actual coefficients and between the coefficients in different countries and at different times. Because of the widespread use of the capital/output ratio and its strong grip on habits of thinking in the field of development planning, we consider a detailed immanent criticism justified, in spite of the transcendental criticisms we have advanced. Experience shows that exposure of the inadequacy of the assumptions on which a model is based is rarely convincing. Facts rarely refute theories. The transcendental criticism therefore has to be complemented by criticism that accepts the assumptions and exposes logical difficulties and weaknesses within the model.

Despite the ambiguities and confusions to which the use of these procedures has given rise, let us now assume, for the sake of the argument in this part, that they are legitimate. We therefore assume that attitudes, institutions, and policies are constant, that changes in levels of living have no effect on output, and that secondary *dynamic* effects on other investments can be ignored. Aside from these assumptions, both the theoretical master model and the assumption of a constant ratio have certain faults that make them particularly

---

[1] It should be noted that not all negative *ex post* incremental 'capital/output ratios' indicate waste. It may be sensible to modernise and re-equip an industry, the demand for whose product is falling. Capital expenditure may reduce costs per unit of output, while output is reduced. Simple-minded students of the capital/output ratio might conclude that output could be raised by reducing the stock of capital. See Section 4 below.

misleading when applied to the problems of development in under-developed countries.

1. The master model[1]

Let Y be income (or output),
   S savings and
   I investment.
Define

$$s = \frac{S}{Y} \text{ (the savings ratio)}$$

$$k = \frac{I}{\Delta Y} \text{ (the } ceteris\ paribus \text{ investment/incremental output or the incremental capital/output ratio)}$$

$$g = \frac{\Delta Y}{Y} \text{ (the rate of growth of income or output)}$$

[1] A clear statement of the assumption of a constant capital/output ratio can be found in Gustav Cassel's *Theoretische Sozialökonomie*, published in 1922. The quotation following is from the English translation by Joseph McCabe:

'The meaning of the continuous formation of capital is seen most clearly in the evenly progressive economy. This may now be defined in more general terms. In the monetary economy economic progress, assuming unaltered prices, can be measured by the increase of the abstract total capital, and may be regarded as uniform when this capital increases annually by a definite and invariable percentage. Let us call this capital C, and suppose that C increases annually by p per cent, p being constant. This increase of capital is, as we have seen, only possible on condition that there is a certain amount of saving. Let us call the annual income I, and suppose that annually the proportion $1/s$ – in absolute amount I/s – is saved. We will call this quotient which arithmetically expresses the community's thrift, the "degree of saving". Clearly $I/s = (p/100)C$, and consequently $I = (sp/100)C$. If we further suppose that the degree of saving $1/s$, or the relative saving of the community, is constant, which clearly harmonises best with our assumption of an even development, we find that the total income is in an invariable ratio to the total capital. From this we get the important principle that in the evenly progressive economy *the income increases in the same percentage as the capital.* This principle is approximately correct for every economy if we take long periods into consideration. It is only during periods of transition that there will be any material difference in the rate of increase of capital and income. This result is important because it affords us standing ground for a critical examination of statistical data as to the increase of income and capital. We find also that it is possible to estimate the income of an evenly progressive exchange economy by multiplying the capital by the product of the percentage of increase and the reciprocal value of the degree of saving. This should be borne in mind in statistical calculations and estimates.

'If we assume, for instance, that the percentage of progress is equal to 3, and that, therefore, the Capital (C) increases annually by 0·03 C, and further suppose that one-fifth of the annual income is saved, the income is, according to what we have said, equal to 15 per cent of the capital. These figures must be about right

Then, if the incremental capital/output ratio, k, is assumed to be constant[1] and if savings equal investment (either as an *ex post* identity or as an equilibrium condition), it follows that

$$\frac{\Delta Y}{Y} = \frac{\Delta Y}{I} \cdot \frac{S}{Y} \tag{1}$$

or

$$g = \frac{s}{k} \tag{2}$$

Alternatively, we may assume that output per worker is growing at an annual percentage rate, p, and that the labour force increases by r per cent per annum. Full employment of the labour force will then require that aggregate demand grow at an annual rate of $p + r$.

If both assumptions are made simultaneously (and if the Δs become infinitesimally small), full employment of both the labour force and the capital stock will require that these growth rates be identical, i.e.

$$g = \frac{s}{k} = p + r \tag{3}$$

Should this condition not be fulfilled, the full employment of labour or the full utilisation of the stock of capital, or both, will be impossible. On certain assumptions about the investment function, such models can illustrate a state in which chronic inflation is accompanied by growing unemployment.

2. Definitions

The following definitions will help to clarify the subsequent discussion.

---

in the case of Sweden, where the national wealth and national income in 1908 were estimated at about 14,000,000,000 and 2,100,000,000 kronor. An official commission of national defence, in fact, estimated the annual percentage of increase of the national wealth during the period 1885–1908 at 3·18 per cent. Such figures can, of course, never be precise, but the figure given must be a fairly correct estimate.

'For the countries of Western Europe we may assume for modern times (before the [First World] War) that the normal advance was about 3 per cent. Although the figure is only approximate, it is as well to have some standing ground for comparisons, and to be reminded that on the whole, and for long periods, the increase of both capital and income must be indicated by the same figure.' Gustav Cassel, *The Theory of Social Economy*, trans. Joseph McCabe, I (London: T. Fisher Unwin, 1923) 62–3.

[1] One could, alternatively, assume that the marginal capital/labour ratio ($c = I/\Delta L$) is fixed and k the dependent variable. If $w = \Delta Y/\Delta L$ is defined as the marginal productivity of labour, $I/\Delta Y = c/w$ and $g = s.w/c$.

1. *Marginal, incremental, and average capital/output ratio.* The marginal capital/output ratio is the *infinitesimal*, the incremental the *non-infinitesimal*, addition to capital divided by the addition to income over a given period. The average capital/output ratio is the *total* stock of capital divided by *total* income per unit of time.

2. *Ceteris paribus, historical, and projected capital/output ratio.* The *ceteris paribus* ratio is the ratio of capital to output based on the assumption that other productive factors and all other conditions, such as knowledge, tastes, attitudes, and institutions, remain unchanged and that changes in levels of living have no effect on output. Historical ratios are derived from observed past changes in capital and in income. Projected ratios are derived from projected changes in the labour force and in other resources and, possibly, improvements in knowledge.

3. *Net* v. *gross capital/output ratio.* The net ratio excludes depreciation from output. Depreciation can be calculated either as the loss of *productive capacity* due to the wearing out of existing capital, or as the *cost* incurred in replacing it. With technical progress the two measures will diverge.[1]

4. *Project, sectoral, and global capital/output ratio.* The differences in these ratios depend on the extent to which the project under consideration (i) inflicts costs on or (ii) yields benefits to other enterprises not included in the project. The ratio for a given type of project is likely to vary from place to place, from time to time, and according to what other projects are executed and what other products are produced.[2]

5. *Short-term* v. *long-term capital/output ratio.* The distinction here is based on the length of time over which costs and yields are considered, and the weights attached to net output at different times.[3]

6. *Ceteris paribus* v. *mutatis mutandis capital/output ratio.* The *ceteris paribus* ratio assumes all other plant and equipment, technical knowledge, tastes, attitudes towards savings, work, and venture, and institutions to be constant and adapted to output increases. The

[1] With technical progress in the machine-making sector, the same *cost* (however measured) as that incurred for the original machine will provide *capacity* for greater output. Measuring capital in terms of its output capacity would normally give a different result from measuring it in terms of the *inputs* required to reproduce it.

[2] This distinction, if applied to the *ceteris paribus* ratio, would correspond to Pigou's distinction between social and private marginal net product, were it not for the fact that not all costs and benefits can be 'brought in relation to the measuring rod of money'. It should be noted that the *global* ratio, as here defined, is *not* the country-wide or aggregate ratio, but the ratio relating to the sector or the project, with allowance for external effects.

[3] Since the capital/output ratio is the ratio of a stock to a flow, it has a time dimension. Hence the oddity of calling a 'ratio' short- or long-term.

mutatis mutandis ratio, if it could be calculated, would take into account changes in these conditions induced by the investment.[1]

7. *Current* v. *technological capital/output ratio.* The technological ratio is dictated by the capacity of completed projects to yield output (assuming a normal degree of utilisation). It differs from the ratio of work currently under construction to output when starts differ from completions.

8. *Incremental* v. *decremental capital/output ratio.* The ratio will normally differ according to whether capital is increased or reduced.

9. *Aggregate (or country-wide)* v. *sectoral capital/output ratio.* The aggregate ratio is an average of all sectoral capital/output ratios, with sector outputs as weights. It can be an average of the average ratios or of the marginal ratios.

10. *Ex ante* v. *ex post capital/output ratio.* The former is the planned, intended or expected ratio, the latter simply an observed statistical residual.

11. *Investment/marginal output ratio* v. *investment per time-unit/ marginal output ratio.* The former disregards the length of time over which capital is added to the existing stock, and the latter takes it into account.

Some relations to familiar concepts are: Keynes's *marginal efficiency of capital,* like Fisher's rate of return over cost, is the reciprocal of the *ex ante ceteris paribus* marginal gross project ratio, if a constant flow of output per unit of time is assumed.[2] The Pigovian *social marginal efficiency of capital* is the reciprocal of the *ceteris paribus* marginal global net ratio, except that some costs and benefits may resist being 'brought into relation with the measuring rod of money'.

3. *Problems of measurement*

The question of the measurement of 'capital' and 'output' raises a large number of very difficult problems, touched on only briefly here.

The question concerns us at two levels: at the statistical and empirical level and at the level of logic and definition. As for the first problem, in most countries planned public 'development expenditure', not all of it investment in the normal sense, and estimated private investment are lumped together to arrive at capital input. In addition, there is the question of the correct valuation of capital and output in

---

[1] There would exist not one but a very large number of *mutatis mutandis* ratios, depending on the history of the economy, the impact of the investment and its repercussions, and the type of disturbance created. It is not a usable concept, but its function is to point up what we would have to know in order to use it. The ratio that we can know is useless, the one that would be useful we cannot know.

[2] Note also Wicksell's natural rate of interest; see Gunnar Myrdal, *Monetary Equilibrium* (London: William Hodge & Co., 1939) chapter iv.

economies where restrictions and direct controls are ubiquitous. Currency and trade restrictions and licensing and allocation prevent prices from equalising demand and supply. To assert that actual prices are largely arbitrary is not to indicate that 'equilibrium' prices, could they be ascertained, would necessarily be adequate measures for evaluating capital and output. In some instances the discrepancy is obvious. With currency and exchange restrictions, the contribution of exports to development may exceed their market prices and the capital/output ratio in export industries is thus smaller than weighting by market prices would indicate. On the other hand, if imported capital equipment is used in the export industries, the higher valuation appropriate for export-output enters into the numerator as well as the denominator of the capital/output ratio and to that extent cancels out. Similar considerations apply to all inputs and outputs whose market prices are kept low by government policies.

As for the second problem – that of logic and definition – we have already pointed out that the specificity, heterogeneity, complementarity and indivisibility of capital in South Asia make aggregation impossible. Here we shall only enumerate some of the general problems that arise in the measurement of capital.

If there are several items on each side of the capital/output ratio, and if these do not change in the same proportion, we are faced not only with the problem of index numbers, including the indeterminacy introduced by price changes in the planning period and by different income distributions, but with all the difficulties peculiar to the measurement of capital that arise from the fact that:

(a) capital lasts, but does not last for ever;
(b) it takes time to construct;
(c) its quality changes as improvements are incorporated;
(d) replacement and improvement are not distinct acts;
(e) it is utilised to varying degrees at different times;
(f) anything that changes the relative prices of capital goods and consumer goods, or of different goods generally, whether from the demand side or the supply side, will alter the capital/output ratio, even without any change in physical capital, physical output, or technology. In particular, changes in real wages, in the rate of interest, and in the prices of imports will change the capital/output ratio, even though neither the composition of investment nor techniques have changed.

When the productivity of newly constructed capital goods changes, the question arises whether the capital goods should be measured in terms of output or of input. Measurement in terms of output is useless for our purpose, for it would make the capital/output ratio a tautological constant. The difficulty with the input measure, on the other hand, is that despite the increase in the productivity of these capital goods, the value of the resources used in their production may not have changed.

Furthermore, there is the problem of rents and quasi-rents, which arises in connection with the use of scarce inputs in conjunction with capital. Consider two projects with identical initial capital costs. One uses an input that is scarce (from a planning point of view), such as a scarce foreign exchange component or a scarce type of skill, while the other uses labour and raw materials in more plentiful supply. Should rents and quasi-rents be included in valuing output, a procedure that would give a lower capital/output ratio for the first than for the second project? Or should rents and quasi-rents, and thus the opportunity costs of using complementary factors, be excluded in valuing output? The problem is not only the accurate evaluation of rents and quasi-rents, but whether to include them at all. For many large public sector projects, moreover, opportunity costs will not be reflected in any prices, for there are no other 'bidders'. Should capital/output ratios reflect not only the opportunities forgone now but also those forgone later?

4. Confusion between the average and the incremental capital/output ratio

Some writers calculate the prevailing average capital/output ratio in advanced countries and extrapolate it to predict the marginal productivity of capital (whatever this may mean) in underdeveloped countries. Quite apart from other problems, the fallacy in this argument is the confusion of the average capital/output ratio OA/AB ($= BD/CD$) with the incremental ratio BD/ED (Fig. 6.1), assuming with traditional theory that OBE is the function relating capital to total product, all other things remaining equal, and BD the (non-infinitesimal) investment.[1] The marginal ratio BD/FD lies between the other two.

5. Confusion between theoretical, 'ceteris paribus' and historical statistical ratios

Here, the average capital/output ratio is calculated for certain years in the past. Since the ratio is found to be fairly constant over long

[1] See, for example, A. Shonfield, *British Economic Policy since the War* (Harmondsworth: Penguin Books 1958) p. 109, and *The Economist*, 26 Mar 1960, quoted in Colin Clark, *Growthmanship* (London: Institute of Economic Affairs, 1961) p. 18.

periods, it is concluded that the marginal and the incremental ratios, being identical with the average, can be extrapolated for increases in capital.

But this statistical time series can give no clue to the relevant incremental capital/output ratio. First, even assuming that we were concerned with a single functional relationship, as in Fig. 6.3, the fact that a ratio is constant for three observed points does not necessarily mean that it will remain constant for smaller or larger increases in capital. But, more important, both labour and capital have in the past improved and increased, so that the *ceteris paribus* productivity curve has shifted upward (Fig. 6.2). Secondly, the data collected incorporate the effects of economic progress and of improvements in technical knowledge, which are at least partly autonomous and would have occurred even without additional labour and capital.[1] Hence productivity would rise in any case, though at a limited rate, and a large addition to capital cannot be relied on to raise total output proportionately.[2] The slope of a *ceteris paribus* curve might decline steeply. Yet it is the avowed purpose of the plans to raise the savings and investment ratios.

The difficulty with historical observations is that they cannot tell

[1] If the curves in Fig. 6.2 represent upward shifts resulting from improved equipment, they assume perfect adaptation of the whole stock of capital to the new knowledge. In fact, there will always be 'old' pieces coexisting with improved ones and the productivity of capital will thus depend on its age composition. The curve relating output to an increase in investment will therefore be steeper than the total adaptation curve for the old equipment, but less steep than the straight line. If the marginal productivity of the new equipment is the same as it would be if the whole stock consisted of new equipment, it will have the same slope as the curve showing full adaptation to the new equipment, which lies vertically above it. Thus, starting at the point of intersection of curve 2 with the straight line, it would show the same slope as curve 3 vertically above it and would lie between the line going through 2 and the straight line.

[2] Several studies have attempted to show that 'technical progress' has been responsible for 80 to 90 per cent of the growth of output per unit of labour, and capital for only 10 to 20 per cent. But since 'technical progress' is a catchall for economies of scale, external economies, improved health, education and skill of the labour force, better management, changes in the composition of output, and other improvements, as well as for technical progress in the strict sense, Moses Abramovitz's term 'measure of our ignorance' or Evsey Domar's 'residual' would be more appropriate. Cf. E. Domar, 'On the Measurement of Technological Change', *Economic Journal* (Dec 1961). Others, including Kaldor and Solow, have abandoned the notion of a 'real' stock of capital, measured in physical terms, and have combined technical progress and changes in the 'stock' of capital, thus abandoning the distinction between movements along, and shifts of, the production function. Marvin Frankel has shown how a micro-economic Cobb-Douglas type of production function can be combined with a macro-economic Harrod-Domar model, so that, in our Fig. 6.2, each firm believes it is moving along a curve of diminishing returns, whereas all are moving together up the straight line. See n. 1, p. 72 above.

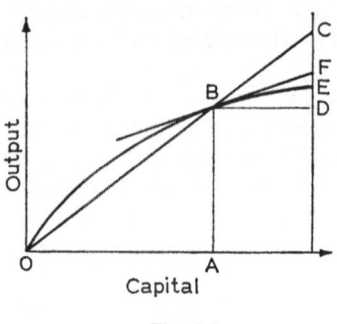

Fig. 6.1

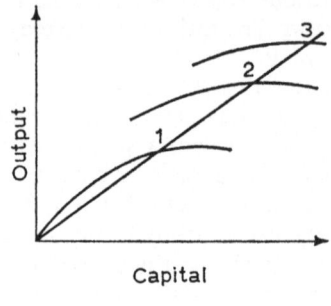

Fig. 6.2

Fig. 6.3

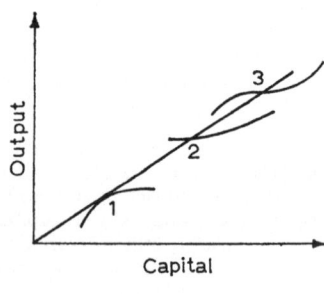

Fig. 6.4

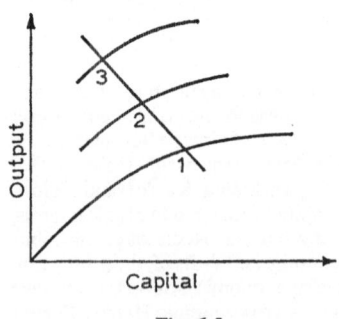

Fig. 6.5

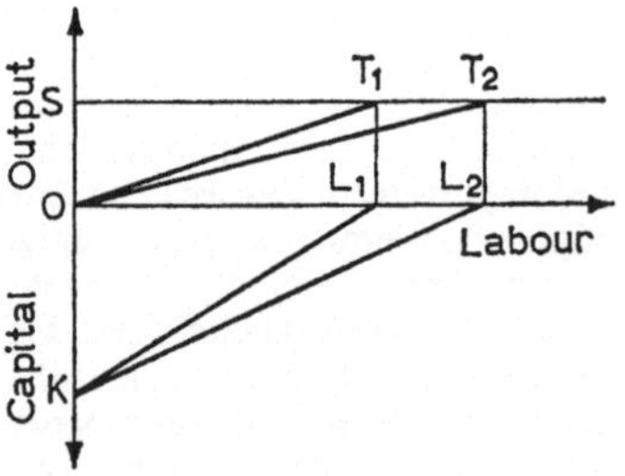

Fig. 6.6

Capital/output ratios under different assumptions

us whether the situation we are facing is like the one in Fig. 6.2 or 3 or 4.[1] The absurdity of the procedure is brought out clearly if we assume observations as in Fig. 6.5. Technical progress, combined with a substitution of other factors of production for capital, has led to changes from position 1 to position 2 to position 3. A capital/output ratio deduced from a line drawn between them appears to be negative, suggesting that by reducing the stock of capital, output can be increased!

The capital/output ratios used in development planning do, however, assume a certain rate of increase in the labour force and are therefore not to be interpreted as *ceteris paribus* ratios. If there are no obstacles and inhibitions to the employment of extra labour other than the absence of capital, if both the ratio of men to machines in the production of all products *and* the product mix are rigidly fixed, and if all other factors of production are in abundant supply, then the extra capital needed to equip a given percentage increase in workers employed can be calculated. But no conclusion can be drawn from this ratio to the additional capital that would be required to equip each worker so as to raise output and income per head. Yet these two distinct notions are not ordinarily separated.[2]

6. The pattern of investment and different techniques

The aggregate (or country-wide) incremental capital/output ratio is the average of the sectoral ratios, weighted by the output increases, assuming techniques in each sector to be rigidly fixed. If an investment of £100 is divided equally between two sectors, one of which has

[1] Cf. T. Balogh and P. P. Streeten, 'Domestic versus Foreign Investment', *Bulletin of the Oxford University Institute of Statistics*, vol. 22 no. 3 (Aug 1960) and chapter 5 in Paul Streeten, *Economic Integration* (Sythoff, 1964).

[2] 'More generally, to raise income per head by 3 per cent a year requires an investment program of at least 2 and perhaps 4 times $(x+3)$ per cent of national income, where x is the rate of increase in population.' (Tinbergen, *The Design of Development*, p. 14.) This is based on the view that 'It would seem often safe to assume that for development programs a capital coefficient of 4 is needed, but we will also consider the consequences of lower values, even down to 2' (p. 13). And: 'Any reduction in percentage population increase means a two- to four-fold reduction in the rate of savings needed to achieve a given rise in the standard of living' (p. 15). 'Suppose that the expected population increase is 1·5 per cent a year, the saving ratio 6 per cent, and the capital-output ratio 4. This will leave the standard of living unchanged, and represents the minimum rate of investment . . . If the *per capita* national income must increase by, say, 2 per cent a year, the national income must increase by $1·5 + 2·0 = 3·5$ per cent every year. This means that, with the same capital-output ratio, the savings ratio must be increased from 0·06 to 0·14, requiring a considerable adjustment in policy measures.' (UN, *Programming Techniques for Economic Development: With special reference to Asia and the Far East*, p. 12.)

a capital/output ratio of 5 and the other of 2, total extra output will be $10 + 25$, and the total ratio will be $100/35 = 5$ times $10/35 + 2$ times $25/35 = 2·8$. In general, if there are several sectors with capital/output ratios of k_1, k_2, k_3, etc., respectively, and if the share of each sector in total output is λ_1, λ_2, λ_3, etc., then the average aggregate ratio will be $\lambda_1 k_1 + \lambda_2 k_2 + \lambda_3 k_3 + \ldots = k$.

A constant aggregate ratio therefore presupposes that, for given sectoral ks, the distribution of investment between sectors will remain the same. Such an assumption is quite unwarranted, as changes in the pattern of investment are bound to occur, whether because of changes in income elasticities of demand or in tastes or because of general policy decisions. If the constancy of the aggregate ratio is the result of offsetting trends in the sectoral ratios, its significance is greatly reduced. On the other hand, since the weights are the shares in *output increases* and not the shares in *investment*, exceptionally high capital/output ratios in certain sectors do not affect the total ratio very much, if these sectors account for only small increases in output.[1] Assume, for example, that an economy with a capital/output ratio of 2 decides to allocate half its total investment to a project with a capital/output ratio of 50. Its countrywide ratio will not rise to 26 but only to 3·8.

Attempts have been made to formulate multi-sector models with different capital/output ratios in each sector. Perhaps the most influential of these are Mahalanobis's two-sector and four-sector models.[2] These models have been criticised both on empirical grounds – that the sectors do not correspond to 'fillable boxes' – and on logical grounds. Mahalanobis assumes that investment is distributed between two sectors, consumer goods (e.g. looms) and capital goods (e.g. machine tools). We thus have two capital/output ratios: the investment/extra consumer goods ratio and the investment/extra capital goods ratio. The former is assumed to be lower than the

---

[1] Cf. W. B. Reddaway, 'Some Observations on the Capital-Output Ratio', Reddaway (ed.), *The Development of the Indian Economy* (London: Allen & Unwin, 1962) p. 209. The appropriate average is the harmonic mean, defined as the reciprocal of the arithmetic mean of the reciprocals of the capital/output ratios. Thus in the above example $k = \dfrac{1}{1/2.1/2 + 1/5.1/2} = \dfrac{1}{14/40} = 2·8$. The arithmetic mean would be $\dfrac{5+2}{2} = 3·5$. In other words, the correct average is the reciprocal of the average output/capital ratio, namely, $\dfrac{10}{50} \cdot \dfrac{1}{2} + \dfrac{25}{50} \cdot \dfrac{1}{2} = \dfrac{35}{100}$, the reciprocal of which is 2·8.

[2] P. C. Mahalanobis, 'Some Observations on the Process of Growth of National Income', *Sankhyā*, vol. 12, pt. 4 (Sep 1953), and 'The Approach of Operational Research to Planning in India', *Sankhyā*, vol. 16, pts. 1 and 2 (Dec 1955).

latter, but the *rate of growth* of investment depends now on the rate of growth of output in the 'capital goods' sector and thus on the allocation of investment between the two sectors. There is an implicit assumption that foreign exchange resources for importing capital goods are strictly limited, so that 'foreign trade productivity' is zero. Thus *the proportion of total investment allocated to the capital goods* sector (together with its capital/output ratio) becomes the crucial variable determining the long-term rate of growth of consumption goods.

This model has been criticised from various points of view.[1] It has been argued that no empirical meaning can be given to the distribution of investments between the two sectors, since most industries supply products to both. The model has also been criticised for implicit and unwarranted assumptions about exports; for neglecting supply limitations other than capital goods; for ignoring depreciation, raw materials, and all intermediate goods; for confusing a technological capital coefficient with an economic choice as to how much of the product of the capital goods sector should be used for investment; for treating the productivity of investment and the capital/labour ratio as independent; for inadequately considering the relation of demand to supply; for assuming labour/capital ratios to be constant; for neglecting the benefits to development that arise from expanding some types of consumption; for not distinguishing between capital goods in general, machine-making goods and heavy and basic industries; and for implicitly assuming a closed economy. When all criticisms are taken into account, certain valid conclusions remain. In the absence of all other limitations on production, if there is a machine that can either reproduce itself or produce other kinds of products, the production of other kinds of products can be raised at some later date by a greater allocation of capital now to the reproduction of the machine.[2] Alternatively, if other limitations on production

[1] See, for example, Shigeto Tsuru, 'The Applicability and Limitations of Economic Development Theory', *The Indian Economic Journal* (Apr 1962); K. N. Raj, 'Growth Models and Indian Planning', *The Indian Economic Review* (Feb 1961); K. N. Raj and A. K. Sen, 'Alternative Patterns of Growth under Conditions of Stagnant Export Earnings', *Oxford Economic Papers*, 13, 1 (Feb 1961); the contributions in *Oxford Economic Papers*, 14, 1 (Feb 1962), and the reply by Raj and Sen, ibid. (June 1962). See also Evsey D. Domar, 'A Soviet Model of Growth', Essay IX in *Essays in the Theory of Economic Growth* (New York: Oxford University Press, 1957), which discusses the very similar model of the Soviet economist Feldman.

[2] K_c The stock of capital that produces consumption goods

    K_m The stock of capital that produces machines.

       A machine can either reproduce itself or produce a machine that makes consumption goods. Machines live for ever.

    I Investment, i.e. additions to the stock of capital

are postulated, the tautological proposition is left that if the growth of an economy is limited by a bottleneck in the production of capital goods (however defined), removal of this bottleneck will accelerate growth. In India's First Plan, emphasis was placed on the marginal propensity to save. It has been healthy to distribute the emphasis among other constraints, such as availability of capital goods, and to show that these may prevent the savings potential from materialising. To raise the investment/income ratio is obviously not enough. Decisions will also have to be taken as to how the investment is to be *distributed* among different activities. Not only the aggregate of savings but also its distribution is important. But any bottleneck – skilled labour, administrative ability, foreign exchange – could be selected as a constraint and the proportion of expenditure (or effort) devoted to reducing this constraint could be made the determinant of development.

But Professor Mahalanobis and some of his predecessors and followers have advocated more 'roundabout' methods of increasing production, in the sense of increasing the allocation of investment to the capital goods sector. These methods are vulnerable to a criticism

---

C Consumption goods

k $= \dfrac{K_c}{C} = \dfrac{K_m}{I}$ The capital/output ratio k is the same in each sector and the average is equal to the marginal.

p The proportion of investment I allocated to K_m

(1) $K_m = I.k$

(2) $K_c = C.k$

(3) $\Delta K_m = pI$ i.e., the part of investment allocated to making more machines

(4) $\Delta K_c = (1-p)I$ The remainder of investment increases the stock of machines making consumption goods.

(5) $\dfrac{\Delta K_m}{K_m} = \dfrac{p}{k}$ dividing 3 by 1

(6) $\dfrac{\Delta K_c}{K_c} = \dfrac{(1-p)K_m}{kK_c}$ dividing 4 by 2

Hence, the smaller p and the larger K_m/K_c, the greater the rate of increase of machines making consumption goods. But the larger p is *now*, the larger K_m/K_c will be *later*. If $p = K_m/(K_m + K_c)$, i.e. if the proportion of machines allocated to making machines is the same as the ratio of the stock of machine-making machines to the machines, $\Delta K_m/K_m = \Delta K_c/K_c$. If $p > K_m/(K_m + K_c)$ the rate of growth of consumption will be smaller than the rate of growth of investment and vice versa.

If we assume that all machines can produce either consumption goods or more machines, K_m and K_c then stand for the number of machines producing more machines and for those making consumption goods, respectively. And p then reduces to the marginal propensity to save, and the growth rate depends only on the savings ratio and the capital/output ratio.

Oscar Braun of the University of Buenos Aires assisted in formulating this note. Mr Jagathpath, of Hindustan Steel Ltd, detected an error which has here been corrected.

that Wicksell advanced against Böhm-Bawerk.[1] The features criticised are not identical, for more 'roundaboutness' is not the same as increased allocation to the capital goods sector, and Wicksell's lengthening leads to a once-for-all increase in income later, whereas reallocation leads to a permanently increased flow. But the parallel brings out the assumptions about Pareto optimality.

To translate Wicksell's bewilderment into the language of the Mahalanobis model, one may begin by asking: if it is the distribution of investment between machines and machines making machines that is the key to rapid growth, why not invest in machines making machines making machines and achieve a still higher rate of growth, and so on? It is irrelevant in the present context to reply that time preference is not zero and that there are political difficulties in the way of such postponement. The present question focuses on the technical possibilities, and Wicksell's reply was that

> ... technically advantageous roundabout methods of production are profitable only to a limited extent economically. If by sacrificing 50 crowns or 50 labour units now I can receive in return 100 from a one-year production process, but 150 from a two-year one, then it is obvious that I ought to choose the *one*-year alternative, even if I intend to wait two years for my returns, because by repeating the one-year production process the next year on double the scale (since I then have 100 crowns or labour units at my disposal), I will obtain 200 at the end of the second year instead of 150. In other words, if a successive lengthening of the production process is also to be economically profitable, the production must increase at a more than geometric rate of progression, as time is increasing at an arithmetic rate. In general this can only be so to a limited extent through newly occurring changes. (If the sacrifice necessary to obtain the same product had been 75 crowns instead of 50, the two-year production process would have been the more profitable, because it would have led to a doubling of the capital, whereas two successive one-year productions would have given an increase in the ratio $\frac{3}{4} \cdot \frac{3}{4} = 9:16$).[2]

---

[1] Wicksell, too, found the problem a tricky one. He writes: 'The *technical* superiority of present goods (including present productive forces) over those of the future is probably the part of ... [Böhm-Bawerk's] reasoning which has set his readers pondering most, at least it has been so for me. I do not know how many times I have returned to this point without being clear *why* it was that Böhm-Bawerk's treatment did not satisfy me, until, particularly by reading Bortkiewicz's criticism ("Der Kardinalfehler Böhm-Bawerks," *Schmollers Jahrbuch*, Bd xxx), I think I definitely found the solution.' Knut Wicksell, *Selected Papers on Economic Theory* (London: Allen & Unwin, 1958) p. 182.

[2] Ibid., p. 183.

In the language of the Indian plan, Wicksell's criticism can be stated thus: ploughing back seeds (presumably consumption goods) *may* yield the same future results and leave more to be eaten now than constructing machine tools to make steel mills to make fertiliser plants to make fertilisers to produce more seeds. Methods of production that are 'inefficient' in the Pareto sense must be ruled out. That is, if by adopting some other method of production, output at one time could be increased without reducing output at any other time, the present method is unambiguously inefficient. If for an infinite time-horizon we substitute a flow of output to the horizon plus a final capital stock, the criterion for inefficiency is that output could be increased at some time without decreasing it at any other and without decreasing the amount of any item in the final capital stock. It is frequently assumed in the discussion that all methods of production using more and more capital goods are 'efficient' in the sense of not being unambiguously inefficient. But only after it has been determined what are 'efficient' methods can it be asked which of these efficient methods should be adopted in view of technological limitations, the need to enforce savings, and the political value judgements about time.

The Mahalanobis model also adds a constraint set by savings. If it is assumed that savings can be raised only by introducing capital-intensive methods of production, then emphasis on heavy industry and capital goods becomes a means of enforcing savings. In terms of the Harrod-Domar model, in which the growth rate (g) equals the savings/income ratio (s) divided by the capital/output ratio (k), s becomes a function of k, and k is a function of the distribution of investment: by changing the direction of investment we can increase the average k, thereby raising s more than proportionately and thus raising the growth rate g. But before choosing this method of increasing g we should be certain that there are no ways of reducing k that would reduce s less than proportionately.

So far we have discussed the distribution of investment between sectors, assuming techniques in each sector to be given. But if it is assumed that one sector supplies inputs to another, a change in sector composition of investment is the same as a change in the technique of producing the final output. Within each sector, techniques of production can often be varied, so that more or less capital can be used per unit of output, with less or more of other factors. Since $k = c/w$ (p. 78, n. 1), any non-proportional change in c and w will affect k. All ks can be assumed to be constant only if the neo-classical assumption of substitutability is replaced by the assumption of complete fixity of coefficients, so that the marginal productivity of labour is zero.[1] Many writers assert that the marginal productivity of labour in many areas in South Asia is in fact zero. If no other inputs were required, we could then postulate constant returns to capital. But the latter assumption is not justified and we criticise the former in detail elsewhere. The allocation between labour and capital will depend, among other things, on time preference, on relative factor prices and, if there is disequilibrium, on availabilities. Any change in prices and availabilities will therefore tend to affect the capital/output ratio.

We have discussed and criticised a number of different models in this section. First, we criticised models that neglect differences in sectoral coefficients, pointing out that the average capital/output ratio is a weighted average of sectoral ratios. Secondly, we discussed a two-sector model in which one sector produces machines and the other consumption goods. We showed that in this type of model a technological restraint on the growth rate is added to the savings restraint. We also showed that the proportion of income saved is not the only consideration; how these savings are allocated between the two sectors is also important. Thirdly, we mentioned a quasi-political constraint on the savings ratio that makes it dependent on the capital coefficient. The introduction of realistic constraints on the growth rate other than low aggregate savings ratios and high aggregate capital/output ratios is useful – more, however, to show the limitations of accepted models than to illuminate new relationships.[2] Fourthly, we discussed models in which an increasing amount of capital is used in combination with limited supplies of other factors. The two-sector model can be of this type, if it can be assumed that the machine-making sector works with a constant labour force. But the assumption of fixed coefficients is inappropriate if the ratio of capital to other factors can be varied.

We may conclude that, far from being constant, the capital/output ratio will depend on the size of additional output, on income and

---

[1] This is illustrated in Fig. 6.6. OK is the amount of capital invested. If the capital/labour ratio falls from OK/OL_1 to OK/OL_2, the capital/output ratio OK/L_1T_1 will remain constant only if the curve relating output to labour inputs is horizontal, i.e. if the marginal productivity of labour is zero. Yet this appears to be the assumption of the Mahalanobis model. See Tsuru's article, 'The Applicability and Limitations of Economic Development Theory', *The Indian Economic Journal* (Apr 1962) p. 375. Mahalanobis is quoted: 'Let us suppose that the values of all θ's [the marginal and average productivity of labour] are doubled but β's [the marginal productivity of capital] remain the same, ...' ('The Approach of Operational Research to Planning in India', *Sankhyā*, vol. 16, pts. 1 and 2, Dec 1955, p. 43.)

[2] The main function of some models is to demonstrate the inadequacy or falsity of another model, for one cannot easily dislodge a theory from the minds of its supporters by facts but only by another model.

price elasticities of demand for and supply of products and factors, and on political choices.[1]

7. *Irreversibility*

Using additional capital always means doing things in a different way, often a new way, and this in turn implies learning, acquiring skills, and perhaps changing a way of life. The capital/output ratio depends on the direction of the change and on past peak output, so that the ratio would not always be the same for an increase in capital as for a reduction. A reduction in capital would not cause a commensurate reduction in output – a fact of special importance in underdeveloped countries, where the initial level of skills is low. This point is entirely separate from the more familiar one that the lumpiness of capital equipment makes a perfect adaptation of the capital stock to a changing output flow impossible and that the durability of capital equipment introduces asymmetry into the capital/output ratio: because, once full capacity is reached, increases in output require increases in the capital stock, while decreases in output will not be accompanied by a corresponding scrapping of capital equipment. The present criticism concerns the notion of reversibility, even if perfect adaptation of the capital stock were assumed. Movements along the 'production function' inevitably, because of the effects of learning, involve shifts of the so-called function. Increases in capital and improvements in knowledge cannot be separated. This is why attempts to separate productivity increases due to capital accumulation from those due to improvements in knowledge are particularly misleading for underdeveloped countries. It also points to one of the dangers of extrapolating the capital/output ratio observed in times of post-war recovery or reconstruction to long-term development. The coefficient may be very low as income rises to the pre-war level, but it will be higher when income rises beyond that level. Similar considerations make it impossible to apply ratios derived from increases in capital to a sectoral decline in capital.

The notion of a stable capital input/output relationship, which is the pillar of thinking about planning, rests on a tacit assumption that such a relationship is independent of time. A hypothetical functional input/output relationship must assume that each point has existed in the past and that all other variables, particularly expectations, have become fully adjusted. It is logically impossible to transfer reasoning

[1] A further difficulty, discussed in Section 9, is that capital/output ratios of particular projects, industries and even sectors are not independent. Capital requirements for a given output depend partly on what other outputs are produced.

applicable to a hypothetical function, all points of which have a full equilibrium history behind them, to an actual movement in the real world. For such a movement is bound to involve a shift of the whole function that destroys its stability.[1]

8. The role of time

The capital/output ratio is clearly not in the same family as other 'great ratios' – the savings/income, the consumption/income, or the investment/income ratios, for example. These are ratios between flows and therefore have no time dimension. The capital/output ratio, as normally defined, on the other hand, is a ratio between a stock and a flow, and therefore has a time dimension. We must specify whether we have in mind one year, or the period of the plan, or some other time span. So much is generally recognised. But it is not equally recognised that the ratio cannot be treated as if it were independent of the period of accumulation of the additional capital stock to which the incremental output flow is related. Time distribution is relevant for several reasons.

(i) Consider a specific project representing a given addition to the capital stock. Much depends on whether the construction period of this project is spread over one year, two years, or five. The shorter the period, the more likely it is that shortages will develop, which will be reflected in rising costs, bottlenecks, hurried improvisations, and substitution of inferior materials or expensive imports. Construction is therefore likely to be less efficient if compressed in time, though the project will, of course, yield output sooner. (The resulting shortages in *other* enterprises are discussed below in Section 9.)

(ii) Differences in construction periods for projects with the same capital input clearly affect the aggregate capital/output ratio when the mixture of projects in the plan changes.

(iii) The fact that construction takes time means that there is a lag between capital expenditure and increases in output.[2] This lag can be assumed to be constant if (1) the construction period for each project, (2) the composition of investment with respect to projects of different construction periods, and (3) the proportionate rate of change of investment per unit of time remain constant.[3]

---

[1] This kind of objection applies, of course, to numerous functional relationships in economic theory in which the roles of time, memory, expectations, and other factors are not specified. But this is not our concern here.

[2] There are also lags between the initiation of inquiries or applications and final decisions, and between the latter and the start of expenditure, particularly if waiting for replies to applications for import licences is involved.

[3] Reddaway deals with this problem in 'Importance of Time Lags for Economic Planning', *The Development of the Indian Economy*, Appendix A (London, 1962).

In a lagged system

$$\frac{I_t}{\Delta Y_t} = \frac{I_t}{B_{(t-1)} \dfrac{\Delta Y_t}{B_{(t-1)}}} = \frac{I_t}{B_{(t-1)}} \cdot \frac{B_{(t-1)}}{\Delta Y_t} = \frac{I_t}{B_{(t-1)}} \cdot k = f.k$$

where 1 is the average construction period and B is projects started, k is the technological incremental capital/output ratio, that is, the ratio between extra *completed* machines and extra output at time t, at a constant degree of capacity utilisation. $I_t/B_{(t-1)} = f$ is the coefficient by which k has to be multiplied in order to get the ratio of current total investment to current extra output. From this it can be seen that (1) if investment grows at a constant percentage rate, $B_{(t-1)}$ will grow at the same rate and the lagged coefficient will be constant. The lagged ratio will be greater than the technological ratio, if $I_t > B_{(t-1)}$; (2) if the percentage rate of growth of investment rises, the lagged ratio also rises: if the percentage rate of growth of investment declines, the lagged ratio also declines. This may be illustrated by a simple table. Assume a two-year construction period, a capital/output ratio of 2, and a uniform spread of starts through the year.

TABLE 6.7

Lags due to Construction Period

Year	Starts (B)	Completions	ΔY_t	Under construction at end of year	$I_t{}^a$ (approx.)	$\dfrac{I_t}{\Delta Y_t}$	k	$\dfrac{I_t}{B_{(t-1)}} = f$
0	1	0	0	1	$\frac{1}{4}$			
1	2	0	0	3	$1\frac{1}{4}$			
2	4	1	$\frac{1}{2}$	6	$2\frac{1}{2}$	5	2	$2\frac{1}{2}$
3	8	2	1	12	5	5	2	$2\frac{1}{2}$
4	16	4	2	24	10	5	2	$2\frac{1}{2}$
5	32	8	4	48	20	5	2	$2\frac{1}{2}$

^{a} Investment is equal to $\frac{1}{4}$ of the starts in the same year plus $\frac{1}{4}$ of the starts in the previous year. See Reddaway, 'Importance of Time Lags for Economic Planning', *The Development of the Indian Economy*, p. 196.

It is difficult to estimate the average lag for a growing economy; the longer the lag, the higher the ratio will tend to be.

(iv) Any given addition to capital equipment can result in a variety of different time distributions of final output; sometimes the pattern of output will show large initial yields followed by small yields, sometimes the reverse. If the stream of returns has an irregular time pattern, the capital/output ratio will not be clearly defined. Either the irregular flow has to be discounted at the 'social rate of time discount' and this discounted value compared with the capital cost, or the rate that equates the discounted value to the capital cost has to be determined and compared with the 'social rate of time discount'. Once the 'social rate of time discount' and the composition of final output are determined, it may be argued that it would be wise to minimise the capital/output ratio, when 'output' stands for the current discounted value of a given composition of commodities. But it would be foolish to deduce from this that a lower capital/output ratio would be preferable if it could be achieved only through a different time distribution or a different composition of future output. The desirability of low capital/output ratios implies neither that the Indians should not produce capital-intensive producer goods nor that they should go in for mass barbering. A reduction in the ratio bought at the expense either of lower future output or of more useful commodities requiring a higher ratio of capital to output is not necessarily a blessing. India's First Plan has been criticised on these grounds. Indonesia's 1956–60 plan also falls into this trap.

A particular problem of choice arises if two investments that cost the same and yield the same flow of *net* output have different durability and therefore differ in their flow of *gross* output. The investment with a shorter life will yield greater annual depreciation allowances that can be reinvested in better equipment. Because of this advantage it may be that projects with a small *net* output are preferable to those with a large net output, if the larger *gross* output of the former affords sufficient advantages in flexibility of reinvestment. Formally, the same flexibility of reinvestment can be achieved by reducing the larger net output of longer-lived projects by an appropriate addition to depreciation due to obsolescence. But since the size of the additional allowance cannot be known before the event, the point remains valid, and will be applicable particularly to situations in which a country's investment ratio is increased. For then the average age of the capital stock will be reduced and so will the flexibility permitted by replacement. Countries stepping up their investment ratio will have to pay particular attention to this distinction between net and gross ratios.

(v) Indivisibilities and variations in the degree of utilisation of existing and completed capacity constitute other reasons why the time distribution of output enters into the calculation of the capital/output ratio. These are discussed in Section 9 below.

In the calculation of the capital/output ratio, as normally defined in the plans, neither the time rate at which capital is accumulated nor the period of time over which the increment in output is spread is considered.[1] Clearly, annual ratios are not very meaningful, for

[1] As defined in equilibrium theory, including equilibrium growth, this question does not, of course, arise.

construction periods are often much longer than a year. Even the period of a whole plan is too short for the bulk of the projects. But if one were to consider decades or even longer stretches, the *ceteris paribus* assumption would lose all plausibility, especially since the very aim of the plan is to make 'other things' *un*equal.

9. Capacity utilisation

Changes in the degree of utilisation of existing capital equipment upset the technological capital/output ratio. Output can rise without any investment if capacity is more fully utilised, and capacity can rise without any extra output if investment leads to reduced utilisation because it deprives other sectors of either inputs or demand. Special difficulties arise in the application of the 'capital/output ratio' to underdeveloped countries. The assumption of perfect divisibility of investment projects is particularly inappropriate in these countries, where projects are often large. Indivisibilities are more prominent than in advanced countries and marginalist reasoning is therefore less applicable for several reasons. First, it is important to build ahead of the expected growth in demand.[1] Secondly, since new plant and equipment in underdeveloped countries are often necessarily large, investment in them is high in relation to both the stock of existing capital and total new investment. Thirdly, economic development is directed at industrialisation, a goal that normally results in an increase in the proportion of a nation's capital tied up in indivisible manufacturing units. Fourthly, much of the necessary social overhead capital and the basic structure of industry (power, steel, transport, government buildings) consists of large indivisible units. Fifthly, a given investment is more likely to require complementary and supplementary investments in the meagre economies of underdeveloped countries. For example, a new textile mill requires more cotton, fuel, and transport services, and the whole investment complex, if it is to be successful, will tend to be a large indivisible lump.[2] Thus the application of constant capital/output ratios may be

[1] See paragraph (i) (a) below.

[2] Against the view that the process of development ties up capital in lumpy, indivisible units, it could be argued, transcending the framework of the model, that development aims at increasing transferability of factors and flexibility generally. The education of workers, the provision of transport and housing, the improvement of the means of communication, the increasing share of 'basic' industries whose products can be used in many different lines, and increased earnings of foreign exchange, all tend to reduce the proportion of national capital tied up in specific production units. A steel plant is technically large, but since there are numerous demands for steel, it is less likely to suffer from underutilisation because demand is deficient than, say, a shoe factory of comparable size.

upset both because of the indivisibility of the investment project under consideration and because of the indivisibilities in the rest of the economy.

(i) *Project capital/output ratio.* If the project itself is lumpy, an incremental capital/output ratio calculated from small additions is clearly irrelevant, and extrapolations from periods or countries characterised by less lumpy projects are misleading. The ratio will depend on (a) the size of the addition to capital and (b) the degree of its utilisation. Small additions, taking the form of extensions of existing plant, sometimes yield a large amount of extra output per unit of capital, whereas the extra output per unit of investment of large additions, involving the construction of new plants, may be considerably less.[1] On the other hand, extensions may involve disturbance and interruption of current production (see (a) below), whereas new plants, particularly if fully utilised soon after completion, may yield more extra output.

Furthermore, utilisation of capacity often increases only gradually. Surplus capacity may be created deliberately, under certain circumstances:

(a) If long-run costs are declining, even if demand is expected to remain constant and there are no indivisibilities, it pays to build a plant larger than that which is optimally adapted to the desired output, and to underutilise it, for the unit costs of production of the optimum plant would be higher than the unit costs of the same output produced by the larger plant. If demand is expected to increase, initial construction of excess capacity may be desirable, even if it results in greater production costs of current output. The amount of excess capacity will depend on a number of considerations. For example, planners will have to consider the future costs of expanding and rebuilding equipment and of interrupting production while expansion is under way. Such costs can be avoided if the initial outlay, instead of being adapted to current demand, is geared to future, larger demand. The choice is between three possibilities: (1) optimum plant for the anticipated output and an additional plant when demand

---

[1] George Rosen found in all cases that the marginal capital/output ratio for extensions of existing plant was lower than for new plant. Cf. George Rosen, *Industrial Change in India* (Glencoe, Ill.: Free Press, 1958) chap. 5.

There are several reasons why the ratio will be higher for large changes. The ratio will tend to be higher for large increments because increasing amounts of capital will be needed to break bottlenecks. In Section 5 we suggested that small additions can incorporate technical knowledge that has accumulated independently over time. In Section 8 (iii) we showed that the higher the ratio of investment to completions, the higher the capital/output ratio. But this is a problem of increasing the rate of investment, not of maintaining it at a high rate. Finally, large additions may require more complementary changes (e.g. more social overhead investment) than small changes.

increases; (2) excess capacity to accommodate a future rise in demand; (3) a plant that is not perfectly adapted to produce the anticipated output, but that can be expanded without excessive disruption of the production process. A political inter-temporal value judgement will be required in weighing the desirability of achieving future cost reductions at the expense of higher current costs.

(b) A temporary labour reserve may be available to build a project before it is needed, as in the Ceylon plan.

(c) Technical indivisibilities may be important. Investments in transport, except in industrially developed, congested areas, are not fully utilised until long after their completion. This is also true of investments in electric power in remote, poor regions and of irrigation schemes in sparsely inhabited districts to which settlers move only reluctantly.

(d) Electric power plants and irrigation and transport projects may provide not only opportunities but also incentives to further development and may therefore contribute to increasing the rate of growth of output. The Tennessee Valley Authority is perhaps the best-known scheme of this kind, though the assumption of its transferability has not been justified.

Excess capacity is, of course, often inadvertently created through miscalculation of demand or supplies, obsolescence, foreign exchange shortages, changes in domestic or foreign policies, or other unforeseen circumstances. The capital/output ratio in the organised industrial and mining sector in India was exceptionally high in the late 1950s and early 1960s, largely as a result of errors and unexpected changes.

(ii) *Ceteris paribus global capital/output ratio.* If indivisibilities are characteristic of the economy, the capital/output ratio may differ substantially according to the *direction* of investment, and the *global* capital/output ratio may differ substantially from the capital/output ratio of an individual *project*. The global ratio will be lower than the project ratio if the project breaks a bottleneck, thus enabling other sectors to make fuller use of their existing capacity. The repair of a bridge bringing back into use an important traffic line, for example, will reduce the global capital/output ratio. The global ratio may be higher than the project ratio if the project creates excess capacity in other sectors by depriving them of resources or demand. For example, the replacement of handloom weavers by a modern textile mill deprives other sectors of demand. The erection of the steelworks in India's Second Plan caused a shortage of railway capacity and thus deprived other sectors of transport facilities and supplies.

The interdependence of several projects, some of them indivisible, can perhaps be seen most clearly when considered in terms of the criteria by which a large firm judges the profitability of its investments.[1] Business firms do not necessarily invest in those projects that promise the highest direct yield, for they realise that some low-yield projects may be necessary prerequisites to subsequent high-yield projects. Long-term expansion of basic capacity or the promotion of improved working conditions and workers' welfare schemes may involve high costs in terms of forgone opportunities for profitable expansion of manufacturing capacity, but in combination with later contingent investment, the high expenditures may prove wise. If these projects were carried out by different firms or by different sectors (for example, public versus private sector) the resulting gains would appear as external economies. Investments with a high project capital/output ratio may pave the way for high-yield projects later.

Thus we have seen that the direction of investment is of crucial importance and that the secondary consequences of the investment may be more important than the primary. There are several more fundamental reasons for this than those discussed here. The inability to add to, or subtract from, investment projects in relatively small doses in underdeveloped countries is one of them.

10. Market imperfections

It is well known that rates of profit vary greatly among firms, industries and sectors in underdeveloped countries:[2] 100 per cent or more can be earned on loans to peasants and 10 per cent on investment in mining. Imperfections in the capital market – ignorance, monopoly, deliberate restrictions, weak incentives and lack of organised trading – are responsible for this. These imperfections are significant in the present context for two reasons:

(i) If there is neither interdependence nor indivisibility and there is a fairly perfect internal capital market, the rate of profit will be roughly the same for projects of similar risk. For a given share of profits in domestic product, this could be accepted as an indication that the marginal productivity of capital, and therefore its reciprocal, the *ceteris paribus* marginal capital/output ratio, is roughly the same for different projects. But the absence of a functioning capital market

[1] As Göran Ohlin pointed out in commenting on a draft of this section, the problems of planners are often analogous to those of private investors. The principles expounded by Western management and business economists may be better guides than those of the pure economists who might advocate equating marginal returns. To assume independence where interdependence in fact prevails is a professional weakness. But the problems faced by planners are old ones that have been present, though perhaps in different contexts, since economic activity began.

[2] See 'Gross Margins in Indian Industry', *Monthly Abstract of Statistics* (New Delhi) vol. 14, no. 1 (Jan 1961).

renders the aggregate marginal capital/output ratio (calculated as a weighted average of projects with widely different ratios) useless, both for evaluating a specific project and for making or criticising a plan.[1] Once again it is the *direction* rather than some aggregate *amount* of investment that matters. Redirection of a given amount of resources for investment may have more spectacular results than increasing the resources.

(ii) So far, we have assumed the imperfections to be given. But an important objective of capital expenditure is to *alter* and *reduce* these imperfections. An investment that breaks or weakens a foreign or a domestic monopoly will be much more productive than one that adds to output in an already fiercely competitive industry. Changing the degree of monopoly in an economy changes the degree of utilisation of existing equipment and the *rate* and *direction* at which equipment is added in different sectors. But it also changes relative prices and therefore the relative weights of different products and the relative price levels of capital and consumer goods.[2]

11. Investment in working capital

Discussion of the capital/output ratio tends to be focused on investment in fixed capital equipment; little attention is paid to investment in working capital (inventories and work-in-progress). Thus the capital/output ratios for certain projects – railways, canals, telephones, telegraphs and warehouses, for example – may be exaggerated unless the reduction in inventories and work-in-progress made possible by these projects is taken into account. Amartya Kumar Sen has found that if working capital is included, the capital/output ratios for cotton weaving in India and for the cottage hand-spinning wheel (the *ambar charkha*) are considerably higher than is commonly supposed.[3]

---

[1] The objection to the use of a marginal ratio, which is the average of different project ratios, for accounting purposes is subject to the same criticism that Böhm-Bawerk directed against Marx's use of the notion of an 'average' in his formulation of the law of value: 'We might just as well try in this way to prove the proposition that animals of all kinds, elephants and May-flies included, have the same length of life; for while it is true that elephants live on an average one hundred years and May-flies only a single day, yet between these two quantities we can strike an average of fifty years. By as much time as elephants live longer than the flies, the flies live shorter than the elephants. The deviations from this average 'mutually cancel each other', and consequently on the whole and on the average the law that all kinds of animals have the same length of life is established!' Eugen Böhm-Bawerk, *Karl Marx and the Close of His System*, trans. Alice M. Macdonald (London: T. Fisher Unwin, 1898) p. 79.

[2] Section 3(f), p. 81.

[3] Amartya Kumar Sen, *Choice of Techniques* (Oxford: Basil Blackwell, 1960) Appendix C, pp. 110–13, and Appendix D, p. 118, n. 7.

But fixed-capital-intensive projects, such as the construction of a steel plant, also often require large additions to working capital, and confining consideration to fixed capital results in an understatement of the capital/output ratio.

As one would expect, the ratio of working capital to output changes as development proceeds, though it is not clear whether it declines, as is commonly assumed. First there is the change in the composition of output. Because agricultural output is produced at one time of the year and consumed evenly over the whole year, larger inventories of agricultural products than of manufactured products are required (though not necessarily in the agricultural sector). Hence, as the composition of demand changes from the predominantly agricultural to a greater emphasis on manufactured products, even if the proportion of each type of product required for inventories is constant, the average proportion of inventories in the economy will decline. On the other hand, requirements for working capital depend not only on technical factors, such as production lags, but also on institutional factors, such as the system of payments.[1] In a peasant society the lag between wage payments to labour and the arrival of the product of labour is absent, and work-in-progress is thus an unimportant factor. Peasants must, of course, eat to survive, but additional effort does not elicit immediate additional remuneration, as it might if wages were paid by an employer. Only when the extra crop is harvested are the extra efforts rewarded. This involves large economies in incremental work-in-progress if the peasant sector is important to the economy. It is often argued that the wage sector in both agriculture and manufacturing industry expands with development. If this argument is accepted, this economy in work-in-progress in the agricultural sector disappears, and additional hours worked call for an immediate increase in the demand for wage goods. For this reason, the shift from household-based production to wage labour in both agriculture and manufacturing will tend to raise the requirements for work-in-progress. Furthermore, if harder work requires more consumption of food, the requirement for an increased stock of food will also raise working capital. It is therefore not clear that the shift from a household-based to a wage-based economy, if it occurs, reduces the need for working capital.

Secondly, the increase in the size of the manufacturing firm will make internal economies in inventory possible. Thirdly, enterprises

---

[1] A. K. Sen, 'Working Capital in the Indian Economy: A Conceptual Framework and Some Estimates', chapter 6, pp. 128–31, in *Pricing and Fiscal Policies, A Study in Method*, P. N. Rosenstein-Rodan (ed.), (London: Allen and Unwin, 1964); *Studies in the Economic Development of India*, no. 3 (Center for International Studies, Massachusetts Institute of Technology).

will enjoy external economies in the form of more efficient and cheaper transport facilities, a higher degree of specialisation, fuller utilisation of waste products and greater skill in avoiding waste, all of which will greatly reduce the inventory/output ratio. Possibly the most important effect of the construction of railways and roads is the substantial saving in inventories.

12. Work shifts

Certain types of reorganisation, such as the introduction of additional work shifts, have very low incremental capital/output ratios, which may in extreme cases fall to zero.[1] Assuming that the additional shift requires no additional investment, and that labour and material are abundant, two distinct benefits accrue from it.[2] First, assuming that all depreciation is user cost, so that doubling the use of machinery leads to twice the depreciation, the capital/output ratio will be halved. If Y_g is income gross of depreciation, and d is depreciation,

for one shift: $\dfrac{I}{\Delta Y_g - d} = k_1$

for two shifts: $\dfrac{I}{2\Delta Y_g - 2d} = k_2$

therefore: $k_2 = \dfrac{k_1}{2}$.

If no additional wear and tear is inflicted by the second shift, a further gain accrues:

$$\frac{I}{2\Delta Y_g - d} \text{ which is smaller than } \frac{k}{2}.$$

Normally, however, depreciation will rise but not double. If the non-user cost element in depreciation is n, the ratio for two shifts will be

$$\frac{I}{2\Delta Y_g - (2d - n)} \text{ where } n < d.$$

On the other hand, the widespread resistance to this apparently obvious and simple solution of the problem of capital scarcity suggests that there may be serious obstacles to the introduction of

---

[1] Multiple work shifts are, of course, a particular means of fuller utilisation of capacity, discussed in Section 9 above. The subject is treated separately because, unlike a simple increase in the supply of some input or in the demand for the output, multiple work shifts appear to involve more deep-seated changes in organisation, attitudes and policies.

[2] Cf. P. K. Sen, 'Use of the Capital-Output Ratio in Economic Planning', *The Indian Economic Review*, v 1 (Feb 1960).

multiple shifts. An interesting paper by David Granick[1] makes the point that, though the Russians had enthusiasm for three-shift, seven-day work weeks in the early 1930s, they had to revert to the single shifts general in Western Europe.[2] His explanation is that multi-shift operations require better work organisation than was possible, tighter scheduling and fewer bottlenecks. Flexibility was enhanced by working general equipment on one shift and only equipment that might cause bottlenecks on more. Flow-production of a limited number of products makes smaller demands on the labour force. Also, working single shifts requires lower skills, because there is more time to repair damaged machinery and less need for careful timing of processes. Single shifts are therefore more effective for training large numbers of 'raw farm youths'. Although the physical output was less than it would have been from multiple shifts, the principal gain was in training an industrial labour force.[3] No doubt, underpricing of capital and overpricing of labour also contribute to the absence of multi-shift working.

There are means other than multiple work shifts that management and organisation can use to reduce the capital/output ratio. Instruction in better care and maintenance of machinery to prolong its life reduces the net capital/output ratio without any investment. The ·steady introduction of small, often routine, improvements in machines, and the skills acquired from experience in working them, reduce the capital/output ratio without a spectacular rise in investment and even without marked organisational changes. Some improvements yield very high returns up to a point, but none beyond. Extrapolations from periods in which temporary effects of innovations have been experienced can therefore be misleading. Increased output in agriculture often depends more on improved techniques (fertilisers, seeds, pesticides, rotation) than on substantial investment.

13. Summary, conclusions and the impossibility of salvage

In the introduction we distinguished between transcendental and immanent criticism of the capital/output ratio. But the distinction between them is to some extent artificial. A distinction cannot always

---

[1] 'On Patterns of Technological Choice in Soviet Industry', *American Economic Review, Papers and Proceedings*, LII 2 (May 1962) 149–57.

[2] 'Even today, the United States is most exceptional among capitalist industrialized countries in the extent to which it employs multishift operation in industries other than those where technical requirements force its adoption' (ibid., p. 152).

[3] Granick adds that multiple work shifts encourage irresponsibility by individual workers in the care of their equipment since they do not bear sole responsibility for it. This argument is more important for a raw labour force than for one with a tradition of pride. Finally, he stresses that an increase in the number of industrial workers is an ideological aim of Soviet planning, irrespective of economic efficiency.

be clearly drawn between assumptions that are logically valid but unrealistic and assumptions that are logically faulty. If the criticism is made that the introduction of a piece of equipment adds to the skills of the workers as they learn how to use it, thus gradually reducing the capital/output ratio, it can be regarded as pointing up the unrealism in assuming 'given skills and responses' or the logical invalidity in ignoring the influence of the passage of time. Changes in work shifts were discussed in our immanent criticism, but the discussion of these and other changes in organisation and management could be regarded as questioning the assumption of 'given organisation'. Similarly, model-builders and model-users might be quite ready to incorporate in their models the effects on the capital/output ratio of changes in expenditure on education, health, nutrition, housing and other 'consumption' items. Indeed, this addition is vaguely accepted by including in the development budget, along with public investment, additions to (but not the total of) certain types of expenditure on these items. As we show elsewhere, however, this procedure is not logically defensible.[1]

Not only certain forms of public expenditure for what is normally regarded as 'consumption', but private consumption expenditure, too, may affect the capital/output ratio, and it may be held that allowance for this could, in principle, be made in the model. First of all, improvements in nutrition increase both the ability to work and, by reducing apathy, the willingness to work. Secondly, certain incentive goods (e.g. bicycles), introduced at strategic points, increase the desire of workers for consumer goods and make them work harder to obtain them. If one is inclined to think in terms of supply curves, these incentive goods can be said to twist the backward-sloping supply curve forward.[2] Resultant increases in output may occur without any investment, but could be attributed to fuller utilisation of *human* capital, just as fuller utilisation of physical capacity might result in increased output without added investment.

Furthermore, for the calculation of an aggregate capital/output ratio it is important to know not only the effects on output in the organised sector of the economy but also what happens in the traditional sector. Part of the problem is that changes may occur in the traditional sector that raise output but could not be classified as 'investment', even if the statistics were available. Also, the effects of investment in the organised sector depend partly on spread effects and backwash effects in the traditional sector – unrecorded direct changes in output and repercussions on levels of living, attitudes and

---

[1] *Asian Drama*, Appendix 4, section 3.
[2] Gustav Ranis, 'Economic Development: A Suggested Approach', *Kyklos*, XII (1959) fasc. 3, p. 444.

institutions that only indirectly affect output. The problem is that these effects do not appear in any accounts anywhere. Nevertheless, investment in the organised sector affects directly and indirectly both the demand for the products of, and the supply of raw materials and labour in, the traditional sector.

Finally, government policies affect the capital/output ratio, both by giving rise to problems of correct valuation[1] and by affecting the degree of capacity utilisation, investment incentives and other conditions.

In view of such considerations, it may be asked whether the capital/ output ratio could be modified by adding the influences of these various factors and thus making it more adequate to the reality studied. An interesting attempt to refine the capital/output ratio in this way has been made by W. B. Reddaway.[2] In order to illustrate why this kind of attempt must fail, let us follow his refinement with a few small modifications and extensions.

We begin by considering the capital/output ratio at *sector level*. This allows for the fact that there are wide variations in the sectoral capital/output ratios, that the aggregate ratio is affected by the composition of investment and output, and that, unless further refined, the sum of the weighted sectors cannot take into account the interdependence of sectoral ratios. In spite of these limitations, it may be argued, the formula indicates the questions we need to ask and the information we need to collect, and we should therefore attempt to separate various influences affecting investment and changes in output for each separate sector.

Investment in a specified period in a particular sector will consist of I, plus any capital expenditure designed to save labour and other scarce resources without increasing output (M for 'modernisation').

As for the increase of output in a particular sector between two specified dates, we may distinguish between the following influences:

1. I/fk, the increase in output resulting from I, given the technological capital/output ratio k and the coefficient f expressing the lag of completions behind starts. Thus if the technological capital/output ratio $= 2$ and $f = 6$, a current annual investment outlay of 12 will yield extra output in the same year of 1.[3] There are difficulties about f. If growth does not proceed geometrically, f has to be replaced by a term in the numerator that indicates the lag between expenditure on construction and completions.

[1] Section 3.
[2] 'Some Observations on the Capital-Output Ratio', *The Development of the Indian Economy*, Appendix C.
[3] See Section 8, iii.

2. An increase due to better methods applied to old plant, involving little or no capital expenditure (T for technical progress not embodied in capital).
3. Increases (or decreases) due to fuller (or lower) utilisation of old plant, as a reflection of changes in demand (called U).
4. Changes due to better management and organisation, as, for example, more work shifts (called S).
5. Changes due to weather (W).
6. Changes due to improvements in attitudes and responses, better nutrition, education, training, health, etc. (A).
7. Changes due to improved institutions (N).
8. Changes due to revisions in domestic and foreign policies, as, for example, changes in the terms of trade (P).

One might then attempt to construct a modified formula for a sectoral capital/output ratio of the kind

$$\lambda_1 \frac{I+M}{I/fk + T + U + S + W + A + N + P}$$

where λ_1 is the sector's share in total extra output. And one could get a coefficient for the whole economy by adding the coefficients of all sectors weighted by their share in extra output.

Those who believe in the usefulness for planning of a technological capital/output ratio implicitly assume that $f = 1$ and that all terms except I are negligible. Once the other influences are recognised, it would be possible to maintain a modified capital/output ratio (no longer equal to the technological ratio k), if the other terms were (a) fairly stable and (b) independent of each other.

There are, however, difficulties in attempting even to attach a meaning to the now emaciated technological capital/output ratio k. It assumes a large number of conditions to be independently determined, including the number of shifts, the degree of capacity utilisation, labour supply and other inputs, attitudes, institutions and policies. If any of these is itself affected by investment, the assumption is unwarranted. In the service sector, increases in output can vary widely for a given investment; it is not possible to speak of a technologically 'fixed' ratio. Even in the industrial sector there are numerous difficulties – discussed in previous sections – such as differences between increases and decreases, differences according to whether existing facilities are expanded or new ones are built and how big the new or expanded facilities are.

Few other conditions can be assumed to be stable or independent of each other. The purpose of the development effort is precisely to change some of them drastically (for example, to raise f, T, and S).

And scarcely any one of them is a wholly independent variable. Many depend on historical factors. All are asymmetrical for upward and downward moves. And the valuation of output and of its flow in time involves political judgements. Labour-saving installations M depend partly on the rate of growth of demand and thus on I; T depends on $I + M$, for knowledge is acquired in the process of capital accumulation; I/fk depends on the size of I, and so on.

Then there is the problem of combining the sectoral ratios into an aggregate ratio. We can allow for greater or smaller capacity utilisation in any one sector as if it were an exogenous influence, but without further complicating the formula we cannot allow for the fact that changes in investment and/or output in one sector affect capacity utilisation in another. Similar interdependence applies also to other conditions. Nor would the problem be solved if allowance were made for simple interdependence. The size of aggregate investment and the timing of sectoral investment will make important differences in the degree and form of interdependence.

In the light of these difficulties and ambiguities, it is apparent that the 'capital/output ratio' can be of no assistance to the planner in deciding where, when, how, and how much to invest. In particular, the illegitimate isolation of a set of conditions and their misplaced aggregation neglect the importance of complementary policies and of all types of external economies and diseconomies. The concept can be used neither to calculate investment requirements for given output increments nor to estimate additional output from given investment. If sectoral capital/output ratios were meaningful and calculable, aggregate ratios would be unnecessary; if sectoral ratios are not known, aggregate ratios cannot be known. The ratio is thus either unnecessary or impossible to calculate.

When a factor – in our case capital – is singled out as the generator, or as a strategic instrument of growth, it is implicitly assumed that this factor can be used to overcome every other impediment. Thus a shortage of skilled labour, of administrative talent, or of foreign exchange must be capable of yielding to a sufficient application of capital. We showed in our transcendental criticism that this assumption is not justified. Complementarities between specific pieces of capital, between capital and other factors, and between investment and other policies may be so strong that substitutability is ruled out. The very concept of contrasting 'capital' with 'labour' on the one hand, and 'investment' with 'consumption' on the other, abstracts from the relevant relationships and cuts across the relevant dividing lines.

Supposing we accept the proposition that more capital per unit of output can surmount the impediments to a higher growth rate that are represented by shortages of natural resources and managerial skills and pressure of time. Given these impediments, we may ask, what is the minimum amount of capital required to generate a million units of additional output, defined as a combination of outputs at base year prices or some set of shadow prices determined by the planners. We assume a choice of techniques for calculating each of the various outputs, the sum of which constitutes additional output. Granted the assumptions about substitutability and assuming we have all the required knowledge, we can discover the minimum capital requirements. Suppose these are two million units. We then have an incremental capital/output ratio of 2. But what will the capital requirements be if the desired increment in output for the same period is doubled? Clearly, this problem cannot be solved in the same way as the first one. In so far as capital can be substituted for resources that are becoming increasingly scarce and have to be used less intensively, the use of capital will have to be more intensive, and the new capital requirements will thus be larger than 2.

Even on the assumptions implicit in the model, then, the capital coefficient can have no use. On the other hand, if we possessed all the required micro-economic information, the aggregate ratio would be unnecessary. The capital/output model is thus either useless or unnecessary.

Until more useful concepts are available, it would therefore seem more sensible to specify as best we can the anticipated effects – immediate and long-run, direct and indirect, primary and secondary – of each project than to conceal a host of suppressed valuations, ambiguous observations and defective analyses under the blanket expression 'capital/output ratio'.[1] It may be said of the efforts made in this essay to reach this conclusion: *parturiunt montes, nascetur*

[1] W. B. Reddaway states his conclusions admirably:

'For my own part I would hesitate to do more than put tentative questions, which would not necessarily be couched in terms of capital-output ratios. "Do you really think that better methods in agriculture will produce such rapid results? Will you *both* have so much fertilizer available in the time *and* induce the peasants to use it?" "Have you allowed enough for the teething troubles of new industrial plants, as well as the period of construction?" "Is it not likely that *both* investment *and* the increase in output will be lower, through administrative delays, difficulties over sites, etc.?"

'This sort of approach seems to me to get down to examining the real reasons why output will rise, which are not confined to the increase in the capital supply. ... discussions about the capital-output ratio, and assumptions made about it by model-builders, seem in danger of diverting attention from other factors.' ('Some Observations on the Capital-Output Ratio', *The Development of the Indian Economy*, p. 212.)

ridiculus mus. But a tiny real mouse may be better than a mythological beast, however elegant and splendid.

APPENDIX: A NOTE ON THE CAPITAL/OUTPUT RATIOS IN THE PLANS

The purpose of this note is to document very briefly what we say about the use of the 'capital/output ratio' in the plans and to illustrate the arbitrariness of the concept and its uselessness for planning. Use of the 'capital/output ratio' in the development plans takes various forms. It is not always clear in the plans whether planned investment or planned output increases come first. Some plans project a 'hoped-for' level of national income at the end of five years, and then decide how much investment is 'needed' to obtain it. Others apparently start with how much investment they can undertake and project the income from this.[1] The first two Pakistan plans and the plans for the Philippines and Thailand appear to estimate output increases and probable investment independently, without using the 'capital/output ratio' at all.

[1] Soviet planning in the past appears to have been based on the implicit assumption that the capital/output ratio must be raised in order to achieve rapid growth. The plans provided for a faster growth of capital goods than of consumption goods. This is, theoretically, compatible with a constant or even a declining capital/output ratio. The share of gross investment in gross national product can rise, while the rate of growth and the capital/output ratio are constant. This is so because a larger share of gross investment may mean a shorter average life of capital. This means that a higher proportion of workers are equipped with new capital, and since output per worker is higher with new than with old capital, average labour productivity will rise. Although in the transition period from the longer to the shorter life the rate of growth of output rises, once the capital stock is fully adjusted to the shorter life the rate of growth (at higher levels of output) will return to its initial level. Thus, after a period of adjustment, the faster growth of capital goods than of consumption goods will be accompanied by a higher proportion of gross investment to gross national product and a constant capital/output ratio.

Moreover, in the Soviet Union, the capital/output ratios could have remained constant in spite of increasing *capital/labour* ratios, if labour productivity had grown at the same rate as the capital/labour ratio. Stakhanovism, incentives to peasants and massive effort in health and education show that much was done to raise labour productivity. But it seems improbable that the effectiveness of 'investment in labour' equalled that of investment in equipment. More recently planning in the USSR and in China has placed less stress on raising capital intensity. In the Soviet Union the importance of reducing the capital/output ratio by various methods has been emphasised. In China, labour-intensive techniques and social change have been stressed in contrast to capital intensity and industrialisation. Inefficiency in the form of unintended excess capacity and unnecessarily high inventories because of inefficient distribution also make for a high, and if increasing, for a rising capital/output ratio.

(*footnote continued on next page.*)

India's First Plan begins with a discussion of the 'needed' rate of net investment. After looking at the situation in developed or rapidly developing economies, such as Hungary, Poland, Norway, Finland, Japan, the USSR, the United Kingdom and the United States, the plan concludes that 'in underdeveloped countries with low standards of living and rapidly increasing population, a rate of growth commensurate with needs cannot be achieved until the rate of capital formation comes up to around 20 per cent of the national income'.[1] Thus 'the question is in what manner and how quickly the rate of capital formation is India can be stepped up, consistently with other objectives, from about 5 per cent of the national income to, say, about 20 per cent'.[2]

The rate at which development can proceed is deemed to depend on (1) the rate of population growth and (2) the increase in national income likely to 'follow a given increase in the capital stock'.[3] These two factors determine how much of the additions to national income can be added to the stock of capital.

After this emphasis on the aggregate capital/output ratio, it is acknowledged that 'There is no unique capital-output ratio applicable to all countries at all times. Much depends not only on the stage of economic development reached but also on the precise forms of further expansion.'[4]

On certain key assumptions:

  (a) population growth = 1·25 per cent per annum
  (b) marginal capital/output ratio = 3·1 (with a time lag of 2 years)
  (c) average savings/income ratio (1968–69 onwards) = 20 per cent
      (initial, i.e. 1950–51, average ratio = 5 per cent); marginal
      savings ratio from 1956 to 1957 = 50 per cent

it is estimated that '*per capita* incomes can be doubled by about 1977, i.e. in about twenty-seven years'.[5] It is clear that this estimate is based on the experience of Japan. 'In Japan, with the population growing at an average annual rate of about 1¼ per cent, *per capita* income is estimated to have been doubled between 1878 and 1912; it was doubled again between 1913 and 1938.'[6] Thus Japan achieved a

---

N. M. Kaplan and R. H. Moorsteen reach the 'highly tentative and provisional' conclusion for the Soviet Union that 'The ratio of capital to output has increased ... monotonically and substantially over the observed years from 1927/28 through 1950, but the change is ambiguous ... through 1957.' ('An Index of Soviet Industrial Output', *American Economic Review*, L 3 (June 1960) 317.)

[1] India, Government of, Planning Commission, *The First Five Year Plan* (New Delhi, 1953) p. 14.
[2] Ibid., p. 17.   [3] Ibid., p. 18.   [4] Ibid.
[5] Ibid., pp. 20–21.   [6] Ibid., p. 14.

doubling of national income over successive periods of thirty-four and twenty-five years, respectively, with a rate of population growth identical with that assumed in India's First Plan. But the First Plan estimates that Japan's investment rate fluctuated between 12 and 17 per cent from 1900 to 1929,[1] and uses a capital/output ratio appropriate to 'some of the relatively more developed countries of the world'.[2]

Japan's achievement seems to represent the Indian goal, and the First Plan is based on assumptions that generally fit the Japanese experience. The 'needed' rate of investment postulated is comparable to that of Japan's second period, while the rate of population growth is taken as equal to Japan's. The capital/output ratio, however, is nearer to the United States and the United Kingdom experience.

In the Second Plan most of the assumptions were revised:[3]

(a) The rate of population growth was kept at 12·75 per cent per decade for 1951–60, but raised to 13·3 per cent for 1961–70 and 14 per cent for 1971–80. (This would have resulted in a population of 408 million in 1960–61; it was in fact 438 million at the beginning of 1961 and is now over 500 million.)

(b) The incremental capital/output ratio was revised downward in the light of experience in the first quinquennium but was assumed to be rising. The values established were: 2·3 for the Second Plan, 2·6 for the Third, 3·4 for the Fourth and 3·7 for the Fifth Plan. Numerous qualifications to a simple use of the capital/output ratio were mentioned, including good monsoons, full utilisation of capacity, technical advance, efficiency in handling new investment, quality of managerial and organisational skill, co-ordination of programmes, avoidance of business cycles, composition of investment. It is also pointed out that non-monetised investment had not been included in capital inputs.[4]

(c) The estimated rate at which savings and investment could be increased was lowered. The ratio was now assumed to go up from 7 per cent of national income in 1955–56 to about 11 per cent in 1960–61, 14 per cent in 1965–66, 16 per cent by 1970–71 and 17 per cent by 1975–76. From this it was concluded that *'per capita* incomes would be doubled by 1973–74'.[5]

In the Introduction to the Second Five Year Plan it was stated that Professor Mahalanobis's work determined the basic approach. His

---

[1] Ibid., p. 13. However, the Second Plan states that in Japan the net investment rate averaged 16 to 20 per cent between 1913 and 1939. (India, Government of, Planning Commission, *Second Five Year Plan*, New Delhi, 1956, p. 10.)

[2] India, *The First Five Year Plan*, p. 19.

[3] India, *Second Five Year Plan*, pp. 8–10.

[4] Ibid., pp. 9, 10.   [5] Ibid., pp. 10, 11.

model, as we have said, departs from the Harrod-Domar model.[1] There can be no doubt that the Mahalanobis model strongly influenced the Second Five Year Plan. It served a useful purpose in deflecting emphasis from the savings ratio and in stressing other limitations, such as lack of foreign exchange and the inadequate share of a *given* savings ratio being allocated to investment goods, and in suggesting, if only implicitly, a possible interdependence between the savings ratio and the capital/output ratio. In so far as it loosened the grip of the crude capital/output model it presented a move towards flexibility, though the particular division into sectors was a move away from rather than towards reality and operational meaning.

In the Third Plan the capital/output ratio as an explicitly formulated concept was dropped altogether. But there is still evidence of a prior determination of output growth, implying a certain rate of 'needed' investment. The aim, as stated in the Draft Outline, is 'to secure during the third plan a rise in national income of over 5 per cent per annum'.[2] 'For achieving a cumulative rate of growth of over 5 percent per annum, it will be necessary to undertake net investment to the extent of more than 14 percent of the national income as compared to the present level of about 11·5 percent.'[3] The needed investment is, however, analysed on a sectoral basis in the Third Plan. Nevertheless, there is a tendency to neglect some of the problems we have discussed in this part, and one gets the impression that the output projection is little more than *past* growth rates slightly raised.

The plans in India and elsewhere do not always show that much detailed analysis goes on behind the scenes. Although attempts have been made – at least in India and Pakistan – to get away from aggregate capital/output ratios and to undertake project planning, some of the objections discussed apply, as we have seen, also to project and sector ratios. And these attempts apply only to the public sector. A common method is to start with an aggregate capital/output ratio, stipulate a certain amount of public investment and a certain rate of income growth, and then derive the required private investment as a residual. However sensible this approach to public investment may be, the plan is vitiated by the lack of control over the private sector. There is a slide from 'needed' to 'planned' to 'pro-

[1] Mahalanobis, 'Some Observations on the Process of Growth of National Income', *Sankhyā*, vol. 12, pt. 4 (Sep 1953), and 'The Approach of Operational Research to Planning in India', *Sankhyā*, vol. 16, pts. 1 and 2 (Dec 1955). See above, Section 6.

[2] India, Government of, Planning Commission, *Third Five Year Plan, A Draft Outline* (New Delhi, June 1960) p. 11; cf. India, Government of, Planning Commission, *Third Five Year Plan* (New Delhi, 1961) p. 48.

[3] India, *Third Five Year Plan*, p. 51.

jected' investment, creating the illusion that the private and the public sectors have been treated symmetrically.

Most of the plans use the country-wide incremental capital/output ratio as a rough guide to the amount of investment required in order to achieve the rise in national income that is planned or expected or hoped for – it is not always clear which of these is being estimated. The importance attached to this ratio justifies the presentation of a table showing the explicitly or implicitly assumed (*ex ante*) and the actual (*ex post*) ratios. According to Table 6.8, there are wide divergences not only between the countries of the region (ranging from an assumed low of 1·26 for the Philippines to an actual high of nearly 5 for Pakistan) but also between the assumed and actual ratios where they have been calculated, as for India and Pakistan. Such variations reflect more the weaknesses of the concept as a tool of planning and forecasting than any fundamental differences between the economies or in the degree of success in planning.

It should be noted that even quite small errors in the calculation of the capital/output ratio have large effects. Thus if a coefficient of 3·1 is used when it is in fact 3·2, additional output will have been overestimated by more than 3 per cent; and if 3 is used when 4 is correct, the overestimation is one third for the first year and more later.

We present the figures as an illustration of the argument in the preceding parts of this essay, and not as constituting valuable evidence in their own right. The following points are worth noting:

1. *Climate.* In India the low actual ratio in the First Plan was the result of favourable monsoons in the last two years of the plan period, whereas in Pakistan poor weather was responsible for the high actual ratios at the end of the First Plan.

2. *Gestation period.* Only India's First Plan makes an explicit assumption about this. The others generally ignore it. Yet many projects will not yield output until some time after the normal planning period. Problems of phasing seem generally to be ignored.

3. *Working capital.* Its treatment is quite inconsistent and obscure. Some plans do not say whether it is included or not (Burma I, Thailand, South Vietnam, and Indonesia). Some exclude it explicitly (Burma II, p. 36; Philippines, pp. 14–15). India's First Plan is vague and has no provision for working capital. The Second and Third Plans provide for increases in inventories, but the Second Plan does not say whether public investment includes working capital; it assumes working capital to be 6·5 per cent of total net investment. The Third Plan includes an estimate of Rs. 200 crores for investment in inventories in the public sector (total investment 6,300 crores) and Rs. 600 crores for this purpose in the private sector (total investment

TABLE 6.8

Implied and Actual Incremental Capital/Output Ratios

Country	Plan	Plan Period	Output Concept	Investment Concept	Incremental Capital/Output Ratio (I: Implied; A: Actual)
Pakistan	I	April 1955– March 1960	NNP fc	Gross	(I) 3·51 (A) 4·42 (A) 4·90
	II	June 1960– July 1965	GNP fc	Gross	(I) 3·69
India	I	April 1951– March 1956	NNP fc	Net	(I) 3·00 (A) 1·83
	II	April 1956– March 1961	NNP fc	Net	(I) 2·31 (A) 3·12
	III	April 1961– March 1966	NNP fc	Net	(I) 2·31
Indonesia		Jan 1956– Dec 1960	NNP fc	Net	(I) 2·10
Burma	I	Oct 1956– Sep 1960	GDP mp	Gross	(I) 3·69 (A) 3·26
	II	Oct 1961– Sep 1965	GDP mp	Net	(I) 3·10
South Vietnam		Jan 1957– Jan 1961	GDP mp	Net	(I) 2·00
Philippines		Jan 1957– Dec 1961	GDP mp	Net	(I) 1·26
Thailand		Jan 1961– Sep 1966	GDP mp	Gross	(no estimate priv. inv.)
Ceylon		Jan 1959– Dec 1968	GDP fc	Gross	(I) 2·85
			NNP fc		(I) 2·30
Malaya	II	Jan 1961– Dec 1965	GNP mp	Gross	(I) 3·84

Note: The incremental capital/output ratio is defined as 'investment' divided by the increase in national income over the plan period.

GDP = gross domestic product
GNP = gross national product
NNP = net national product
fc = at factor cost　　　mp = at market prices

Pakistan: The First Five Year Plan says: 'We do not know what the incremental capital-output ratio in Pakistan is, nor is it useful to attempt to apply ratios calculated from the very different experience of other countries.' (*The First Five Year Plan 1955–60*, p. 67.) The two estimates of the capital/output ratio in the

(*Notes continued on following page*)

(Notes to Table 6.8 continued)

First Plan reflect the two separate figures given for 'total development expenditure'. No explanation for the difference is given. (Pakistan, Government of, Planning Commission, *The Second Five Year Plan, 1960–1965* (Karachi, 1960): at p. 3, Rs. 9,715 million; at p. 28, Rs. 10,780 million.) Since the investment figures are in current prices and GNP figures in constant prices, we deflated the former by national income deflators. (Institute of Development Economics, Monographs in the Economics of Development, No. 4, *A Measure of Inflation in Pakistan 1951–60* (Karachi: Mar 1961) p. 21.)

India: In the First Five Year Plan the capital-output ratio was taken as 3, *with a time lag of 2 years between the increase in investment and the increase in output.* (*Second Five Year Plan*, p. 8.) Unadjusted, the capital/output ratio would have been 3·5–3·6. Apparently no such time lag is assumed in the Second Plan, which gives the capital/output ratio as 2·3. (Ibid., p. 9.) The Third Plan provides for a rise in national income of Rs. 4,500 crores and investment of Rs. 10,400 crores in 1960–61 prices, which yields a marginal capital/output ratio of 2·31. (*Third Five Year Plan*, p. 28.)

Indonesia: The Indonesian plan says: 'It must be emphasized that the marginal capital-output ratio of approximately 2 applies only to the First-Year [*sic*] Plan (1956–1960) . . ., after which it will rise to 4.' (Indonesia, Government of, State Planning Bureau, *Broad Outlines of the Five-Year Development Plan 1956–60* (Djakarta, 1958) mimeographed, p. 3.)

Burma: Reckoned at the current prices assumed in the First Plan, the anticipated capital/output ratio would be 3·69; reckoned at constant prices (according to another plan assumption), the ratio would be 3·28. The Second Plan says: 'Net investment requirements during the Plan period are worked out . . . assuming a gestation period of one year, and marginal capital-output ratios of 3:1 and 2·9:1.' (Burma, Government of, Ministry of National Planning, *Second Four Year Plan for the Union of Burma 1961–62 to 1964–65*, A Draft Outline (Rangoon, 1961) p. 26.) Of the two, the Second Plan prefers the latter: 'If a marginal capital-output of 2·9:1 is accepted for the Plan period, total net investment in 1959–60 prices required to produce a 5 per cent growth in three years within the Plan period (1962–63, 1963–64 and 1964–65) and one year outside (1965–66) would be K 96·0 crores, K 100·8 crores, K 105·9 crores and K 111·3 crores respectively for the four plan years. . . .' (Ibid., p. 27.) The plan does not 'include any provision for employment of the presently unemployed . . . [nor does it] contemplate any more modern and therefore more productive methods of production than exist at present.' (Ibid., p. 31.)

Ceylon: The Ten Year Plan gives capital/output ratios for different sectors of the economy. These 'have been computed by dividing the respective amounts of expansion investment (viz. investment which increases gross domestic product as distinct from replacement investment which is required for maintaining the existing level of gross domestic product) by the corresponding increase in gross domestic product.' (*The Ten Year Plan*, pp. 80–81.) For the economy as a whole, the capital/output ratio thus defined – gross investment, including non-monetised investment minus depreciation divided by increase in gross domestic product – is 2·6. (Ibid., p. 110.) The ratios in the table relate gross investment to GNP and net investment to NNP at factor cost. It seems that the sectoral ratios have not been used for planning purposes. After a discussion of the advantages and disadvantages of investing in industries with high and low capital/output ratios, the plan says that 'a compromise has been adopted and provisions have been made for an expansion of sectors with a low as well as high capital output ratio'. (Ibid., p. 82.)

(Notes to Table 6.8 continued)

Malaya: The Second Plan explicitly assumes 'a ration of investment to output of about 4:1 which is about one-third higher than similar ratios in many other countries'. (*Second Five Year Plan 1961–1965*, p. 24.) The length of time required for investments to mature is given as the reason for this difference; otherwise it appears that no use has been made of the concept in the plan.

4,100 crores).[1] A. K. Sen, however, estimates that the working capital requirements for just the five sectors he considers will be well above Rs. 1,800 crores – considerably more than twice the amount actually provided for. The requirements of manufacturing alone will be considerably greater than the total provided for in the Third Plan.[2]

4. *Municipal overhead capital.* This is an important component of capital expenditure, particularly when development is attempted. Although sewage, water, gas, and municipal housing absorb scarce resources, the plans do not always clearly account for them.

5. *Private investment.* Since only public investment is under the direct control of the governments, it is not always clear how the aggregate ratio, which includes private investment, is calculated. One method, as we have seen, is to start with an aggregate ratio, stipulate public investment and a certain rate of income growth, and then derive the required private investment as a residual. The distinction between 'required', 'hoped-for' and 'planned' investment is not clear. Alternatively, one starts with public investment, adds to this guesses about private investment and output growth, and then derives the capital/output ratio as a residual.[3]

6. *Non-monetised investment.* This is particularly difficult to estimate. Pakistan's First Plan says it 'may be of the order of 1,500 to 2,000 million . . . rupees during the Plan period',[4] but no estimate is given in the plan and no indication of what significance such an estimate can have. Pakistan's Second Plan does not even mention it. The Ceylon plan, however, includes it as a big item (Rs. 855 million out of total gross investment of Rs. 13,600 million).[5]

[1] India, *Third Five Year Plan*, p. 59.

[2] A. K. Sen, 'Working Capital in the Indian Economy: A Conceptual Framework and Some Estimates', chapter 6, p. 146, in Rosenstein-Rodan (ed.), *Pricing and Fiscal Policies, A Study in Method.*

[3] For example, this appears to be the procedure employed in the Second Plan of Malaya. (Malaya, Government of the Federation of, *Second Five Year Plan 1961–1965* (Kuala Lumpur, 1961) pp. 22–5.)

[4] Pakistan, Government of, National Planning Board, *The First Five Year Plan 1955–1960* (Karachi, 1957) p. 16.

[5] Ceylon, Government of, National Planning Council, *The Ten Year Plan* (Colombo, 1959) p. 78.

7 An Institutional Critique of Development Concepts

A CRITICAL examination of economic models soon leads to the examination of concepts, which are the bricks of which the models are built. Such an examination reveals that the bias in our view of economic and social reality enters before the model building begins, at the level where concepts are formed. The formulation of any concept, as I have tried to argue in my chapter on 'The Use and Abuse of Models in Development Planning',[1] presupposes two procedures: aggregation of one set of items and isolation of this set from other sets. When we speak of a 'tree' we aggregate birches, beeches, elms, firs, larches, etc., into one category and, at the same time, differentiate them from bushes, shrubs, flowers, ferns, etc.

A chief criticism of some concepts used in economics is that this aggregation and isolation is carried out along misleading or unhelpful lines. The distinction between 'consumption' and 'investment' or between 'employment' and 'unemployment' may be useful in one setting but inappropriate in another. It is the essence of what is sometimes called the institutional approach to probe into the psychological, social, political and cultural justification for the formation of certain concepts. I have attempted to subject the concept 'capital output ratio', which forms a pillar of development models and development plans, to such an institutional criticism in Appendix 3 of Gunnar Myrdal's *Asian Drama*[2] reproduced as Chapter 6 of this book.

The main conclusion of that discussion is that the postulate of a fairly constant relationship between inputs of capital and the flow of production attributed to them is completely unwarranted, but, at the same time, supports strong vested interests which would suffer from the measures to which a deeper probe would give rise.

Even accepting the framework of conventional economic analysis,

---

[1] In Kurt Martin and John Knapp (eds), *The Teaching of Development Economics* (London: Frank Cass, 1967), Chapter 5 in this book. I am grateful to Michael Lipton for helpful comments.

[2] (Hardmondsworth: Pelican Books, 1968), vol. III.

the notion of constant incremental capital-output ratios is untenable. First, the ratio depends upon the distribution of investment between sectors, the bulk of which do not contribute directly to production (housing, public utilities, schools, hospitals, roads). Second, even the technological ratio in commodity production is not fixed. Much depends upon the techniques and processes used, and the collectiön of commodities produced. Third, the ratio depends upon the rate of investment itself. The more rapid is the accumulation of capital, the higher will be the proportion of the most up-to-date machinery. Fourth, it depends on the availability of other factors of production and their quality, especially land and labour. Fifth, it depends upon population growth and population density, the level and rate of growth of unemployment and the policies pursued to reduce unemployment.

But the framework of the analysis must itself be subjected to criticisms. The common assumption that social institutions and human attitudes and aptitudes are either fully adapted to economic change or speedily adaptable is unfounded. The ratio will crucially depend upon institutional arrangements (agricultural output from irrigation depends on land tenure; industrial output on public and private administration). It will depend upon motivation and skills. The degree of capacity utilisation of a large steel plant can vary from under 50 per cent to nearly 100 per cent, depending on the quality of management, while capital (and other) inputs remain the same. Workers learn by doing, farmers and peasants acquire new motives, managers organise things differently with time and experience. In each of these cases the relationship between capital inputs and the flow of production will be tenuous. To postulate a constant relationship merely detracts from the need to focus on the institutional and human changes required to fuller utilisation of resources and serves as an elaborate smokescreen.

In a critique of the concepts used in development planning, two distinct problems arise: first, a concept may be appropriate for one set of circumstances, say those of advanced industrial countries, but inapplicable to underdeveloped countries. Just as it makes sense to ask in Delhi 'Where is the University?' but not in Oxford, so it may make sense to ask 'What has been the growth of income per head?' in Sweden but not in Kuwait.

Second, the same concept might be appropriate in both sets of circumstances if we knew what it meant when applied to a situation of underdevelopment. The point can be illustrated by the distinction between consumption and investment. If investment is defined as 'abstaining from consumption now for the sake of higher consumption later', the first problem may arise: the concept is inapplicable in conditions in which *higher* consumption *now* can lead to *higher* consumption *later*, through better feeding, reduced apathy, improved health, greater resistance to disease. But if investment is defined as any input which yields higher output later, in other words as 'development expenditure', the question as to whether 'abstaining' is involved does not arise. The second problem then arises: which activities should we group under 'investment' in underdeveloped countries which, in advanced countries, would be classified as 'consumption'. The debate about investment in human beings can be regarded as a widening of the concept 'investment' rather than as its dismissal.

It is possible to widen the concept 'capital' even further so as to include anything that yields a stream of production and income over time. All forms of income- and product-yielding activities can be interpreted as creating 'assets' whose value can be determined by capitalising the expected production stream at an appropriate rate of interest.

Investment in 'human' capital is already generally treated in this fashion. Raising levels of living by better feeding, education and health measures, and reforming some human attitudes by the creation of incentives, are nowadays treated as investment, although, as in the case of physical investment, the need for an appropriate composition is sometimes neglected in the act of aggregation and the need for complementary activities is occasionally forgotten. The question remains whether the reform of institutions of all relevant attitudes and of policies can be approached in the same way – i.e. as the creation of 'capital' in an even wider sense than that embracing both physical and human capital.

The answer depends on whether these measures require the application of current resources and whether the costs incurred can be subjected to the economic calculus. It can be argued that the implementation of a land reform or of an effective birth control campaign depends only to a small extent on the amount of money spent and that such propositions as 'a pound invested in birth control is a hundred times as effective as a pound devoted to physical investment' are pointless. One can admit that costs in the widest sense must be incurred in order to reform attitudes and institutions, but that these costs are largely social and psychological and cannot be subjected to the measuring rod of money.

Such costs may be regarded as the risks of failure to achieve the intended goals, such as effective land reform or population control. If each outcome is multiplied by its probability (taking institutional obstacles fully into account), the sum of these products may be regarded as the true economic yield of the money costs involved. The danger is that a spurious air of confidence is given to probability estimates, which are bound to remain largely matters of judgement or guessing.

To the criticism of the unmeasurability of yields a number of replies can be made. First, even if these psychic and social costs were entirely unmeasurable, usually some resource costs are involved and it is of interest to planners what these costs are. Second, the fact that these 'investments' are not embodied either in physical or in human capital does not *ipso facto* preclude calculation. Investment in some branches of knowledge has become a matter of routine and its returns can be estimated. Firms try to make estimates of the yield of their expenditure on advertising and the creation of goodwill – activities directed at changing human attitudes. Similarly, a rough estimate of the returns on the reform of attitudes, institutions and policies may be possible, at least in some cases.

Third, the main difficulty arises not because investment is not 'embodied' in a visible asset, but rather because the concept 'investment' assumes substitutability between different forms of investment, both in production and in consumption – so that the investment yielding the highest returns can be selected – whereas many investments are complementary – e.g. equipment, training for a skilled labour force, social overheads, breakdown of caste prejudices and reform of trade union structure. It may be argued that this is not a conceptual difficulty but merely a reason why calculations are more complicated. For one could argue that the return on a particular investment is a vector, depending on investment volumes A, B, C or even A, B, $A + B$, $A + C$, $A + B + C$, etc. The choice of a constrained optimal investment set is still possible, just harder. But the point is that the stronger such complementarities and their interaction with other complementarities, the less can be said about particular acts of investment in isolation and the more important does it become to compare whole strategies or alternative packages, appropriately phased.

At the same time, the institutional approach to development in the above sense avoids certain kinds of fault: it is no longer possible to say that labour is a plentiful factor in underdeveloped countries and capital is scarce, when it is seen that people have to be trained, educated, motivated, and given the institutional framework before they become productive agents and these forms of investment may be even more costly, and may yield lower returns than investment in certain types of equipment.

While the 'returns to investment' approach tends to overemphasise the opportunities for substitution (a bias it shares with marginal productivity theory), the manpower planning approach has the opposite bias. By assuming fixed coefficients between skills, other factors of production and output (and often also between teachers and pupils), it transfers all the errors of using fixed capital coefficients from planning physical to planning human investment. A generalised approach to capital accumulation may help to correct both biases. It may help to approach different investment complexes (the components of which are complementary) as substitutes in the strategy for development. The returns of such complexes or packages could, in principle, be compared. But it would amount to the evaluation of different large strategic decisions, not of marginal or infinitesimal moves.

Rather than continue at a general and abstract level, I should like to give another illustration of an institutional critique, using this time the concepts 'employment' and 'unemployment'. The argument elaborates the reasoning in *Asian Drama*.[1] It has the incidental advantage of dealing with a problem which will become increasingly serious in the next ten to fifteen years.

Employment and unemployment

Most less developed countries have what is commonly described as a serious and growing problem of surplus labour, unemployment, disguised unemployment and underemployment. Whatever the precise interpretation of these somewhat vague and ill-defined terms, there can be no doubt that development policies must give a high priority to a fuller mobilisation and utilisation of what is sometimes thought to be their most abundant factor of production – unskilled labour. It is worth considering briefly the notions of unemployment, disguised unemployment and underemployment.

Unemployment, underemployment and disguised unemployment are often considered both a cause of poverty and a potential source of development. Approaches in terms of 'employment', 'unemployment' and 'underemployment' are misleading because they suggest that an increase in effective demand and the provision of equipment are all that is needed to absorb labour and raise production, while all other conditions are adapted or easily and quickly adaptable to full labour utilisation. In fact, a number of other measures are necessary for a full mobilisation and utilisation of manpower: better feeding, improvements in health, training and education, transport and housing, and fundamental attacks on prevailing attitudes to life and work (e.g. women's participation, a contempt for certain kinds of work, the desire to minimise work, lack of discipline) and on institutions (introduction of standard working week and working day, creation of labour market, provision of information, readiness to

[1] Op. cit., especially vol. II chap. xxi.

move from one place to another or to change one's occupation, etc.).

As a first step, it is helpful to break down the multiplicity of dimensions of Income (or Product) per Head of the Population into four categories. These should aid the collection of data, the organisation of thought, and the formulation of policies.[1]

$$\frac{Income}{Population} = \frac{Production}{Hours\ Worked} \cdot \frac{Hours\ Worked}{Labour\ Force} \cdot$$

$$\frac{Labour\ Force}{People\ of\ Working\ Age} \cdot \frac{People\ of\ Working\ Age}{Population}$$

The identity brings out four distinct aspects of the Level of Living (= Income per head) on which more information would be useful for framing policies for the multidimensional aspects of labour utilisation. It is important to note that the ratios are not independent of one another.

(1) $\qquad \dfrac{Production}{Hours\ Worked}$ or *hourly productivity*

depends, in any given activity in any given sector, on a large number of factors, including other terms in the identity, such as: hours worked and participation rate (see below (2) and (3)); also on equipment, fuel, raw materials and other complementary productive factors; education and training; health affecting work such as intestinal parasites, amoebas, onchocerciasis or schistosomiasis, intensity of application, itself a function of morale; industrial relations; motivation; incentives, etc.; organisation of work, management, etc.

This category covers numerous aspects, some of the most important of which are difficult to measure. It should be analysed in greater detail. For the country as a whole, it is an average of all sectors, each weighted by its share in the total number of hours worked. If we denote the sectors as 1, 2, 3, etc., and their shares in total working hours as h_1, h_2, etc., we can write:

$$\frac{Output}{Hours} = h_1 \frac{Y_1}{H_1} + h_2 \frac{Y_2}{H_2} + \ldots$$

Hourly productivity can be raised if all other things remain constant, either by transferring workers from low-productivity to high-productivity sectors, or by raising productivity within sectors.

[1] A similar identity was first used by Michael Lipton in a working paper for Myrdal's *Asian Drama* in April 1961. See also W. J. Barber, 'Some Questions about Labour Force Analysis in Agrarian Economies with particular reference to Kenya', *East African Economic Review* (June 1966), and Myrdal, op. cit.

(2) $$\frac{Hours}{Labour\ Force}$$ or *working time rate*

depends on organisational and institutional factors; whether there
is a standard working day and working week; whether overtime is
worked; whether multiple shifts exist; whether time is wasted in
idleness, waiting for materials and components, or spent on holidays,
weddings, funerals and at feasts. It also depends on natural factors
such as the weather and the requirements of harvest seasons. The
ratio will depend both upon the level of demand and on the availability of essential supplies. A shift of rural labour to urban industry
raises output not only by changing the weights attached to low- and
high-productivity sectors, but also by raising hours per labour force.
Unemployment of people both willing and able to work will show
up as low hours/labour force. But the distinction between ability
to work and willingness to work in any occupation outside the home
may not always be easy to draw or even logically legitimate (e.g.
Moslem women). Much time is spent in an underdeveloped country
moving from one place to another: peasants walk from one piece
of their land to another; women walk back and forth to draw water;
migrant workers walk from one region to another to collect the harvest, etc. In so far as these movements are necessary to carry out
specific tasks, given the prevailing institutions, transport facilities
and co-operating factors, it is a factor accounting for low hourly
productivity. But if the movements are in search of work, they come
under low working time.

(3) $$\frac{Labour\ Force}{People\ of\ Working\ Age}$$ or *participation rate*

depends on attitudes to work and to gainful activities (their dignity
or ignominy) housing and transport facilities, legislation about
minimum working age, compulsory full-time education, etc. Removal
of the objections to certain kinds of work, increased incentives to
earn money, emancipation of women, improved mobility, etc., will
raise participation rates.

Education is by no means necessarily an investment with positive
returns. It can result in reduced labour force participation. The
educated unemployed, a widespread phenomenon in South Asia,
figure prominently in unemployment statistics. While their geographical mobility between urban areas is high, their occupational
mobility is small. They are not prepared to accept manual work.
From a sample survey of unemployment in Calcutta in 1953 it
appears that only ten per cent of the unemployed were illiterate and

27 per cent had enjoyed higher education. Only 43 per cent of the total sample were seeking work involving manual labour.

The attitude to work appropriate for one who has enjoyed education is rooted in traditional attitudes and reinforced by the colonial heritage and possibly even by technical assistance. It is by no means just a matter of the wrong curriculum, for there is large and growing unemployment of engineers in India. It is estimated that there were about 50,000 fully qualified engineers unemployed in 1970. The shortage exists in the same occupation for less qualified people, e.g. for semi-skilled technicians.

Both in Asia and in Africa, education reflects and instils an anti-rural bias; indeed the pressures for education arise from a desire on the part of parents and teachers to free their children from the miseries and hardships of rural life.

Attitudes towards work among the educated – often ill-educated – are deeply rooted in the social structure and cannot easily be elimi-nated by restoring 'equilibrium' between supply and demand, by changing curricula or by exhortation.

There are parallels between the participation rate of the unemployed and the participation rate of women. Non-participation of women is linked with status and prestige, particularly in the higher strata of society.

(4) $\dfrac{\textit{People of Working Age}}{\textit{Population}}$ is a *demographic ratio*

and will depend on the age structure of the population, which can be predicted with a fair degree of accuracy. All those of working age in fourteen years' time are already alive and only mortality and migration rates have to be allowed for.

Since each of our four categories, viz. (1) hourly productivity, (2) working time rate, (3) participation rate and (4) demographic ratio, is an average of sectoral ratios, each sector appropriately weighted, the identity can be rewritten as:

$$\frac{Y}{P} = \left[h_1 \frac{Y_1}{H_1} + h_2 \frac{Y_2}{H_2} + \ldots \right] . \quad \left[l_1 \frac{H_1}{L_1} + l_2 \frac{H_2}{L_2} + \ldots \right] .$$
$$\left[p_1 \frac{L_1}{W_1} + p_2 \frac{L_2}{W_2} + \ldots \right] . \quad \left[s_1 \frac{W_1}{P_1} + s_2 \frac{W_2}{P_2} + \ldots \right]$$

where Y is total income (output)

H is total hours worked

L is labour force

W is working age group

P is population

h is share in total hours worked
l is share in labour force
p is share in age group
s is share in population

and the suffixes indicate the different sectors.

The conventional presentation suffers from the fact that intensity of work, skill, organisation, education, health, labour markets, transport, information, etc., are assumed given. Thus the only variables are demand and equipment. Furthermore, the assumption is usually made that unemployment and underemployment are 'involuntary'.[1] This implies that willingness and ability to work are present. It also presupposes Labour Exchanges or some other objective test of voluntariness. Without such a test, it is impossible to tell. Some men work with dysentery, others don't. Some may not seek work because they know or believe that none is available. In the absence of an organised market for labour, the distinction between voluntary and involuntary unemployment breaks down. Unemployment and underemployment must also be defined with reference to some standard of working hours per day and working days per week. But such standards do not exist in large parts of traditional societies and are therefore introduced, usually implicitly, from outside. The whole set of questions relating to participation and organised work

TABLE 7.1

Compulsive, Permissive and Persuasive Measures

	Compulsive	*Permissive*	*Persuasive* *(incentives)*
Output/Hour	Make pay depend on minimum output	Forbid trade union restrictions	Piece rates
Hours/Lab. Force	Fix 8-hour day	Improve diet	Overtime rates
Lab. Force/ People of Working Age	Lock up workless, conscript, poll tax	Raise demand, provide equipment	Raise wages, supply incentive goods
People of Working Age/ Population	Draconian measures against large families, forced late marriage	Birth control advice and contraceptives supplied	Birth control campaigns, a transistor for a vasectomy, child tax

[1] L. Currie, *Accelerating Development* (New York, 1966) p. 168: '[. . .] there is a great deal of idleness, voluntary, and involuntary' [in Colombia]. In the Ivory Coast, the essence of the primitive methods of producing coffee is described by Prof. Barna as minimising the amount of work necessary for obtaining a coffee crop of any sort.

is thereby begged and a number of important relationships are concealed.

Once the relevant distinctions are drawn, policies can then be classified according to whether they use compulsive, permissive or persuasive measures.[1] The table on p. 125 provides illustrations.

The main lesson of this brief discussion is that the utilisation of labour in developing countries has many dimensions and it is not warranted to assume that attitudes, aptitudes and institutions are adapted to full labour utilisation or that consumption at low levels of living has no effect on productivity. Measures which raise labour productivity may reduce hours worked or participation rates[2] and measures which raise participation rates may lead to work-spreading and less intensive or to otherwise less productive work. Only a simultaneous attack on several of the relevant variables can bring about fuller utilisation of labour.

The analysis also bears on the argument that there is a surplus of unskilled labour to draw on for any alternative activities and that labour opportunity costs are therefore low or zero. If these alternatives require attitudes, motivations, responses, work habits or institutions different from those to be found in, say, coffee growing, the fact that coffee growers dispose over spare time is irrelevant to the availability of labour supply for these alternatives. It would be dangerous to argue from the premiss that coffee growing does not take up all the potential working hours of the farmers to the conclusion that alternative work opportunities, either elsewhere or in the place of residence, would automatically be taken up and result in larger production. Proposals for alternatives must be accompanied by detailed specification as to what measures of reform with respect to human attitudes to work and life and to social and commercial institutions, such as land reform, or reform of the civil service, or the creation of a labour market, or of credit channels, or of marketing outlets, have to accompany this shift in resources.

The main causes of the gross underutilisation of labour are to be found in rural underemployment, combined with an industrial sector which, though often growing very rapidly in terms of production, is too small and often uses techniques inappropriate to absorb even a

---

[1] The distinction is due to P. Sargant Florence, *The Logic of British and American Industry* (London: Routledge and Kegan Paul, 1953). The application to the theory of controls was suggested by Michael Lipton to Gunnar Myrdal. Further subdivisions are possible by combining the general-specific and positive-negative distinctions with those in the table.

[2] Currie, op. cit., p. 156: '[. . .] The relative high productivity of the machine, and the use of better techniques in commercial farming lower the return the colonial-type farmer can gain and make it even less practical for him to do all the costly things that would increase his productivity.'

fraction of the rapidly growing potential labour force. Under-utilisation reflects the attitudes and institutions of a backward society and can therefore not be treated as a source for its transformation.

Conclusions

The main conclusion is to beware of the simple transfer of fairly sophisticated concepts from one setting to another, without close scrutiny of the institutional differences.[1] Liberation from the powerful legacy of intellectual traditions is extremely difficult. Although Myrdal asserts that 'facts kick', it is my experience that the power of the crust of intellectual tradition is stronger than the kicks. It takes a model to kick out a model, as is shown by the dominance of Say's law in the face of mass unemployment, until Keynes' *General Theory* appeared. Scientific research and its dissemination by teachers is characterised by standard models: by certain established grooves which determine the questions asked, the categories by which we order the empirical material and the methods we use in deriving answers. These models are at once a crutch and a prison, since it is in their nature that they focus on some aspects of reality at the expense of others. The material which remains intractable is presented as anomalies, exceptions, modifications. Only when a new model is constructed along radically different lines do these anomalies come into their own. Perhaps the best answer to the question: how are we to choose between models, was given by Kaldor:[2]

A theoretical model consists of certain hypotheses concerning the causal interrelationship between various magnitudes or forces and the sequence in which they react on each other. We all agree that the basic requirement of any model is that it should be capable of explaining the characteristic features of the economic process as we find them in reality. It is no good starting off a model with the kind of abstraction which initially excludes the influence of forces which are mainly responsible for the behaviour of the economic variables under investigation; and upon finding that the theory leads to results contrary to what we observe in reality, attributing this contrary movement to the compensating (or more than compensating) influence of residual factors that have been assumed away in the model. In dealing with capital accumulation and economic

[1] According to Myrdal's definition of the institutional approach it means that 'history and politics, theories and ideologies, economic structures and levels, social stratification, agriculture and industry, population developments, health and education and so on must be studied not in isolation but in their mutual relationships' (*Asian Drama*, I, p. x).

[2] N. Kaldor, 'Capital Accumulation and Economic Growth', ch. x, p. 177, in *The Theory of Capital*, ed. by F. A. Lutz and D. C. Hague (London, 1961).

growth, we are only too apt to begin by assuming a 'given state of knowledge' (that is to say, absence of technical progress) and the absence of 'uncertainty', and content ourselves with saying that these two factors – technical progress and uncertainty – must have been responsible for the difference between theoretical expectation and the recorded facts of experience. The interpretative value of this kind of theory must of necessity be extremely small.

But the choice of concepts and models is itself determined by social forces. The irrelevance of concepts like 'capital/output ratio' and 'unemployment' appeals to the forces resisting development. Their critique is a task as much of social policy as of intellectual clarification.

8 Economic Development and Education[1]

THE first section is a brief introduction to the history of thought on this subject; the second section discusses measurement, projections and planning of qualified manpower. The third section is devoted to a critical survey of three approaches attempting to calculate returns to educational expenditure. The fourth section briefly summarises the main requirements of educational planning and the fifth section applies some of the conclusions to the area of rural education and rural reform. Sections 1 and 2 cover both advanced and underdeveloped countries, while sections 3 to 5 apply to underdeveloped countries only.

I. ECONOMICS AND EDUCATION: SCOPE AND LIMITATIONS

At least since the days of Adam Smith, economists have tried to analyse systematically the contribution which education makes to the working of the economic system. The classical economists in the nineteenth century considered the creation and improvement of human skills as much part of raising production as the accumulation of physical capital.[2] Adam Smith, both a moral philosopher and an economist, considered education as fundamental to social peace, self-improvement and economic progress. Ricardo and Malthus saw in education a way of inculcating providential habits, which would lead to family limitation. John Stuart Mill develops the idea of education as a means of creating habits of prudence, providence and self-improvement. Education, in the view of the classical economists,

[1] I am indebted to Clive Bell for valuable assistance, to Richard Jolly for valuable comments, and to the *Bulletin of the Oxford University Institute of Economics and Statistics* and the *Journal of Development Studies* for permission to use material published there. My main intellectual debt is to Lord Balogh whose contribution to thought on this subject has been pioneering.

[2] For a good summary, see John Vaizey, *The Economics of Education* (London: Faber & Faber, 1962) chap. 2, to which this section is indebted.

develops not only aptitudes but also attitudes conducive to economic progress.

Although Ricardo emphasised the accumulation of physical capital, McCulloch includes 'the dexterity, skill and intelligence' of the mass of the people in his definition of national capital. Alfred Marshall said that 'the most valuable form of capital is that invested in human beings'.[1] He believed that 'the older economists took too little account of the fact that human faculties are as important a means of production as any other kind of capital . . .'[2] and concludes 'that the wisdom of expending public and private funds on education is not to be measured by its direct fruits alone. It will be profitable as a mere investment, to give the masses of the people much greater opportunities than they can generally avail themselves of.'[3]

Sidney Webb sounds particularly modern when he writes:

> The leaders of all the political parties unconsciously absorbed the idea that national efficiency depended on our making the most of the capacities of the whole population, which form, after all, as truly part of the national resources as our iron and coal. Indeed, as we now see with painful clearness, we have, in the long run, for the maintenance of our pre-eminent industrial position in the world, nothing to depend on except the brains of our people. Public education has, therefore, insensibly come to be regarded, not as a matter of philanthropy undertaken for the sake of the individual children benefited, but as a matter of national concern undertaken in the interest of the community as a whole.[4]

Marx stood firmly in the classical tradition and saw in education a way of combating the alienation of man from his own economic activities, which the division of labour under capitalism had brought about. Marx called man 'the most productive force of all'; in particular he regarded all acquisitions of skills as investment. Occasionally, Marx went even further and emphasised that all consumption had a productive aspect. His insistence on this detracts from the value of his insight and merely leads him to conclude: 'Hence, it is the simplest matter with a Hegelian to treat production and consumption as identical'.[5]

[1] Alfred Marshall, *Principles of Economics* (London: Macmillan, 1880: 6th ed., 1910) p. 564.
[2] Alfred Marshall, op. cit., IV 8.   [3] Alfred Marshall, op. cit., IV 7.
[4] Sidney Webb, *London Education* (London: 1904) p. 9, quoted by John Vaizey, op. cit., p. 7.
[5] Karl Marx, *A Contribution to the Critique of Political Economy*. Translation 2nd German ed. by N. L. Stone. With an appendix containing Marx's introduction to the Critique recently published among his posthumous papers, 2nd rev. ed. (New York: The International Library Publishing Company; London: Kegan Paul, Trench, Trübner & Co., 1904) p. 282.

Marx's followers have tended to neglect the productive aspect of education. Soviet practice, though not Soviet theory, has not conformed to the 'Marxian' view that only capital accumulation is productive. In addition to their investment programmes, Soviet plans always contained sections devoted to huge expenditures on the creation of skills and the transformation of human attitudes. It is now evident that the Soviet Union's high growth rates were partly due to this investment in man, for which there was no theoretical basis in Marxian theory, and that earlier underestimates by Western observers of Soviet growth rates may have been due to their neglect of the effects of these expenditures. 'Marxian' theory itself, with its emphasis on physical capital accumulation, contributed to these erroneous estimates by Western economists.

In neo-classical writings, which concentrated on how to optimise the allocation of given resources, considerations of education as investment were neglected until they enjoyed a renaissance in the 1950s and 60s. This occurred under the influence of full employment, a renewed emphasis on growth and development and the experience of European post-war recovery, in which capital for the purpose of reconstruction turned out to yield much higher returns than had been expected, and than were found elsewhere, largely as a result of the existence of a skilled and appropriately motivated and organised population.

It is now part of the theory of economic policy that the provision of trained manpower – scientists, engineers, technicians, administrators, managers – contributes to the growth of the national product. In order to be effective, education must be part of a wider plan, so that skills can be matched by opportunities to work. The supply of capital equipment, the demand for skilled labour and the demand for the goods produced by the factors of production must fit into the supply of manpower with specific or. adaptable skills. The use of general knowledge and the specific skills of the worker are now treated as the returns on an investment in his education and training. These take the form partly of the development of general capacities which enable him to participate in the co-operative process of production and partly of specific skills required for his particular job. The money for this investment comes sometimes from the State, sometimes from the employer and sometimes from the worker himself. The appropriate source of this finance has been a subject of discussion. It is now generally accepted that labour services, like the services of capital equipment, are produced means of production and that the methods of producing these means are training and education.

II. THE NEED FOR QUALIFIED MANPOWER IN ECONOMIC DEVELOPMENT

A. Conceptual Framework

Two of the most important indicators of the level of development of an economy are the complexity of its structure and the level of its technology. The economic structures of poor countries and the techniques of production employed are comparatively simple and there is little interaction between sectors. By contrast, the economies of rich countries possess structures the components of which are highly interlinked, and which make widespread use of advanced techniques – both in the sense of a high degree of mechanisation, and in the technology which is embodied in them. It follows that rich, complex economies require a more highly qualified work force than simple, poor ones.

However, advanced economies are not distinguished from underdeveloped economies only by structures which are more complex. In addition, the pattern of output and of employment changes radically as development proceeds. As Professor Chenery has shown,[1] a typical country with a per caput income of $100 derives about 50 per cent of its gross national product from the primary sector, about 35 per cent from the services sector and the remaining 15 per cent from the industrial sector. The corresponding figures at a per caput income level of $1,000 are about 15, 45 and 40 per cent respectively. The proportions of the work force employed in these sectors are different from the proportions of income generated in them, because there are differences in productivity per man between sectors. However, the sectoral composition of employment moves in the same direction as that of income and output and the proportion of the labour force in agriculture is initially even higher and declines more rapidly than the proportion of gross national product generated in agriculture.

Suppose now that there are two 'typical' economies – A, which has a per caput income of about $1,000, and B with a per caput income of about $100. For simplicity, we assume that their working populations are of the same size. It is clear that A will have many more engineers, scientists and technicians than B, simply because its industrial sector is so much larger. This applies *a fortiori* in so far as the technologies in A will be more advanced than those in B; for an advanced technology requires greater inputs of skill than does a backward one. This is likely to be reinforced further by the fact that the range of

[1] Hollis B. Chenery, 'Patterns of Industrial Growth', *American Economic Review*, 50, 4 (Sep 1960) pp. 624–65.

goods produced will be different, even within the two industrial sectors. Production in A may be concentrated on sophisticated machinery and durable consumer goods, while B's industry produces largely simple semi-manufactures and consumer goods such as textiles. Similar arguments also apply to the demands for the products of the primary sector and for skilled manpower. Although the absolute number of people working in the tertiary sectors of A and B are not likely to be very different, the composition of skills embodied in these people is radically so. Most of the people employed in B's service sector are petty traders and low-level clerks, together with a whole host of under- or pseudo-employed middlemen who scarcely fit into any occupational category. On the other hand, the phenomenon of underemployment and low labour utilisation is largely absent from A, while the occupational structure is marked by a relatively high proportion of highly qualified administrative and allied professional workers. A complex socio-economic system generates a greater demand for competent decision-making than a simple one. The greater proportion of highly qualified administrators in A than in B is a response to this need. Even the primary sector is subject to the same influences. Although its importance in terms of share of employment and output declines relatively to industry and the services, its demand for qualified manpower is likely to be at least as high in A as it is in B (relatively, of course, it will be much greater). The farmers in A will be better educated than their counterparts in B; their employees will be able to operate and maintain machinery, whereas those in B can drive only teams of oxen and may not be able to read instructions. The former will have at their disposal the services of teams of experts ranging from veterinary surgeons to ecologists, while the typical farmer in B must rely largely on his own experience and may be suspicious of advice offered – at an experimental station away from his own plot.

An advanced country, therefore, needs a far greater proportion of qualified manpower than does a less developed country for three main reasons.

1. As between the primary, secondary and tertiary sectors, those sectors requiring more skills are larger.
2. Even within corresponding sectors, the pattern of output is more skill-intensive in the advanced than in the underdeveloped economy.
3. The prevailing technologies for the same occupations and outputs make greater demands for inputs of skilled labour.

But the problem is not quite so tidy as the above argument suggests. There are some categories of highly qualified workers for which demand is not rigidly linked to the level of development. Obvious examples are doctors, dentists and nurses. To some extent their services are inputs because the level of the national product (and, as we shall see below, its rate of growth) depend on the health of the labour force. But health is also an end in itself and the demand for medical services stems from popular pressure. If A has more doctors than B, it is partly because its educational system has a greater capacity and its resources for training doctors are more plentiful – not because gross national product requires them. The demand for skills is partly derived from productive requirements, and partly reflects final demands. The demand for teachers also has this dual origin. Again, popular demand for 'universal education' is an important factor, but this is most acutely felt at the primary level. The demand for education at this level is mainly a demand for literacy. At the secondary and higher levels of education the demand for qualified teachers is determined by the need to satisfy the skilled manpower requirements described above, although there is also political pressure for secondary and tertiary education. For at any given level of income, a certain flow of newly qualified workers into the existing manpower pool is required, and in its turn, this implies a fairly well-defined stock of teachers to produce it. At the highest level, a rich society can afford more scholars engaged in pure research, without obvious or direct usefulness for production.

So far we have discussed in general terms how the need for qualified manpower changes with the *level* of development. A further question is: 'How does the need for qualified manpower depend on the *rate of growth* of national income?'

Clearly, if two economies start from the same level of national income and income per head, the one with the faster rate of growth will need to expand its output of engineers, technicians, mechanics, etc., more rapidly than the slower growing one. But there are less obvious differences. First, because teachers produce school and university graduates, a higher flow of output of the latter requires, assuming the productivity of teachers to be constant, a larger pool of teachers. Moreover, the educational system produces not only qualified manpower for others but also more teachers, and for this reason, too, the stock of teachers and students will have to be larger for a higher rate of growth. The second point is that a higher rate of growth entails a more rapidly changing economic structure. The earlier obsolescence of skills will impose greater difficulties of adaptation, though much depends upon the rate of growth of the labour force. For the same aggregate growth rate, high growth rates of income per head combined with a slowly growing labour force create greater problems than lower rates of growth of income per head combined with faster growth in the labour force. Rapidly changing patterns of output and employment, therefore, place a premium on flexibility and a heavier administrative load on decision-makers. Retraining schemes are in vogue at present, but they do not provide the whole answer. In rapidly changing economies it is also important to design vocational training systems which are not excessively specialised, though it must be admitted that the precise content of 'not excessively specialised' may have to be determined by trial and error. Ability to acquire new skills can be taught, at the expense of expertise in specific skills, and may show higher long-run returns. In a changing world the costs of greater flexibility have to be compared with the forgone benefits of greater specialisation, although flexibility and specialisation are partly complementary.

The experience of China provides a pertinent example in this context. During the great initial drive towards industrialisation in the middle and late 1950s, the educational system was geared to produce many specialists – particularly engineers. A graduate from a certain specialist school might know virtually everything about bridge construction, but virtually nothing about other fields in civil engineering. This worked well enough for a time, but rapidly changing needs began to render many of these qualified workers redundant. If heavy specialisation is one side of the coin, the other is likely to be inflexibility; the cost exacted for retraining at this level can be heavy.

There remains the question: how are the benefits and costs of training and education related to the stage of development? At very low levels of income, the impact of a few highly trained people can be very significant. Many African countries which are suffering from severe shortages in these occupations are cases in point. At this level an increase in the number of trained and educated beyond a fairly low level results in unemployment if the educated insist on getting the jobs and salaries which they expected. The paradoxical situation of unemployment of educated and trained people in underdeveloped countries is a common one.[1] One reason for this is the lack of absorptive capacity: absence of management, capital equipment, foreign exchange, etc., to put the skilled manpower to productive use. Another is the wage structures and the wage levels, and a third is the excessive aspirations of the educated.

As development proceeds and accelerates, shortages and bottle-necks of skills become more marked. The wrong kinds of skill may still be in surplus while there are deficiencies of others, but these structural imbalances tend to yield, after a time, to the growing demand for educated manpower if the necessary reforms of human attitudes and social institutions are carried out. If rapid changes in

[1] See pp. 124, 143.

the composition of output and demand are coupled with sticky political and economic responses, shortages will be prolonged. The more flexible the skills and attitudes of the political and technocratic élites, and the more responsive the educational system to the demands placed on it, the easier is the transition from a simple to a complex economic structure likely to be.

B. Methods of manpower projection

In the above section, the problem has been treated conceptually. We now need to discuss the operational methods which are used in manpower projections. At present, the state-of-the-art is still relatively primitive. There are three main types of forecasting procedures.

1. The first is based on the extrapolation of past trends. This requires time series of output and employment, preferably disaggregated into a number of key sectors and categories of the occupational structure in each. If the target year is then set, and past trends in output, labour productivity and occupational structure are maintained, the stocks of different categories of qualified manpower can be derived. Moreover, if changes in participation rates, and withdrawals from the labour force through retirement or death can be predicted with tolerable accuracy, the output of the educational system necessary to hit these targets can be deduced. This method suffers from fundamental drawbacks. Its use demands access to high quality, disaggregated data which stretch some way back into the past. Yet very few countries and virtually no less developed country possess such data. Even at this stage, the validity of the method can be contested on the ground that past trends resulted from conditions which will not continue in the future. For example, a high rate of increase of labour productivity in the past, based on a shift of men from agriculture into industry, must slow down as surplus agricultural manpower is exhausted. In addition, the targets set need not be compatible with the total labour force in the terminal year, for the crude extrapolation of past trends may imply either a manpower shortage, or a high level of unemployment. Finally, this method does not question the efficiency of past trends and contains no provision for improving on past performance. The present structure of employment and its future trends are treated as inviolate. The less disaggregated the categories, the less liable to faults is the system, but the less guidance does it provide for training and education.

A variant of the above method which goes some way towards meeting these criticisms involves *setting*, as opposed to *projecting by extrapolation*, gross national product in the terminal year. It is then possible to work backwards to check for inconsistencies, so that a target gross national product which implies full employment without imposing impossible or unacceptable demands on the educational system, can be derived by a process of trial and error. This variation is essentially the same as method 2.

2. In the absence of time series data of the kind referred to above, a fair procedure for projection is that employed in a study[1] made in 1957 of Puerto Rico's manpower needs for 1975. This implied that certain goals were incorporated in the plan so that unlike the first variant of method 1, some normative elements had been incorporated. The critical assumption of the present method was that the levels of productivity in Puerto Rican industries would be similar to those ruling in 1950 in the same US industries, and that the same would apply to the occupational structure. The US Census of 1950 could then be used to give manpower targets for each occupational category for Puerto Rico in 1975. Granted the right sort of data, educational targets could then be set as indicated above in method 1.

An alternative approach consists in examining the occupational composition of employment in the most advanced domestic firms in various industries. These manpower structures are then assumed to be the shape of things to come. For example, the National Team for Greece of the Mediterranean Regional Project assumed that the *increase* in employment in each sector between 1960 and 1975 will possess the occupational structures of the most advanced firms in each sector in 1960.[2] Several refinements can be added to this method.

3. One of the most sophisticated approaches to the problem is due to Tinbergen and Bos.[3] In spite of its limitations, this model has two features which confer on it a considerable advantage over the methods described above. First, it tackles with some success the point raised above[4] that manpower needs depend not only on where one wants to go, but also on how and how fast one wishes to get there. It does this by integrating into the same formal structure both the educational supply over time and manpower targets. Secondly, it points the way – albeit crudely by dealing with supply alternatives –

[1] Commonwealth of Puerto Rico Planning Board, Bureau of Economics and Statistics in co-operation with the U.S. Department of Labour Bureau of Employment Security, *Puerto Rico's Manpower Needs and Supply* (San Juan: Commonwealth of Puerto Rico Planning Board, 1957).

[2] Herbert S. Parnes, *Forecasting Educational Needs for Economic and Social Development* (Paris, OECD, 1962) p. 35.

[3] Jan Tinbergen and H. C. Bos, 'A Planning Model for the Educational Requirements of Economic Growth', pp. 9–31. In: OECD, *Econometric Models of Education*. Some Applications (Paris: OECD, 1965) p. 99.

[4] See pp. 133–6.

towards an optimising procedure and does not accept past performance as a datum.

In its simplest form[1] the model assumes two levels of education – secondary and higher. The supply of primary school graduates is assumed to present no bottleneck for the expansion of other levels. The unit time period t is taken as six years. The following notation is introduced omitting the time index t:

Y, volume of production

N^2, the labour force with a secondary education

N^3, the labour force with a higher education

m^2, those who have entered the labour force N^2 within the previous six years

m^3, those who have entered the labour force N^3 within the previous six years

n^2, the number of students in secondary education

n^3, the number of students in higher education

The following relationships are assumed to hold:

(1) $N_t^2 = y^2 Y_t$, where y^2 is a constant

(2) $N_t^2 = (1-x^2)N_{t-1}^2 + m_t^2$, where x^2 is the proportion of withdrawals from N^2 over the previous six years,

(3) $m_t^2 = n_{t-1}^2 - n_t^3$

(4) $m_t^3 = n_{t-1}^3$

(5) $N_t^3 = (1-x^3)N_{t-1}^3 + m_t^3$, where x^3 is similarly defined with respect to withdrawals from N^3.

(6) $N_t^3 = y^3 Y_t + p^2 n^2 + p^3 n_t^3$, where y^3 is a constant and p^2, p^3 are teacher-student ratios at secondary and higher levels of education.

From these simple assumptions and equations, the authors develop a more general model which can deal with the problems generated by accelerating the rate of growth, or by switching rapidly from expatriates to nationals in former colonial countries.

The chief limitation of these methods of manpower projection lies in the rigidity of their linear structure, i.e. the assumption that the relationships between the strategic variables remain rigidly proportional. Some substitution between labour and capital is undoubtedly possible. Yet present projections adhere to the assumption that if one wants X, Y and Z at any time, then one must have precisely P, Q, R and S amounts of different sorts of labour to get them and that the

---

[1] Jan Tinbergen and H. C. Bos, op. cit., pp. 10–12.

coefficients remain constant. The most casual observations of the real world refute this assumption.

Part of the problem is a technical one. The present method leans too heavily on simple statistical techniques which seek to express the demand for labour as being dependent on only one or two controlling variables – e.g. the level of output. This approach is obviously inadequate. What is required is a statistical analysis which can accept many variables and deal with the difficulty that some of them may be related to each other.[1] But a residue of uncertainty would still remain. This is not to imply that manpower planning is futile, but rather that methods must be evolved which would enable planners to find the range of values manpower targets are most likely to take, and to keep that range as small as possible.

III. EDUCATIONAL EXPENDITURE AS A FORM OF INVESTMENT IN UNDERDEVELOPED COUNTRIES

Carefully directed social expenditure in general and on education in particular can have a much higher total yield (including all secondary effects) than types of expenditure which may result in some imposing visible structure, but whose effects on present and future output in other sectors of the economy are zero or negative. Expenditures on education can raise output considerably, if properly directed and linked with improved equipment and appropriate institutional reforms. But these expenditures have for long been recalcitrant to theoretical treatment because

(1) they are permissive, creating opportunities for output growth without being its sufficient condition;
(2) their direct output is often not easily measurable;
(3) their effects are widely diffused;
(4) their effects are spread over a long time;
(5) there exists no determinate functional relationship between inputs and outputs, partly because success is contingent on complementary measures;
(6) independent value, as well as instrumental value, is attached to both the initial expenditure and the resultant flow of satisfactions;
(7) considerations of 'deserved social rewards' enter into the determination of costs (e.g. teachers' salaries);
(8) they cut across the traditional distinction between investment and consumption (on which many growth theories are built),

[1] Russel G. Davis, *Planning Human Resource Development*. Educational Models and Schemata (Chicago: Rand McNally, 1966) p. 334.

according to which a sacrifice in current consumption can make future consumption greater than it would otherwise have been;

(9) they are frequently correlated with other causes of higher productivity from which they are not easily separated statistically;

(10) they are largely borne by the Government and therefore removed from the tests of the market.

Although many of these considerations apply, perhaps to a lesser extent, also to expenditure on physical capital, they are more glaring when expenditure on education is considered and therefore these expenditures have been, until recently, unpopular with model builders. But the bias which emphasises allegedly measurable, separable and determinate relationships, and neglects other types is unwarranted. Actions about whose results it is possible to make only vague or only qualitative guesses may be more important than actions whose trivial quantifiable effects are precisely foreseeable. The challenge of estimating the returns on educational expenditure has been accepted, but in the process of analysing them certain difficulties have become apparent.

There are three main approaches to the measurement of the returns to educational expenditure. First, the macroeconomic approach attempts to relate increases in aggregate production to increases in physical factors such as labour and capital. Whatever is then left over, the 'residual', is attributed to a variety of forces improving the quality of human beings as productive agents, and some part or the whole of this is identified with education. A second approach calculates the life-time excess earnings of people who have undergone various lengths of education over those who have not, estimates the costs incurred in their education and derives a rate of return on individual education. A third approach attempts to relate all social benefits, made commensurable in a single measure, with all social costs of expenditure on education. The third method is essentially the same as the second, except that it allows for benefits enjoyed by others than the educated individual.

Those using the first approach have constructed models which attempt to isolate the contribution to growth made by expenditure on education. The starting-point has usually been the addition of one term to the Cobb-Douglas production function:

$$Y = aK^\alpha L^\beta H^\gamma,$$

where Y is national income, K capital, L labour and H is a ragbag term for 'human factor', including 'improved knowledge', improved health and skills, better organisation and management, economies of scale, external economies, changes in the composition of output, etc., a, α, β and γ are constants, and $\alpha + \beta = 1$.

These models have a certain value for advanced Western countries and the attempt to get away from a preoccupation with physical investment is welcome. But their application to the problems of underdeveloped countries is fraught with difficulties.

The reasoning behind these new models can be briefly summarised in this way: the increased use of one factor of production, while others are kept constant and 'knowledge' and 'skills' are given, will yield diminishing marginal returns. If the growth of national product over several decades is such that the expansion of land, labour and capital does not account for the whole increase, the remainder must be due to 'investment in human beings'.

But the reasoning is open to a number of criticisms. In the models of an aggregate production function a relationship, based on static economic models, is *assumed* between capital, labour and output; the historically *observed* relationship in *advanced* countries is seen to diverge widely from the *assumed* relationship, and the difference is *postulated* to be due solely to 'improvements in knowledge' or 'education'. This conclusion is then bodily transferred to a totally different technical, historical, cultural, religious, institutional and political setting. Even if education were a necessary condition for production growth, it might yield output only if incorporated in machines, exploited in specific ways, or combined with other factors or policies, but not if occurring in isolation. Nor is education a homogeneous input. The teaching of Sanscrit has different results from the teaching of land cultivation. The teaching of book-keeping may increase the efficiency of manual labour, while the teaching of certain religions may reduce it. Isolation of 'education' from other measures including other forms of investment in human beings like health, ignores the importance of co-ordinating policies, and aggregating all types of 'education', obscures the type of education required for development.

The second approach attempts to estimate the returns in the form of higher earnings to the educated persons in relation to expenditure on their education in the USA or other advanced industrial countries. This approach also seemed to show that the returns to this type of 'investment' are above or similar to the returns to physical investment.[1] The conclusion is then drawn that expenditure on education and on other ways of improving knowledge and skills should be carried out by planners in other countries, and particularly in underdeveloped countries.

[1] But see below, p. 145 n. 1.

The calculations of the returns to education, based on correlating income with educational attainment in the USA or other advanced countries, cannot be applied to underdeveloped countries for at least three reasons: first, differences in earnings do not reflect differences in productivity but institutional arrangements (e.g. foreign enterprise) and tradition; second, even if they did, education is highly correlated with other causes of higher productivity, such as intelligence, motivation, environmental influences and co-operating factors such as expensive equipment; third, it cannot be assumed that an underdeveloped economy can absorb the educated irrespective of the type of education and irrespective of a host of other measures, and in particular agricultural modernisation and industrialisation. The marginal returns on higher education in India and primary education in Africa may turn out to be negative, while average returns may be high. The American data, which are mostly used, do not provide evidence as to whether expenditure on education is *cause* or *effect* of superior incomes; they do not show, even if we could assume it to be a condition of higher earnings, whether it is a *sufficient* or a *necessary* condition of growth (industrialisation in Britain preceded general compulsory education), and they do not separate *monopolistic* from *other forces* influencing differential earnings which are correlated with, but not caused by, differential education.

The calculations based on these data ignore both the indirect (financial and non-financial) returns accruing to others than the educated individual, and the direct non-financial returns to the individual. On the other hand, they pay a good deal of attention to income forgone during study which constitutes a large proportion of the costs of 'investment'. But neither the income forgone by other groups in society (housewives, voluntary workers, even some university teachers – who accept a lower income than they could get in other occupations), nor the non-financial benefits enjoyed during education are estimated. Since the time-flow over a lifetime of the earnings of the educated, moving up to a much later peak, is quite different from that of the uneducated, lifetime earnings in the 1960s must be calculated as returns on education in the 1920s. To conclude from these returns anything about returns from expenditure today is like identifying a crystal radio set with Telstar.

Assuming that the ratio of returns to costs reflected something significant, it would be rash to attribute it to education. Expenditure on education is highly correlated to income and wealth of parents, to ability, perseverance and motivation, to educational opportunities such as urban residence and proximity to educational centres, to access to well-paid jobs through family and other connections, any one of which could, either by itself or in conjunction with any of the others, account for the superior earnings. So also could the fact that more physical capital or other types of human investment (health, on-the-job training) are characteristic of occupations requiring education.

Monopolistic elements are sometimes concealed as requirements of professional qualifications of, e.g., lawyers and doctors. Some of the higher earnings of those who happen to enjoy them are not a return on education but a monopoly rent resulting from restrictions on members permitted into a profession in which privileged members have a financial interest in maintaining scarcity. These institutional arrangements can be reflected in vast differentials between average and marginal returns to education. The calculation of returns to education, unsupported by institutional analysis, provides no clues to policy.

If anybody attempted to use these models for calculating the returns to education in many underdeveloped countries, he would discover that pay scales in the Civil Service, in universities and in the professions are governed by the traditional standards of a feudal or colonial oligarchy, by demand in an international market and by natural or artificial restrictions. On the other hand, the conditions under which higher education has to be provided raise its costs above those in much richer countries. The resulting rate of return would provide no clue as to how public money ought to be distributed between 'investment' in 'physical capital' and in 'people'.

The main weakness of that type of returns to education approach, which aggregates all types of education and isolates it from complementary measure, is that it singles out one item, either as the necessary and sufficient condition, or as a principal strategic variable of development. But the wrong kind of education, unaccompanied by the required complementary actions, can check or reverse the process of development. An unemployed or unemployable intelligentsia can be a source of reactionary rather than economic activity, and young people brought up to despise manual work can reinforce the resistances to development.[1] Growth rates derived from the experience of the United States cannot be used to calculate the returns on education in the entirely different setting of underdeveloped countries.

[1] Wilfred Malenbaum, for instance, found that unemployment in India varies directly with the degree of higher education. See Wilfred Malenbaum, 'Urban Unemployment in India', *Pacific Affairs*, 30, 2 (June 1957) p. 146. Quoted in Gustav Ranis, 'Economic Development: A Suggested Approach', *Kyklos*, 12, 3 (1959) p. 445.

In Mexico experiments have shown that investment in rural schools may not result in increased production or changed attitudes. For a discussion of the hostility to development generated by education and intellectuals see Joseph A. Schumpeter, *Capitalism, Socialism and Democracy*, rev. 2nd ed. (London: George Allen & Unwin, 1947) pp. 152 ff.

The same 'input' could result in refusal to work on farms, an increase in urban unemployment, subversion and collapse. The wrong type of education can also produce a ruling élite which gives the wrong kind of advice, as well as setting up ideals that stand in the way of development. It can encourage ignorance of and contempt for the professional and technical qualifications which are a condition of economic development.[1]

Aggregation of all 'investment in human capital' and its separation from 'investment in physical capital' not only obscures the complementary nature of most subgroups of the two, but also serves as an intellectual and moral escape mechanism from difficult and unpleasant social and political measures. An approach which separates different types of education and incorporates complementary factors and measures is more promising.

The third approach, which is really an extension of the second, attempts to quantify and relate the benefits attributable to expenditure on education to the social costs of education. The method is the same as that which is used to calculate the returns on the construction of roads, underground extensions, or irrigation works. The economic value of a proposed investment is expressed as the present value of the future stream of net benefits accruing to all affected by it (whether they pay for it or not), divided by the present value of its costs over its life. Alternatively, the value is equal to the net future benefits expressed as a rate of return on the capital costs. This method is sound in principle, on the assumption that future benefits can be attributed to educational expenditure without complementary measures. Even with this proviso, the calculation is very difficult in practice. Many benefits are difficult to assess and the attempt to quantify them merely opens the door for the pseudo-scientific expression of value judgements or mere prejudices.

When we compare the manpower planning approach discussed in the previous section and the various returns to educational expenditure approaches discussed here, we see that the two make diametrically opposite assumptions about the way in which educated and skilled labour enters into the functional relationship between productive inputs and output (the production function). According to the returns to education approach, different types of labour of

---

[1] The importance to the *type* and *composition* in contrast to the *total* of social expenditure is particularly glaring in the field of health: expenditure on death control, which simply reduces mortality rates may have a negative effect on per caput growth rates in many underdeveloped countries, whereas expenditure on birth control and improved health, which raises vigour and reduces apathy has a positive effect. The same is true of expenditure on education. Education which breeds religious aversion from work and snobbery produces a selection mechanism and policies which have income-depressing effects.

different quality can be perfectly substituted for one another. In competitive conditions their earnings then reflect the marginal productivity of education. According to the manpower planning approach, on the contrary, different skills are necessary in fixed proportions to achieve certain results. Where the former school emphasises substitutability, the latter stresses complementarity. In the manpower planning approach, earnings do not reflect marginal productivities, which are determined by other forces. Both the proportions of different types of labour, and those between educational capital and output are assumed to be fixed and constant.

It is paradoxical that, on the one hand, planners who aim at removing deficiencies such as inadequate human capital formation are bidden by the manpower planners to assume past trends to hold good in the future, while, on the other hand, the marginal productivity school ignores the importance in planning of a concerted and simultaneous attack on several fronts. Yet, a judicious combination of the two approaches is likely to yield useful results.

A number of critics have attacked what they consider the sordidly mercenary and banausic approach to activities of high intrinsic value, saying that it is a perversion of values to calculate rates of return on what is, or should be, the ultimate purpose of all production. But these criticisms miss the point. The chief conclusion of some of the recent researches is that not enough is spent on education. The high independent value of education itself and of the consequent flow of independently (i.e. not instrumentally) valued satisfactions may be used as an argument against not spending enough, but it cannot be used as an argument against spending at least as much as would yield a return equal to that on physical capital. It could, of course, be said that once mercenary calculations are admitted, the relative values of *different kinds* of education will be assessed by the wrong standards, and that the sense of the *value* of education will be lost, the more accurately its *price* is known. It might also be used as an argument for giving higher priority to the education of a skilled élite than to general education of the mass of the people. Furthermore, some authors argue already that the returns on education in certain countries are lower than those on physical capital.[1]

But the fact that we attach both independent and instrumental value to certain activities and that we attempt to estimate, when this is possible, the instrumental value, does not detract from the

[1] Arnold C. Harberger, 'Investment in Men Versus Investment in Machines: The Case of India', pp. 11–50. In: C. Arnold Anderson and Mary Jean Bowman (eds.) *Education and Economic Development* (Chicago: Aldine Publishing Co., 1965) p. 436.

independent value. If the two reinforce each other, there can be no cause for complaint, and if they don't, it is surely rational to wish to discover the costs of policies promoting independent values.

The objection to the models is therefore not that they degrade education and equate human beings with machines. Better knowledge of the productive potential of human beings would raise, not lower, human dignity, rational human choice and human freedom. The objection is that some of the models approach the problem in the wrong way.

A criticism of the isolation of one tributary to the stream of production and the aggregation of different channels, some of which flow in opposite directions, some of which are stagnant and some of which do not contain any liquid, does not imply a disparagement of the need for detailed quantitative planning, including the planning of education, which has particularly long gestation periods. Whether a particular theoretical model is worth constructing depends upon whether we can give sufficient precision to the definition of the parameters and the variables and whether we can estimate the numerical relations between them. The rigour which is claimed for mathematical models is an illusion if the terms which they contain have no clear reference to the relevant items.

In the process of criticising misplaced aggregation, such as that which lumps all education into a single category, we are led to the formulation of less general questions and concepts: education is subdivided according to where it takes place, in what subjects, at what level and to whom. The purpose of such decomposition, disaggregation and subdivision is not to restrict analysis to less general concepts. We are, indeed, first trying to get rid of ragbag terms which do not correspond to anything observable and to replace them by 'boxes' that can be 'filled'. But as the boxes are being filled and we gain fuller empirical knowledge, we may look forward to the formulation of new aggregates and to the reconstitution of the decomposed material in a different form. The new 'packages' or 'boxes' will differ from the old. Some of the new distinctions will cut across the old ones. Thus when we examine the forces determining labour utilisation in underdeveloped countries, we shall discover that certain forms of education improve the quality of work and its efficiency, as well as, by improving hygiene and sanitation, the duration of work. Capital equipment may extend its duration and efficiency. Instead of separating 'equipment' from 'labour' and aggregating each, we may arrive at a new abstraction in which skill and knowledge are infused through the introduction of machines.[1]

[1] An interesting attempt to construct a model in which all productivity change is embodied in new investment was made by Professor Robert M. Solow, who, in

IV. EDUCATIONAL PLANNING

The formulation of long-term plans of economic development for underdeveloped countries which must incorporate the planning of education, müst meet, in addition to these conceptual, certain other requirements.[1]

1. A long-term plan must embrace a study of how and how far traditional educational patterns have contributed to the failure of social and economic progress in the past. The study must discover whether the attitudes which are hostile to economic progress have been the result of a specific structure of education, and what modifications of that structure are needed to accelerate development. In both the formerly British and the formerly French territories a disdain of technical education prevails which has been strengthened by the low status of technical schools and the restricted openings for their pupils. So long as the Civil Service and the appointments controlled or influenced by it are the preserve of the non-technically educated, the best ability will be diverted into non-technical education. This will both justify and strengthen the initial disdain and render progress more difficult. On the basis of this study of obstacles a new educational structure can be planned which will raise the status of those who meet the requirements of accelerated growth. Thus both diversion of the best talent and an increase in the supply of the required skills will be achieved.

2. The second requirement is a concrete idea of the size and composition of long-term development, based upon knowledge of the concrete endowments of the economy and a clear formulation of specific objectives and ideals. From these the future pattern of manpower distribution can be derived and thus an indication of the

---

the words of Arthur Smithies, 'is like a Pied Piper who can play different tunes'. This particular tune is the exact opposite of those which separate 'disembodied' knowledge and other improvements from capital accumulation. (Robert Solow, 'Technical Progress, Capital Formation and Economic Growth', *American Economic Review*, 50, 2 (May 1962) pp. 76–9.)

Professor Kenneth J. Arrow and Messrs. Nicholas Kaldor and James A. Mirrlees also have developed a model in which men learn by doing work with equipment: Kenneth J. Arrow, 'The Economic Implications of Learning by Doing', *Review of Economic Studies*, 29, 80 (June 1962) pp. 155–73. Nicholas Kaldor and James A. Mirrlees, 'A New Model of Economic Growth', *Review of Economic Studies*, op. cit., pp. 174–92.

[1] Starting with a critical appraisal of the conceptual framework for planning economic and social development in underdeveloped countries, Myrdal describes the main characteristics of the new approach. See Gunnar Myrdal, *Asian Drama. An Inquiry into the Poverty of Nations* (New York: Pantheon, 1968) p. 2284, in particular Appendices 2 and 3 in vol. III.

measures and the timing needed for educational development. The long gestation period of much education and training requires that starts are made now in order to reap results after 15, 20 and 25 years. Neither general formulae of ill-defined and irrelevant aggregates, nor the occupational composition of the population experienced at comparable stages of development in advanced industrial countries are of much use.[1] Past experience of non-Soviet countries relates to spontaneous growth (or its failure). It cannot be assumed that deliberate efforts to accelerate growth by a series of policies would show the same requirements. The problem is to overcome *specific* difficulties, which *differ* from country to country and from time to time, while historical experience from now advanced countries points to broadly *similar* categories. From the long-term plan the quantities and types of educated personnel in detailed categories can be derived. Since changes in technology, demand, international policies, etc., will continually change these requirements, the long-term plan should be a 'rolling' plan, reviewed continually and at least annually, and adapted in the light of new information. It should provide the framework for the 5-year (or 7-year) plans and for the annual budgets, so that policies which will not bear fruit until after more than five or seven years will not be neglected. To avoid superimposing new rigidities upon often already rigid economies, all three plans, the annual budget, the 'plan' and the perspective plan should be reviewed continually, and carried forward, so that they apply always to the next year, the next five years, the next fifteen years.

3. A number of measures will have to be taken which lie outside the scope of conventional economic considerations. Thus if training takes place abroad, the return of the trained men will have to be ensured; if they have acquired the required skills, it will be necessary that they use them in isolated rural areas and reluctance to live there has to be overcome; the type of training provided must fit the available

[1] The most promising approach is that adopted by Mr Pitambar Pant of the Indian Planning Commission: 'To conclude, planning for education involved careful analysis of a number of issues . . . the planning of education should be approached from the point of view of long-term objectives of the society. In other words, the objectives and programmes of education should be related to the requirements of the future plans. Secondly, it is not very meaningful to talk in terms of aggregates, when the equation of supply and demand has to be worked out for each separate category of personnel. For only to a limited extent are these variously qualified graduates interchangeable. A comprehensive plan should identify clearly the various categories of trained manpower required, and it is the main function of the education process to give to properly selected boys and girls the best education and suitable environment to fit them for creative endeavour in future' (Pitambar Pant, 'Manpower Planning and Education', *Indian Journal of Public Administration*, 7, 3, July/Sep 1961, p. 330.)

current and expected future technology and not be appropriate to a more advanced form.

4. Because of the narrow margins of tolerance and the closeness of many underdeveloped countries to misery and starvation, it is crucially important that minimum needs are estimated and that the required combination of measures is planned and executed. Failure to execute complementary measures, properly phased, can spell disaster. The isolation of 'educational' expenditure may distract attention from the urgent need, not only to select the right type of education, but also to combine it with the provision of better seeds, drainage, irrigation and fertilisers, with land reform and price stabilisation, with improvements in transport and birth control, with a reform of recruitment to the Civil Service and business management.

5. Detailed planning of education and training presupposes explicit political judgement about the distribution of the benefits between classes and over time. One of the costs of raising output later above what it would otherwise have been is the use of resources now to support the educational system required at a later stage. Since the social rate of time discount will tend to be high in countries where many are on the verge of starvation, extreme care is required in the choices of expenditure on education. Financially conservative advice will be politically difficult and unpopular and may in some areas give rise to accusations of racial discrimination. Efforts are therefore needed to remove prejudices against quick-yielding and applied types of education and to avoid excessive expectations. In particular, choices will have to be made between (1) quality and quantity, (2) science and arts, (3) vocational training in school and on the job, (4) education emphasising modern and applied content and education in indigenous history and anthropology, which may prevent a reaction to primitive tribalism, (5) regulation of salaries and consequently incentives by the State and by the market (including the international market for professional services), (6) the desires of the individual and the needs of the community, (7) education in the country and in towns, (8) education of men only or of men and women, (9) education of children and youth and education of adults, (10) expenditure on brick and mortar and on flesh and blood, i.e. the balance between capital and recurrent expenditure, and (11) the proper balance between primary, secondary and higher education.

Having made these choices or compromises correctly, in the light of both economic and non-economic objectives, education has to be used to get the right kind of education accepted. The larger the area for which collective planning can be initiated, the greater will be the scope for large, highly specialised institutions which are expensive, not directly related to current progress, but imposing and prestige-yielding. The division of labour, in this field too, is limited by the extent of the market, and the larger and richer the area the more scope is there for specialised units conducting 'basic' research and breeding 'pure' scholars. Although it is true that the practical use of 'pure' research is unpredictable and that conscious direction of education and research to 'applied' fields does not always yield higher returns earlier than some initially 'pure' research, it remains true that it takes time between a discovery, its technical application by engineers, its commercial exploitation by innovating entrepreneurs and its imitation and marketing on a large scale by their followers. Only a large and rich economy with a low rate of time discount can afford to devote much energy to basic or pure scholarship. The adaptation of known techniques, which admittedly requires qualities similar to those of innovation, by poor developing countries could raise substantially their real income.

The choice of the distribution of benefits over time is related to the choice between types of education with a high ratio of instrumental to independent value and those with a low ratio. The pursuit of knowledge for its own sake, wherever it may lead, is highly valued in many cultures, and makes itself an indirect contribution to development by encouraging rational questioning of traditional ways and of authority. It is also a fact that pure research is necessary in order to keep and attract good scholars, including those working in applied fields. But it is not costless. The choice will depend upon the political judgements made about the rate of growth of real income compared with that of leisure and the form in which leisure is to be enjoyed. These political value judgements will not be unalterable, but will themselves change as the plan is executed. But without a specification of concrete objectives and concrete manpower requirements, the calculation of 'returns to education' suppresses these value judgements in a pseudo-scientific formulation, buries the factual judgements in misplaced aggregation and severs crucial connexions by illegitimate isolation.

V. THE ROLE OF EDUCATION IN RURAL REFORM

A strand of current doctrine has moved away somewhat from the highly aggregated approach in which all expenditure on education is considered to yield high social returns; impressed by agricultural stagnation or slow growth in the majority of underdeveloped countries, it has awarded the highest priority to agricultural, vocational and technical education. It insists that the main task is to link education with agricultural improvement: to make farmers literate will raise their productivity. Progress in primary education does not, however, according to this doctrine, guarantee literate farmers. In Africa rural children, educated at rural primary schools, will seek jobs in towns, which are paid twice or three times as well as what they could hope to earn if they returned to their farmstead. But not enough town jobs are available. To attract them back to the country, the modernisation of agriculture and the growth of rural schooling must be kept in step. The conclusion is then reached that one should concentrate on agricultural, vocational education and restrict universal primary education.

There is a danger that the doctrine of the high priority to be attached to agricultural, vocational and technical education is about to become vulgarised into the *simpliste* belief that more expenditure on this kind of schooling and a reform of the school curriculum are a *sufficient*, a *basic*, or at any rate a *strategic*, condition of development.

First, the provision of vocational, agricultural and technical education is certainly not enough to accelerate development. Equally important is the provision of employment opportunities for technicians and agriculturists, both in the private and in the public sector. The present fault lies not only, and perhaps not mainly, with the type of training provided, but with the educational requirements of the public service. As long as the public sector rewards 'academic' qualifications and penalises technical, the wrong incentives will be perpetuated in the educational system. The appearance of white-collar unemployment must not be taken as *ipso facto* evidence of unfilled vacancies in technical and agricultural activities. It may simply be a symptom of general unemployment – or under-utilisation of labour – which would be shared by those educated technically if more were turned out by the educational system.

Second, changes in schooling must be accompanied by higher relative pay and status of technicians and agriculturists. Even if employment opportunities existed, the attractions to clerical jobs of higher prestige, status and pay will continue, unless fundamental reforms are instituted. In order to enable higher wages and salaries to be paid, productivity must rise. Although, therefore, vocationally trained men will be more productive, productivity and pay must be raised in order to provide the incentives for such training.

Third, facilities and amenities in rural and technical occupations must be improved. Like status and pay, these are necessary to create the correct incentives. Mr Kiichi Aichi, chief Cabinet Secretary to Mr Sato, the Japanese Prime Minister, is reported[1] to have seen one

[1] *The Times*, 13 Sep 1966.

of the most important problems in agriculture in its failure to attract good brides – thus adding to the general gloom of the countryside. The Government proposed a series of social welfare and amenity reforms to stimulate an 'influx of desirable brides' into the countryside.

Fourth, even more important than changing the content of education is research into crops and animal and plant diseases and the dissemination of its results. It is interesting to note that the contribution of the American land grant colleges lay mainly in this field and not in training farmers.

Fifth, in view of the unreliability of projections of manpower requirements and of the continual advance of technical and agricultural knowledge, schools must lay the foundations for the ability to acquire and use further knowledge. They should provide the general basis for specialist training, but not the actual training. They should train for mental flexibility and insure against intellectual obsolescence.

Finally, there are social, political and long-term economic reasons for universal primary education of a fairly general type.

The conclusion is that the solution of the problem is much more complex than a change in curriculum, however important educational reform itself is. The solution depends upon a concerted attack on a system of interdependent factors determining agricultural and industrial productivity. An isolated attack on education may be as wasteful or counter-productive as the 'academic' curriculum which has, rightly, been criticised. Although the need for balance between schooling and agricultural reform is obvious, the conclusion points towards more rapid and more radical agricultural reform, rather than less and a totally different kind of schooling.

CONCLUSIONS AND QUESTIONS

I have attempted to show that calculations of the returns to education, based on correlating income with educational attainment in the USA, cannot be applied to underdeveloped countries for at least three reasons: first, differences in earnings do not reflect differences in productivity; second, even if they did, education is highly correlated with other causes of higher productivity, such as intelligence, motivation and environmental influences; third, it cannot be assumed that an underdeveloped economy can absorb the educated irrespective of the type of education and irrespective of a host of other measures, and in particular agricultural modernisation and industrialisation. The marginal returns on education by itself may often turn out to be negative.

For the rest I propose to set down only a number of questions:

1. Are we justified in continuing to support efforts for better remuneration and higher status for teachers? This is a complicated question, which raises other questions about the general level of Civil Service salaries (including teachers'), the relation between qualification of teachers, quality of teaching and salaries and the desirable scale and distribution of the educational effort.
2. What is the correct balance between capital expenditure on building and recurrent expenditure on staff? Does capital budgeting and project aid-giving reinforce waste and attitudes hostile to development by drawing a false distinction between 'investment' (brick and mortar) and 'consumption' (teachers' salaries)?
3. What are the causes and cures of over-education?
4. Should university students be sent to Britain or America (or Moscow or Peking) to be educated or should they be educated, often at greater cost, locally?
5. What is the correct strategy for a literacy and numeracy campaign? Should it be directed at children or adults or both?
6. Where and how has the search for emulating educational standards of the West – whether in content or in length and quality of training – been detrimental to development?
7. Should research be pure or applied? How should its results be disseminated? What are the barriers to acceptability?

9 Economic and Social Rights and the Developing Countries

THIS chapter attempts to put forward some ideas on how an economist might tackle the interpretation of economic and social human rights in the context of the present efforts of developing countries to lift themselves out of poverty and to give every citizen an opportunity to the full development of his personality.[1] While an economist can present only a partial view, which will have to be supplemented and complemented by other approaches, all approaches have economic aspects. The scarcity of resources for development imposes choices. It would be quite mistaken to interpret the economist's approach as inspired by a desire to subordinate all values to production and economic growth. Economists are sometimes regarded as monsters who can see no values except material ones. I should like to suggest that the economist's role is quite a different one. By pointing to the implications of our choices, he brings out the costs, in terms of alternatives forgone, of insisting on the attainment of different objectives. Thus, most of what I shall have to say does not raise problems of rights versus development, but rather rights for some now versus rights for others, later. If I criticise some interpretations of the right to education or the right to collective bargaining or the right to free choice of job, it is not because I wish to reduce man to a beast of burden for the greater glory of material development, but because I believe that premature insistence on certain rights involves greater sacrifices of the attainment of possibly more important rights for more individuals in the future.

I think it will be generally agreed that an interpretation of economic and social rights cannot be made irrespective of the stage of development of a country, of its available physical and human resources and of competing claims on these resources. It may be useful to distinguish between *aspirations*, which are ideals we hope to attain eventually, and *rights*, which have to be implemented immediately. It is

[1] I am indebted to Frances Stewart for helpful comments.

surely proper that we should aspire to opportunities for a full development of the human personality, including rights to the best medical treatment, the best education, the best provision for injury, sickness, old age and widowhood, free choice of employment, etc. But it is obvious that immediate implementation may be highly undesirable, because it may be achieved only at the expense of other rights and aspirations or at the expense of the rights of some sections of the community.

The logic of rights

In the Middle Ages scholars enunciated a system of natural law and natural rights. Both law and rights were thought to have religious sanction and moral certitude outside the realm of purely human thought and activities. More recently the use of the term *rights* has come to imply a peculiar moral authority for the objective delineated. By calling some human aspiration a *right*, the objective in question has been given a moral and categorical supremacy, irrespective of the nature of the right, its appropriateness to the circumstances in which it is proclaimed or to the possibilities or costs of achieving it. The use of the term has attempted to achieve what since Hume many have thought to be impossible – to derive an *ought* from an *is*; and more than this, to derive from the ought, itself *derived*, a will. Man is human; therefore he has the right to x; therefore we will give it to him. But the rights in question are just objectives like other objectives with independent and instrumental values; like other objectives, they confer benefits but also incur costs. Like others, they are also subject to economic analysis.

The right to education

Consider 'the right to universal, free, elementary education' (Article 26).[1] First, the implementation of such a right in many countries would be enormously expensive. Poor countries have, typically, perhaps 1/10 of the national income of rich countries. On the other hand, the proportion of the population aged 5 to 15 and to be educated (primary and secondary education and hence wider than the Declaration) is perhaps twice as large as in rich countries (25–30 per cent compared with 15 per cent) and teachers' salaries, which are near or below the national average in rich countries, are four or five times (or in Africa seven times) the average in poor countries. This means that a vastly greater share (typically eight–ten times as much)

[1] *Universal Declaration of Human Rights*, UN Office of Public Information, 1948.

of a much smaller national cake would have to be devoted to education, with the inevitable result that less would be left over for the implementation of other objectives.

Quite apart from the constraints set by available resources, one has to consider the social and economic results of such a programme. In Africa and Asia the experience has been that a very high proportion, sometimes four fifths, of those educated in primary schools drop out or forget what they learn soon after, so that educational efforts on them are wasted. Those who remember what they are taught seek to escape the miserable rural existence and hope to find employment as clerks in the towns. Administration cannot offer jobs to all of them and, far from becoming a source of productive activity, they are liable to become a source of disruptive activity. Far from being fulfilled, they are frustrated.

In order to make sense of the right to education, employment opportunities would have to be provided. Since the large majority of school-leavers will have to make their living in the countryside, this means that rural productivity, rural incomes and rural amenities would have to be improved so as to attract the school-leavers to remain and work in the countryside.

This in turn may mean a concentration of effort on agricultural extension services, including adult education of farmers, even, if necessary, at the expense of rural primary schools. Education without regard to the consequences on income distribution, relative salaries, distribution of the population between town and country and job opportunities not only has effects hostile to development, but must ultimately rebound to an infringement of human rights and human dignity. Case studies are now available of large advances of primary education without the accompanying measures in the field of job creation and rural advance. Kerala has the highest literacy rate of any state in India, but incomes are substantially below the Indian average, there is continued political unrest and the state is a victim of the brain drain. The drive to universal literacy has resulted in a denial of human rights and human opportunities to the mass of the people.

In the previous chapter I have argued that educational planning, like all planning and policy making, involves priorities and choices. The language of human rights, on the other hand, seems to deny the need for such choices. 'All or nothing' often will mean nothing. The striving for the best will lead to a state worse than the third best. Without a specification of concrete objectives and concrete manpower and other resource requirements, insistence on abstract rights suppresses the underlying value judgements and blurs the factual issues.

Social security and health

Another illustration is the attempt to implement social security (Article 22) and the right to health and medical care (Article 25). In fact this usually amounts to a reinforcement of urban bias, a concentration of medical training on producing completely trust-worthy, highly qualified doctors, at the expense of the medical ancillary personnel, less well educated but much more useful, which is desperately needed in the villages to cure communicable diseases, and teach hygiene and birth control. A false interpretation of human rights in the medical field has led to excessive emphasis on *curative* medicine in *towns*, in often splendid hospitals with highly trained doctors and modern equipment, at the expense of *preventive* medicine *in the country*, carried out by nurses and auxiliaries, requiring much shorter training. The beneficial impact of curative facilities is narrow: most of the benefits go to a small, relatively well-off part of the population within a small radius. The urban facilities also contribute to the drift to the towns.

Related to this is the question of the level of medical training and the number of personnel. What is needed is the modern equivalent of the medieval barber ('leech') who, besides cutting hair, put leeches upon people to reduce their blood pressure. Advocates of such a policy are sometimes accused of wishing only the 'second best' for poorer countries. But the desire for the best is here, as elsewhere, the enemy of the good.

At present, the balance between curative and preventive health measures is biased too heavily in favour of the more expensive, urban, middle-class orientated curative measures. Within the curative area, more could be done to promote rural health posts, without in-patient facilities, instead of expensive hospitals.

Health, like education, is both an end, valued for its own sake, and a means that contributes to development and hence to other ends. There is nothing banausic, philistine or degrading in looking upon health measures as ways of improving the productive capacity of human beings. At present, health measures both reinforce inequality and contribute little to manpower development. Expenditure on health can be productive in several ways:

(i) by lowering *mortality* in the age group entering the labour force, it raises the yield to the community of bringing up children (assuming employment is found);

(ii) by lowering *morbidity* (i.e. the time a man is off work because of illness) it increases the number of hours worked;

(iii) by lowering *debility* (i.e. reduced intensity of work because of ill-health) it improves the quality of work, both mental and physical, by reducing apathy and lethargy (malaria, sleeping sickness, dysentery and bilharzia), it raises attentiveness, vigour and motivation and strengthens the muscular power of the body;

(iv) it increases the use of natural resources by clearing otherwise uninhabitable land.

Since resources are scarce, their use for one purpose involves forgoing others. It is relatively cheap to control death rates through the reduction of cholera, typhoid and dysentery, through improvements in environmental sanitation, leading to control of malaria, yellow fever and tuberculosis and through vaccinations against diphtheria and polio. These successful public health measures contributed to the population explosion. The ends are important and the means relatively cheap. The real problem arises, not in the area of public health, but in curative medicine, especially hospitals and clinics.

These are more visible to the public, more prestige-yielding, but also much more costly and much less productive. While it is agreed that health is good, it does not follow that budgets should carry expensive urban hospitals with highly and expensively trained doctors. Lavish expenditures in these directions now may benefit only a small section now, at the expense of accelerated development which would benefit many more citizens later.

Labour

A third, possibly more controversial, area is the subject of labour standards applying to safety, hours, collective bargaining and anti-forced labour conventions (Article 23). The reluctance to use compulsion in order to increase labour utilisation is frequently sanctified by not entirely relevant political memories. Memories of forced colonial labour, slave labour, indentured labour or labour on orders of tribal chiefs, on the one hand, and references to Soviet labour camps, and Soviet treatment of labour generally, reinforced by misguided ILO Conventions, have prevented less developed countries from mobilising the rapidly growing masses of unemployed and rural underemployed for the construction of rural public works such as feeder roads, drainage, irrigation, school buildings or rural education. Political vested interests opposed to mobilisation of labour should not be encouraged by pseudo-moral arguments which, ultimately, condemn the masses to continued starvation, malnutrition, misery and and ill-health. An appeal to human rights can be a cloak behind which hides what Gunnar Myrdal has called 'the soft state'.

Just as in industrial technology great harm has been done by the thoughtless transfer of highly capital-intensive techniques from labour-scarce, capital-abundant, rich countries to the entirely different conditions of developing countries, so in the area of social services and trade union legislation, inappropriate institutions, justified in the light of misguided ideals, have been transferred and imitated (Article 23[4]). Present union aspirations were formulated *after* industrial revolutions had occurred and when labour was scarce. Collective bargaining, in such conditions, benefits both the workers and the community, by giving an impetus to mechanisation. In pre-industrial societies with populations increasing at 2–3 per cent per year and a large proportion of people of working age without hope of a job, collective bargaining and minimum wages are most irresponsible policies, aggravating social inequality, unemployment and poverty. While parading as an implementation of a human right, it is a flagrant denial of such a right to those outside the fortunate labour aristocracy who happen to have found a job. Some of these themes are taken up in the next section.

Standard-setting

It is in the field of standard-setting that the assertion of human rights is open to criticism. The 'international demonstration' effect has been much discussed in international trade and in the transfer of modern and large-scale technology. It has been shown how the desire to emulate standards and behaviour of advanced industrial countries can, without proper adaptation, harm development efforts. But relatively little attention has been paid to the inappropriateness of transferring standards, values, practices and legislation in the field of industrial relations. Standards which are suited for advanced industrial countries have been transferred to the entirely different environment of the developing countries.

In an economic setting like that of the rich countries of the West, where, at certain periods, progress may have been impeded by lack of effective demand, a rise in real wages may accelerate growth. A rise in industrial wages in an advanced industrial economy reduces, rather than increases, inequalities and encourages, rather than discourages, productive investment.

But the situation is quite different in developing countries. There can be little doubt that the adoption of Western labour standards has damaged the development efforts of the developing countries. Thus the creation and encouragement of trade unions, which increase and equalise opportunities in industrial countries, when transferred to traditional economies, can turn into an obstacle to progress and an impediment to opportunity.

The contract to work is nowadays restricted in a number of ways, which reflect the growth of awareness of the need to protect the weak. Certain contracts are forbidden, such as the employment of children or of women in mines. Sometimes maximum hours, minimum wages or maximum burdens are stipulated. Apprenticeship may be regulated and the rights of trade unions are protected. All these represent solid social achievements. If in a particular instance these prohibitions impede economic development, this is not necessarily an argument against them. There are costs of development which a community may not be willing to pay. But there are also other instances in developing countries in which the restrictions fail to contribute to the social justice at which they aim. Where they both impede development and fail to achieve their social aims, these restrictions should be abandoned.

The most important influences of these ideas have been upon:

(a) trade union growth;
(b) collective bargaining;
(c) minimum wage legislation;
(d) 'forced' labour.

Trade unions in developing countries

In general it is reasonable to assume that the stimulation of mass participation in the development effort will directly encourage development. No development planning in a free society can be successful without the enthusiastic co-operation of wide sections of the population. In this sense it is right to encourage the formation of trade unions representing the working people; first, the people participate directly in development and secondly, if represented adequately, they will see to it that they share in the benefit from any increase in national wealth.

However, the establishment of trade unions by itself does not mean that development will be promoted. Trade unions generally represent sectional interests: workers carrying out specific economic functions in particular trades or industries or districts. This is certainly true of the British model and it is true to a large extent of trade unions in developing countries.

Trade unions in developing countries have the following characteristics:

1. Only a small percentage of the working population belongs to the trade unions. Of a total labour force of over 150 millions in India probably only 3 or 4 per cent are unionised. There are normally hardly any fee-paying members, although workers

are prepared to follow the lead of the union and will pay their dues when a dispute is imminent or has just been handled satisfactorily.

2. Trade unions are strongest among urban workers especially in large industries and government. There is little or no union activity in the rural areas.

3. Trade unions (and even more their teachers) tend to be very closely associated with political parties. In India the All-India Trade Union Congress was formed in 1918 through the initiative of prominent members of the Congress Party. The present central labour organisation, the Indian National Trade Union Congress, was established (in 1947) with the official support of the ruling Congress Party. In Africa the development of national government has been evolved largely out of trade union activities. In Tanzania via TANU and in Ghana it had become difficult to distinguish between the Convention People's Party and the trade unions.

While the proportion of the working population organised in unions is very small, the influence and significance of these unions are substantial. Trade unions, far from being the organisation of the weak and exploited that they were in eighteenth- and nineteenth-century England, have usually more power than either the middle classes or the farmers. They tend to be concentrated in the growth sectors of the economy and particularly in the small industrial sector. They often have considerable political power and they exercise influence in many spheres. By creating and perpetuating pockets of privilege, they impede the movement of labour from low to high productivity employments.

Wages are raised highest in the industries which can pay most – often the foreign-owned petroleum or mineral sector – and the rest of the wage structure is pulled up. The 'leading' industry's investment and competitiveness is not affected, but the repercussions on the rest of the economy can be disastrous. The consequential wage increases (a) damage the profitability of established industries and especially export industries and reduce their ability to invest; (b) reduce the incentives to set up new industries in competition with foreign firms, (c) turn whatever investment continues in the direction of saving labour, and (d) reduce agricultural production by making industrial incentive goods more expensive.

Collective bargaining and minimum wage fixing

Collective bargaining and minimum wage fixing are often regarded as part and parcel of the same process. In relation to developing countries the regulation of terms and conditions of employment have been precisely set out. Particularly, the ILO Convention of 1947 on Social Policy in Non-Metropolitan Territories (developing countries) required responsible governments to subscribe to these articles:

(14.1) The fixing of minimum wages by collective agreements freely negotiated between trade unions which are representative of the workers concerned and employers or employers' organizations shall be encouraged.

(14.2) Where no adequate arrangements exist for the fixing of minimum wages by collective agreements, the necessary arrangements shall be made whereby minimum rates of wages can be fixed in consultation with representative organizations, where such exist.

In 1955 the ILO's Committee of Experts on Social Policy in Non-Metropolitan Territories asserted: 'Collective bargaining constitutes the method of determining wages and conditions of employment which is in the best interests of all parties. . . .'

Despite ILO pronouncements on collective bargaining in developing countries, genuine collective bargaining is usually not significant. Most developing economies have a systematic procedure for wage regulation in at least the industrial and public sectors. But this is usually a system of legal regulation and although the actual machinery varies from country to country, it seems important enough to influence the general wage-level, especially in urban and industrial areas.

Even where wage-fixing by collective negotiation appears to be important, the appearance is often illusory. In the former British West African countries, for example, negotiations in individual firms have very largely waited on decisions made about the pay of government employees, which though themselves formally subject to joint discussion have in most cases of major wage-adjustments been submitted to Commissions of Enquiry, and in any case been effectively made by the Government.

It is doubtful whether this system of wage-fixing has any bearing on the real problems of development. Public authorities have been highly susceptible to the pressure of organised groups – which means urban and industrial workers, as well as civil servants. It is doubtful whether collective bargaining as we know it is likely to develop at all in these countries. The conditions for a general development of collective bargaining do not exist and may never emerge. If the public sector will remain the dominant force in economic development in many of these countries, it seems almost inevitable that other organisations will follow the Government's example.

Minimum wage principles are of more importance to wage-policy in developing countries than in developed countries. First, minimum wages often have a greater effect on the total wage-structure. Second, minimum wage principles and procedures have occupied a central place in international discussion (for example, the ILO's attempts to influence national legislation and wage policy). And, third, the lowest level of wages is particularly important in underdeveloped countries because, for the worker, this level represents the threshold from the traditional to the modern economy.

The basic standard for the minimum wage level should be the living standard of cultivators in the traditional sector of the economy, allowing for extra costs incurred by taking up industrial work. In fact, the minimum wage is not thought of in these terms. More frequently it is adjusted for political purposes, or automatic increases are granted as the cost of living index rises and the minimum wage is often regarded as if it were in fact the normal wage level, and not a wage which ought generally to be restricted to one category of workers, who represent new and inexperienced recruits to the labour force.

On the whole it cannot be said that the development of the present wage-fixing procedures has done much either to promote the general development effort or to reduce the social injustices that arise from the existing anomalies and inequities in income distribution.

1. Inflation has been encouraged by automatic upward adjustments of wages, led by a few firms.
2. The diversion of scarce investment resources towards labour-saving and capital-using equipment, processes and products has been encouraged and the absorption of the growing labour force has been impeded.
3. The gains from the economic development that has been achieved have benefited a small proportion of the total population. In certain African countries almost the whole gain appears to have gone to raise consumption of a limited aristocracy of urban industrial workers. The effect has thus been to create or perpetuate an urban labour élite to the detriment of the mass of people.
4. More generally these policies have led to an income distribution which is both economically unsound and socially unjust: the drift from country to town has been accentuated, unemployment has increased, differentials have been narrowed and consumption has risen faster than savings.
5. Finally, the procedures have contributed to the fragmentation of markets (because industry has to cater for a very uneven income distribution with differentiated purchasing power and tastes), the high costs of agricultural inputs and incentive goods

and the low purchasing power of the rural sector. In these ways full labour utilisation has been prevented and production growth impeded. In the name of human rights, these rights have been violated.

To say that union behaviour and labour standards should not be simply transferred from advanced to developing countries does not mean that unions have no function in developing countries. They have a *different* function. They should act as a channel of communication between the Government and the wage earners (as well as between employer and workers); they should organise training and productivity campaigns; they should reduce industrial tensions and unrest. They can also promote social services, organise cheap holidays and welfare facilities, etc. In the United Kingdom, trade unions behaved in this sort of way during the war. A concerted effort for mobilisation, whether for war or development, calls for different functions of unions.

Forced labour

One of the most serious obstacles to development is the absence of effective utilisation of labour in developing countries. Labour utilisation has many dimensions. It embraces not only demand by employers for labour and equipment, but also willingness and ability to work, readiness to be subjected to discipline, minimum educational, nutritional and health standards, motivation and intelligence, and many others. What is commonly described as growing unemployment, underemployment and disguised unemployment really amounts to a growing demoralisation of large and growing numbers of people, the majority of them young men entering the labour force, and a disintegration of whole communities. One aspect of this problem is the attraction of urban living standards and promise of employment for those leaving the countryside. This deprives the land of many of its most promising potential innovators and thus contributes to the perpetuation of rural poverty. It swells the population of the shanty towns some of whom, after a time, become so demoralised that they are unemployable.

The mobilisation of rural labour for rural public works, where necessary seasonal or part-time, would support the successes of the Green Revolution at minimum cost to the economy. There is great need for the construction of feeder roads, irrigation works, storage facilities, schools, rural housing and rural works of conservation and rehabilitation. Such mobilisation could be used to improve rural amenities, make rural life more attractive and reduce the flow of migrants to the towns. It can prevent a slow-down in the disintegration of rural communities and the growth of urban misery.

One difficulty is the provision of wage goods on which the additional incomes, paid to the workers thus mobilised, is spent. The public works programme must be organised so as to increase investment and at the same time either raise food production to feed the men engaged on the programme, or enforce the spread of existing food supplies over those employed on the public works.

This is where compulsion can meet a need. It can be used to economise in the extra supply of food as a wage good. The workers continue to live with their families and to be maintained by them while rendering their services.

It has been proposed that this form of service should be conscripted in a manner similar, or as an alternative, to national service. Five reasons can be advanced for this. First, there is a crying national need both for the investment and the mobilisation of labour, which might otherwise not be met. Second, labour tends to be immobile and is not always responsive to economic rewards. Financial or other material inducements may also be inadequate, or if adequate too costly. Third, compulsion can harness the necessary labour services with less inflationary results than a system of economic incentives. Fourth, certain burdens are more readily shouldered if there is certainty that others will be called upon to share the contribution fairly. Fifth, there is psychological advantage for the population to be directly engaged in the development effort. Without compulsory general national service, employment on public works, especially if organised for relief, will endow those engaged on them with an inferior status. It is essential that the privileged educated youth should also be mobilised and promotion and eligibility for attractive jobs later in their career be made dependent on periodic national service in the countryside. Only then can prejudices be broken down and the ignominy of manual rural work be eradicated.

Two objections have been raised to schemes of this kind: that they are inefficient ways of mobilising labour because work done under compulsion is never as good as work done out of free choice; and that they infringe human rights. The International Labour Conventions on Forced Labour of 1930 and 1957 provided for the abolition of any form of forced labour or compulsory labour, for five specific purposes, including 'as a method of mobilising and using labour for purposes of economic development'. In 1961 the ILO Committee of Experts on the Application of Conventions and Recommendations called attention to the infringement of 'human rights' which many of these schemes presented.

This attitude, entirely proper in the conditions of a developed cash economy, in which communal obligations can be discharged by money payments in the form of compulsory income tax, is neither morally nor economically appropriate in a society in which the use of compulsion may be the only way to secure collective action and in which abstinence from compulsion can perpetuate injustice, privilege and underdevelopment.

With regard to the efficiency of work, research is needed about motivation, morale and incentives. Even in the least favourable circumstances, such as prisoner-of-war camps or penal institutions, useful work has been carried out. Safeguards are necessary to prevent, on the one hand, oppression and exploitation, benefits accruing to a small group and discrimination and, on the other, deterioration of the quality of work. But there is evidence that the appropriate organisation and a fair distribution of burdens can achieve remarkable results.

The reluctance to use compulsion in order to increase labour utilisation is frequently concealed behind politically palatable slogans. Memories of forced colonial labour, slave labour, indentured labour or labour on order of tribal chiefs on the one hand, and of Soviet labour camps are used to justify the reluctance to recruit a national service corps. The sanction of 'human rights' gives this resistance moral blessing. Fear to use such an organisation is hidden behind the pretence that democratic government does not permit such compulsion. An appeal to democracy is used to justify the soft state in its reluctance to tackle the hard task of development.

Conclusions

The correct way to look at a strategy of implementing human rights is to construct a time profile, showing who achieves *what* rights, *how* effectively, at *what* time and at *what sacrifices and costs*. Premature attempts to aim at the best now may lead to sacrifices later and in some cases to sacrifices by others now. A more modest, partial attack on literacy, health or work standards is likely to lead to a fuller realisation of these rights than an attempt to transfer at once alleged universal principles from rich to poor countries.

This can be illustrated by Article 23(1), the right to employment. It is plain that there is no prospect, for a considerable time to come, of full employment in developing countries. The strategic questions that arise are:

1. To what extent does the employment objective conflict with other goals of policy, e.g. free choice of employment, more production now or later, higher living standards, greater independence from foreign assistance, etc. ?

2. To what extent can more employment *now* be achieved only by sacrificing employment *later* and vice versa? What is the preference of policy makers with respect to the time profile of employment growth?

3. What social and institutional reforms are necessary to achieve higher employment? Are there serious social objections to multiple-shift working? Are trade union objectives compatible with higher employment? What incomes policy is required to absorb additional labour and reduce the gross imbalance between urban and rural incomes?

But a simple time profile for the achievement of human rights is not enough. A further complication arises because the achievement of certain rights may create 'second generation problems' in the attainment of other rights. Death control raises population growth and all the well-known difficulties that stem from it. Technical progress creates problems of the preservation of the environment and hazards to health and safety. Progress on one front may spell regress on others. A proper intertemporal strategy must allow for these new threats and challenges which arise from the attainment of aspirations.

One difficulty in this area is that the specialised agencies of the UN were set up at a time when development was not a main objective and when the implications of their policies for low-income countries had not been thought through. The ILO, for example, founded in 1919, was at least partly inspired by the desire of advanced industrial countries to check industrialisation of the (then) less advanced countries, like Japan, and to limit competition for selling manufactures in world markets. Its role in the international field was parallel to that of the craft unions which attempted to assert differentials for skills and to fight the erosion of their privileged position that resulted from growing competition. It is ironical that some of these principles have been transferred wholesale to the developing countries of the post-war period, whose own interests are diametrically opposed to these principles.

As a result of their origin, the specialised agencies have tended to see themselves, at least until recently, as the guardians of certain principles which were appropriate for rich industrial countries, but are quite inappropriate for developing countries. ILO has insisted on collective bargaining, labour standards, anti-forced labour conventions and the transfer of trade union objectives, all principles and practices which are not conducive to development or to the human aspirations to which lip service is paid. UNESCO preached universal literacy, raising the pay and status of teachers and encouraging liberal arts courses, which reinforced the costly alienation of élites and the brain drain from developing countries. WHO refused to consider birth control which should form part of any integrated village health programme and emphasised curative rather than public health preventive measures. FAO stressed the technocratic approach to agriculture and minimised the human, institutional and political obstacles to better feeding. In each case, rivalries between spheres of competence prevented the concerted, joint, multipronged attack which a development strategy requires. Pleas for human rights were used to bolster up the vested interests and justify the poor results in terms of development. Much of this has begun to change and the focus on development has corrected some old errors. While development is not everything, indeed is only a means to the attainment of other goals, without development the rapidly growing masses of the third world will remain condemned to live without some of the most important rights.

The economist, if he knows anything, knows that scarcity imposes choice and that choice has to lay down priorities. Rather than advocating the immediate implementation of long-term aspirations, the economist will be biased in favour of getting better value from the existing system. He will emphasise improvements in the quality and efficiency of a going educational system before rushing into rapid quantitative extension of the system. He will examine what complementary actions a multi-pronged attack on poverty requires to enable the educated, the healed, the employed, to make full use of their opportunities, and he will pay some attention to balance: balance between the various sectors of education, balance between technical and liberal education, balance between country and towns, balance between workers and farmers, balance between skills and jobs, balance between present and future. Once again, balance implies priorities and forgoing less important alternatives, at least for a time. The economist will reduce abstract appeals to concrete choice. But, by laying bare disagreeable choices, he paves the way for a more rational move forward.

Part Two

International Movements of Capital, Money and Goods

10 International Capital Movements[1]

I. DEFINITIONS AND MEASUREMENT

INTERNATIONAL capital movements are normally registered in the capital account of the balance of payments. Table 10.1 illustrates some of the items entered on both sides of the account.

TABLE 10.1

Balance of Payments

Capital Account

Receipts (Credits)	*Payments (Debits)*
Long-term: Government	
Long-term borrowing from foreign governments (in cash or kind)	Long-term lending to foreign governments
Borrowing from international organisations	Lending to international organisations
Capital repayments by foreign governments	Capital repayments to foreign governments
Sale of other assets to foreign governments	Purchase of other assets from foreign governments
Unrequited receipts (grants, reparations, indemnities) received from foreign governments	Unrequited payments (grants, etc.) paid to foreign governments or international organisations
Long-term: Private	
Long-term borrowing from foreign individuals or firms	Long-term lending to foreign individuals or firms
Direct investment by foreign firms (i) plough back profits (ii) new investment	Direct investment abroad
Portfolio equity investment from abroad	Portfolio equity investment abroad

[1] I am grateful to Sir Roy Harrod, Dr Keith Griffin, Mr Vijay Joshi, Professor Walter Newlyn, Mr Akbar Noman and Mrs Frances Stewart for valuable comments and help.

(Table 10.1 *continued*)

Receipts (*Credits*)	Payments (*Debits*)
Short-term capital and monetary movements	
Short-term borrowing from foreign governments	Short-term lending to foreign governments
Trade credits received (short-term private borrowing)	Trade credits extended (short-term private lending)
(i) government guaranteed	(i) government guaranteed
(ii) non-guaranteed	(ii) non-guaranteed
Decrease in sterling and dollar assets, gold and convertible currencies	Increase in sterling and dollar assets, gold and convertible currencies
Decrease in holdings of non-convertible currencies	Increase in holdings of non-convertible currencies
Drawing on account with IMF	Repaying debt to IMF

The relation of the capital account to the other items in the balance of payments can be seen in Table 10.2.

The balancing item in Table 10.2 covers errors and omissions in other items and is introduced to balance the accounts. It also conceals illegal and not reported transactions and can therefore be an indication of illegal capital flight.

The main distinctions are those between short-term and long-term capital movements, official and private, multilateral and bilateral, loans and grants, autonomous and accommodating, and, within private, between direct and portfolio and between bond and equity investment. Short-term lending and borrowing has two aspects: the length of time that passes before maturity of the loan and the expectation as to whether the movement is likely to be reversed soon or whether it is expected to continue. Bank deposits, Treasury Bills, commercial bills and long-term securities in their last year before

TABLE 10.2

Balance of Payments Accounts

Current account	
1. Current balance of receipts over payments	....
Long-term capital account	
2. Balance of long-term capital receipts over payments	....
3. Balance of current and long-term capital transactions (1 + 2)	....
4. Balancing item	....
Short-term capital and monetary movements	
5. Balance of short-term capital and monetary movements	....
6. Total balance (algebraic sum of 3 + 4 + 5) =	0

maturity are short-term assets because they mature quickly. But they may be renewed at maturity, and the loans may, in that case, be expected to continue.

Short-term capital movements used to be determined by interest rate differentials. In the peaceful and stable world before the First World War, when exchange rates were fixed, foreign exchange restrictions unknown and confidence abounded, a rise in Bank Rate, followed by other short-term interest rates, attracted funds and increased the reserves. In our own more disturbed days, such a rise may be thought to herald weakness and devaluation and it may lead to withdrawal of funds. It is, however, possible to insure against the risk of devaluation by simultaneously selling forward the currency acquired to earn a higher interest rate. A skilful combination of interest and forward exchange rate manipulation by the Government may therefore be thought to be able to counteract the perverse effects of interest rate policy. It has been argued that the support by the Government of the rate at which the acquired currency is sold forward, combined with a sufficiently high interest rate, should make it possible to attract short-term funds even if there is lack of confidence in the currency. But such a policy would not work if there was lack of confidence in continued freedom to transfer capital. From the Government's point of view, it would mean the gain of reserves in exchange for the acquisition of short-term liabilities to foreigners. If the Government did have to devalue, its support of the forward rate may involve it in large losses. For these reasons the flow of private short-term capital can no longer be relied upon by itself to be a stabilising force, helping governments to tide over periods in which more fundamental adjustments are carried out.

The volatility of short-term capital movements is aggravated by rumours of political upheaval, war or any other event which might lead to restrictions of transfer. Bank Rate increases still play a part in attracting capital, but more by raising general confidence than by the promise of higher commercial yields. They therefore often have to form part of a larger package, containing deflationary measures and other actions designed to restore confidence abroad.

An important element in the large movements out of and into a major world currency is due to world trade being invoiced and settled in that currency. If devaluation is expected, imports are ordered in advance and payments for imports are speeded up, while exports are delayed. One has to distinguish these precautionary transactions from speculative ones, although their effect on the reserves is the same. Traders with future liabilities in foreign currencies try to cover their exchange risk by purchasing the currency they want by means of a forward exchange contract. The bank which sells them forward foreign currency covers its risk by buying 'spot' foreign exchange at once, holding it to maturity of the contract. In this way, the country's foreign exchange reserves are depleted. Similarly, foreigners with a future claim to sterling sell sterling forward to avoid the risk of devaluation. Other foreign traders who have future commitments to pay in the suspected currency, who normally cover these, cease to do so when devaluation is expected. They prefer the chance of buying a devalued currency later cheaper to having to buy the currency forward now. All these movements are known as 'leads and lags' and are motivated by precaution, not by speculation. All three types of movement increase the supply of forward currency relatively to the demand for it. The excess supply of forward sterling has to be covered by the purchase of foreign currencies spot and this constitutes a drain on the reserves.

In addition to covering and uncovering by those who invoice trade in the currency, foreigners holding balances of the currency which has come under suspicion will wish to hedge by selling their currency forward with a view to repurchasing it spot when the contract matures and devaluation has taken place. This may be important for the large, multilateral corporations. Finally, there are straight speculators who seek not protection but sell the suspect currency forward in the hope of making a profit by buying it spot after devaluation.

The reduced ability to rely on private short-term capital movements to stabilise disequilibria and the increased importance of sudden changes in confidence have led to greater reliance on intergovernmental borrowing and lending. Claims on the International Monetary Fund (IMF) are based on subscriptions of currencies; additional currencies were provided for the IMF under the General Arrangements to Borrow (GAB) and monetary authorities have made arrangements to swap currencies. The IMF is supposed to look after basic deficits, while swap arrangements look after leads and lags.

Factors similar to those determining the movement of private short-term capital also determine *private long-term capital movements*. Higher interest rates and the expectation of high rates of return, after deduction of a risk premium, both attract old capital from countries where returns are lower and attract new savings from everywhere. The composition of private investment has radically changed since the nineteenth century. Whereas then 70 per cent of world foreign investment took the form of bonds and only 30 per cent of equity, today bond investment is very small (though it has recently shown signs of reviving) and the majority of long-term capital takes the form of direct equity investment.

The distinction between direct and portfolio investment cuts across the distinction between bond and equity investment. Most bond investment is portfolio investment, though it is possible to envisage an invitation to a foreign firm to invest but to confine some of its capital participation to fixed-interest lending. This would contribute a form of direct bond investment. Direct investment is normally equity investment with control and management of the operations of the firm. Bond investment and equity investment without management are forms of portfolio investment. The balance of payments reporting of the IMF and of the Organisation for Economic Co-operation and Development (OECD) provide the main sources of information on international capital flows. These statistics, though greatly improved in the last few years, still fall far short of what is needed. Ideally, we should require a world-wide complete and detailed matrix of trade and payments, showing flows by countries, terms, sectors and types. At present no reconciliation is possible between recorded outflows and recorded inflows. Definitions and categories are not consistent. The standard of accuracy of reporting varies greatly between countries and some do not report at all. Illegal transactions are also concealed by these inconsistencies.

Starting with the balance of payments reporting of the flows from and to developed countries, Table 10.3 regroups the items in order to bring out the resource flows.

Table 10.3 covers only changes in *assets* of the capital-exporting countries and not liabilities, resulting from operations of the multilateral agencies or residents of developing countries. Table 10.3 also omits interest and other income receipts on current account, which are directly related to the capital transactions. In order to get a full picture of the *net* transfer of resources, these current account items must be included. Net, in this context, means not only after deduction of repayment of principal and reverse flows of capital, but also net of payments of interest, profits and dividends arising from past investment. The table also excludes changes in assets maturing in one year or less.

Official flows of long-term capital, which have largely replaced the private bond market, will be discussed below.

II. THE MECHANISM OF ADJUSTMENT

In this section we consider the question: how does voluntary international capital transfer, and in particular lending and borrowing, affect the balances of payments of the lending and borrowing countries?

A good deal of theoretical ingenuity has been devoted to an analysis of the mechanism of adjustment to capital transfers. It is

TABLE 10.3

Summary of Movement of External Resources (other than Military Grants) from Developed Market Economies to Developing Countries and to Multilateral Agencies

	Flow of developed countries' resources		
Resource flow	*From developing countries and multilateral agencies*	*To developing countries and multilateral agencies*	*Net flow of developed countries' resources*
Grand total			
Total official			
Bilateral			
Central government transfer payments:			
In cash:			
Local currency			
Other			
In kind:			
Technical assistance			
Other			
Central government capital transactions:			
Loans:			
Local currencies			
Other			
Securities			
Changes in local currency holdings			
Other			
Government agencies[a] capital transactions			
Central monetary institutions capital transactions			
Multilateral			
Central government:			
Contributions to and payments from multilateral agencies			
Grants to multilateral agencies			
Subscriptions and transfers of supplementary resources to multilateral agencies			
Loans and securities of multilateral agencies			
Government agencies[b]: securities of multilateral agencies			

| | Flow of developed countries' resources | | |
	From developing countries and multilateral agencies	To developing countries and multilateral agencies	Net flow of developed countries' resources
Resource flow			
Multilateral (contd.)			
Central government (contd.)			
Central monetary institutions: securities of multilateral agencies			
Total private			
Bilateral			
Private institutional transfer payments:			
In cash			
In kind:			
Technical assistance ⎱			
Other ⎰			
Private non-monetary sector's capital:[b]			
Direct investment:			
Undistributed profits			
Other			
Portfolio investment			
Loans and trade credits			
Other			
Private monetary institutions			
Multilateral			
Private non-monetary sectors			
Private monetary institutions			
Total bilateral, official and private			
Total multilateral, official and private			

[a] Covers public corporations, which are treated in the IMF system as part of the private non-monetary sector, and publicly owned monetary institutions (other than central monetary institutions) which in the IMF system are grouped with private monetary institutions.

[b] Including local government where applicable.

Source: *Measurement of the Flow of Resources to Developing Countries*, a report on methodological problems by a group of experts (United Nations, 1967) pp. 11–16.

ironical that most actual transfers have in the past turned out to be less problematical than one would infer from the literature on transfer mechanisms. This divergence between theory and practice is due partly to preoccupation in the past with tributes and reparations fixed in terms of money and partly to the assumptions of full employment and comparative statics.

In the past, there were two schools of thought which attempted to explain how the real transfer, i.e. the export of commodities and services, was affected by the lender country after a loan had been made. We shall consider both under fixed and under variable exchange rates.

J. S. Mill and Taussig assumed that the reciprocal demand curves (the demand for imports as a function of the supply of exports) remained unaltered as a result of the extension of a loan and that therefore a change in relative price levels must occur in order to secure, on favourable elasticity assumptions, an export surplus from the lender country. In its crudest form, this theory holds that a gold flow from the paying to the receiving country raises prices in the latter and lowers them in the former. Elaborations stress the changes in relative interest rates and their repercussions on the credit structure. A purchase of foreign securities will tend to lower the rate of interest abroad, lead, it was thought, to expansion and price rises abroad and thus create favourable conditions for the generation of an export surplus by the lender. The reverse movements would occur at home.

An obvious objection to this theory is that, if the borrower wants to buy what the lender does without, so that the extra demand generated by the loan is directed at precisely those goods and services which are released by the lender, there will be no need for relative prices to change.

This is the starting-point of what used to be called 'modern' theories (Bertil Ohlin, Carl Iverson) though they now look as dated as other past manifestations of modernity. In any case, they go back at least as far as Ricardo. Although the criticism of the 'modern' school is valid, in an international system which uses money and not barter, it is most unlikely that those who sell securities will spend their receipts on the things left on the shelves by those who bought these securities. Even if the transfer were not one between financial assets but an act of new saving, and even if total aggregate demand remained unaltered, it is most unlikely that the composition and direction of demand and supply would be so nicely matched.

If there is not precise matching, we must consider the domestic cost conditions and import propensities. If long-term costs per unit of output are constant, if both countries have a marginal propensity to import of zero, and if exports are not substitutable for domestic goods, either themselves or by shifting factors of production, Mill's theory remains correct. The terms of trade will then have to change sufficiently to effect the real transfer of the loan. But if the borrowers do not spen d the *whole* proceeds of the loan on domestic goods, and if the lenders do not confine their expenditure reductions to domestic goods, and if domestic goods and exportables are substitutable or factors of production can move from domestic goods to exports in the lender's country and from exports to domestic goods in the borrower's, the terms of trade need change correspondingly less, or not at all. Any other relative sectional price changes within a country will lead to factor transfer and restoration of prices to the *status quo*. This follows from the classical assumption of perfect mobility of factors within, and complete immobility between, countries.

If constant costs do not prevail and/or if the marginal propensity to import is positive and large and/or if domestic goods and exportables are substitutable either themselves or by factor transfer, other price movements, in addition to those envisaged by Mill and Taussig, will ensue. The terms of trade may even move *in favour* of the lending country. This will be the case if the transfer increases total demand for its goods and decreases demand for those of the borrower.

Both the classical and what then was known as the 'modern' theory assumed that total purchasing power was preserved. The only difference between them was that the classical theory assumed foreign trade purchasing power to be constant in each country, while the modern theory assumed a transfer of purchasing power from lender to borrower. When the assumption of perfect internal mobility of factors is dropped, the direction of the movement in the terms of trade becomes even less predictable. For the 'modern' theory, terms of trade movements, however, are of only secondary importance, for the primary causes of the transfer are the *shifts* in the demand curves, not movements along constant demand curves. Demand of the borrower will be greater at the same, or even at higher, prices of the lending country's goods. No gold, price or interest movements are necessary, although they may in fact occur.

Where exchange rates are freely adjustable, the classical school argued that the foreign exchange rate of the lending country will fall (i.e. fewer units of foreign currency will buy one unit of domestic currency) and – elasticities being assumed favourable – the lender's balance of trade will improve until the transfer is accomplished. Once again, the 'modern' school pointed out that exchange rates may not move, or may move in favour of the lender whose rate appreciates, and transfer will yet take place. Short-term accommodating capital movements from the borrowing to the lending country will tide over the transitional period. These 'equalising' movements will be the result partly of interest rate differentials, partly of expectations that the fall in the exchange rate (if it does fall) is only temporary. They would reduce the depreciation of the exchange rate but, to that extent, they would also fail to bring about the intended long-term transfer of purchasing power. But unless there is complete equalisation by reverse capital flows, borrowers have acquired purchasing power from lenders and neither the amount nor even the direction of the change in exchange rates can be determined without additional information about the pattern of demand and costs.

Both theories have serious empirical and theoretical weaknesses. Historically, foreign lending was accomplished much more easily than the cumbersome mechanism of the theory would suggest. It was normally not reflected in a see-saw mechanism – one country raising prices while the other lowered them – but by simultaneous movements of employment, income and prices in the lending centre and the borrowing periphery.

Analytically, Keynes's *General Theory* introduced variations in employment and real income which greatly raise the speed and ease of adjustments. In this analysis, the preservation of purchasing power, whether jointly or separately, can no longer be assumed. If the international capital market were perfect, so that only one rate of interest could rule at any one time, and if exchange rate parities were fixed, changes in international lending, like changes in domestic lending, would tend to lead to simultaneous changes in world incomes and employment, unless governments pursued offsetting expenditure policies. An increase in the desire to lend may merely reduce income and employment, while a reduction may do the opposite. If, however, the international capital market is imperfect and different interest rates prevail in different centres, increased foreign lending will tend to reduce the rate of interest of the borrowing country relatively to that of the lending country. This may elicit equalising short-term capital movements or it may lead to credit expansion in the borrowing, and credit contraction in the lending country.

Alternatively, it can be assumed that the lending country creates a budget surplus equal to the foreign loan, while the borrowing country creates a budget deficit of the same amount. The lending country will then experience a decline in income, employment and imports, depending on its propensity to consume, invest and import, while the borrowing country will experience a rise in income, employment and imports. The outcome will be different according to whether such fiscal policies are pursued symmetrically in the two countries or only in one and whether either or both countries are stable or unstable (i.e. whether the sum of the propensities to consume and invest is less or greater than one).[1]

The discussion so far has not considered the question why the initial act of foreign lending (or investing) occurs. This question can be ignored in decisions to pay reparations or tributes, which are not determined by variables within the system. They can be treated like acts of God. It is these cases to which the analysis is best tailored. But normally, the act of new lending or investing is the result of more remunerative investment outlets in the borrowing country. Sir Alec Cairncross, in his analysis of British experience between 1870 and 1913, concluded that '. . . it was upon the terms of trade that the distribution of investment between home and foreign, as well as the course of real wages ultimately depended'.[2]

When the terms of trade moved against Britain, so that import prices rose relatively to export prices, British capital was attracted abroad. Professor Brinley Thomas criticises this view, suggesting that it is not consistent with the evidence. In the later phases of foreign investment booms, the terms of trade turned in favour of Britain. Brinley Thomas's explanation for the long swings in foreign investment is the uneven rate of development, the so-called Kuznets cycle, largely caused by population movements and construction, which attracted capital. 'One may summarize the process as an interregional competition for factors of production within the Atlantic economy, with the Old World and the New World alternating in the intensive build-up of resources.'[3] Movements of the terms of trade, according to Brinley Thomas, are a consequence, rather than a cause of the distribution of capital between home and foreign investment. But these movements are not induced by the attempt to transfer capital across the exchanges: they are the result of the interplay of demand and supply in the main industries. In neither case are movements in the terms of trade the medium of transfer. On the Cairncross view, they cause capital movements; on the Thomas view they reflect them.

A special case to which the analysis of tributes and reparations may be thought to apply is the transfer of foreign aid. There are, clearly, a number of differences. Much foreign aid is tied to procurement from donor (creditor) countries, although the possibility of switching reduces the effectiveness of such tying. The use of sterling and dollar balances as liquid assets by recipient countries implies

[1] Lloyd A. Metzler, 'The Transfer Problem Reconsidered', chap. 8 in *Readings in the Theory of International Trade*, ed. Howard S. Ellis and Lloyd A. Metzler (Homewood, Ill., 1949).

[2] A. K. Cairncross, *Home and Foreign Investment 1870–1913* (1953) p. 208.

[3] Brinley Thomas, 'The Historical Record of International Capital Movements to 1913' in chap. 1 in *Capital Movements and Economic Development*, edited by John H. Adler (1967) p. 19.

that, instead of gold flowing to recipients in the first place, long-term loans are accompanied by short-term reverse borrowing, until the transfer is accomplished.

Nevertheless, the impact of aid on the terms of trade and balances of payments has not received the attention that it deserves. It is obvious that a real transfer of resources can be brought about only through an export surplus of donors and a matching deficit of recipients. We know that large and unaccounted for reverse flows of capital from poor to rich countries occur and that much aid is simply a compensation for this form of lending by poor to rich countries. But what is the effect of aid-giving on the terms of trade? The classical doctrine, as we have seen, suggests that lenders' terms deteriorate while borrowers' improve, so that there should be a secondary gain to recipients, over and above any primary gain from aid. To some extent, aid, like direct investment, involves direct exports and therefore raises no transfer problem. But there remains a transfer problem for untied aid. Partly for the reasons given above and partly for others, the classical mechanism does not operate. Assume, for instance, not unrealistically, that the transfer is brought about, not by lowering the prices of exports – an uncommon procedure with manufactured products – but by import restrictions imposed by aid donors or by 'voluntary' restrictions of the exports of aid recipients. These may take the form of 'voluntary' quotas, as for textiles, or of import duties or other restrictions. Such measures will lower the prices of the exports of the developing countries, unless suppliers can reap the scarcity value of the reduced demand. As to the export prices of donors, the result of tying and their near-monopoly position in capital goods markets enables aid donors to raise prices against the purchasers or, at any rate, to sell at uncompetitively high prices. Estimates put this rise as high as 20–25 per cent. For these reasons, aid is more likely to worsen than to improve the terms of trade of the recipient and to detract from the real benefit of aid to him.

An analysis of the effects on the terms of trade of aid-giving would be valuable. There can be little doubt that it would show that the net transfer is reduced by the deleterious effects on recipients' terms of trade.

The situation would be eased if the service of aid loans reversed the process and debtors could then improve their terms of trade. But this, unfortunately, is not the case. While much aid is tied, repayments have to be made in convertible currency. This means that more exports have to be sold competitively in world markets. In the absence of effective international commodity agreements, this is liable to worsen the terms of trade of debtors. On the other hand, import restrictions by debtors on manufactured products from industrial countries will not lower their prices. It thus appears that a terms of trade burden is carried by aid recipients *both* when they receive *and* when they service debt.

So much for changes in the balances and terms of trade resulting from changes in international lending and borrowing. But the causal links are more complex. International capital movements may be the result, as well as the cause, of divergent domestic levels of activities and divergent balance of payments movements. Countries generating export surpluses as a result of purely domestic conditions will tend to lend and countries running balance of payments deficits will tend to borrow. There will be a tendency for voluntary lending to follow surpluses and borrowing to follow deficits. A country with a surplus in its balance of payments registers an excess of its total *ex post* savings over its domestic investment. This will lead to lower interest rates at home and encourage more foreign lending than would otherwise have been the case. Foreign lending will reduce the interest differential between foreign and domestic capital markets which would have occurred in the absence of international capital flows. A similar movement may be expected in the exchange rates which will tend to move against the lender and in favour of the borrower.

The less imperfect the international capital market, the stronger will be the tendency for long-term capital movements to follow payments imbalances. It is precisely this mechanism (of compensating private and public capital flows) which maintains balance between regions within a country, where exchange rate adjustments are ruled out.

This was approximately the situation in the nineteenth century. The English-speaking world and the Atlantic community formed a fairly unified region within which capital moved freely and restrictions on the movement of labour were much smaller. Fixed exchange rates were widespread, though not universal. Surpluses and deficits between the periphery and the centre were accommodated by balancing capital movements. New borrowing in the form of capital issues quickly led to transfer of real resources to finance deficits of borrowers and deficits of borrowers quickly led to balancing capital issued and long-term loans. Both deficits and loans reflected increased investment opportunities in the periphery. The large and free capital market in London, in which money could be borrowed at rates only slightly above those prevailing on domestic securities, enabled equilibrium to be restored painlessly and quickly.

III. THE PRESENT SITUATION

It would be an understatement to say that the situation today is very different. While the required adjustments were smaller in the nineteenth century, the scope for making them was much larger. There are a number of features which distinguish modern international capital flows and the modern adjustment mechanism from those in the last century.[1]

First, countries no longer use the automatic adjustment mechanisms of the balance of payments which existed in the nineteenth century. They are now able and determined to maintain high levels of employment, so that variations in employment cannot take the brunt of adjustments. Price deflation in advanced manufacturing countries is now ruled out because money wages are inflexible downwards. Exchange rates are kept fixed for long periods, without adherence to the principles of the gold standard. For these reasons, a greatly increased weight would have to be borne by capital movements as almost the only remaining equilibrating force. As far as short-term capital movements are concerned, they could, in principle, play an equilibrating part, in the short run, were it not for disequilibrating speculation. But they would not be a substitute for adjustments. Some writers see in long-term capital movements a possible equilibrating mechanism. No doubt, in certain situations they can fulfil this function. Europe's post-war balance of payments disequilibrium was partly remedied by American capital inflow. The structural balance of payments disequilibria of some developing countries can be eased by long-term capital inflow. The terms of America's capital to Europe under the Marshall Plan were excessively soft – more than 90 per cent in the form of grants – and today's terms of aid to developing countries are too hard; in 1969 the grant element of total loan commitments and grants received was only 45 per cent but, whatever the terms, aid can contribute to the restoration of equilibrium. But there are other forms of disequilibria to whose cure long-term capital flows make no contribution; they may even be aggravated by them, because fundamental adjustments are postponed.

Second, the world economy, in spite of the remarkable buoyancy of total world trade, is no longer the *same kind* of 'engine of growth' which it was in the last century. Britain, which had a high propensity to import primary products without restrictions, and which provided the capital and the men for the expansion of the production of primary commodities abroad, had been replaced as a centre by the USA with a considerably lower import propensity. The USA is a much more self-sufficient economy, protects heavily its domestic

[1] See P. N. Rosenstein-Rodan, 'Philosophy of Foreign Investment in the Second Half of the Twentieth Century', chap. 4, and George Borts, p. 65, in *Capital Movements and Economic Development*, Proceedings of a Conference held by the International Economic Association, edited by John H. Adler and Paul W. Kuznets (London: Macmillan, 1967).

market, particularly of labour-intensive and of processed products, and absorbs a much higher proportion of its savings at home. Europe, though more dependent on trade, is even more protectionist. Political uncertainities have further reduced the flow of international investment. As a result, the transfer problem for underdeveloped countries created by servicing debt and investment is much more serious than it was in the last century.

Third, the international monetary system, from having been the oil which lubricated the 'engine of growth' by facilitating trading and lending, has become grit in the engine and a major obstacle to the expansion of international trade and investment. Recent reforms have alleviated the situation, but we are still far from an international monetary system which facilitates trade, growth and the fullest use of the world's resources.

Fourth, much international lending is no longer guided by profitability. Intergovernmental lending in the form of aid occupies now an important place. Whatever the merits and defects of international aid, there is little to be learned from the nineteenth-century pattern, except that successful development often requires soft loans, whether *ex ante*, as today, or *ex post* (with debtors defaulting as a result of depressions and wars), as in the nineteenth century.

Fifth, the movement of capital is no longer accompanied by the emigration of people who propose to settle overseas. In spite of the growth of technical assistance, migration of skilled, highly motivated people, representing a large transfer of human capital, is rare and their integration into the developing societies is much more difficult.

Sixth, default on foreign debt, which was common in the nineteenth century, is hardly ever allowed to occur today. While default on private debts made the effective terms of lending much softer than the anticipated or nominal terms, it also had a healthy effect on the distribution of new loans. Today's complex machinery of rescheduling and refinancing debt, often incurred by rash traders regardless of borrowers' ability to repay, both diminishes the amount of aid which can be given to those who need and deserve it most and removes the incentive of private lenders for caution. Even if exchange control, devaluation and nationalisation are considered as modern equivalents to default, there are fewer defaults today, unless continuing debt rescheduling is regarded as a form of default.

Turning now to private capital movements, seventh, we have already seen that, whereas in the nineteenth century 70 per cent of world foreign investment took the form of bonds and only 30 per cent that of equity, today bond investment is very small (although middle-income countries like Mexico, Argentina and Israel have floated large bond issues in recent years and a revival of the bond market may be possible) and, disregarding trade credits, the majority is in direct equity.[1] This has changed not only the rates of return and the services rendered by private foreign investment, but also the nature of the relationship between investor and host country. In the nineteenth century a handful of countries confronted numerous businesses and an even larger number of anonymous lenders; today, numerous countries, the majority of them quite small, inexperienced and weak, confront a handful of powerful, large, transnational companies. Compared with the speed with which these giants grow fewer in number and larger in size, the pace of progress of international co-operation and integration between sovereign countries is slow. The value of the output of the overseas subsidiaries of American companies alone is probably greater than the gross national product of any country other than the USA and USSR (although a comparison of gross output and GNP is not a proper comparison). The overseas subsidiaries of European and Japanese companies are probably half the size of American corporations. By 1968 there were more companies than countries with incomes greater than $2,500 million. This is probably the most important change, affecting not only private investment and its returns, but also trade relations, the transfer of technology and even government policies and international relations in a number of other spheres.

Eighth, equity investment in the nineteenth century carried the risk of cyclical fluctuations in demand from the industrial countries. In bad years no dividend would be paid out. Such fluctuations are less important today and there is, therefore, less justification for a reward for this kind of risk-bearing. Fixed interest borrowing is therefore often a cheaper way of achieving the same purpose.

Ninth, as a result of the more rapid spread of knowledge, certain, although by no means all, types of technological and managerial knowledge are nowadays much more widespread and standardised than they were in the nineteenth century. It is sometimes cheaper to hire foreign engineers and to borrow capital at fixed interest rates than to encourage equity investment. In those areas where hired skills plus fixed interest borrowing can achieve the same results more cheaply than foreign equity investment, the latter puts an excessive burden on the host country. But some forms of modern technology are ill-adapted to the conditions of developing countries and technical progress continues even in the area of public utilities, e.g. desalination, nuclear power plants, hovercraft. It is not easy to lay down general rules about the most appropriate combinations of know-how, capital and management, but new thinking is needed and historical experience is only of limited value. The main lesson is that terms of

[1] P. N. Rosenstein-Rodan, loc. cit.

transfer intended to accelerate development must be soft, that soft aid and private overseas investment are often complementary, and that thought must be given to new forms of the cheapest and most effective combination of capital, know-how and management.[1]

IV. CAPITAL REQUIREMENTS, GAP ANALYSIS AND ABSORPTIVE CAPACITY

The conventional approach to the aid requirements of developing countries attempts to calculate a gap, either between required investment and domestic savings, or between required foreign exchange and earnings from exports. In the calculation of the investment-savings gap, also called the resource gap, the required investment is normally derived from a target rate of growth of national income and a constant or systematically varying capital/output ratio. Given a target rate of growth and a capital/output ratio, the investment/income ratio can be derived. Domestic private and public savings are then deducted from the required investment and the difference emerges as the resource gap, to be filled by foreign capital. Similarly, in calculating the foreign exchange (or the trade) gap, import requirements are geared to growth of national income, likely export receipts are deducted and the difference appears as the foreign exchange gap. Both models are based on a Harrod-Domar model with structural constraints added in the model of the foreign exchange gap. The limit on growth is set by whichever gap is larger. *Ex ante*, the resource gap is said to precede, historically, the trade gap as the 'dominant gap' in a country's development. The gap between the gaps can be inferred only from projected requirements. *Ex post*, it always disappears and the two gaps are identical, since the accounting identity: [excess of imports over exports = excess of domestic investment over domestic saving] must hold.

This highly aggregated analysis can be disaggregated. The model can specify a set of consistent relations between production, consumption and trade for any number of commodities and services into which the national product is divided. Such an intersectoral analysis of the structure of production, consumption and trade can be used to determine the level of gross national product, gross investment, exports and imports and aid corresponding to each solution. But this model is static and refers only to one point in time, usually the last year of the Plan. It also omits effects of price changes.

The dynamic model, which analyses growth patterns and gaps over time, relates growth of GNP to savings, investment, imports and exports. It can be made more flexible by the introduction of

[1] See pp. 219–22.

assumptions about (a) the cost of aid relative to the value of increased consumption and (b) absorptive capacity and other limitations on the economy's ability to invest and shift resources into import substitution.

The *investment-savings gap* or the *resource gap* has the following weaknesses:

1. The growth rate of national income does not depend primarily on the investment/income ratio, i.e. on the extent to which the people are prepared to sacrifice present consumption in favour of greater future consumption. Growth depends as much on factors other than capital in the narrow sense, particularly administrative, technical and managerial skills. At times this point is made in an extreme manner by postulating limited 'absorptive capacity' (see below), but the general point is simply the law of diminishing returns in a growth setting. The preoccupation with capital makes the solution of the development problem appear both easier and more difficult: easier, because it suggests that if only more capital were provided from abroad, growth would be accelerated; more difficult, because it neglects the numerous ways in which output can be raised without any, or without substantial, capital expenditure.

2. The capital/output ratio cannot be assumed constant or a stable function of income, or of the rate of growth of income. It depends on a large number of variables, including climate, human attitudes and social institutions, as well as conventional economic variables such as the degree of capacity utilisation and the construction period. In particular, it depends on the policies pursued by the Government.

3. The distinction between consumption and investment is false. Much development expenditure is directed at health, education and even feeding. Consumption in many less developed countries has a positive marginal productivity. On the other hand, much investment makes no contribution to development (palaces), or is wasted (unused irrigation, under-utilised industrial capacity, some luxury housing).

4. The attempt to calculate a single gap is pre-economic. Even on the assumptions of the model, domestic savings cannot be assumed to be a given function of income. Therefore, the aid requirements for a given growth rate cannot be expressed in a single figure, but are the function of domestic savings and other variables. Domestic savings will also depend on the trade-aid mix.

In addition, both types of gap calculations use quite unreliable data to arrive at misleading aggregates. Projection of past trends neglects policy changes, while the attempt to incorporate such changes endows personal judgement with an air of mathematical certainty and feeds false confidence.

Men of goodwill face a dilemma in the present aid crisis. On the one hand, it is evident that there is no correlation between the amount of aid per head received and economic growth of the recipient. All sorts of reasons or excuses can be advanced to explain or to explain away this (to the aid lobby) unpalatable fact, but it remains an awkward fact.[1] On the other hand, it is surely a basic creed, not only of economics but of common sense, that if aid, defined as the provision of additional resources, is used effectively, it must lead to greater production than would have been possible without it. And if economic growth is desired, greater production can be allocated to yield more growth.

The conflict between the (non-conclusive) evidence of absence of a relationship between aid and development (as measured by growth rates) and the logical force of the proposition that more means more, can be used as a challenge to developers to ensure the effective use of aid.

In the conventional gap analysis domestic saving is added to foreign saving to give the total resources available for investment, which, in turn, determine the addition to national income and therefore the growth rate. In Fig. 10.1 the line GG_1 shows alternative combinations of foreign and domestic savings rates required for a growth rate of, say, 6 per cent, on the assumption that they are, dollar for dollar, perfectly substitutable. The line will have a slope of minus one, cutting the two axes at angles of 45 degrees. If foreign funds show a tendency to flow into projects with higher capital/output ratios than domestic funds, the line will be flatter, like GG_2. If, on the other hand, recipients are fonder of capital-intensive projects than donors (like moving capital cities or constructing large steel plants), the line will be steeper. If we start from a point E, a crude gap analyst might say that foreign savings must rise by FF_1 in order to achieve 6 per cent growth. But domestic savings are not independent of foreign savings, though the precise nature of the dependence is not altogether clear. The relationship may be as pictured in the three S functions:[2] domestic savings might rise with foreign savings

[1] Some explanations are given in the Pearson Report, pp. 49 ff. (*Partners in Development*, report of the commission on international development, 1969). Perhaps one might also add that food aid should be deducted before correlating aid and growth.

[2] Alternatively, savings could be traced on the two axes. It is the savings *rate* which is relevant to the growth rate, but it must be remembered that income and

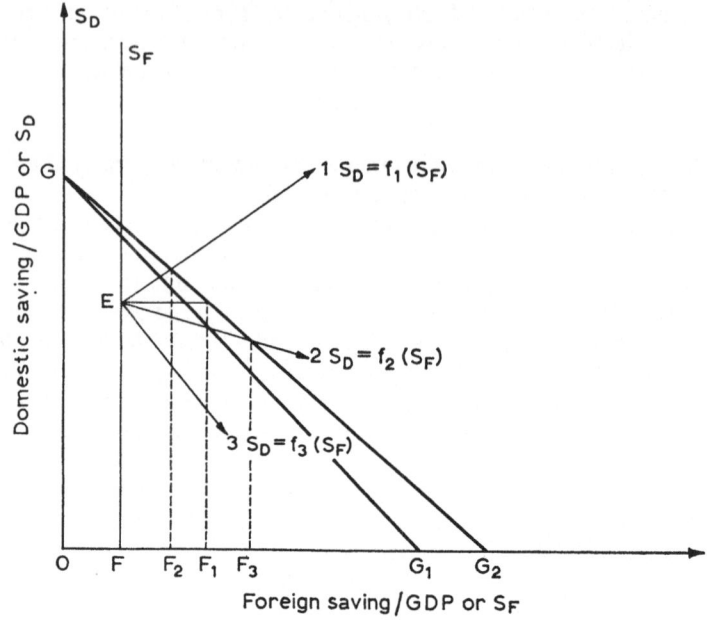

Fig. 10.1

Relation between domestic savings and foreign aid under different assumptions

if the country generates higher savings rates out of the higher incomes made possible by aid or if it responds to 'performance criteria'; or they may fall, but less steeply than the growth line, as in line 2, or they may fall more steeply, as in line 3. If the domestic savings rate rises as the foreign savings rate rises, the gap will be smaller, viz. only FF_2. This could be the result of greater private and public efforts, or simply of the higher incomes generated by foreign savings. A fall in the domestic savings rate may result from increased foreign capital either because domestic inflation leads to higher consumption and, in real terms, reduced investment; or because investment opportunities are thought to be limited, so that foreign finance simply replaced domestic finance; or because fiscal efforts to raise public savings are relaxed. The analysis could be carried into the political sphere. The argument would then be that

---

savings can go up as a result of an inflow of foreign aid, while the savings rate remains the same or even declines. Whether we trace savings or the savings rate, aid can contribute to an increase in *consumption*. If the terms of aid are sufficiently soft, this must be reckoned a benefit even if neither the savings *rate* nor even *savings* are increased.

foreign support enables a government to remain in power which is unwilling to, or incapable of, carrying out the structural reforms to raise the savings rate.

If domestic savings fall, a *sufficient* increase in foreign savings to F_3 will still achieve 6 per cent, but it will be more than is suggested by the crude gap, because domestic slackening has to be offset. But if the situation is as in line 3, additional foreign savings can make the growth prospects only worse and the way to achieve 6 per cent may be to *reduce* foreign funds.

The supply of foreign savings may in turn be a function of domestic savings (e.g. when performance criteria are applied seriously). In this case the EF line will be positively sloped and the equilibrium point of intersection E can be shifted to the target rate of growth only through bargaining and agreed changes determining the behaviour of the curves.

This formal presentation may clarify one aspect of the dispute between the aid and the anti-aid lobby,[1] even although it is grossly oversimplified and exceedingly crude. Foreign savings must be scrutinised for the terms on which they are supplied. Domestic savings should be an expression which is intended to cover all, and only, developmental expenditure, which includes a good deal of what is normally classified as consumption (health, nutrition, education) and excludes resources saved and invested in projects which make no contribution to development. Growth rates are imperfect and misleading indexes of development. Capital/output ratios have limited value. And so on. But the lack of a relationship between aid and growth remains even if we count aid net of repayments or in terms of the grant element and if we use any other development indicator, such as greater equality, more employment, proportion of the labour force in industry, etc.

The point which the diagram makes is that special attention must be paid to the *net* contribution of aid to development, allowing for a relaxation or an increase of domestic efforts, both private and public, including changes in attitudes and institutions.

In calculating the resource gap, all forms of capital inflow are aggregated and added to domestic savings. But just as in trade gap calculations (see below) export receipts have a different significance

---

[1] Perhaps the diagram raises more questions than it answers. Implicit in the presentation is the argument that, while there may not be a correlation between aid and growth, growth is positively correlated to investment/income ratios. Yet, the evidence shows only very weak correlation. It might therefore be that it is the absence of a relation between investment and growth which accounts for the absence of a relation between aid and growth. Further, the data of the critics are taken mostly from cross country studies. Time series for particular countries might show stronger correlations.

from loans and grants, so in resource gap calculations private capital differs from official capital granted or lent on concessional terms. The two are often complementary, even at the margin, for a number of reasons (see below). Hence filling a given aggregate gap has a very different significance according to the composition of finance between private and public capital.

While the relation between aid and growth is tenuous, the Pearson Report says that there is 'a close link between growth and import capacity . . . all the fast growers in the developing world received substantial amounts of foreign financing of all kinds . . .' (p. 50). The Pearson Report does not make it clear what items are intended to be covered by 'import capacity'. A link between import capacity and aid does not reveal which is cause and which effect, or whether there is mutual causation or whether both are effects of a third factor. Fast growth could lead to high rates of growth of exports and could attract foreign capital, thereby raising import capacity; or import capacity may provide the foreign exchange which is used to promote growth; or both causal links may be at work; or entrepreneurial ability or high investment may cause both. Unless we know the direction of the causal link, no conclusions can be drawn for aid policy. Many of the criticisms which we have made of the resource gap apply, *mutatis mutandis*, to the trade gap.

The trade (or foreign exchange) gap assumes, misleadingly, that aid, trade and private foreign investment are substitutes in the provision of finance for development. But this is not so. First, aid on concessionary terms provides additional resources, trade and private finance do not in themselves do so. Aid and private finance provide additional resources *now*, trade does not. Trade converts domestic into foreign resources and may thereby raise national income. It is remunerative if the alternative domestic employment of the resources absorbed in exports shows lower productivity. The second difference is that trade raises real incomes and domestic savings, and therefore reduces foreign exchange requirements below what they would have been (for any given level of aggregate demand), had the same amount been received through aid. An increase in trade therefore removes the basis on which the gap is calculated. Third, the effects of trade, aid and private foreign investment on skills and technical knowledge are different. Only if imports are required in fixed proportions in the production of national output and cannot be supplied from domestic resources can a situation arise as pictured in Fig. 10.2, where E shows the amount of foreign exchange available and the distance from GG shows the dominant trade gap.

It can be seen that a reduction in domestic savings in response to an inflow of foreign savings now *may not* affect the trade gap or again

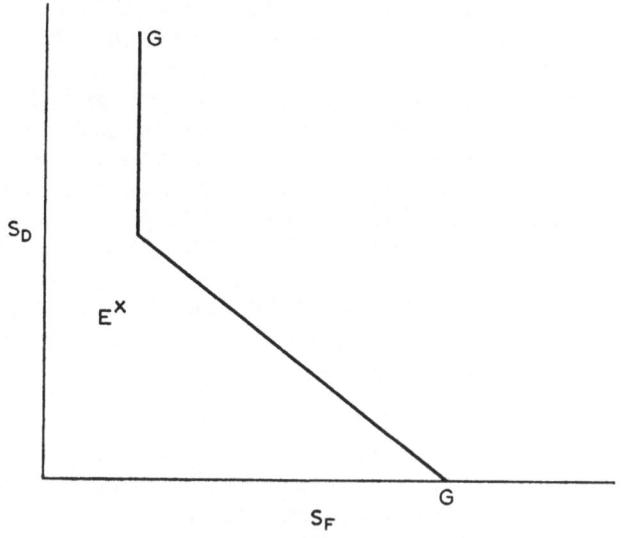

Fig. 10.2
Dominant trade gap

it *may*, depending on the location of point E and the slope of the function.[1]

It may be said that all the above discussion is beside the point. The function of gap projections is not to analyse but to pressurise. Any self-respecting country must draft its national plan so that a gap appears which it can then ask to be filled with foreign capital. The World Bank, members of aid consortia, partners of consultative groups and bilateral donors ask to have 'needs' and 'requirements' served up in a pseudo-scientific form. If a first draft of a plan does not yield a gap, the growth rate can always be raised until the Harrod-Domar mechanics produce a plausible gap. This gap should be large enough to exploit fully all possible capital provisions, but small enough not to look utopian.

In spite of the above criticism, the gap approach has a certain analytical merit, if its limitations are borne in mind. Underdevelopment is tantamount to inflexibility, immobility and inability to co-ordinate the numerous activities which have to be planned simultaneously. For these reasons, progress in development is therefore often held up by specific bottlenecks, though these are not

[1] It might, of course, be argued that extra aid merely replaces other forms of foreign exchange receipts and, in particular, exports. This would be one way of accounting for the absence of a relation between import capacity and growth. The impact of aid on import capacity would always be negligible, because cancelled out by offsetting movements of other credit items.

always measurable in terms of financial or even physical resources. But in so far as external resources can break these bottlenecks, whether they take the form of raw materials and spare parts, of fuel and power, or of certain skills, they can contribute a multiple of their nominal value to economic growth. In so far as gap analysis identifies these structural imbalances and bottlenecks, it serves a useful purpose, though the essence of the exercise is to get away from macroeconomic aggregates and to identify specific needs. It is also in those circumstances that the foundations for ability to service debts are laid. Contrariwise, projects which inflict high recurrent costs and deprive the rest of the economy of scarce factors are to be avoided, for they aggravate the structural imbalances which impede progress.

Absorptive capacity

The gap approach is often replaced by an approach which emphasises the limited absorptive capacity of developing countries for capital assistance and occasionally even for technical assistance. 'Absorptive capacity' is a concept which appeals to the instincts of donors. It saves money and thought. But it is an exceedingly nebulous concept and is hardly more useful than the concept of the 'gap'.

Sometimes it is used as if it implied a zero marginal productivity of capital, so that additional foreign assistance would yield no returns. Sometimes this is rationalised by assuming not a maximum level of investment, but a maximum investment/income ratio. Even if the marginal productivity of investment were zero, it would not constitute a case against additional assistance which could be used to subsidise consumption. In a vaguer sense, lack of 'absorptive capacity' may refer to delays or absence of suitable projects. But such delays in loan applications or loan disbursements or absence of suitable projects or inefficiencies in the execution of projects may be the fault of donors' terms and conditions, or they may be the result of inadequate technical assistance in project preparation and loan negotiations, or they may be due to inadequate administration and management.

In an even more general sense, 'absorptive capacity' refers to a wide range of presuppositions of effective planning and policy-making. It covers surveys and knowledge of available physical and human resources; an identification of specific bottlenecks of finance, manpower, skills and foreign exchange; identification of priorities and the design of a balanced, properly phased, development programme, with consistent programmes for sectors. Moving down to the project level, it implies not only sound project selection, preparation and presentation, but also efficient execution and assessment, so that faults can be identified and avoided in future. It also suggests a careful weighing of the costs of particular strategies and a planning framework. Interpreted in this wider sense, 'absorptive capacity' means much more than careful project identification, selection and preparation. It implies that the projects themselves are part of a well-designed development strategy, that they are properly phased, fit well into sectoral advance and mutually support one another and that errors are identified and corrected.

It is clear that many countries lack 'absorptive capacity' in this sense; but so do many highly developed and sophisticated countries with considerably greater reserves of skilled manpower, administrative talent and experience.

For the purposes of a narrower working definition of 'absorptive capacity' it is important to note that absorptive capacity is a function of the form of aid. Certain forms of technical and capital assistance can raise absorptive capacity. While there are, of course, also limits to absorbing knowledge and skills, these limits depend upon the composition and quality of technical assistance. 'Absorptive capacity' also depends on the composition of aid as between project and programme aid.

Concretely, 'absorptive capacity' depends on the rate at which the required number of entrepreneurs, production engineers, managers, foremen, designers, accountants, agronomists, health workers, teachers, etc., can be made to grow. 'Absorptive capacity' is therefore continually changing.

The use of the misleading concept 'absorptive capacity' has served as a convenient rationalisation for limiting aid and even more for limiting thinking about the required types of aid. Instead of asking by what extra technical assistance and improved preparation, selection and management of projects can we raise the productivity of investment and other development projects, donors have rested content in telling themselves and one another that 'absorptive capacity' was strictly limited and that therefore more aid was not needed.

If the intention is to design an effective policy for international co-operation, it is necessary to identify jointly shortages, bottlenecks and needs and to see how these can be overcome, broken and met. A blanket term like 'absorptive capacity' conceals rather than reveals the strategic problems.

Suppliers' credits

A special problem is presented to developing countries at an early stage of development by suppliers' credits, which are used to promote exports of equipment, are often but not always guaranteed by a government agency, and are extended at high interest rates for short or medium terms. When the day of reckoning comes, they cannot always be repaid and refinancing is necessary. Such refinancing involves concerted action amongst all creditors, lest anyone fears that his concession merely goes to service the loans of the others. The refinancing operations channel aid resources not necessarily to those who need them most or manage their affairs best and provide no incentives for greater caution in the future. It is for these reasons that restrictions on this type of credit should be imposed jointly by creditor-exporters and, if possible, by debtor-importers. The goods bought with these credits often do not have a high development priority and the exercise of negotiating debts that cannot be repaid does not contribute to fruitful international co-operation. This is not to deny that there is a place for short and medium-term commercial credits, but their proportion to other debt and their place in the development efforts as opposed to the export lobbies of industrial countries should be carefully considered. And there is no case in semantics for calling them 'aid'.

International capital flows and the problem of debt service

The external public debt of the developing countries rose by about 14 per cent per year in the 1960s. By the end of 1969 the recorded public debt stood at $59 billion. Service payments on official debt amounted to $5 billion in 1969. In the last ten years, these payments rose by 14 per cent per year. In several countries, the ratio of public debt service to export earnings exceeds 20 per cent.

The outflow of interest and amortisation can also be expressed as a percentage of new loan disbursements. If we include in these suppliers' credits, private and official loans and loans of international agencies, but exclude grants and private investment, the ratio for 1965–67 was 87 per cent for Latin America, 73 per cent for Africa, 52 per cent for East Asia and 40 per cent for South Asia and the Middle East.

The experience of the World Bank (IBRD) in 1967 illustrates the kind of situation which could develop over time if multilateral hardterm lending by the World Bank, the Regional Development Banks and others increases, without a simultaneous rise in soft loans and grants. Although gross disbursements of the IBRD to Africa, Asia and Latin America rose in 1967 to $510 million, a 22 per cent increase over the average level of the previous three years, disbursements net of amortisation fell by $10 million. To maintain disbursements net of repayments constant, an increase of 25 per cent in gross disbursements would have been necessary. To attain an expansion of, say, 15 per cent, an increase in gross disbursements of over 35 per cent would have been required in 1967.[1]

It should be noted that payments of interest on multilateral lending have not been taken into account. If they were, the actual transfer of resources to LDCs from the multilateral agencies would of course be seen to be much less. For example, gross disbursements by the World Bank group amounted to about $870 million in 1967, whereas disbursements net of amortisation, subscriptions and contributions,

TABLE 10.4

External Public Debt outstanding and Debt Service Payments

(Billions of US dollars)

Debt outstanding		Total[a]
31 December 1961		21·59
,,	1962	25·94
,,	1963	29·71
,,	1964	33·17
,,	1965	37·06
,,	1966	41·05
,,	1967	46·20
30 June	1968	
Total		47·54
Disbursed		36·01
Undisbursed		11·53
Service Payments—		
	1961	2·31
	1962	2·58
	1963	2·75
	1964	3·18
	1965	3·28
	1966	3·78
	1967	3·97
	1968[b]	4·02

[a] Includes 79 countries   [b] Projected

and of changes in holdings in developing countries of the funded debt of the IBRD amounted to $545 million. Interest received by the World Bank group amounted to over $200 million in 1967 (23 per cent of gross disbursements). Thus the real net transfer of resources amounted only to $345 million or about 40 per cent of gross disbursements.[2]

---

[1] UNCTAD, *External Development Finance: Present and Future*, TD/B/C.3/61.
[2] Ibid.

The tendency to focus attention on gross flows of capital or on flows that are net only of amortisation and capital repatriation is thus liable to obscure the important question: how much do foreign resources contribute to the capacity of the developing countries to import? It has been estimated that approximately half of the gross flow to developing countries is offset by amortisation, interest and dividend payments and that the gross flow will continue to be offset by these payments at an accelerating rate if present terms continue.

TABLE 10.5

External Public Debt outstanding (including undisbursed) and Debt Service Payments of 80 Developing Countries, by Region

| | Debt outstanding 12/31/69 ($ million) | Debt-service payments in 1969 ($ million) | Average annual rate of growth 1960–9 (%) | |
			Debt outstanding	Debt-service payments
Africa	9,184	725	13	13
East Asia	7,876	436	17	17
Middle East	4,883	475	13	5
South Asia	13,154	618	17	19
Southern Europe	6,228	532	13	8
W. Hemisphere	17,618	2,183	11	6
Total	58,943	4,969	14	9

Source: *Annual Report of the World Bank, 1971.*

Over the period 1970–5 developing countries will be required to make service payments of nearly $20,000 million on the debt of about $43,000 million outstanding to bilateral official and multi-lateral creditors at the end of 1969 – a ratio of required debt service over that six-year period to debt outstanding of 46 per cent. Debt service due on the debt of about $15,530 million to private creditors, on the other hand, is expected to total nearly $13,000 million, a ratio of 84 per cent. In some countries (such as Argentina, Brazil, Mexico, Peru, the Philippines and Yugoslavia) the ratio for private debt is expected to be close to, or even higher than, 100 per cent.

Some general considerations

While the literature on the burden of the debt service in developing countries is mounting, it is worth stepping back for a moment in order to ask: what is the 'burden of development debt?' A hostile critic may say that any debtor who talks of a 'burden' when it comes to the obligation of repaying his debt deserves little sympathy. In what sense, if any, can debt service then be regarded as a burden? If the yield of a loan exceeds the interest rate and amortisation, there

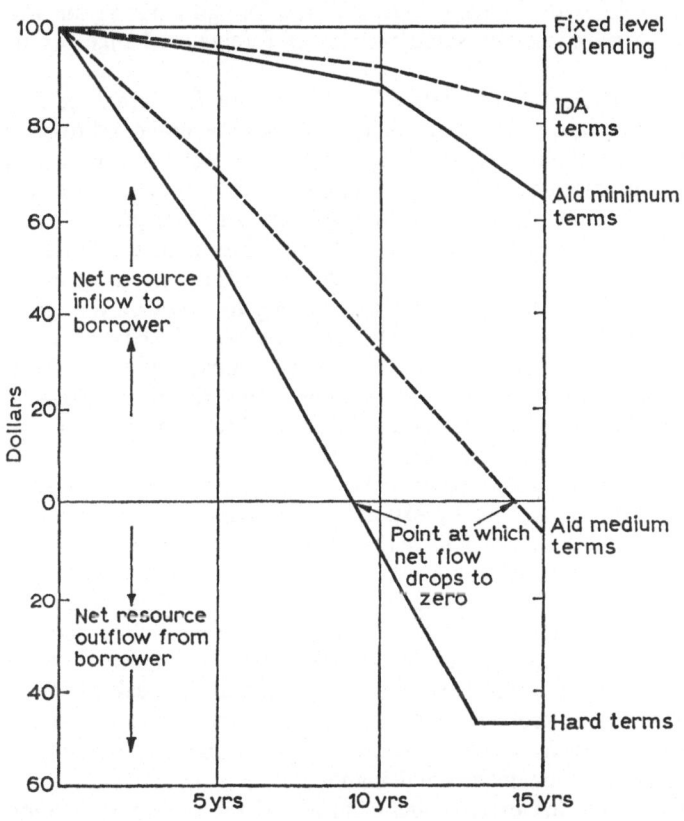

Fig. 10.3

Decline in net flow of resources if gross lending is maintained at a fixed level of $100 per year

(Harder terms mean less real impact for each dollar of assistance)

remains a net benefit to the borrower; if not, there is no case for borrowing. This is how a prudent debtor would look at the problem. The analogy from the individual domestic borrower is, however, misleading. In international lending, the payment of interest and amortisation must be effected by the generation of a surplus of exports over imports. This so-called 'transfer burden' of the debt service may be, theoretically, positive or negative, depending, amongst other things, upon the trade policies pursued by the remitting and receiving countries. To give only one illustration of a negative burden, if the borrower pays interest and principal by raising the prices of his export commodities in the face of an inelastic foreign demand, he will be able to purchase the same volume of foreign exchange for fewer exports.

The 'problem of debt service' arises because there are three distinct hurdles to be overcome by the borrower and several conditions to be fulfilled by the lender. While it is true that a loan normally supplements investment and other development resources and contributes to accelerated capital formation and growth, this growth may, in some conditions, be less than the effective cost of the loan, if full allowance is made for tying, for repayment in convertible currency and for the secondary effects of servicing the loan on the terms of trade. Even if the total domestic returns exceed the cost of the loan, the service payments have to be collected in taxes and the inadequate administrative machinery of developing countries is not always able to cope with this fiscal requirement. Even if domestic returns, properly calculated, are adequate and even if the fiscal conditions are fulfilled, the service payments have to be remitted through the balance of payments, by stepping up exports or by saving on imports.

The conditions which have to be met by the lender are readiness, in spite of existing indebtedness, to continue to finance development where the fructification period of the investment is long, and to accept payment by granting freer access to domestic markets, when service payments fall due. It will be seen that it is rare that these conditions are fulfilled. Hence it is legitimate to speak of an international debt problem, even though we should have no sympathy with a domestic borrower who complained about a 'burden' when interest and repayment are demanded.

The mounting external debt burden of the developing countries brings out the need for soft term loans. Furthermore, if development loans are made on soft terms rather than hard, the job of development will be finished sooner and donors will have to furnish less total aid in order to achieve firm development objectives.

This follows from the fact that, as loan terms harden, the net flow of resources decreases. And a decrease in the net flow of resources has two effects: it lengthens the time necessary to do a given job of development, and it increases the amount of aid required to do that job.

This is illustrated by Figs. 10.3–5, taken from an AID study which brings out clearly the relationships between loan terms and aid requirements. The figures compare the effect of making loans on the following terms:

1. IDA:[1] ¾ per cent interest, 50 years' maturity including a 10-year grace period;
2. *AID Minimum*: 2 per cent interest, 40 years' maturity including a 10-year grace period with 1 per cent interest;
3. *AID Medium*: 3 per cent 20 years including a 3-year grace period;
4. HARD:[2] 5½ per cent, 13 years including a 3-year grace period.

Fig. 10.3 assumes a steady level of lending at the rate of $100 per year. It shows that the net flow will vary substantially depending upon the loan terms that are used. The harder the terms, the less the net flow. After the eighth year there is no net flow on loans made on hard terms – annual debt service charges exceed the $100 aid level.

Fig. 10.4 compares the gross cost of maintaining a continued net flow of $100 on various loan terms. As loan terms harden, debt service charges mount and more aid must be provided each year to maintain the same net flow. For example, to produce $100 of net flow in the tenth year, $270 of gross aid is required on hard terms, $195 on AID medium terms, $115 on AID minimum terms, and $109 on IDA terms.

Fig. 10.5 assumes that the development objective of a given country can be achieved with an annual net flow of $100 over a 10-year period and that the country's repayment capacity will improve fairly rapidly thereafter. The Chart shows that in order to achieve this objective on IDA terms, gross aid of $1,040 will have to be provided over a period of 11 years. On AID medium terms a total of $4,475 will be required over 45 years. The additional amounts over $1,000 are the extra assistance needed to cover debt servicing until the country's repayment capacity can do the job. Finally, the Chart shows that the cost of trying to achieve development on hard terms is clearly excessive – if indeed, it can be achieved at all.

Fig. 10.6 shows debt service as a per cent of exports on various assumptions.

Various debt service projections for the period 1966–75 have been

---

[1] The International Development Association, the affiliate of the World Bank (IBRD) which makes loans on soft terms.

[2] These terms are generally in line with those extended a few years ago by the World Bank, the Export-Import Bank and others. International lending now takes place on even harder terms, though accelerated inflation overstates the real interest rate.

made by the UNCTAD secretariat.[1] The interest and amortisation payments falling due from 1966 to 1975 have two components:

(i) payments on the initial debt outstanding on 1 January 1966;
(ii) service payment on new loans contracted during the projection period itself. The time profile of service payments on new gross

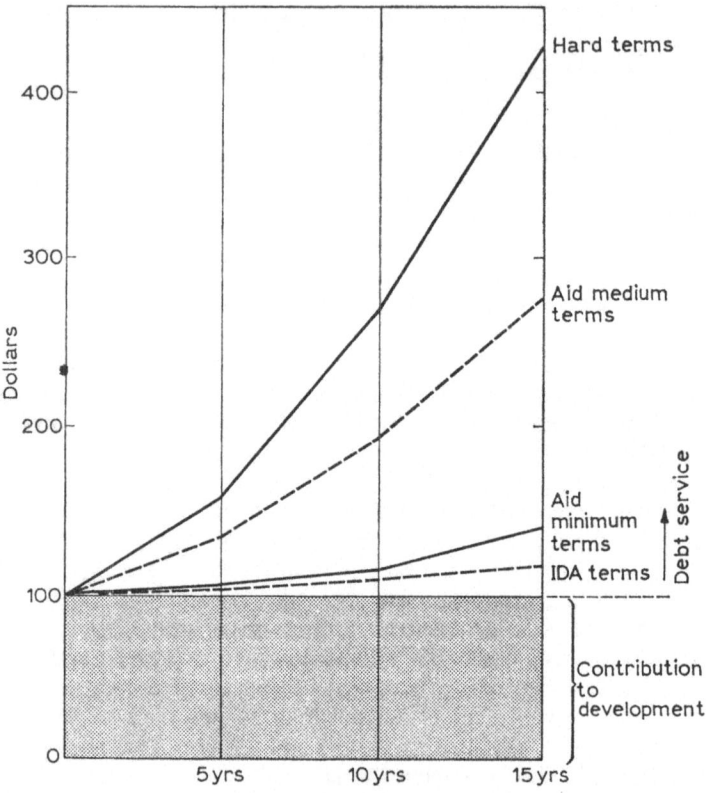

Fig. 10.4

Gross lending per year required to maintain an annual net flow of $100

(Harder terms mean that more aid is needed to do the same job)

---

[1] *The Outlook for Debt Service*, TD/7/supp. 5; *The Terms of Financial Flows and Problems of Debt Servicing*, TD/7/supp. 3; *The Terms of Financial Flows*, TD/B/C.3/35; *The Terms, Quality and Effectiveness of Financial Flows and Problems of Debt Service*, TD/B/C.3/35.

inflows of grants and loans for the years 1966–75 would depend on the volume of such inflows, as well as their composition and terms.

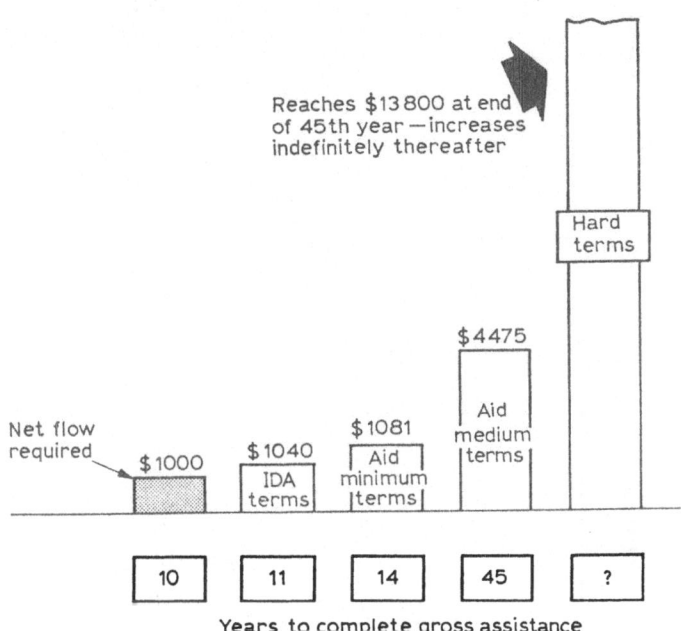

Reaches $13 800 at end of 45th year — increases indefinitely thereafter

Hard terms

$4475

Aid medium terms

$1081

Aid minimum terms

$1040

IDA terms

Net flow required $1000

| 10 | 11 | 14 | 45 | ? |

Years to complete gross assistance

Fig. 10.5

Gross aid required to finance $100 of net flow for 10 years

(Harder terms mean substantially longer and larger assistance programmes)

Note: Assumes moderately rapid improvement in debt servicing capacity after the 10 years of net flow.

By 1975, debt servicing is expected to pre-empt 23 per cent of the export earnings (excluding petroleum exports) of all LDCs on the following assumptions:

(i) terms and composition of new gross inflows would be the same as in 1965;
(ii) net inflow of grants and loans was maintained at the 1965 level;

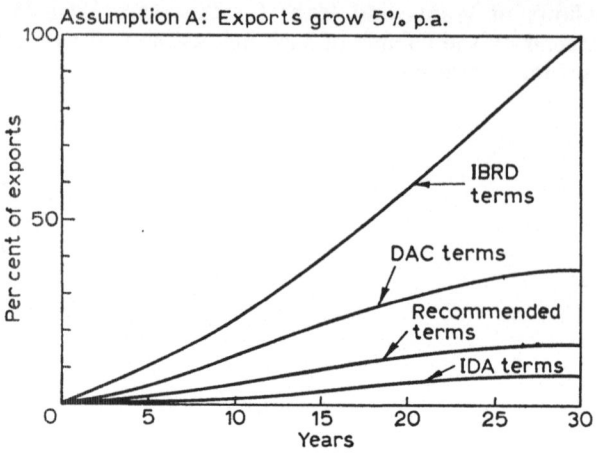

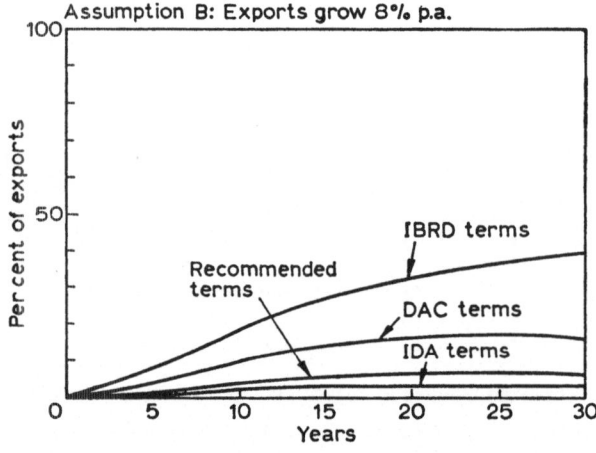

Fig. 10.6

Debt service as per cent of exports under alternative assumptions

Note: The net flow of external lending is assumed to be 40% of exports in year zero, increasing by about 2% per annum up to year 15, and then remaining unchanged.

Source: Pearson *et al.*, *Partners in Development*, p. 161.

(iii) export credits grow at 5 per cent per annum and
(iv) exports grow at an average of 4 per cent per annum.

It can be seen from Table 10.5 that, for each region, debt service as a percentage of gross inflow is projected to rise considerably from

1966 to 1975. Debt service as a percentage of exports is also seen to rise.

Another set of projections shows the net inflow of resources and net lending on the assumption that the gross inflow of grants and loans to each region were to remain constant at its 1965 level throughout the projection period.

It can be seen from Table 10.6 that total net lending would decline by more than $2 billion during the period 1966–75, and would become negative in 1970.

For some of the less developed countries the debt servicing burden reached such proportions as to necessitate rescheduling of debt. The projections for debt servicing indicate that an increasing number of rescheduling operations will have to be launched in the future as a matter of necessity; the number of such operations that would be desirable is even greater. So far debt has been rescheduled only as a rescue operation in the face of imminent disaster, carried out *ad hoc*.

There is a pressing need for institutionalising rescheduling operations and particularly for an early warning system, so that the problem can be tackled before it becomes a crisis. Institutionalisation and an early warning system would seem necessary in order to avoid any adverse effects on, or disruption of, the long-term development plans of a developing country as a result of debt servicing problems.

Fuller information and proper budgeting for debt service with an early warning system is also a necessary condition for a rational presentation of the problem to donors and for improved relations with donors. Each country should have a clear and up-to-date picture of its debt situation and should attempt to make projections of future liabilities on various assumptions.

There is need for a general overhauling of aid-giving machinery, in particular for a greater co-ordination between different donors, on the one hand, and between donors and recipients on the other. A primary aim should be the avoidance, in the first place, of situations demanding rescheduling. Another important objective is to stabilise the flow of aid and reduce uncertainty as to amount of aid in the future and for a correct assessment of needs and priorities. All this can best be done within the perspective of a country's long-term development plan and potential.

The mounting debt problem is now recognised to present serious difficulties for aid recipients. On the other hand, budgetary appropriations for aid present many donors with difficulties. The following proposal is an attempt to contribute to the solution of both problems simultaneously.

Repayments of principal and interest payments on previous loans should be credited to a separate aid budget, instead of returning to

TABLE 10.6

Developing Regions: Projected Estimates of Gross Capital Inflow and Debt Service 1966–75, corresponding to a Constant Net Inflow of Resources[a]

($ billions)

	Africa			Asia & Middle East			Latin America			Total[c]		
	1966	1970	1975	1966	1970	1975	1966	1970	1975	1966	1970	1975
(1) Net capital inflow[b]	2·3	2·3	2·3	3·5	3·5	3·5	0·8	0·8	0·8	7·1	7·1	7·1
(2) Gross capital inflow	3·1	4·1	4·9	4·9	6·0	6·7	3·0	3·3	4·0	12·2	14·9	17·5
(3) Total debt service	0·8	1·7	2·6	1·4	2·5	3·2	2·3	2·5	3·2	5·1	7·8	10·4
(4) Debt service as % of gross capital inflow	26	43	53	29	41	48	75	77	81	42	52	60
(5) Debt service as % of exports assuming exports grow at 4% p.a.[d]	11	20	25	12	18	19	23	21	22	16	21	23

[a] The net inflow of resources is held constant at the 1965 level and the composition and terms of net inflow are assumed to be the same as during 1965 except that supplier's credits are assumed to grow at an annual rate of 5 per cent.

[b] Grants and lending net of amortisation and interest payments.   [d] Excluding petroleum exporters.

[c] Including European developing countries.

Source: UNCTAD, *Growth, Development Finance & Aid*, TD/7, p. 17.

TABLE 10.7

Annual Net Inflow corresponding to a given Gross Inflow of Financial Resources, 1966–75

($ billions)

	Africa			Asia & Middle East			Latin America			Total[a]		
	1966	1970	1975	1966	1970	1975	1966	1970	1975	1966	1970	1975
(1) Gross inflow	2·9	2·9	2·9	4·6	4·6	4·6	2·6	2·6	2·6	11·0	11·0	11·0
(2) Total debt service[b]	0·8	1·6	1·8	1·4	2·2	2·4	2·3	2·3	2·4	5·1	7·0	7·5
(3) Net inflow[c]	2·1	1·3	1·1	3·2	2·4	2·2	0·4	0·3	0·2	5·9	4·0	3·6
(4) Net lending[d]	0·7	-0·1	-0·2	1·1	0·2	0·1	-0·2	-0·3	-0·4	1·8	-0·1	-0·5
(5) Debt outstanding	5·8	8·5	9·7	12·2	17·0	21·2	10·2	11·8	13·5	31·5	41·8	49·9

[a] Includes projection for Southern Europe.

[b] Includes estimates of debt service on old debt as well as new gross lending.   [d] Net of interest and amortisation.

[c] Grants and grant-like contributions plus net lending.

Source: UNCTAD, *The Outlook for Debt Service*, TD/7/supp. 5.

the Exchequer. In this way, the budgetary requirements for new aid appropriations would be reduced. If donors are not willing to contribute aid, it would be open to them to reduce new appropriations to the same extent as the separate aid budget grows. But if they are serious in saying that it is a budgetary, not a real resource, constraint which prevents from doing more, such an arrangement would make it possible to give a greater volume of aid without additional budgetary appropriations.

11 New Approaches to Direct Private Overseas Investment in Less Developed Countries[1]

HAND in hand with the current disenchantment with official aid for development has gone a reappraisal of the role of private overseas investment (POI). Several writers have argued that developing countries should rely much more on POI, especially on the operations of the multinational corporation. At the same time, a number of obstacles stand in the way of greater participation of private overseas investment in the development process. New thinking, new policies and new institutions can contribute to overcoming these obstacles.

The obstacles are partly economic, arising from the difficulties of operating in countries with shortages of skilled manpower, foreign exchange and basic utilities, and partly political. The latter include the sometimes ambivalent attitudes of the governments of developing countries and the resulting political risks faced by private enterprise.

Drawbacks of private overseas investment

Private overseas investment, since about 1950, has played a smaller part in the transfer of resources to underdeveloped countries than official aid. Net direct private investment in less developed countries fluctuated between $2,000 million and $3,400 million per annum from 1956 to 1970, while private investment by rich countries in other rich countries was considerably larger and increased substantially. The British contribution to direct investment in less

[1] I am grateful to Frances Stewart, J. P. Hayes and James Theberge for many ideas and helpful comments. For a more critical view of the impact of private overseas investment on development, see Frances Stewart, *Venture* (Mar 1970) pp. 23–8.

developed countries fluctuated between $200 million and $480 million.

POI, with all its merits, can probably not achieve a large and sustained transfer of *foreign exchange* resources to developing countries. Only if the percentage rate of growth of accumulated foreign capital is higher than the rate of return òn accumulated foreign capital is there a current net addition to the foreign exchange resources available for development.

It has been said that this way of looking at the foreign exchange contribution of POI is based on a misunderstanding.[1] It is argued that a comparison of new inflow plus retained profits with the profits earned on the accumulated foreign investment fails to account for the impact of foreign investment on export promotion and import-saving. The critics usually go on to quote the example of the oil companies, the bulk of whose production contributes to export earnings. According to this line of argument, the maximum contribution of POI to the balance of payments of the host country is given by all additional sales made possible by the investment project, minus the imported inputs into the project. This would be a true maximum if all resources employed in the project were previously unemployed, all sales were either exports or import substitutes, or all additional income generated were saved or if the marginal propensity to import were zero or if fiscal policy kept consumption constant (although any other project would also generate income and demand for inputs).[2] Otherwise, there will be some reduction in the maximum foreign exchange earnings and savings, depending on the amount of extra imports or reduced exports. The lower limit of the maximum would then be no change in the balance of trade, as the marginal propensity to save becomes zero or the marginal propensity to import unity.[3]

[1] See, e.g., *Partners in Development*, Report of the Commission on International Development (London: Pall Mall Press, 1969) pp. 100–1. The Pearson Commission's alleged clarification of a number of misunderstandings about POI only adds to the confusion. See also a number of documents produced by the Development Assistance Committee of the OECD.

[2] It is necessary to specify the assumptions made about government policy. Clearly the maintenance of a fixed exchange rate is required for any analysis of balance of payments effects. In addition, one could choose between the Government maintaining by fiscal and monetary measures full-capacity utilisation and therefore compensating for any inflationary or deflationary effects of POI. Alternatively, one could assume the Government to remain passive in the face of expansionary or contractionist impulses.

[3] The improvement in the balance of trade is given by the expression

$$I_{VA}\left(1 - \frac{1}{1 + s/m}\right)$$

But there are two faults in this analysis. First, the characteristic feature peculiar to POI, as distinct from domestic investment, is that privately owned foreign exchange first flows in for the construction of the project and later flows back in the form of remitted profits. The indirect effects described in the previous paragraph arise from *any* investment, not specifically from POI.

Thus, if, say, Tanzania wishes to build a cement factory, she can invite Portland Cement to do it for her, or she can build it herself, hiring experts and managers, hiring or buying machinery, borrowing capital, etc. Or she may do without the cement for a time. Institutionally, this may be done by the Government, by government agencies or development corporations or by delegation to the private sector. It may, of course, be that the foreign investor will erect and manage a factory more efficiently or more cheaply than if it had been all done at home or if it had been done by borrowing capital and hiring skills. (Though it can also work the other way.) Then the differences in costs and returns should be credited (or, in the opposite case, debited) to POI. But the economics of investment is not the same as the economics of POI, and to credit all indirect effects to POI is to confuse the two. Historically, POI may often have been the only way of getting the investment and it would then be correct to identify the total effects with the differential effects. The typical case here is investment in oil. The oil exports would not have occurred had it not been for the foreign company's investment and total oil export earnings should therefore be credited to the balance of payments contribution of the investment. But analytically (i.e. for the purpose of analysis) and operationally (i.e. for the purpose of policy), the two are quite distinct.

What matters is not what historically preceded the foreign investment, but what the next best alternative would have been for analysis, or ought to be, for policy. Any operational assessment of the potential contribution of POI must start from an assumption about this alternative. If a country wishes to evaluate the costs and benefits to be derived from setting up an additional cement plant, it is irrelevant to compare the established plant with the situation before its establishment. What is relevant is a comparison between the following possibilities:

where I_{VA} is the domestic value added by POI, s is the marginal propensity to save and m the marginal propensity to import, because the increase in imports equals

$$m.\Delta Y = \frac{m.I_{VA}}{s+m}$$

The formula is due to Frances Stewart.

   (i) to raise the capital and other resources domestically and set up an indigenous cement plant;

  (ii) to borrow money abroad, hire engineers and managers and buy the know-how through a licensing arrangement;

 (iii) any partial combination between (i) and (ii), including joint ventures with foreign firms, management contracts, etc.;

 (iv) to import the finished product;

  (v) not to carry out the investment now nor to import the product, but to do without it for the time being.

A clear formulation of the alternatives is an essential prerequisite to the proper appraisal of the value of foreign enterprise. The important point for analysis and policy is to free oneself from ideological bias and historical precedent, and to exercise one's *institutional imagination* upon the various alternatives, against which any *operational* assessment has to be made.

The second flaw of the analysis is that it assumes not only that the resources employed in the project were previously *unused* and, as is argued above, *unusable*, but also that they represent *net* additions in that they do not replace resources in other sectors of the economy. Even where supply is freely available, demand may be such that previously employed resources now become unemployed. The production may neither earn nor save foreign exchange, but simply displace other sources of supply, which now become unemployed or underemployed. Not only must there be no limitations of *supply*, *demand* limitations also must be absent.

There is a further objection, not to the analysis but to the assumption of total unemployment of *all* resources. If any of the resources employed in the project are taken away from activities which earn or save foreign exchange, the foreign exchange contribution is reduced and may become negative.

The analysis which runs in terms of capital inflow (including retained profits) and profit outflow, crude though it is, has therefore, at a general level of discourse, stronger logical validity and operational use than the analysis based on 'indirect' effects and can be defended against the criticism that it neglects the so-called indirect effects of POI. The much-quoted oil companies, which carry out investment that could not have taken place otherwise, which export the bulk of their product and which make hardly any claims on domestic resources should not be taken as the paradigm for balance of payments analysis. Their experience should not be applied to foreign investment in manufacturing or services.

At a less general level, there is no escape from a thorough examination of available alternatives. These are bound to be different from case to case, country to country and period to period. Any government, faced with a request to admit a foreign company, cannot avoid such concrete investigation if it is to choose rationally.

The capital/profit flow approach, however, leads to the horns of a dilemma, wreathed in a vicious circle. It is sometimes said that additional new investment and the retention of current profits in the host country can indefinitely offset and more than offset the return flow of profits and dividends on old capital and of capital repatriation. But if the rate of return on foreign capital (after local tax and depreciation have been deducted) exceeds the rate of growth of national income – a quite realistic assumption because the former is likely to be at least 10 per cent and the latter at most 5 per cent – the rate of growth of foreign capital must be higher than that of national income. This implies, assuming a constant average ratio between capital and output, that foreign capital ownership grows at a faster rate than domestic capital and therefore an ever increasing proportion of the domestic capital stock will be owned by foreigners.[1] This is particularly serious if, initially, little locally owned capital exists, as in many African countries. Even if such alienation of the capital stock were politically acceptable (and it rarely is), the process must come to an end when *all* capital is owned by foreigners. After that further postponement of repatriation and of remittances will not be possible, unless the rate of return is brought into equality with the rate of growth of national income.

Remittances abroad may also, sooner or later, grow faster than export earnings, since these are not likely to grow much faster than income. For a constant investment base, remittances may be expected to be constant and therefore, with growing export earnings, represent a shrinking proportion. But fixed interest bearing capital may be raised locally and the growing gearing ratio be reflected in a rising profit rate.[2] Then growing profits will be remitted on a constant investment stake. Growing remittances may also reflect growing investment in the past and profit retention may place a growing future burden on the balance of payments.

For these reasons, private investment is not likely to make a sus-

[1] If the capital/output ratio for foreign investment is higher than that for domestic investment, the rate of growth of foreign capital can exceed the rate of growth of national income, without a change in the distribution of ownership. But the average capital/output ratio for the whole economy, weighted by the shares of the two sectors in increased output, will rise.

[2] Local borrowing creates its own dilemma. The borrower may be accused of draining the limited local pool of financial resources to enrich himself. On the other hand, if he borrows abroad, he may be accused of adding to the balance of payments burden when repayment and interest payments have to be made. The expansion of foreign banking in LDCs may sharpen this dilemma in future.

tained and substantial net contribution to foreign exchange earnings or savings. To say this in no way implies that foreign investment may not make a contribution to economic growth. Numerous factors which accelerate growth lead to a deterioration of the balance of payments. It is, for example, quite possible that the worsened balance of payments position occurs at a higher level of foreign trade and real income than would have been attainable without the foreign investment. All that is argued here is that no large and sustained net contribution to *foreign exchange* can be expected.

But even during the period when a net inflow of foreign exchange is possible, because the rate of growth of foreign capital exceeds the rate of return on foreign capital, less developed countries are faced with a dilemma: either they permit or even encourage this growth of foreign capital, in which case they will be faced with growing foreign ownership of their capital stock. Or else they limit this process of alienation, in which case a part of their export earnings will be mortgaged to remitting profits and repatriating capital. It is small wonder that this ineluctable dilemma has led to ambivalence and hostility towards foreign investment.

The reaction to this dilemma is feared to be expropriation (without adequate compensation) to prevent alienation, or restrictions on remittances abroad, to lighten the burden on the balance of payments. This fear of expropriation or restrictions on profit remittances adds to political risks and raises the rate of return required by foreign companies before they invest. The fact that expropriations and interferences with remittances are in fact rare does not necessarily eliminate or reduce the subjective fear in the minds of investors. But these high rates of profit sharpen the dilemma: alienation versus balance of payments burden. The host governments accuse the companies of taking out of the country more than they put in. The foreigners accuse the host countries of creating political risks which raise the required rates of return. The high profits, intended as an insurance against risks, tend to lead to those dreaded events for which the high profits seek to compensate. This gives rise to the demand for even higher profits and the vicious spiral is given another twist.

It is clear that mutual gains could be derived from measures which lower these risks, lighten the balance of payments burden, reduce the rate of profits required by the company and dispel fear and suspicion. Private investment in uncertain conditions is not a zero-sum game and both investor and host country can gain from such mutually agreed 'disarmament'.[1]

[1] The argument here is different from Charles P. Kindleberger's, which is based on bilateral monopoly, where the reserve prices of the two parties are far

Neither the 'crude' analysis, which runs in terms of new investment versus profit outflows, nor the 'indirect' analysis, which takes into account the effects on export earnings and import savings, make any allowance for the complex political effects of the pressures of POI upon the economic policies conducted by a host country. The range of policies that might be affected in this way cover tariffs, import licensing and other protective measures, foreign exchange rates, monopoly legislation, taxes and other measures.

It may be objected that this lengthy discussion of the balance of payments effects of POI is beside the point. Policies towards POI, which is a long-term problem, should not be guided by short-term considerations relating to the balance of payments. In any case, it might be said that it is the function of proper government policy to keep the balance of payments in order through exchange rate variations and appropriate monetary and fiscal measures. Whatever the merits of this line of reasoning, developing countries will wish to know what the effects on their balances of payments are likely to be, so that they can take corrective action. For this purpose, the above analysis has a place in an examination of the impact of POI.

The effect of POI on the balance of payments is only one amongst a number of factors to be considered in evaluating the drawbacks and costs of POI. Foreign companies are sometimes accused of sacrificing the national development of the country to their desire for profits.[1] It would be both unreasonable and possibly undesirable to expect foreign companies to act altruistically in promoting local development. Within the constraints set by competition, legislation, morality and public opinion, there is a presumption that they are best employed in seeking profits, as long as they take a long-term view.

These and similar considerations, quite apart from political fears of domination or foreign influence, suggest that a framework should be created which would reduce the costs of foreign investment to the host country, without reducing its benefits. A high share of equity investment imposes two kinds of burden on the host country. First, a high share of the increase in production, which the investment makes possible, must return to the foreign investor in the form of profits. Secondly, these resources must be transferred through additional foreign exchange earnings or foreign exchange savings.

---

apart. See *American Business Abroad* (Yale University Press, 1969) pp. 149–51. My argument is based on the removal or reduction of mutual fear and suspicion.
[1] See p. 233.

Advantages of private overseas investment

Private investment is frequently lumped together with official aid as a quantum with which to fill the 'resource gap', and with official aid and receipts from visible and invisible trade, as a quantum with which to fill the 'foreign exchange gap'. It has been argued above that private investment cannot be expected to make a substantial contribution over a sustained period of time to filling the foreign exchange gap. But while the additions to the *volume* of total available foreign exchange may not be substantial, private investment may provide capital in a particularly productive form, so that the *efficiency* of the resources transferred is high. The particular contribution of private investment may lie, not in the transfer of foreign exchange so much as in helping to lay the foundations for further growth in the economy and in strengthening the base from which domestic savings and foreign exchange are generated. In particular, private overseas investment can bestow substantial benefits on the host country where domestic management skills and entrepreneurship are embryonic and there is no other way of organising large-scale manufacturing industry.

Its merits then lie not so much in contributing to filling the *foreign exchange gap*, or even the *savings gap*, as in the following:

(i) it may contribute indirectly to filling the savings and the foreign exchange gaps by contributing to tax revenue. This contribution to filling the *budgetary* gap is particularly important in countries where effective taxation of the domestic sector is difficult. It can, however, be eroded by tax concessions extended by less developed countries to attract foreign companies;

(ii) it helps in the *transfer* of technology (know-how) and skills;

(iii) it provides management and training of *local managers*;

(iv) it can help in the *training* of workers and the creation of indigenous skills in administration, marketing and other business techniques;

(v) in appropriate forms and with appropriate safeguards, it can contribute to the growth of *local entrepreneurship*, by subcontracting, by the encouragement to repair shops and other ancillary enterprises;

(vi) it may, by changing the market structure, contribute to more vigorous *competition*;

(vii) it helps in establishing *contacts* with overseas banks, capital markets, markets for products, sales organisations and other institutions and it opens a previously closed society to world-wide influences;

(viii) it may create, directly and indirectly, *employment* opportunities;

(ix) it may raise domestic *wages*, or improve the terms of trade.

While all these contributions are possibilities rather than certainties, since under each heading negative as well as positive results can be listed, they point the way to solutions which will maximise the net gains.

A challenge to the institutional imagination

The organisational structure and motivation of the international corporation, with subsidiaries and branches in many countries, which can militate against the interests of development in a particular country, is for the same reason capable of responding more effectively to technological, political and economic changes in switching to new products, closing down inefficient lines, cutting costs by shifting to new sources of supply, etc. The pressure for greater local participation in ownership and control may impede or prevent these operations in much the same way in which nationalism and autarky prevent the most efficient international specialisation. Adam Smith's invisible hand has a strong cosmopolitan bias. It ignores nationalistic aims and, in seeking profits wherever they arise, transcends national boundaries. Whatever may be true of the *national* corporation, what is good for the international equivalent of General Motors is *not* always good for America. It is this dilemma between, on the one hand, international allocation in the service of efficiency and, on the other, greater local participation and commitment, which must be resolved.

The problem is to invent the modern, orderly equivalent to the more cataclysmic methods of transfer to local ownership – liquidations and expropriations in wars, default and bankruptcies in depressions – common in the nineteenth century and until the last war. We must find ways of easing this transfer in an age when national default is rarely permitted and when anonymous transfer through local purchases of foreign bonds no longer can play an important part, because of the dominance of direct foreign investment and the large international corporation. Albert Hirschman has proposed *international divestment companies* for this purpose.[1]

In the first place, the argument points to an additional reason for the complementarity between soft-term official aid and private

---

[1] See Albert O. Hirschman, *How to Divest in Latin America, and Why*, Essays in International Finance No. 76, Nov 1969 (International Finance Section, Princeton University, 1969).

investment. The reason usually put forward is that official aid goes into physical infrastructure projects – ports, roads, irrigation, public utilities, transport – or social infrastructure projects – education, health – which cannot normally recuperate as profits the full benefits which they bestow upon an economy. Private investment, on the other hand, goes into directly productive forms, which are facilitated and made more productive by the physical and social infrastructure. The additional argument derived from the considerations sketched out above is that private investment normally imposes a burden on the balance of payments of the host country and official aid on soft terms contributes to easing the transfer burden of the remittances. Official aid thus can be regarded as safeguarding for private investors in rich countries the receipts of their profits. Were it not for the aid, many developing countries would have to do without the private investment or would be forced to restrict remittances.[1]

Secondly, private investment may be conducted by public corporations like the Commonwealth Development Corporation, which, being specifically charged with contributing to development, combine the virtues of efficient management and know-how with relatively soft term lending.

Third, more thought should be given to methods of assembling the 'package' which is claimed to be the particular virtue of POI (finance plus management plus know-how plus contacts) in the cheapest and most effective manner. By way of illustration, it would, for instance, be possible to offer a management contract to a foreign investor who may also be permitted to hold a substantial minority of shares.[2] The foreign investor would construct and manage the plant and would receive a management fee. This fee can take the form of a percentage both of profits and of foreign exchange savings realised. At the same time the managing firm may be expected to offer a credit at a fixed rate of interest to the local firm.[3] This credit should cover either the foreign exchange costs or a certain proportion of the total investment costs of the project. The duration of the loan would be the same as the duration of the management contract.

Fourth, many more experiments should be conducted with various forms of joint ventures, especially those which provide for a gradual and orderly transfer to local ownership and management. I shall return to this in the last section.

[1] A third argument for the complementarity of aid and POI is presented in the last section of this chapter, 'A new form of joint venture'.

[2] Cf. P. N. Rosenstein-Rodan, op. cit.

[3] Hans Singer calls this a form of direct bond investment. Cf. Rosenstein-Rodan, op. cit., p. 182.

Areas of common interest

A policy which aims at maximising the positive impact of private foreign enterprise on development may begin by tracing the interest spheres of the foreign company and attempt to identify areas of common interest, where progress benefits both the foreign company and the host country, and areas of interest clashes, where bargaining encroaches upon the interests of either party.

The foreign investor is interested in profits and growth. His risks are reduced by clear terms, informed negotiators, speedy decisions. Then the companies who come know what they are coming to, the companies which do not come make their decision with the minimum of hard feelings. The charge for real risk comes down, the charge for risks which exist only in the investor's imagination disappears.

Assuming that agreement has been reached on the type of product, both foreign company and host country have an interest in growth, which adds to production, and in higher profits, though their division between taxes and dividends raises interest conflicts. Both are interested in a growing, skilled labour force and better trained local managers who replace expensive overseas personnel. Both are interested in reducing risks due to subjective fears in the mind of the investor. Such risk reduction lowers the required rate of return on foreign investment and, as a result, removes some of the forces that may justify the fears. Several measures contribute to risk reduction: investment guarantees, free remittance of profits, ready availability of information, speedy administration of licences. As risks are reduced, the required rate of return falls; and as the rate of return falls, the burden on the balance of payments of foreign remittances falls or the rate of growth of foreign ownership falls and the contribution of the foreign enterprise to the domestic economy rises and is seen to rise.

On the other hand, there are areas in which the company's gain is the country's loss or vice versa. In these areas the task will be, once it has been decided to attract the foreign company, to negotiate so that that share of profits is permitted to accrue to the company which induces it to remain and expand and encourages new companies to enter, while the remainder accrues to the Government as revenue.

Suggestions for planners

The following suggestions are illustrative only. The main point of this chapter is to emphasise the need for exploring new institutional approaches, which should attempt to combine the best features of public and private operations.

The private sector's commitment to national development is

likely to be far greater if some of them are consulted both in the formulation of the development plan and in occasional exploratory discussions of new policies affecting foreign exchange control, re-investment, trade and transport regulations, etc. Small, informal exchanges are likely to be most fruitful. Sometimes the private sector's understanding of what is needed and why, and the willingness to con-tribute to it are likely to be enhanced with such participation. The private sector can in turn provide the Government with information about their plans for existing and potential productive resources, present and anticipated market demands, inventory accumulations, prospective need for capital and credit, and bottlenecks. In every development plan, much is required of the private sector: given its acceptance as part of the economic order, it may be wiser, therefore, to plan with and not only for private business, and to exchange ideas. Private sector planning has often been the weakest link in the chain of planning.

In many developing countries there are few officials who have had experience in negotiating a project with foreign investors. This experience is often accompanied, understandably, by suspicion of the motives of the 'outsider' on the one hand, and of the competence of the Government, on the other: attitudes which do not work towards amicable negotiations. Frequently the civil servants need training and background information on how such enterprises have worked in other countries, where to obtain assessments of foreign firms, what points need to be covered in analysing and negotiating a private project, and where to collect information on specific types of industry.

Far too few foreign enterprises have undertaken to build up local entrepreneurs or co-operatives which could provide their supplies or service their equipment. More have trained distributors and retailers of their products. Such an effort requires the establishment of specifications, training in how to meet these, help in defining and maintaining quality control, possible assistance in opening links to overseas suppliers, and obtaining local sources of credit, etc. Con-siderable expenditure of time is necessary for these measures and they are unlikely to be undertaken by the larger enterprise unless specifically encouraged by the Government.

A new form of joint venture

The above discussion has emphasised the dilemma between growing foreign ownership and balance of payments burden. Anything that reduces risks and the required rate of return, helps to reduce the conflict. The dislike of growing foreign ownership must be accepted as a psychological and political fact, however much internationalists may deplore it. The following proposal aims at reducing political risks and replacing measures that inspire apprehension and hence the need for large and quick returns by agreed, peaceful, negotiated procedures. In this way free remittance can be combined with reduced balance of payments burden, and foreign investment with growing local ownership. It assumes the possibility to build up mutual trust in a manner which would survive a succession of governments.

A private firm would establish a joint enterprise with a local government or a government agency, such as a local development corporation. The foreign firm should put up not more than 49 per cent of the capital, but enough to benefit if the enterprise succeeds, and of course suffer if it fails. It should have a substantial minority interest, while the local Government or agency has the dominant interest.

Such a holding would often be sufficient to secure a decisive role in management. But it might be possible to arrange in special circumstances that, in the initial phase, the foreign investor should hold a higher percentage of the equity, as long as the arrangement for eventual transfer to local ownership is clearly stated. The foreign firm might also provide some of the money on a fixed interest basis or in the form of preference shares.

The equity interest of the foreign firm would be bought out by the local Government at the end of a prearranged period. This period could be ten years, with provision each year after say seven years to extend for a further five years up to say fifteen years or longer in the case of, e.g., plantation enterprises. Other forms of rolling extensions could be devised, such as periodic reviews with stated period of extension. Alternatively, the period might be longer, but there could be options at fixed points when either the local Government can buy out or the firm can sell out. An evaluation procedure to determine the price would have to be agreed.

Managerial and technical staff would initially be provided almost exclusively by the foreign firm, perhaps under a management contract, but with the obligation to train local replacements within the specified period before buy-out. The rate of replacement could not be specified contractually, but the local Government would be able to use its representation on the board to ensure that it went foward at a satisfactory pace.

Housing and other community services should be provided by the local Government or appropriate local statutory body set up for the purpose. In view of the relatively short period of ownership participation, the foreign firm's capital should be concentrated on directly productive activities.

Official aid may provide the finance for participation of the local Government. It might be possible to provide a long-term loan on soft terms to enable a host Government to participate in a venture. No subsidy to a particular private firm would be involved, for the Government's terms of on-lending could be commercial. Only the secondary foreign exchange burden would be lightened. Governments can also support such joint ventures with buying-out options either by investment guarantees or by including a clause in the contract of the loan that in case of expropriation without proper compensation the whole outstanding loan would fall due for repayment immediately. The force of such a clause would lie in the fear of loss of credit standing if default occurred.

Arguments against such proposals are based partly on the need to repatriate capital paid to buy out a firm and the consequential strain on the host country's balance of payments, and partly on the fear that limited participation is bound to reduce the involvement of the foreign firm in the host country and to reinforce its enclave nature.[1] The reply to both points is that companies should be encouraged to reinvest their funds in new ventures in the same country. Where this is impossible, the costs of repatriation and short-term involvement would have to be compared with the benefits of increased local participation.

Arrangements of the kind sketched out above would attract foreign capital and know-how to the activities where they are most useful, but would release them, when the host Government buys out the firm, for new ventures elsewhere. Thus good use would be made of the finance and experience of foreign companies by keeping them in a revolving fund. Teams could be kept working together and political friction and transfer burdens would be minimised.

The climate for international investment and for new forms of joint ventures would be greatly improved if a set of rules for the remittance of profits, capital and capital gains could be agreed upon and obeyed. It is important that profits earned by foreign capital should be allowed to be remitted home. Restrictions, except those imposed temporarily in emergencies, would only discourage the future flow of investment, and are as much against the interests of the investor as they are against those of the host country. But if the foreign firm borrows local capital, which it can often do very cheaply in view of its good credit standing, profits earned on this local capital need not enjoy the same freedom. The same rules should apply to these profits as those which apply to local firms.

While it may be sensible to aim at a certain proportion of equity to fixed interest investment for foreign capital in an underdeveloped

[1] See Hans Singer, in Rosenstein-Rodan, op. cit., p. 185.

economy as a whole, the proportions of specific sectors and firms may, of course, vary widely from the country-wide average. Some sectors, like transport and power, can be wholly financed on a fixed interest basis. Others, where entrepreneurial initiative is important, may be financed wholly by direct equity investment, while others again may show a variety of gearing ratios of equity to bond capital. Again, a variety of arrangements can be made for the transfer and adaptation of know-how. Individuals can be hired, management contracts can be concluded, and participation in profits can be arranged. It is the purpose of such arrangements to minimise both the cost to the host country of the transfer of capital and know-how, and political frictions, while safeguarding the interests of those who are willing to conduct this transfer.

If our main concern is the social and economic development of less developed countries, the contribution of private overseas investment must be assessed in the light of a variety of methods of mobilising indigenous resources, skills and know-how. Our task is to explore the most effective and the cheapest way of attracting foreign resources, skills and knowledge and the best way of combining them in order to bring about such a mobilisation. This requires the examination of new institutions, arrangements and forms of contract.

The objectives of the new arrangements would be, first, to reduce the political tensions that arise from large foreign-owned enclaves in less developed countries and the fears of expropriation which deter foreign enterprise by an agreed upon and institutional form of divestment, which would replace the cataclysmic form of the past; second, to establish a framework which would change the policies of foreign companies so that they do not necessarily subordinate the policies of the local companies to the interests of the parent companies; third, to induce spread effects, so that the beneficial activities of the foreign companies spill over into the less dynamic sectors of the rest of the economy; fourth, to set free, after a period, the scarce foreign capital and skills so that these can be re-employed in pioneering new ventures rather than continuing to be employed in existing activities.

12 The Multinational Corporation and the Nation State

THE multinational corporation (MNC)[1] has been acclaimed as an agent of development and has been condemned as a weapon of exploitation. Those who have acclaimed it have argued that what they believe to be the likely future decline of official aid makes it even more advisable than before to switch attention to direct private foreign investment as an external source of development finance. Those who have condemned it point to the small or negative resource transfer, and some advocate expropriation.

Most advocates and opponents agree that the MNC can be a most potent agent of innovation, a ruthless cutter of costs and a wily harnesser of resources. Attention has recently shifted from the contribution that the MNC makes through the transfer of capital to the contribution that it makes through its ability to draw on a fund of not freely available knowledge, subject to economies of size, on a network of information, on managerial and technical skills, including those of marketing the product (again subject to scale economies), and on the institutionally built-in propensity to adapt and innovate.[2] In the current jargon, it is the software as much as the hardware that counts.

The knowledge that goes with the investment may relate to production or to marketing. *Production* knowledge may refer to a

---

[1] The term is used in this chapter in the widest sense. It comprises in the loaded terminology of the Task Force *Foreign Ownership and the Structure of Canadian Industry*, the national company with foreign operations, the multinational corporation in the narrow sense, which is sensitive to the local needs of the countries in which it operates and the international (or the transnational) corporation, which is guided largely by standards transcending those of any particular nation state; cf. C. P. Kindleberger, *American Business Abroad* (Yale University Press, 1969) p. 179n. I am grateful to Frances Stewart, Vijay Joshi, J. P. Hayes and F. B. Rampersad for helpful comments.

[2] Cf. Jack N. Behrman, 'Promoting Free World Economic Development through Direct Investment', *American Economic Review* (May 1960) pp. 271–81.

specific and *stable* process of production or to a *changing* flow of varying processes. Specific and *stable* processes can again be subdivided into stable and *simple* recipes and stable and *complex* processes. The former can be patented or sold through licences. The latter require experts to go along with the process, at least initially and possibly continually. Access to a flow of changing knowledge is less easily bought.

Marketing knowledge may refer to (1) access to an existing network of outlets or (2) quality guarantee or goodwill attached to a brand name or (3) access to economies of scale through a marketing organisation.

These distinctions are relevant to three questions: can the knowledge be purchased separately? what is the value of the knowledge? how are any gains distributed between different countries and the world as a whole?[1]

The ability to purchase the information separately will depend upon its separate transferability. Where the advantage lies not in any specific formula, but in a complex network of information gathering, filtering, processing, feedback and application, a separate transfer may be impossible. When parting with the knowledge would be detrimental to the company, a separate transfer would be possible but will not occur. And there are numerous intermediate cases.

If advantages of information shade, on the one hand, into advantages of institutional relations, mutual trust and co-operation, they shade, on the other, into monopoly power. The line between the efficient network of communication and the old boys' network becomes blurred. Where does 'knowing' markets end and carving up markets begin? Where does a brand name advertise special characteristics and where does it prey on ignorance or anxieties? Where are private risks only reduced and where social risks? Whatever the reasons, the MNC has a special advantage over the local firm in producing and selling.

It may then be true of certain cases, but it is irrelevant – the advocates argue – that capital could be borrowed more cheaply and information bought separately. The higher returns earned by the MNC reflect exploitation, not of the country, but of the opportunities

---

[1] Several people have made to me the fairly obvious point that one should distinguish between MNCs operating in extractive industries, in production for the domestic market, for exports and in services. While these distinctions are clearly important for many purposes, I did not find them useful for the purpose of this chapter. Much more useful would be a typology along the lines suggested above, for it is these categories which determine how the components of the private foreign investment 'package' should best be bought and assembled, what the benefits from buying them are and how these benefits are distributed between countries and throughout the world.

which the firm itself discovers or creates. In spite of declarations of public relations men to the contrary, the proponents of the MNC admit, indeed boast, that the creation of profitable opportunities pays little heed to social considerations; to justice, to equality, to even or balanced progress or to national sentiments. The profit-motivated approach, the tougher proponents of the MNC say, is incompatible with an approach emphasising social planning. The operations of the MNC will accentuate inequalities in the distribution of income because rewards will go to the most productive. They will increase unemployment of the unskilled, for the technology which the MNC uses has been developed in societies where labour is scarce and capital abundant. They will aggravate regional inequalities, for location of plant in the service of efficiency will conflict with regional, provincial or state claims for fair shares. They will accentuate sectoral inequalities and reinforce dualism, for modern technology is suited only for certain types of industrial activity. They will draw on outside resources and men, and will draw resources and men outside, guided only by costs and returns, without regard to national sentiments or social needs.

Between the Schumpeterian protagonists and the socialist-nationalist antagonists of the MNC there are those who advise the developing host governments to harness the beneficial effects of the MNC and to control or curtail the damaging effects. Three sets of problems arise here. First, even if the will and the political power to control were present, to what extent is it feasible for a host government to control the MNC effectively (i.e. to what extent has it the necessary expertise and non-political power)? Second, even if it had the political power, does it have the will? Third, even if it had the will, the knowledge and expertise and the non-political power, does it have the *political* power?

Ability to control

If the centre of decision-making is located in the parent country, while subsidiaries and branches are located in many overseas countries, the technical ability of a host government to control is greatly reduced. The MNC will be less responsive to exhortations and requests. There may be doubts about which legal system applies. The MNC will be less responsive to monetary policy, for it can draw on alternative sources of funds, both from abroad and from internal accumulation. While this ability to draw on funds from outside may be in some respects an advantage, it, together with its reputation and size, also increases the firm's borrowing power in the host country, with consequential effects on the allocation of domestic resources and on the balance of payments. Fiscal policy can be circumvented by adjusting prices charged between stages of a vertically integrated firm, by the allocation of overhead and other joint costs, by the conversion of what should be regarded as profits to management fees, royalties or other 'costs'. Trade policy may be determined by marketing considerations of the parent firm or by political conditions imposed upon it by the parent Government, such as the prohibition of American firms to trade with Cuba and China.

Against this, it is sometimes argued that because the foreign firm is large and visible and its accounts published and accessible, it has less scope to evade the law than smaller domestic firms. It has also been said that in granting concessions, or generally permitting entry, the host Government can exercise more influence on the decisions of foreign firms, say with respect to where the plant should be located. In Britain, for example, it was easier to steer foreign than domestic firms into depressed areas, possibly because they were more responsive to financial incentives.

In spite of these considerations, the balance of the argument for less developed countries seems to be on the other side. Economic control will tend to be less feasible and therefore less effective. While illegal evasion of the law is more difficult for the foreign firm, it has more scope for legal avoidance. It is larger and more powerful than the domestic firm, it is less dependent on the goodwill of the Government and it can always go elsewhere.

Will to control

There is a wide area of policies, supported by entrenched vested interests, including, ironically, many of which both the host Government and the foreign firm are most proud, which are hostile to development. This unholy harmony of interests is reinforced by the high prestige which institutions, practices and ideas in advanced industrial countries enjoy and by the inertia which makes their transfer to societies with utterly different conditions and problems so tempting.

The transfer of trade union objectives from industrial to underdeveloped countries, the introduction of collective bargaining, the setting of high labour standards, minimum wage legislation, short working hours, resistance to multiple-shift working and the adoption of expensive social welfare services are a potent source preventing the beneficial effects of the MNC from spreading. The principles which these practices reflect are enshrined in declarations of human rights, in international conventions and in the sermons of officials and managers. The foreign firms pride themselves on the high labour standards which they introduce into less developed countries, the high wages they pay, the short hours their workers work and the generous welfare services which they provide. In fact, all these are detractions from, not contributions to, the development effort. It is precisely in the area where host Government and foreign firm seem to pursue common interests, where the profit motive and national aspirations seem to coincide, that most damage is done, particularly if these benevolent activities are accompanied by tax concessions.

In the acceptance of wage-increasing union activity, the MNC does not necessarily sacrifice profits. Where it can pass on wage increases in higher prices, inflationary pressures are communicated to the rest of the economy. Even where it absorbs wage increases, it benefits from improved labour relations and ability to attach a more contented and privileged labour force to the firm. The small domestic competitor, who is unable to match the higher wages, is squeezed out or is not given an opportunity to set up in business. The differentials between the privileged labour aristocracy attached to the MNC and average incomes are very large. In Jamaica, an unskilled worker earns at least three times as much in the bauxite industry as in the sugar industry, and a fraction of this in indigenous rural employment. The same differentials exist in Zambian copper mines and in Mauritian and Guyanan sugar plantations. The practices reduce the incentive to develop unskilled-labour-intensive methods of production and management and they aggravate unemployment and social inequality. While there was a case for a high wage policy in colonial times, when the foreign company was not taxed, the payment of higher wages was the only method of transferring some of its profits to the indigenous population, and higher wages were a condition of an efficient labour force, today it would be more sensible to tax profits directly, rather than indirectly by imposing conditions on the use of local supplies, local labour, local share capital or by imposing on it welfare costs for the benefit of a small labour aristocracy. If it is decided to admit the MNC, the host Government does best to encourage the MNC to lower costs by drawing resources from wherever in the world they are cheapest. It is here that its particular virtue lies. It is not sensible to transfer income by attempting to transform the MNC from what it is – a profit-seeking animal – into something it is not – a public service.

Autonomy of policies

Anglo-Saxon welfare economics tends to be conducted on the assumption that the government of a country is the custodian of the social interest (which is sometimes tacitly or explicitly equated with the national interest) and has supreme and autonomous power although not perfect knowledge) to implement policies in pursuit of this objective. In fact governments everywhere, and particularly the governments of less developed countries, are neither monolithic nor fully autonomous. They represent a conglomeration of ideals and interests, usually susceptible to outside pressures, which may reinforce some local interest. A proper theory of foreign investment must therefore be integrated into a political theory of the sources of policy. The point has become increasingly important. For in the nineteenth century a host of small and anonymous lenders and businesses confronted a handful of large governments. Today, a handful of powerful, large companies confront a host of small, competing, weak and not always single-minded governments. The large and powerful MNC can draw on a pool of skilled and experienced manpower and, on occasion, on the support of the Government of the parent company. The officials of the host Government, by contrast, are typically inexperienced. The MNC will tend to demand privileges with regard to taxation, relief from duties on imported products necessary for its investment and production (sometimes at overvalued exchange rates), low bank interest rates and protection against foreign competition. If these concessions are granted, there is no longer a presumption that the MNC will contribute to the resources of the host country.

Consider a protective tariff. In conditions of free trade, the MNC sells its product at world prices – say at $100. If imported inputs cost $50 and local costs amount to $30, the remaining $20 profit is a net contribution to production, which can be divided between foreign shareholders, ploughed back profits and taxes. But assume a 100 per cent tariff enables the firm to sell the product at $200. Private profits no longer are an indication of gains in production, for imported inputs may now swallow up more than what is added to social product. Even 100 per cent taxation of profits would not reduce this loss to the host country and any tax concession would increase it. An allowance could be made for a shadow wage rate below actual wages, but the danger often remains. Moreover, as Harry Johnson has shown,[1] technical progress or the accumulation of factors of production in the protected industry may further reduce the country's real income.

Tax concessions to foreign investment not only deprive the host Government of development revenue, they also encourage methods of production which are less capital-saving than if the concession took the form of a wage subsidy. Such a subsidy may be justified if

---

[1] H. G. Johnson, 'The Possibility of Income Losses from Increased Efficiency or Factor Accumulation in the Presence of Tariffs', *Economic Journal* (Mar 1967) pp. 151–4.

the shadow wage is lower than the money wage and if there is a choice of technique. Arguments have been advanced that labour may be an inferior good and that such subsidies would then reduce the demand for labour.[1] They are based on fallacious reasoning, for it is always possible to tax directly the extra income, generated by the wage subsidy, and thus restore the pre-subsidy real income level, leaving the firm only with the substitution effect in favour of more employment.

However great the contribution of the MNC to development, which stems from its advanced techniques in production and marketing, its training of local labour, of suppliers and of purchasers and its encouragement of ancillary business through subcontracting, its operations require a number of complementary or compensating activities to which the MNC does not normally contribute. Above all, there are the necessary complementary investments in physical and social overhead capital: roads, harbours, utilities, education, health, nutrition. The MNC has normally no reason to make a substantial direct contribution to these. Then, finance is needed to conduct pre-investment, design and feasibility studies which prepare the ground for the private foreign investment. Third, where a transfer problem exists, finance is needed to service the payment of remittances and possibly repatriation of capital across the exchanges. Fourth, a country may wish to finance a gradual and agreed transfer of equity to indigenous (public or private) ownership.

But more important than any of these reasons for complementary sources of finance is the desire of a country to correct some of the violations of social objectives inflicted by the MNC. Wherever the MNC operates unchecked, it perpetuates and aggravates inequalities of income and wealth, it creates new oligarchies and it destroys a sense of participation of the less productive masses. Its operations are also liable to sudden and large changes over time. The host country may therefore wish to restore balance in the face of this uneven impact of the MNC, by reducing extreme inequalities, as between income by size, or between regions, even when these do not give the unproductive groups or regions a better opportunity to become productive.

For any or all these reasons, complementary sources of finance will be required when the green light is given to the MNC. These might take the form of aid funds contributed on soft terms or of tax revenue. The deficiencies of aid are by now well known and adequate collection of tax on company profits is essential if the MNC is to be

[1] Michael P. Todaro, 'A Theoretical Note on Labour as an "Inferior" Factor in Less Developed Countries', *The Journal of Development Studies* (July 1969).

used as an agent for development. I have argued that political and economic pressures weaken the political and administrative power to tax adequately. Lack of information about taxable capacity further reduces the bargaining power of the host Government. In conditions of bilateral oligopoly or bilateral monopoly, the maximum tax that can be levied without deterring investment and the minimum tax that will still make it appear worth while to the host country to attract the investment will be some distance apart, sometimes quite far apart. The pressures to reduce taxation and to grant concessions do not come only from the MNC but also from competing developing countries trying to attract the investment. The elasticity of supply of total direct overseas investment is probably low, so that competitive tax concessions lead to beggar-my-neighbour policies. Companies often declare that concessions, though welcome, do not make much difference to their decisions to invest if expected profits are adequate (or threatened losses from not investing are serious), if the continuation of the concessions is uncertain and if the company expects to be subjected to other forms of restriction. The study carried out by the Institute of Development Studies and Queen Elizabeth House on private overseas investment has shown that few of the twenty-nine foreign firms interviewed in Kenya and Jamaica considered inducements offered by host governments to be of major importance in their decisions to invest. The size of the tax concessions and the height of protective tariffs appeared to be in most cases excessive.

It is difficult to interpret these declarations in the light of rational behaviour, attempting to equate continuously varying marginal revenues to marginal costs. But it must be remembered that the relation between companies and host governments is often one of bilateral oligopoly. The firms would be prepared to carry out the same investment even with smaller concessions, while the countries would be willing to attract the investment even at the cost of granting larger concessions. This situation creates an area of bargaining within which concessions can vary without affecting any decisions.

Assistance is therefore required in enabling a host country to identify the bargaining area and to determine the range of optimum taxation. One set of obstacles to the imposition of the optimum tax would be removed if several host countries combined in eliminating competitive concessions. Although gains from such co-operation could be substantial, they face the danger of all such agreements that an outsider can damage the scheme. Benefits to individuals from corruption would also remove their incentives to co-operate. Another possibility would be an expert advisory service, either in the form of an international agency or of an independent group of consultants. What is needed is information and technical assistance in negotiation.[1] There would be several considerable advantages in more expert handling of the taxation of the MNC. A greater contribution through tax revenues would reduce the need for development aid. At the moment, taxpayers in donor countries subsidise, to some extent, the operations of the MNC by providing aid for infrastructure projects which make these operations profitable. It would also make for the quiet style in resource transfer for which some have pleaded. It would remove international co-operation for development from the noisy area of annual budgetary appropriations, performance criteria, confrontations and recriminations, and assure a fairly regular flow of resources on which recipients could rely in their forward planning.

A more radical solution has been proposed by Professor Edith Penrose.[2] Her proposal is that international firms should be incorporated under international law and subject to a single international income tax. In this way all distortions and conflicts which arise from different income tax rates would be eliminated, as well as the incentives to grant competitive tax concessions. Information and expertise could be concentrated in the international tax authority. While Professor Penrose does not propose this, an obvious next step would be to use the tax revenue for development aid. It could take the form of grants, thus avoiding the laborious stage performance of loan agreements, debt relief, rescheduling, etc. The distribution of the revenue could be guided by genuine criteria of development, rather than by the accident of the geographical distribution of oil resources.

The conclusion of this part of the argument is that those who hope for a substantial contribution to development by the MNC, particularly if they are also pessimistic about soft aid prospects, should emphasise the importance of strengthening the power and willingness of host governments to tax. This involves detailed research into optimum tax levels, which should take into account both ability and incentive of the MNC to continue investment; it involves co-operation between less developed countries; and it involves strengthening the basis of information on which decisions are made. A rational system of company taxation might go a long way to save the tax payers in rich countries money for aid programmes and at the same time make the expenditure more effective.

---

[1] See Dudley Seers, 'Big Companies and Small Countries: A Practical Proposal', *Kyklos*, vol. xvi (1963) fasc. 4.

[2] Edith T. Penrose, *The Large International Firm in Developing Countries* (Cambridge, Mass., 1969) p. 273.

The alternatives before the host Government

The characteristic feature of foreign investment by the MNC is that it transfers a whole complex set of productive factors, some amenable to conventional economic analysis like capital and technical skills, others less easily comprehended by it, like executive capacity, management, know-how, goodwill and a network of relationships giving access to supplies or markets and feeding back information gleaned. From the point of view of the host country, though not from the point of view of the MNC, the question is whether, assuming the investment is wanted, these factors and conditions can be assembled more cheaply in some other way. Any operational assessment of the potential contribution of the MNC must start from an assumption about an alternative.[1]

A clear formulation of the alternatives is an essential prerequisite to the proper appraisal of the value of foreign enterprise. The important point for analysis and policy is to envisage the various alternatives against which any operational assessment has to be made and to assess the benefits and the costs of each, measuring what is measurable and judging what is not.

This formulation of the problem has come under considerable attack, both from academic colleagues and from businessmen. It is said that administrative talent is scarce and it is quite unrealistic to hope that such investigations can be conducted; that no lessons can be learned from a particular evaluation in one country at one period for other countries or other periods; that the best alternative may be impossible and hence irrelevant.

My reply is that the opposite view leads to no conclusions. From complete ignorance, nothing follows. I should certainly not wish only first-best alternatives to be considered, but should be content with either second-best possible or first-best feasible alternatives. I have more faith in the profitability of investigating case studies of similar industries put up in different ways in similar countries, subject to the costs of administering the investigation. The typology suggested on pp. 223–4 will be a help. No one proposes today to use direct foreign investment for railways or public utilities. Many would agree that it might be suited for petrochemicals. Intermediate cases, like fertiliser or cement plant, do not seem to raise impossibly difficult problems.

Once the problem is viewed in this manner, new possibilities arise. Foreign or international development corporations may be invited or created, domestic development corporations may be created or expanded, an indigenous base for research and development may be

[1] See Chapter 11, p. 211.

built up, an altogether different pattern of final consumption or of productive techniques may be adopted, etc.

Here again, as in the formulation of tax policies, technical assistance in assessing the alternatives and in creating and providing the alternative institutions will be necessary.

Areas of conflict and harmony

Conflict between the MNC and the host Government may derive from four sources: from the fact that the MNC is *private* and hence may clash with the social and national goals; that it is *large* and oligopolistic and hence possesses market and bargaining power which may be used against the interest of the host country; that it is *foreign*, particularly if it is American, and hence may be serving the national interests of a foreign nation; and that it is '*Western*' and hence may transfer inappropriate know-how, technology or management practices, or products, designed with characteristics not needed in less developed countries.

The MNC is sometimes accused of sacrificing the national development of the country to its desire for profits. It would be both unreasonable and possibly undesirable to expect foreign companies to act altruistically in promoting local development. Within the constraints set by competition, legislation, morality and public opinion, there is a presumption that it is best employed in seeking profits, as long as it takes a long-term view, not giving excessive weight to quick profits at the expense of future profits and as long as it assesses correctly the constraints set by political action and public opinion.

More serious is the charge that the local company sacrifices its own profits to the interests of the parent company or sister companies in an advanced industrial country or indeed to the interest of the group of companies as a whole, and that this, rather than any lack of nationalism, charity or altruism, damages local development. Such restrictions on local profit maximisation can have different reasons. The company may charge higher prices for its products in order to prevent the elimination of inefficient sister or parent companies in the investing country. But the reverse may also be true: the parent company pricing its products so as to keep an inefficient subsidiary in business. In the former case the high prices of primary products may lead to faster innovation in synthetic substitutes, in which the parent company may be engaged. The problem here is not monopoly pricing by the subsidiary, for price reductions would increase local profits, but the foreign locus of ownership and control. Or again, local 'profits' may be minimised rather than maximised, by underpricing output and overpricing inputs, if by this device tax liabilities can be shifted from a high-tax country to a low-tax country, or losses can be set off against highly taxed gains. Another cause of conflict is to be found, as we have seen, in the high wages and fringe benefits which the foreign company can offer to local workers and which do not reflect the cost of alternative uses of the labour forgone. While this policy ensures that some of the profits of foreign enterprise are retained by citizens of the host country, it can play havoc with the wage structure in the rest of the economy, aggravate social inequality, perpetuate unemployment and encourage the wasteful use of capital.

Conflicts may arise, as I have suggested, between profit-seeking and social objectives, between the uneven progress imposed by the profit-orientation of the MNC and the balanced progress desired by the country, between the dualism created and deepened by the MNC and the need for spread effects.

First, the impact of the MNC will be strongest in those sectors in which the know-how of the foreign firm can be applied. Sectors like tropical agriculture, small-scale production, traditional crafts, the processing of local raw materials, the use of local by-products, subsistence farming, have no parallels in advanced industrial countries and will therefore remain untouched by the MNC, or may be destroyed by it, except in so far as their transformation feeds the activities of the MNC.

Second, the MNC will use not only the capital-intensive, often inappropriate technology which it transfers from its parent company, but it will also employ labour-saving management techniques and practices. Its interests lie in minimising industrial relations with a foreign labour force, which may be unskilled, underfed, unhealthy, unreliable, undisciplined and perhaps hostile, and dealings with which may give rise to political difficulties. How much easier to rationalise this reluctance behind a 'decent wages' and generous industrial welfare policy, where the standards of decency and generosity are taken from the economic and social conditions prevailing in the parent country.[1]

Third, while the MNC will have an incentive to borrow locally, it will prefer fixed interest loans to equity and will tolerate local equity participation only to the point where the parent company maintains control. This means that a high proportion of earnings will accrue to foreign equity holders. If ploughed back, they will further raise the foreign stake; if remitted abroad, they will burden the balance of payments.[2]

---

[1] For evidence of limited local training see J. N. Behrman, 'Foreign Investment and the Transfer of Knowledge and Skills', in R. Mikesell (ed.), *U.S. Private and Government Investment Abroad* (University of Oregon Books, 1962).

[2] See pp. 212–14.

A conflict of a different kind arises for a developing country when it has to choose between benefiting from the power of the MNC by gaining stable and monopolistic outlets for the products whose raw materials are extracted from its soil but at the same time sacrifice national control, and, on the other hand, gain national control through indigenous operation or joint ventures, but sacrifice the advantages of market outlets which only the MNC can offer.

Political risks, such as expropriation without adequate compensation, restrictions on remittance of profits and repatriation of capital, multiple currency practices or devaluation are often cited as factors which make it necessary to earn high rates of profit to compensate for these risks. The high rates earned then cause suspicion and hostility in the host country and tend to lead to the events for which the high profits seek to compensate. High profits, required because of risks, also impose a heavy balance of payments burden, tending to lead to restrictions on remittance and repatriation, and once again strengthen the demand for higher profits to compensate for the risk of the imposition of such restrictions.[1]

There are other vicious circles of a similar nature. If, for instance, the firm estimates the risks as high and anticipates to leave the country before very long, it will have no incentive to train local labour. But the absence of such training schemes reinforces the desire on the part of the host Government and local opinion to push out the company, because it contributes little to long-term development. Once again, these sentiments reinforce the company's desire to quit soon.

It is clear that mutual gains could be derived from measures which lower these risks, lighten the balance of payments burden, reduce the rate of profit required by the company, increase the time horizon and the incentive to train local labour, and dispel fear and suspicion. Private investment in uncertain conditions is not a zero-sum game[2] and both investor and host country can gain from such mutually agreed 'disarmament'.

Against these conflicts between the aims of the MNC and national and social objectives must be set the benefits that flow from the urge to make profits. This primary urge can have a number of incidental spread effects, beneficial to development in the host country. We have already discussed the need to avoid tax concessions, to gather full information about profits and about the range within which bargaining power can be used and to make tax revenue contribute fully to development expenditure.

[1] See Chapter 11, p. 213.
[2] The expression is applied to a different state of affairs from that envisaged by C. P. Kindleberger in *American Business Abroad*, pp. 150 ff. See also this book, p. 213.

Apart from taxation, the firm itself may have incentives to generate spread effects. It has an incentive to train and improve the performance of local suppliers and to spread information and skills among its potential customers. A firm processing or tinning fruit may teach fruit growers to grow and supply the required kinds of fruit (although firms are known to have imported fruit and even sugar from their parent country, on the ground that it could not be grown or be properly refined in the host country). A firm may have an interest in encouraging the growth of efficient local repair shops or supplies of components and spare parts. A firm producing for the domestic market fertilisers or farm equipment will have an interest in training farmers in their proper use, as Esso in the Philippines and Shell and Standard Oil of California in India are doing. To the extent to which it pays the firm to employ local labour, it will be in its interest to train it. It will also wish to train local managers and technicians, if its time horizon is sufficiently long. The cost of trained labour transferred from the parent country is substantially higher than training local labour, because both investment in teachers and earnings forgone by the taught are much greater in a rich country. This diffusion of incentives, knowledge and skills amongst suppliers, users and employees will be beneficial to indigenous development.

There are clearly limits to these spread effects and there are, as we have seen, backwash effects, such as the possible discouragement to indigenous production, skills and entrepreneurship. The power of the MNC to increase competition and to force cost reductions on hitherto inert local competitors has sometimes been a beneficent force in old-established advanced industrial countries. The arrival of the American subsidiary in Western Europe has often shaken up a sleepy entrepreneurial clique. But in underdeveloped countries the bracing effect of the cold wind of competition may be so harsh as to kill or prevent indigenous growth.

National integration and international disintegration

So far we have discussed the relations between the MNC and the host Government. Different problems arise in the relations between host Government and Government of the country in which the parent company is located over their different attitudes to the MNC.

The growth of the integrated nation state has created problems for the developing countries which the now industrialised countries did not face in their pre-industrial phase. Advance has meant national progress and national consolidation in the industrial countries. But the benefits of the welfare state are largely confined to its citizens.

National consolidation in rich countries has tended to lead to international disintegration.[1] By its general welfare policies the national welfare state inhibits or frustrates the internationally integrating power the MNC would have in conditions of free trade and free movement of men. In the absence of these restrictions, the MNC, recruiting wherever it can, irrespective of colour, nationality, creed or caste (except at the top level), and selling wherever it can, might be guided by the invisible hand to promote something not too different from the cosmopolitan interest. What then should be the response of the less developed countries?

One way is that suggested by Gunnar Myrdal. Though by conviction an internationalist, he says:

> The road to international integration must go over national integration; nationalistic policies by the poor countries and an increase of their bargaining power, won through these policies and through increased cooperation between them as a group, is a necessary stage towards a more effective world-wide international cooperation.[2]

The thesis has to be negated by an antithesis before a synthesis is reached. Option for the nationalist solution is not necessarily motivated by nationalistic or xenophobic ideals. It is quite consistent for a genuine internationalist to argue that national consolidation is a necessary stage in progress towards internationalism in our present world economy. The other option for the LDCs is to lay themselves open to what integrating forces prevail in the world economy, adopting free trade, free migration, and a welcome to investment from abroad, accepting the protectionist policies of the rich like natural obstacles.

It may be said that the international economy offers benefits which a small, weak developing country cannot afford to forgo and that the way to national strength and consolidation is through full participation in the international division of labour, by adopting free trade and unrestricted investment policies. Just as the internationalist can advocate national policies as a step towards the ultimate goal, so the nationalist can advocate outward-looking policies. Little can be inferred about ultimate ideology from the path proposed, or about the path from ideology. It may well be that either path is possible. History has certainly shown that successful development can be achieved by both types of policy. But history's lessons are of limited value here. For it makes a crucial difference to the development

[1] Gunnar Myrdal, *An International Economy* (London, 1956) and Chapter 1, p. 9, of this book.

[2] *Reshaping the World Economy*, edited by John A. Pincus (Englewood Cliffs, N.J., 1968) p. 90.

prospects what happens in countries in the lead. Coexistence of rich and poor, for good and ill, has made a vital difference to the efforts of the poor.[1]

Conclusions

A main theme of this chapter is that we should not contrast the MNC and the nation state, but that the important alignments cut across this distinction. Firstly, the nation state is not monolithic. Different interests within it align themselves differently with the MNC. Among those who will side with it are bribed officials, the small employed aristocracy of workers who enjoy high wages and security, the satellite bourgeoisie to whom world-wide mobility and prospects are opened and the domestic industries producing complementary goods who benefit from the concessions which the MNC has achieved for itself. On the other side of the fence are the masses of unemployed, non-employed and underemployed, those who suffer from the higher costs, the competitors, actual and potential, and those who dislike foreigners. In view of this division, it is misleading to speak of the interest of the nation state.

Secondly, the interest of the ruling élite in the nation state should be viewed in relation to the interests of other élites in competing or neighbouring developing countries. Many policies damaging to a particular country and its interest groups result from competitive concessions, ignorance and weak bargaining power. The gathering and dissemination of information, the pursuit of joint policies and similar forms of co-operation promise gains for the developing countries as a group. On the other hand, the existence of such co-operation gives a premium to any one country staying outside, or breaking away; and the fear of such break-away may reduce the cohesion of the alliance. Sanctions may be required to enforce participation. What institutional forms these alliances should take is not under discussion here. It may be that a separate UN agency is desirable or that intergovernmental co-operation suffices. The main point is that with the expansion of the MNC and with the possibility of trade union action becoming international, the nation state must look beyond its boundaries if it is to match the new forces.

Thirdly, MNCs pursue different objectives which sometimes clash. To group them together as a single force for world integration or world domination, undermining the nation state, is misleading. Exciting generalisations, often a symptom of the infancy of research, are intoxicating but they share some of the aftereffects of intoxication.

---

[1] See Chapter 1.

13 Killing Two Birds with One Stone

IT may be true that nobody has ever killed two birds with one stone. But there are many occasions on which two separate aims have been achieved by one policy instrument. Progressive rates of income tax redistribute income from rich to poor and, at the same time, stabilise the economy in the face of booms and slumps. Higher interest rates attract funds from abroad and reduce investment at home. Devaluation encourages exports and discourages imports. And so on.

The proposal I wish to discuss here is to link the creation of new international reserves with development aid. The Hon. Maxwell Stamp proposed this as long ago as 1962. A distinguished group of experts, called together by the United Nations Conference on Trade and Development (UNCTAD), recommended a modified version of the Stamp plan in 1965[1] and another international group of experts met in September 1969 and produced a report on *International Monetary Reform and Cooperation for Development*.

The Board of Governors of the International Monetary Fund (IMF) in Rio de Janeiro in 1967 agreed on a scheme of Special Drawing Rights (SDRs), by which either these or the equivalent currencies could be used to buy bonds of the World Bank (IBRD) or to replenish the funds of its soft-loan affiliate, the International Development Association (IDA). The World Bank or the IDA would use these funds for development aid. Each developed country would then have to compete for the additional orders to which the World Bank's investment gives rise and would earn additional reserves. The SDR amendment to the Articles of Agreement of the IMF was ratified on 28 July 1969, and the activation of the SDR scheme was announced at the September 1969 meetings of the IMF and the IBRD.

At the 1968 annual meeting of the IMF the Italian Governor and Minister of Finance, Signor Colombo, put forward a proposal that

[1] United Nations, *International Monetary Issues and the Developing Countries*, Report of the Group of Experts. UN Sales Number 66 II D.2.

the main industrial countries should use part of their reserves corresponding to a portion of their Special Drawing Rights allocations for the replenishment of IDA or for a subscription to World Bank bonds.

The US Congressional Subcommittee on International Exchange and Payments, under the chairmanship of Henry S. Reuss, recommended that at the 1969 meetings a resolution along the following general lines be introduced and discussed by the Governors of the two institutions:

> Resolved, that the Executive Directors of the International Monetary Fund and the International Bank of Reconstruction and Development promptly consider an amendment to the IMF Articles of Agreement, supplementing the Special Drawing Rights amendment ratified on July 28, 1969, whereby those 18 IMF members who have previously contributed to the International Development Association would direct that 25 per cent. of their Special Drawing Rights allocations be retained by the IMF to finance expanded IDA development assistance.

The main advantage of the proposal to link new international reserves with development aid is that it makes it possible for donors to increase aid without anxiety about their balances of payments. This fear has been a powerful force restricting the growth of aid and worsening its terms. In particular, it has led to tied aid and thus reduced the value of aid by between 10 per cent and 20 per cent. The link also meets the problem of those countries which feel unable to appropriate public funds for more aid, because it makes it possible to give more aid without additional budgetary appropriations. Furthermore, the link would meet the widespread desire of rich countries to run export surpluses in exchange for reserves. It would therefore enable all rich countries to enjoy surpluses, without depriving one another of liquid reserves and so would improve the working of the international monetary system.

What are the benefits and drawbacks of the proposal from the point of view of the less developed countries (LDCs) themselves, and of advanced, industrial countries in need of reserves, like Great Britain?

The adoption of such a proposal would be of considerable advantage to the LDCs. They would, initially at least, obtain a substantial accretion in the flow of development aid on easy terms. (It would be on easy terms since there would be no necessity to charge the IBRD/IDA anything for currencies, or more than a 'moderate rate of interest', perhaps 1·5 per cent per annum, on the SDRs transferred.) International monetary reserves are now about $70,000 million. The increase in international liquidity through the creation of SDRs will be $3,200 million per year for the next three years. If the proportion distributed by means of the link were to be 50 per cent of the allocation to rich countries rather than the excessively modest 25 per cent proposed by the Congressional Subcommittee, this would produce an annual increment of over $1,000 million in capital aid, a substantial amount in relation to the current world flow of aid. It would greatly increase the lending capacity of IDA. At the same time, this would be considerably less than one *per mil* of the demand for output in all the rich countries, which amounted to $1,700 billion in 1968.

Development aid is in a bad way. At a time when needs and abilities to make effective use of aid have risen in LDCs, donors, especially the larger ones, have tightened their purse strings. The international commission headed by Lester Pearson has called for bigger efforts by donors. Taking this wider point of view, the case for the link is that it would enable an internationally agreed objective, whose urgency has been vividly demonstrated by the Lester Pearson Commission – the increase in the flow of aid to the LDCs – to be achieved, while safeguarding the donor countries against the danger, which most of them fear, that increased aid will damage their international liquidity position. That there is widespread fear of the effect of aid on the balance of payments is shown by the prevalence of tied aid. Even countries with strong reserves and persistent surpluses tie their aid, thereby increasing the inflationary pressures whose effects on their economies they continually bemoan. The greater the extent to which any one advanced country makes real resources available to the LDCs through the link, the greater the extent to which it will share in the ultimate distribution of the newly created reserves.

These considerations are of particular importance to any country (like Britain) which has emphasised that the volume of its aid is restricted by balance-of-payments considerations substantially below the level which it should otherwise like to see it attain. That they are relevant to such a large part of the whole field of aid has a bearing on one argument which is often used in criticism of the link proposal, namely, the assertion that monetary reform and increasing aid are logically separate objectives which can and should be separately pursued. The fact is that concern about national balances of payments, which is a symptom of a world economy suffering from liquidity shortage, is also a powerful constraint upon, and inhibitor of, aid policy. And from a practical point of view, though it is true that any international monetary reform which brings about a general increase in liquidity will tend to cause a liberalisation of aid policies, it is exceedingly doubtful whether this process would ever have the same effect on the flow of aid as would a scheme which linked the two things together right from the start. To put the same point another way round, it may be true that if a link were adopted, some donors would say that the existence of this new aid channel made it unnecessary for them to go on giving so much directly and would reduce the scale of their bilateral aid. But it seems most unlikely, for practical reasons and because of the changed aspect of the balance-of-payments problem, that this could produce more than a fairly small offset to the direct effect of the proposal on the volume of capital aid.

There is another reason for expecting that the link would lead to an increase in the total flow of aid. This is that, once agreement has been reached, it could provide an automatic and unquestioned method of sharing the burden of the additional aid. It would thus avoid the disputes about burden-sharing which have tended to occur in international aid operations – especially in the discussions on replenishing IDA, and which tend to make any such operation small-scale and slow-moving.

The adoption of the link would not only increase the total flow of aid; it would also lead to a higher proportion of the flow being channelled through the IBRD and its affiliate. This must be reckoned as a considerable advantage, implying better administration of the aid on average and better value in relation to the aid given – probably quite a lot better. But it would be possible to attach the link to any other aid scheme. Thus SDRs could be linked with Supplementary Financial Measures, the scheme which proposes to insure LDCs against unexpected shortfalls in export earnings, with commodity price support, with regional development banks, or with regional payments unions.

It seems clear, therefore, that the adoption of the link would bring substantial economic advantages to the LDCs. We have next to consider whether, and to what extent, this gain to the LDCs would be matched by a loss or cost to the advanced countries. It is conceivable that an advanced deficit country might find itself in the position of having to buy back its own currency from an advanced surplus country, on whose exports the currency had been spent, and so of failing to share in the liquidity gain. At the worst, the country concerned might be no better off in terms of total liquidity than it was before the allocation of a portion of SDRs to aid. But donor countries as a group are likely to receive all the SDRs initially distributed, except to the extent to which LDCs increase their own reserves. While the total of newly-created SDRs will remain unaffected, the ultimate distribution will be different from that which would have occurred according to IMF quotas. The advantages derived from the liberalising effects on trade and payments policies will remain and only the distribution of the new assets may be altered.

Deficit countries with balance of payments problems might increase their reserves by raising their development orders, and surplus countries with budgetary problems might increase their aid, without aid appropriations in the budget. In both cases, of course, additional real resources (engineering goods, lorries, wagons, etc.) would have to be made available.

Some of the advanced countries, notably some Continental European countries, might not find the effect of the proposal so much to their taste as other countries. They would see it as facing them with the prospects of increased pressure of demand on their economies, already overemployed and suffering from inflation. They could only avoid this by not taking any share in the new development orders, and if they did this they would not gain any of the additional liquidity distributed through the link. It is clear that it would not be reasonable for a country to support the proposal unless it was prepared to make an additional transfer of real resources in favour of the LDCs. If it is so prepared, however, it should also be willing to take action to reduce domestic demand to the extent necessary to prevent an overloading of the economy. Clearly, the proposal has no chance of being adopted unless there is a sufficient number of countries, which, like Britain, are willing to make a greater real transfer to the LDCs so long as their balances of payments and reserve positions do not suffer thereby. If this is the case, then the difficulty about inflationary pressure, which in any case is, as we have seen, likely to be very small, is not insuperable. And the need to *earn* reserves, in exchange for real resources, should provide a safeguard against excessive expansion of reserve assets and should appeal to those concerned by the inflationary dangers of the link.

An objection which has been made to the link is related to the time pattern of the two operations which it is desired to link. It has been said that the long-term commitment needed for development aid is incompatible with the flexibility required for the creation of international liquidity.

This criticism has little substance. The volume, timing and distribution of SDRs would be determined solely by the estimated needs of the world economy, not by development needs. A proportion of these newly created SDRs would be put at the disposal of the IBRD, and the size and timing of this provision would be designed to meet the needs of development policy. It should be possible to achieve quite a satisfactory degree of continuity from the point of view of IBRD/IDA planning; indeed, the situation with 'link' finance might well be an improvement on the types of finance available to the IDA at the moment, particularly if it is remembered that this would be a supplementary source of finance.

It is a common objection to the link that liquidity and aid are entirely separate problems which cannot and should not be packaged together. If a group of countries – the argument runs – wish to give each other credit, or create additional liquidity for one another, there is no reason why they should not be entitled to create the necessary instruments for themselves without linking this scheme with the provision of real resources to LDCs.

The reply to this argument, given by Professor Machlup, is that the creation of new liquidity presents a saving compared with the acquisition of gold. When new gold deposits were discovered, those who wished to acquire gold had to give up real resources. The introduction of international 'paper' money (or 'paper gold', as it is sometimes called) amounts to a technical invention which creates gold without costs. It is sensible, and many would say just, that this saving should accrue to those most in need, the LDCs, and that richer countries should have to earn at least part of it. It would be a manifestation of international solidarity, an auspicious beginning of the second Development Decade and a visible response to Lester Pearson's appeal, if the rich countries declared that the saving derived from this innovation should go to the poor countries.

There remains the question as to the most suitable form of the link. There are two possibilities: an 'organic' or institutional and a 'non-organic' or voluntary link. In an organic link an agreed proportion of SDRs would be withheld by the IMF and directly handed over to the IDA, which could immediately convert them into national currencies so as not to sterilise the newly created reserves. In a non-organic link, national currencies corresponding to SDRs allocated would be pledged by national governments to subscriptions to the IDA. The difficulty about an organic link is that the Articles of Agreement of the IMF, as now amended and ratified, unfortunately rule out the holding of SDRs by multilateral institutions engaged in development assistance. A re-negotiation of these Articles may be arduous at this stage and, in any case, would take time.

Even a voluntary link might be possible without budgetary appropriations, though much depends upon institutional arrangements in contributing countries. Since monetary authorities will be receiving an asset without having to pay for it, Treasuries or Exchange Funds can sell it to their Central Banks for currency which could be paid to IDA without a budgetary appropriation. Against the costless acquisition of the SDRs as assets the books will have to show some liability, possibly in the form of a contingent liability upon withdrawal from, or liquidation of, the scheme. In order to balance the outflow of cash an asset would have to appear, say in the form of an IDA bond. But Central Banks might find such IDA bonds not sufficiently liquid and mobilisable to be acceptable in exchange for cash. In any case, the route which would avoid budgetary appropriations would also require legislation, and it might be simpler to let the Treasuries rather than the Central Banks handle the whole set of transactions.

If budgetary appropriations were necessary, national legislatures would be tempted to regard these appropriations as part of their regular aid budget and so to cut down on other forms of aid. Disagreements on burden-sharing might also be reopened at every round of pledging unless the pledge is for a long period. That form of the link should be chosen which is found politically most acceptable. Voluntary pledging could be an interim solution until the Articles are appropriately amended. The important thing is a long-term forward commitment to provide assurance for the continuation of interest-free, multilateral development aid.

Acceptance of the proposal would give a substantial encouragement to the development of the LDCs, while providing donor countries with an opportunity to earn reserves. Developed deficit countries could strengthen their reserves by making a special effort to fill the development orders which the scheme would generate, and developed surplus countries could continue their surpluses without forcing others to restrict trade or without denuding them of reserves. SDRs present an imaginative innovation in international relations. A parallel step forward in development co-operation would be a suitable start for the second Development Decade. If the British Government were to put forward or to back such a proposal, it could combine doing well and doing good. It could kill the two birds with one stone and put their feathers into its cap.

14 The Developing Countries in a World of Flexible Exchange Rates

THE bias built into the politics of many countries against changes in parities of their exchange rates has meant that the degree of flexibility provided by the Bretton Woods system has not been fully used. Governments have thus deprived themselves of at least one instrument of policy in their attempts to reconcile internal and external objectives of policy. The result has been restrictions, protection and, in some cases, inhibitions of growth. These have had detrimental effects on the flow of trade and capital to the developing countries.

The present mood is more receptive to policies of limited exchange rate flexibility, whether in the form of a crawling peg, a widened band, a combination of the two, or managed floating rates. From the point of view of devising appropriate international monetary policies for developing countries, two questions arise. First, how would any proposed changes in exchange rate arrangements affect, directly and indirectly, the development prospects of these countries? And second, what would be the implications of such arrangements for the policies to be pursued by these countries? Should the new arrangements be adopted or adapted, or are quite different arrangements appropriate for their different problems?

If greater flexibility liberalises trade, capital and aid policies in the West, this will indirectly benefit the third world. This benefit indeed is one of the most powerful reasons for the adoption of such arrangements in the West. But the more specific effects of frequent small changes in the relative values of major currencies are more difficult to predict. One must ask how do they affect the value of reserves held in the form of dollars, sterling or francs, liable to changes in their value and how do they affect the burden of debt service, the terms of trade and the ability to pursue domestic stabilisation and adjustment policies. The increased difficulties of managing asset holdings whose relative values are uncertain constitute a strong argument for a generally acceptable international reserve asset. SDRs are a step in the right direction and the adoption of limited exchange rate flexibility would strengthen the case for a more rapid advance in this direction. The real burden of debt service would also vary with fluctuations in the relative value of the creditor's currency.

Terms of trade problems arise if certain primary products are sold largely in one market, while imports come from another. Thus, if, say, Ceylon devalues with sterling and sells tea in London but buys machines in New York, the dollar price of exported tea falls, while the dollar price of imported machinery does not. Much will depend upon the geographical pattern of trade and the way in which prices are determined. In view of the small (though growing) importance of foreign trade, the small (though possibly frequent) changes in exchange rates and the possibility of using the London forward exchange market, the effects of limited flexibility in the West on large developing countries (like India, Pakistan or Brazil) are likely to be, on balance, favourable and will not present the difficulties which they might present to smaller developing countries. To the extent that flexibility of their own exchange rates is useful to certain developing countries, a move in this direction by the West will also help them.

Dual exchange rates

The second question relates to the appropriate currency arrangements for the developing countries themselves. It will be conceded even by passionate advocates of flexibility that such flexibility can make only a small contribution to the much deeper-seated problems of poverty, structural change and development. But there is one type of exchange rate arrangement which may, together with other measures, contribute to the solution of some of the problems of certain developing countries. One method of adjusting the persistent tendency of import requirements to outpace export earnings in some developing countries is the adoption of a dual exchange rate: one fixed and higher (i.e. more units of foreign currency for one unit of domestic currency) for traditional primary exports, and essential imports such as certain capital goods, industrial raw materials and food; the other lower (i.e. fewer units of foreign currency for one unit of domestic currency) and possibly floating or frequently adjusted, for new, especially manufactured, infant-industry exports and inessential or less essential imports. The low rate might be left to equilibrate the forces of supply and demand and might rise as export earnings from manufactures rise with growing production and competitiveness.

The case for a dual rate rests on certain peculiarities of the economies of many developing countries.[1] It is well known that manufactured import substitutes will normally have to face the initially high costs of infant industries. Cost ratios between manufacturing and agricultural production will be initially less favourable than they will be after economies of scale have been established and industrial attitudes and aptitudes created. If protective devices are adopted in an attempt to bring internal price ratios in line with internal cost ratios, the size of the market will be restricted and incentives to raise efficiency will be blunted. This will result in further claims for protection. Even apart from these cost-raising and efficiency-reducing tendencies, the attempt to set up import-saving industries will raise, for a period, import requirements relatively to export capacity. Import substitution has then to be accompanied, initially, by *higher* rather than lower foreign exchange expenditure. This tendency will be aggravated and prolonged if the protective devices raise costs and discourage efficiency. Since import substitution was embarked upon in order to save foreign exchange, it is frustrating to find that it appears to be self-defeating. This frustration often manifests itself in an accentuation of nationalistic and autarkic measures.

To avoid these results, the need to increase exports has been stressed. But if these consist of manufactured products, the common difficulty, as with manufactured import substitutes, is that these activities are conducted at too high a cost to be competitive with the established manufacturing exports of advanced industrial countries. The traditionally advocated remedy – a depreciation of the exchange rate – does not solve the problem. The traditional exports of primary products will tend to be in inelastic supply in the short run (and demand will be inelastic in the long run for large countries) and depreciation, unaccompanied by an increase in export taxes, will inflate prices and incomes in this sector. This may be justified if expansion of production or re-equipment and modernisation are wanted. But world demand is normally not such as to warrant expansion of primary products, except by small countries which encroach upon the market shares of large ones. The inflation of the incomes of the primary exporters (e.g. jute or cotton) following devaluation will raise their demand for food and may, in some cases, reduce its supply (e.g. by transfer of land from food to jute or cotton production). In addition to this, the higher domestic costs of imported industrial outputs and the resulting wage-cost inflation, will soon

[1] See N. Kaldor, *Essays on Economic Policy*, vol. II, chap. 19 and 'Dual Exchange Rates and Economic Development', *Economic Bulletin for Latin America* (Sep 1964). Kaldor has cogently argued the case for dual rates.

tend to wipe out the cost advantages gained by devaluation. Conventional anti-inflationary policies of restriction of domestic demand cannot tackle this type of inflation. If pursued vigorously enough, they create unemployment without touching the imported inflation in the traditional export sector and lead to the co-existence of unemployment and inflation.

The appropriate solution is to apply different remedies to staple exports, the prices of which are largely determined by world demand, and to manufactured exports, whose prices are determined by costs of production. This can be done in three ways: by introducing a system of dual exchange rates, by indirect taxes and subsidies or by centralised marketing. It is not the purpose of this chapter to compare in detail the merits of these different methods but to focus on the effects of dual exchange rates.

By the employment of a dual exchange rate export prices could be rendered competitive, while inflation of the income of the growers of primary products would be avoided. This would also prevent the inflation from being communicated to the prices of home-produced food and to industrial wages, and thus avoid the danger of wiping out the benefits of exchange rate depreciation.

A purist might argue that multiple rates (or better still a set of indirect taxes and subsidies) should be chosen so as to reap the maximum benefits for the nation of different demand and supply inelasticities. But, quite apart from the rules of the IMF and possible foreign retaliation, it would not be desirable to proliferate the number of exchange rates because avoidance and evasion would be made easier, particularly as the dual rate can be supplemented by a system of indirect taxes and subsidies.

While the high rate would be chosen for primary export commodities, the low rate, which could be more flexible and allowed to float, would apply to all those imports which do not qualify for a currency allocation at the official rate. Importers would obtain an import licence by purchasing the necessary amount of foreign exchange. The range of goods which would be covered by this rate could be varied by the Government from time to time and the free rate could thereby be influenced. Manufacturers unwilling to shoulder the risks of the variable rate would be able to buy foreign exchange forward. The Government may have to set up a purchasing agency or a Marketing Board in order to ensure that the foreign exchange proceeds of the primary exports are surrendered at the official rate. To avoid foreign exchange allocations for the specified imports being used for other purposes, the Government could ask for advance deposits in local currency.

Some disadvantages

Against the advantages of a system of dual exchange rates must be set at least three disadvantages. If they were designed to stimulate manufacturing, the stimulus to manufacturing industries would not be uniform, but would favour those making plentiful use of the imports admitted at low prices. Thus if all primary products were allowed into the country at the favourable rate chosen for 'essentials', oil refineries, for example, would benefit; cotton spinning would be favoured compared with weaving and clothing. If capital goods were permitted at the low rate, this would give an undesirable encouragement to imported-capital-intensive methods of production. Exports using much of the favoured imported inputs would be encouraged, compared with those using fewer or none. On the other hand, to keep the price of imported food low will favour labour-using industries and this will be desirable. A second possible objection is that dual exchange rates, which permit imports of food and raw materials at low prices, discourage the local production of these goods, unless special measures are taken to subsidise local producers, e.g. by a system of deficiency payments. It has been argued that domestic agricultural production should not be penalised in this way. Although for some countries, like India and Pakistan, food imports will be of decreasing importance as development proceeds, the case for a dual rate is probably weaker on the import side than on the side of exports. The argument then reduces to a case for subsidies to exports or manufacturing industry or particular factors of production or activities or services.[1]

A third difficulty, on a different plane of reasoning, which explains the reluctance to move away from import controls which are recognised to be inefficient, is the existence of tied aid. This forms a significant proportion of available foreign exchange in some developing countries, like India and Pakistan. There are ways of matching supplies of inconvertible currencies and demand in a system of dual exchange rates.[2] But aid-tying should not be accepted as an unalterable fact.

The increased competitiveness of manufactured exports derived from a lowering of prices to foreign buyers achieved in this manner has a number of additional advantages. If the low rate is allowed to float and thus to equilibrate the demand for and the supply of non-essential imports with demand for and the supply of manufactured exports, the discount of the floating rate (i.e. the premium on buying

[1] See Paul Streeten, 'The Case for Export Subsidies', Chapter 18 in this volume.
[2] 'The Implications of Economic Controls and of Liberalization', p. 92, in *Economic Survey of Asia and the Far East 1968* (Bangkok: United Nations, 1969).

foreign exchange over the official rate) will reflect the balance between the demand for inessential imports and the supply and the competitiveness of manufactured exports. The lower the rate, the greater the encouragement to exports. If the response is an increase in the supply of exports, this will tend to reduce the discount and bring the two rates nearer together.

Such a system would also meet a number of difficulties which arise from the different levels of development at which different developing countries find themselves. Differences among less developed countries, which have tended to increase in the last few years, can present problems similar in nature to those between less developed and developed countries. A system of simple preferences for manufactured imports, without a number of safeguards for the least developed, may simply award the lion's share of the markets to those less developed countries already more advanced and therefore least in need of assistance.

A system of dual rates, with one rate floating to equilibrate the demand for foreign exchange for less essential imports with the supply of foreign exchange earned by manufacturing exports, would automatically adjust the handicap to the level of industrialisation. The least developed countries at the earliest stage of industrialisation would enjoy the greatest price advantages for manufactured exports, while those whose cost conditions approximate those of the industrial countries would find their discount dwindling away.

In addition, it would encourage trade between developing countries without, once again, jeopardising the chances of the least developed countries of participating in industrialisation. It is a common failing of schemes of regional integration among developing countries that some member countries not only fail to share in the benefits of industrialisation, but are deprived of the opportunities which protection would have given them. The proposed system would combine the benefits of regional integration with those of participation in the industrialisation process of the least developed and would thus remove what has been a main obstacle to plans of integration between countries. While it is not normal to assume exchange rate flexibility between members of a customs union, it might overcome some of the obstacles which presently stand in the way of co-operation between developing countries.

A system of indirect taxes and subsidies can be used to achieve the same effects as a dual exchange rate. On grounds of economic theory it can be argued that it would do this more efficiently. But it is likely to be more difficult to administer. Traditional exports and inessential imports are taxed and the tax revenue is used to subsidise manufacturing exports and essential imports. Institutionally, raising indirect taxes through a Treasury is probably more difficult than gathering a larger domestic currency equivalent for a unit of foreign currency by a Central Bank; and subsidies may be more difficult to administer than permitting purchases of imports at lower prices in terms of domestic currency.

Finally, the same objective can be achieved by a national central marketing agency which buys primary products at low prices and sells them at higher prices in world markets. The agency would have to have the right of monopoly purchase from the farmers. The agency may also provide other services to the farmers. The case for such marketing agencies is stronger, the more important it is to fix different prices for different primary exports, and the weaker the case for admitting imports at a high rate.

The infant industry argument, often interpreted to justify protection, can be interpreted as an argument for subsidies in the first place or for dual exchange rates if subsidies are administratively difficult. Although both protection and subsidies tend to bring nearer together the price ratio between manufactures and primary products and their cost ratio, protection does it by raising the prices of manufactures, while subsidies and dual rates do it by lowering their costs.

Countries like India and Pakistan, with export bonus and import entitlement schemes, are, through a system of indirect taxes and subsidies and through other regulations and controls, in fact employing a system of *de facto* multiple exchange rates. The proposal in this case is to simplify this complex administrative apparatus and to replace it by a system of dual exchange rates, possibly modified by indirect taxes and subsidies. Argentina, Brazil, Ceylon, Taiwan and the Philippines have, at some time, used multiple exchange rates, though the lessons are not clear. The establishment of dual exchange rates has been called a wrong step in the right direction. This is to damn with pained phrase. If the above arguments are accepted, the unfavourable verdict would have to be revised.

Our conclusions on monetary arrangements for developing countries are these:

1. A move towards limited exchange rate flexibility among the advanced industrial countries is likely to benefit, on balance, the developing countries, although it presents them with some difficult choices with regard to portfolio management of their international assets and with regard to the pegging of their own exchange rates. Much more thought should be given to the repercussions of limited flexibility among industrial countries on the development prospects of developing countries.

2. Limited flexibility has not much to offer to exchange rate management of the developing countries, but the advantages and

drawbacks of dual exchange rates are worth exploring more fully. While many of the arguments for dual rates can be reduced to arguments for specific subsidies which might do the same job better, administrative considerations weigh in favour of dual rates.

15 Overseas Development Policies under the Labour Government[1]

(with Dudley Seers)

IN some obvious ways the world seems to be much more 'one family' than it was over thirty years ago. Jet aeroplanes have brought us together and television has destroyed old images. An advertisement for the Concorde airliner said: 'The world is about to be halved in size'; Marshall McLuhan tells us 'the new electronic interdependence recreates the world in the image of a global village'. The numerous activities of the United Nations, the stupendous growth of the multinational business corporation, the attempts to weld continents into common markets, the flourishing voluntary organisations have provided us with an institutional framework for international co-operation.

But this framework is unused. In many ways we have turned inwards, with an increasingly short-sighted view of the interests of our own nation and its citizens. The socialist parties of the industrial countries of the West were pioneers of international solidarity before the First World War, but now friendly references to international matters in national plans, publications, manifestoes, speeches and other declarations are considerably less common (as well as less convincing) than they were sixty years ago. The phrase 'workers of the world unite' would have no appeal, almost no meaning, to a modern British factory worker and is not likely to be voiced at a Labour Party Conference. It would in fact not be easy to say unambiguously whether the Conservative or the Labour Party is more 'international-minded'.

[1] This is a chapter from *The Labour Government's Economic Record 1964–1970* edited by Wilfred Beckerman (Duckworth, 1972). The authors are indebted to Miss Diane Elson and Ron Brigish for material used in this chapter and for help in writing it, and to a number of friends and colleagues for comments.

The pre-election policy

International policy is, however, a moral issue. If the Labour Party is to have any capacity to inspire people, especially the young, it has to be rooted in humanism, ultimately in the recognition of the essential brotherhood of man – and thus in a revulsion at the scale and nature of world poverty, a revulsion which does not stale with the familiarity and intractability of the problem.

Labour leaders once saw this. They were, when in opposition, committed to the relief of world poverty and to the creation of an integrated world community. This is especially true of Harold Wilson, who in 1953 wrote *The War on World Poverty*, a book pervaded by a sense of outrage at the world's social evils, and urging that aid flows should amount to 3 per cent of national incomes, more from richer countries. Through the whole period from 1945 to 1964 he returned again and again to the need for large capital flows as part of an international plan.

Even as late as 1964, in an article for the *Britannica Book of the Year*, entitled 'The Relevance of British Social Democracy', he proposed a solution to the problem of international liquidity which would harness the industrial capacity of the advanced countries 'to increase aid to the underdeveloped areas to the utmost'. In the section on trade policy, he stressed the need for world-wide commodity agreements, to be negotiated under the aegis of the UN Conference on Trade and Development (UNCTAD) and said:

> Commodity agreements, a world food plan, have always been central to our thinking . . . we must recognise that it is idle to talk of world development or of containing communism in the contested areas of the world, if we are prepared to see the earning power of these countries, through their sales of primary produce, subject to sudden and periodic collapse through price instability.

In particular, he suggested that

> in addition to existing UN or national plans, we might provide that the IMF be empowered to assign credit certificates, to the tune of say £200,000,000 – £300,000,000 a year, to an international investment fund which might be set up in conjunction with, or in replacement of, the existing International Development Association. These credit certificates would be allocated for spending in fully developed debtor countries which at the same time have unemployed resources – such as Britain and the United States in present circumstances.
>
> What is urgent is that western nations should regard [an

international economic summit meeting to discuss this type of plan] as a matter of primary importance.[1]

Similarly, Mrs Castle, in the debate on 3 February 1964 on the International Development Association (IDA) Bill,[2] made an impassioned plea for more aid and for a more effective and better co-ordinated aid strategy. She castigated motives for giving aid – 'which have nothing to do with the prime purpose of securing the economic development of the recipient countries of the world'. Development aid had miscarried, because those providing it had done so 'for reasons of national prestige, or for political motives to sustain certain regimes as against others, or for reasons of rivalry in the cold war, or for reasons of their own internal economic self-interest'.[3]

The manifesto on which the Labour Party fought the 1964 election was a good deal more cautious, but it showed awareness of the indivisibility of poverty, wherever it occurred in the world. The party promised that, if elected, it would

discuss with other countries proposals for expanding the trade of the developing nations;

increase the share of national income devoted to essential aid programmes, not only by loans and grants but by mobilising unused industrial capacity to meet overseas needs;

revive the concept of a World Food Board for the disposal of agricultural surpluses.

To give a dynamic lead in this vital field Labour will create a Ministry of Overseas Development to be responsible not only for our part in Commonwealth Development but also for our work in and through the specialist agencies of the United Nations. This new Ministry will help and encourage voluntary action through those organisations that have played such an inspired part in the Freedom from Hunger Campaign. We must match their enterprises with Government action to give new hope in the current United Nations Development Decade.

The manifesto also undertook that a Labour Government would strengthen Commonwealth ties. Migration limits would be 'negotiated', a Commonwealth Consultative Assembly established, joint projects (e.g. satellites) adopted and a career service created for experts working in the Commonwealth. All this would be in the context of the creation of a 'genuine world community' with (eventually) a world government.

[1] Harold Wilson, *Britannica Book of the Year* (1964), pp. 35–6.
[2] IDA is the 'soft-loan' affiliate of the World Bank, designed for very poor countries.   [3] *Hansard*, 3 Feb 1964. col. 831.

This chapter will attempt to contrast the hopes with the realisations, the election promises with the performance in office. It would be too easy to blame the Civil Service or the inheritance from the Tories or economic adversity or the limited scope set by outside pressures for the gap between promise and fulfilment. These are all – as we shall see – elements in the picture. But the central theme is one of political sociology; how, with the assumption of power by Labour, 'responsibility' made for nationalism.[1]

It is perhaps worth pausing momentarily to discuss what steps were actually implied by the Labour Party's proclaimed policy. Certainly it would have been unrealistic to rush to carry out the promises in the manifesto. There was a wide measure of public support for lofty ideals, but this would soon have evaporated if these had been made specific, for example, by handing Aden over to the United Nations for decolonisation, or shifting the emphasis from military expenditure to development aid in the Persian Gulf.

Yet public opinion is not inflexible. To do what the manifesto said clearly provided a perfectly feasible role for Britain, as a middling power with trading and cultural links throughout the world. A great bonus of goodwill still awaits the first industrial nation that shows by its actions genuine sympathy for, or even understanding of, the problems of the world's poor countries. What was necessary was a strong and consistent lead from the centre to help keep this view of our role before not only public, but also official, opinion. Political leadership meant insisting on this international strategy, whatever temporary retreats and compromises might be necessary.

The first steps needed (and possible) were, however, organisational. An enlightened international policy – even an enlightened aid policy – was out of the question so long as a group of somewhat archaic but intelligent officials in the Foreign Office (and in the Commonwealth Relations Office, as it then was) determined strategy in all its essentials. It would have required politicians of much greater capacity and moral conviction than those the Labour Party had at their disposal to induce them to accept a decisive change in approach to foreign affairs.[2] The key move would have been the creation of a

---

[1] See Gunnar Myrdal, *An International Economy* (London: Routledge & Kegan Paul, 1956).

[2] A particularly memorable occasion was when a member of the foreign service was explaining to a committee how much better it would be to expand bilateral aid than to join in a move for a big replenishment of the resources of IDA. Sir Andrew Cohen pointed out to him that a rise in our contribution to IDA would be a means of obtaining eight times as much in additional funds from other donors; and that India was the chief beneficiary. He paused to consider this. 'Well,' he said, 'our masters' (the traditional ironic term for Ministers) 'would rather India received £1 from us than £9 from an international agency.' (One wonders whether

political and economic staff inside the Office, brought in from outside, to provide an alternative source of advice for Ministers, with access to all the papers of officials and to their meetings. The measure needed to complement this was the appointment of an unofficial committee – perhaps a few months later – to suggest how the diplomatic service should be reorganised (as the Fulton committee did later for the home Civil Service).[1]

Still, such moves would not have been enough in themselves. It would take many years to reform the Foreign Office (and the other overseas departments). A separate Ministry was needed, at least in the meantime, to take account of the interests of poorer countries in their dealings with us, over a wide range of policies, including aid.

This Ministry was in fact established, and in a way that showed how the Foreign Office too might have been handled.

The creation of the Ministry of Overseas Development

One of the first acts of the Labour Government was, as promised, to centralise the administration of aid in a single department. The previous position had been vividly described by Mrs Castle:

> We have no fewer than seven Departments with a finger in the pie, six of them with other responsibilities – the Treasury, the Board of Trade, the Colonial Office, the Commonwealth Relations Office, the Central Africa Office, the Foreign Office and the Department of Technical Co-operation, to say nothing of those Departments which have also a general oversight over the relationship with the work of the specialised Agencies, such as the Ministry of Agriculture, which deals with the FAO and with international commodity agreements in food, and the Ministry of Education, which deals with UNESCO – and so we could go on.[2]

Many of those working in the field – William Clark of the Overseas Development Institute, for example – had been promoting the idea of a single department for some time. The precise shape of the new Ministry of Overseas Development (ODM for short – to avoid confusion with the Ministry of Defence – MOD) was determined by a working group of Fabians set up early in 1964, with Thomas

---

Labour Ministers had entirely lost influence on some aspects of policy – or had they really been brainwashed?)

[1] The Plowden Report (Cmnd. 2276) had already considered many organisational questions, but had not raised the basic issues of the sort of service Britain would need in the closing decades of this century. The Duncan Report (Cmnd. 4107) was to raise some of these issues subsequently in 1969, but in a superficial and unenlightened way, especially so far as the Third World was concerned – see below.　　　　　　　　　　　　　　　[2] *Hansard*, 3 Feb 1964, col. 845.

Balogh as Chairman. The central idea was that poverty should be attacked by a coherent strategy, in which the various forms of aid complement and reinforce one another.[1] Moreover, they need co-ordinating with many other types of policy – in trade, migration, international monetary reform. ODM was not seen as just an aid Ministry but (as its name implied) a department concerned with all aspects of policy affecting the Third World.

The fact that it was a Ministry outside the Foreign Office reflected the view that development policies should not be subordinate to our own political interests. Making it a Ministry of Cabinet rank underlined the importance attached to its work, and a belief that development policy was something worth while.

The first Minister was Barbara Castle, a Minister of outstanding determination and energy, and a close confidante of the Prime Minister. Her Permanent Secretary was Sir Andrew Cohen, previously Director-General of the Department of Technical Co-operation (DTC), set up in 1960. Andrew Cohen, a man larger than life-size in a number of senses, was an open Labour supporter and keenly sympathetic to the aims of the new Minister. The Ministry soon and inevitably acquired the nickname the Elephant and Castle and the tiny Minister and her huge Permanent Secretary were described as a well-balanced team.

Round the old DTC, which had been formed mainly from superannuated colonial servants, were grouped administrators from the Foreign Office, the Commonwealth Relations Office, the Colonial Office, the Treasury and other departments. But the most radical innovation was the creation by Mrs Castle (on the advice of Dr Balogh) of an economic planning staff of twenty economists and statisticians, under the authors of this chapter.

This consisted of three divisions. One was statistical (the descendant of the old Colonial Office statistical department), one dealt with general economic policy issues, and the third consisted of a group of economists with considerable overseas experience, each working in a geographical department. Through ourselves, who were

---

[1] Aid may be given in the form of technical assistance, or goods (e.g. food aid) or money to buy goods (capital aid); for specific investments, such as a steel mill or a dam (project aid) or for general purposes in the context of an overall plan (programme aid). It may be transferred directly from donor to recipient (bilateral aid) or through an international agency like the United Nations Development Programme or the World Bank Group (multilateral aid). These forms of aid are not, however, true *alternatives*, although they are often presented as such in controversies: thus only a well-worked-out programme can provide the framework for useful projects; capital aid can be more effectively utilised if it is accompanied by technical assistance; multilateral co-ordination should draw on the political will behind bilateral aid, etc.

given very senior positions (perhaps excessively so) this staff had direct access to the Minister.

The overt purpose of its creation was to introduce professional expertise into an area of policy where it had been conspicuously lacking. (The Commonwealth Relations Office had been lending or granting more than £100 million a year, allegedly for purposes of economic development, without the help of a single economist.) In addition to that, however, one motive was to bring into Whitehall those who were sympathetic to the Government's approach to overseas problems, and who saw Britain's role not just as the dispenser of financial and technical help to former colonies but as a pioneer in creating a more equitable world system.

The digestion of this relatively large group of outsiders was naturally not achieved without some difficulties, both outside and inside the Ministry. The Treasury took the idea in its stride, but the overseas departments, which were in any case resentful of the arrival of a new sister, found it embarrassing to meet 'outsiders' on interdepartmental committees.

One line of public criticism was that where economic expertise was really needed was not in London but in the field, especially in our embassies and high commissions, both to help improve policy and also to assist governments. There was something to this, though perhaps the first task was to create a nucleus in London big enough to affect policy. Its work was supplemented in this field by a number of missions, drawing on non-official economists, to assess aid needs and to advise on development policy (*inter alia* to Tanzania, Malawi, Southern Africa, the Caribbean). In any case, the attachment of economists to overseas posts was resisted by the overseas departments. (There were two economists in the Middle East Development Division in Beirut, one in the Caribbean and one was later appointed to work in the high commission in New Delhi.)

Inside the ODM a *modus vivendi* was fairly soon established. This was partly due to the Minister, who went out of her way to ask for the views of the economists. (Indeed, every submission had to show whether they agreed with the advice she was offered.) But it was also due to the determination of the Permanent Secretary to make the arrangement work and to see that these foreign bodies, unaccustomed to the ways of the Civil Service, were quickly integrated into the regular machinery. The decisive step was a conference in February 1965 (at Buscot Park, the home of Lord Faringdon) where the leading administrators and economists met for a whole weekend going over all aspects of policy, with the Minister herself taking a very active part. Most administrators, especially those with geographical responsibilities, came not only to accept but even to welcome the economists.

A very senior official went so far as to say, 'I cannot imagine how we ever managed to operate without the advice we get from the Economic Planning Staff'.

The 1965 White Paper and the volume of aid

The idealism evident in the election manifesto and in the creation of the new Ministry seemed to be confirmed by the Ministry's first White Paper. It was published on 3 August 1965, on the same day as an appalling fall in the gold reserves, a conjunction of events that did not augur well.

The White Paper, more than most such documents, reveals signs of multiple parenthood, reflecting the views of officials of many departments. Whenever an assertion is made which appears to commit the Government to a definite moral position, it is immediately withdrawn, contradicted or softened. 'The basis of the aid programme . . . is a moral one' but: 'the provision of aid is to our own long-term economic advantage'. Or: 'it is in the nature of aid that we should accept an economic sacrifice when giving it' but 'we give aid because in the widest sense we believe it to be in our interest to do so as a member of the world community'. Or: 'aid is not a means of winning the friendship of individual countries', though 'we are glad to offer aid to our friends'. And so on. Political security; altruism; commercial advantage and profit seeking; they are all grist to the mill and everyone can take his pick. The variety reflects the then unresolved political conflicts within government, and between Ministers and officials.

Yet, despite these equivocations and despite frequent references to constraints set by the balance of payments and the 'strength of the economy', the White Paper was positive and struck a completely new note. Unlike previous White Papers in this field, which were largely descriptive, it provided statistical and economic analysis; whereas former documents had been somewhat apologetic, it sounded optimistic and independent. Development aid was intended to accelerate development. The need for forward planning of aid, to avoid disruptive uncertainties for recipients, was emphasised, as well as support for regional co-operation, so vital for the formation of wider markets, and rational investment policies in areas where the political boundaries bear no relation to the needs of development. Greater efforts would be made to co-ordinate aid with other donors; and top priority was given to technical assistance. Stress was laid on the need for multilateral aid, which has the advantage of less direct political pressures, and, unlike most bilateral aid, is not tied to purchases in a particular country.

An important step foward in the White Paper was the announcement that 'in appropriate cases' (which are explained later) countries would in future receive interest-free loans. The decision had been a difficult one. There had been considerable opposition in Whitehall because of the anticipated objection of European creditors. Yet it was clear from the known liabilities of overseas countries that the burden of debt service which was accumulating would soon prove unmanageable.[1]

It might be argued by a hostile critic that debt service can hardly be regarded as a 'burden'. If the yield of a loan exceeds the interest rate and amortisation, there remains a net benefit to the borrower; if not, there is no case for borrowing. However, this ignores certain other factors relevant to aid. For instance, even if the total returns to the recipient exceed the cost of the loan, after making full allowance for tying,[2] the debt servicing payments have to be collected in taxes; the fiscal machinery of many less developed countries is not able to cope with this task. Moreover, in international lending, repayments can be made only by generating a surplus of exports over imports, which depends upon (among other things) the willingness of creditor countries to open their markets to goods and services from their debtors. Furthermore, a relatively long period of net resource inflow is required to permit the structural changes essential if development aid is to be successful and provide the means of servicing itself. The harder the terms (i.e. interest rates, grace periods, maturity dates, etc.), the smaller is the *net* flow of resources, the longer therefore the time necessary to do a given job of development, and the more aid is required to do that job.[3]

A lead in the direction of softer terms seemed necessary. The British initiative in making loans interest-free would have favourable

[1] The public external debt of all 'developing' countries had risen from $8 billion in 1956 to $33 billion by the end of 1964, an average annual growth of over 15 per cent, while the annual growth of their GNP was on average 4 per cent. (As a percentage of GNP this debt rose from 6 per cent in 1956 to 15 per cent at the end of 1964.) Total debt service in 1965 was $4·2 billion (including private investment and non-DAC aid) and constituted over 11 per cent of export earnings of 'developing' countries and more than half of the gross capital transfers from all sources. The growth of debt service between 1962 and 1966 had been 10 per cent per annum, while exports grew by 7·3 per cent annually. Moreover, projections made by the Agency for International Development (AID) of debt service to 1975, on various assumptions about loans and their terms, suggested that debt service might by then be claiming up to 22 per cent of export earnings. See D. Avramovic and associates, *Economic Growth and External Debt* (IBRD, 1964) and P. Lieftinck, *External Debt and Debt-Bearing Capacity of Developing Countries* (Princeton Essays in International Finance, No. 51, Mar 1966).

[2] In 1967, for instance, only 16 per cent of official aid flows remained untied. This has been estimated to reduce the real value of aid by at least 20 per cent. See *Partners in Development* (Pall Mall Press, London, 1969) p. 77.

[3] See Chapter 10.

effects on the aid debate in the American Congress and possibly on other donors. In actuality, the hoped-for decline in interest rates on aid loans did not take place (though the British initiative may have checked a tendency for them to rise), but the decision was clearly justified in itself.[1]

But there was a darker side to the picture. Very little was said in the White Paper about other policies (notably trade) affecting development. Moreover, it was silent about the future volume of aid, in spite of its declaration that, to be effective, aid should be planned ahead. All the Ministry was allowed to say was that 'ultimately the amount of aid we provide will depend on the amount of our total resources which we are willing to sacrifice'.[2]

Anyone looking for an indication of what this really meant had to turn to the National Plan[3] published soon after the White Paper and while the Minister of Overseas Development was still a member of the Cabinet. They would have had a shock: British policy towards the 'developing' countries there appears in a very different light.

The Plan shows what the Government's intentions were *on the assumption that economic developments after 1965 would be favourable.* A total growth of 25 per cent was envisaged between 1964 and 1970, or an annual average of 3·8 per cent; somewhat less in the early years, but accelerating to 4 per cent 'well before 1970'. The Plan provided for a 21 per cent rise in personal consumption over the period 1964 to 1970, and a 27 per cent rise in social and other public services.

After allowing for correcting the balance of payments and increasing investment in private and nationalised industry, the rest of the extra production was to be shared between personal consumption and public services. Out of every extra hundred pounds, 25 would go to improve the balance of payments and raise investment, nearly 20 to housing, defence, health, education, roads, etc., and over 55 to personal consumption – i.e. to cars, television, travel, drink, pet foods, cosmetics, etc., etc. The total addition between 1964 and 1970 was to be £8,000 million (in 1964 prices).

---

[1] For the sake of the record, it should be made clear that position papers favouring interest-free loans were prepared in the Treasury before the 1964 election, although one wonders whether this change would have been implemented without the existence of ODM, and the persuasive powers of Mrs Castle. (The reason for the Treasury position may interest students of administration. They resisted concessionary interest rates on overseas loans because they feared that public authorities in Britain would demand that the same rates be applied to themselves; the Treasury felt confident that no authority would be bold enough to demand interest-free loans!)

[2] HMSO, op. cit., para. 61.

[3] *The National Plan*, Cmnd. 2746, HMSO, Sep 1965.

How was aid to fare in this opulent world? The lengthy plan document contains three brief references. While always paying lip-service to the importance of aid, 'the amount we give must be subject to restraint while our balance of payments difficulties persist, and we have to plan our aid so that the foreign exchange cost of the programme is kept to a minimum'.[1]

The second reference has an even leaner look:

The Government have decided to restrain two major items of their overseas expenditure. First, they intend to restrict the Defence Budget. . . .

The grants and loans which make up the Government's programme for economic aid also place a burden on the balance of payments. . . . The Government are fully aware of the importance of aid to the developing countries, and are taking steps to increase the effectiveness of what aid is given. It will, however, be necessary to scrutinise the aid programme with particular care so long as the United Kingdom balance of payments is under such great strain and we are faced with the need to repay the overseas indebtedness recently incurred.[2]

The third passage says that 'the Plan makes provision for only a small rise over the levels of the current financial year' and that 'the reduction in military expenditure will more than offset the increase in aid'.[3] In fact, although no figure was quoted, a ceiling had been clamped on aid.[4] There was no intention to add many million pounds of the extra £8,000 million of output to the £100 million of grants and £90 million of official loans transferred to the 'developing' countries in 1964.

It was – and is – often argued that to give money away while we are in debt was both wrong and absurd. The Chancellor asked repeatedly 'How can I give away a deficit?' Such objections to more aid would have sounded more convincing if repayment of debts had been given priority over all other claims on resources, i.e. if personal and public consumption had been similarly restricted. As Professor Thomas Wilson put it:

We are in the position of a man who has got into debt by over-spending. He is still living comfortably, is exerting himself no more than he did, and expects his income and consumption to continue

---

[1] HMSO, op. cit., para. 25 p. 6.
[2] HMSO, op. cit., para. 16 p. 71.
[3] HMSO, op. cit., para. 3 chap. 7 p. 75.
[4] ODM was also singled out as the *only* department for which expenditure targets had to be set in current prices without automatic adjustment for inflation.

to rise. But the fact is he is in debt. What a fortunate opportunity for reducing his modest annual subscription to Oxfam![1]

The record

The August White Paper and the September National Plan express the two souls of Labour:[2] one generous and far-sighted, conscious of international responsibilities and opportunities – the other narrow, nationalistic, materialistic; one looking outward – the other inward; the long-hairs against the skinheads.

The levelling off of British aid was more conspicuous because it followed a rapid rise over the previous decade – despite periodic foreign exchange crises. Gross aid which had been running at about £50 to £55 million in the early 1950s climbed to £150 to £160 million, or three times that level, in the early 1960s, much more rapidly than the national product, and reached £207 million in 1966. There it stuck for the next three years. Meanwhile, amortisation was rising, and so were prices. So the real value of net aid declined for the first time since the war. Expressed as a percentage of GNP at market prices, net aid fell from 0·48 in 1965 to 0·39 in 1969, back to the level of the mid-1950s.

Aid was subjected to a number of assaults. A ceiling of £205 million was imposed, without adjustment for a fall in the value of money, which other spending departments enjoyed. Then a cut of £20 million (10 per cent) was made in 1966, when other public expenditure was planned to rise by 5 per cent. A loss of about 10 per cent in the real value was suffered due to the rise in export prices after devaluation in 1967. These are indications of the priority the Government gave to aid compared with its other concerns.

Parallel with these slashes at the aid programme were a number of political changes in the Ministry's standing. Barbara Castle was succeeded by Tony Greenwood and Arthur Bottomley. In January 1967 the Minister was removed from the Cabinet – an act of both symbolic and genuine significance.

It is true that gross aid disbursements continued to rise until 1966 (see Table 15.1). But the Government cannot claim much credit for these figures. They were largely determined by commitments entered into under the Conservatives. The point is that a tight rein was kept on *current* commitments. New commitments in 1965 were the second

---

[1] The *Statist*, 4 Feb 1966, p. 282.

[2] There was in fact a political deadlock over the publication of the ODM White Paper, which was put on ice for some weeks. It was only brought out of cold storage (rather hurriedly) to offset the very bad impression that was expected to be created abroad by a policy statement on immigration.

lowest since the late 1950s. The aid levels of 1967, 1968 and 1969 are better evidence for the intentions of 1965 and 1966 than the then current disbursements. Table 15.1 summarises the figures of disbursements during the period of the Labour Government.

TABLE 15.1

Total Gross and Net Disbursements of Aid to
Developing Countries

(£ million)

	1964	*1965*	*1966*	*1967*	*1968*	*1969*	*1970*
Aid Programme							
Gross	191	195	207	201	203	211	214
Amortisation	18	26	34	28	30	31	28
Net of Amortisation	173	169	174	173	173	180	186
Interest	22	24	26	27	27	24	24
Net of Amortisation and Interest	151	145	148	146	146	156	162

Source: HMSO, Ministry of Overseas Development, *British Aid Statistics 1964 to 1968* (London, 1969) p. 8, *1965 to 1969* (London, 1970) p. 15, and *1966 to 1970*, p. 12 (London, 1971).

The increase in gross aid between 1964 and 1969 by 10 per cent, small though this figure is, can be misleading. We must allow for the mounting repayments of old loans and interest payments (shown in the table) and for the rise in prices. If we set it against the growth of gross national product, the proportion of net official flows fell from 0·53 per cent in 1964 to 0·39 per cent in 1969. Public expenditure over the same period grew by over 50 per cent. Aid showed the smallest increase of expenditure by any government department, except defence.

Balance of payments: reason or excuse?

Balance of payments difficulties, and in particular the much publicised £800 million deficit inherited from the Tories, figured prominently amongst the explanations for the restraint of aid. This represented a return to an earlier Whitehall view on the treatment of the balance of payments costs of aid. The White Paper issued in 1963 had said that government overseas expenditure 'is a massive charge on our balance of payments, and aid to developing countries is one of the biggest items in the account'.[1] Yet subsequent calculations showed that

[1] HMSO, *Aid to Developing Countries*, Cmnd. 2147, para. 24.

in 1963 the burden of the balance of payments amounted to approximately £50 million, less than one third of total gross aid.[1] Even this figure exaggerates the burden. It was obtained by looking at British aid in isolation; if effects on the aid programmes of other donors are taken into account, the British balance of payments, far from being burdened, may well benefit from aid. Britain provided about 7½ per cent of the total flow of aid, but received nearly 12 per cent of the orders for the goods imported by the 'developing' countries from the industrial ones. (See the Annex on the 'true' cost of aid, pp. 292–6.)

It may therefore be asked whether balance of payments difficulties were the *reason* for the severe constraint imposed on the aid programme during the years of the Labour Government, or whether they served as an *excuse* for the lack of political will of some Labour politicians.

We have already quoted the National Plan and the 1965 White Paper, both of which emphasised the constraint of the balance of payments. In his speech to the meetings of the World Bank and Fund in October 1965, the Chancellor, Mr Callaghan, said:

> We naturally regret that in the immediate future we shall not be able to increase our aid as much as we should like to, although we shall continue to improve its quality and effectiveness. Putting it bluntly, we feel that countries with strong balances of payments could and should do more to raise the volume of aid; and we intend to do so as soon as our position permits it.

In view of Britain's large accumulated debt obligations, this position lay safely in the distant future.

Aid in perspective

In spite of repeated incantations of the balance of payments, the reason for the retreat from idealism – or perhaps rather a more realistic view of the post-war world – lies deeper. The test can be found in the Government's attitude to policies which would have been beneficial for the balance of payments (or, at worst, neutral), though they would have imposed a sacrifice in real resources. Studies by ODM economists showed that international agreements to support

---

[1] 'British Aid and the British Balance of Payments', by A. Krassowski, *Moorgate and Wallstreet: A Review* (Spring 1965). The order of magnitude was confirmed by more detailed studies by the Ministry's Planning Staff, initiated by Robin Marris. There was a good deal of resistance to the publication of these estimates, which are inconvenient for those speaking from Treasury briefs. Eventually a revised and more thorough set of estimates was printed under the title 'Aid and the Balance of Payments', by Bryan Hopkin and associates in the *Economic Journal* (Mar 1970) vol. LXXX, no. 317.

prices of certain commodities, such as cocoa, would probably on balance earn Britain foreign exchange.[1] The same is true of the 'link' between Special Drawing Rights (SDRs) and development aid. It seems clear that the Government's lack of enthusiasm for these measures was due to its unwillingness to give up the engineering goods or tractors or railway wagons provided under the aid programme and that the balance of payments was, to a large extent, a pretext. Whenever a policy with a beneficial impact on development could be shown to be also beneficial for the British balance of payments, objections were raised by the Treasury and the DEA that it cost real resources or that it was inflationary.

This came out explicitly before the Estimates Committee, when a representative of the Treasury said: 'It really is not true that it is simply because of the balance of payments impact that a ceiling has been placed on aid. This is misconceived. The Government has to decide what resources it is going to devote to aid, and all the other things within its care.'[2]

Further evidence, if this were needed, that aid is available when political pressures are mobilised (for ends other than development) are the items in the so-called 'additional aid programme', over and above the ceiling. This includes the increased contribution to IDA under the second replenishment (it was finally accepted in Whitehall that the British interest in foreign exchange and in development obviously coincide in IDA replenishment), special aid for Malaysia and Singapore (to induce them to acquiesce in reductions in military expenditure), food aid under the International Grains Agreement (which had to be swallowed as part of the Kennedy Round 'package') and contingency aid to Zambia (to offset the damage done by Rhodesian independence).

There is a reply to those who criticise the aid programme along these lines. In the crisis atmosphere of the Government's first two years, when planned public expenditure was cut and taxation raised, a slightly growing aid programme, though it may look feeble compared with its past growth, was not really so immoral. In 1966 both

---

[1] The calculation on cocoa was made by Miss Peter Ady. In brief, the reason for the beneficial effect is that Britain's share in world purchases of cocoa is smaller than her share in additional imports of cocoa-exporting countries, generated by their higher earnings. When cocoa-producers get higher prices, what in effect happens is that other consuming countries contribute to larger purchases from Britain. Similarly, Britain's contribution to IDA is smaller than her share in the orders generated by total IDA disbursements. It is because Britain plays such an important part in world trade that she stands to gain in higher export earnings from most policies that increase the total contributions of industrial countries, whether directly or through commodity agreements.

[2] HMSO, *Seventh Report from the Estimates Committee Session 1967–68, Overseas Aid*, para. 1410.

gross and net aid were at record levels; even expressed as a proportion of GNP, the official net flow did not fall in that year. To cut aid drastically would certainly not have been politically difficult. There were few votes in aid, no powerful lobbies for development. It is the considerable achievement of Barbara Castle (the case for the defence goes) to have defended the programme against such attacks. The cuts in US aid are an example of what can happen when anti-aid forces predominate.

But a plateau of disbursements may conceal the forces making for future decline, when new commitments are severely controlled. (See Table 15.2.)

TABLE 15.2

Commitments of Bilateral Financial Aid

(£ millions)

	1964	1965	1966	1967	1968	1969	1970
Total bilateral financial aid	236·3	114·9	129·6	149·9	175·0	130·4	143·9

Note: The surprisingly large figure for 1964 is explained partly because it was the last year before a ceiling was imposed and partly by a few large long-term commitments, such as that to Malta.

Source: HMSO, Ministry of Overseas Development, *British Aid Statistics 1964 to 1968* (London, 1969) p. 16, *1965 to 1969* (London, 1970) p. 19, and *1966 to 1970*, p. 19 (London, 1971).

After commitments were cut by £20 million in the deflationary measures of July 1966, the alliance between the Department of Economic Affairs, concerned with British economic growth and firmly anti-aid, the Treasury, resisting all forms of public expenditure and overseas expenditure in particular, and the Board of Trade became almost invincible in suffocating the goodwill, idealism and talent assembled in the ODM, which only got half-hearted support from the (unreformed) overseas departments.

In addition, there are of course powerful voices on the Right against aid. Two voices supporting Labour policy may serve as an epitaph on this period. The Governor of the Bank of England in a speech (in May 1969) attacking aid as a major factor contributing to our deteriorating balance of payments, said: 'This has been extremely worrying and I am glad that at last the increase has been checked and is beginning to give place to a modest fall'.[1] If the first voice comes from the core of the Establishment, the second is that of a

[1] Bank of England, *Quarterly Bulletin*, vol. 9 no. 2 (June 1969) p. 170.

Conservative backbencher, Mr Cranley Onslow. At the Select Committee on Overseas Aid he said to the Treasury witnesses:

> Since our Chairman said in her introductory remarks how much she agreed with the cut in defence expenditure, perhaps I could say that I find the standstill in aid since 1966 one of the few sensible things the Government has done.[1]

In 1969, the last full year of the Labour Government, Britain's net *official* transfer to less developed countries was somewhat smaller (at £150 million) in money terms (and considerably less as a proportion of national income or in real terms) than the amount which the Labour Government had inherited from the Conservative Government in 1964 (£153 million). Ironically, the net *private* flow in 1969 at £299 million, due to some freak financial items, was substantially larger than the £152 million inherited in 1964 and larger than the official flow. These results, especially the figure for official assistance, but also the figure for private investment, far from being declared Labour policy, ran counter to all declarations and intentions. It is a reflection on the gap not only between words and deeds, but also between intention and result. And it might well be argued that the second gap, the one between intent and outcome, mitigates any charge of insincerity or hypocrisy levelled on grounds of the first gap, the one between words and deeds. The complexities of implementing economic policies, particularly in the private sector, are such that inability rather than unwillingness may account for the discrepancy between Labour promise and fulfilment.

There was, moreover, a marked change of attitude in 1969. A White Paper on public expenditure published in early 1969 gave a target figure of £227 million for overseas aid in 1969–70 and of £235 million in 1970–71. Excluding Britain's special aid to Singapore and Malaysia, because of the defence element, economic aid was planned at some £219 million in 1969–70 and some £227 million in 1970–71.[2]

Judith Hart, the new Minister, revealed a more optimistic picture in November. From 1971–72 all economic aid was to be consolidated into one official aid programme (comprising both the basic aid programme and the special items). The gross aid ceiling was to be raised from £227 million in 1970–71 to £245 million in 1971–72, £265 million in 1972–73 and £300 million in 1973–74, the last year of the Public Expenditure Survey. Including the defence element in special aid the figure for 1972–73 is £270 million; £305 million for 1973–74.[3]

[1] HMSO, Select Committee on Overseas Aid, *Minutes of Evidence*, Sessions 1968–69, 1969–70, Monday, 10 Nov 1969, 348.

[2] *Overseas Development*, no. 20 (Jan 1970).

[3] Statement in Parliament by the Minister of Overseas Development on 27 Nov 1969, cited in *Overseas Development*, no. 20 (Jan 1970).

Taking what was called a 'high estimate for private flows', the Minister hoped that Britain would reach the UNCTAD 1 per cent target not much after 1975 but added 'we recognise the element of uncertainty which is bound to attach to estimates of private flows six years hence. So we shall keep the progress of both official and private flows under review.[1] In any case, the Government intends, unless our balance of payments position should preclude it, to reach the target of 1 per cent total flow not a moment later than the end of the Second Development Decade' (i.e. by 1980).

This response to the Pearson Report, to pressures of aid supporters inside and outside the Government and to the improvement in the economic situation, somewhat made up for the bleak years that had gone before. But, judged against the magnitude of the problem, against the Pearson target of 0·7 per cent of GNP for *official* aid, against Britain's wealth and allegedly strong balance of payments, and against past declarations, the response was disappointing, especially if one allows for the accelerating price inflation. Moreover, after the experience of 1965–69, one must wonder what pledges are worth. At the first sight of another economic crisis, would not another George Brown have appeared to convince the Cabinet that a ceiling should be set to such electorally unprofitable expenditures?

The effectiveness of British aid

A stereotyped formula, repeated whenever restraint of the volume was mentioned, was the need and the intention to increase the effectiveness of British aid, or to improve its quality.

The meaning of 'effectiveness' is elusive in the absence of a clearly stated set of objectives. But even on the assumption that we know what is meant, it is plain that effectiveness can hardly be improved without increasing staff overseas, and ensuring that they are capable of judging how British resources can most effectively be mobilised to help a country's development – which means that the aid administrator overseas must understand the country's problems and the general lines of their solution (not necessarily the lines that suit British interests). With that understanding, and sufficient staff, he can guide London on the way to respond to requests – what sort of aid 'package' would be most helpful, what types of people are needed

[1] Private overseas investment, however useful to development, should, for semantic as well as for political reasons, not be counted as aid. Like trade, it is a transaction into which both parties enter in the expectation of gain, whereas aid, properly defined, involves an economic sacrifice. The UNCTAD 'one per cent' target, which includes net private flows, has therefore, on these grounds alone, little meaning. It is curious that the actual turnout of 1969 is almost on the target which Mrs Hart promised for 1975, or at least 1980: total net financial flows were 0·97 per cent of GNP.

for technical assistance, etc. In some cases he could usefully ask questions about projects, since usually it is too late to alter a project by the time it comes to London. A man in an overseas post can also often help steer students to the right courses at home.

The number of people engaged full-time on aid administration in all our embassies and high commissions overseas amounted to 23 at the start of 1965. This number excludes the Middle East Development Division, a regional pool of advisers who include among their duties assisting governments with project preparation and administering aid policy for the area, and also those British officials in the colonies (that still existed) who were in effect working on aid administration. Still it is a very small figure in relation to aid of more than £100 million to independent countries. And it says, by implication, a good deal about the motives for British aid. A programme consisting of rewards for political and commercial favours needs very little administration compared with one designed to help a country's development. One result of understaffing, in fact, is that the same person is often responsible both for promoting British exports and for aid – making it extremely difficult to separate the two functions (especially in the eyes of recipients).[1]

By February 1968, the number of full-time staff had risen to 55, and another regional Development Division had been created (in the Caribbean). But this number was still very small in relation to their tasks, especially if one allows for the fact that a number of colonies had become independent in the meantime. To take a rather extreme example, one man in Zambia in 1967 placed over 700 technical assistance personnel, and helped 100 Zambian students and trainees visit Britain – such a man can be little more than a postbox. The Duncan Report estimated that in 1968 there were altogether 120 officials (in full-time equivalent) of executive officer and above administering British aid in the field.[2]

The situation does not seem to have changed dramatically in the meantime. The British Council has taken over much of the administration of the training programme, but the advice of the Duncan Committee has been followed – it 'could not accept that there is an urgent need for an increase in the Diplomatic Service resources devoted to aid administration'. Apart from being based on a very cursory examination of aid administration,[3] this position faithfully

---

[1] In Nairobi, where there are enough officials for a separate aid section, trade and aid administration have for many years been run by a combined group.

[2] *Report of the Review Committee on Overseas Representation*, 1968–9, Cmnd. 4107.

[3] This is shown in a special number of the *Bulletin of the Institute of Development Studies* (vol. 2, no. 1) devoted to the Duncan Report and the questions of the adequacy and balance of aid administration.

reflected the Government's attitude by this time, not merely its views on the amount it was prepared to spend but also on the weight it was prepared to give to the problems of world poverty. In the absence of a genuine overseas development policy, with political and financial resources behind it, the scope for improving effectiveness is narrow, and the declarations of the intention to do so ring rather hollow.

The pattern of aid

The other way of making aid more effective would be to improve its pattern, steering it deliberately towards governments with the intention and capacity to achieve development. This too would not have been easy to achieve in a static programme.

Official declarations by the Ministry of Overseas Development had a tendency to endow with a *post hoc* rationality a programme that had grown out of history, pressures and short-term responses. We yield here, we give in there and, lo and behold, the result is a grand design! Inability to cast off the millstone is displayed as pride in the adornment by a pearl necklace; inability to cast off the past, as 'the importance of continuity'.

The pattern is difficult to discern anyway, because of the multiplicity of forces at work. British business interests are in various ways pressing for aid to back up their export drive and their investment overseas, and this is reflected in the positions taken by officials of the Board of Trade and other departments.[1] The military, with the backing of the Ministry of Defence, are concerned with such matters as alliances, bases and over-flying rights. The diplomatic service makes its own amalgam of these into the 'national interest' in some higher sense. There is a welfare lobby, centred on the voluntary agencies, heavily concerned with relieving poverty, and this may converge with commercial and strategic interests in urging the support of colonies (or former colonies) that have limited development prospects. The somewhat lonely voice of the economists in ODM draws attention (*inter alia*) to the development potential of various countries. Lastly there are the influences outside Britain – the big say of the United States, the pressures exerted by potential recipients and the way they play their own hand (an influence which is by no means to be underestimated),[2] and the forces in the General Assembly and other international fora. The pattern of aid is the

---

[1] There is no suggestion here that officials consciously favour interests of particular firms – after all, increasing exports is a national requirement. (But it would be interesting to investigate how many senior civil servants in recent years have moved into business after their retirement.)

[2] We have seen delegations depart from ODM with far less generous arrangements than the Ministry had decided to concede to them – simply because they had not done their diplomatic homework.

TABLE 15.3

Gross Disbursements under Aid Programme,
by Type of Aid, 1965 and 1969[a]

(£ millions)

	1965	1969	1970
Total	*195*	*211*	*214*
Multilateral	*19*	*32*	*20*
IDA	12	20	6[e]
UNDP[b]	5	6	6
other	3	6	8
Bilateral	*176*	*179*	*154*
of which *primarily strategic motivation*	29	20	21
Turkey	7	3	5
Jordan	3	2	1
Non-Commonwealth Asia[e]	3	6	6
Aden and South Arabia	9	—	—
Cyprus	2	—	—
Malta	6	4	1
Singapore	—	4	8
primarily welfare motivation	25	30	30
Malawi	10	7	8
Former High Commission Territories[d]	9	12	7
Caribbean Associated States	2	3	7
Oceania	3	8	8
other bilateral	*123*	*130*	*143*
India	28	34	45
Pakistan	10	11	11
Indus Basin	4	2	—
Malaysia	4	3	11
Kenya	17	8	11
Tanzania	5	2	2
Uganda	4	4	4
East Africa (regional)	3	2	1
Ghana	1	6	6
Nigeria	10	6	11
Remainder	37	52	41

[a] Includes advances to CDC.
[b] Includes UNICEF.
[e] Indonesia, Laos, Thailand, South Vietnam, etc.
[d] Botswana, Lesotho, Swaziland.
[e] It should be noted that the 1970 IDA figure of £6 million is misleadingly small because it represents exceptionally low drawings from the IDA and for this item the 1969 figure would be more representative.

Source: Ministry of Overseas Development, *British Aid Statistics 1965 to 1969*, pp. 26 ff. (London 1970), and *1966 to 1970*, pp. 26 ff. (London 1971).

resultant of hundreds of individual decisions within and between departments – to treat this country well, another badly. Still, we should at least look at it for clues on government motivation.

Table 15.3 shows the general geographical pattern for 1965, which reflects the outcome of the decisions of several Conservative administrations – who, as we have seen, increased the aid programme and were thus able to shape it as it grew. One striking feature of this pattern is the high share of bilateral aid in 1965. This itself suggests that political and/or commercial bias was considerable. When we ask what countries were being aided under the bilateral programme the impression is strengthened; a large share was going to a group of half a dozen countries which were on the edge of the Communist sphere of influence, mostly in or near the Middle East, and were thus considered by the British Government (and usually by the United States Government as well) to be highly aid-worthy. One can surmise that aid to these countries would have been drastically reduced, possibly eliminated altogether, if there had been a complete *détente* between East and West; it was essentially Cold War aid.

The rest of the bilateral programme shows a heavy concentration on the Commonwealth, i.e. colonies and ex-colonies. But this is hardly an explanation in itself – we have to recognise the fact that, apart from sentimental ties, there are trading links and British investments built up in the colonial era.

Within the Commonwealth, there is one group where the balance of motives has been somewhat different. This consists of countries which have been receiving financial assistance not only with capital spending but also with their current expenditure. Britain had in fact not built up their economies to the point where they could, unaided, maintain even a bare minimum of services – a task which geography had in some cases made difficult. If Colonial Office policies of the 1950s had been maintained, these would in fact never have been considered 'ready' for independence, but the political pressures of the 1960s compelled the viability criterion to be set on one side. Of course trade and strategic interests (and the wish to avoid the world's opprobium) exert their influence here too. Mere destitution, without British colonial links (and all that goes with them), does not play a big part, otherwise our aid would have been flowing to countries like (say) Honduras and Upper Volta – more especially to North Vietnam. But still, we would be justified in saying that the motive for this category of aid was primarily 'welfare'.

A comparison between the patterns of aid in 1965 and 1969/70 might throw some light on the changes in motivation, though we must remember that the official ceiling on aid meant that there was not much room to manœuvre.[1]

[1] This suggests an interesting speculation: was the ceiling imposed partly because of a subconscious desire not to have to face the choices that would otherwise have emerged?

When one makes a summary comparison of the 1965 and 1969 programmes one notices some improvements. Above all, in accordance with declared policy, there was a shift towards multilateral aid. Within the bilateral programme, which fell in real terms, the fall was concentrated on the countries where the motivation appears primarily military.

However, on this point interpretation is not simple. In part it is due to withdrawal from military commitments (Aden), yet this is balanced by increases to offset withdrawal (Singapore), and the rise in aid to South Vietnam and its neighbours might be regarded as a sort of substitute for the regiment to support the US operation there, for which Lyndon Johnson and Dean Rusk pressed so hard. The decline in the case of Turkey (a weak link in the NATO chain) could be attributed to an economic boom rather than to any reduction in the Foreign Office's desire to use aid for strategic purposes.

On the other hand, aid primarily for welfare was increased, despite a reduction of aid to Malawi – where internal revenue rose sharply.

There was only one major new recipient, and this itself throws some light on motives, because the country was Ghana. The resumption of aid to Ghana (this also happened to Indonesia and Ceylon) represented a gesture of support to a regime considered more helpful to British interests, in various senses, than its predecessor. (In these cases, it could also be argued that the new governments could make better use of aid, but this hardly can be a very weighty argument if one considers how much aid certain administrations receive.)

The story behind the sharp decline in aid to Tanzania is even more revealing.[1] Tanzania broke off diplomatic relations in December 1965, in response to the failure of the British Government to stop the Smith' regime in Rhodesia declaring independence. The British reaction reflected – as so often – a departmental compromise. No new aid agreement would be negotiated (and a loan agreement already drawn up remained 'frozen'), but drawings on existing loans continued and so did technical assistance. By comparison with US reaction in similar circumstances (e.g. to Arab countries when the 'June war broke out) this was civilised, but nevertheless it revealed an element of spite (the Commonwealth Office still tended to expect grateful compliance from the former colonies). After all, there was no real break;[2] in fact many RAF personnel and other British experts

---

[1] The other big decline, to Kenya, is due to the fact that in 1965 substantial sums were paid under settlement schemes (in effect to buy out British farmers).

[2] The traditional significance of breaking off diplomatic relations is a prelude to war, but Tanzania had no such intention. The origin of the Tanzanian gesture was a meeting of the Organisation of African Unity which voted to break off

began arriving at this time to help maintain supplies to Zambia.

This rather anomalous aid relationship with Tanzania survived the nationalisation of British businesses early in 1967, but not the announcement in July 1968 that Tanzania would cease paying pensions to British administrators who had served there before independence – even though diplomatic relations had now been restored. It is odd that any British Government should have expected this burden to be carried by newly independent countries – and in fact much aid was in effect a way of financing it. It is even odder that the Labour Government waited so long to take over these pensions, which were a perpetual source of petty friction with all countries (aggrieved pensioners were continually mobilising their MPs to ask questions in Parliament) especially since President Nyerere had given twelve months' notice of his action. Britain's immediate and petulant response to the blow when it fell was to end aid to Tanzania, though those in technical assistance posts were allowed to serve out their contracts. In March 1970, ODM at last took over responsibility for *all* colonial pensions, a move for which Nyerere must be given the chief credit; by implication not only was Tanzania's lost virtue restored but the general principle underlying his action was conceded.[1]

There is another plane on which the composition of aid can be judged – the proportion spent on technical as opposed to financial assistance. Table 15.4 shows that technical aid has certainly grown in accordance with policy priorities; the 1965 White Paper stressed the importance of skills. But this rise is to some extent illusory. The increase in expenditure on supplying experts, which is responsible for about half of technical assistance outlays, is in large part due to general salary increases (and perhaps to the use of more highly paid types of expertise); the number of experts overseas has not greatly

---

relations with Britain if action were not taken to crush the Rhodesian rebellion. Nyerere's action seemed at least partly designed to stop the OAU voting for resolutions which its members had no intention of implementing.

[1] It was done very grudgingly. On 11 March Judith Hart said in Parliament that 'the Government had decided that as part of its policy of aid to development it is willing at the request of any government concerned to *consider* assuming responsibility for the cost of pensions to expatriate officers in respect of pre-Independence government service. The assumption of such a responsibility would be *taken into account in determining the total amount of aid* such a country might receive . . .' (our italics). Aid to Tanzania was not actually resumed, however, until the Conservatives took office. An ODM official visited Dar-es-Salaam at the end of June 1970 (though this visit had been planned before the election), and put forward a proposal, accepted in principle, to resume technical assistance immediately and to make a loan on which drawings could begin in April 1971 (the month when Britain would be starting to pay other colonial pensions).

TABLE 15.4

British Technical Assistance Disbursements,
1965 and 1969

(£ millions)

	1965	1969	1970
Bilateral			
Education and training programmes in Britain	3·5	7·8	8·3
Education and training in country of origin	0·9	0·3	0·4
Total education	4·4	8·1	8·7
Experts on technical assistance[a]	14·1	20·4	21·9
Compensation to expatriate officers	7·2	3·0	0·7
Research	2·3	3·1	3·7
Other[b]	3·7	9·0	10·6
	31·7	43·6	45·6
Multilateral	4·6	6·5	6·8
Total	36·3	50·1	52·3

[a] Includes those receiving supplements under OSAS, etc., as well as wholly financed experts.

[b] Consultancies, surveys, equipment, grants for volunteers (and to IUC and TETOC) and (for 1969) expenditure within the British Council's own budget.

Source: HMSO, Ministry of Overseas Development, *British Aid Statistics 1965 to 1969* (London, 1970), from Table 9 p. 23, and *1966 to 1970* (London 1971), from Table 12.

changed, nearly 3,000 a year being recruited in Britain each year (financed from public funds).[1]

There has also been a big increase in the provision for students and trainees. In this case the rise is in some degree a real one, though it is partly due to increases in fees, such as that made in 1967 for university students from overseas.[2] In any case, a serious question is raised by the combination of the increased expenditure on students to come to this country (largely recurrent expenditure) with the reduction in provision for training them in their own countries (largely capital expenditure).[3] Although the two sets of figures are not strictly

[1] One campaign promise has been kept, the creation of a 'career' for experts, by giving them long-term contracts – though not many contracts have in fact been issued.

[2] This, however, mainly affected overseas students financed from other sources; these outnumber those assisted out of British public funds.

[3] The rise in disbursements for overseas education levelled off (at about £5 million) in 1967. This implies a downward trend in real terms since then, which will continue, judging from a fall in commitments. A very dubious policy is the running down of support for research by overseas institutions, and offering instead the services of British consultancy teams, which is presumably believed

comparable, the comparison indicates a shift in the wrong direction. It may be explicable in balance of payments terms but undoubtedly the most helpful type of education in many cases is education in one's own country; much of what is taught in Britain and against a British background is of limited relevance to local problems.

The increased reliance by Britain on imported skills must in any case be considered to have offset any rise in the exports of skills under technical aid. Attention is usually focused on the racialist implications of British immigration policy, especially of the Common-wealth Immigration Act of 1968, which in effect discriminated in favour of white holders of British passports who reside in East Africa and want to migrate to Britain. But there is a development aspect too. The effect of successive changes in the past five years has been to make it easy for doctors and others with professional qualifications to migrate to Britain, very hard indeed for anyone else (except rela-tives of those already here). Now we have an immigration structure designed primarily to meet the needs of the *British* economy.

Terms of aid

On terms of aid, the record is more encouraging, especially the decision, mentioned earlier, to make most loans interest-free. This did not apply to all loans. In the 1965 White Paper the Government stated: 'In offering these concessions we shall have regard to the economic position of the country concerned. We believe that this, rather than the nature of the project or other purpose of the loan, should be the decisive economic criterion for the terms of aid.'[1] In practice, the 'economic position' has been interpreted as poverty (with the IDA limit of $250 a year per capita income as obviously a big influence).[2] Since 1965, rather over 80 per cent of the money loaned has been interest-free.

The weighted average rate of interest on British loans had already fallen from 5·8 per cent in 1962 to 4·1 per cent in 1964, largely as a result of the introduction in 1963 of (temporary) waivers of interest on

---

to create more goodwill. (A conspicuous case here is the fast reduction in British support to the regional research programme of the Department of Agriculture of the University of the West Indies, a sad contrast with all the effort that earlier went into building it up, as the Imperial College of Tropical Agriculture; it also seems inconsistent with declared priorities, both for agricultural development and for regional schemes.)

[1] HMSO, *Overseas Development: The Work of the New Ministry* (London, Aug 1965).

[2] But subject to the additional test, for countries below that level, of whether (e.g. because of oil reserves) the balance of payments outlook was such that debt servicing would be easy.

TABLE 15.5

Average Terms of Official Assistance

	Weighted average maturity periods (years)					Weighted average interest rates (percentages)				
	1964	*1965*	*1966*	*1967*	*1968*	*1964*	*1965*	*1966*	*1967*	*1968*
UK	24·0	22·2	23·9	24·1	24·0	4·1	3·3	1·0	1·1	1·0
All DAC countries[a]	28·6	22·6	25·1	24·0	26·0	3·1	3·6	3·1	3·8	3·6

[a] Countries which are members of the Development Assistance Committee of the OECD.

Source: OECD, *Resources for the Developing World* (Paris, 1970) p. 283.

certain loans. The provision of interest-free loans resulted in a further steep fall in the average level of interest rates to 1 per cent (see Table 15.5). The effect was, however, partially offset by a sharp decline in grants (from £46 million in 1965 to £24 million in 1969), due partly to a big decline in budgetary assistance.[1]

British financial terms started therefore to comply with one of the OECD Development Assistance Committee's recommendations in the 1965 resolution on the terms of aid.[2] However, there has not been any significant lengthening of either maturities or grace periods (before repayment starts). Indeed because of our rather short average grace period (see Table 15.6), Britain continued to be technically a defaulter on this resolution. Still, as can be seen from Tables 15.5 and 15.6, the best that can be said about the general performance of donors (in which the United States has of course a heavy weight) is that it has not actually worsened since this resolution was passed – the practice of voting for resolutions and then ignoring them is not confined to the OAU.[3]

[1] The *total* aid going to countries in receipt of budgetary assistance has, however, risen – see above.

[2] The DAC resolution of 1965 which Barbara Castle supported effectively, required either that 70 per cent of aid should be in the form of grants, or that *all three* provisions relating to loans and grants are fulfilled. The provisions are: (i) 81 per cent of total commitments as grants and loans at 3 per cent interest or less; (ii) 82 per cent of total commitments as grants and loans with maturity of 25 years or more; (iii) a weighted average grace period of at least 7 years. A subsequent resolution put forward alternative targets to 70 per cent in grants – either *each* transaction in at least 85 per cent of all official commitments should have a 'grant element' of at least 81 per cent, or 85 per cent of commitments should have an *average* grant element of at least 85 per cent. (The 'grant element' is a statistical device to bring out the concessional element in commitments: in a loan, the 'grant element' is the amount of the loan less the discounted payments of interest and principal.) Britain satisfies both of these alternatives.

[3] The same has happened to many rich-country votes on UNCTAD resolutions.

TABLE 15.6

Progress of DAC Countries on Terms of Aid

	Grants as percentage of total commitments					Grants and loans at interest rates of 3% or less as percentage of total commitments				
	1964	*1965*	*1966*	*1967*	*1968*	*1964*	*1965*	*1966*	*1967*	*1968*
UK	54	55	50	57	46	61	70	93	90	91
DAC countries*a*	60	61	62	56	51	84	78	85	78	81

	Grants and loans with maturity of 25 years or more as percentage of total commitments					Weighted average grace period of loan commitments (years)				
	1964	*1965*	*1966*	*1967*	*1968*	*1964*	*1965*	*1966*	*1967*	*1968*
UK	92	84	95	96	96	5·1	4·8	6·0	5·5	5·6
DAC countries*a*	85	76	81	77	78	6·5	4·6	5·8	5·5	6·0

a Countries which are members of the Development Assistance Committee of the OECD.

Source: OECD, *Resources for the Developing World* (Paris, 1970) p. 282.

'Developing' countries, with reason, object to the 'tying' of aid so that it can be spent only in the donor country. This means it buys less. It also cannot be used for local expenses, with the result that highly mechanised projects, requiring expensive imported equipment, are easier to finance than those giving a lot of local employment.[1] British performance has been relatively liberal. About two-thirds of the total of British grants and loans are tied in whole or in part to the supply of British goods and services (capital assistance to Asia, Latin America and Turkey being generally wholly tied to procurement in Britain). But budgetary support and investments by the Commonwealth Development Corporation (CDC) are not formally tied, and capital assistance to certain countries (mainly in Africa) can be applied in part to finance 'local costs' of projects – 33 per cent to 40 per cent in East Africa, and there is 'no fixed limit' for Malawi, Botswana or Lesotho. Rather under a half of British aid is tied to particular projects (which normally implies tying to the source of

[1] It is odd that to our knowledge no recipient of aid loans has proposed that repayments should be tied to purchases from *its* country (though repayment in local currencies has been specified in some US food aid agreements under Public Law 480, and Soviet aid agreements in effect provide for this).

procurement as well). But there was no trend in this ratio while the Labour Government was in office.[1]

The Confederation of British Industries (CBI) in evidence before the Estimates Committee on overseas aid criticised the Ministry of Overseas Development for inadequate 'commercial orientation' of the aid programme. (This phrase means, of course, more than just 'tying'.)[2] Government departments – the ODM, the Treasury and the Board of Trade – did not regard this criticism as valid. In fact the Committee felt that there had recently been some increase in commercial orientation. It could 'find no evidence to support the criticisms made by the CBI. These may have been valid two or three years ago, but they do not appear valid now. Those responsible for the aid programme are aware of the needs of British industry, and they must continue to be so.'[3]

'The Permanent Secretary of the Ministry of Overseas Development admitted that in the early days of the Ministry there might have been a tendency to pay insufficient attention to British commercial and trading interests, but claimed that this was no longer the case.'[4]

Other development policies

The Ministry of Overseas Development has in reality been largely an aid Ministry. This itself says something about the Government's approach to the problems of overseas development. After all, aid is only one of the policies affecting overseas development; as we have already seen, immigration policy also has its effect, though ODM has had very little, if any, influence here. The truth is that many, especially in parts of ODM itself, look on British policy for development overseas as a sort of rearguard action in the recall of the legions of the Colonial Service. There is still a strong ex-colonial flavour about ODM, and many of its officials naturally see it not so much as a Ministry concerned to make British policy in many fields helpful to development but rather as a sort of jumbo version of the old Colonial Development and Welfare operation. At its worst this means shoring up the positions of commercial advantage in the former colonies: at its best it represents an attempt to provide financial compensation for our failure to develop them in the past, or even to create the infrastructure that would have enabled them to develop themselves once they had become independent. One must add that neither the Cabinet nor individual ODM Ministers (at least since the departure

---

[1] There was a temporary jump in the proportion of commitments tied in 1968, but this was then reversed.

[2] HMSO, *Seventh Report from the Estimates Committee*, Session 1967–68, *Overseas Aid*, House of Commons Paper No. 442 (London, 1968) p. xxvi.

[3] HMSO, op. cit., p. xxvii, para. 78.   [4] Ibid., p. xxvii, para. 77.

of Barbara Castle) did much to discourage either of these attitudes, each in their different ways misleading as a guide to policy.

Even if we parochially confine our attention to the former colonies, the most important British policies are not usually in the aid field. The British bungling of the Rhodesian rebellion (remember how the Smith regime was going to fall in a matter of weeks?) had far more effect on the development of neighbouring African countries, especially Zambia, than the aid that was provided subsequently.[1] Indeed some of the work of ODM has turned out to be sweeping up after parties in other departments.

Another area where British policy seriously (and adversely) affected development prospects was in South-East Asia, by supporting American military operations in Vietnam – and indeed in a fairly large area around it. If one is to credit the previous Government with schools and houses it helped to construct in Africa, one must enter on the debit side those which were destroyed, with its diplomatic support, in South-East Asia.

Indeed, if we mean by 'development' more than just 'economic growth', if we allow for the social dimensions which are far more important (and in the long run, we would argue, necessary for growth), then the whole question of the stance of Britain *vis-à-vis* different types of government is relevant. There is always a danger that the Government of a rich industrial country will (as the United States did in Cuba) base its relations on the treatment of 'its own' companies, or upon whether the other Government is friendly with those who happen to be its own enemies. We have already seen that this influences the pattern of aid, but it also affects development less directly through, for example, treaties, sales of arms and support in international disputes. The Labour Government inherited an odd collection of allies from the past. Portugal was one; there were also the various treaty organisations such as CENTO and SEATO. It was the natural practice, especially during the worst blizzards of the Cold War, for Britain (like the United States) to attempt to prop up, by other measures besides aid, governments which were anti-Communist, often precisely those resisting, or merely paying lip-service to, tax reform, land reform, educational reform and other essential ingredients of development in a wider sense. One cannot in honesty say that Labour had abandoned this practice before it lost office, or that it changed our role in the United Nations as a defender of Portugal and even South Africa.

[1] Perhaps the most revealing of all the Cabinet's decisions on Africa was to entrust the *economic* campaign against the Smith regime to the *administrative* side of the *DEA*, which was singularly lacking not merely in economic expertise but even in experience of Southern Africa.

Private British investment overseas also has an impact on development – what sort of impact depends (*inter alia*) on the sector concerned, the extent to which foreign governments or individuals share in the profits and control, the amount of income and employment generated locally by purchases of materials. A government of a rich country that says it wants to co-operate in ending world poverty has therefore to draw certain conclusions for its policy on overseas investment (or stand exposed as hypocritical).

This potential inconsistency appears most clearly in its attitude towards the taxation of its own companies by the governments of poor countries. It looks somewhat odd if Britain is handing out aid to a government at the same time as it is backing the particular and narrow interests of British companies, especially those threatened by nationalisation. The practice of hinting that aid will be easier to come by if British companies are well treated links the two together[1] and one can see the combined implications. What this amounts to is offering money which gains goodwill, which has to be spent in Britain and which has to be repaid, in place of a foreign exchange flow which the recipient government could spend freely and as of right.

The question is really one of the nature of the support. One hopes we will never again see a Labour Government (or indeed any British Government) behaving as the previous one, the Attlee administration, did in backing a petroleum company's fight against higher taxes (and later nationalisation) in Iran – to the point of organising an international boycott. Indeed diplomatic pressure in support of the interests of British companies is hardly compatible with development objectives or with the political philosophy of the Labour Party, tempting though it may be in terms of short-run politics.

Any company has of course the right to the advice of 'its own' embassy on legal questions. In practice, however, the big petroleum and mining companies and the large multinational corporations are usually well able to look after themselves, and indeed are already at a decided advantage in dealing with foreign governments. An industrial country that was really sincere about development policy would in fact be offering objective technical help to governments in their negotiations with foreign companies, including companies based in Britain.[2]

[1] Governments which are sympathetic to foreign investors appear in any case as more 'aid-worthy'.

[2] It might be argued that governments in petroleum and mineral economies rarely need British aid. But some of them would certainly welcome *this type* of aid, in spite of the success of OPEC. On the other hand, bilateral advice and help offered to host governments might be suspect, and this is clearly an area for multilateral action. (The Commonwealth Secretariat has made a small start in rendering this type of technical assistance.)

There was one measure of the last Government that did have a big effect on private investment in the Third World, the introduction of the corporation tax. This change removed what had previously been favoured treatment of overseas investment. From a *national* point of view, returns from overseas investment *after* foreign tax should be equated, at the margin, to returns from domestic investment *before* tax; in the case of overseas investment, only the returns net of foreign tax accrue to Britain, whereas in the case of domestic investment, the whole return accrues to Britain, either as tax to the Exchequer or as profit to the investor. The old provisions, however, before the introduction of the corporation tax, enabled British companies to offset foreign taxes fully against British income tax and profits tax liabilities. This led to a situation in which, from a national point of view (quite apart from considerations of the balance of payments), too much private capital was invested abroad. At the same time, there was some evidence that, in spite of wide dispersions, the rate of return on foreign investments in underdeveloped countries was higher than that in overseas industrial countries.[1]

The corporation tax removed this favoured treatment of foreign investment by permitting the company to offset overseas tax against British tax liability only up to the limit of British corporation tax liability. Those hit by it looked on the change as a form of unfair discrimination against overseas investment. Transitional arrangements were made to ease its impact, but the new arrangements were designed precisely to deter the outflow of capital. The opposition to the tax demanded general and permanent relief from personal income tax for the British dividend receiver to the extent to which the foreign company tax exceeded the UK corporation tax.

The developmental implications of the corporation tax are complex. In so far as overseas investment is regarded as beneficial to development, a deterrent to such investment is unhelpful and should be opposed. Probably on balance the effect of continuing to what amounts to a subsidy to foreign investment in 'developing' countries is positive, since it means that lower operating profits are needed to justify any act of investment. But private overseas investment in 'developing' countries is only a small proportion of total private overseas investment and only a fraction, though a sizeable one, of the total flow of resources to 'developing' countries. The United Kingdom's large capital outflow in 1963–64, mainly to other rich countries, was a principal cause of its economic crisis and necessitated restrictive short-term measures. To the extent to which a measure

[1] See John H. Dunning, *Studies in International Investment* (London: Allen & Unwin, 1970) Table 4 p. 57 and W. B. Reddaway, *The Effects of U.K. Direct Investment Overseas* (Cambridge, 1967 and 1968).

strengthens the British balance of payments and the British economy, that measure must be supported by those wishing to promote development, for it makes possible more aid and more liberal trade policies.

There are reflex actions in Whitehall. The ODM, almost automatically, was tempted to align itself with the other overseas departments and with the Ministry of Fuel and Power, in opposing the tax. But it was clear to many, including some of the economists in the ODM, that the corporation tax made good economic sense, taking all its repercussions into account.[1] In any case, the Ministry could and did argue that, whatever the general merits, special provisions should be made for private investment in 'developing' countries, especially those with high nominal tax rates (although even there actual taxes paid are reduced by numerous exemptions and special allowances). It would, for instance, not have been difficult to extend the investment grants to certain types of investment in the 'developing' countries.[2] Alternatively, a Labour Government might have increased the flow of official aid to compensate for the deterrent effect on private investment. Or an investment guarantee scheme could have been introduced such as almost all other industrial countries have now adopted. The National Plan had said that it recognised 'the part which private investment can play in overseas development' and the Chancellor of the Exchequer had promised in his budget statement 'to keep the impact on developing countries of all these various measures under review' – this seems, however, in retrospect, to have been merely a sop to quieten the opposition.

In addition to changes in taxation, the Government introduced more severe exchange controls on private foreign investment, though so far as poor countries were concerned this affected mainly those outside the Sterling Area. (The 1966 scheme for voluntary restraint

[1] On a different plane, it could be argued that the irrational system of decision-making in Whitehall justified a retention of the old tax system, amounting to a general subsidy on company profits. Tax alleviation does not count as 'aid', and therefore does not have to compete with other forms of assistance where there is a ceiling on 'aid'. But we are raising questions about the way in which policy issues are posed and would not accept the treatment of aid in isolation, still less the imposition of an aid 'ceiling', as necessary constraints on rationality.

[2] In the event, the change from investment allowances to investment grants penalised overseas investment. Investment allowances had applied to British equipment installed at home or abroad, whereas investment grants applied only to equipment used in Britain. Thus a British company whose direct overseas investment consisted largely of the direct supply of British machinery lost a tax concession. This loss was only partially offset by the fact that assets obtained in Britain for use overseas were still eligible for initial allowances, which were raised from 10 per cent to 30 per cent. As a result of these changes, far from applying grants to investment in 'developing' countries, the new investment incentives reduced the inducement to invest in these countries.

on investment *inside* the Sterling Area specifically excluded 'developing' countries.)

Partly as a result of all these measures private foreign investment (net of disinvestment) in 'developing' countries declined from £157 million in 1965 to £70 million in 1968, with a recovery to £188 million in 1969 and £136 million in 1970. The recovery, however, appears to be the result of a number of financial transactions of oil companies which led to an upward revision of the published figures for 1969 of over two-thirds.[1] The revisions resulted from the failure of anticipated disinvestments or sales of assets to take place. A better picture of the trend is therefore provided if oil investment is excluded; then overseas investment (net of disinvestment) in 'developing' countries moved from £40 million in 1964 to £46 million in 1968. In real terms, whether oil is included or excluded, the figure for the last available year is lower, though not substantially lower, than for 1964.

More deplorable than the tax changes has been the unconstructive attitude of British delegations in international discussions on trade expansion. Britain declared her willingness to participate in suitable commodity agreements, such as cocoa and tea, but when these were negotiated, the delegation included British trade interests, and often excluded the ODM.

Our own national economic policies showed similar lack of concern with the problems of the Third World. The surcharge on imports hurt some poor countries disproportionately; exemptions or earlier reductions *in favour* of them were *refused*. On cotton textiles, discrimination *against* trade with developing countries was introduced through formal quotas in 1966, due to be replaced by a tariff from 1 January 1972. Beet sugar protection continued and attempts were made from time to time to dismantle the Commonwealth Sugar Agreement, which provides long-term guarantees of purchases at agreed prices. These attempts have failed but, in the renegotiations of the CSA, its term was shortened so as to provide room for manœuvre in negotiations with the EEC.

British attempts to enter the European Common Market have posed a clear danger that the trade of many 'developing' countries would be threatened, especially the exporters of sugar and textiles. Lip service has been paid in British documents and speeches to the protection of Commonwealth interests, but there is little evidence that the needs of 'developing' Commonwealth countries have been thoroughly considered. Labour's White Paper on the Common Market contained no analysis of this consequence of Britain's joining.

[1] Cf. Judith Hart, 'Public Aid or Private Investment?', *Venture* (Nov 1970) pp. 8–11.

This failure of the Labour Government to advance on the trade front is more difficult to explain, except simply as yielding to vested interests.[1] The strictly national advantages of increased aid are at least arguable, but an enlightened trade policy would beyond doubt be economically beneficial to Britain. A restructuring of British industry so as to draw men and capital from out-of-date, semi-stagnant sectors and move them into those which are expanding was one of the great domestic aims: it is part of modernisation, technology, growth, redeployment. Reduced protection of beet sugar and of cotton and jute textiles would have contributed to growth in Britain, as well as in the Third World. It would have created a supply of recruits for engineering and electronic industries, which is (as European experience shows) a condition of economic dynamism – apart from providing employment for the rapidly increasing masses of unemployed in the 'developing' countries. Increased imports of cheap cotton textiles are, from the point of view of the British consumer, equivalent to technical progress in synthetic fibres, but with beneficial instead of detrimental effects on poor countries. Even from the most selfish British point of view, the continued protection of the cotton textile industry is unwise. If the same resources, instead of defending and re-equipping an uncompetitive industry, had gone into the more dynamic sectors, clamouring for skills and capital, levels of living and growth would have risen faster, to the benefit of all, except a small, well-organised pressure group (including, of course, trade unions).

On international monetary reform, Britain supported – after some equivocation – the right of the 'developing' countries to participate in the negotiations leading up to the creation of SDRs, against those European countries that wished to confine the discussion to the inner circle known as the 'Group of Ten'. But since there was a clear harmony of interests among all chronic-deficit countries, including Britain, this concern for the interests of others was interpreted, perhaps over-cynically, less as a regard for the needs of the poor than as an attempt to get support for expansionist or – as the opponents would say – inflationary, policies. Britain did not, in any case, back 'the link' between SDRs and aid very strongly, and in fact only gave lukewarm support to the idea, even after the activation of the SDRs. Until this had been done, 'don't rock the boat' was given as the reason for this reluctance, afterwards fear of 'killing a tender plant'.

The conception of the Ministry as a *development* Ministry rather than an *aid* Ministry, with a voice and representation in all issues affecting development, never really took hold in Whitehall. The

[1] Though in fairness one must point out that its record is not worse than that of other industrial countries (especially the United States).

Board of Trade in particular considered the charge levelled against the Ministry of being a lobby for the 'developing' countries as sufficient condemnation, certainly not as a justification for fuller representation on the key inter-departmental committees. Treasury officials, in particular, rejected the Government's expressed philosophy (which had, in any event, very little conviction behind it). A Treasury witness before the Estimates Committee, asked about the relations between British trade interests and aid, criticised the Government's conception of ODM in the following terms: 'If I can say so frankly, there has been a little bit of a tendency in an aid Ministry to say our prime responsibility is towards the recipient country'.[1]

As a result, when there were negotiations on immigration, the Kennedy Round, the scheme for generalised preferences for manufactures, agreements for commodities such as cocoa, cotton textiles, entry into the Common Market, or international monetary reform, ODM was either not represented at all, or only very meagrely. Often it was not even consulted. The Economic Planning Staff, which was created to keep an eye on these wider issues, was kept too busy on aid problems and in any case had not the armoury to keep up the unequal battle against the powerful combination of the rest of Whitehall.

Key representational posts, in the field of development, were kept out of ODM's reach. A notable example is the British Executive Directorship in the International Bank, a post in which there is in practice much discretion for policy-making. One of the few battles Barbara Castle lost in the early weeks of the Ministry was the retention of this post by the Treasury. This has ensured that the British voice has been conservative (with a small 'c') on the major policies, and that the substantial British vote has been used to help allies and friends, rather than to hasten the gradual conversion of the Bank to a more development-orientated role. The same could be said of British briefs for meetings of the Directors of the Fund, which showed such enthusiasm for monetary orthodoxy as a cure for the problems of 'developing' countries that it became embarrassing as our own foreign exchange problems grew more acute – apart from casting a Labour Government in the role of an opponent of development.

The other key international post, that of leading the delegation to UNCTAD (and providing representation on its Board), remained with the Board of Trade. UNCTAD would have provided the forum for constructive initiatives towards a more integrated world economy, but is treated by Whitehall with considerable suspicion. Ministerial pressure was strong enough to get a bid made for London as the site of the UNCTAD secretariat, against heavy pressure from the

[1] *Report of the Committee on Estimates*, 1377.

diplomatic service ('The Americans would boycott UNCTAD if it were not in New York; besides, it would mean another couple of hundred wogs in London with duty-free privileges' – to run together two separate quotations). But the bid was put forward very feebly – the British delegation hardly bothered to hide their disagreement with their brief.

In the 1968 UNCTAD at New Delhi, British policy was in fact much less sympathetic than it had been in 1964 in Geneva, when the delegation was led by Edward Heath (and produced the proposals for 'supplementary financial measures' to enable development plans to proceed despite unexpected shortfalls in export earnings). The New Delhi Conference took place soon after the 1967 devaluation and there were no signs of improvement in the British balance of payments. Some people argued that since the British crisis was as acute as ever, if not worse, Britain was not in a position to give a lead. But seen in conjunction with all that went before, it is impossible to argue that the British feebleness in New Delhi can be explained wholly by economic difficulties.

Conclusions

On the whole, Labour's record was discreditable, especially in contrast to the promises before the election (which some of us were naïve enough to believe). Particularly damaging was the rejection of any attempt to lead public opinion to accept a more international, development-orientated strategy.

This is not to say that all British international policy (including aid) is always just an imperialist plot, necessarily damaging to the Third World. Some types of aid involve a genuine sacrifice, and much of it is on balance constructive in its effects; many countries, notably India, would face a challenge that could well prove catastrophic if aid were withdrawn.

Nor is it to say that the Conservatives would have produced a more defensible set of policies if they had won the 1964 election. Judging from their own record (and allowing for known shifts in attitudes), the history of the past five years would probably have been only marginally different.

It may be that they would also have cut the aid programme after 1964 as they entered a period of inevitable economic difficulties. Our belief, however, is that they would have continued to expand it slowly, because the cuts were due more to Labour's parochialism than to economic difficulties, real though these were. A Conservative administration would have felt less constrained to demonstrate their 'respectability'. On the contrary, Conservatives like to show how enlightened they are – within, of course, the natural limits of their policies. We must not forget that if the Conservatives had won the 1964 election (the hypothesis here), the Labour Party would have still been in opposition and therefore still vocally internationalist. Tories are, in any case, less easily taken in (because less willing to be) by 'balance of payments' arguments and might have had fewer inhibitions about devaluing sterling, the main requirement for easing the payments problem. It is difficult to believe, once the argument was posed squarely in terms of real resources, that they would have given such an overriding priority to the increase in personal consumption, already so high by international standards.

On immigration, too, Conservatives might have been less influenced by pressures from the Right-wing press, and therefore possibly more enlightened. Many of the improvements which Labour did make would have presented, in fact, little difficulty for the Conservatives – the shifts towards multilateral aid and technical assistance, even interest-free loans; one can reasonably conclude that these did not depend on which government was in power.

The great question is whether they would not have made aid policy even more political and commercial than it was, especially if we assume that they would have expanded the programme and thus gained increased room for manoeuvre. The pattern of aid might well have reflected even greater support for British political and trade interests.

Patience with Tanzania would have been even shorter, one guesses, and it is quite possible that aid to the United States in Vietnam would have been less indirect. However, one cannot fairly deduce what the Conservatives' policy on such matters would have been from their statements in opposition. In *office* they might well have grasped more quickly than Labour did the impracticability of maintaining large military bases East of Suez. One even wonders whether Smith would have tried his breakaway – or have succeeded so completely – with Conservatives in power (though ancestral memories of Carson and Ulster make one hesitate to give them the benefit of the doubt).

Trade policy, however, would hardly have been much better from a 'development' point of view, under Conservative management. Indeed, the post-election withdrawal of the government grant to the Consumer Council suggests that any interest alignments between British consumers and exporters of low-cost products from 'developing' countries would have been sacrificed in favour of vocal and well-organised British producer interests clamouring for protection.

'Untying' of aid would have created obvious problems with their backers. But (as can be inferred from Edward Heath's own strong support of legislation to control Resale Price Maintenance) doctrinal belief in the merits of competition might have opened their eyes to what could be gained from a determined British initiative to achieve an international agreement to untie.

These are not purely historical speculations. They are a way of asking about policy in the 1970s. And we shall soon see the shape of the answer. One thing is certain – the Conservatives would not have made an attempt to take the interests of the poorer countries of the world *institutionally* into account. In other words, they would not have created an independent Ministry with a planning staff with political and economic functions. They would presumably have produced earlier a semi-autonomous unit for co-ordinating aid – probably within what was then the Commonwealth Relations Office.

It has been argued, e.g. when this unit was in fact formed in 1971, that aid policies are weakened, not strengthened, by being handled by a separate Ministry, especially a new one. This vulnerable area of policy needs a powerful sponsor – even if the sponsor does not really approve of, or even understand, the rationale of what he is sponsoring. The same argument has been used against the creation of a separate Department for overall economic growth policy. The almost spectacular divergence between Labour promise and fulfilment, both in development and in domestic growth policies, raises this institutional question. Everything seemed to be set up for aid in 1964 – a new Ministry, a tough Minister, professional expertise, the right support from some of the most powerful people. If, in spite of these good omens, things went so wrong, an explanation is required.

The question was not at root one of institutional change. Setting up an independent Ministry becomes merely an empty gesture unless there is real support within the Government for its policies – support strong enough to withstand, and in time change, a public opinion that expects immediate, tangible, national advantages from the proceeds of taxation. When it comes to the pinch, Labour is really very parochial.

ANNEX: THE TRUE COST OF AID

In order to grasp the full implications of the discussion of how much aid we can afford, let us look at the 'true' cost of aid. The simplest reply to the question: 'What is the true cost of aid?' is: 'Its nominal cost'. It is simple, but not very enlightening. Any attempt, however, to introduce corrections involves making hypothetical assumptions which are bound at best to be largely unverifiable guesses – or an opportunity to introduce hidden prejudices, at worst.

If our balance of payments were in equilibrium and we had adequate foreign exchange reserves, if we suffered from neither inflation nor deflation and neither bottlenecks nor surplus capacity, if costs indicated forgone alternatives, and if we gave away the aid as grants, the nominal cost of the aid programme would be a rough guide to its true cost to the British economy. Divergencies between the two arise because:

(1) a £ worth of foreign exchange is worth more than one £ if there is disequilibrium in the balance of payments and if we are very short of foreign exchange;

(2) a £ worth of aid is worth more than one £ if the item is 'rationed' (e.g. reflected in lengthening domestic order books) and less than a £ if we have surplus capacity in the industry producing it or surplus stocks;

(3) a £ worth of aid is worth more than one £ if the domestic benefits exceed the nominal costs and less if they fall short of them;

(4) a £ worth lent (instead of given away), will yield a return in the future and this has to be appropriately deducted.

1. The main point to note on the divergence between the cost to the balance of payments and the nominal cost is this. If we are short of foreign exchange reserves, the official exchange rate does not reflect the real value of a loss of foreign exchange. While a good deal of aid is spent on British goods and services, some – it has been estimated about a third – constitutes a claim on foreign exchange reserves.[1] A foreign exchange cost occurs if either goods could have been exported for cash (or short-term export debits), had they not been delivered to aid recipients or if, although the aid is tied, recipients buy with tied aid goods they would otherwise have bought with untied foreign exchange and use the money thereby set free to buy from other countries. The latter reason for a foreign exchange cost is known as *switching*; the former might be called *diverting*.

It is sometimes argued that the import content of aid is also a charge on the balance of payments. But to the extent that either 'switching' or 'diverting' occurs, no *additional* output is necessary over and above what would have been produced otherwise. Therefore, no extra imports are required. Only if *neither* switching *nor* diverting occurs, so that the aid exports necessitate *additional* output, will there be *extra* imports. But these import requirements arise from *all* increases in British production and are not a valid reason for cutting aid rather than, say, industrial investment, in order to save foreign exchange. Suppose, on the other hand, the increase in aid-financed exports is *at the expense of* some other *domestic* activity,

[1] The references are given in the text, p. 267 n. 1.

then no additional imports are required. (This argument assumes that the import content of aid is no higher than that of the displaced activity.)

Aid can also be beneficial to the balance of payments. Thus aid to transport systems in countries with British-owned mines and plantations can generate a much greater increase in profit remittances to this country. Since countries of this type receive an abnormally high share of British aid (in relation to their population), and since British embassies and high commissions favour precisely the types of project that have this effect, the point is of more than academic significance. In addition, the supply of British equipment in aid programmes makes purchasing departments overseas familiar with their characteristics and thus inclined to place orders outside the aid programme – so the goods financed by aid can have the same commercial significance as 'samples'. A further significant help to exports is that the supply of equipment leads to orders for spare parts – which are rarely financed by aid.[1]

In any case, to say that one third of the aid is a cost to the balance of payments comes nowhere near to answering the important question, what the cost actually is. For, in so far as the loss takes the form of a reduction of foreign exchange reserves, there is no immediate real burden. (The real burden falls on those countries that make this possible by accumulating reserves or extending credits to us.) Only when corrective policies are applied in Britain and the exchange loss is thus halted is a real burden imposed. These corrective policies may take the form of a worsening of the terms of trade, or of domestic deflation with unemployment and loss of production, or of import restrictions with a resulting loss in the form of a less desirable composition of imports – and perhaps of retaliation by foreigners in the form of controls on our exports. The size of this secondary burden may be larger than that of the primary sacrifice although it could, in exceptional circumstances, be negative (e.g. a surcharge on imports that improves our terms of trade).

In order to calculate the 'real' cost, one needs a 'shadow' exchange rate. Since this rate, however, depends on the hypothetical policies that would or will be pursued to put the balance of payments in order, there cannot be a single correct answer. If we have to deflate in order to correct a chronic deficit, the cost is different from what it is if we devalue and again different from what it is with an import surcharge or import restrictions.

Estimates of this shadow rate ran as high as five times the official

---

[1] There are even further complications, though perhaps of theoretical rather than practical significance. Thus if other industrial countries increase *their* exports at our expense, for any of the reasons given, they will buy more from us.

rate. The argument goes like this: if the propensity to import is one fifth of income, we have to deflate national income by £5 in order to reduce imports by £1, so £1 loss of foreign exchange imposes a loss of £5 on the economy. Actually, the 'equilibrium' exchange rate before the most recent devaluation was hardly more than 14 per cent above the current official rate (i.e. hardly more than the devaluation that did occur), and the difference between 1·14 and 5 can be ascribed to the stubborn refusal to devalue rather than to the aid programme.

2. Divergences between nominal and true costs also arise because of bottlenecks and surplus capacity. If an item is in scarce supply but the scarcity is fully reflected in the price, the nominal cost is raised to the true cost. But in manufacturing industry this is not customary. Order books lengthen, i.e. supply is rationed. The true cost exceeds the nominal cost, since some buyers would be prepared to pay more for speedier delivery.

Against this, aid given from surplus capacity costs less than the nominal cost, for the productive factors would not otherwise have been employed. This has been important for the USA, which supplies surplus food as aid, but is probably not very significant in our aid programme (though more use of second-hand machinery could be important). Even if aid could be given from surpluses in, say, railway wagons or ships, it could be argued that this only prolongs the life of an industry that should contract and release labour, skills and capital to industries that are expanding. Therefore only *temporary* surplus capacity, such as occurs from time to time in the steel plant manufacturing industry, can be regarded as a legitimate reason for marking down the cost.

Special problems arise in respect of the services of certain types of scarce skilled manpower (e.g. economists and statisticians) supplied under technical assistance. The salaries of these men often fall short of their true scarcity value (firms say they just cannot recruit certain people) and therefore the apparently low cost of certain forms of technical assistance understates the true cost of the aid programme. (This is, of course, not the same as their value to the recipient country.) Against this, experience overseas may be regarded as a form of human investment which stands the British economy in good stead when the man returns to base. Moreover, even if he is completely unbiased in his advice, his recommendations are likely to lead to orders for equipment from Britain rather than from other industrial countries, simply because he knows British equipment best and the techniques he recommends may require that any capital goods needed be bought here.

So far we have talked about *specific* shortages and surpluses in *particular* industries. Some might argue that adjustments should be made if *general* inflationary conditions prevail or if *general* under-employment exists. True costs exceed nominal costs in inflation and fall short of them in deflation. But the excess of true over nominal costs exists for *all* forms of expenditure in inflationary conditions and there is no reason to pick on the aid programme. Nor is it right to mark down the costs in conditions of general underemployment, for this will normally be the deliberate result of government policy.

3. There may be other reasons why true costs exceed nominal costs. If a very high priority domestic objective, whose true value exceeds its nominal costs, has to be curtailed or abandoned solely because of the claims of aid, it would be fair to attribute the excess cost to the aid.

4. Finally, much aid is not given away but must be repaid, some-times with interest. There is a simple method of reducing to a common factor the rag-bag of soft loans and hard loans, short-term and long-term loans, at commercial and subsidised rates of interest, together with free gifts and private investment, which appears now in aid statistics, sometimes gross and sometimes net of repayments. We calculate the nominal value of all forms of financial flows disbursed (or committed) in a year and deduct from this sum the discounted present value of interest payments and loan repayments, discounted at a rate of interest that reflects the alternative employment of long-term public capital. In this way all forms of financial flow are reduced to their equivalent value as a grant (or gift or subsidy). The longer the term of the loan, the lower the interest rate and the later pay-ments start, the greater will be the aid component thus calculated. There is, of course, some doubt as to what is the appropriate discount rate to use – this could vary between periods.[1]

---

[1] The appropriate rate may in any case not be the same for borrowers (and may differ between different borrowers).

16 A New Look at Foreign Aid

The origins of our concern with development

SOCIAL scientists rarely investigate the social origins of their own interests and doctrines. Yet, such investigations not only are intrinsically interesting but also contribute to purging research of bias and thereby to restoring perspective and objectivity. It is for this reason that I shall start by examining the social and political origins of our interest in development, which has culminated in the Pearson Report,[1] hailed by some as the most important document on development of the post-war years or even the century.

Awareness of the existence of a problem of development is remarkably recent. The academic literature, the public debate, voluntary and official agencies and institutions and policies are not more than twenty years old. The Aid India Consortium, which marks the departure of a new approach to foreign aid, was created in 1958. There are, I believe, four quite distinct reasons for this rapid growth of interest.

First, awareness that poverty is not the inevitable fate of the vast majority of humanity is quite new. It is itself the result of the rapid and continuing post-war economic growth in the West and in Japan, combined with the spread of communications. The transistor radio in the distant village has brought home to millions of poor people that their poverty need not be their ineluctable fate. As a result of the education or propaganda of politicians and economists, economic growth has come to be regarded as a human right.

A second, quite different reason has been the Cold War. Marshall Aid for Europe was aid to win and strengthen allies. Later, in the 'Third' World, the other two worlds, Western capitalism and Soviet communism, vied with one another for the goodwill of the 'non-aligned'. Growth, according to their respective Western and Eastern

[1] *Partners in Development*, Report of the Commission on International Development under the chairmanship of Lester B. Pearson (New York: Praeger and London: Pall Mall Press, 1969).

recipes, was held out as the reward for keeping out of the other camp. The second cause reinforced the first, by adding an element of competition to the propaganda that growth was a human right. It is a sad reflection, not only on the limits of economics, but on the limits of human generosity and wisdom, that the thawing of the Cold War (if this is the right metaphor, bearing in mind its heating up in some places) in the 1960s did not lead, as economists might have predicted, to more development aid. It might have been thought that resources previously devoted to defence could now be diverted to development. But availability is of no avail if the political will is absent. To say that nations that can afford to spend between 10 and 20 per cent of their national incomes on defence should be able to afford 1 per cent for development is raising an irrelevant alternative. It is like the story of the boy who announced proudly to his father that he had saved ten cents by walking home from school instead of taking a bus. 'You fool,' his father replied, 'why didn't you not take a taxi and save two dollars?'

A third and again quite different reason is the radical change in the balance between men and resources created by rapid and accelerating population growth. World population grew from the dawn of human history to 1850 to 1,000 m. By 1960 it had more than trebled and by 2000 it will have reached between 6,000 m. and 7,000 m. As a result of this stupendous change in the dimensions of the population problem, development became necessary to prevent a decline into abject misery. The problems raised by the introduction of modern death rates into societies with primitive birth rates are not primarily the result of pressures on land and food, though these can be serious in certain regions, but of the difficulty of generating a sufficiently high savings ratio for investment and allocating out of this smaller savings ratio enough to productive investment rather than to welfare investment – schools, hospitals, etc.

The fourth reason is the large number of countries that have achieved political independence and with it development aspirations. In the last twenty years 65 countries have become independent. In the past decade alone more than 200 million Africans in 33 newly independent countries are seeking nationhood with economic development as a main objective. UN membership has grown from the original 51 to 130. Inevitably, this has produced new political pressures to concern ourselves with development and the structure of the UN system has been adjusted to handle these issues.

The psychological, political and even military origins of our interest in development have coloured the approach and the content of development studies. They are part of international diplomatic relations and hence polite and flattering diplomacy, intentionally or unintentionally, has entered not only the terminology ('developing nations', 'take-off', 'self-sustained growth', 'the free world') but also the substance. Economic targetry can serve as a focus for political will. It can also serve as an escape mechanism.

The limits of Pearson

The Pearson Report is, of course, a political document, to be understood against this background. Perhaps it is unfair to expect such a highly praised public document to come to grips with deep-seated intellectual and political difficulties. Perhaps the commissioners had to be diplomatic and had to tread carefully. But can one make omelets in this particular kitchen without treading on toes? Effective policies create dilemmas involving choices. Private foreign investment creates a dilemma between, on the one hand, reinvestment of the foreign profits in the host country and consequential alienation of the capital assets of a nation, and, on the other, remittance home with the consequential burden on the balance of payments. The bilateral aid relationship creates the dilemma between doing only what national governments ask for (thereby avoiding the charge of paternalism or neo-colonialism) and what maximises the impact on development. Budgetary aid, considered necessary to prevent collapse, often gives rise to padding of unproductive employment in the government service. Aid to new industries, intended to save foreign exchange, gives rise to *larger* import requirements. Transfer of responsibilities to local staff may mean employing, for a time, *more* expatriates. There are gentle references in the Pearson report to these disagreeable dilemmas, but the main line of reasoning is not a presentation of the choice between sound and unsound uses of aid that arises from particular applications – a discussion which might have reduced resistance amongst the hard-headed if not the hard-boiled, on the left and on the right – but it is largely a confrontation of 6 per cent growth by recipients with 1 per cent contribution by donors in 1975.

Similarly, the chapter headed 'Development Debts' does not draw a sufficiently clear distinction between *commercial* debts and *development* debts, between the problems of, for example, Ghana and India. Debt relief which does not draw such a distinction encourages the running up of commercial debts on hard terms in the expectation that relief will be given later. Such relief might then be at the expense of worthier aid recipients in favour of unworthy exporters and their bankers.

There can be no doubt that the spirit of the report is generous, the argument lucid and well presented and most recommendations sensible. But one is left with certain doubts. These do not relate to the lack of originality. It was right that the report should underline the conventional wisdom, particularly where it *is* wisdom. The doubts relate rather to certain presuppositions. Is it not naïve and pious, as well as ultimately damaging, to assume that morality and national self-interest coincide? Is it not futile to build the case for aid on international interdependence? Is not the fundamental presupposition of the strategy of the report – that the need for aid should subside in thirty years – unrealistic, lacking in vision and inconsistent with the claim to reduce international disparities in income? Does not the enthusiastic support of a scheme of generalised, non-reciprocal preferences for manufactured and semi-manufactured products from underdeveloped countries, compared with a lukewarm hypothetical paragraph on the link between Special Drawing Rights and the replenishment of the International Development Association, display a curious lack of a sense of priorities? Are not aid, trade and private foreign investment treated in a political vacuum? Are not the targets of 6 per cent growth, 1 per cent capital transfer and 0·7 per cent official aid either meaningless or, if meaningful, unwarranted? (There is the odd result that in 1975 Japan is expected to contribute $2,062 million while Britain only $853 million, in spite of the fact that income per head will still be 50 per cent higher in Britain than in Japan. Should there not be, as with income tax, a lower exemption limit, or rates of contribution progressing with income per head?) Does not the preference for multilateral aid (the commission calls for raising it from 10 per cent to 20 per cent of official aid) fail to take full account of the present limitations and deficiencies of some of the international agencies spelt out in detail by the Jackson Report?[1] Are not the 'Green Revolution' and private foreign investment oversold, inviting a backlash of disenchantment? The commissioners and the secretariat are obviously aware of these dilemmas and difficulties. But a political document has to be diplomatic.

Why aid?

The report does not succeed in providing a good reason for rich countries to give aid to poor countries. It veers from moral duty to national self-interest and from there to the irrelevant fact of interdependence. But the report does make an interesting start in attempting to reconcile national self-interest and moral duty.

'There is also the appeal of enlightened and constructive self-interest. . . . The fullest possible utilization of all the world's resources, human and physical, which can be brought about only by

[1] *A Study of the Capacity of the United Nations* (UN, Geneva, 1969).

international cooperation, helps not only those countries now economically weak, but also those strong and wealthy.'

But then the report goes wrong. It does not explain how aid and international trade, which it specifically mentions, promote the harmony of interests.

A more promising approach might have been to point to the growth of applied and commercially exploited scientific knowledge as the factor which ultimately sets a ceiling on economic growth. Since the scientific revolution in the seventeenth century, it has been knowledge, applied in technically feasible forms, commercially exploited and spread through imitation, which has permitted the productive capacity of societies to advance. The basic knowledge from which economic progress springs is a free, public good. Its enjoyment by one does not deprive another. But its commercial exploitation is partly naturally, partly artificially, rendered scarce. Now it is clearly in the interest of humanity as a whole that no potential contributions to the stock of knowledge be wasted. It is not only a *moral* duty to enable human beings, wherever born, to develop their faculties, but it is in the *interest* of all that these human resources should be fully developed, so that, instead of being a drain on the world's resources, they may contribute to their growth. It is in this way that one might think that aid-giving can be shown to be in the long-run enlightened interest of donor countries, and not because it is a particularly effective form of export sales promotion, peace-mongering or democracy-touting.

Unfortunately, this most promising line of identifying national self-interest with international solidarity does not succeed either. The direction and content of applied research has not contributed to a wide spread of benefits. On the contrary, it has been concentrated on the problems of the rich and much of it has been detrimental to the development efforts of the poor. It has also left vast gaps in our knowledge of how to solve the problems thrown up by development. Knowledge, like trade and capital flows, tends to benefit those who have and is either neutral or detrimental to the problems of the have-nots.

The point which few men in authority have recognised, or at any rate openly admitted, is that a disinterested concern with development and the promotion of national self-interest are incompatible. The current crisis in aid – the reluctance of the large donors, the USA and the UK, to expand or even continue the aid programme – is the inevitable result of false attempts to base aid on self-interest. When the senators began to see, what others have known all the time, that aid does not buy gratitude, nor trade, nor democracy, nor peace, nor votes, nor military support, they were understandably disappointed.

On the other hand, many smaller countries, such as the Scandinavian countries, the Netherlands, Canada and others, which based their programmes on moral and humanitarian grounds, expanded their aid in the late 'sixties and early 'seventies. Americans are no less open to moral and human appeals than Danes. But these appeals were not made sufficiently unequivocally in America and the programme is therefore in danger of collapse. A clearer sense of motivation and objective may lead to less aid, but it would be built on a firmer base.

The gap

The treatment of the income gap between rich and poor in the report is economically and logically unsatisfactory. The report opens with this sentence: 'The widening gap between the developed and developing countries has become a central issue of our time.' This proposition and the justification of aid that is built upon it is quite inconsistent with the emphasis on aid to get rid of aid and its anticipated demise in the near future. This emphasis again springs from a false bow to what is regarded as hard-headed American attitudes. In discussing 'Why Aid?' the report says:

> What, then is the objective of cooperation for international development? It is not to close all gaps and eliminate all inequality. That would, in any case, be impossible. It is to reduce disparities and remove inequities. It is to help the poorer countries to move forward, in their own way, into the industrial and technological age so that the world will not become more and more starkly divided between the haves and the have-nots, the privileged and the less privileged (pp. 7–8).

But reducing the gap is inconsistent with aid to end aid by the end of the century. The gap in income per head today is at its extremes more than $3,000. Present projections show that it will widen to between $7,000 and $9,000 by the year 2000. Income per head in the USA is expected to reach then $10,000, in Brazil $500 and in India $200. This at a time when the Pearson Report envisages aid to cease.

The Pearson Report does not analyse the significance of the gap. It does not raise the question: Does the widening gap matter? One can answer this question at three levels of sophistication. An immediate reaction is 'Of course: this is what aid, international co-operation and development is about.' But, on reflection, it seems to be the need to eliminate poverty, rather than the need to reduce an income gap, that should guide our policy. If we could choose between, on the one hand, rich countries growing at 7 per cent and poor countries at 6 per cent, and, on the other hand, the rich growing at 2 per cent and the poor at 3 per cent, should we not all prefer the first alternative, even though the gap would widen, to the second, which would narrow the gap? Should we not hesitate to reduce the gap in income per head by recommending faster population growth in rich countries, which, after all, is one way of narrowing the gap? Do we not view envy as a deplorable emotion, not to be heeded by planners and policy makers?

But at a third level of sophistication, we note that differential growth rates must not be considered in isolation. There are, for good and ill, numerous repercussions of higher growth rates of the rich on the prospects of the poor, depending upon whether the rich grow because their incomes *and* their numbers grow rapidly, or because their incomes per head grow rapidly. The demand for the staple exports and the new manufactured products of the poor, the availability of spare capital to be invested in the developing countries, the rate and direction of technical innovation, the flow of international migration, of skilled and unskilled manpower, and other forces crucially affecting the development prospects of the poor depend upon growth rate and income level differentials. Even if all dogs in the manger were kept on chains, gaps could not be ignored, because no country is an island, entire of itself.[1]

The ideology of aggregation

It is a weakness of the report, which stresses the fact of international interdependence, that it neither probes into the specific economic problems created by the coexistence of rich and poor nor even, in any detail, identifies those problems in underdeveloped countries to whose solution international co-operation could make a particularly effective contribution. Much of the discussion is conducted in terms of vast aggregates of gross national products, savings, investment and their growth rates. Many sins can be concealed by such aggregations. They are sweet music to the ears of the vested interests which can shelter behind global expenditure ratios. A brief discussion early in the report of the need to eliminate *internal* inequality, as much as *international* inequality, is soon lost sight of when we move on to growthmanship. In order to eradicate the roots of poverty and in order to win the support of those who believe that aid is wasted, one must point to actually or potentially successful applications of aid (research, food, population, jobs, slums), as well as to ways of avoiding failure. As in Mr McNamara's speech to the assembled bankers in Washington in 1969, one must say what should *not* be done, as well as what *should* be done (for example, in education less 'bricks and mortar' and more functional literacy for adults).

[1] See Chapter 1.

The arithmetic of the Pearson Report is simple. The target 6 per cent growth rate of the poor countries requires a contribution in aid and private foreign investment of 1 per cent of the gross national product of the rich countries. In 1969 the growth rate of the poor was 5 and the contribution 0·72 per cent. If the Pearson targets are hit, with population growth of, say, 3 per cent, income per head can then grow by 3 per cent annually. This means doubling income per head in 23 years. If population growth can be reduced to 2 per cent, income per head can grow by 4 per cent and double in 18 years. This type of arithmetic is a source of comfort. Pour in the capital, turn the handle of the machine called capital/output ratio, and out flows sweet extra growth-juice.

This picture is false for three reasons. First, development is not a matter of aggregates such as financial flows, capital/output ratios and growth rates, but involves the painful transformation of social institutions and human attitudes. The link between a given volume of expenditure and an effective land reform, a policy of population control or the establishment of an honest and efficient Civil Service is tenuous. Second, the task of bringing about such a transformation can be tackled only if specific obstacles are identified and removed. This means digging beneath the aggregates. Third, while rich countries can make an important contribution to co-operative solutions, their contribution must be the net result of all their policies bearing upon the development efforts of the poor. To isolate financial flows is at best irrelevant, at worst escapism or hypocrisy.

All three criticisms of the arithmetical approach question the value of large aggregates and invite disaggregation and digging beneath the economic appearance to the human and institutional reality.

The Pearson Report contains much that satisfies the need to pay attention to social transformation, to identify specific problems and embark upon their international co-operative solution, and to take other policies into account. But, being cast in the framework of target rates of growth and percentage contributions, the focus is on the aggregates and the picture of the reality is therefore blurred.

The framework cast in aggregates has been discredited by the lack of correlation between aid and development. Numerous excuses can be and have been advanced for this. The reason is inadequate insurance that aid is used for development because it was made the servant of too many other masters simultaneously. Confused objectives, bad selection of projects, allocation to the wrong sectors, and corruption are among the causes of the failure of aid. The policies other than aid pursued by the rich countries have often taken away with one hand what was given with the other.

The need now is to identify problems and set about solving them together. Rural development, population control, prevention of growing mass unemployment and underemployment and of the spread of slums and urban misery, improved nutrition and the right type of education – these are the issues to be tackled in the 1970s; '1 per cent' can aggravate, as well as alleviate these problems.

Development has a Hydra-like characteristic. As fast as you cut off heads, they grow again. We reduce death rates and prolong mortality, a basic human objective, and we are faced with an unprecedented problem of population growth. We introduce mechanical contraceptives, and medical complications speed up the rejection rate by women. We introduce new high-yielding varieties of grains, only to find that rural inequality and unemployment, market surpluses and political riots result. We set up an educational system and find that it leads to an exodus from the countryside, where the educated are most needed, and from the country, swelling the brain drain. Science may eventually present the solution to every problem. But each solution presents new problems.

The third deficiency of the Pearson Report is its emphasis on aid. Of course, even the Pearson Commission cannot talk of everything at once, and there is much talk of trade and investment. But targetry provides an easy escape from assessing the impact on development of the whole range of a rich country's policies – foreign policy, military policy, fiscal and monetary policies, immigration, as well as science policy, trade and private foreign investment. Just as private charity can be more than wiped out by a stroke of the Chancellor's pen, so the beneficial effects of aid on development can be cancelled out by military interventions or other acts of foreign policy, trade restrictions, restrictions on capital flows and migration or new technological inventions. Not until development enters as one objective into *all* acts of government that have a bearing on it, and is fitted into the *whole* development process, can we honestly speak of 'partners in development'.

Lessons

The lessons that the 1960s have taught us are different ones for the donors and the recipients. The donors must clarify their motives and objectives and abandon the notion that military, political or commercial ends can be bought through aid. Three conditions must be fulfilled: a sufficiently large quantum of aid must be transferred; it must be applied and used efficiently; and it should be removed from all the many frictions created by intergovernmental confrontation. In some way, the goodwill and the basic decency of the citizens of the rich country must be harnessed and backed by the powers of the State, without the intervention of diplomats. An imaginative proposal has been made by Albert O. Hirschman and Richard M. Bird.[1] Reform will have to be sought along such lines as these.

It is neither easy nor promising for recipients to appeal to the conscience of the rich. They must identify much more clearly where their bargaining power lies and exploit this power to the utmost. The Organisation of Petroleum Exporting Countries has begun to show the way. Instead of appeals to advanced countries to reduce their trade barriers and abolish protection, the interests of the consumers and of independent retail chains in low-cost products should be harnessed to the interests of low-cost producers and exporters from poor countries. The power to withhold the supply of minerals and tropical beverages, the power to withdraw money balances or default on debt, the power to tax private foreign investment, these and similar powers have hardly yet been used. Admittedly, the use of such powers requires solidarity between groups of poor countries and such solidarity is not common. But other powerful pressure groups have started off weak and disunited. Strength and success, like weakness and failure, are self-reinforcing.

[1] *Foreign Aid – A Critique and a Proposal*, Essays in International Finance, no. 69 (July 1968).

17 A Primer for Aid Recipients

'Because I am witty you must not imagine I am frivolous, and I will not imagine that because you are pompous you are therefore serious.' (Sidney Smith to a bishop.)

THIS short guide is written for aid recipients who wish to find their way through the political and bureaucratic jungle of donors' prejudices, myths, idiosyncrasies and more sensible requirements.

The kings of Siam are said to have ruined obnoxious countries by presenting them with white elephants that had to be maintained at vast expense. In the modern setting this can be achieved best by tying a high-interest loan, called 'aid', to projects and to donors' exports and to confine it to the import content or better still some part of it, of the project. But even untied aid on soft terms can be used to promote projects of a white elephantine nature, because capital grants do not cover the subsequent recurrent expenditure which the elephant inflicts on his owners. Receiving aid is not just like receiving an elephant but like making love to an elephant; there is no pleasure in it, you run the risk of being crushed and it takes years before you see the results.

Economists have correlated aid received per head with a number of characteristics of the recipient country. Valuable lessons can be learned from this exercise. If you wish to maximise aid received per head, you must become a very small country. If you are a member of a Federation, break away. If you have an irredentist movement, encourage it. You must register a low temperature in the cold war, belong to NATO, CENTO, SEATO and as many other military pacts as possible. You must have a regime that *declares* that it is favourable to private enterprise. The fact that the public sector is in fact much larger in the countries that preach the virtue of private investment than it is in yours is quite irrelevant. You must attempt to get a high score on the check list of performance criteria – except when it comes to population policy when it is non-performance that counts.

The final incidence of much aid is such that it benefits the donor, not the recipient. Aid, by raising demand for the exports of donors and by reducing demand for the exports of recipients, while increasing their supply, tends to improve donors' terms of trade. Salaries of expatriate managers, technicians and administrators flow back into the countries from which they come. The CBI never fails to point out how private investment overseas generates a stream of demand for components, spare parts and materials from the investing country. Tied loans are extended for goods at uncompetitive prices, but have to be repaid, with interest, in convertible very hard currency. Charity therefore may begin abroad, but sometimes ends up at home.

If aid is not given to benefit pressure groups in the donor countries, it is given to undo the harm done previously. According to a news item in *The Times* (16 Feb 1966): 'Vice-President Humphrey of the United States announced a $50 m. loan for Pakistan to reduce pressure on the national economy caused by the suspension of American economic assistance.' Much and a growing amount of aid is given to finance repayments of past loans and interest payments on them. Gross figures for aid have grown, while the only relevant figure – the net transfer of resources, has declined.

A simple test is this: whenever an overseas firm comes to you for a concession with the promise that it will raise your exports or encourage import substitution, and therefore be splendid for your balance of payments, check carefully what story it has told the authorities guarding the foreign exchange position in its mother country. Often you will find that the very same firm received permission to spend money abroad on the ground that the investment would strengthen the balance of payments of the capital exporting country. It may be the same firm that promises in its company reports to export more from Britain, which also promises you to import less from Britain.

Many forms of aid received turn out, on closer inspection, to be aid *given*. Aid is, for this and other reasons, a three-letter word. Donors may lend you at 8 per cent and you hold sterling or dollar balances at 4 per cent. Aid from donors' surplus capacity means that you, the poor, are helping to reduce unemployment and to raise profits in the countries of the rich. The acceptance of food aid helps the party in power in the donor country to keep the farm vote, sometimes at the expense of your indigenous agriculture. Purchases of fertilisers keep important branches of the chemical industry in business. Aid-tying enables producers to raise prices against you and to acquire a captive market. Sending young and promising men to be trained, helps donors to staff their hospitals, factories and universities with the best of your brains.

Always look a gift horse in the mouth, for it may turn out to be

Trojan. Or, as Ernest Bevin used to say, when you open the Pandora Box, it's full of Trojan 'orses.

Many donors have promised to provide 'financial resources . . . of a minimum net amount approaching as nearly as possible to 1 per cent of (their) national income' (UNCTAD Recommendation A.iv.2). You must beware lest they will hit this target not by inflating aid, but by deflating their national income. The British Government has said 'we shall hope . . . to be in a position to increase our aid to foreign countries . . .' (Cmnd. 2736, para. 5). The hope may be realised as a result of the break-up of the Commonwealth.

Much of what donors call 'aid' is really aid to their own citizens. This does not only cover loans and equity investment yielding handsome rates of return, though tabulated by the Development Assistance Committee of OECD as 'aid'. (It is rather as if, when buying a share of ICI, I enter the transaction as a charity.) In addition to this, aid covers part of the compensation paid to former colonial civil servants for loss of career when they retire when a country attains independence. Aid covers compensation to individuals and companies who had claims to money, property or land in newly independent countries, which these countries did not meet. Compensation of British farmers in Kenya and of the British South Africa Company in Zambia is counted as aid. If exporters, over-eager to sell, have acquired debts which cannot be repaid, and if their foolishly incurred debts are paid off by the British taxpayer, the payment is called aid to developing countries. Those who lost the war and pay reparations are also encouraged to count these damages paid to developing countries as aid.

There are a few simple rules which may help you to get aid.

First, potential donors have to be identified and their peculiarities and idiosyncrasies have to be studied, so that proper requests can be made and the right types of representative be sent out. In order to make the right impression on aid agencies, their motives and methods must be studied. Send out, for aid negotiations, representatives who resemble the donors, or rather resemble the image that donors have of themselves. The representative should speak the same language, literally and metaphorically, appear to accept the same values and have the same manners as the donor. To appeal to Englishmen, he must show common sense, be able to engage in small talk, not be too serious, too clever, too articulate or too learned, laugh at the Englishmen's jokes, which will suggest that he has a sense of humour, not be too successful with women and not have oily hair. To appeal to Americans, he must be frank, manly, unpompous, good at facts and figures and appear professional. To appeal to Germans, he should be hard-working, keen on private initiative and capable of formulating ideas in a coherent philosophical system with numerous categories, spelt out in long words with classical derivations. (A subsequent primer will be devoted to what appeals to Russian and Chinese donors.) The more the representative approaches the image that each donor nation has of itself, while remaining properly deferential, the better his chances of success. It is useful to know the jargon: always say, and, more important, write: 'absolute increases in income and income per capita are highly positively correlated with initial levels of income and income per capita' when you wish to say: The rich get richer. It is also useful to be familiar with the latest intellectual fads. To those who are impressed by the need to reform agriculture and limit population growth you must present programmes of land reform, large fertiliser purchases and cost/benefit calculations of the marginal sperm diverted. Others, eager to embark on thorough evaluation exercises, will be impressed if you can produce an evaluation of evaluaters. Whatever you propose to do, be ready with an evaluation.

But to send out acceptable negotiators, who can play golf, or drink beer or be prepared to picnic, and who can talk of trade matrices, systems analysis, and gaps is not enough. They must be well briefed, documents must be ready on time and letters must be answered.

Amongst the projects, some of the best ones will stand little chance of success, while some of the worst most. Agricultural, fishing or forestry projects may show low rates of return, sometimes long delayed, but can make large contributions to the economy as a whole. They will not be very popular with donors. Projects with a small import content make good use of local resources but, because of the local cost theology of donors, will not attract much foreign aid. Large residential universities, preferably on fertile agricultural land, planetariums, auditoria and other monuments to which labels can be attached, may have no (or negative) development impact but are dearly loved by donors. Administrative buildings, police houses and even, in some cases, prisons may be essential but to ask for them is a pretty hopeless quest.

In matching projects with your donors, you must also pay attention to their balance of payments position. It is easier to persuade surplus countries to finance the domestic content of a project than deficit donors. Projects with a high import content should therefore be sold to those with balance of payments deficits. Make good use of the skills which donors can supply. It is not much use asking a Catholic country for the pill, or one without a chemical industry for fertilisers, however important both pill and fertiliser may be. There is no point in asking for a project which requires for its execution managers whom the donor country is not able or willing to release. It is useful to employ knowledgeable aid consultants, preferably men who are familiar with the procedures of donors.

You do not have to know whether aid is given for military, altruistic, Machiavellian or profit-seeking reasons. But it is a great advantage to know something of the power games played in the corridors of the offices of the donor country and of the bargaining between different Civil Service departments concerned with the distribution of aid. If the recipient can add his weight at a crucial moment and at a crucial point in the process of decision-taking into a balance of considerations and power, he may be able to make a substantial difference. Such knowledge may have less to do with the merits of a case than with the idiosyncrasies of ministers and their senior officials and with the state of bargaining on quite different fronts.

You must try to maximise the number of donors and aid channels. Although this adds to your administrative work, it makes it possible to play one against the other and to encourage them to compete. The larger the number of channels, the greater the number of vested interests and therefore the larger is likely to be the flow of aid. Always oppose efforts to co-ordinate, streamline, or integrate aid-giving activities and institutions. More difficult is the creation of the right kind of political climate. To the Americans and to the Germans, you must convey the impression that you are helping yourself; then Uncle Sam and Onkel Michel may wish to push the car you have started. To the World Bank and other donors, you must present consistent national plans. National planning, irrespective of the plans of other nations and sometimes inconsistent with these plans, is the modern equivalent of nineteenth-century *laissez-faire*. You may be forced to repeat and perpetuate myths, such as that your borrowing is only for import of capital goods, that it is only for projects that yield exportable goods, or for projects that 'pay for themselves'; that all the money will be spent on the donor's products, and on his chosen projects, etc. Most important of all, you must perpetuate the myth that you will 'take-off' within a specified period and that all aid will then come to a happy end.

If you have a good agricultural engineer or a good expert on fisheries, and you wish to do him a good turn, recruit him for a UN technical assistance programme and ask for a similar expert from another underdeveloped country. Admittedly, both will be less effective in the foreign land, but their multiple salaries will be untaxed and paid for mainly out of rich countries' UN contributions. The more swapping of this type you can engineer, the higher the standard of living of your experts, though admittedly their contribution to development is reduced.

It is useful to know the prevailing mythology of aid.

There has been a good deal of discussion of the harm done by project and procurement tying. No doubt, a combination of these two forms of tying can greatly reduce the value of aid of recipients, and either of the two by itself can be harmful. But success either in project tying or in procurement tying is limited, the limitation depending on a number of factors such as the stage of development of your country, the volume of your trade with the donor, etc. Project tying is limited by the fact that the donor's money only apparently finances a high priority project, while in fact it would have been carried out in any case with funds which are now freed for some low priority activity. Similarly, the possibility of switching always exists with procurement tying. Free foreign exchange earned through exports can be diverted to purchases from other countries, while the tied loan is used to buy what would have been bought in any case.

Another myth is the notion that, to achieve development, aid-financed imports must be capital goods. It is of course true that many underdeveloped countries cannot produce capital goods themselves, or only at excessively high costs. But the development problem is how to feed the workers who do the construction of investment goods, while consumption levels generally are very low. And to finance this surplus by importing food from abroad may make as great a contribution to development as importing the capital goods.

It is also said that you should borrow only for projects that yield exportable goods. Even where balance of payments relief is the main consideration, the whole balance of payments position must be considered. Any contribution to domestic production which, directly or indirectly, reduces dependence on imports, is just as useful as the production of exports.

It is further said that you should borrow only for projects that 'pay for themselves' so that revenue collected is sufficient to service the debt. But again, it is not the revenue collected from the aid-financed project but the total public revenue position that matters. If taxation from other sources can be raised sufficiently, there is no reason why a non-self-liquidating project, such as many agricultural or educational projects, should not be undertaken.

The donors' jargon of 'taking-off' into self-sustained growth serves psychological and political needs, but not analysis. As long as it is merely a rationalisation of donors' hopes to be rid of aid before too long, no great harm may be done. Even then, it may be better to educate opinion gradually by getting it to accept not only the permanent justification of capital flows across national boundaries, for there is no reason why each nation should be self-sufficient with respect to its capital requirements, but also towards the international solidarity which would enable it to envisage the possibility of an international system of taxes and subsidies on a pattern which has become generally accepted within advanced nation states. But the notion of 'take-off' can carry misleading implications for current policy. It may give the impression that there is something inevitable or very easy in sustaining growth, once a critical point has been reached. Even when we adhere to the aeroplane metaphor, we must remember that crashes can occur. There is nothing automatic in sustaining development once certain savings and investment ratios have been achieved. Equally, 'preparing the runway', by gradually building up local institutions, a skilled and honest administrative service, an entrepreneurial class interested in building large-scale enterprises and in producing rather than trading, a reform-minded peasantry, etc., may be an essential prerequisite for development, but show slight or no returns in terms of the ratios normally used to indicate distance from 'take-off'. There can be a good deal of development without any growth, just as there can be growth without development. The metaphor taken from aeronautics can be adapted, but it is usually wiser to touch down from motoring or flying analogies and to ask who does what to whom when and why. Eschatology is no substitute for policy.

18 The Case for Export Subsidies[1]

IN the code of international economic morality which has evolved since the end of the war and is embodied in our international economic institutions, export subsidies are regarded as especially naughty. Import restrictions are explicitly permitted for balance of payments and other reasons. Increases in tariffs are permitted in certain circumstances, such as when low-tariff countries join a customs union, as a defence against dumping and in some cases to protect infant industries. Devaluation is an entirely proper mode of behaviour if there is a fundamental disequilibrium. Only export subsidies are beyond the pale.

On reflection, this is odd. For there are clear merits of export subsidies which other measures, conventionally considered more legitimate, do not have. Part of the explanation may be found in the fact that, since countries are normally more specialised in their exports than in their imports, the impact of 'damage' inflicted by export subsidies will tend to be more concentrated. For a developing country in particular, the degree of concentration by products and destination is likely to be great, and opposition from entrenched interest groups in importing countries therefore strong.

While it is generally agreed that, on certain assumptions which need not be spelt out here, a uniform change in the exchange rates would give the optimum solution, we may assume that this is ruled out or, if a devaluation occurs, that it would be accompanied by other measures affecting trade.[2]

1. In the first place, export subsidies increase the volume of world trade. International trade is generally regarded as 'a good thing' and one is sometimes even exhorted to 'maximise world trade'. If this exhortation were taken seriously, it would imply subsidies to all

---

[1] I am indebted to Michael Lipton for helpful comments.

[2] If, as recent UK and Indian experience suggest, the volume of imports is less responsive to devaluation than the volume of exports, devaluation operates like export subsidies, with the added advantage of a possible reduction in the (foreign) price of imports.

transportable domestic production, so that it could be sent abroad and swapped for all required purchases, to be imported from abroad. This would clearly produce a situation which is worse than no trade and, since restricted trade is better than no trade, a situation worse than restricted trade. Less extreme cases can easily be constructed to show that excessive subsidies are worse than restrictions. Clearly, subsidies can be too large. But as long as subsidies are kept within a critical limit, it is desirable that a country in balance of payments difficulties should correct its deficit by increasing trade and making fuller use of international specialisation, whereas a country resorting to import controls and tariffs would reduce international specialisation. Given the prevalence of restrictions on international trade, there is a presumption that measures designed to increase such trade are, *ceteris paribus*, likely to be beneficial.

2. Compared with devaluation which, of course, is similar to an *ad valorem* tariff on all imports and an *ad valorem* subsidy to all exports, export subsidies are more easily reversible. If the balance of payments difficulties are temporary, the subsidies could be removed later, whereas appreciation may prove difficult.

3. From the point of view of the country buying the subsidised exports, subsidies have the advantage of improving its terms of trade, whereas quantitative import restrictions and tariffs imposed by the exporting country will tend to worsen them. If it, therefore, has to accept the reduction of a given balance of payments surplus, this will be achieved with a bigger gain in its real income. From the point of view of the exporting country, while export subsidies worsen its terms of trade, the benefits from international specialisation will outweigh the losses from worsened terms of trade if trade restrictions were, initially, above those required for optimum tariff policy. In view of general foreign exchange shortages, this is often likely to be the case.

4. From the point of view of the subsidising country, export subsidies show up clearly the costs of protection. If they are imposed to protect an infant export industry, it will be clearly seen how much the nursing costs are. If they are imposed to correct the balance of payments, again costs will be apparent and can be compared with those of other measures. Not only the amount but also the locus will be open instead of concealed. It will also be easier to oppose vested interests when subsidies are reduced than when import restrictions are removed.

5. The fact that export subsidies normally involve the raising of additional revenue means that no country will resort to them lightly, as it might to imposing import restrictions. It will be forced to weigh more carefully the cost against the advantages expected from them.

From the point of view of a developing country with a weak apparatus for tax collection, tariffs appear to have the advantage of raising revenue easily. But rarely are the long-term diffused costs to the economy as a whole counted against the administrative advantages. A method of correcting the balance of payments which is administratively difficult will force governments to pay greater attention to its costs, as well as its benefits.

6. Export subsidies will tend to be less inflationary than import restrictions, tariffs or devaluation. Import prices will not be raised and there will be no cause for wage demands on the ground that the cost of living has risen. Hence cost inflation will be avoided.

7. Whereas devaluation affects the value of debts incurred in the past and therefore impairs the free international mobility of capital, export subsidies (like tariffs and quantitative restrictions) do not suffer from this defect. It is true that it is not easy to subsidise the prices of exported services directly, but grants to the service industry would enable it to reduce prices.

8. It might be argued that receiving countries are worried by the effects of dumping. But if a surplus of a given size in the balance of payments has to be reduced, some domestic industry is bound to suffer a reduction in demand. If foreigners impose quantitative restrictions, the export industry will be hurt. If, on the other hand, subsidised imports are received, industries producing substitutes for these imports are hit. It would, of course, not be wise to move resources out of the industry if the subsidy is temporary. But the same problem arises for an export industry against which restrictions have been imposed.

9. Export subsidies, unlike quantitative import restrictions (but like tariffs and devaluation), combine the virtues of planning with those of the price mechanism. While they can be used as instruments of public policy, they operate through market incentives (which quotas do only if they are auctioned by the Government) and are, therefore, more conducive to an efficient allocation of resources. Import licences are normally allocated at best 'fairly', according to a base period, and therefore hamper the most dynamic firms, or, at worst, by bribery and corruption. There is no guarantee that licences granted to importers will go to those who can make the best use of them, whereas there is a presumption that the most efficient exporting firms would benefit from export subsidies. The higher profits can then be devoted to further sales promotion, marketing efforts and cost reductions.

10. For any given price reduction, export subsidies will yield additional foreign exchange only if the price elasticity of foreign demand is greater than one. A selective system of export subsidies

could concentrate on subsidising those exports for which foreign demand elasticities are high and avoid subsidising exports on which foreign exchange losses would be suffered, because elasticities are low. Since a tariff *always* saves foreign exchange, the scope for selecting the best system of tariffs on *other* grounds is greater than the scope for selecting the best system of subsidies. Moreover, even where foreign demand is elastic, the *extent* to which export subsidies can be used to raise foreign exchange earnings depends on the supply elasticities of exports and these are often quite low, at least in the short run, in less developed countries. These considerations tell against the use of export subsidies.

The above arguments for export subsidies have been misinterpreted as arguments for export subsidies as second-best solutions when uniform changes in the exchange rate are ruled out.[1] They are clearly nothing of the kind. It has been shown above that subsidies can yield situations worse than autarky and, since restricted trade is better than no trade at all, subsidised trade must then be worse than restricted trade. All that is shown by the above considerations is that moderate export subsidies may in certain conditions be preferable to restrictions and especially to additional restrictions when trade is already restriction-ridden. Since the respective merits of subsidies and restrictions will depend upon the particular circumstances, no universal rules can be laid down. It follows that it is desirable to review the rules of GATT, the articles of the IMF and the general ban on export subsidies as a weapon in the armoury of international trade policies.

Considering the position of less developed countries, it must be emphasised that export subsidies, though probably a necessary component of foreign trade policy, are certainly not a sufficient condition for raising foreign exchange earnings. Above all, the additional supply must be made available. This implies ensuring the necessary equipment, power and transport. Further, quality improvements, export promotion, the provision of information and a series of other carefully thought-out measures must form part of a 'package', of which any one component, used in isolation, will probably be ineffective or may be harmful. Price reductions will have to be supplemented and complemented by those other measures. But the demand for nontraditional exports is highly price elastic, while there are indications that even the total demand for some of the traditional exports is more elastic than is often assumed.

A fuller analysis would also have to consider the differential impact

[1] Jagdish Bhagwati, *The Theory and Practice of Commercial Policy: Departures from Unified Exchange Rates*. International Finance Section, Princeton University, Special Papers in International Economics, no. 8 (Jan 1969) p. 12.

on industrial and agricultural production, paying attention to differential supply elasticities and infant industry arguments. Protection of manufacturing industry tends to turn the agricultural/industrial terms of trade against agriculture and discriminates against exports. Whereas subsidies align the internal cost structure to the international price structure, tariffs align the internal price structure to the internal cost structure. The higher the degree of protection, the greater the divergence between the internal price ratio of primary to industrial products and the international ratio.[1] This hampers agriculture, exports and ultimately development. The infant industry argument points to subsidies, not protection.

In the light of all this, it is worth giving careful consideration to a system of selected export subsidies to increase foreign exchange earnings and build up export markets. They would have to be frequently reviewed in the light of changing conditions of world demand. They should form an element in a complex of measures directed at improving the balance of payments at minimum cost to domestic living standards and to the development effort.

[1] N. Kaldor, *Essays in Economic Policy* (London, 1965) vol. 2, ch. 19.

Part Three
Projects and Technologies

19 Conflicts between Output and Employment Objectives in Developing Countries[1]

(*with Frances Stewart*)

NEITHER of the objectives, maximum output and maximum employment, is unambiguous. The output objective is ambiguous because output at any time consists of a heterogeneous collection of goods. Types of employment, in duration – daily, weekly, and seasonally – in effort and by regions, etc., also differ. In addition, both output and employment occur over time. Current levels of output and employment may influence future levels. Weighting therefore both intra- and inter-temporally is crucial to the *definition* of the objectives. However, we shall begin by ignoring these ambiguities and assume that our sole concern is with current levels of output and employment, and that maximising current levels automatically leads to achievement of future objectives, or put more formally, that maximising the present value of the entire streams of output and employment over time. We shall also begin by assuming that there is a single index for output and one for employment.

Conflicts resulting from scarce complementary factors of production

We can then rephrase the question and ask: Is maximum current production compatible with maximum employment? On the face of it, the answer seems to be an obvious 'yes'. More men must surely be able to produce more. It is hard to picture conditions in which it is impossible to find anything useful to do for extra hands.

At a given time, with a given stock of capital equipment (inherited

[1] We are grateful to Gavan J. Butler, M. FG. Scott and Professor H. W. Singer for helpful comments.

from the past), the employment of more men on that equipment may, up to a point, increase output, although it could be that, as a result of the reorganisation of the work, of less efficient production methods used, of people standing in one another's way or of a fall in efficiency for some other reason, the extra workers do not add to, and may subtract from, production. However, the choice facing a country is not simply a question of employing additional men with the existing capital stock but of the type of new equipment to install, and in this decision about the nature of new investment there can be a conflict between output and employment. Given that the total funds available for new investment are limited, using the funds for equipment to employ people in one way will inevitably mean *not* using the same funds for some other equipment which may involve *less* employment but might also produce more output. Maximising output involves using scarce resources as efficiently as possible. If capital is the scarce resource, it involves minimising the capital/output ratio. The type of production this requires may be, but need not be, consistent with maximising employment.

Suppose in the textile industry the minimum capital/output ratio is associated with fairly modern-style industry. If £100,000 is available for investment in textiles, if the capital/output ratio is 2·5, and if the capital cost per work place for this type of factory is £1,000 (assuming a given degree of utilisation of capacity), then investing all funds in this modern factory will involve extra employment of 100 and extra output of £40,000. An alternative way of investing the funds might be to introduce handspinning. Suppose for this the capital/output ratio was 5·0 and the cost per work place £100; then the extra output resulting from using the funds for handspinning would be £20,000 and the extra employment generated 1,000. In this case there is a fairly dramatic conflict between employment and output maximisation. It should be noted that this conflict (which is a fairly realistic one if one examines actual figures for costs, etc., in the textile industry)[1] arises because the more labour-intensive method in the sense of the method which uses a lower capital/labour ratio or shows lower cost per work place, actually involves *more capital per*

---

[1] A. S. Bhalla, 'Investment allocation and technological choice – a case of cotton spinning techniques', *Economic Journal* (1964), suggests that the capital/output ratio (including working capital as well as fixed capital) using factory methods in cotton spinning is about three-quarters of that using the hand Ambar Charkha methods. Bhalla's analysis of rice-pounding, 'Choosing techniques: handpounding *v.* machine milling of rice: an Indian case', *Oxford Economic Papers* (Mar 1965), suggests a similar conflict here; the technique which maximises employment (or has the lowest cost per work place), the pestle and mortar, requires nearly twice the capital per unit of value added compared with the large sheller machine. The latter requires investment per work place about 100 times as great as the former.

unit of output than the capital-intensive method. Some theoretical models assume this can never happen. It would be true that it could not, if all techniques of production were invented and developed simultaneously, since the labour-intensive methods which use more capital would never be developed. But in fact methods of production are developed over a historical period with the more labour-intensive methods generally originating from an earlier period. One reason why this sort of situation develops is the existence of economies of scale; as machinery has been adapted for larger-scale production the capital costs in relation to output have tended to fall, so that for large-scale production the later and more capital-intensive methods tend to economise on capital in relation to output. For small-scale production the older machinery may remain efficient.[1]

Implicit in this example is the assumption that there is a specific level of employment associated with each technique, and thus that it is sensible to talk of a 'cost per work place'. In fact, the number of people employed with any given machine may vary. The variation can take the form of using the machine more hours per day, or of employing more workers on the machine, directly or indirectly, at any one time, or reducing the number of hours worked by each worker. Since greater utilisation of machinery and greater employment arising from using machines more hours per day can normally occur with any type of machine, it does not affect the comparison or conflict. If a machine is used at all there is normally some minimum amount of employment required to operate it (e.g. one man to drive a bulldozer). Above this minimum, employment may be variable. For some types of production output levels may be unaffected by the amount of 'free' or variable labour employed. For others output may be increased – normally by speeding up the pace of operations. But there is almost always an upper limit to the output level attainable as more labour is employed. When the machine is working at maximum pace additional workers may reduce the efforts of other employees rather than increase output. So long as output is responding positively to additional workers the level of employment associated with a given machine may depend partly on the level of wages. Even where output is invariant with respect to employment the actual employment associated with given machinery may depend partly on real wages since managerial effort may be substituted for employment as real wages rise. Thus the employment level associated with any given

---

[1] The importance of scale in determining the efficient range of production possibilities is emphasised by many empirical studies, including G. K. Boon, *Economic Choice of Human and Physical Factors in Production* (North-Holland Publishing Co., 1964), and W. P. Strassman, *Technological Change and Economic Development* (Cornell University Press, 1968).

machine may not be independent of the wage rate.[1] In the examples above some wage level is implicitly assumed in associating each machine with a unique output and employment level. A range to represent output and employment at different wage levels would have been a more realistic representation. If one assumes that continuous variations in output are associated with continuous variations in employment, for each machine, but that there is diminishing marginal product as employment is increased, one is back in a neo-classical world where there are variable factor proportions and any amount of capital (or any machine) may be associated with any level of employment. In this neo-classical world the limit to employment is set by the real wages workers demand. There can be no conflict between output and employment because every type of machine can be associated with any amount of employment. Thus if the modern factory methods were employed in spinning, the extra 900 workers could be employed in the factory and would each add to output. At least as much employment and more output could result from choice of the factory alternative. We do not believe that this is a realistic assumption. Though some variation in employment is possible with any given machine, there comes a point at which the machine is operating at its maximum pace, when additional workers do not increase output. There is thus a limited range of employment possibilities associated with each machine, which means that there can be a conflict between output and employment. Put in another way, for *any* positive real wage there comes a point at which it is no longer worth while employing extra workers with a particular machine. This point may be reached at a lower employment level and a higher output level for one machine than for another. In this case there is a conflict between output and employment, which is independent of any institutional or other lower limit on the level of real wages.

Just as some economists assume that such a conflict between output and employment cannot arise, others assume not only that it has arisen in the past, but also that it necessarily must arise. The capital-intensive methods of production, it is claimed, will always involve lower capital costs per unit of output (and higher costs per work place) than the labour intensive methods.[2] This position is as extreme as the

---

[1] What matters is *relative* wages. In a two-factor world, trade union action to prevent a fall in money wages is not an obstacle to wage flexibility. The relative cost of *capital* can be raised so as to encourage the absorption of all workers, were it not for the other difficulties mentioned in the text.

[2] See, for example, N. Kaldor in Ronald Robinson (ed.), *Industrialisation in Developing Countries*, published by the CUP Overseas Studies Committee (1965) pp. 28–9: 'There is no question *from every point of view* of the superiority of the latest and more capitalistic technologies' (our italics). Similar emphasis on the overall superiority of capital-intensive techniques is found in S. Amin, 'Levels of

other. There is considerable evidence that in many industries, and in many processes, the more labour-intensive methods also save capital per unit of output.[1] In these cases maximising current levels of employment and output are consistent. Probably of more significance is the possibility of devoting research and development (R & D) efforts to the labour-intensive methods (in the sense of low capital cost per work place) so that they become efficient as compared with capital-intensive methods. Present possibilities reflect the fact that almost all R & D is concentrated on producing methods suitable for the developed world, in which labour is scarce; the labour-intensive methods currently available are generally the products of earlier and less sophisticated science and technology.

The questions at issue can be illustrated diagrammatically (Fig. 19.1). The neo-classical assumption of substitutability between

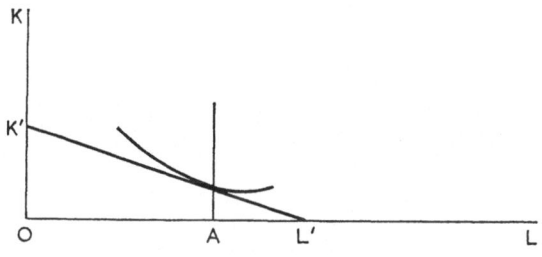

Fig. 19.1

Capital/labour ratios under neoclassical assumptions

capital and labour as represented by the continuous convex isoquant excludes the possibility of a conflict between current levels of output and employment. The relative wage level determines the employment associated with a given output level. With a sufficiently low relative wage level, represented by K′L′, full employment OA may be achieved. Deficiency of employment opportunities is to be attributed to excessive

---

remuneration, factor proportions and income differentials with special reference to developing countries', in *Wage Policy Issues in Economic Development*, ed. A. Smith (Macmillan, 1969) pp. 269–92.

[1] A. S. Bhalla, *Economic Journal* (1964) suggests that the capital/output ratio for traditional spinning methods, as opposed to the Ambar Charkha, may be lower than for factory methods. A. K. Sen, *Choice of Techniques*, Appendix C, suggests that in cotton weaving the capital/output ratio is the lowest for the most labour-intensive technique, the fly-shuttle hand loom, and highest, nearly $2\frac{1}{2}$ times as big, for the automatic power loom (again including working capital). Evidence for the existence of a range of efficient techniques in a number of industries below a certain critical scale of output is also contained in G. K. Boon, op. cit.

relative wages. The neo-classical model is sometimes applied only to new investment decisions – with the assumption that there is limited (or no) substitutability between labour and existing machines (the putty-clay model); and sometimes to all capital including existing machines (putty-putty). Clearly freedom of action and possibilities of achieving desired employment levels are greater with the latter type model; for the former the burden of generating desired employment is entirely on new investment.

The alternative view, which produces the conflict between output and employment described above, is that techniques available are limited and opportunities for labour/capital substitution correspondingly narrow. Production possibilities can be more accurately described by a few points on the diagram, than by a continuous curve; some of these points consist of inferior techniques requiring more of both factors, as in Fig. 19.2. Here a conflict arises between output and

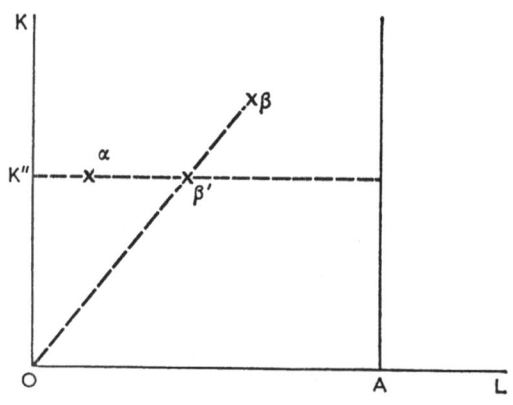

Fig. 19.2

Capital/labour ratios under non-neoclassical assumptions

employment for any given quantity of capital available. Technique α represents the factory alternative; technique β the handspinning alternative. Output is the same at α and β; β' is a smaller amount of technique β, involving less output than α. If α and β are the only techniques available and investment resources are limited to, say, OK'', no level of real wages will bring about full employment OA. However, choice of β will increase employment as compared with α, but for the same investment will mean sacrificing output, as at β'.

In the hypothetical example the hand technique involved 900 additional employees compared with the capital-intensive technique. Apart from simply maximising output, going for the capital-intensive technique and ignoring the employment implications, three possibilities are open. First, there is what we might describe as the Gandhi solution of adopting the hand technique despite halving of output. Second, there is the Nkrumah solution of introducing the modern factories and 'employing' the additional 900 workers in some minor and possibly completely useless capacity in the modern factory. Problems here are first that the extra workers might reduce output as a result of getting in each other's way and diverting administrative personnel (though probably output would not be reduced by as much as if the Gandhi solution were adopted and administrative difficulties might also be less). Secondly, if the modern factories also pay modern (i.e. relatively high) wages, as they generally do, the wage cost may be exorbitant. This has implications for savings and also for the viability of the enterprise if it is in private ownership. The Gandhi solution would probably allow lower wages per head. Thirdly, in a mixed economy it may be impossible to get employers to take on such useless labour. Voluntary agreements to increase employment by as little as 10 per cent have been notoriously short lived. A third solution is to adopt the modern methods and to use some of the extra output to employ the non-employed[1] on public works, etc. The difficulty here is that if any equipment is involved in the public works, employing workers on them will again divert capital equipment from other parts of the economy where the impact on output might have been bigger – in fact we are back at the initial problem.

The dilemma arises from the existence of scarce resources (in the above case capital, but it could have been entrepreneurship, administration or some other input), which all forms of employment require. Sources of employment which do not use scarce resources will not present this dilemma. If, for example, the non-employed can make their own tools from local materials that are not scarce, and if their employment does not require the diversion of scarce administrative personnel, their employment will increase current output.[2] The same is true of employment which makes fuller use of the existing capital equipment, e.g. shift working, though some scarce resources of organisation, administration, skills, etc., are almost always involved.

The aggregate level of organised employment depends not only upon the labour-intensity or capital-intensity of the methods of production adopted, but also on the level of real wages in relation to

[1] We use the expression 'non-employed' to distinguish them from Keynesian 'unemployed'.

[2] It was this type of employment Nurkse was considering in discussing the underemployed as a source of savings, in *Problems of Capital Formation in Underdeveloped Countries* (Blackwell, 1953).

the consumption goods available to meet these real wages. If real wages in organised employment are higher than the levels of consumption of the non-employed, transferring workers from non-employment to organised employment will involve a net increase in consumption. An upper limit to this process is set by the resources available for the transfer. With a given real wage (and a given distribution between wages and other income) the maximum level of employment is determined by the consumption resources available, which depends on the level of output and the proportion of output saved. The labour-intensive alternative may therefore be ruled out, if the total consumption generated by those additionally employed is greater than available consumption resources. If real wages are flexible downwards or if redistribution is possible this problem does not arise.

Reasons for preferring employment to output

If a conflict between maximising current output and employment were inevitable, why should we wish to sacrifice output to employment? Four possible answers occur to us, though others might think of additional reasons. First, employment creation and the consequential wage payments may be the only mechanism by which income can be redistributed to those who would otherwise remain unemployed. With an efficient fiscal system, taxation combined with unemployment relief, free social services, and other forms of assistance to the unemployed could be used as an engine of redistribution. In an underdeveloped society, loyalty to the extended family may induce the employed wage earner to share his wages with his often large extended family. But if neither fiscal system nor family provide a systematic channel of redistribution, job creation may have to be used for this purpose. Production will then be sacrificed for better distribution and, as a means to this, greater employment.

Second, unemployment is demoralising. To feel unwanted, not to be able to make any contribution, lowers a man's morale and makes him lose his self-respect. The preservation of self-respect is worth sacrificing some production. As Barbara Ward has said, 'of all the evils, worklessness is the worst' – clearly not only and even not mainly because and if it lowers national product. It is worth sacrificing production to reduce this evil.

Third, it might be thought that work is intrinsically good, whatever its impact on morale, self-respect and other subjective feelings. The Puritan ethic may command job creation as valuable, irrespective of its contribution to production. Puritanism played a valuable part in making desirable the necessary but unpleasant sacrifices which promoted the Industrial Revolution in Britain. Whether this ethic, where it has been adopted in the developing world (and it is notable that most Puritan-like statements tend to come from expatriates), should be encouraged and where it has not been adopted should be promoted, if it leads to a situation which impedes rather than speeds up growth by requiring the adoption of inefficient techniques to compensate for the masochistic value placed on work, is another question. Other aspects of Puritanism are certainly conducive to development; to the extent that Puritanism is a package deal, this aspect may have to be accepted along with the rest.

Fourth, there are obvious political disadvantages and dangers in widespread unemployment and non-employment. This is an important reason for valuing employment since, in so far as anyone does, it is the politicians who lay down 'the objective function' of society. Political instability resulting from heavy unemployment may, in any case, eventually endanger output levels and growth.

The value placed on employment as such is likely to depend partly on the type of employment. This is not just a question of the pleasantness or unpleasantness of the work, though nobody would value some types of sweated labour. Work which leads to ill health, shortens lives, or breaks spirits may sometimes be a necessary cost of output; it *is* a cost and not a benefit. Besides this aspect the location of work may also be relevant. If it is their failure to deal with the urban unemployment problem that is worrying politicians, urban employment may be valued more than rural. The feeling of worthlessness arising from unemployment is also likely to be more closely tied to long-term urban unemployment than to labour underutilisation in the rural areas, which has a long and respectable history. More rapid expansion of urban employment opportunities may have little impact on the number of urban unemployed in so far as the expansion of employment opportunities adds to the flow of migrants from the rural·areas seeking employment, and hence leaves the visible pool of unemployment unchanged. None the less, it seems likely that the situation would be less explosive if employment opportunities were expanding at, say, 10 per cent per annum, than if they were static, or, as in many countries, actually declining. The desire for employment which is so apparent in many countries cannot be entirely divorced from the desire for higher incomes. Many of those seeking urban employment are looking for work *at the going wages* in the organised industrial sector, where wages are generally considerably higher than incomes obtainable elsewhere. Discussion of the need for rural employment opportunities to reduce the underutilisation of labour normally takes place in the context of the need to create opportunities for increasing incomes through fuller labour utilisation. Again the need is for incomes as much as for work. It is unlikely that the unemployed, or those scratching a living in the rural areas, would be prepared to suffer some loss in *their* incomes for the sake of more work. What is wanted is increased opportunities to work *and* earn higher incomes. Because both work and higher incomes are required it is difficult to disentangle the two. Clearly, the desire for redistribution of income is of prime importance. To achieve this redistribution, employment opportunities may be needed but the sacrifice, or trade-off, involved may be of the income of the better-off for the sake of that of the worse-off, rather than of output for the sake of employment. However, it can be argued that it is not just a question of income redistribution but of providing a chance to *earn*, not simply receive, the higher incomes.

These are the only reasons we can think of as to why the employment objective might conflict with the output objective, and sacrifice of output to employment, *properly defined*, is justified. But what are the proper definitions? As argued in the first paragraph, objectives are ambiguous. Two types of ambiguity are relevant. First, national product consists of a heterogeneous collection of goods, 'of shoes, and ships and sealing wax, of cabbages' (and possibly of the services of kings) and it accrues to different people, in different regions, with varying needs. In putting all these together we must use a system of weighting the different items and different sets of weights may lead to contradictions. One set may give the impression that we are sacrificing product for employment, another may not.

Another ambiguity arises because both production and employment occur in time and stretch into the future. An infinite number of time profiles within any horizon that we care to consider can be drawn up. Any profile for either of our two objectives that lies all the way below another profile of the same objective can be dismissed as inefficient. But in order to choose between those that intersect at some moment of time, we must make additional choices in the light of our policy objectives. What if 5 per cent less employment now gives us 15 per cent more employment in two years' time? What if a rise of 10 per cent in employment now prevents us from employing an additional 5 per cent of a vastly larger labour force in ten years and after? We must turn to the problems of *weighting* and *timing*.

Weighting: distribution

Assume a mini-community produces and consumes whisky and milk. Whisky is drunk by the few rich, milk by the many poor. In the first year national income consists of 2 pints of whisky and 5 pints of milk, in the subsequent year of 1 pint of whisky and 10 pints of milk.

National income is the sum of whisky and milk, weighted not by pints, but by the appropriate prices. But the relative prices registered in the market are partly the result of income distribution. On the demand side, they depend upon the purchasing power of milk- and whisky-drinkers. The relative prices derived from an *unequal* income distribution are (let us say) 100*p*. per pint of whisky and 10*p*. per pint of milk. With these weights, income has *fallen* between the two years from 250*p*. (100*p*. × 2 + 10*p*. × 5 = 250*p*.) to 200*p*. (100*p*. + 10*p*. × 10 = 200*p*.). A *more equal* income distribution, putting more money into the pockets of milk drinkers relative to whisky drinkers, would give weights for whisky of 50*p*. per pint and for milk of 20*p*. per pint (on the assumption of increasing unit costs with increasing output). The income, weighted by these prices, would have *risen* from 200*p*. (50*p*. × 2 + 20*p*. × 5 = 200*p*.) to 250*p*. (50*p*. + 20*p*. × 10 = 250*p*.).

Let us assume that the second year's production results from employing more men which raises the share of wages relative to profits and hence the demand for milk relative to whisky. A national income accountant, using the first set of weights, would register a fall in national income. People interpreting his statistics would say that we have sacrificed income for the sake of higher employment. But from the point of view of someone using the weights appropriate to the more equal distribution that results from greater employment, income is seen to have risen. There is a conflict between production and employment only if we use the wrong set of weights, assuming we prefer the more egalitarian income distribution.

Weighting other than by market prices should be introduced to reflect the different values of bundles of goods purchased by those at different income levels. Since the marginal utility of income is higher for a poor man than for a better-off man, greater weight should be attached to what goes to the poor than what goes to the better-off. Similar differential weighting might be attached to the expenditure of people in poorer regions within a country.

One difficulty in such an approach concerns the question of what weights to use. In the above example it was suggested that the prices emerging from the more equal income distribution should be used; these involved higher prices (and therefore weights) for the low-income good – milk – and lower prices and weights for the high-income good. This was only the case because of increasing costs for both goods. With elastic supply and constant unit costs the relative prices would have remained the same. With decreasing costs the relative price of the low-income good would have declined as incomes became more equal. Thus to use the prices emerging from the more equal income distribution is not sufficient to deal with the problem of including the value attributed to income distribution in the measure of income. This may be so even in the case of increasing costs, when the resultant change in prices may not be enough to allow for one's judgement about the distributional implications of the change. The weights attached to the different goods need therefore have no relationship to the pattern of prices that might emerge with the desired income distribution.

Attaching different weights to different goods (e.g. milk and whisky) according to who consumes them is effective as a means of incorporating judgements about the income distribution only if the pattern of consumption differs among consumers of different income levels. At one extreme if all consumers consumed only one good, say maize, and differed only in the amount of that good they consumed, the value attributed to output would not be affected by the distribution of income whatever the weight given to the single good. In this case maize itself must be weighted or valued differently according to who consumes it. This is an unrealistic extreme. But there are many goods that are consumed at all income levels. So long as the pattern (i.e. proportion of income spent on different goods) of consumption differs according to income level a revised weighting system can, in theory, incorporate distributional judgements. Its calculation would be highly complicated, and would change over time as patterns of consumption changed.

An alternative is to attach weights to the income, according to the level of income of the recipient, rather than to goods; this is broadly the system adopted by Marglin[1] where the value attributed to the demand for any good is weighted more heavily the poorer the consumer. For judgements about macro-income changes this approach has much to recommend it in terms of simplicity. It does not, however, rule out ambiguity in real output changes consequent upon changes in relative prices. With such a system 'income' would be increased simply by improving the distribution of income without any change in the output of goods and services.

Weighting according to the value of expenditure to the individuals and groups who benefit from it raises certain philosophical problems. One may not wish to define 'income' and 'growth of income' in such a way as to incorporate all distributional value judgements in the definitions, so that no conflict could ever arise between 'income', its distribution and employment. A narrower definition is useful, in order to bring out the choices. On the other hand, so long as the conventional definitions are accepted and countries placed in league tables according to them, the arbitrary nature of national income

[1] S. A. Marglin, *Public Investment Criteria* (London: George Allen & Unwin, 1967).

measurement tends to be forgotten and virtue gets associated with movements in this arbitrary figure. Policies as well as value judgements may be influenced by the form of measurement adopted. There is much to be said, therefore, for even a crude and arbitrary adjustment in the direction of incorporating judgements about income distribution.

Weighting: time

Another serious ambiguity arises from the fact that sacrifices now may yield gains in the future. We must consider two opposite sets of circumstances: first, where less production and more employment now leads to more production later than would otherwise have been possible; second, where less employment and more production now lead to more employment later than would otherwise have been possible.

In order to illustrate the first case, let us return to the situation where men were demoralised by unemployment. We then regarded self-respect and high morale as ends in themselves. But we may also regard them as necessary for the continued employability of men. If men remain unemployed for long, their skills as well as their attitudes deteriorate and they are incapable of producing as much later. This situation cannot be remedied by unemployment assistance, for it is only on the job that ability to work and motivation are maintained. Just as machines sometimes have to be kept going in order to prevent attrition or rust, so workers and teams of workers have to be kept busy to prevent them from becoming rusty or apathetic. Current employment, even where there is nothing to show for it, can be regarded as a form of investment – human maintenance – which prevents future deterioration of productivity. In addition men's productive capacity, their ability to work, their initiative and organisational ability, and their concentration may not merely be maintained but may actually be increased by working. This form of learning by working means that the greater current employment opportunities, the greater is future productive capacity.

The second case works in the opposite direction and is possibly the most important way in which an apparent conflict between employment and output arises. Here we maximise production in the short run, even though it means tolerating more non-employed now, because the extra production enables us to generate more jobs later than would otherwise have been possible. If there is a current conflict between output and employment, it must be remembered that output is useful not only for itself, but can be used to generate more employment.

The inter-temporal 'trade-off' between employment now and employment tomorrow arises because, by tolerating more unemployment now for the sake of producing more, we can provide the men (and their children) with more jobs later. This is only partly a matter of investment, i.e. producing now the machines, or resources with which to buy the machines, that will give jobs tomorrow. A greater volume of food which provides better nutrition for the workers and their children, of health measures and of certain forms of education can also contribute to greater employment (and fuller labour utilisation) in the future. The point leads once again to income distribution, but this time not valued independently as desirable, but as instrumental to faster growth. The choice between maximum employment and maximum output reduces to one between jobs now or later, because more output now can promote more, and more effective, employment in the future. To raise employment means sacrificing not only output now (and, on our assumption, the rate of growth of output) but also the rate of growth of employment. This means that at some future date the level of employment will be lower than it would otherwise have been. To go back to the example discussed earlier, suppose in each case, modern factory and hand-spinning-wheel, 20 per cent of income generated is saved. The factory solution will involve £8,000 investment available in the next year, while the hand-wheel alternative will involve £4,000. The divergence will get greater in subsequent years. The factory alternative will lead to an annual growth in income (and assuming the same £1,000 a work place technology is adopted, in employment) of 8 per cent per annum while the handspinning-wheel alternative will lead to 4 per cent annual growth in output and employment. (This ignores the impact of extra consumption on growth.) Fig. 19.3 illustrates the possibilities.

The choice now presents itself as one between different time paths of output and employment. It is thus partly a question of our time preference towards both output and employment: i.e. the basis on which we should make our choice for given possible time paths, as the one illustrated in Fig. 19.3. But the situation is somewhat more complicated than this because there are other ways in which current choices of output and employment levels may affect the future pattern of both.

As to the right choices, a good deal will depend upon our time horizon and on uncertain future developments. As far as employment is concerned, the life span of one generation and perhaps its children will be relevant, but few would be prepared to tolerate widespread unemployment over two generations to improve the job prospects of their great-grandchildren. This is not only because we show less

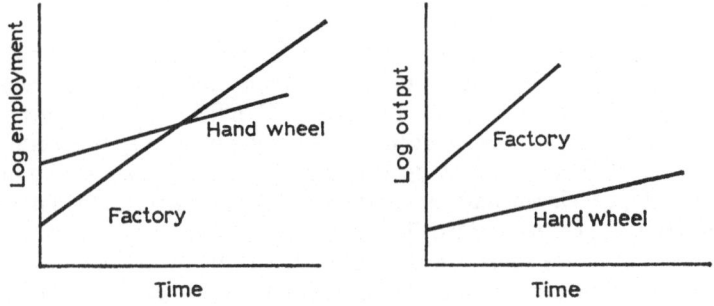

Fig. 19.3

Growth rates of employment and output

concern for our great-grandchildren, but also because we may rightly hope that their prospects will improve for other reasons, such as the development of more appropriate technologies, improvements in motivation, administration, education, etc. Within such a time horizon we might argue that, on the one hand, the richer society of tomorrow can look better after its unemployed and to be unemployed then will be a smaller hardship. On the other hand, with present trends of growth of the labour force in less developed countries and likely opportunities for jobs, the total number of unemployed is increasing rapidly. While the lot of a given number of unemployed will therefore be better in the future and the burden of maintaining them lighter, the number to be looked after will be larger. In the more distant future, however, we may assume that population control will have become effective or new scope for migration will have opened up. In view of all this, it seems right to discount future jobs and to give more weight to more jobs now and in the near future.

But, though the discount rate that we should apply to employment should be positive, it may be less than the one we apply to output or to consumption. The main argument for applying a discount rate to output is that the marginal utility of income is less for a richer society. This does not apply in the same way to employment – i.e. the value of extra employment generated does not decline as the level increases – though increasing *incomes* per head may make employment in the future less important as a means of income redistribution. On the other hand, the contrasts between those employed and those not employed and the accompanying resentment may work the other way. Poverty in the midst of affluence is worse than plain poverty widely shared. This, and the question of numbers, suggests that it may be correct to give greater relative weight to future as against current employment than to future as against current output.

Planners must know not only their preferences between the present and the future, for both output and employment, but also what opportunities there are for trade-offs. Conflicts between current levels and growth rates of output and employment may arise either because growth rates are determined by savings rates (or, more generally, developmental expenditure rates), savings rates by income distribution and income distribution by employment levels, or because growth rates are determined by the allocation of a given savings ratio between sectors and this allocation influences the level and growth of employment.

It is common to assume in this context that a capital-intensive technique leads to a higher savings ratio for the same income level than a labour-intensive technique. On this assumption, lower employment now can give faster growth of both output and employment. Those who make this assumption[1] assume

(a) that a higher proportion of profits is saved than of wages (at its most extreme the assumption is that all profits are saved, all wages consumed); and that consumption makes no contribution to future growth;
(b) that wage rates do not depend on techniques;
(c) that the Government is incapable of securing the savings ratio it desires by taxing wage earners and generating adequate public savings or using inflation to reduce real wages.

Since the growth rate is the product of the savings ratio and the output/capital ratio, the effect on the growth rate of raising the savings ratio by increasing the capital-intensity of technique adopted will depend on the consequences for the output/capital ratio. Fig. 19.4 illustrates the implications for growth of neo-classical assumptions as the capital-intensity of techniques is increased. With such a production function the most labour-intensive technique maximises current employment, for any given capital expenditure. On the diagram, as one approaches the origin, labour requirements per unit of output rise while capital requirements fall. Techniques to the left of h involve negative savings and are therefore unlikely to be feasible. But for any given capital-intensity of techniques and in the absence of technical progress (or in the presence of neutral technical progress) the growth of employment is determined by the growth of output.

[1] For example, A. K. Sen, op. cit., and I. M. D. Little and J. Mirrlees, *Manual of Industrial Project Analysis in Developing Countries*, vol. ii, p. 42, Development Centre of the OECD (Paris, 1969).

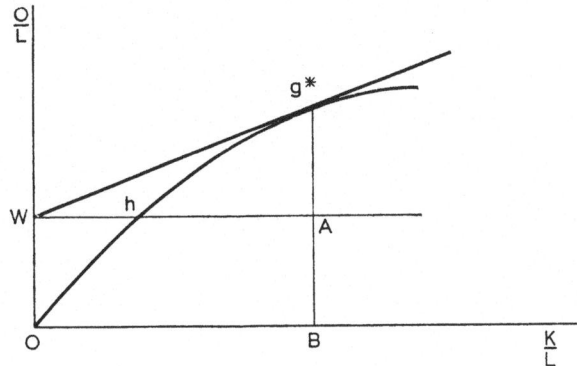

Fig. 19.4

Conflicts between employment (output) and growth of employment (growth of output) under neoclassical assumptions

Assuming all wages are consumed and all profits saved, the technique which maximises the growth of output (and also employment) will depend on the wage level. With wages per employee OW, which do not vary according to the technique adopted, the growth rate (s/v) is represented by the slope of the line from W to the production function.[1] This is maximised when it is tangential to the production function as at g* in the diagram. Here there is a conflict between maximising current employment (which involves choosing the technique nearest to the origin for a given capital stock) and maximising the growth of output and employment at g*. However, there is no conflict between maximising the growth of employment and output, both of which involve the same technique. The conflict between current employment and the growth of employment worsens as the wage level increases, as illustrated in Fig. 19.5. As the wage increases from OW^1 to OW^2, the capital-intensity of the technique which maximises the growth of output and employment increases (increasing the conflict between current and future employment), while the maximum attainable growth rate declines. If we drop the neo-classical assumption of rising capital/output ratio as the capital-intensity of techniques increases, the most capital-intensive technique available maximises the growth rate, irrespective of the wage rate.

[1] $s = \dfrac{g^*A}{g^*B}$, where all wages are consumed, all profits saved.

$$v = \frac{OB}{g^*B}.$$

$$\frac{s}{v} = \frac{g^*A}{g^*B} \div \frac{OB}{g^*B} = \frac{g^*A}{OB} = \frac{g^*A}{WA} = \text{slope of line from } W \text{ to the production function.}$$

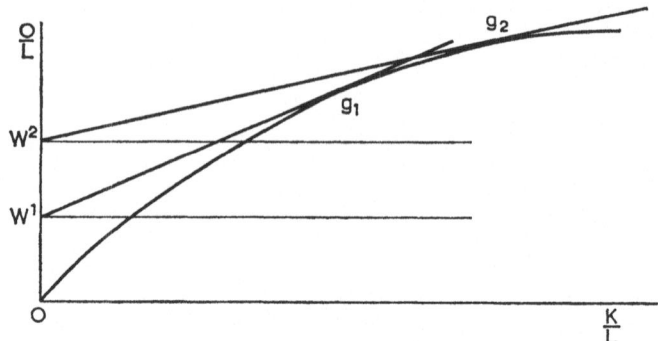

Fig. 19.5

Conflicts between employment and growth of employment with
rising wages

Additional employment of the kind discussed earlier which is costless in terms of present output since it does not require any scarce
resources as additional inputs – neither capital nor administration
nor skilled manpower – may impede growth on these assumptions
because the extra consumption of those additionally employed will
reduce society's propensity to save.

If the rate at which we discount future output is higher than that at
which we discount future employment (an assumption which we
argued was reasonable), we get the perverse situation that a strategy
of optimum employment growth might require greater current
unemployment than a strategy aiming at optimum income growth.
The former would involve more capital-intensive techniques, higher
savings rates, and greater income growth.[1]

The assumptions of this model are questionable: first, there is
evidence[2] that the wage rate is linked to labour productivity and the
choice of technique, so that the more labour-intensive methods

[1] For a precise formulation, we would have to know not only the two rates of
time discount, but also the preferences between employment and output. A lower
rate of time discount for employment than for output might be offset by a lower
preference for employment. The values of the respective discounted streams would
have to be traced on an indifference map.

[2] There is considerable evidence that wages are related to the scale of the enterprise, while the smaller the enterprise the more labour-intensive (in terms of
capital per worker) the technique tends to be. See, for example, E. N. Dhar and
H. F. Lydall, *The Role of Small Enterprises in Indian Economic Growth* (Delhi:
Asia Publishing House, 1961); M. C. Shetty, *Small-scale and Household Industries
in a Developing Economy* (Asia Publishing House, 1963); Saburo Okita, 'Choice
of techniques: Japan's experience and its implication', in *Economic Development
with Special Reference to East Asia*, ed. K. Berrill (Macmillan, 1964).

involve lower wages per man than the more capital-intensive ones. Secondly, all profits are not saved and it may not even be warranted to assume that a higher proportion of profits is saved than of other incomes. Profits remitted and retained overseas, even if saved, will not add to the investible resources of the developing economy. Thirdly, there is the rather asymmetrical assumption that the Government is incapable of enforcing the saving it desires by wages or taxation policy, but is capable of enforcing it through choice of technique, despite the fact that this choice, in a mixed economy, is not directly in its hands in many cases, and involves, if made effective, a lower level of employment. The sacrifice of employment, in this case, is not so much a sacrifice for the sake of future levels of output and employment, but more a sacrifice on the altar of government inability to pursue effective taxation policies.

So far we have focused on the aggregate savings ratio. If it is determined by the distribution of income between wages and profits and if this distribution in turn is determined by the level of employment, a conflict may arise between maximising current employment and maximising the growth of employment and income.

Now let us consider the case where a given ratio of savings to income can be invested in either of two sectors:[1] one making capital goods that make capital goods (machine tools), the other making capital goods that make consumer goods (looms). The higher the proportion allocated to the machine tool sector, the faster the rate of growth of total output and the higher consumption at some point in the future and after, though the lower the initial increase in consumption. Assuming employment requirements, in relation to investment, are the same in both sectors, maximum *current* and *future* employment will be achieved by maximising the proportion of investment allocated to the machine tool sector. This choice also maximises current and future levels of *output*, but involves the lowest initial increase in consumption, though eventually consumption will be highest with this path. Hence there is no conflict between output and employment, but there may well be conflicts between consumption objectives and employment. If the labour requirements of the machine tool sector are lower than those of the loom sector, a conflict between employment (and current consumption) and growth arises. The proportion allocated to each sector which is optimal from the point of view of income and consumption growth may conflict with the ratio which is optimal from the point of view of employment growth. It should be noted that this two-sector model implicitly assumes that over a period of time the Government is able to enforce

[1] This is the Feldman model as described by E. Domar, *Essays in the Theory of Economic Growth*, ch. ix, 'A Soviet Model of Growth'.

any savings ratio it likes, and equally any level of real wages per head of the employed. The only limitation on the savings ratio is the productive capacity of the machine sector and not the propensity to save and consume. This is in complete contrast to the earlier model where the Government was explicitly assumed incapable of enforcing the savings ratio or real wages per employee that it considered desirable by any of the usual means, and the choice of technique therefore also assumed the role of determinant of the savings ratio. If the same assumption is made for the two-sector model it alters the nature of the choices available since employment can then never rise faster than the output of consumption goods and thus the main source of possible conflict is removed.

This type of two-sector model has been criticised for rigidity of assumptions – particularly the assumption that the capacity of the 'machine tool' industry limits the investment possible, which denies the possibility of expanding investment by increasing imports of machinery. However, the model is more generally applicable than that; it applies to any sector which is holding back development, and which could be expanded by devoting sufficient resources to it. Resources devoted to the bottleneck sector will increase the rate of growth of the whole economy, and ultimately of *all* sectors of the economy at the temporary cost of the development of those sectors from which resources are diverted. Thus conflicts in timing emerge; they may be relevant to the employment question, as suggested above.

Technical developments

Until now we have assumed that the technical choices available remain unchanged, and that output and employment grow at the same rate if a technique of particular capital-intensity is adopted and adhered to over time. In practice the technical possibilities available change over time. Generally technical progress takes a form which involves increasing labour productivity, so that the rate of growth of employment is less than the rate of growth of output. This phenomenon – output increasing faster than employment – has been observed in many developing countries. The increase in labour productivity is partly a question of improved management techniques and greater labour efficiency as a result of learning by doing and the spread of education. In this respect it is probably unrelated to the rate or type of investment (it could be classified as 'disembodied technical progress') and therefore does not affect the choice of technique or the basic comparison between techniques: the technique which maximises the rate of growth of output will also maximise the rate of growth of employment, though the latter will be lower than the former.

But the increase in labour productivity is also partly due to the installation of new machines (both as net additions to the capital stock and as replacements of old machinery). Technical developments which take the form of new machines and new products may affect the terms of conflict between output and employment. Such developments are likely to affect some techniques more than others. In particular, research, development, and use of techniques in developed countries are virtually confined to techniques of high and *increasing* capital-intensity. For these techniques, labour productivity, and often capital productivity as well, may rise over time, while the more labour-intensive techniques may be unaffected by technical progress. The labour-intensive techniques may therefore become inferior over time and their use may then involve a sacrifice of output as compared with the use of the later, more capital-intensive techniques.

The earlier arguments of this paper might suggest choosing the later more capital-intensive techniques where they result in more output and therefore savings than the labour-intensive techniques on the grounds of maximising future employment as well as current and future output. (Indeed, if we assume savings are inversely related to employment, for any given output, the more capital-intensive techniques may maximise the rate of growth of employment even where they result in no greater output than the labour-intensive methods.) It might therefore appear that, from the point of view of long-run employment, it would be correct to adopt the output growth maximising tactic of adopting techniques of successively greater capital-intensity which are developed as time proceeds. But the increasing capital-intensity (defined in terms of capital requirements per worker) means that a given amount of savings generates progressively fewer jobs. If the proportionate increase in the savings available for investment as a result of moving to techniques of greater capital-intensity, which lead to higher output and savings, is less than the increase in capital requirements per worker, then the growth in employment will be *less* with the output-maximising technique than if the older, more labour-intensive techniques, leading to lower output, were adhered to.[1] In an extreme case, the adoption of successively more capital-intensive techniques, if applied to replacement as well as net investment, might lead to a fall in employment despite rapid and

[1] For the employment generated by new investment is the product of labour per unit of capital invested multiplied by investment

$$\left(L = \frac{L}{I} \cdot I\right).$$

accelerating output growth. In such situations it makes sense to talk of a conflict between output and employment.

There is a paradox here. The later, more capital-intensive techniques, it is postulated, are more efficient (i.e. lead to higher output) and therefore generate more savings. This means that if chosen they would allow greater employment at a subsequent date than the earlier labour-intensive techniques, for any comparable type of employment in terms of capital cost per work place. (E.g. more public-works-type employment would be possible because the savings required to finance such works would be greater.) If our concern is with to-morrow's employment as much as today's we should choose the more capital-intensive technique which will allow potentially more employment tomorrow. But when tomorrow comes the development of techniques extends the choice to yet more capital-intensive techniques. If chosen, these will lead to lower employment levels than if the now inferior techniques previously chosen continue to be adopted. On the grounds of maximising the surplus available for future employment, the more capital-intensive techniques should again be chosen. This may continue indefinitely. Choice of the later more capital-intensive technique is always justified on grounds of output maximisation and future potential employment. But this leads to a persistently lower level of employment than would occur if the capital intensity of methods adopted did not rise continually. The potentially greater employment will be realised in actual employment levels only when this argument is rejected and the accumulated savings or some of them are used for less capital-intensive employment. When they are so used, there will be a sacrifice of output for employment.[1]

[1] (1) ... $L = L/K.K$, or K/c,
        where L = employment;
            K = capital stock;
            c = capital per man.

(2) ... $DL = DL/DK.DK$ or DK/c^*,
        where $c^* = DK/DL$, or additional capital in relation to additional
            employment.

(3) ... Rate of growth of employment, $DL/L = DK/K \div c^*/c$.

(4) ... $DK = I = sY$,
        where s is average propensity to save; I = net investment;
        Y = output.
        $K = vY$,
        where v = average capital/output ratio.
    Therefore $DK/K = s/v$.

(5) Therefore, in (3), $DL/L = s/v \div c^*/c$.

In the absence of technical developments, assuming a single technique is chosen and adhered to over time, then v^* (marginal capital/output ratio) = v; and $c^* = c$; $DL/L = s/v = DY/Y$; whatever maximises growth of output maximises growth of employment.   (*footnote continued*)

The application of this argument can be exaggerated. Only in special circumstances will the use of successively more capital-intensive techniques actually involve a fall in employment. In many cases their use may still maximise the rate of growth of employment. Observations[1] of the relationship between the growth of output, employment and labour productivity over a large number of countries suggest that generally there is a positive association between the growth of output, employment and labour productivity. The path which maximises the growth of output will also maximise the growth of employment but the output growth will be greater than the employment growth.

Greater use of labour-intensive techniques may also bring about various improvements in their costs and performance, including a fall in their cost simply as a result of economies of scale in their production. Labour-intensive techniques may be easier to produce in the developing countries, because they are often of simpler design and more (in number) are required in a particular country so that some of the economies of scale may be exploited. Current relative costs and efficiency of different techniques may therefore fail to reflect potential relative costs after technical progress through use has been

---

Now assume technical developments such that each year new techniques involve a reduction in v, and a rise in c. (Developing countries may ignore, if possible, those developments that involve a rise in v, or constant v, assuming s is unaffected by changes in v.) This means that if the new techniques are adopted each year, growth of output accelerates since v continuously falls and we are assuming s constant. The change in employment is given by formula (5). This will be greater or less than the change in employment achieved by adhering to the old technique according to whether,

(6) ... $s'/v' \gtrless s''/v'' \div c^*/c,$

where s', v' is average propensity to save and capital/output ratio of old technique, s'', v'' of new technique.

Since, by assumption, $s' = s''$, (6) may rewritten,

(7) ... $v''/v' \gtrless c/c^*$. Adhering to the old technique will thus involve greater employment than *continuous* switching to new techniques according as the decline in capital requirements per unit of output (on average) is less than the increase in capital intensity represented by c^*/c. However, if one switches to the new technique and *then sticks to it*, employment growth and level will ultimately be greater with the new technique than the old. If $v'' = v'$, $c^* > c$, then employment is less with switching while output is no greater. This, very broadly, appears to be what has happened in some countries. The analysis above is complicated if the new techniques affect the propensity to save, s, because, for example, they lead to reduced labour requirements per unit of output, and hence possibly a reduced wage bill. Then the initial formulation (6) applies, $s'' > s'$, and with constant or even rising v, output growth may be greater with the new technique than the old.

[1] See 'Wages and Employment', C. St. J. Oherlihy, ILO contribution to the Meeting of Directors of Development Training and Research Institutes, July 1970 (mimeo), Table 2 and Chart II.

realised. They may also fail to take into account the differing possibilities for local production and repair of the different techniques. This means that current possibilities may understate the likely implications for output of labour-intensive techniques; the conflict between employment and output may therefore be less in reality than at first appears.

The product-mix

So far we have assumed the composition of consumption goods to be determined and have varied only the techniques of producing them and the allocation of investment between sectors. If different consumption goods require different proportions of labour and capital, we can raise the level of employment without varying the techniques of producing any product by enlarging the share of labour-intensive products at the expense of capital-intensive products. If there are opportunities for international trade on favourable terms, this is an obvious solution. If, however, a changing composition involves changing the products consumed at home, the question is whether, with a proper system of weighting, losses in consumers' welfare would arise. If the labour-intensive products are also those largely demanded by the poor, we have already seen that a fall in output may be an optical illusion and that the weights derived from a more equal income distribution might show a rise. There may also be external diseconomies of consumption, or buying as a result of created wants or of habits. If a product is wanted (1) because others buy it or (2) because it was bought in the past or (3) wants are created through advertising, and if these features are peculiar to the capital-intensive product, its elimination may lead to smaller welfare losses (in cases 2 and 3 after a time) than the expenditure values would indicate or it may lead to welfare gains.

The scope for changing the consumers' product-mix in a labour-intensive direction is generally considered somewhat limited, apart from possibilities of international trade, by the need for a reasonable balance in the composition of demand. We cannot expect people to consume all food and no clothes, for example, or to have more haircuts at the expense of bicycles. But the conclusions drawn from this, in terms of the narrow scope for product substitution, arise partly from a mistaken definition of product. Any given need may be fulfilled by a number of different products: nylon or cotton shirts fulfil the need for clothing, wooden houses, mud huts, reinforced concrete multi-storey buildings fulfil the need for shelter. While maintaining a reasonable balance in terms of needs (clothing, housing, shelter, etc.), there is considerable scope for substitution towards more labour-intensive products for the fulfilment of each need. The possibilities of concentrating more on labour-intensive products to fulfil each need may therefore extend the scope for using the product-mix to increase employment opportunities.

Conclusion

On examination the possible conflicts between output and employment objectives appear more complex than might be supposed from the increasingly fashionable assertion that 'we must sacrifice output to employment'. The measure of output is itself ambiguous, depending on the weighting attributed to different components of output. Not only current but also future employment levels as well as output must be taken into account. In many cases higher current output levels, and lower employment levels, may lead to higher future levels of employment as well as output. The potential conflict between output and employment is thus likely to be a question of different preferences for an entire time profile of output and employment, with the preferred output path being associated with a rejected employment path. It is unlikely that this conflict could be accurately described as a desire to sacrifice output for employment or vice versa. It is a more complex question of, for example, the weight given to current as against future output being greater than that given to current as against future employment. The terms of a potential conflict of this kind may also be alterable by a shift in the pattern of R and D leading to a shift in the alternatives available; greater government control over the savings potential of the economy would also alter the pattern of conflict.

In this chapter we have been concerned to illuminate the conditions under which it is meaningful to talk of a conflict between employment and output. The conclusion we reach is that, in many cases, the path which maximises the growth in output is also that which maximises the growth of employment. This might appear to be in strong contrast to the general dissatisfaction currently felt with recent developments in the developing countries, where, it is often argued, output growth has been taken as the overriding objective irrespective of the unfortunate consequences for employment. To some extent (in many Asian countries) recent experience bears out our theoretical contention, that output growth and employment growth are not in conflict as objectives. The dissatisfaction felt appears to have its origin in the unsatisfactory rate of employment creation, in relation to the desire and need for employment, rather than in some sacrifice that has taken place of employment for output. But elsewhere (parts of Latin America, the West Indies, and Africa) it appears that rapid rates of growth of output have been realised with minimal or no increases in employment. Here the increasing capital-intensity of production may have more than offset the additional resources available for investment in their effects on employment creation. In addition the potential savings available from the higher levels of output were not always channelled into investment, as a result of rising real wages, and repatriation of foreign owned profits. The simple model used earlier in the paper (pp. 334 ff.) assumes that savings are a function of the level of output; in reality who gets the output and how and where it is spent is also of importance. Dissatisfaction with performance in these and other economies is also a reflection of dissatisfaction with the distribution of income, and the meaningfulness therefore, of conventional measures of income and income growth.

20 The Little–Mirrlees Method and Project Appraisal

(*with Frances Stewart*)

Economic welfare is a subject in which rigour and refinement is probably worse than useless. Rough theory, or good common sense, is, in practice, what we require. It is satisfying, and impressive, that a rigorous logical system, with some apparent reality, should have been set up in the field of social sciences: but we must not let ourselves be so impressed, that we forget that its reality is obviously limited; and that the degree of such reality is a matter of judgement and opinion. (Concluding sentences in I. M. D. Little, *A Critique of Welfare Economics*, Oxford: Clarendon Press, 1950.)

... for the man of education will seek exactness so far in each subject as the nature of the thing admits ... (Aristotle, *Nicomachean Ethics*, 1094b).

IT IS not uncommon in the history of positive and normative economic doctrine for a new law or a new rule to be announced which is interesting and appears to reveal something important. Under the impact of criticisms (including self-criticisms), the law or the rule is qualified, refined, redefined and reformulated until it becomes a tautology. The original, non-tautological proposition is now seen to be false, though illuminating; the reformulated, redefined, qualified proposition to be true, though tautological. Yet, the proposition and others derived from it survive because they draw strength from swinging in an indeterminate manner between falsehood and tautology. In the area of positive economics, the assumption of profit maximisation, the equation of marginal revenue to marginal cost, and the theories of the firm derived from these premises, may serve as illustrations. In optimising theory the L–M (Little–Mirrlees) method of project appraisal in some respects resembles this procedure. When it has 'body' and substance, when it is applicable and practical, it is open to certain objections, most of them seen by the authors themselves. When it is provisos, 'footnotes' and qualifications, it tends to retreat into tautology.[1]

The paradigm, to which L–M methods[2] apply perfectly, is a project which has its impact on international trade and local labour, but does not affect production elsewhere in the economy. The impact of such a project may then be assessed in terms of extra imports or reduced exports (for the direct inputs of the project and extra consumption of those directly employed) and additional exports or reduced imports (output) caused directly and indirectly by the project. The position is complicated by the introduction of non-tradables, but so long as constant returns prevail, their cost may, by a process of iteration, be translated into international prices. In such a case the application of L–M methods requires prediction of shadow wage rates, the Accounting Rate of Interest (ARI) and international prices. Infinite elasticities are not necessary but *ascertainability* is and anything less than perfect elasticities destroys the neat distinction between tradables and non-tradables since whether a good is traded or not will not then be independent of production decisions, depending only on transport costs, but will also depend on the quantities concerned. There is room for disagreement about the values to be attributed to the shadow wage rate (as, for example, in the discussion below) and the ARI – but this is not disagreement about the principles of the method but the judgements to be embodied in that method. The free trade zones to be found in some countries, like Taiwan, Mexico or the Irish Republic, most nearly resemble the above paradigm. The claim made, in applying such methods more widely, is that the paradigm also applies on a wide – possibly universal – scale; i.e. that for traded goods (which are defined to include all goods that 'would be traded' given 'optimal' trade policies) the impact of a project is on trade and not on domestic activities; for non-traded goods constant returns prevail and the impact may also be ultimately split into the effect on labour and on international trade.

Those who feel that L–M methods do not contain the whole answer to project selection and development do so because they believe the paradigm does not universally (or even in most cases) apply. The L–M methods may themselves be stretched to cover some (possibly

[1] For another example, viz. theories of stages of growth, see Gunnar Myrdal, *Asian Drama*, vol. III, appendix 2 p. 1855.
[2] *Manual of Industrial Project Analysis in Developing Countries*, vol. II by Ian M. D. Little and James A. Mirrlees (Development Centre of OECD, Paris, 1969).

all) of the exceptions; in practice, as the Manual is written and applied, it is unlikely that they will be so interpreted. The controversy is as much about *balance* as about Right or Wrong. For this reason L–M may almost always answer their critics by pointing to the small print. Much of the criticism would be met by a different balance and emphasis in a second edition.

Domestic activities

The main way in which it is felt that the paradigm does not apply is that many projects affect local activities, and not international trade only. Consequently their impact on local activities must also be assessed. Local activities will also be affected:

(a) if the consumption of the extra workers induces additional local production of consumer goods (multiplier);

(b) if the project uses additional amounts of locally produced inputs whose supply increases (backward linkage);

(c) if the output of the project stimulates further local processing, or alters the terms on which further industries receive inputs (forward linkage);

(d) if the project induces additional production locally of some complementary good (horizontal linkage);

(e) if the project eliminates or prevents local production of some competing good (anti-linkage);

(f) if the project alters the pattern of consumption (tastes);

(g) if the project provides training for peasants, workers or managers, who subsequently move elsewhere, and leads to wider managerial, administrative or technological diffusions, etc. (externalities).

Most of these possibilities are excluded if one assumes full capacity operation throughout the economy and an unchanging tariff structure. If capacity is fully used, local production cannot increase, so that (a), (b), (c) and (d) above are eliminated in the short run, though linkages may operate in the long run through induced investment, economies of scale or increased specialisation. Production can decrease, so that (e) remains a possibility. However, low capacity utilisation is a well-established phenomenon in many developing countries.[1] The Manual adopts the assumption of full capacity. 'It,

[1] Almost all the evidence suggests substantial industrial excess capacity in developing countries. Some industries show rates of capacity utilisation of 50 per cent and below, while rates between 60 and 80 per cent are common, where the rate is defined as percentage use of *customary* number of shifts. If 2 or 3 shift use is taken as the standard of comparison, a very large number of industries fall below 50 per cent, not only in highly controlled economies. Some evidence is

therefore, appears, that the only reasonable assumption to make is that the economy will operate without more than occasional lapses from full capacity working: for obviously this is the only efficient way of working' (p. 90).[1] With indivisibilities it is not obvious that this is the only efficient way of working; and in view of the absence of full capacity operation for prolonged periods in many developed countries, as well as almost all developing countries, the full capacity assumption is quite unrealistic. Absence of full capacity utilisation does not mean that all industries could costlessly expand in response to an injection of Keynesian demand. With the many imbalances present in developing countries an increase in effective demand would very rapidly run into bottlenecks of various types, and an overflow into imports and/or inflation might be unavoidable, with any *generalised* increase in demand. But increases in demand directed at particular industries of the kind that a project may generate, for example for inputs, will often meet a positive supply response. The factors responsible for excess capacity may (though many would question that this was the whole story) be irrational and inefficient in Manual terms, and might even, given determined and longlasting pursuance of what the Manual describes as 'rational' policies, eventually be eliminated. But, whatever the eventual outcome, we start in an irrational and inefficient world and project evaluation must take *prevailing* conditions into account, including excess capacity, if it is accurately to portray current opportunity costs.

Many industrial products are *de facto* non-traded (i.e. neither imported nor exported) given the large band between import and export prices due to transport costs, tariff protection and non-tariff

---

summarised in I. Little, T. Scitovsky and M. Scott, *Industry and Trade in Some Developing Countries* (OUP 1970) ch. 3. They conclude that the figures show a 'lower average utilisation of productive capacity in the developing than the developed countries'. Further evidence is provided in G. C. Winston, 'Capacity Utilisation in Economic Development', *Economic Journal* (Mar 1971) and *Industrialisation and Productivity*, Bulletin no. 15; National Council of Applied Economic Research, *Underutilisation of Industrial Capacity* (New Delhi, Oct 1966); and for Algeria, H. Joshi, *The Use of the Little–Mirrlees Method of Project Evaluation for Developing Countries:* an Algerian Case Study (B.Litt. Thesis, Oxford, 1970); for Taiwan and Indonesia see *Economic Survey of Asia and the Far East* (ECAFE, 1969). The ECLA Report, *Basic Equipment in Brazil* (UN, 1963), calculates ratios of demand to capacity in the capital goods industries. For two products among the heavy engineering products demand was estimated to exceed supply, in one case substantially. For the other six products capacity utilisation was below 50 per cent.

[1] To make an assumption about an aspect of government policy which is of critical importance to the method on the ground that it is believed to be the 'only efficient' one, displays a certain naïvety in the light of the history of economic policy in developed and developing countries. But see below, pp. 359–60.

trade barriers. If a project affects the demand for the products of such industries, for any of the reasons described above, then it is not international trade[1] but local production and/or prices which are changed. Such changes in local production/prices may affect other local producers or consumers by altering the terms (in price and/or quantity) on which they receive the goods and hence induce changes in their production. With quantitative import restrictions a project may alter the terms on which other local consumers receive the product even given the assumption of inelastic local production since an increase in demand for the product subject to rigid quotas will then raise prices all round, while a decrease will lower them. If tariff and import restrictions change as a result of the project – not an unusual situation – further local repercussions are inevitable.

L-M accept that their method, and particularly the use of border prices, is most suitable for application where trade only is affected:

> In short, the greater the extent to which it affects only trade, the better will border prices measure its social costs and benefits. . . . In general, only trade – rather than domestic production or consumption of the commodity – will be affected if internal prices are not changed as a result of the project.[2]

The point is that the 'trade only' assumption often cannot be made, and therefore that the other effects must also be assessed. Development consists of a number of complementary projects, many of which are justified only in the presence of the other projects, and projects should not be viewed in isolation. Many empirical studies suggest the important and varying incidence of linkages of one kind or another.

Linkages and externalities

Linkages are often negative. The negative impact of modern production on traditional markets and output in India, for example, is well testified.[3] Other forms of negative linkage occur when production of one good leads to successful pressure for protection to produce

---

[1] For many industries trade *and* local production may be affected – e.g. if some extra local production is forthcoming at less than import prices (including tariffs), but then local production becomes inelastic in the short run and additional demand overflows into imports.

[2] L-M, 'Further Reflections on the OECD Manual of Project Analysis in Developing Countries' (mimeo, May 1970) p. 5.1.

[3] Jaipal P. Ambannavar, 'Changes in the Employment Pattern of the Indian Working Force; 1911-1961, *The Developing Economies*, vol. VIII (Mar 1970) no. 1 summarises the impact of the development of factory methods of manufacture in the processing of food grains, bakery, vegetable oils, textiles and the leather industry on employment in the small-scale traditional sector.

another 'uneconomic' good. Thus bread manufacture has led to the manufacture of flour at higher cost and lower quality than that previously imported.[1] Vehicle assembly is often the first step that leads to manufacture of tyres and other parts under heavy protection. Positive linkages also occur when, with the establishment of one industry, some other industry is able to acquire inputs, or sell output, on more favourable terms. This is most frequently the case with a supply based industry. For example, two way linkages between canning and fruit cultivation, and fruit cultivation and canning, and forward and backward linkages from the manufacture of sisal ropes and bags to sisal production (backwards) and improved and cheaper storage and transport of other agricultural products has been established in East Africa.[2] Linkages between complementary goods are seen in the relationship between beer and bottle manufacture, and subsequently between bottle manufacture and bottling other soft drinks.[3] Another very common linkage is that between electricity and electricity using industries, between production and packaging and between transport and the repair and eventual partial manufacture of vehicles and subsequently machinery.[4]

The assumption that projects affect trade only and not local activities is justified only in the complete absence of linkages if linkages are understood to imply the mobilisation, creation or destruction of domestic resources. However, given uniformly positive (or uniformly negative) linkages the L–M method which ignores them would understate (or overstate) the value of all projects equally and hence might not mislead too much for the selection of projects. But reality is more complex than this. Some projects have no linkage

[1] See P. Kilby, *Industrialisation in an Open Economy* Nigeria, 1945–1966 (CUP, 1969), and *African Enterprise: the Nigerian Bread Industry* (Hoover Institution Studies, 1965).

[2] Examples shown in D. S. Pearson, *Industrial Development in East Africa* (OUP, 1969).

[3] Small-scale bottle manufacture can be uneconomic and the bottle industry may be established only with protection, raising (not lowering) prices to the bottle users. See the history of the bottle industry in Nigeria, P. Kilby, op. cit., p. 100.

[4] Further evidence for linkages of these and other types are to be found in P. Kilby, op. cit., and D. S. Pearson, op. cit. J. T. Thorburn has established important linkages in tin mining and rubber in West Malaysia. The tin dredging and gravel pump tin mining industries 'have generated substantial investment opportunities elsewhere in the economy, particularly in electricity supply and petroleum refining'. In addition the tin industry is responsible for the development of a Malaysian light engineering industry. Rubber displayed less significant linkages, though it encouraged the local production of chemical fertilisers and contributed to training of the labour force, but to a lesser extent than tin. See J. T. Thorburn, 'Export Expansion and Economic Development', ODA Report (1971).

effects, others positive and others negative. Hence they can be of critical importance to project selection. Linkages merge into externalities. Any distinction is somewhat arbitrary. 'Externalities' are here used to describe unpriced benefits and costs, such as benefits taking the form of the acquisition of workers' and administrators' skills, and costs in the form of the spread of corruption, while linkages describe the direct impact of one local production decision on another.

Two different points of method are raised. First, interdependence between projects locally limits the validity of the use of international prices, which is discussed further below. Secondly, in so far as a project has external consequences, these consequences, as well as its direct impact on output and input, must also be included in any assessment. To some extent the latter point is independent of the question of international prices, as externalities, if significant, could presumably also be measured in international prices. The main point is that they should be included. But the two questions are not completely independent since by using international prices local linkage effects are automatically excluded, while some at least of what we have described as linkages would be included if local prices were adopted, since they do begin to reflect the *local* opportunity cost of resources used.

Externalities are not taken very seriously by L–M, partly because there is 'little chance, anyway, of measuring many of these external economies' (p. 37) and partly because the authors believe 'that differences in those external effects, which are not in any case allowed for in our type of cost-benefit analysis, will seldom make a significant difference' (p. 219). It is difficult to get very far in discussing these issues at a general level.

It is well known that project appraisal within a large firm is not made by equating the marginal returns on each product in isolation. Investment planners are conscious of the fact that one type of investment will add to the net returns of another, or will prevent a reduction, another type of investment will detract from them. This is sometimes known as the 'organic' theory of investment decisions.[1] The operations of the firm are regarded as an interdependent 'system'. Interdependence between different activities is taken into account and destroys the neat separation into isolated projects whose rates of return can be equated.

[1] See, e.g., John H. Dunning, *Studies in International Investment* (George Allen & Unwin, 1970) pp. 65 and 125. The theory was put forward by the US National Industrial Conference Board, *US production abroad and the US balance of payments* (New York, 1966). The same point was made in Paul Streeten, 'The Taxation of Overseas Profits', *The Manchester School* (Jan 1957) p. 99.

While this is, of course, one of the justifications for bringing various activities under the umbrella of a single firm, similar interaction is well known to occur between investments of different firms. They constitute an important argument for economic planning. They may be positive or negative, but there is no presumption that they add up to zero for every single project. Such interaction becomes especially important if projects are large, both relatively to the stock of capital in existence and to the total investment decisions taken in a period. This is often the case in underdeveloped countries. Whenever such interactions are present, externalities must be allowed for by the planner. They may, of course, be small, but there is no presumption that they always are.[1]

In the detailed study of the Commonwealth Development Corporation's Kulai project by Little and Tipping,[2] the importance of three types of externality is either neglected or minimised (half a page in the book). These are the facts: that for the first time in Malaya smallholders were taught to grow oil palms; that a novel method of combining a modern processing factory, marketing and extension services (some functions of a 'nucleus estate') were combined with smallholder plots; and that a substantial number of Malaysian administrators were trained for management on the estate, many of whom worked later for the Federal Land Development Authority. It so happens that the results, even without regard to these externalities, are favourable to the project. But had they been unfavourable, the neglect of external economies could have been seriously misleading.

In justification of their belief in the insignificance of externalities L–M cite two pieces of evidence: first that one of the authors visited an industrial project 'which had been operating for more than two years, pointed to an adjoining empty area apparently reserved for some industrial use and asked what it was for. He was told that it was reserved for the industries which would grow up to supply the project' (p. 217). The statistical insignificance of this evidence is outdone by some further down on the same page when an entirely invented arithmetical example is used to suggest that 'this does make one wonder whether it is worth spending a lot of time trying to estimate external economies. It may be far more important to spend the time improving the ordinary estimates of sales and costs' (p. 218).

Externalities (or indirect effects), whether positive or negative, are

---

[1] Some interesting illustrations, using investment in the Kabyle mountains and the Bou Namoussa project in Algeria as case studies, are given by Keith B. Griffin and John L. Enos, in *Planning Development* (London, 1970) ch. 7.

[2] I. M. D. Little and D. G. Tipping, *A Social Cost Benefit Analysis of the Kulai Oil Palm Estate West Malaysia*, Development Centre of the OECD, Paris, 1972.

ubiquitous.[1] But L–M are inconsistent on this score. They allow for one type of externality, the effects on savings and the propensity to reinvest, but hardly for others.[2] The conventional way (partially) to ward off externalities is to say that they could or should be the 'internalities' of some other project that aims directly at training labour, encouraging entrepreneurs, strengthening management, or, negatively, eradicating corruption, etc. Yet, there can surely be no *general* rule either about the relative importance of different externalities or about the probability that action will be taken to bring the desired effects independently.

Border prices, domestic values and exchange rates

If the impact of a project is on international trade alone then international prices[3] clearly correctly reflect the opportunity cost of resources used (extra inputs) and benefits of output (exports or reduced imports). But with interdependence between projects, as in the presence of linkages, the L–M criterion is valid only if it is adopted for *all* projects. If non-optimum policies are pursued in other sectors, for other projects, *and* if there is interdependence, the criterion ceases to be valid. In the paradigm there is *no* interdependence in the relevant sense. Facing infinite elasticities, full domestic capacity and constant costs for non-tradables, each project may be treated in isolation and optimised in isolation. However, even in this case projects compete for scarce resources (savings). The ARI is supposed

[1] 'It is generally recognised that besides the output of goods and services which is their primary raison d'être, projects have a variety of more subtle, yet perhaps highly important and powerful effects, from the acquisition of new skills to greater readiness, on the part of the consumers of the project's outputs, to produce for the market; from the stimulation of entrepreneurship to the learning of cooperation and discipline; from backward and forward linkages to greater propensity to engage in family planning; from increased literacy to greater confidence in the ability of one's country to achieve progress – not to forget negative effects such as new or heightened social and ethnic tensions, fresh opportunities for spreading corruption, etc. Should and can these multifarious non-output effects of projects be thoroughly canvassed and taken into account in making investment decisions? Albert O. Hirschman, *Development Projects Observed* (Brookings, 1967) p. 160.

[2] It has for example been claimed that more capital-intensive projects not only raise savings and reinvestment ratios, but also dampen population growth and are more conducive to the incorporation of technological innovations. Cf. W. Galenson and H. Leibenstein, 'Investment Criteria, Productivity and Economic Development', *Quarterly Journal of Economics*, vol. 69 (Aug 1955) pp. 343–70, and H. Leibenstein, 'Technical Progress, the Production Function and Development', in W. W. Rostow (ed.), *The Economics of Take-Off into Sustained Growth* (Macmillan and St Martin's Press, 1963) pp. 185–200.

[3] Or rather marginal export revenue, marginal import cost with less than infinite elasticities. The question of elasticities and border prices is discussed in the next section.

to confine the number of projects undertaken to the resources available. If the ARI which ensures the correct overall balance involves a different discount rate in the optimised (L–M) sector from the rest of the economy, savings may be misallocated.

Assume two sectors (or two projects), one private, the other public. The public sector applies L–M, the private sector actual market prices. Assume further that an imported input is required in both sectors and that the quantity of this imported input is fixed. The opportunity cost of this input in the public sector is then the higher value attached to it by the private sector, reflected in its market price, or the value attached in the home market to other imports that have to be reduced in order to make room for the allocation of the imported input to the public sector. But it is not its international price.

The criterion is also invalidated if the public and the private sector produce competing non-traded products, say electricity and gas, or use the same non-traded input, for which costs are not constant. As long as the private sector uses market prices, the application of international prices to the public sector only will not reflect the correct opportunity costs.

Similar qualifications apply if foreign elasticities are not infinite. Neither the ordinary foreign supply elasticity of imports nor the foreign demand elasticity for exports (for which the Manual formally makes allowance) is sufficient to give the correct opportunity costs. The domestic supply elasticities and output elasticities must also come into play. For when the country's opportunity cost curve is shifted outward as a result of the project (or the complex of projects) the terms on which international goods can be exchanged in the new situation will depend on the change in the willingness to trade.[1] In the Fig. 20.1, illustrating a two-commodity model, this willingness is shown by the relation between the two trading triangles CDR and C'D'R'. If the two triangles are the same size (or, if different sizes, if the international elasticities are infinite, so that the terms of trade remain constant in spite of increased willingness to trade), there will be no change in the terms of trade. If C'D'R' is larger than CDR, the terms of trade will worsen. The extent to which they will worsen will depend upon the shift of the transformation curve, the slope of the transformation curve (i.e. the bias in the growth of productivity) and the slopes of the terms of trade lines. If C'D'R' is smaller than CDR, the terms of trade will improve, the extent again depending on the variables mentioned. Domestic opportunities forgone, as well as international prices, ought to determine the proper valuation of the project.

In the paradigm inputs and outputs are either actually imported or exported or indirectly traded internationally, and it is relatively easy

[1] See Paul Streeten, *Economic Integration* 2nd ed. (Sythoff, 1964) Appendix 1.

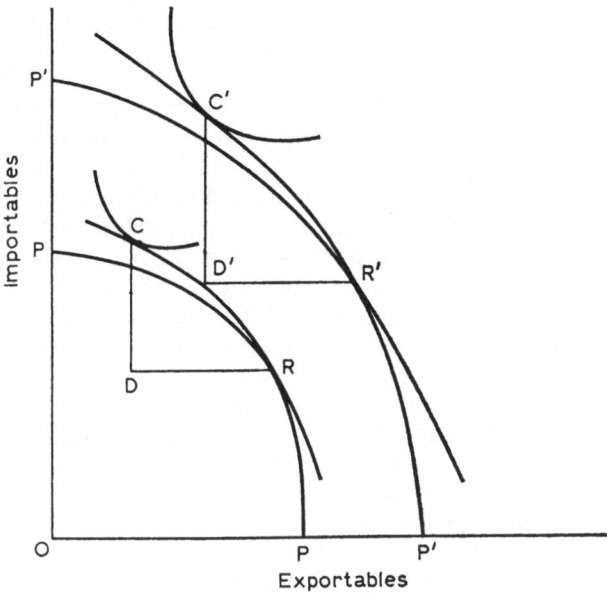

Fig. 20.1
Productivity Growth and Terms of Trade

to establish their prices. With infinite elasticities and the local production of goods that can be converted at constant unit costs into others that are traded, this is so. But if the locally produced goods differ in quality, type, etc., from those internationally traded, and/or if elasticities are imperfect it may be very difficult – and in some cases impossible – to establish their price.

Export markets may be broadly classified into two types: the 'homogeneous', chiefly primary products, where perfect elasticity of demand would be a sensible assumption for a small producer, but where concentration of production, quotas and other market restrictions, make demand inelastic in many products for many countries. Secondly, manufactures where products are differentiated by type, quality, etc., where demand is not perfectly elastic and considerable advertising and promotion costs, as well as transport costs, and/or price reductions have to be faced if the market is to be extended. For both types, the border price is ambiguous, depending on the quantity and quality in question and also on the actions and reactions of buyers and other producers. Receipts depend upon the trade policies pursued by rival supplying countries and by importing countries. Many international prices are formed in oligopolistic markets, where interdependence arises not only from individual producers' reactions but also from government policies, such as the imposition of import restrictions on successfully expanding LDC exports. Changes in exchange rates overseas may change the relative (and absolute) prices of internationally traded goods. Bilateral trading agreements with Eastern block countries, which represent a sizeable option for many developing countries, further reduce the area in which international prices are known, unambiguous and relevant.

The adoption of L–M methods renders a shadow exchange rate nugatory because valuation at international prices takes the place of converting domestic prices at a shadow exchange rate. The shadow wage rate translates local prices into international prices. But this does not solve the problems of how to deal with disequilibria in balances of payments. If actual exchange rate changes (or, for that matter, any other method) are used as instruments for correcting disequilibria in the balance of payments of the country concerned, the relative prices of labour and traded goods change, and consequently the value of different projects. The Manual says that if successful devaluation is anticipated this should be taken into account by adopting a different (lower) shadow wage.[1] However, the device of using a shadow exchange rate is more commonly used where devaluation is needed but *not* anticipated. In such a situation, if the alternative to devaluation is deflation, or costly forms of import restriction, foreign exchange-saving or -earning projects may be considerably more valuable than they appear with current exchange rates. L–M would argue that their method, since it involves maximising foreign exchange earnings, cannot be improved upon. This is true only in a situation where domestic capacity is fully used. But overvaluation is very often accompanied by excess capacity in a number of industries, caused by import restrictions following on the overvaluation. Where there is some excess capacity, gearing projects towards the use of such capacity will make a greater level of expenditure possible for a given balance of payments position. In that case, border prices do not consistently represent the foreign exchange cost of the resources used.

The apparently simple system of using international prices is in practice difficult to apply, as argued above, because international prices are not known, fluctuate unpredictably[2] and depend on the

[1] *Manual*, p. 138. The multiple changes in exchange rates, import taxes, etc., since President Nixon's announcement on 15 August 1971 highlight some of the problems that arise from relying on international prices in project evaluation. The term 'international prices' has lost a precise meaning. It could, of course, be argued that what matters are *relative* prices, but the recent realignments will not leave terms of trade unchanged.

[2] Some of the difficulties of ascertaining current and predicting future international prices are well illustrated in an actual case in H. Joshi. op. cit.

volume of trade. This system is made increasingly cumbersome as more exceptions are allowed for. The exceptions which require some valuation of domestic gains and losses, because the 'trade only' assumption is illegitimate, raise difficulties of principle as well as of practice. The basic philosophy behind the L–M method is that production and consumption patterns may be divorced: an efficient pattern of production may be translated into any desired consumption pattern through international trade. Hence the international and not domestic values are relevant for productive efficiency. The well-known difficulties of arriving at sensible and objective measures of domestic costs and benefits are apparently avoided. But for the exceptions, such measures are required, and so the problem of how to arrive at a correct evaluation, which L–M appear to avoid by the use of international prices, then requires solution.

Assumptions about government policy

The Manual assumes a certain rationality, consistency and uniformity in government policy. Doubts about this fundamental assumption have already been raised in relation to full capacity, exchange rate policy and linkages. One of the ways in which linkages operate most obviously in practice is through one project generating pressures for another project which is linked (through inputs, outputs or consumption). The second project may be uneconomic by L–M criteria, but profitable if sheltered by tariffs or quantitative restrictions. The first project cannot be assessed without also assessing the second project – the use of international prices for all traded goods (defined as traded given 'optimal' policies) would exclude consideration of the second project[1] since the projects are linked by political and institutional pressures, not by technology and cost. An apparently economic project considered in isolation may be undesirable because of these pressures. Conversely, an apparently uneconomic project may be desirable *if* it uses the product of some white elephant previously erected and covers its variable costs. Therefore, what is justified by L–M may in fact not be justified and vice versa. Possibly (though by no means certainly) if one has to make *one* assumption about government policy it is better to assume rationality and efficiency than irrationality and inefficiency. But there is no need to make a single assumption. A more flexible method[2] would allow for a greater

[1] This point is made by A. K. Sen in 'Accounting Prices and Control Areas: An Approach to Project Evaluation' (mimeo).
[2] Such flexibility is one of the advantages of the proposed UNIDO method as compared with the L–M approach. See A. Sen, S. Marglin and P. Dasgupta, *Guidelines for Project Evaluation*, UNIDO, United Nations (New York, 1972).

variety of government reactions, and hence make fewer mistakes. Part of the difficulty here is the dual role the Manual plays. At times it is trying to influence government policy in what L–M believe is a desirable direction. But it is also designed to be an operational guide to project selection. For the former role, relevant government policies are those the authors consider right: for the latter, actual policies. Unless the Manual achieves 100 per cent success in its first role, actual and 'rational' policies will diverge. The Manual makes no allowance for such divergence.

Strategies

The Manual rejects strategies: 'such hunches often carry the euphemistic name of "strategies" . . . Our belief is that such hunches have no general value. . . .' 'The arguments on both sides usually have some validity: in practice though everything depends on how much validity – and this can only be determined by a proper system of cost benefit analysis' (p. 59).

The point of a strategy is that the whole is argued to be larger than the parts, so that piecemeal cost-benefit analysis is very difficult to apply, and, indeed, by its nature will not do justice to the whole. Yet cost-benefit analysis cannot normally be applied to the whole because the necessary *ceteris paribus* assumptions cannot be made. In assessing why some societies have developed and others not, the answer tends normally to be framed in terms of strategies – which is as true of the analysis of Little, Scitovsky and Scott[1] as of others. Whether or not strategies are considered valuable, it remains true that governments have strategies and hence selection of projects must take their contribution to the general strategy into account, as well as that towards income creation. For example, in Kenya an important objective of government policy is to increase the cash crops grown on smallholdings:[2] hence the scheme for tea smallholdings cannot be fully assessed without taking its contribution to this objective – or

[1] In *Industry and Trade in Some Developing Countries*, op. cit.
[2] For a variety of reasons: to monetise the previously largely subsistence African small-scale farmers, to encourage specialisation and so raise agricultural productivity, to replace European estate methods by African farms and spread the benefits to large numbers. Elsewhere R. E. Baldwin has shown that family-size farm units lead to a more equal distribution of income than plantations and therefore permit earlier the setting up of manufactures to serve the local market. 'Patterns of Development in Newly Settled Regions', *Manchester School of Economic and Social Studies*, vol. 24 (May 1956) pp. 161–79. Albert Hirschman pointed out the complementary nature of the Galenson–Leibenstein and Baldwin analyses of growth impulses in industry and agriculture. *Development Projects Observed*, p. 163 n.

strategy – into account. The very interesting study by N. Stern[1] assesses it with L–M methods without allowing for this factor. Since his calculations suggest a high rate of return without making any such allowance it might be argued that in this case it does not matter – or that it is for the Government to make its own assessment of this sort of objective. It can also be argued that the contribution, if quantified in some way, can easily be handled within the L–M framework. All this is true. The point is that the tenor of the Manual and the framework suggested would generally lead to omitting such contributions; again it is a question of emphasis.

The implicit strategy

Although, as we have seen, the Manual rejects strategies, it contains implicitly its own strategy. The paradigm supports a policy of free international trade modified by the use of a shadow wage rate. It is now conventional wisdom that (with the exception of the terms of trade argument for protection) free trade produces the best results in the sense that it produces a Pareto optimum. Any deviations caused by 'distorted' prices or factor rewards should be corrected, not by protective devices, but by taxes and subsidies, which themselves should not have distorting effects. The Manual cannot consistently subscribe to this line, because it assumes that fiscal policies are incapable of raising savings rates. If project selection is used as a method of raising savings, it is hard to see why it should not be used also as a method to pursue any of the other legitimate aims of fiscal policy, since the latter is deemed to be impotent.

But no other aim is admitted as legitimate. If, for example, international markets are imperfect, whether for reasons of demand and supply in markets or of government policy, the paradigm is no longer applicable. But the use of international prices biases the results in favour of export-orientation and free trade. For judgements on such matters as the ease or difficulty of new market penetration, of the likelihood of the invocation of market disruption clauses by importing countries when exports go up or of external changes in exchange rates influence crucially the decision whether exports or import substitutes are favoured. It is possible that much industrialisation has, in the past, been based on excessive trade pessimism. On the other hand, it is plain that the application of L–M criteria biases the results in favour of trade optimism. Would it not then be preferable to espouse openly free trade policies, laying bare the judgements of value and

[1] N. H. Stern, *An Appraisal of Tea Production in Kenya. An Experiment with the Little–Mirrlees method*, Development Centre of the OECD (Paris, 1972). We are indebted to Judith Heyer of the University of Kenya, Nairobi, for comments.

fact that underlie them, rather than to conceal these value and factual judgements behind a set of shadow prices and in an apparently 'scientific' method of project appraisal?

The implicit strategy is also unacceptable to those who believe that the development of appropriate products and technologies, diversification and independence, cannot be achieved without seriously modifying the free trade strategy.

Shadow wage, savings and income distribution

L–M share the view of others[1] that project selection should be used to generate savings which, in many developing countries, should be valued more highly than consumption. The justification of this view is that (i) savings are suboptimal; and (ii) the Government is incapable of enforcing adequate savings through the other instruments available – taxation, public expenditure and pricing decisions, or exchange rate policy. The implication of valuing savings more highly than consumption is to raise the shadow wage above its marginal product in agriculture and towards the actual wage, and hence to direct investment decisions towards more capital-intensive and less employment-generating projects than if consumption and savings were regarded as equally valuable.

It is easy to justify the view that if savings are left entirely to individuals the total may be suboptimal for society as a whole.[2] This suboptimality provides the justification for government saving through the tax system. But it is much more difficult to see how one can justify the view that savings are sub-optimal in the presence of a government sector which is free to tax, etc. Optimality is normally defined with reference to community preferences. It is always difficult to know what is meant by community preferences, and how they can be ascertained. The theory of revealed preference might suggest that community preferences are expressed in government actions. On the savings front, government tax, pricing policies, etc., would therefore reveal its savings preferences. It can be argued that the Government does not represent the community: this position is a difficult one for foreign experts to take, and is not that proposed in the Manual. It believes that the Government may be constrained from raising taxes, etc., but none the less want more savings. In practice this may be a

[1] E.g., A. K. Sen, *Choice of Techniques*, 3rd ed. (Blackwells, 1968), S. Marglin, *Public Investment Criteria* (Allen & Unwin, 1967).

[2] See the discussion of the Prisoner's Dilemma in A. K. Sen, *Choice of Techniques*, op. cit., William J. Baumol, *Welfare Economics and the Theory of the State* (Longmans, 1952) and J. S. Mill, *Principles of Political Economy*, book v, chap. xi §12.

position a government adopts since policies are normally decided in a public and democratic context, while decisions on project analysis are regarded as part of the technical branch of government and outside the purview of public discussion. The implications for the allocation of savings and consumption of using project selection, as against taxation should be appreciated before this view is accepted. Using project selection to generate savings involves employing less people, and hence the saving (i.e. non-consumption) come from those who would be employed but are not – from the unemployed or very low productivity workers. The implications of raising savings through taxation depends on which taxes or other means are used, but the burden is almost certain not to fall solely on the would-be employees. It is true that the non-employed often lack obvious or immediate political force.[1] But this does not seem a reason to systematise this lack of power in project selection.

If income distribution between contemporaries is weighted in an egalitarian way in the project analysis this may offset the implications of weighting savings more heavily. However, while the Manual provides systematically for the weighting of income distribution over time, justifying the use of a Consumption Rate of Interest (CRI) with reference to rising consumption standards and diminishing utility, it does not introduce the same systematic weighting system into contemporary income distribution. Hence the method may encourage governments to put the interests of present taxpayers and future generations above those of the currently unemployed. Politically, this may prove to be a short-sighted policy, although, to the extent that the shadow wage is lower than the actual wage, the application of the Manual will involve more employment than the use of market prices.

Appraisal before and after project execution

The outcome of a project depends upon a set of inputs, valued at one set of prices, and a set of products, valued at another set of prices. The transformation depends, amongst other things, on the quality of management, which is not normally treated as an input. Let us grossly simplify matters (ignoring for this purpose demand and other deficiencies) and say that the degree of capacity utilisation is a function of management. It clearly depends upon labour relations, on fitting and phasing inputs to requirements, controlling stocks, etc. Then the success of a project will depend upon the degree of capacity utilisation, which will determine capital costs per unit of output. But how is

---

[1] This view is forcefully argued by D. Turnham in 'Political and Social Aspects of Employment Policies and Choices', a paper presented to the Cambridge Conference on Employment, 1970, in *Prospects for Employment Opportunities in the Nineteen Seventies*, ed. by Ronald Robinson and Peter Johnston (HMSO, 1971).

the project evaluator to know what degree of utilisation to assume? The differences made to the project according to whether it is evaluated at shadow or market prices may be quite small, compared with the differences made by varying degrees of capacity utilisation. The steel mill constructed at Durgapur in India by British aid reached 95 per cent of capacity utilisation under the brilliant management of Sir Douglas Bell, who thereby drastically reduced unit costs of production. Under his successors (though not entirely through their fault), standards of management fell, capacity utilisation dropped drastically to 25–40 per cent and unit costs shot up. How does one evaluate Durgapur at international prices?

The Brazil textile industry provides another example. The productivity of different cotton spinning mills ranged from less than 500 grammes per man/hour to more than 6,000 according to the ECLA study.[1] A similar range was found in weaving:

> what might be called physical factors of production characteristics do not explain the sharp variations in productivity levels in Brazilian mills. Consequently, after studying the limited data available, it must be concluded that the explanation of that part of the variation in productivity not attributable to the physical factors involved *must be looked for in the human factors in the production process. The most important is mill management.* . . . An estimate prepared for the cotton industry, which is the largest sector in the Brazilian textile industry as a whole, shows that approximately one-third of the total operational deficiency is due to the obsolescence of the machinery, while *under-utilisation of the existing machinery (irrespective of its age and technical characteristics) as a result of defective internal organisation accounts for the remaining two-thirds* (our italics).

There are other reasons besides management why the same or very similar inputs can yield different outputs. Amongst these are changes in government policy, and changes in the relative bargaining position of those executing the project and those setting the various constraints.

Since these influences cannot easily be incorporated in project appraisal, there is a systematic weakness in any *ex post facto* project evaluation. It is bound to attribute to those factors which it selects and quantifies influences due to factors (such as the ones mentioned above) which it neglects. (Albert Hirschman makes a good deal of this point in his book *Development Projects Observed*.)

[1] ECLA, 'The Textile Industry in Latin America. II: Brazil' (United Nations, Oct 1963), quoted in J. Bergsman, *Brazil, Industrialisation and Trade Policies* (OECD and OUP, 1970) ch. 6.

General versus specific criticisms

It is true that some (though not all) of the questions raised above apply to *any* known method of project appraisal, not to L–M specifically (though the Manual is peculiarly open to most of these criticisms because of its presentation, emphasis and likely interpretation). The usual reply to such criticisms is: 'what else can you put in its place?' We do not question that good methods of project appraisal, used by intelligent and sensible men, have a useful place in the wider context of policy making. And we would agree that the L–M international price prescription has helped to highlight the costs of excessively protected industries – which can easily be disguised as highly profitable if domestic prices alone are considered. At the same time, we believe that the method presents difficulties, both in practice and in theory. In *practice* there are dangers of (a) excessive confidence in instruments of limited value, to the neglect of more important considerations; and (b) sub-optimisation in the sense that things will be done very well that should not be done at all, or things dismissed altogether that should be done. Complete rationality about a sub-system can be worse than sub-rationality about the whole system. A particular instance of this danger is the L–M assumption that the Government pursues 'sensible policies' in other sectors. Something that is sensible on this assumption may be stupid on the opposite assumption and vice versa. The dismissal of strategies and the concentration on individual projects confirms one's fear that in the hands of epigones the method is liable to abuse. In *theory* and at a more fundamental level, it may be asserted that in general the appropriate social valuation of costs and benefits must be derived from the domestic opportunities forgone, and the domestic benefits derived, rather than the border prices of internationally traded goods.

L–M introduce an apparently simple innovation into cost-benefit analysis: the replacement of domestic prices, that are distorted by taxes, tariffs and income distribution and hence do not reflect the social value of costs or benefits, by net foreign exchange earnings, a measure independent of these distortionary factors. But for the reasons discussed here, the objectivity, unambiguity and accuracy of the suggested measure is often spurious, while involving the appraisers in unnecessary complications. The attempt to objectify cost-benefit analysis that began with Dupuit has not yet met with success.

Summary

L–M methods are best suited to the selection of projects whose sole impact is on international trade, for commodities whose export demand and/or import supply elasticities are infinite. The method leads to the neglect of local effects and requires substantial modification to deal with the many projects which also affect local activities as a result, for example, of linkages and externalities. In such cases the valuation of inputs and outputs at border prices does not correctly represent local opportunity costs. The absence of full utilisation of domestic production capacity, the presence of 'irrationality' in government policies, and the use of L–M methods in one sector only are likely to produce cases where strict adherence to L–M principles may lead to misallocation of resources. Less than infinite trade elasticities invalidate the pure border price approach, while modification presents theoretical and practical problems, and if widespread, makes the method impossibly cumbersome.

The Manual rejects the use of strategies in economic policy while containing its own implicit strategy, itself questionable. Likewise multiplicity of objectives is rejected and consumption over time taken as the sole maximand, with one exception, a premium to be placed on savings. The justification for making this the sole exception is not obvious, particularly as it may conflict with employment and income distribution objectives. Here, as elsewhere, there is confusion as to whether L–M are trying to influence or interpret government policy. On both counts they may be faulted, but if faulted on one they may retreat to the other and thus appear impregnable.

In any project the actual outcome, and hence the desirability of the project, will depend on factors such as management which are outside the framework of L–M and similar project analysis. To the extent that the outside factors are more important than those included, selection of projects on this basis may systematically suboptimise.

L–M methods *can* be interpreted to allow for all these objections. But there is a real danger that in practice the necessary modifications and qualifications will not be made, a danger that is borne out by some of the studies already made.

21 The Political Economy of the Environment: Problems of Method[1]

A COLLEAGUE of mine has a name for those whose heads are as soft as their hearts. He calls them Goody-Woollies. These Goody-Woollies have their fashions, and preserving the environment is currently a strong candidate for the top goody-woolly cause of the decade. As a reviewer of one of the flood of books on the subject pointed out, it has many of the ingredients beloved of women's magazines – animals, a strong medical interest and a readily identifiable villain. It performs the difficult feat of appealing to the most advanced sociologists and to those who detest change in any form, to old women of both sexes and to the revolutionaries of unidentifiable sex, to the silent majority and the screaming minority, to the young swingers and the old danglers.

Economists have not been slow to jump on to the bandwagon. The smoke and sparks emitted by a factory chimney, which had been a curiosity in Pigou's *Economics of Welfare*, now pervaded the atmosphere and set alight social cost-benefit analysis, which swept like a wildfire through articles, books, commissions and reports. Ministries in particular welcomed the opportunity to shift the burden of political choice on to a set of mathematical formulae. Peter Self, Professor of Public Administration at the University of London, has borrowed Bentham's description of natural rights and applied it to some of the products of the growth industry of cost-benefit analysis: nonsense on stilts.

The problem

'Cost-benefit analysis is a practical way of assessing the desirability of projects, where it is important to take a long view (in the sense of

[1] I am grateful to Diane Elson and Nicolas Lethbridge for help in the preparation of this paper, and to Frances Stewart and Wilfred Beckerman for stimulating discussions.

looking at repercussions in the further, as well as the nearer, future) and a wide view (in the sense of allowing for side-effects of many kinds on many persons, industries, regions, etc.), i.e. it implies the enumeration and evaluation of all the relevant costs and benefits.'[1] A stream of future social benefits and of future social costs, properly adjusted for uncertainties, are discounted by a social rate of time preference and then compared.

Applied to the environment in underdeveloped countries, the problem is how to strike a balance between the benefits of raising the level of living of the mass of the people in poor countries, and its costs in terms of the deterioration of the environment. The basic criterion for deciding how much to spend on reducing the deterioration of the environment, e.g. by choosing a more costly site for a dam, can be stated as follows. The deterioration should be reduced to the point where the costs of doing so are covered by the benefits from this reduction.[2] This formal statement – being a tautology – is immensely easier than its practical application. Two points of elaboration are in order. First, there are many aspects of a deteriorating environment, and these are spread over time. It is therefore important not to apply the analysis to one aspect in isolation. Intertemporal and interspatial interdependence must be allowed for, so that, for example, a programme designed to bring water does not later lead to excessive salination, or a programme to increase electricity supply to the excessive spread of schistosomiasis, or chemical pest control to the excessive killing of the destroyers of the pest. Second, priorities relating to the desirable objectives must be supplemented and modified by consideration of costs. Thus a high priority objective of environmental improvement which is very costly may have to give way to a lower priority one which imposes lower costs.

Applied to, say, river development projects, the need is to identify options and to estimate the benefits and costs in the light of social priorities. Environmental safeguards, such as the preservation of fishing facilities, of farming land for existing tribes, the avoidance of canal-borne diseases, of aquatic weeds or of secondary poisoning of the killers of pests, are costly. These additional costs are acceptable if, but only if, the added benefits exceed them.

Plainly, planning the environment and balancing control of the environment against other objectives of policy, require a comprehensive analysis and calculation of the costs and benefits involved. After a brief discussion of 'Growth *versus* environment', the rest of

---

[1] A. R. Prest and R. Turvey, 'Cost-Benefit Analysis: A Survey', *Surveys of Economic Theory*, vol. III (Macmillan, 1966) p. 155.

[2] First Report of the Royal Commission on Environmental Pollution, Cmnd. 4585, HMSO 1971, para. 20, p. 6.

this paper, except for the last two sections, is devoted to showing some of the limits and dangers of such calculations, particularly when applied to underdeveloped countries.

Growth versus environment

Some writers have presented to us a choice between preserving the environment and promoting economic growth. Growth, the argument goes, pollutes. As normally calculated, the growth of GNP does not allow for these social costs of growth. A more welfare-orientated policy would decelerate growth – some even argue for zero GNP growth – in order to preserve or restore a purer environment.

Many things are wrong with this argument. Perhaps the most basic objection to it is that growth, *properly composed and properly weighted*, can be complementary with environmental protection. Industrial anti-pollution devices and the technology that produces them are part of the GNP. And faster growth renders obsolescent more rapidly such polluting agents as the motor car. It is true that both pollution and the reduction of pollution are a function of the level of 'income'. The argument presented here depends upon the condition that the proportion of income devoted to anti-pollution devices or pollution-free innovations exceeds the proportion of income adding to pollution. If the appropriate social weights are attached to the components of income, measured 'income growth' will show up as genuine growth only if the condition laid down in the previous sentence is met.

On the other hand, there is almost certainly some trade-off between environmental objectives and growth in the short- and medium-long run. The following diagrams illustrate possible temporal growth paths of GNP and of something to be measured by an index of the preservation of the environment (or of reduced pollution). H is the high growth path, L the low growth path.

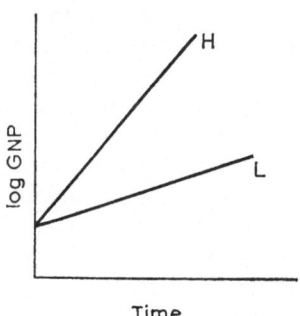
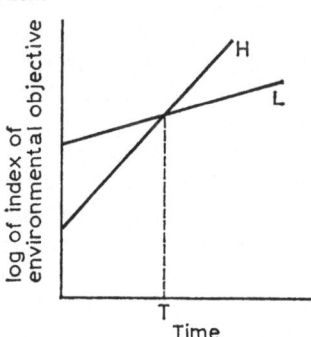

Fig. 21.1
Growth and pollution over time

Until time T the high growth strategy sacrifices the environment. But at T and for ever after, high growth promotes a purer environment.[1] Which path is chosen will depend upon the rate of time discount for environmental purity, compared with that for GNP. Since the marginal utility of consumption declines with rising income, whereas the relative value attached to reducing pollution increases with rising income, the rate of time discount for the environment is likely to be lower than that for GNP. If this is so, those who lay much store by the environment ought to advocate a *higher*, not a lower, growth strategy than that dictated by optimising consumption over time. Only then can devices to protect the environment (a new growth industry) and the technology that evolves anti-pollution techniques, processes and products develop sufficiently rapidly.

Even this way of posing the problem greatly oversimplifies it. In fact, four choices are open. First, we may abstain from producing as much as we otherwise would in order to reduce pollution. Second, we may devote resources that might have produced goods to produce products that combat pollution. Whether this means stepping up national product, slowing it down or changing its composition depends on conventions of national income accounting.[2] Third, we may step up the production of ordinary goods, notwithstanding the fact that they aggravate pollution, to a degree that compensates for the growth of pollution. Finally, we might produce different products, not as attractive as those that would have been produced without regard to pollution, but with the compensating merit that they carry with them less pollution. Zero growth would be not only a blunt, but an ineffective, instrument for achieving a better environment.

The use of mathematics

All cost-benefit analyses must use mathematics. Its scope and limitations depend on the problems treated. It is sometimes said that mathematics permits rigour, though possibly at the expense of relevance. In fact, much mathematical economics is vague, but for quite different reasons than those that give rise to vagueness in literary treatments. This is so because it is not made clear what real entities the mathematical symbols stand for, or, if it is made clear, the assumptions about the symbols do not apply to the concrete entities. While a, b and c lend themselves to rigorous manipulations, the identifications of a with an individual, b with a farm household and c with a firm constitute large logical jumps. Rigour is lacking because the symbols are not identified or are ill-defined.

[1] The argument is adapted from an article by Frances Stewart and Paul Streeten, Chapter 19 in this volume.
[2] Much that is counted as part of GNP should be deducted as intermediate goods.

One danger of the use of mathematics is that it lulls its practitioners into a false sense of certainty. The temptation for the mathematical economist, and even more his mediocre disciple, is to mistake logic for economics or validity for truth, i.e. the correct deduction of logical conclusions for the discovery of facts about the real world. For a minimax player it may be professionally comforting that the damage done by the computer in economics is less than in defence analysis. In both it can lead to disastrous decisions. According to the well-known principle of GIGO – garbage in, garbage out – results can be no better than assumptions. Mathematics is no substitute for thought or for values. Of course, all good mathematical social scientists know this.

Another well-known danger in mathematical decision-making is sub-optimisation. What is best for part of a system may not be best for the whole. The temptation is to proceed with those parts that can be treated mathematically and to neglect the rest. We then may do perfectly something that should not be done at all. Practitioners try to select the quantifiable, identify it with the important and happily proceed to sub-optimise. The result may be the worst of all possible worlds. As Kenneth Boulding has emphasised, rationality about a sub-system can be worse than sub-rationality about the whole system.[1] Decision-models, based on a set of explicit and quantified assumptions (the framework discussed in the next section), often cover such a sub-system, whereas decisions based on vague judgements and intuitions, with all their well-known faults, may take into account the whole system. This is particularly important in development studies in the light of the strong relationships between sub-systems and the lack of relationships within any given sub-system. It is also very important in arms control. It is the tendency to sub-optimisation that leads to the neglect of factors to which a mathematically less sophisticated but good policy-maker (admittedly an even scarcer resource than mathematical sophistication) would pay more attention.

Choosing the framework

Benefits are just benefits. There is normally no distinction between benefits that contribute to positive happiness, those that reduce misery that is inflicted by God or nature and those that reduce man-created misery. The blackmailer creates a nuisance, for the removal of which he extracts payment. Depending upon the assumptions and the terms of reference of the framework, the benefits derived from the

[1] K. E. Boulding, 'Economics as a Moral Science', *The American Economic Review*, vol. LIX no. 1 (Mar 1969).

removal of man-created nuisances count in the same way as the benefits that add to the net enjoyment of life. Social life is full of situations that can be comprehended only by the economics of blackmail: desires created by envy, by advertising, by habit formation, by the conspicuous consumption of others, by the prevailing income distribution; or needs generated by emissions of noise, dirty air or dirty water or just dirt. On the other hand, clearly not all man-created desires fall into the blackmail category. It is the purpose of education to generate desires for truth, goodness and beauty, which can never be fully satisfied. Both the highest and the lowest wants are the result of want creation, of the generation of a void for whose filling someone can extract a charge that may count as a benefit. The point is that benefits cannot be aggregated without a series of value judgements in addition to the simple one that it is good that people should have more of what they want. The wants and their causes themselves must be subjected to a critical evaluation before we can apply a true cost-benefit calculus. If, as J. S. Mill thought, it is better to be Socrates dissatisfied than a satisfied pig, it may, in some cases, be better to widen the gap between 'bads' and 'goods'. In other cases, the production of 'anti-bads', to abate the nuisance caused by the generation of 'bads', does not add to welfare.

Cost-benefit analysis must be conducted within a framework which selects certain relationships by putting them into equations, and involves moral, political and social considerations. This means that valuations enter; that they have to be selected, and then quantified. In locating an airport, for instance, such disaparate considerations as surface travelling time, loss of agricultural land, differential impact of losses on rich and poor, the value to future generations of historic churches and houses, the loss of wildlife, as well as the more obvious capital construction costs and revenues collected, all have to be brought together. It is quite true that cost-benefit methods help to establish a logical framework for decision-making. The framework determines the outcome. It is bound to be less than fully comprehensive and by selecting some and leaving out other considerations biases the results.

Partial versus general equilibrium analysis

Formally, cost-benefit analysis can be made to fit all cases. In practice, it ceases to be usable for decisions that change what are normally taken as parameters of the system. This means that, if decisions affect the values of the variables in the rest of the economy, the partial equilibrium approach or the micro-approach, on which the analysis is based, breaks down and only a general equilibrium analysis will do.

This sets severe limits to its application to underdeveloped countries. Suppose that a river development project depends for its benefits not only on expenditure on investment and the external costs that became evident in the Aswan dam, but also on the incentives of farmers, in turn a function of the system of land tenure, and on their willingness and ability to adopt new methods of cultivation. These may be functions of the speed of modernisation of the whole economy, itself partly dependent upon the river development project.

Conversion of political choice into technical

Cost-benefit analysis has a tendency to convert political, social and moral choices into pseudo-technical ones. Hence its psychological appeal to administrators, but also hence its logical flaw, evident to those trained in the analysis of choice. If two objectives conflict, say the requirements of industrial growth and the protection of the environment, someone will have to choose. The choice may be democratic or dictatorial or oligarchic, but choice it must be. It is possible to make the conflicting objectives commensurate by attaching numerical weights to them and then estimating how these weighted values are affected by different courses of action, allowing for interdependences, cross effects and intertemporal connections. Different values can thus apparently be reduced to a single value: the maximisation of the numerical excess of 'benefits' over 'costs'. But the clash has not disappeared. It has been concealed in the relative values (often highly arbitrary) attached to the objectives. The judgement is no more 'objective'. On the contrary, I would argue that policy makers should be fully aware of the choices and should not be confronted with fudged, predigested and prejudged pseudo-technical results. It is, for instance, formally possible to lump together the effects of a project on (a) income distribution, (b) the balance of payments and (c) the growth of industrial production. Shadow pricing of inputs and outputs can embrace all these objectives. But unless there is a clear and precise consensus upon the relative weights to be attached to these objectives (e.g. to an extra dollar that goes to a rich and a poor man), a planner has a clearer picture by having the issues set out separately rather than being served with single figures that conceal the preferences. A decomposed set of indices will lead to better decisions than a composite index.

When exchange values are non-operational

One of the characteristics of cost-benefit analysis is that it attaches money values to choices that have never been and never will be subjected to the test of an exchange situation. In the first place, the money calculus cannot be applied if objectives are not commensurable; if we are not prepared to give up any amount of one thing for a little more of another. 'Everything has its price' is just not true. If we regard human slavery or prostitution as incompatible with human dignity, or if we regard them as incompatible with certain inalienable human rights, the proof that these institutions come out well in a cost-benefit analysis is irrelevant. Secondly, even where there is commensurability, to attach values to choices that will never be put to a test is essentially arbitrary. Sensitivity analysis can determine what difference would be made by varying the values and, if we are lucky, certain variations will make little difference to the outcome. But others will be crucial. Interviews and hypothetical questions about what value we attach to time saved or beautiful flora and fauna preserved do not help much. We all know about the gap between words and deeds, particularly if we can never be faced with the deeds. Thirdly, whenever ends are not given but explored, modified or discovered in the process of allocating resources, the model that confronts given competing ends with scarce means does not fit the facts.

The cost of information and uncertainty

A full cost-benefit analysis requires not only a carefully constructed analytical framework, but also a vast amount of quantitative data. The construction and gathering of this knowledge take time and skilled manpower, which is very scarce in underdeveloped countries. The costs of acquiring the information and knowledge to maximise net benefits must be weighed against the extra benefits to be derived from them. It may then be perfectly *rational* to stop short of being *perfectly* rational.

Allowances for uncertainty can be made in three ways:

(1) in the assessment of annual levels of benefits and costs; (2) in the assumptions about length of life; and (3) in the discount rate. The first is most appropriate if the risk dispersion of outcomes (or inputs) is irregularly, rather than regularly, distributed with time. If the main risk is that there may be a sudden day of reckoning when benefits disappear or costs soar, the second type of adjustment is needed. The third correction, a premium on the discount rate, is appropriate where uncertainty is a strictly compounding function of time.[1]

Professor Shackle has rejected orthodox probability theory for situations that cannot be repeated many times. Even if chances of

[1] Prest and Turvey, op. cit., p. 171.

success and failure could be calculated actuarially, disastrous outcomes put an end to further 'trials'. Professor Shackle has proposed to replace probability distributions by his highly original concept of 'potential surprise'. Ignorance as to which of many possible events will occur is reflected as a low potential surprise value of each, not, unwarrantedly, as a low 'probability' of each. He has substituted for mean value and dispersion his concepts of 'focus gain' and 'focus loss' – the most attractive and the most repellent outcomes, thus rejecting the addition of mutually incompatible hypotheses.

It might be argued that these innovations do not apply to public investment projects. Many of these will have only very small effects on average incomes per head of the population or on those of a particular group. It may therefore be thought that, where a probability distribution is known, actuarial risk can be applied. On the other hand, the kind of projects that we are concerned with will be sufficiently large and localised to have considerable effects on groups of people and the possibility of disastrous outcomes may be important. Focus values of the type proposed by Professor Shackle will then be more appropriate than adjustments to actuarial risk. Furthermore, in conditions of uncertainty, flexibility will be appropriate. Even though costs for any given outcome will be higher or benefits lower than they would have been, had this outcome been expected with certainty, costs will be lower or benefits higher if outcomes deviate from the expected values. No method that uses certainty equivalents can deal correctly with this phenomenon.

Implications for aid-giving

By looking at aid-giving in isolation, we have not taken into account the possible harmful effects on the environment in poor countries which are caused by the transfer of our technologies. I have tried to enumerate some of these in *Development in a Divided World* (Pelican Original, edited by Dudley Seers and Leonard Joy, February 1971).[1] The most important is the introduction of cheap and effective methods of reducing death rates, without a correspondingly cheap and effective technology to reduce birth rates. This has upset the population equilibrium and has vastly contributed to the difficulties of development. Other examples are the capital-intensive techniques of production which aggravate the unemployment problem, the transfer of Western institutions such as trade unions and modern social services, and most recently the new seed varieties. Not only have we isolated aid-giving from its total effects in recipient countries, but we have also isolated it from our other national policies which have an impact on development. Vast sums are spent on research and development which

[1] See Chapter 1.

make the primary products obsolete, on whose exports developing countries depend; we prevent them from selling more manufactured products in our markets by cascading tariffs, rising with the stage of processing, and impose quotas on imports when they show signs of being successful; we encourage the immigration of scarce professionals whom these countries have trained, while shutting our frontiers to unskilled immigrants; we conduct our foreign policy in a manner which imposes added burdens on the poor countries. No cost-benefit analysis has yet embraced these highly relevant considerations.

The need for interdisciplinary studies

There are two good reasons for conducting interdisciplinary studies, one obvious, the other less so. The obvious reason for interdisciplinary work arises from the requirements of applied research. The solution of particular practical problems, such as urban congestion and slums, pollution, location, river development, nutrition, population control, labour utilisation and many others, requires the contributions of different disciplines and their application to the specific issue. The prevalence of government planning at all levels has contributed to the co-operation between, and sometimes the integration of, different disciplines. The planner has to draw on all relevant knowledge and skills, without being bound by conventional boundaries. This practical need to bring all relevant methods and data to bear on the solution of a specific problem does not affect the method used in the contributing discipline. It is because they are specialists in their fields that the different members have a contribution to make to an integrated solution.

There is, however, a second and deeper reason for interdisciplinary research.[1] The justification for having separate disciplines and for specialising in them is that between the variables encompassed by one discipline and those treated by another there are few interactions and the effects of any existing interaction are weak and damped. Only then are we justified in analysing problems in one field, without always and fully taking into account others. As Michael Lipton has argued in a stimulating and valuable article,[2] the need for interdisciplinary studies does not arise because people in underdeveloped countries, particularly in subsistence households, perform many

[1] Some people object to terms like 'multi-disciplinary' or 'interdisciplinary'. It is true that they sound somewhat pretentious and abstract. I have not been able to think of a better expression for this type of work.

[2] Michael Lipton, 'Interdisciplinary Studies in Less Developed Countries', *Journal of Development Studies*, vol. 7 no. 1 (Oct 1970).

functions normally separated in rich countries, but because there is 'interdependence between variables normally analysed separately Lack of specialization among the people being studied in no way. justifies lack of specialization among the students. A student of Michelangelo could well confine attention to his sculpture, while caring little for the architecture and painting in which Michelangelo also excelled.'[1] The fact that functions in underdeveloped societies are less differentiated does, of course, have a bearing on the interdependence.

If interdependence between variables normally studied separately is strong, or, though weak, if reaction coefficients are large, or, even though small, if they change size for moves above a certain critical size, interdisciplinary studies are indicated. The situation can be illustrated diagrammatically.[2]

Figure 21.2 illustrates the absence of interdependence between the

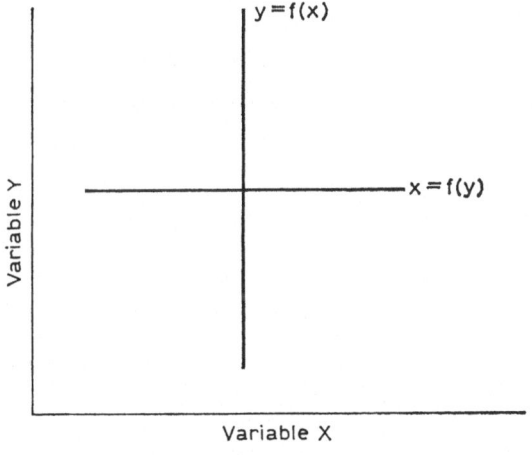

Fig. 21.2

Non-interdependence

variables X and Y. Figure 21.3 shows interdependence, but it is weak and damped, so that if one variable diverges from the stable equilibrium point S, the system will tend to return to it. Whether we are justified to neglect such interdependence will depend upon the size of the reaction coefficients (the comparative slopes of the lines) and on the time lags in the adjustment process. Figure 21.4 shows a cumulative process away from the unstable equilibrium at U. Clearly, we must not neglect such interdependence in our studies. Figure 21.5 shows that stability and instability may be the function

[1] Loc. cit., p. 6.   [2] See Chapter 5.

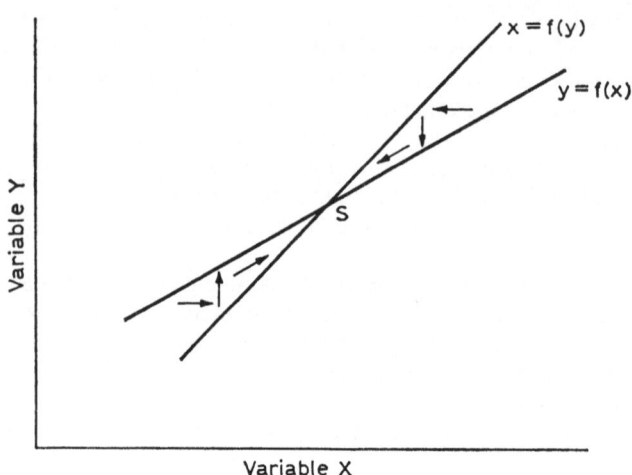

Fig. 21.3
Damped interdependence

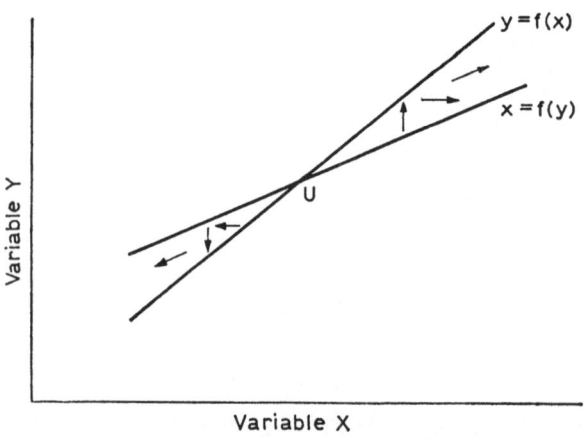

Fig. 21.4
Explosive interdependence

of the size of the move, so that for small moves interdependence is damped and for large ones explosive. Theories of the large push or the critical minimum effort are based on such non-linear relationships.

There are numerous illustrations of such interdependence in the field of development studies. One is the relationship between income per head and population growth. High rates of population growth

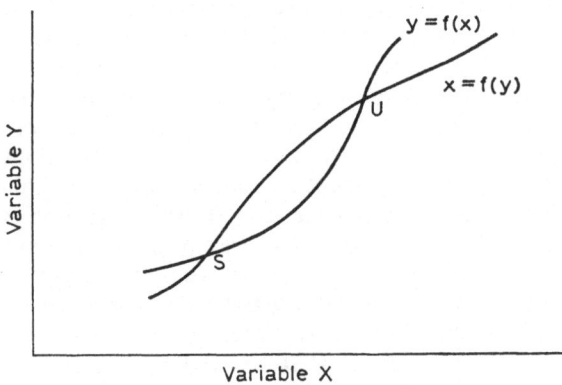

Fig. 21.5
Non-linear interdependence

may be assumed to reduce income per head and higher income per head may be assumed, in certain conditions, to reduce population growth. Or take the relationship between the level of living of a deprived minority group, e.g. a low caste or a racial minority and an index of prejudice against it. Prejudice will be a function of the level of living – the less educated, the less healthy, the stronger the grounds for prejudice – and the level of living will be a function of prejudice – the stronger prejudice, the stronger discrimination in jobs, education, etc. Or consider the relationship between productivity per man and the investment/income ratio. The higher productivity, the higher will tend to be the savings and hence the investment ratio, but the higher the investment ratio the more capital per man and hence the higher productivity. There is also interdependence between the quality of interdisciplinary studies and the quality of the scholars they attract. One can go on.

Strong interdependence, or weak interdependence with cumulation, or weak interdependence without cumulation within certain limits but cumulation beyond these limits, constitute a case for interdisciplinary studies, where the variables under consideration belong to different conventional disciplines.[1]

It is possible to draw two quite different conclusions from this. On the one hand, it may point to the need, not so much for

[1] A third justification for defining a discipline is that it uses certain assumptions and methods, that it employs, in the jargon, a kit of tools (e.g. maximising behaviour). The danger of this justification is to be found in the 'law of the instrument', according to which a small boy, given a hammer, will find everything worth pounding. The subject is then determined by attractive weapons that are used to shoot at anything in sight, rather than at suitable targets.

interdisciplinary studies, as for a *new discipline*. I do not mean some kind of super-politics-economics-sociology, but a discipline that builds with concepts and models appropriate to the physical and social conditions of less developed societies. Alternatively, the framework of the established disciplines may continue to be used but some of the substance may be provided from outside these conventional fields. Thus the concept of a production function or of capital may be adapted from economics but we may operate with non-economic inputs such as educational or health levels or distance from towns in an agricultural production function, or we may widen the concept of capital to comprise national integration or improvements in the quality and attitudes of the labour force, if these 'investments' raise the flow of production above what it would otherwise have been. In either case, we may in the process incidentally gain new insights into social phenomena in advanced industrial countries. Studies of the caste system may throw light on trade union behaviour; scrutiny of the capital/output ratio may change our view of the production function; a wider concept of capital may throw new light on incentives and management; a study of underdeveloped countries will improve our methods of dealing with underdeveloped regions in advanced countries. If this happens, it will be a bonus over and above what we had bargained for.

22 Technology Gaps between Rich and Poor Countries[1]

The causes of international inequality

THE growing inequality in the international distribution of income is of relatively recent origin. It is a phenomenon of less than 200 years. It started towards the end of the eighteenth century when inventors combined engineering skills and entrepreneurial ingenuity, while a social and technical revolution in agriculture released the men and the food for industrialisation. Its twin causes are (a) the appearance of a new condition which permits the income and production of some countries to grow at much faster rates than those of others, and (b) the existence of obstacles to the spread of the benefits from the fast-growing to the slow-growing countries. We do not have far to seek for this permissive condition. It is neither the discovery of natural resources nor, as was thought at one time, the accumulation of capital as such. Accumulation of capital, without improvements in knowledge, could not have brought about the substantial increase in income per head that occurred. The ceiling that this condition sets is determined by the stock of scientific knowledge (know-why and know-that) and technology (know-how), by its application to production and organisation in industry, trade and agriculture and by its commercial exploitation.[2] It is the continuing interaction between a succession of scientific, technological and industrial revolutions

[1] I am indebted to Jonathan Hughes, Constantine Vaitsos, Michael Sharpston and Hans Singer for helpful comments and particularly to Frances Stewart who has contributed to and clarified my ideas.

[2] 'Technology' in this paper is used not in the sense in which the engineer might use it but in the economist's sense: it means the same as the production function which specifies the relation between inputs of all factors of production, including skills and organisation, and outputs. As a result, the discussion in this lecture is unaffected by such common assertions as 'there is no technological gap; there is only a management gap'; or 'the technological gap is entirely a research and development problem'.

and the human, economic, political and social conditions that create and use these revolutions, that sets the upper limit to economic growth.[1] According to the assumptions of economic theory, the fruits of economic progress tend to be widely spread and to 'trickle down', through competition, specialisation and public policy, from the rich to the poor. This has been largely true *within* already advanced countries as they progressed further. Whether competition and specialisation worked for a trickling down or a polarisation of benefits, the policies of the modern state have, on the whole, worked towards reducing domestic inequalities. But it has not been true *between* different countries nor within many underdeveloped countries. Clearly, no international government and therefore no international redistributive machinery exists. Other reasons why the spread has not occurred internationally will be considered later.

What matters in this context is neither the *proportionate* difference (of, say, income per head or product per worker), nor the *differences in magnitudes* at the start, but the growth factor.[2] A simple example illustrates the point. Call A_1 and A_2 the initial magnitude of the gross national product per head in two countries. The initial ratio of these two magnitudes $R = A_1/A_2$; the final ratio (F) after a number of years (t) will depend on the initial ratio (R) and the respective rates of growth (r_1) and (r_2).

$$F = \frac{A_1(1+r_1)^t}{A_2(1+r_2)^t} = R\frac{(1+r_1)^t}{(1+r_2)^t} = R.k, \text{ where } k = \frac{(1+r_1)^t}{(1+r_2)^t}$$

The following table shows k for different annual growth rates over 5, 10 and 20 years.

It can be seen that, if two countries started with equal income, one

TABLE 22.1

Growth Factor for Different
Annual Growth Rates

	$t = 5$	$t = 10$	$t = 20$
$r_1 = 2\%, r_2 = 1\%$	1·05	1·10	1·22
$r_1 = 20\%, r_2 = 10\%$	1·55	2·39	5·70

[1] Although the bulk of this chapter is devoted to a discussion of the growth of scientific knowledge and its application, attitudes such as those towards entrepreneurs and the cultural, social and political institutions that provide the stimulus for the growth of knowledge and that makes it possible to absorb it are equally important, though less visible, less well understood and therefore often neglected. Understanding the atom is child's play compared with understanding child's play.

[2] The argument was put forward by Simon Kuznets in a seminar at the Johns Hopkins University in 1956. It can also be found more subtly developed than here, in his *Economic Change*, chapter 8 'International Differences in Income Levels' (Heinemann, 1954) and *Modern Economic Growth, Rate, Structure and Spread* (Yale University Press, 1967).

growing twice as fast as the other, a difference of 10 per cent between 20 per cent and 10 per cent would make income in the faster growing country 5·70 times that in the slower one after twenty years. If, with the same proportional advantage, the difference were only 1 per cent, i.e. one growing at 2 per cent, the other at 1 per cent, the income ratio of the two countries would hardly have been altered. If the faster country started with 50, the slower with 100, and if the former grew

TABLE 22.2

Rate of Growth per Decade of Product per Head
(per cent)

England and Wales – United Kingdom	
1. 1700 to 1780	2·0
2. 1780 to 1881	13·4
3. 1855–59 to 1957–59	14·1
France	
4. 1841–50 to 1960–62	17·9
Germany – West Germany	
5. 1851–55 to 1871–75	9·2
6. 1871–75 to 1960–62	17·9
Netherlands	
7. 1900–04 to 1960–62	13·5
Switzerland	
8. 1890–99 to 1957–59	16·1
Denmark	
9. 1870–74 to 1960–62	19·4
Norway	
10. 1865–74 to 1960–62	19·0
Sweden	
11. 1861–65 to 1960–62	28·3
Italy	
12. 1861–65 to 1898–1902	2·7
13. 1898–1902 to 1960–62	18·7
United States	
14. 1839 to 1960–62	17·2
Canada	
15. 1870–74 to 1960–62	18·1
Australia	
16. 1861–65 to 1959/60–1961/62	8·0
Japan	
17. 1879–81 to 1959–61	26·4
European Russia – USSR	
18. 1860 to 1913	14·4
19. 1913 to 1958	27·4
20. 1928 to 1958	43·9

Source: Simon Kuznets, *Modern Economic Growth* (Yale University Press, 1966) pp. 64–5.

at 20 per cent, while the latter at 10 per cent, the fast would have caught up with the slow within ten years. But if the fast grew at 2 per cent and the slow at 1 per cent, the latter would still be substantially ahead after twenty years. In fact, over the last 200 years, different countries' growth rates of product per head varied widely, between nearly zero and over 25 per cent *per decade*. The post-war period has witnessed an even wider spread of growth rates. Some growth rates of product per head per decade over long periods for different countries are given in the Table 22.2.

The transfer of knowledge

If we are interested in the wide spread of the benefits of science and technology (S & T) and in policies which promote this, we must ask ourselves whether the knowledge is transferable from country to country or whether it is tied to a particular place. Where knowledge is transferable, we must ask how best it can be transferred, and to what extent different methods of transfer are substitutes or complementary. If they are substitutes, the question is whether transfer should be carried out through local subsidiaries of international corporations, or through imports or through licences, joint ventures or collaboration agreements, or through hiring experts, or whether it is not better to rely solely on an indigenous scientific capability, by training students at home or possibly by sending them to be trained abroad, in order to build up indigenous institutions later. If they are complementary, the question is what are the best combinations and what the appropriate phasing?

In order to answer these questions, we have to construct a typology of S & T. The following questions are relevant:

1. Is the knowledge physically transferable or is it tied to a particular locality?
2. Is it freely available or do patents or other property rights impose a cost on those wishing to acquire it?
3. Is the knowledge of the process or product stable or changing?
4. Is it separable from other activities of the firm, such as using sources of supply or seeking market outlets or is it inextricably tied up, through feedbacks and 'feed-forwards', with knowledge or information drawn from these other activities? Is it, in other words, an integral part of the whole system or parts of the system of the firm's activities?

The answers to these questions will determine the most effective way of acquiring the knowledge. Thus, if the knowledge is transferable, free and separable, the solution is to look it up; if property rights are attached to it, it may have to be bought; if it is changing or integrally linked to other activities, direct foreign investment may be invited. The problems arising from this last type are more fully discussed below.

A good deal of S & T is freely available, though even then 'absorptive capacity' is required in the sense that there must be people willing and able to understand and apply the knowledge. Without a receptive indigenous S & T capability and a social structure adapted to receiving its fruits, even freely available and communicated knowledge remains unused.

There is, of course, no hard and fast line between knowledge that is freely available and knowledge that is tied to individuals or institutions. Like a recipe, anyone can look it up (if he knows that it is worth looking and where to look), but everyone is not an equally good cook. 'Knowing that' is different from 'knowing how'.

Output gaps and technology gaps

When we say that there is a technology gap between rich and poor countries we *may* mean no more than that output per worker is greater in rich countries than it is in poor. Alternatively, we may wish to draw a distinction between an output gap and a technology gap, so that it would be possible, in principle, to have low output per worker and an advanced technology, or high output per worker and a backward technology. The distinction can be illuminated by separating different influences on output per worker.

Output per worker can be analysed as consisting of two components: output per unit of capital, multiplied by capital per worker.[1] Productivity may be high either because workers are backed by a lot of capital or because the productivity of the capital with which they work is high, or both. Knowledge and skills embodied in workers can be regarded either as a form of capital or as a way of raising labour productivity for a given amount of capital. Aggregate differences in productivity per worker may again be due to four factors:

1. Sectors with different productivities may have a different relative weight in the economy of different countries. Thus richer countries have a larger industrial sector in which productivity is higher than in agriculture in poor countries.

---

[1] The relation between income per head and the various factors bearing on the technology gap is this:

$$\frac{\text{Income}}{\text{Population}} = \frac{\text{Output}}{\text{Labour Force}} \cdot \frac{\text{Labour Force}}{\text{Population}}$$

$$= \frac{\text{Output}}{\text{Capital}} \cdot \frac{\text{Capital}}{\text{Labour Force}} \cdot \frac{\text{Labour Force}}{\text{Population}}$$

2. Within a sector similar enterprises vary substantially with respect to their productivity. The proportion of enterprises following the best practice (with respect to engineering or organisation) will vary and will determine the average productivity in the sector and hence in the economy.
3. The 'best practices' themselves will vary from country to country and differential standards will mean that some societies show in their 'best practice' firms in similar sectors higher productivity than others.
4. Differences in productivity may be due to economies of scale.

This fourfold division refers to output per worker and must again be subdivided in the first three cases into differences of output per unit of capital and those of capital per worker. Either capital or workers may embody technical and organisational knowledge.

Technology gaps may then be of one of two types: they may be due to imperfections in communicating and transferring existing technologies (call this the Communications Gap) or they may be due to absence of appropriate technologies (Suitability Gap).[1] A Communications Gap means that existing knowledge is only partly or imperfectly communicated. It may be responsible for any of the output gaps (1) to (3). It may lead to a relatively small share of high productivity sectors, or to a low proportion of enterprises practising 'best practice' techniques or to the 'best practice' techniques themselves being of a lower standard.

The Suitability Gap

But the Communications Gap cannot explain *all* the factors responsible for the output gap, because the adoption of 'best practice' techniques developed in industrial countries by less developed countries is likely to involve such a high ratio of capital and sophisticated skills to unskilled labour and such a large scale of production (factor 4) that, even with the best communications, poor countries simply do not have the resources. Compared with the rich countries, poor countries have to provide about three times the number of jobs with about one-twentieth of investible resources per worker. These are rough orders of magnitude that show that only about one-sixtieth of the investible resources per worker of the rich countries is available for the creation of jobs in poor countries, if only additions to the labour force are to be employed. The ratio is even lower if jobs are to be created for all those already unemployed and underemployed. This

---

[1] I am indebted to Mrs Taya Zinkin for coining this term.

alters the scale of the whole problem of job creation and makes historical comparisons with the adaptation of existing technologies by industrialising Japan or Germany quite irrelevant.

This is partly what is meant by saying that rich men's technologies are inappropriate for the poor countries. It is for this reason that we must identify the second type of technology gap, the Suitability Gap. It is a gap in the development of the appropriate technology and of the resources devoted to the discovery of such a technology. The problem here is that techniques with low ratios of physical and human capital to labour but high ratios of output to capital just do not exist (perhaps do not exist any longer), so that the low capital-labour ratios, inevitable for a large proportion of the labour force, lead to extremely low workers' productivity. In many countries many workers have zero capital to work with: they are 'non-employed', rather than 'unemployed'. Resources devoted to closing the Suitability Gap would raise the productivity of labour-intensive techniques and would thereby help to close the output gap.

Inappropriateness is only partly a matter of differential capital availability. In many underdeveloped countries not only labour but also capital is underutilised. Technologies developed in the industrial West are also inappropriate because physical and social conditions differ. Many agricultural and some industrial technologies have been developed for countries in the temperate zone, whereas most underdeveloped countries are in the tropics. Again, technologies depend upon economic, social and political features that may be quite different in the two types of country. Even such a simple implement as a spade is not suitable for bare-foot diggers. Adaptation requires ingenuity and invention. It is not enough to add a simple wooden platform to the top of the spade, for earth would adhere to it. The same is true with much greater force of more complicated production processes which may depend upon large markets, hierarchical management structures, impersonal administration, or labour relations or cultural attitudes which differ in the country to which the technology is transferred.[1]

[1] At the same time, there are strong pressures from the underdeveloped countries themselves to seek only the most modern, most sophisticated and often most capital-intensive equipment, even where simpler and lower-cost items are available. Even, or perhaps especially, the smallest countries feel they must have a Boeing 707 if they have an airline or go without it. Many countries prohibit the import of used or obsolete equipment. Sterling International, a Californian pulp, paper and board exporting firm, reported that there had been a change from manufacturing lavatory paper with perforations with a sawtooth edge to perforations in a series of straight lines, like a Morse code. Machinery to make the former cannot be converted to the latter and this made all saw tooth perforating equipment obsolete in North America and available for next to nothing. The firm shipped out three such machines to plants which they had established in Hong

'Scientific discoveries, and particularly their practical counterparts in inventions and technical improvements, are often the solution to a specific problem in a specific country adapted to the resources it possesses.'[1] To the extent to which this is true, the impression of universal availability of scientific knowledge is an illusion. The agricultural revolution met the needs of agriculture in eighteenth century England with plentiful land and a temperate climate. The improvements of the USA were adapted to a large market of mass consumers and less suitable for smaller countries with more differentiated markets. The factory organisation in Western Europe and North America, with its system of hiring and firing labour, is adapted to a set of human relations quite alien to other cultures.

It is still often said that there is no lack of knowledge as to how to develop, only a lack of will to apply it. This view combines two deep-seated nineteenth century biases. One consists in the abstraction of economic theorising from scientific innovation and from technical progress. In its nineteenth century guise the assumption is that the 'state of the arts' is constant; in its twentieth century guise that a simple transfer of existing technologies to underdeveloped societies is possible. The other ideological element is to put all the blame on the inability or unwillingness of the people in underdeveloped countries to make use of existing facilities. This comes near to the prejudice about the 'ignorant and idle native'. But to anyone who has worked in this field, it is clear that even the adaptation of existing knowledge to the different physical and social needs and conditions of less developed countries requires creative and imaginative innovation comparable to new discovery so that there is no hard and fast line between the Communications Gap and the Suitability Gap.

But in many areas there is not even a technology which can be adapted. The technology has to be invented; in some cases, possibly reinvented, for technical knowledge decumulates as well as accumulates, and things once known and now forgotten may be useful; but invention or discovery there has to be.

The absence of technologies appropriate to the low-income countries is the result, partly of the high incomes and the corresponding pattern of demand in advanced countries, and partly of the high ratios of saving and investment per head, to which these high incomes give rise. They are therefore doubly inappropriate: over a wide range of products it is nearly true to say that what the rich consume, the

Kong, Singapore and Beirut. In each case, marketing pressures in the areas compelled them to re-equip the plants to produce the more elaborate perforation adopted in North America. To have less elaborate perforation than the Americans, even in such private places as lavatories, was regarded as undignified.

[1] S. Kuznets, *Economic Change*, p. 244.

poor do not produce, and what the rich produce, the poor do not (or should not) consume.

The situation may be even worse, because the technologies and products for the rich may compete for scarce skills and capital with the technologies for the poor. Fast private transport, space exploration and catering for sophisticated consumers' choices may prevent or impede the development of technologies for efficient public transport or public health services, for low-cost construction, for mass literacy or for an improved basic diet. In addition, the technologies that meet the most sophisticated demand are also more exciting intellectually, more glamorous professionally, and more closely linked with advanced science. Stuart Hampshire put this point vividly in a review of C. P. Snow's *Public Affairs*.[1]

So faith in technology may result in ever better methods in Massachusetts General Hospital and ever greater medical poverty in outlying places, which lose their few remaining doctors to the centres where progress is made: or, more frivolously, the journey from London to New York becomes shorter and shorter, and from Oxford to Cambridge longer and longer, until after a few more years of 'advance', the first will be shorter than the second. The super-highway and aerodrome come near the village just as the train and bus services are phased out. The older technologies had their corresponding social forms; as they are replaced by the new, those who live at the bottom of the scale of opportunity are left out of the social progress. . . . Just as much modern architecture is fun for the architects, but leaves the mere populace depressed; so much very advanced technology is fun for the technologists, and its few beneficiaries, but leaves the world's villagers just where they were before. As a social scientist, Ludd was inclined to over-simplify; but we still do not have an adequate theory to put in the place of his.

Relation between the two gaps

The common factor in the two technology gaps is that the acquisition of technology is costly though the method of acquisition differs for the two gaps. Imperfect communications and other obstacles to transfer raise the costs of acquisition. But for bridging the Suitability Gap, non-availability rather than high cost is the problem. The implications for analysis and policy of high cost are different from those of non-availability.

The two types of technology gap, Communications Gap and

[1] *The Obesrver Review*, 31 Oct 1971.

Suitability Gap, have different causes and call for different measures.
Closing one may even open up the other. The Communications Gap
can be narrowed by improving communications, compiling cata-
logues, establishing clearing banks, easing patent laws, facilitating
licensing, encouraging training of engineers abroad, changing the
balance of bargaining power, etc., as well as by better scientific and
technological education and training. But the more and the better
advanced technology is communicated, the less likely it is that a new
and more appropriate indigenous technology will be developed.
Better communication reduces both the opportunity and the will to
invent an indigenous technology. Closing an economy off against
foreign influences and particularly against the multinational corporation, may be the correct policies if we wish to close the Suitability
Gap.[1] Attempts to close the Suitability Gap by devoting resources
to the development of an appropriate technology may be frustrated
by the increasingly well-communicated foreign technology, producing
'better' goods more 'efficiently'.[2]

At a deeper level, the question arises whether societies developing
with different methods and making different products can be properly
compared for the purpose of 'gap' calculations. A poor country
neither can nor should fully and uniformly adopt the technologies of
a rich country, not only because it has different factor endowments,
different social and physical (including climatic) conditions and
different patterns of demand, but also because it has different objectives. To develop special technologies, appropriate to the economic,
social and physical conditions of the poorer country, involves accepting permanently some kind of differences between the two

[1] Everett E. Hagen in his book *On the Theory of Social Change* (Tavistock
Publications, 1962) considers Indonesia, India, China and Japan. The country
with the greatest degree of contact with the West is Indonesia, where the Dutch
were present for 300 years. Next comes India where the British gradually expanded
their footholds; then China, where trade along the coast created enclaves from
which trade with the interior was forced on the country; last Japan where the
Tokugawa enforced a policy of no contact with the West except through a small
Dutch trading group. Yet, Japan started to grow first and made rapid progress;
China is well on the way; India comes next and Indonesia last. The order of
economic advance is the reverse of the order of contact (pp. 24–5).

[2] In discussing ways of building up local technical capability, Charles Cooper
writes: '. . . governments may simply refuse to allow local companies to sign
licence agreements and demand predominantly local development of the technology. . . . Japan, for example, has been able to follow restrictive policies in
certain cases where local technical capability is highly developed. It appears that
the Indian government has also limited technical agreements from time to time
and *de facto* stimulated some local development in various fields of process
technology.' 'The Mechanism for Transfer of Technology from Advanced to
Developing Countries' (mimeo) and 'Instrument Industry in India' (Bombay,
1970).

societies. Whether these differences are properly understood as 'gaps' or just as varieties is a matter partly of semantics and partly of valuations. The measurement of output gaps is difficult enough when it is remembered that these will depend upon how different components of measured output are weighted and how unmeasured costs and benefits are treated. The difficulties are similar and even greater when we attempt to define and measure technology gaps.

A possible objection

A recent trend in the location of labour-intensive processes by vertically integrated multinational firms in low-income countries may appear to contradict what I have been saying so far. Especially in electronics and electrical components, but also in garments, gloves, leather, luggage, baseballs, watches and other consumer goods, and in electrical machinery, machine tools, accounting machines, typewriters, etc., processes that require much labour and initially limited capital and skills have been located in South Korea, Taiwan, Mexico, Hong Kong, Singapore, the West Indian islands, Mauritius. In one sense, the doctrine of comparative advantage seems to be vindicated, though in a manner quite different from that normally envisaged. It is foreign, not domestic, capital and management that are highly mobile and combined with the plentiful immobile domestic labour. Specialisation is not by commodities but by factors: the poor countries specialising in low-skilled labour, leaving the rewards for capital, management and know-how to the rich. Cost advantages are not passed on to consumers in lower prices and the profits accrue to the parent company. The continued operation of this type of international specialisation depends upon the continuation of substantial wage differentials (hence absence of trade union action to push wages up), continuing access to the markets of the parent companies (hence stronger pressure from importing interests than from domestic producers displaced by the low-cost processes and components including trade unions in rich countries) and continuing permission by host countries to operate with minimum taxes, tariffs and other regulations. The bargaining power of host countries in this situation is likely to be weak and the question is whether such a division of gains between parent and host, between capital and labour, remains acceptable. The gains to the host country are confined to the wages of those employed if the alternative is unemployment. While such a strategy has attractions for some countries faced with labour surpluses and foreign exchange shortages and poorly endowed with natural resources, the potential gains may not be considered worth the social costs.

Obstacles to the spread of benefits

Why, then, is there such a wide and widening gap between potential and realisations, between the S & T of the most advanced and of the least advanced countries? Why are there technology gaps? There are (at least) three reasons for the gaps.[1]

First, scientific attitudes and institutions in many less developed countries are weak or absent and there are obstacles to the use of S & T in the social structure of these countries. They often lack a fully rational, experimental and scientific outlook and are not adapted to the introduction or acceptance of systematic change. This explains partly why no use is made of so much S & T that already exists and is available. (This is relevant to the Communications Gap.) The absence of institutions refers not only to institutions directly concerned with S & T, such as research and training institutes. All social institutions may bear on the acceptability of S & T. Thus an antiquated system of land tenure may prevent the use of modern seeds or irrigation to improve crops. A system of sharing earnings with family members may prevent the growth of an innovating entrepreneurial class. Bureaucratic red tape may discourage business men from innovating. A system of social values may attach low status to engineers and entrepreneurs. There is a vicious circle: S & T are necessary for development, but equally, development, with the disruptions that it brings, is necessary for the growth of S & T. Only those who already have an indigenous S & T capability can successfully absorb new S & T. It can be very hard to break out of this mutually reinforcing low-equilibrium trap.

The second reason is the heavy concentration of expenditure on research and development (R & D)[2] in developed countries and the wrong orientation and emphasis of this expenditure there: wrong, that is, from the point of view of solving the problems of the poor countries and contributing to a wider sharing of the benefits of S & T. The orientation of most R & D expenditure is either irrelevant to these problems (like space research) or positively detrimental to their development efforts (like the concentration on improving temporate

[1] The following owes much to a paper 'Science, Technology and Under-development: The Case for Reform' by the Sussex Group under the chairmanship of Professor Hans Singer, 'Science and Technology for Development – Proposals for the Second UN Development Decade' (United Nations, New York, 1970), Sales No. E.70 I.23 pp. 18–41.

[2] R & D, though clearly related to, is not the same as S & T. Many techno-logical innovations are done by small inventors or are the by-product, intended or unintended, of other activities or are imported. Again, innovation overlaps with, but does not coincide with, narrowly interpreted S & T. Some of the most important innovations relate to changes in organisation, marketing, accounting, personnel management, etc.

zone agriculture at the expense of tropical agriculture or the $1,000 million per year research on synthetics which knocks out many exports of the developing countries). (This is relevant to the Suitability Gap.) Of the total expenditure on R & D, which is an important and relatively easily measurable part of S & T, only 1 per cent is specifically directed at the solution of the problems of the poor countries. The wrong orientation has, in turn, three results. Firstly, it leads to a misorientation of efforts in the less developed countries themselves, because standards and interests are prescribed by what goes on in the most prestigious centres in rich countries. This might be called the internal brain drain: the diversion of talent inside the developing countries to problems irrelevant to their development.

Secondly, it leads to the (external) brain drain, so that the scarce professional manpower, educated and trained in poor countries, contributes to augmenting the S & T of the rich countries. The flow of scientists and engineers from poor to rich countries now exceeds the flow of technical assistance from rich to poor. The inability of the developing countries to find employment for these people is both cause and effect of their loss of professional manpower.

Thirdly, the wrong orientation leads to a composition of the stock of knowledge that may be harmful to the development efforts of the poor, like the concentration on synthetics already cited. Another instance of the wrong direction of existing R & D is the industrial technology, developed in conditions of labour scarcity and capital abundance. There is also the concentration on *products* that meet the needs of high-income, labour-scarce societies, while gaps remain in the range of products that meet the needs of low-income societies in which labour is abundant.[1] Transfer of inappropriate technologies and products aggravates the large and growing under-utilisation of labour from which all underdeveloped countries suffer and it increases inequality in these countries. This is especially relevant to the obstacles to closing the Suitability Gap. As a result, the international technology gaps are matched by domestic technology gaps inside the poor countries. The existence of such gaps within poor countries would not matter if the countries proceeded, like Japan or China in their different ways, 'on two legs', so that modern technology co-existed with traditional and intermediate technology, each supporting

[1] Celso Furtado in *Development and Underdevelopment* and Frances Stewart have emphasised the inappropriateness of many *products* introduced into developing countries, in contrast to the usual emphasis on inappropriate *processes*. If the costs of thermal and other pollution, and the use of irreplaceable, exhaustible raw materials were to be fully taken into account, the appropriateness of many sophisticated products would become more doubtful even for rich, industrial societies. In any case, appropriate costing would lead to a different international division of labour and location of production.

the other. But in many countries the modern technology destroys the traditional one and eliminates opportunities and incentives to invent a substitute. International inequalities in job opportunities and income distribution are thus matched by internal inequalities. The modern technology, with its sophisticated products, distributes the lion's share of incomes to profit earners and the small, employed labour aristocracy. These groups in turn provide the market for the high technology products, make the investment profitable and constitute vested interests for its perpetuation. Inequality is both the result and the cause of the misapplied high technology.

In these ways, the small share of 2 per cent of total world R & D that poor countries spend on R & D is (through the internal brain drain) rendered less productive than it otherwise would be and the large share of 98 per cent is either irrelevant or harmful. Of the 98 per cent, 45 per cent is spent on defence and space and another 7 per cent on atomic energy. Even with the most generous allowance for unexpected spin-offs, this is a fantastic waste of world resources.

It is important not to make false claims. Statisticians have found no correlation between R & D expenditure and economic growth. Indeed, there is evidence of a negative correlation between growth and the proportion of GNP spent on R & D. The negative correlation may partly be due to the fact that countries that spend a lot on R & D also spend a high proportion of it on defence, space and allied projects. The links between R & D, S & T and growth are subtle and complicated. In addition to the fact that much innovation is not S & T and that much technology is not the result of R & D, the effective application of innovations usually requires capital and the right type and attitude of people. Large expenditures on R & D can remain unproductive for lack of capital or of engineers and business managers, or absence of a receptive social climate. But equally there is no doubt that problem-orientated research pays off handsomely. Quite small sums devoted to research into the new varieties of rice, wheat and maize showed how the identification of a problem and research directed at its solution can yield high returns. It also, incidentally, illustrates the obstacles put into the path of the spread of progress by the nation state. Only non-governmental institutions like the Ford and Rockefeller Foundations could devote money to a purpose that would benefit others than those in whose country the work was done. The much larger sums of national aid have to be used for purposes that the recipient nation states conceive as in their own interest, which tends to be rather narrowly interpreted.

The third reason for the gap is the prevalence of obstacles to access by less developed countries to whatever relevant and useful S & T exists in the world. Communications in this area are poor, institutions absent or weak and the wheels of the transfer mechanism are badly oiled. This is relevant to the Communications Gap.

Why has the market not closed the gap?

We now turn to policies. The first question that occurs to an economist is to ask why has the market system not provided incentives for the appropriate direction and utilisation of S & T? Though underdeveloped countries are poor, they are potentially large and growing markets. Why have there been so few inventions of low-cost, simple, agricultural or industrial machinery? Why has there not been more progress in low-cost construction or transport? Why do those industrial countries that have a comparative advantage in manufacturing industry, protect, often at high cost to themselves, their agriculture, instead of exchanging low-cost machinery and durable consumer goods (say a £10 refrigerator) for the agricultural exports of underdeveloped countries? Henry Ford announced in 1909 that his aim was to produce and sell a cheap, reliable model 'for the great multitude' so that every man 'making a good salary' could 'enjoy with his family the blessing of hours of pleasure in God's great open space'. The mass production of the model T Ford ushered in a major industrial and social revolution, the cars of which have, incidentally, destroyed the 'great open space'. Why has no-one initiated a corresponding revolution to raise and tap the purchasing power of the world's teeming millions? Insufficient foresight in the face of still small markets (small in terms of purchasing power) and over-estimation of risks or a divergence between private (including political) and social risks may be part of the explanation but it cannot be the whole.

It is easier to see why the market in complex, specialised, often secret or patented, modern technology is different from the market for turnips or even for land. Technical and managerial knowledge and its commercial and industrial application cannot easily be assimilated to the treatment of the conventional factors of production: land, labour and capital, for at least five reasons.

In the first place, knowledge, although clearly not available in superabundance, is not scarce in the sense that the more we use of it in one direction, the less is left over for use in another, or the more I use it, the less is left for you. The use of knowledge is subject to indivisibilities and average costs diverge widely from marginal costs. The result of this is that it is much cheaper for the multinational corporation to use what it already has: the existing but inappropriate technology developed in high-income, labour-scarce countries than to spend money on developing a new technology, more appropriate for the conditions of the developing countries.

Secondly, there is the well-known difficulty of appropriating the fruits of efforts devoted to increasing knowledge and the need either to treat it as a public good or to erect legal barriers to appropriation by others, in order to create and maintain incentives for research and invention. This leads to the divergence of social from private benefits and costs.

Thirdly, knowledge is, in a sense, substitutable for other productive factors, so that an improvement in technical knowledge makes it possible to produce the same product with less land, labour or capital, or with more capital but a more than proportionate decrease of labour or land, or a better product with the same amount of other factors. But its costs fall under those of either labour (especially trained employees) or capital (purchase of patents or research laboratories or equipment or intermediate products or other assets embodying the knowledge). As a result, the market for knowledge is normally part of the market for these inputs. If the owners of the inputs that embody knowledge command monopoly power, they can exercise this power over the sale of the knowledge component of the whole package.

Fourthly, the accumulation of knowledge is only tenuously related to expenditure on its acquisition. Indeed, useful knowledge can be accumulated without any identifiable allocation of resources for this purpose and, conversely and more obviously, large resources can be devoted to research without any productive results. There is, in the nature of discovery, uncertainty about the outcome of efforts devoted to inventions. This uncertainty cannot be removed by insurance, for insurance would also remove the incentive for research. A common way of reducing it is through diversification of research activities. Only large corporations are capable of this. In a private enterprise system the large multinational corporation has an enormous advantage in reducing the risks attached to research.[1]

A fifth and even more fundamental difference lies in the absence of the justification of the common assumption about the 'informed' buyer. Where technology is bought and sold, as it often is, through the purchase of an asset (or through admitting direct private foreign investment), the underdeveloped recipient country as 'buyer' of the technology is, in the nature of things, very imperfectly informed about many features of the product that it buys. The common assumption

[1] Cf. K. J. Arrow, 'Economic Welfare and the Allocation of Resources to Invention', in *The Rate and Direction of Inventive Activity: Economic and Social Factors* (National Bureau of Economic Research, Princeton University Press, 1962) pp. 609–26; reprinted in *Economics of Information and Knowledge*, Penguin Modern Economics Readings, edited by D. M. Lamberton.

about an informed buyer choosing what suits him best is even less justified here than is usual. If the country knew precisely what it was buying, there would be no need – or considerably less need – to buy it. Knowledge about knowledge is often the knowledge itself.[1] Part of what it buys is the information on which an informed purchase would be based. As a result, the recipient Government will be in a weak position *vis-à-vis* the investing firm when it comes to laying down terms and conditions. Excessive 'prices' paid by recipient Governments for capital equipment or imported components and technologies inappropriate from the country's point of view, or acceptance of excessively onerous conditions must therefore be the rule rather than the exception in a market where information embodied in equipment is bought by ignorant buyers.

The five features characteristic of the market for technical knowledge – (i) indivisibility, (ii) inappropriability, (iii) embodiment in other factors, (iv) uncertainty and (v) impossibility to know the value until the purchase is made – go some way towards explaining the absence of a free market in which the low-income countries could buy this knowledge.

The situation is quite different from that of an 'equilibrium price' reached in a competitive market. It is more like that of a bilateral monopoly or oligopoly where bargaining theory applies. There is a vast gap between the incremental cost to the owner of the technology of parting with it and the value to the country or firm wishing to acquire it. The cost to the seller is either zero, since the investment has already taken place, or the small amount required to adapt it to the circumstances of the developing country. The value to the buyer is the large amount that he would have to spend to start inventing and developing from scratch and to 'go it alone'. The final figure in the range between these two limits is determined by bargaining strength, which is very unequally distributed.

Here again, international inequality and internal inequality in the poor countries reinforce one another. Unequal income distribution is both effect and cause of inappropriate technologies and products. It is an effect because capital-intensive methods and products raise the share of profits and of rewards for sophisticated skills and reduce that of unskilled labour; and markets for sophisticated, differentiated products require a small élite with high incomes. And it is a cause,

---

[1] Constantine V. Vaitsos, 'Bargaining and the Distribution of Returns in the Purchase of Technology by Developing Countries', *Bulletin of the Institute of Development Studies*, vol. 3, no. 1 (Oct 1970). Arrow writes: '. . . there is a fundamental paradox in the determination of demand for information: its value for the purchaser is not known until he has the information, but then he has in effect acquired it without cost.' op. cit. (Penguin) p. 148.

because the existence of a market for differentiated luxuries deprives enterprises of an incentive to produce low-cost, more appropriate products for a mass market. Henry Ford had the advantage not only of imagination but also of relatively high real wages.

Four policies for closing the gaps[1]

Policies for closing the gap suffer, as we have seen, from the dilemma that measures that narrow the Suitability Gap *may* widen the Communications Gap and vice versa. There may, therefore, be alternative routes to technological independence. Nevertheless, a carefully selected combination of measures for narrowing both gaps is possible. But they have to be seen as a package and have to be adopted together. The adoption of any one of these policies without the others may be worse than not doing anything. The first three types of policy and the need to strengthen bargaining power are relevant to the Suitability Gap; the first also and the fourth policy to the Communications Gap.

First, the less developed countries must build up their indigenous S & T by raising their expenditure on R & D above the present 0·2 per cent of their GNP. While the total percentage is not meaningful, it provides a guideline, if combined with the other three policies. At present, not only is the ratio very low, but much of it is spent on research irrelevant to development.

Secondly, a higher proportion of development aid should be devoted to supporting S & T. Not all of this need or should be intergovernmental aid. As we have argued, non-government aid can have special virtues.

Thirdly, the advanced industrial countries should devote a larger proportion of their total R & D expenditure (the Pearson Commission recommended 5 per cent), to R & D that is relevant to the problems of the developing countries. Priority areas have been identified and include extension of the Green Revolution to millet, sorghum, tuber crops, etc., pest control, desalination, the development of salt-resistant plants, the use of sea water for irrigation, birth control, cyclone warning and weather control, solar power, production of edible proteins, appropriate industrial technology, use of tropical hardwoods for pulp and paper production, use of indigenous building

---

[1] These are the policies recommended in the paper by the Sussex Group, except that the argument for the fourth policy is strengthened. The targets of 0·5 per cent of GNP for R & D by less developed countries and of 5 per cent of aid for R & D by developed countries have been adopted by the Pearson Commission and are part of the international strategy of the UN Second Development Decade.

materials, exploitation of the ocean and sea beds, irrigation, new forms of transport.[1]

Fourthly, there should be improved access to what is available. An international technology transfer bank has been proposed that would, on the one hand, reduce the risks of those acquiring and wishing to sell S & T, and, on the other hand, reduce the costs for those wishing to buy it. But the basic task goes much deeper than overcoming imperfections of the market: it is to bring about a more equal balance of bargaining power.

Bargaining power is, in turn, partly a function of information and partly of solidarity between countries. Access could be greatly improved by adding to informed knowledge of the buyer, by assisting him in bargaining with the multinational owners of technology, and by joint, rather than competitive action of several buying countries. Potential buyers of knowledge *within* an advanced industrial country are in a much stronger position than less developed buying countries, because the government in the former shoulders a large proportion of the costs of acquiring knowledge, through subsidies, tax deductions and the direct supply of information. No similar mechanism of insurance, subsidy and diffusion is at work internationally. The governments of developed countries are also in a stronger position than those of underdeveloped countries in bargaining with the multinational corporation, because their officials and businessmen can match its information and skills.

How then can we remove this handicap? Since bilateral assistance in bargaining is bound to be suspect, in view of the presumption that parent countries will support their own parent firms, this is eminently an area for multilateral assistance, at any rate until international political institutions have caught up with the multinational company.

Summary

We have started by asking the question: why are there international income inequalities? We have ascribed them to differences in applied knowledge. This raised the question, why can productive knowledge be communicated and diffused within an advanced nation but not between nations or within underdeveloped nations? What are the obstacles to the international diffusion of benefits?

We have found these in two areas: obstacles to communication and absence of suitable technologies. The obstacles to communication can again be divided into those due to costs of transfer and those due to

[1] The priority areas have been spelt out in considerable detail in the UN *World Plan of Action for the Application of Science and Technology to Development*, UN Publication Sales No. E 71. II.A.18 (New York, 1971).

intentional restrictions or the exercise of monopoly power. But even perfect communication would not meet the need for quite different technologies from those developed in high-income countries.

Measures that reduce the Communications Gap might make the Suitability Gap wider and vice versa, but a set of integrated actions attacking both gaps has a chance of success. Technical knowledge cannot be marketed like other products or factors because it possesses the following peculiar features – (i) indivisibility, (ii) inappropriability, (iii) embodiment in other factors, (iv) uncertainty and (v) impossibility to know its full value until bought. Policies for closing the two gaps are interdependent, so that the pursuit of any one in isolation might make matters worse. A set of integrated actions attacking both gaps, combined with other measures, has a chance of success.

Part Four

The Commonwealth

23 A New Commonwealth

THE Commonwealth, too, has its Cavaliers, who are Wrong but Wromantic, and its Roundheads, who are Right but Repulsive: the soft-hearted idealists and the hard-headed realists. According to the Roundheads, the hard facts of geography, or of Britain's economic weakness, or of the hostility of the newly independent Afro-Asians and their reaction against colonialism have made the Commonwealth obsolete: a millstone: an albatross. The sooner we get rid of it the better.

According to the Cavaliers, historical continuity, a common language, common institutions and shared values, a shared respect for democracy and the rule of law and the bridging of the gaps between rich and poor and white and black make the Commonwealth a rare opportunity for international co-operation. I believe that both are wrong.

The continuities of history create illusions. Political independence presents such a radical break with the past that to postulate continuity has proved, and will prove again, misleading and dangerous. The common language is shared only by a small élite, and the Westminster parliamentary model is not appropriate for many countries of Africa and Asia.

If history is out, geography is in. Who would not wish to swing with the regional groupings of Europe, LAFTA, NAFTA, Panafrica, and gain strength through joining? Who does not venerate the so-called facts of geography? But behind the new regionalism there is ignorance, fashion and the search for an ersatz empire. Modern economic facts make for *inter*-continental groupings, because sea freights have fallen compared with land transport costs. In particular, the economic benefits from regional integration between large, rich, industrial countries – as in Europe – are now small or absent, and the political gains dubious.

But one can be hard-headed without being hard-boiled. With an effort of the imagination one can envisage a non-square Commonwealth, proponents of which share neither the old nostalgia with the Cavaliers nor the new brutalism with the Roundheads. Sir Edward Boyle and Michael Lipton have both suggested that this new

Commonwealth should be *multilateral*; that it should be built on growing areas of *common interest*; and that it should be able (however tentatively at first) to commit its members to *decisions*.[1]

This Commonwealth in fact already exists, inconspicuously and practical, in many areas not considered newsworthy. For whether it is true or not that no news is good news, it is certainly true that good news is no news. In the professions, in law, in education and the universities, in medicine, in chambers of commerce, in market development, in tourism, in telecommunications, in the Commonwealth Institute, the Commonwealth Foundation, the Commonwealth Development Corporation, the Commonwealth Parliamentary Association and the Commonwealth Secretariat, individuals and governments co-operate constructively. But the Commonwealth that appears in the headlines is one of *bilateral* relations, radiating outward from Britain at the hub; it is one of *declining* shares of trade, investment and earnings and of sentimental appeals to tradition and goodwill to make up for lack of interest, lack of active salesmanship and lack of policy; and it is one of ministerial or high-level official meetings, where resolutions are passed which *bind no one*.

No wonder that the battle between the Roundheads and the Cavaliers is conducted over the publicised, sentimentalised anaemic Commonwealth, where the whole system of relations is poisoned by any charge which the periphery may wish to raise against a withdrawing Britain (Rhodesia, Tanzania), while the full-blooded multilateral Commonwealth of common interests goes on quietly and modestly, outside the limelight. Admittedly, much of it is only talk. But talk often precedes action.

Does this second Commonwealth provide a basis for further constructive action? I think the answer is 'yes'. Take only one example of how to turn multilateralism to good advantage. Effective co-operation for development will not be achieved, as in UNCTAD (the United Nations Commission for Trade and Development), by confrontation of monolithic blocks (although in UNCTAD too the Commonwealth group can do something to soften the hardening postures of the rich against the poor). Developing countries can learn much from one another's experience. Technical assistance by countries which have only recently tackled problems similar to those faced by others is often more useful than the assistance by countries far removed from these problems. Just as India has much to offer in the fields of family planning and land consolidation, and Hong Kong in industrialisation and export promotion, so the experience of Kenyan

[1] See Michael Lipton, 'Prospects for Commonwealth Co-operation and Planning', in *Commonwealth Policy in a Global Context*, edited by Paul Streeten and Hugh Corbet (Frank Cass, 1971).

tea smallholders is more relevant to poor tropical farmers than is farming experience in Iowa. Development can be a co-operative endeavour in which almost everyone at various stages of development can offer something, and it is both false and psychologically damaging to divide the Commonwealth into the aiding and the aided.

There are other ways in which a multilateral network of relations can greatly improve upon the present bilateral set-up. Larger financing by rich Commonwealth countries of the training of men and women in third countries of the Commonwealth could increase the effectiveness of educational aid and technical assistance. The limited untying of British aid, so as to permit expenditure of funds on goods supplied by other underdeveloped Commonwealth countries, could encourage the now stagnating trade between these countries. Similarly, Britain, Canada and Australia, if willing to give one another credit, could make a start with reciprocal untying of their capital aid. The new Special Drawing Rights could be used to finance regional payments unions between developing Commonwealth countries so as to permit them to expand trade with each other without fear of foreign exchange losses and to embark on more rational investment and industrial location policies.

In private overseas investment, there is scope for joint ventures, between overseas private and home private, between government and private and for other combinations, which would take the nationalistic steam out of the business and gradually transfer ownership and management of firms to the host countries. Joint investment guarantees could reduce political risks and the required rate of return, and thus contribute to a larger flow of investment with a greater development impact.

Such a multilateral Commonwealth, based on growing common interests, would no longer have its fulcrum in London and, for that reason, Britain's contribution could be greater.

Another constructive proposal is Michael Lipton's idea of a Commonwealth Indicative Plan (with strong emphasis on the 'indicative'), in which the present absurd investment and export policies of some countries might be avoided, in which cement and steel plants would be located according to more rational criteria, and in which agricultural diversification by one country would no longer mean diversifying into another country's surplus crops. In particular we could attempt to identify the growth industries and the declining industries of the future and to sketch out dynamic alternatives to the present policy of propping up the decaying sectors by defensive investment. If, instead of supporting cotton textiles, we shift capital, management and labour into engineering products where there is a shortage, we simultaneously open up markets for the cotton textiles of Hong Kong, India and Pakistan and speed up our own progress. Such matching of markets, based on detailed forecasts of industrial change, contains enormous scope for mutually advantageous fruitful co-operation.

We hear often that the Commonwealth cuts across divisions of race, religion and wealth. Equally important, but less publicised, is the fact that it unites industrial and agricultural economies, countries with plenty of capital and labour scarcity and countries with a surfeit of labour and capital scarcity. It is here that the basis for international specialisation lies: in the exchange of low-cost cotton and jute textiles, cane sugar and labour-intensive, low-technology consumer goods and machinery, for sophisticated engineering goods, not in the much touted figures of swapping Renault Dauphines for Morris Minors. For the gains from international trade are measured not by volumes or values or shares of trade, or by their rates of growth, but by the costs that would be incurred if imported products (like copper or cotton textiles) would have to be produced at home or would have to be done without. By this measure, the Commonwealth is a source of greater gains for Britain than Europe.

Similarly in the field of training and technical assistance, private investment, capital aid and monetary reform, common interests can be identified and co-operatively pursued. There are strong complementarities between rich and poor Commonwealth countries in agriculture, where the rich should, in their own interest, abandon protection and the poor expand production; in family planning, where high returns can be achieved with few resources; in education, where exchanges of teachers benefit everyone; in plugging the brain drain, where lack of co-operation can play havoc with development efforts; and in the co-operation between ageing and increasingly youthful societies.

One reason why the Commonwealth has been, mistakenly, regarded as a liability rather than an asset, is to be found in the nature of present British interest-groupings. If the producers of beet sugar, of Lancashire cotton textiles and of Dundee jute products are better organised and more vocal than the consumers of these products, the great potential benefits from freer access for Commonwealth imports are obscured. Only the cartel arrangements between the industrial giants producing and selling in Europe appear as attractions. But if the Commonwealth links could be used to create or strengthen genuine cross groupings of now diffused and fragmented interests – say between British retailers, interested in low-priced consumer goods and the numerous, small Commonwealth producers of labour-intensive products, like sewing machines, light electric motors, clothes, shoes and of the crops grown by unorganised farmers – then the advantages of expanding Britain's Commonwealth trade would become obvious.

The growth of independent retail chains and of larger and stronger retail shops may produce such a shift in alliances and may weaken the producer lobbies. Much of the reorientation of our trade policies is derived from the illusion that our common interests are with those who shout most. Yet, there ought to be no difference between welcoming technical progress, which lowers the cost of producing synthetic fibres, and admitting into the country more natural fibres from countries which can produce them at lower costs then we do. But the former is hailed as a technical asset of our country, while the latter is decried as a political liability. The chemical industry is articulate and organised, the people who wear the shirts and those who grow the cotton and weave the cloth are inarticulate and unorganised.

The dialectic between the continuities of history and the contiguities of geography, between the 'idealists' and the 'realists', is a sham dialectic. True, one important argument for using the Commonwealth is that it exists. It may be that, if it did not exist, we would not invent it, although I suspect that we should try to invent something rather like it. But the fact is that it does exist. Let us not throw away the advantages we have. Instead of playing unhappy families (who wants Mr Singh, the Asian trade?) let us exploit the heterogeneity of the Commonwealth and make it a force, not a farce, an asset, not a liability.

24 Access to the New Europe for Third World Trade

BRITAIN'S interests and obligations in the Commonwealth are often thought to conflict with her attempts to forge closer links with Western Europe and, in particular, with her repeated attempts to join the European Economic Community (EEC). British membership of the EEC is the most immediate trade challenge to Commonwealth countries and to Britain herself. But just as there may be advantages in joining one trade grouping, so corresponding disadvantages may arise from opting out of others. Any trade advantages to Britain from joining the EEC have to be weighed against the trading disadvantages of exclusion from, or weakened links with, other groupings such as the Commonwealth preference system.

What, then, are the conflicts between Britain's economic interests in, and obligations towards the Commonwealth on the one hand and closer economic association with Western Europe on the other?

This problem, like many other problems of weighing trading interests with different countries, or groups of countries, is usually treated in terms of comparative trade shares. To assess interest or dependence in this way is to fall a victim to trade fetishism: the treatment of trade as if it were a good thing in itself, irrespective of the gains derived. Thus it may be said that in 1968 less than a quarter of British trade was conducted with the Commonwealth, while nearly a third was done with Western Europe, over 20 per cent being with the EEC. Alternatively, the interested reading public is often presented, in the debate over Britain's place in the world, with rates of growth of foreign trade as if they were of special significance in themselves and, of course, it is easy to show that over the last ten years Britain's trade with Western Europe has grown much more rapidly than it has with Commonwealth countries (see Table 24.1).

Regarding the first approach, comparisons between trade values as a way of measuring dependence on markets and supplies, can be very misleading. Trade with one area may be very large, but it may

TABLE 24.1

Changing Shares of UK Exports and Imports, 1957–68

	Commonwealth	*Western Europe*	*EEC*
	%	%	%
Shares in Imports			
1957	38	25	12
1968	25	37	22
Shares in Exports			
1957	38	28	15
1968	23	36	29

be conducted entirely in the exchange of close substitutes. The fact that a large number of engineering goods of one type are exchanged for goods of a similar type does not mean that the countries are very important to each other. Such trade may be further artificially inflated by discriminatory pricing and tax policies, lower prices being charged in foreign competitive markets than in protected domestic markets. The volume of trade subject to such cross-hauling is a misleading guide to the benefits derived from it and substantial reductions can be envisaged which hardly reduce the gains from trade. On the other hand, a small volume of trade may be conducted in essentials without which production (or even life) could not be carried on.

In this context, it is the consumers' and producers' surpluses that matter (or, as some prefer, the divergencies of the transformation ratios and of the substitution ratios between the member countries before tariff reductions); that is, the deprivations caused by reductions in trade, not the total value of trade. By this test Britain depends much more on other Commonwealth countries than on other West European ones. Many European manufactured products could be easily replaced by domestic products. But few Commonwealth products could be replaced without great sacrifices. The question may therefore be asked: should Britain endanger her economically essential connections with the Commonwealth for further enlargement of less essential new links?

The second line of argument cites, not shares in trade, but rates of growth of trade. It is often said that trade between industrial countries has grown much faster than trade between industrialised and primary producing countries and, more particularly, that West European trade has grown more rapidly since 1950 than Commonwealth trade. If Britain looks for her markets of the future (it is said), they are more likely to be in Europe than in Africa or Asia; the sooner she casts off the Commonwealth albatross, the better.

Expanding markets, however, are not necessarily in themselves an indication of increasing importance. First, the statistics of trade growth, like so many others, depend on the choice of the base year. Using a pre-war year as a base, Commonwealth trade has shrunk much less in its importance to Britain than if a post-war year is used.[1] The direction of world trade during the 1930s, 1940s and 1950s was changed by depression, war and then by the post-war dollar shortage, with Britain's Commonwealth trade benefiting from the preferences and later the import licensing arrangements of the sterling area. It is essentially a value judgement whether the pre-1933 or the post-war shares in trade are regarded as 'normal'. On trade growth statistics there is a second point. For rapidly growing trade, precisely like large trade shares, may largely be confined to the exchange of increasing numbers of Renault Dauphines for Morris Minors, of similar products for which the gains from trade are small.

On the question of British membership of the EEC, an argument which is more convincing than the deployment of statistics on comparative trade shares and comparative growth of trade suggests that the scope for mutual gains from complementing each other is greater if countries are producing similar products than if they are already complementary. Free trade with Western Europe, it is argued, is likely to be, on balance, trade-creating, whilst preferential or free trade with the Commonwealth would be trade-diverting, by encouraging the growth of inefficient industries. One could then point to the expansion of coal and steel production in the countries of the European Coal and Steel Community as suggesting that precisely where the same products were produced by several countries inefficiently before free trade, the best opportunity for efficient reallocation of resources exists (although there is no evidence that this has actually happened).

On closer inspection such arguments are found to be not altogether convincing. It is of course true that the rest of the Commonwealth is more complementary to Britain than the rest of Western Europe is to her. Free trade with the Commonwealth, combined with joint protection, may therefore divert production from low-cost suppliers outside to high-cost suppliers inside. But the argument for union with similar countries is valid only if the countries, though actually similar, are potentially complementary. And the argument against union with dissimilar countries is valid only if the countries, though actually complementary, are, as a result of the union, attempting to become more similar. These provisos are not met in the case we are

---

[1] This point has been demonstrated by a number of writers, but see, in particular, John Knapp, 'Would Britain Profit from the EEC?', *The Round Table* (London, April 1967).

considering. There are reasons to doubt that Europe can become very complementary and also that the Commonwealth countries would not in any case try to put up their own industries.

Furthermore, these arguments always assume constant, or diminishing, returns to scale. If, as is probable, the industries in the Commonwealth countries are subject to increasing returns to scale, the switch in trade from outside to inside sources of supply can mean a gain in efficiency. These important qualifications weaken the economic case for union with other European countries and against closer ties with other Commonwealth countries.

In addition, the argument assumes that money costs are a good indication of real costs. This is not so for mainly two reasons. First, money costs include taxes and tariffs on inputs of production which ought to be excluded for a calculation of real costs. Secondly, wages in underdeveloped countries do not reflect the opportunity costs of labour but are institutionally determined and usually higher than social costs. For both reasons, what may look like trade diversion, may in fact be trade creation.

Finally, one might argue, on the side of Europe, that although there are historical connections with what is now the Commonwealth, the connections with Europe are older. In the heyday of Britain's prosperity in the last century she led the way in free trade with Europe, whereas much of the growth of Commonwealth trade is simply the result of the depression in the 1930s (Ottawa and imperial preference), the last war and the post-war period of disturbance and dollar shortage (discriminatory exchange controls, bulk purchase and long-term contracts). On a return to 'normal' conditions one might therefore expect a turning by Britain to the markets of Western Europe (and, it should follow, to the new industrial market of Japan). In any case, it is argued, present Commonwealth preferences are small. The average margin of preference for British goods is about 7 per cent on all Commonwealth trade, itself less than a quarter of Britain's total exports. These preferences, moreover, are being eroded through inflation and general trade liberalisation. But special provisions to safeguard Commonwealth interests are likely to be included, it is added, in any European agreement between the EEC and the 'applicant states', namely Britain, Denmark, Norway and the Republic of Ireland.

To this historical line of argument it can be replied that history is neither a very good nor an unambiguous guide to future prospects. The return of 'normalcy' has seen a number of countries outside Europe in the world of developed economies. But Canada, Australia and, to a lesser extent, New Zealand are interested in diversifying their overseas trade. The dangers of historical illusions need to be pointed out to those in Britain who hanker after the old Commonwealth as well as to those who, in extolling 'the new Europe', are often simply hankering after the old Europe.

Europe and developing Commonwealth countries

But there should be no need for serious conflict between Britain's position and interests in the Commonwealth and her position and interests in Western Europe. The cultivation of Commonwealth trade is not inconsistent with membership of the Common Market. Careful thought and imagination are none the less required in order to resolve spurious conflicts and resist well-organised vested interests. An effort should also be made to ensure that the exercise of such thought and imagination is seen to be made by observers lest fresh antagonisms are needlessly aroused.

Over one-third of the British imports from other Commonwealth countries are raw materials that enter the EEC duty-free. Agricultural products raise very important issues, but are not dealt with here. Other imports from the Commonwealth are manufactured and semi-manufactured goods which benefit significantly from the tariff preferences they enjoy in the British market.

Imports into Britain from developing Commonwealth countries in the process of industrialisation are precisely the kind of goods (labour-intensive, with a low technological content and often based on raw-material industries) in which the potential benefits of trade for Britain are substantial. But vested interests likely to be affected by higher imports of these products into Britain and other West European countries are capable of uttering loud protests. Their loudness is a measure of the benefits to be derived for producers in the developing countries and for consumers in developed country markets from the liberalisation of trade in these products.

The Strasbourg Plan recalled

In searching for a solution to the problem of encouraging the exports of developing Commonwealth countries, while permitting Britain to develop still closer economic relations with other West European countries, the imaginative scheme proposed in the early 1950s under the Strasbourg Plan might be recalled.[1] Its purpose was to improve economic relations between the member countries of the Council of Europe and the overseas countries with which they had constitutional links.

The idea was for the raw material and food producing potential

[1] *The Strasbourg Plan* (Strasbourg: Council of Europe, 1952).

of the Commonwealth to be harnessed to the manufacturing capacity of Europe. It was intended to eliminate quantitative restrictions and to lower tariffs. Instead of proposing a full customs union, it envisaged a two-tier system, in which the member states of the Council of Europe would grant each other tariffs intermediate between those against the rest of the world and those of the Commonwealth preference system. Such arrangements may be rendered acceptable to the signatories of the General Agreement on Tariffs and Trade (GATT), if any outside country were allowed to join the secondary preference system in return for equivalent concessions.

These proposals relating to trade were linked with other proposals aimed at raising and stabilising the supply of, and the demand for, primary products. Among the suggestions were long-term contracts and international commodity agreements covering both quantities and prices, investment in overseas territories by a special bank to which all European member countries would subscribe and which would also finance public works required in the development of new countries, and encouragement to migration.

Although the Strasbourg Plan was rejected by the British Government, its basic ideas are still helpful in resolving the continuing differences between the European and the British approach to integration.

A distinction has to be drawn between the already developed Commonwealth countries and the developing countries. The principle is now generally accepted and enshrined in GATT, that the rules of equality do not apply to relations between unequals and that developing countries should be granted special privileges in protecting growing industries. France persuaded her EEC partners to accept this principle in their relations with their overseas territories. (And it is also accepted for the underdeveloped regions inside the EEC.) It would be a simple logical step to allow the underdeveloped Commonwealth countries to be associated with the EEC on the same terms as the present associated overseas countries of the EEC – permitting them to protect their infant industries with a preferential tariff on European goods, while granting their products free access to the whole European market. Such a scheme would remove discrimination against the Commonwealth, it would remove Britain's alleged privileged position arising from her double advantage of free trade with Western Europe and preferential trade with the Commonwealth, and it would give the underdeveloped Commonwealth the added advantage of free access to the whole European market. The scheme would apply to countries like India, Pakistan, Ceylon, Malaysia, the Caribbean countries, Nigeria and Ghana, but not to Canada, Australia and New Zealand.

Since this proposal would leave outside the preference system only non-associated, non-Commonwealth countries, and would therefore discriminate against the remaining Asian, African and Latin American foreign countries, it raises the question as to the merits of the scheme of generalised tariff preferences which has been discussed within the United Nations Conference on Trade and Development and the Organisation for Economic Co-operation and Development. More specifically it has to be asked what advantages developing Commonwealth countries could derive from the UNCTAD scheme that would make it worth their while giving up Commonwealth preferences.

Commonwealth and UNCTAD preferences

Less developed countries have been urging upon the industrial countries at UNCTAD, first in the 1964 conference in Geneva and then in the 1968 conference in Delhi, a system of generalised preferences for manufactured and semi-manufactured exports from developing countries that is non-discriminatory as between developing countries and non-reciprocal as far as developed countries are concerned. A considerable literature on the subject is now available.[1]

Against preferences there can be ranged a number of strong arguments. First, few products and few countries would be affected. Tariffs on manufactures and semi-manufactures are already low and will be lowered further as a result of the tariff reductions negotiated in the Kennedy Round of GATT negotiations.

Secondly, the main obstacles to better export performance, on the part of developing countries, lie on the supply side. In spite of low wages, it is lack of know-how and of managerial and marketing skills, as well as protectionist policies in less developed countries which tend to limit export growth.

Thirdly, if preferences were to be combined with market disruption clauses, or tariff quotas, as seems highly likely, there is a danger that restrictions might be more severe under a generalised preference system than in the absence of UNCTAD preferences.

Fourthly, if Commonwealth preferences were to be abandoned without any, or without adequate, French concessions then the less developed countries of the Commonwealth would lose.

Fifthly, disruption clauses together with the exemption of textiles and other 'sensitive' items would rule out those exports with the greatest market potential and whose impact, therefore, on the development of poor countries is likely to be most beneficial.

[1] See, for example, Harry G. Johnson, *Trade Policies Toward Less Developed Countries* (Washington, D.C.: Brookings Institution, 1967; and London: Allen & Unwin, 1967).

Sixthly, the Third World is not monolithic. Differences within the group of less developed countries make it likely that a few countries who need help least would benefit most.

Seventhly, preferences are bound to have an opportunity cost, in terms of other forms of concession. They may reduce other forms of aid which may be more desirable. In addition, the efforts developed to implementing the scheme will divert attention from possibly more important matters.

Finally, if they are regarded as a form of aid, they impose costs on donor countries, including balance of payments costs, without permitting control over the volume, timing and direction of the flow of this aid.

In favour of a generalised scheme of preferences there can be ranged on the other hand a strong set of arguments, some of which meet the criticisms outlined above. First, although average tariffs are becoming low – by 1972 they will be down to 11·2 per cent in the United States, to 10·2 per cent in Britain, to 9·8 per cent in Japan and to 7·6 per cent in the EEC[1] – there is a wide dispersion and some tariffs on goods of great export interest to developing countries are still very high. Although the trade of developing countries is small and concentrated it has been growing rapidly and become more widely spread by both producers and countries.

Secondly, while recent GATT negotiations have lowered tariffs of export interest to developed industrialised economies, those of actual or potential export interest to developing countries have often been excluded from the bargaining process and remain high (although this depends on how comparative reductions are measured).[2]

Thirdly, even a low nominal tariff can be a high effective tariff on the manufacturing process of adding value. Its removal can be a substantial encouragement to industrialisation.

Fourthly, the international mobility of business firms makes it possible for them to make use of low wages by locating firms in less developed countries and thus export know-how, capital, management and skills from the advanced home country of the parent firm to the developing countries. Using this favourable factor combination the firm can then sell to its home country and to other industrial countries, thus making the most of the preference system.

---

[1] Maxwell Stamp and Harry Cowie, 'Britain and the Free Trade Area Option', in Johnson (ed.), *New Trade Strategy for the World Economy* (London: Allen & Unwin, 1969; and Toronto: University of Toronto Press, 1969) p. 205.

[2] According to Balassa's calculations, the reductions of tariff rates on imports from less developed countries appear to be larger than those on total imports. But the level of *effective* production remains over twice as high against imports from developing countries (23 per cent) as against imports from all sources (11 per cent).

Fifthly, while irrational elements enter into decisions on the international location of plant, and while the time limit and disruption clauses might reduce the incentive to direct investment in developing countries, tariff concessions may lead to a reappraisal of investment strategy and may draw attention to profit opportunities that would otherwise have been neglected.

Sixthly, even if benefits were concentrated on a few products and countries, indirect gains will tend to spread to others.

Finally, while the balances of payments of the countries making the concession, as a group, will tend to deteriorate, the balances of payments of those countries within the group which already pursue freer trade policies will tend to benefit. For their share in additional exports to less developed countries will be larger than their share in buying additional imports from them. Their foreign exchange earnings will therefore tend to rise.

The preferences that will emerge from the negotiations begun immediately after the Delhi session of UNCTAD are not likely to be satisfactory to all Commonwealth developing countries. Tariff quotas on a number of 'sensitive' items will discriminate against exports of manufacturers from Commonwealth developing countries to the European Community and to Japan. US insistence on the phasing out of reverse preferences before granting preferences will mean losses to Caribbean and other Commonwealth countries. Escape clauses of various kinds will protect importing countries whenever vested interests scream loud enough. The various schemes are therefore no substitute for the continuation of pressures for better access to markets.

Alternative preference schemes

One possibility would be for the rich Commonwealth countries – Australia, Britain, Canada and New Zealand – and the other industrialised countries to make freer access to their markets for the developing countries an integral part of the next major effort to liberalise still further the trade conducted between themselves. Professor Johnson has reviewed the optional negotiating techniques now under consideration in the major trading nations. Among them is the free trade treaty option which could make provision for a generalised scheme of tariff preferences. Under such a treaty it would be possible for developed countries to share responsibility for assisting developing countries.[1]

Early proposals for a free trade treaty approach to the general

[1] This possibility is discussed in David Wall, *The Third World Challenge* (London: Atlantic Trade Study, Trade Policy Research Centre, 1968).

problem of liberalising trade under GATT rules suggested that the initiative could be taken by the United States, Canada, Britain and the other member countries of the European Free Trade Association, as well as the other developed Commonwealth countries and Japan. It was then thought that the EEC might not be ready to eliminate its common external tariff. These industrial countries are already more liberal in their import policies for manufactures than continental Europe and the scope for displacing internal high-cost producers is therefore smaller.

Effective rates of protection are much higher in continental Europe than in the United States.

In 1965 the developed countries of continental Western Europe imported some $560m of [coarse fibres, leather and wood] from all the less developed countries. Only 9 per cent of that total consisted of finished manufactures [Hal Lary has pointed out] and 16 per cent of intermediate products, while 75 per cent was in the crude form of fibres, hides and skins and logs. United States imports of these items from the less developed countries in 1965 totalled somewhat less, $460m, but the proportions were roughly the opposite: 72 per cent finished products, 10 per cent intermediate products and 18 per cent crude materials. If we look at the finished manufactures in more detail, United States imports from the less developed countries in 1965 compare with those of continental Western Europe as follows: Jute fabrics and other products of coarse fibre, $193m versus $24m; shoes, gloves, handbags and other manufactures of leather, $40m versus $13m; plywood, furniture and other manufactures of wood, $97m versus $12.[1]

While the scope for displacing domestic products is therefore smaller in countries like Britain and America where effective tariffs are low, the figures also suggest that supply limitations are not the main difficulty. Less developed countries would be able to benefit from the growth of demand as well as from the lowering of duties.

There are numerous other possibilities for reconciling the interests of developing Commonwealth countries and those of Western Europe, although they presuppose a political will to achieve such a reconciliation. But if there is the political will the following arrangements might be worth considering.

The free entry of specific Commonwealth products into Western Europe could be negotiated. This would be important for countries

[1] Hal B. Lary, 'Tariff Preferences for Less Developed Countries', *A Supplement to National Bureau Report 2* (New York: National Bureau of Economic Research, 1968).

which the EEC would not admit, or which would not wish to be admitted, as associated overseas countries on the same terms as the French, Belgian and Dutch ex-colonies. Or the Commonwealth might extend its preferences to European products in return for Europe admitting British and Commonwealth goods on preferential terms. Britain could waive its claims to Commonwealth preference as a bargaining counter. In this way, the preference system of the Commonwealth would be merged with that of the EEC, although new preferences of less than 100 per cent would have to be admitted. Some of these extensions of a preferential system would not be permitted under the present rules of GATT, but one could attempt to negotiate a waiver. Finally, agreed quotas might give Commonwealth countries specified shares in the enlarged EEC (which is, for agricultural products, a managed market in any case). It ought to be possible, too, for some of the stronger Commonwealth countries to make concessions which would benefit some of the weaker members. Canada might thus reduce her barriers to European manufacturers in return for free entry of cocoa from Ghana into the EEC. The rich Commonwealth countries, which now give Britain the greatest preferences, could thus make concessions to the enlarged EEC in return for favoured treatment of the poor countries.

25 Aid to India: I

(*with Roger Hill*)

I. THE TERMINOLOGY OF AID

AN important distinction is that between *project aid* and *non-project aid*. The former is a specific sum of money which is intended to cover the foreign exchange cost of an identifiable project within the total aid allocation. Such aid need not cover the whole foreign exchange component of the project, though it normally does. Donors provide aid to the Government of India, which makes the funds available, on its own terms, to the authority responsible for the project. Conditions may be attached by the donor to consultancy, supervision, bidding for contracts, shipping arrangements, etc. These 'strings' are of a different nature from the more general 'conditions' relating to performance in the economy at large, although they too can give rise to disagreements between donors and recipients.

Non-project aid refers to all other goods provided under the aid programme: primary products, semi-finished products, spare parts, components, machine tools, equipment, etc., which are needed to keep existing firms going or to start new projects and generally to support the balance of payments. Most of UK non-project aid consists of general purpose loans, which the Indians are free to spend on a wide range of imports from the donor country. The rest is devoted to purposes agreed on with the Indians. For example, the so-called 'Kipping aid'[1] is used to supply components and spares to metal-using industries which look to Britain as their source of supply. Similarly, a loan in 1963 was made for the procurement of steel plate in this country. Other donors, particularly the US, tie their non-project aid to specific commodities, though the range of these may be very wide.

In addition to being tied to projects, aid may be tied to purchases in the donor country. This is *procurement-tying*. At present nearly all bilateral US aid and over half of bilateral UK aid is wholly or partially tied in this manner. Only a small proportion of German aid

[1] Named after Sir Norman Kipping who led a mission which recommended it.

is formally tied, though in effect the proportion is much higher, for the Germans tend to avoid making commitments for projects in sectors in which German firms are not competitive. Donors tie their aid to protect their balances of payments. For the recipient country the main disadvantage is that it cannot buy its imports in the cheapest market, although a certain amount of 'switching', i.e. using aid to buy products on which 'free' foreign exchange would otherwise have been spent, is usually possible. The opportunity to switch will be greater, the larger are the commercial imports from the donor country and the more diversified the tied aid, while the desire to switch will depend on competitiveness of the products of the supplier. Mahbub ul Haq has estimated for Pakistan that aid-tying has raised the average price of all commodities imported under aid arrangements by 15 per cent.[1] In addition, aid-tying complicates the administration of aid.

Double-tying occurs when aid is both project- and procurement-tied. Donors double-tie to make it more certain that aid will produce extra demand for their goods. With procurement-tied aid for programmes, a recipient can select those commodities he would buy from the donor in any case. Double-tying makes such selection more difficult, since it is unlikely that a single donor will be the cheapest supplier of all the goods required for a project.

There are three stages in the process of aid-giving and aid-receiving: pledging, committing, and disbursing. First, each donor *pledges* a total amount at the annual meetings of the Aid India Consortium.[2] Pledges of one donor influence pledges of others, and Britain (giving about 10 per cent of Consortium aid to India) can therefore exercise some leverage on total aid contributions. Non-Consortium aid to India is largely Soviet aid. Not all aid provided by members of the Consortium has been pledged. Thus PL 480 aid was independent of the US pledge until 1967. Pledges are considered binding, although the Americans did not in fact commit aid pledged in 1965 after the Kashmir hostilities.

At the next stage, the pledge aid is *committed, allocated,* or *authorised.* At this stage aid is divided between project and non-project aid. The initiative for suggesting projects lies with the Indians, though representations from industrial and commercial interests are made to the donor country's authorities. The result is a

---

[1] Mahbub ul Haq, 'Tied Credits – A Quantitative Analysis', in *Capital Movements and Economic Development*, ed. J. Adler for the International Economic Association (London, 1967).

[2] It was set up by the World Bank in 1958 and consists of the US, Britain, Canada, Japan, West Germany, France, Italy, Netherlands, Belgium, Austria, the World Bank and, since 1959, IDA.

compromise between Indian wishes and British commercial and prestige interests. The process of committing can take some time. For the UK, after the 1963 pledge it took nine months; after the 1964 pledge only three. Lags have also been reduced for other countries.

The final stage is that of *disbursements* or *utilisation*. The rate of disbursement is clearly faster for non-project aid than for project aid, because the range of imports is wider, and for soft loans than for hard loans, because higher interest rates, payable when goods have been ordered, induce greater caution in giving orders. It is in the nature of a project that it takes time to negotiate, prepare, and execute, and disbursements are bound to be less than commitments. This shortfall rises as commitments increase. But slow disbursements can also be due to inadequate or inefficient administration by the Indians. Most of UK non-project aid is normally spent within the financial year of the pledge, though delays in the disbursements of Kipping aid beyond that have been known. Delays are longer in the disbursement of non-project aid from other donors, including IDA. The lag of disbursements behind commitments creates the *pipeline* which consists of unspent claims arising from past authorised loans. The pipeline permits the continuation of expenditure for a time when new commitments are run down. It creates problems for British economic policy, for it can give rise to unplanned claims on British resources. The size of the pipeline can be reduced by spreading commitments over the period of construction of projects. The lag of disbursements behind commitments, which can also be reduced by raising the proportion of general purpose aid to the total, and by softening the terms of aid, has the added drawback for India that commitments are made in terms of money, and rising prices wipe out part of the real value of the aid.

Gross aid disbursed in a year exceeds net aid by payments of interest on past loans and repayment of capital. *Debt relief* is perhaps the most urgent need. To avoid default, debt can be *rescheduled* or *refinanced*. Rescheduling means lengthening the period of the loan. Refinancing means making new loans to meet obligations on outstanding loans. Loans may be advanced with *grace periods* before interest falls due. This is another way of easing the terms of loans.

The provision of a *bisque*, advocated by some, is modelled on the waiver clause in the American loan to Britain of 1946, which allows Britain to opt out of capital repayments (though not interest) in an agreed number of years.

In tackling the debt problem, one has to distinguish between *new* debt – the problem of the *terms of aid* – and *old* debt, which may be rescheduled or refinanced. The link between the two is that the

TABLE 25.1

Sources of Aid to India until 1966

(Rs millions)

Sources of aid	Aggregate external assistance since independence			
	Authorised up to March 1966		Utilised up to March 1966	
	Amount	% of Total	Amount	% of Total
IBRD/IDA	7,415	12·8	5,815	13·0
US	30,487	52·5	26,052	58·1
USSR	4,855	8·4	2,833	6·3
W. Germany	4,444	7·7	3,417	7·6
UK	3,660	6·3	2,931	6·6
Others	7,154	12·3	3,770	8·4
Total	58,015	100·0	44,818	100·0

Source: Reserve Bank of India, *Report on Currency and Finance 1965–6* (1966) p. 28, Table 28.

attitude to accepting and servicing new debt will be influenced by the manner in which old debts are settled.

II. REVIEW OF PAST AID TO INDIA

Up to the end of March 1966 aid authorisations from all sources amounted to Rs 58,015 million, of which 77 per cent (Rs 44,818 million) had been utilised. Only Rs 290 million, of the authorised aid and Rs 220 million of the utilised aid were received prior to the First Plan.

Table 25.1 shows external assistance by sources. The donors' list is dominated by the US, which provided over half the authorised aid, and a little under three-fifths of the utilised aid. Aid authorisations under PL 480 accounted for 51 per cent (Rs 13,860 million) of US aid. IBRD and IDA, the main multilateral donors, have been responsible for just over 12 per cent of the aid received by India. Table 25.2 provides a more detailed breakdown of the sources of aid.

Table 25.3 breaks down external assistance by form. The outstanding feature here is the decline in grants: from 36 per cent of authorisations in the First Plan to 3 per cent in the Third Plan. Loans amounted to Rs 22,690 million during the First Plan, but the 1951 US Wheat Loan accounted for Rs 9,030 million (40 per cent) of this figure. Over two-thirds of the aid utilised in the Third Plan has been in loan form. Authorisations of PL 480 aid reached very high levels

TABLE 25.2
Sources of External Assistance
(Rs millions)

	Aid authorised up to end of 1st Plan	Aid authorised during 2nd Plan	Aid authorised during 3rd Plan
I. Loans			
(1) Repayable in foreign currencies			
(i) International institutions	572	2,612	4,231
(ii) US	903	1,085	7,917
(iii) Canada	—	157	310
(iv) UK	—	1,226	2,420
(v) W. Germany	—	1,342	3,081
(vi) Japan	—	268	1,381
(vii) USSR	648	3,190	1,005
(viii) Switzerland	—	65	180
(ix) France	—	—	571
(x) Italy	—	—	813
(xi) Poland	—	143	270
(xii) Yugoslavia	—	190	24
(xiii) Czechoslovakia	—	231	400
(xiv) Austria	—	—	85
(xv) Belgium	—	—	114
(xvi) Netherlands	—	—	219
(xvii) Sweden	—	—	22
(xviii) Denmark	—	—	14
Total	2,123	10,509	23,057
(2) Repayable in Rupees			
(i) Denmark	—	—	10
(ii) US	146	2,304	486
Total	146	2,304	496
II. Grants			
(i) US	918	546	200
(ii) Canada	323	571	551
(iii) Australia	111	22	22
(iv) New Zealand	17	17	7
(v) UK	4	4	6
(vi) W. Germany	—	21	—
(vii) Norway	7	19	20
(viii) USSR	—	12	—
Total	1,380	1,212	806
III. PL 480, 665, and Third Country Currency Assistance	169	11,307	4,506
Grand Total	3,818	25,335	28,865

Source: Reserve Bank of India, *Report on Currency and Finance 1965–6* (1966) Statement 82.

TABLE 25.3

External Assistance by Form

(Rs millions)

Form	Authorisations			Utilisation		
	Up to end of 1st Plan	During 2nd Plan	During 3rd Plan	Up to end of 1st Plan	During 2nd Plan	During 3rd Plan
1. Loans	2,269	12,813	23,553	1,264	7,247	19,094
(i) Repayable in foreign currencies	2,123	10,509	23,057	1,241	6,079	17,530
(ii) Repayable in rupees	146	2,304	496	23	1,168	1,564
2. Grants	1,380	1,212	806	702	1,603	877
3. PL 480 and PL 665 aid and Third Country Assistance (gross)	169	11,280	4,506	51	5,423	8,532
4. Total	3,818	25,305	28,865	2,017	14,273	28,503
Debt Servicing Payments	n.a.	n.a.	n.a.	n.a.	1,192	5,470
Net Aid					13,081	23,033
Net Aid at 1965–6 import prices					13,769	25,403
5. IMF	476	952		476	952	
Percentage Distribution						
1. Loans	59·5	50·7	81·6	62·7	50·7	67·0
2. Grants	36·2	4·8	2·8	34·8	11·2	3·0
3. PL 480 and 664 aid and Third Country Assistance (gross)	4·3	44·5	15·6	2·5	38·1	30·0
4. Total	100·0	100·0	100·0	100·0	100·0	100·0

n.a. = not available.

Source: Reserve Bank of India, *Report on Currency and Finance 1965–6* (1966) Statement 82.

during the Second Plan and provided a large 'carry-over' into the Third Plan. For this reason utilisation of PL 480 aid between 1961–6 was nearly double the authorisation during the same period.

III. EXTERNAL DEBT

External debt servicing charges rose from $250 million in the Second Plan (just under 4 per cent of export earnings) to $1,150 million during the Third Plan (about 14 per cent of merchandise export earnings) and to 22 per cent in 1966. During the period 1966–70 these charges are estimated as $3,050 million – 28 per cent of estimated export earnings and 36 per cent of aid requirements. The total outstanding external public debt has risen from $400 million in 1955 to $6,900 million in June 1966.[1] The problem of external debt is a major one in the late 1960s. While debt servicing obligations rose by 84 per cent between 1962 and 1966, exports increased by only 14 per cent. This is the legacy of past loans. However, a marked softening of aid terms has taken place recently. The average rate of interest on new external debt contracted during 1960 was 4·19 per cent, the average grace period 4·0 years and the average term to maturity 16·7 years.[2] In 1965 the corresponding figures were 3·18 per cent interest rate, 7·4 years grace period, and 31·3 years to maturity.[3] This reflects an even greater improvement if account is taken of the general rise in commercial interest rates. Nevertheless, further renegotiations, rescheduling, consolidations and waivers of loans must be expected during the Fourth Plan period, for servicing charges are likely to account for 28 per cent of a very optimistic export projection of Rs 80,330 million (Rs 51,000 million in pre-devaluation rupees).

The problem of debt service has several aspects.

1. In the 1970s the debt servicing problem will become even more serious. From 1966–7 to 1980–1 India will require some $18,000 million of foreign aid but her debt servicing liability will come to $14,000 million. After 1975 the planners expect repayments to outstrip inflows of capital.

2. Next, there are the terms on which loans are incurred and renewed. India herself has in the past declared that she does not wish to receive grants. Some donors believe that soft terms discourage economic use and encourage waste. There cannot be much in this argument because the Government of India can lend on at appropriate interest rates, and can require these rates of return for its own projects. Soft terms are intended to get over the foreign exchange difficulty, and do not reduce the need to calculate adequate domestic returns on expenditure. Whether local currency counterpart funds for interest receipts should be accumulated by the creditor country is another question.

3. Most bilateral aid is tied to procurement from the donor and often tied to projects as well. Repayment, on the other hand, is demanded in convertible currency, and the use of such funds is not tied to Indian exports. This asymmetry introduces an

[1] IBRD, *Ann. Rep.*, *1965–6* (1967) p. 33, Table 5, and *1966–7*, p. 31, Table 6.
[2] Ibid., p. 36, Tables 7 and 8.   [3] Ibid., p. 35, Table 9.

additional element of hardness. The exception is aid from Russia and certain European countries which is usually repaid in the recipient's traditional exports; thus, in effect, repayment is in the borrower's own currency.

4. It is not sufficient to give debt relief when the time for debt repayment arrives. Foreign exchange has to be accumulated in the form of extra reserves, and hence diverted from development imports well in advance of the date when debt payments are due, and debt relief promised in advance is worth more than relief that comes later.

5. From the point of view of any one creditor, debt relief should be given by all creditors. Otherwise the relief given by one can be regarded as being used to pay the obligations to others. (The same applies to giving aid on soft terms.) The World Bank, because of its need to raise money in the capital markets of the West, is in a special position and may not be able to give relief without impairing its impeccable credit standing. But bilateral Consortium donors normally consider that they must act in consort.

IV. THE SLOW UTILISATION OF AID

Until recently, a characteristic of Indian aid was the large proportion authorised but not disbursed. To help remedy this slow disbursement of aid, the Rao Report recommended in 1964 that a larger proportion of aid should be non-project.[1] In the years 1963–4 India received considerable quantities of non-project assistance (apart from PL 480) for the first time. In the years 1965–6 about half the aid pledged was non-project, while for 1967 Consortium members have agreed to about $900 million (Rs 6,800 million) of non-project aid.

However, the causes of slow disbursements are to be found on both sides. In India, slow disbursements may occur because of (a) inadequate project planning, i.e. faulty project preparation, programming, and scheduling, (b) faults in complementary actions, e.g. failure of supplies of raw materials and components, and services like electricity and transport, and (c) failures in aggregate planning, e.g. non-availability of rupee resources, inadequate aggregate demand, wrong choice of top personnel, and other wrong decisions. Even forms of aid which are avowedly the most useful, because they are not tied to projects, have been slowly disbursed. Thus 'Kipping loans' have, astonishingly, suffered from slow disbursements.

But the main reason for slow disbursement is found, the Rao

[1] Ctte on the Utilisation of External Assistance, *Report* (Min. of Finance, 1964)

Committee suggested, in the fact of project aid. Aid geared to the creation of capacity, it is said, is of little use and can be an obstacle if the main bottleneck is imports of raw materials and components, especially fertilisers, and spare parts. The superiority of general-purpose aid over project, and even non-project but specific-purpose aid, has been increasingly recognised, and the change in the composition has contributed to speedier disbursements. The need for non-project aid grows as development progresses. A final reason for delays has been the terms of aid. The harder the terms, the more reluctant the borrower will be to draw quickly on a loan, because interest is charged from the date of drawing, not from the date of commitment. Thus the share of loans tends to be higher in the aid pipeline than in total aid commitments.

However, more non-project aid and softening of terms, together with changes in the administrative machinery, especially in the vetting of import requirements, have produced in 1964 and 1965 a marked improvement in the rate of aid utilisation. This is borne out by Table 25.4.

TABLE 25.4

Utilisation of Loans

(Rs millions)

	Authorised and undisbursed	Used in following year	2/1
	(1)	(2)	per cent
March 1961	6,571	2,296	34·9
1962	8,378	3,058	36·5
1963	11,292	3,918	34·7
1964	11,755	4,831	41·1
1965	11,886	4,991	42·0

Source: Reserve Bank of India, *Report on Currency and Finance 1965–6*, Part I, Table 2.

V. THE IMPACT OF AID

There is a widespread impression that India receives large sums of aid. This is, of course, true in the sense that India is a large country, containing 30 per cent of the population of the underdeveloped world. But it is not true if the relevant measure, viz. aid per head, is used. India received in 1961 $1·5, in 1962 $1·7, and in 1963 $2·1 from OECD countries and multilateral agencies, compared with Pakistan's massive doses: $2·8 excluding Indus Waters Scheme, $4·0 including it (some of this should, however, be credited to India) in 1962; $4·2 excluding, $4·9 including it (1963), and a further rise to about $6·0 in 1964. Stepping up gross aid to $10,000 million for the period 1966–70 would mean raising aid per head to $4 a year, still considerably below the level of Pakistan and of many other aid recipients. Whatever aid criteria one wishes to choose, India should be given much higher priority than it receives now.[1] India is one of the poorest countries. Its development potential is high. It has an efficient administration, a high level of education and skills, and a reserve of potential entrepreneurship. Its plans are well conceived and it has applied stringent import controls and high levels of domestic taxation. There can be no doubt that it has a structural balance of payments problem and considerable absorptive capacity. It enjoys constitutional democracy and has been the victim of an attack by China. What India does will serve as an example to others. Whether one's criteria are cold war, the encouragement of democratic government, the promotion of self-help, good performance, the relief of the needy, or the activation of development potential, India should qualify for massive aid. In fact it is grossly under-aided.

Both the Right and the Left have attacked India's reliance on foreign aid, which both tend to exaggerate. The Right argues that aid, by encouraging central planning and public prestige projects, discourages the growth of private savings and private initiative, frightens away foreign enterprise, discourages economy in the use of capital, and generally destroys the basis of decentralised decision-taking which, on this view, is the prerequisite of development. Aid thus is thought to perpetuate the system which makes aid necessary; some go further and say that it pauperises the country, making it increasingly dependent on external assistance.

The Left attacks aid on the ground that, by supporting reactionary groups in power, it retards the introduction of the institutional and political reforms, particularly effective land reform, which are necessary for development. Aid, on this view, props up reform-resisting oligarchies and conservative and feudal social systems, and again perpetuates the system which makes it necessary.

These arguments, which fit in well with the general disenchantment with aid among donors, are difficult to quantify and to assess. We shall discuss the argument in the context of food aid below. In order to bring out the costs and benefits of aid, and also in order to present clear political choices, it might be possible to draw up two simultaneous plans: one with a somewhat smaller reliance on aid, the other with somewhat more aid and with possible concessions to the donors. The cost of aid in the widest sense, including policies adopted or sacrificed, would thus be brought out clearly.

[1] This is powerfully argued in I. M. D. Little and J. M. Clifford, *International Aid* (London, 1965) pp. 226, 231, 234.

Distribution of Foreign Loans/Credits by Purposes

(Figures in brackets show percentage distribution)

(Rs millions)

Loans/Credits	Authorised				Utilised			
	(1) Up to end of 1st Plan	(2) During 2nd Plan	(3) During 3rd Plan	Total 1 to 3	(1) Up to end of 1st Plan	(2) During 2nd Plan	(3) During 3rd Plan	Total 1 to 3
1. Railway Development	156 (6·9)	1,952 (15·1)	1,392 (6·1)	3,500 (9·2)	156 (12·3)	1,432 (20·1)	1,850 (10·1)	3,438 (12·8)
2. Power Projects	196 (8·6)	623 (4·8)	2,414 (10·5)	3,233 (8·5)	121 (9·6)	293 (4·1)	1,529 (8·3)	1,943 (7·2)
3. Iron and Steel Projects*	786 (34·7)	2,242 (17·4)	2,078 (9·1)	5,106 (13·4)	27 (2·1)	2,541 (35·6)	1,049 (5·7)	3,617 (13·5)
4. Ports and Development	—	205 (1·6)	186 (0·8)	391 (1·0)	—	68 (0·9)	180 (1·0)	248 (0·9)
5. Transport and Communication	—	148 (1·2)	930 (4·1)	1,078 (2·9)	—	90 (1·3)	759 (4·1)	849 (3·2)
6. Industrial Development	193 (8·5)	7,555 (58·7)	15,266 (66·7)	23,014 (60·5)	23 (1·8)	2,554 (35·8)	12,836 (69·6)	15,413 (57·5)
7. Agricultural Development	34 (1·5)	—	621 (2·7)	655 (1·7)	34 (2·7)	—	225 (1·2)	259 (1·0)
8. Wheat Loans	903 (39·8)	157 (1·2)	—	1,060 (2·8)	903 (71·5)	157 (2·2)	—	1,060 (3·9)
Total	2,268 (100·0)	12,882 (100·0)	22,837 (100·0)	38,037 (100·0)	1,264 (100·0)	7,135 (100·0)	18,428 (100·0)	26,827 (100·0)

* Includes Orissa Iron Ore Project.

Source: Reserve Bank of India, *Report on Currency and Finance 1965–6* (1966) Statement 83.

Table 25.5 shows the uses to which aid has been allocated. It adds to the total resources available to the community. It may be used to raise consumption, private investment, or government expenditure. In this general case, the value of aid to India is equal to the value of these additions. But if it helps to break a bottleneck – foreign exchange, particular items of equipment, or particular skills – the value of aid to India exceeds the nominal value of aid given. It makes fuller utilisation of capacities in other sectors of the economy possible. Against this, it is possible that an aid-financed project imposes a burden of recurrent or other contributory expenditure on the domestic economy, and that these resources could have been used more productively in other lines. In such conditions the value of aid to India falls short of its nominal value. In so far as aid is available in freely-spendable foreign exchange, its value is likely to exceed its nominal value. The more it is tied to projects and donor procurement, the less likely will this be.

The conventional approach to analysing the impact of aid is to regard it as filling either of two gaps, depending upon which is larger. If growth is seen as a function of the ratio of investment to national income, aid is seen as filling the gap between target investment and domestic savings. Alternatively, if growth is regarded as constrained by foreign exchange, aid fills the gap between the foreign exchange required to achieve a given growth target, and the foreign exchange earned by visible and invisible exports plus private capital flows.

The weakness of the double gap approach is that it makes assumptions, sometimes justified in advanced economies, which are unwarranted for India. The savings gap approach assumes that the relationship between investment and additional output is fairly stable, that consumption makes no contribution to output, and that home and foreign savings are interchangeable. But in the diagnosis of India it is normal to assume that the dominant bottleneck is not savings, but foreign exchange. And we have certainly witnessed situations in which potential domestic savings have run to waste for lack of foreign exchange. Aid requirements therefore tend to be approached through the trade gap. This analysis assumes that growth of domestic production could be accelerated with more foreign exchange

We see from Table 25.6 that the contribution of external finance to public plan outlay is large. However, the apparently greater dependence on external assistance in the Draft Fourth Plan is due to the rise in the rupee figure resulting from devaluation; in fact, if corrected for devaluation, the proportion of aid-financed public outlay is less in the Fourth than in the Third Plan. It may be that without aid India would have increased its already strong tax efforts even more,

TABLE 25.6
Financing of Public Outlay
(Rs millions)

Sources	1st Plan	2nd Plan	3rd Plan	4th Plan
1. Balance from Current Revenues	3,820	110	– 4,730	33,450
2. Surpluses of Public Enterprises	1,150	1,670	6,960	13,450
3. Capital Receipts	6,860	14,390	21,390	38,800
4. Deficit Financing	3,330	9,540	11,510	—
5. Additional Taxation	2,550	10,520	26,600	27,300
6. Budgetary Receipts corresponding to External Assistance	1,890	10,490	24,550	47,000 (a)
7. Total Resources	19,600	46,720	86,280	160,000
Row 6/Row 7 per cent	9·6	22·5	28·5	29·4 (b)

(a) Post devaluation.
(b) This figure is not comparable with the previous figures because of devaluation (see text).

Source: *MFB*, pp. 117–18, Table FR 2.

but it is impossible to dispute that the Second and Third Plans would have been smaller without aid.

Consider aid as a provider of foreign exchange, assuming that domestic savings are not the dominant constraint. The withdrawal of aid would then have necessitated a combination of four courses of action: non-development import retardation, development import substitution, export expansion, and a shift of plan outlay into areas with low foreign exchange requirements. Since the foreign exchange crisis of 1957–8 India has imposed the most stringent controls on

TABLE 25.7
Imports of Consumer Goods
(Rs millions)

	1st Plan	2nd Plan	3rd Plan
Consumer Goods	8,878	10,742	12,786
Foodgrains	6,015	8,046	10,330
Non-foodgrains	2,863	2,696	2,456
PL 480	51	5,448	8,800
PL 480 as percentage of total foodgrains	1·8	68·0	85·0

Source: *4DO*, pp. 100–2.

imports of consumer goods. Table 25.7 shows that if foodgrains, 82 per cent of which consist of PL 480 imports, are excluded, the total value of consumer goods imports was lower in the Third Plan than in the First. Little foreign exchange can be gained by further restrictions of consumption imports. As for the second course, development-import substitution, raw materials, and equipment are closely scrutinised for possible indigenous replacement. In any case, import substitution of equipment requires, in the initial stages, larger, not smaller, imports. It is the strenuous attempt to set up domestic import-substituting capital goods industries which is responsible for the growth of raw material and capital imports.

There has been considerable unused capacity in Indian industry, largely as a result of inadequate imports of raw materials, components, and spare parts. A change in the composition of imports – a higher proportion of maintenance imports and a lower proportion of imports tied to new industrial capacity – would indeed lead to higher capacity utilisation. But there is little scope for substituting domestic production for imports in such a way as to reduce import requirements substantially in the near future.

Export expansion, unaccompanied by an equivalent fall in unit prices of exports, is the third way of reducing dependence on aid. Indian exports stagnated during the First and Second Plans. They rose between 1960 and 1964–5, but seem to have run out of steam since. Traditional exports (tea, jute, cotton) run into limitations of demand, and non-traditional exports, though they showed impressive increases, are still a small proportion of the total. Exports of engineering goods, iron ore and steel, and chemicals are still less than 10 per cent of total exports. No doubt it is in the expansion of these exports that future earnings prospects lie, but foreign exchange will be needed in order to build up this export potential.

The fourth method of saving foreign exchange is to change the composition of plan outlay in the direction of economising in foreign exchange. This means more for agriculture, less for industry. In the Third Plan public outlay in agriculture and irrigation was Rs 14,600 million, exclusive of industries producing agricultural inputs such as fertilisers, and in medium and large industries Rs 25,700 million. If aid reductions had forced a substantial switch of investment from industry to agriculture, some foreign exchange could have been saved, though limitations of absorptive capacity may have retarded growth. An increase in agricultural inputs such as fertilisers does require foreign exchange, directly if these are imported, and indirectly if domestic fertiliser plants are to be put up.

We conclude that added foreign exchange shortages would have led to even more severe cuts in the Second and Third Plans, even if domestic savings had been available. In addition, it is most unlikely that the Government of India could have raised enough resources to maintain the size of the plans even if structural balance of payments problems had not constituted an obstacle. These considerations suggest that the Second and Third Plans would have been reduced by an amount greater than the aid provided, if aid had been reduced. Or, to put the same point the other way round, in spite of some waste in the preparation, execution, and management of some projects, additional aid enables India to mobilise a multiple of the resources provided by aid.

VI. AID AND THE DRAFT FOURTH PLAN

In the Draft Fourth Plan aid plays a crucial role. Economic planning aims ultimately at a 'steady and satisfactory rate of growth, without inflation and without dependence on foreign aid'.[1] It is planned to bring about a sharp fall in imports in the Fifth Plan coupled with a continued increase in exports, so that by 1977 the balance of payments gap will be closed even after providing for debt repayments, and no more aid will be needed. To do this, the Indians estimate that they will require gross external assistance of between $8,500 and $9,000 million exclusive of PL 480 aid during the 1966–71 period. About $2,000 million was in the pipeline at the end of the Third Plan, so that disbursements of new aid will have to be about $7,000 million. To provide this volume of disbursement, commitments of between $8,000 and $10,000 million will have to be made for the plan period. Since debt servicing during the period 1966–70 is likely to absorb around $3,000 million of gross aid, net aid should amount to about $6,000 million or Rs 45,000 million. This is over 20 per cent of total estimated investment. In addition, external finance is to be the main source of public outlay during the Fourth Plan, accounting for 30 per cent of total planned development expenditure.[2]

But aid needs may be even greater than indicated by these figures. The aid requirements calculations are based on very optimistic assumptions about domestic production, exports, and savings. Already, domestic production of fertilisers and steel shows shortfalls, and higher imports will be required to make up for them. The export earning projections seem over-optimistic, particularly the projected increase in jute and tea exports.

[1] It is envisaged that in the course of the Sixth Plan the stage will be reached when 'further economic growth will no longer require any net increase in our foreign indebtedness' (*4DO*, p. 28).

[2] These ratios are based on post-devaluation figures and cannot be compared with the same ratios for previous plans.

These are India's aid needs, but how much it will actually receive is another question. So far Aid India Consortium members have pledged sums of $900 million of non-project financial aid each year for 1966–7 and 1967–8. To meet the aid requirements of the Draft Fourth Plan, India must receive in addition to the promised Russian aid ($1,000 million for the Draft Plan, or more) about $1,600 million of gross aid per year from the Consortium. The amount of aid India is receiving is therefore well below the aid requirements of the Plan. However, the virtual moratorium on Indian debt repayments during 1967–8 will save it some $400 million of foreign exchange. How much the debt burden will be reduced in the later years of the Plan depends upon the outcome of the bilateral rescheduling negotiations.

In spite of errors and some faulty management, there is no doubt that India could absorb substantially more aid than it receives now. But the solution is more complex than simply changing the composition of aid in the direction of more maintenance imports. The contrast between project- and non-project aid over-simplifies the real issues. Not all capacity which has been created in India is equally valuable from a development point of view, and to under-write maintenance imports for all existing capacity may lead to fuller utilisation of capacity that should not be more fully used and may encourage the creation of undesirable capacity. On the other hand, economic progress, the unequal degree of capacity under-utilisation, and the fact that fuller utilisation of the capital goods industries is possible only if new projects are started, imply that *some* new projects will have to be started, say some new fertiliser plants, while there is still under-utilisation in less important sectors. It is then essential that these projects should be well selected, well prepared, and well executed. Donors should offer assistance in sector and project selection, execution, and planning, as well as raising the proportion of non-project aid. These measures would not only raise the productivity of aid directly, but would also lead to fuller utilisation of existing capacity, thereby raising output indirectly. They would reduce the need for detailed physical controls, economise in scarce administrative talent, and thus contribute to higher productivity and better morale.

But all this is relevant largely for the urban industrial sector. The most serious constraint on development, apart from population growth, is the relative stagnation until recently in many rural areas. Even a substantial speeding up of the already high industrial growth rate is bound to be halted unless food production is raised by much more than it has been in the past. Project the figures for 1961–5 into the future. Industrial output increased annually by 7·4 per cent,

TABLE 25.8
Illustrative Growth Rates Weighted by Sectors

	Percentage of net domestic product at factor cost 1964–5	Annual growth rates 1961–5	Weighted growth
Agriculture	51	2·7	1·4
Industry	18	7·4 (assume 10)	1·3 (1·8)
Services	31	6·7	2·1
All sectors	100	4·8 (5·3)	4·8 (5·3)

services by 6·7 per cent, and agricultural output by 2·7 per cent.[1] Weighting these growth rates by their respective shares in 1964–5 in net domestic product at factor cost, the total growth rate is 4·8 per cent, which is 0·8 per cent per annum less than the projected rate of growth 1964–5 to 1970–1 (see Table 25.8). Even if we assume that industrial output is raised by the planned 10 per cent per annum, the aggregate growth rate is raised, initially, to only 5·3 per cent. The lag of agricultural production constitutes a serious brake on the power of foreign aid to speed up development. Slow growth in agriculture limits essential supplies to industry, demand for mass-produced industrial products, and the savings ratio. Industry can, of course, also contribute to the growth of agricultural output and to rural development, particularly through higher fertiliser inputs, but its efficacy there is more limited than in urban manufacturing industry. It can do relatively little to promote land reform or effective agricultural extension services on the spot. But more recently there have been promising signs that farmers, encouraged by high prices and responding to new techniques, have in some areas substantially increased production. Success will depend upon both sectors advancing together.

VII. FOOD AID FROM AMERICA

Over half the aid India has received from the US and slightly less than a third of the total aid it has utilised has been in the form of commodities. (Part of the non-project aid also takes the form of commodities.) A small amount of this was received under the US Mutual Security Act (PL 665), but by far the greater part has come under the US Agricultural Trade Development and Assistance Act (PL 480), particularly under Title I which authorises the sale of US

[1] Calculated from *4DO*, pp. 62–3.

agricultural commodities for foreign currencies. Between India's first PL 480 agreement with the US in 1956 and the end of the Third Plan, the total sales proceeds of PL 480 imports amounted to Rs 156,730 million. Four-fifths of these counterpart funds were lent or granted to India; 7 per cent were loaned to US private enterprises,[1] the remaining funds (13 per cent) have been retained by the US Government for its own use.

Though self-sufficiency in foodgrains received top priority in the Third Plan, imports of PL 480 foodgrains have increased markedly since 1961–2. And this rise is not solely the result of large imports in 1965–6 following the disastrous harvest; year by year throughout the Plan, cereals imports have increased. Table 25.9 shows that nearly all the increase in imports during the Third Plan can be accounted for by larger quantities of PL 480 imports. Domestic production of foodgrains stagnated during the first three years of the Plan and fell severely in the fifth year, so that dependence on imported food has increased: in 1961 net imports of cereals were just over 5·2 per cent of net production; by 1963 this figure had risen to 7·8 per cent, and by 1964 to over 11 per cent.[2]

But the growing size of US food shipments is entirely contrary to American aid philosophy. US aid, perhaps more than that of other donors, is intended to promote self-reliance, not to undermine it. America has expressed its dissatisfaction with India. The most obvious expression of this dissatisfaction was President Johnson's four-month delay at the end of 1966 in sanctioning new PL 480 agreements with India, but another sign was the American stipulation in 1965 that India must pay in foreign currencies the whole cost of PL 480 freight, not just 50 per cent as previously. This has been followed by the US Food for Freedom Act which is intended to move countries receiving American food aid from soft currency payments to a system of dollar payments on long terms, but the Act is unlikely to be applied in its full rigour to India for some time. The US has in effect indicated to India its reluctance to continue food shipments at the present high levels. For one thing, the Americans feel that others should share the burden of feeding India. It is for this reason that the US has been the major force in getting food and food-related aid co-ordinated through the World Bank Consortium. Also, US Government wheat stocks have in recent years fallen dramatically, largely because of increased food aid, especially to India. This has led to the removal of area limits in order to stimulate US grain production.

[1] Under the Cooley Amendment, Cooley rupees have, according to AID attracted over fifty American investors to India.

[2] Min. of Finance, *Economic Survey of India 1965–6* (1966), Table 1:4.

TABLE 25.9

Total Imports and PL 480 Imports

(Rs millions)

	1961–2	*1962–3*	*1963–4*	*1964–5*	*1965–6*
Total imports	11,071	11,356	12,229	13,490	13,490
PL 480 foodgrains	710	1,120	1,730	2,250	2,680
Net total imports	10,361	10,236	10,499	11,240	10,810

Source: *4DO*, p. 102.

There is, however, a deeper reason for the American reluctance to continue large-scale commodity shipments to India. The Americans fear that dependence on PL 480 food will breed even greater dependence. It is felt by some Indians as well as Americans that US surplus food, available almost for the asking in years of good harvests as well as bad, has undermined India's determination to tackle its agricultural problem seriously. In particular, food management, and especially efforts to draw out the marketable surplus, may have suffered as a result of PL 480 aid. True, self-sufficiency in foodgrains received top priority in the Third Plan. But this was not achieved and has now been carried over to become a major target in the Fourth Plan. Though weather played its part in this failure, it is not yet clear that India has yet hit upon a combination of policies which will ensure a high and sustained rate of growth in agriculture. India has cut the share of investment in agriculture and has not a sufficiently strong policy to get trained personnel into rural areas. Such policies will involve difficult and unpopular choices and changes, and the Indians may prefer to postpone making them as long as possible. Certainly such postponement will be easier the more India can rely upon the US to bail it out of its worst consequences.

But US commodity aid may have had a more direct impact on agricultural production via its effect on cultivator incentives. PL 480 funds have been a major source of aid to the public sector. It is estimated that during the Third Plan funds arising from PL 480 aid financed over 10 per cent of public development outlay. PL 480 aid accounted for 56 per cent of the external assistance to public outlay. Because of the dangers of too much deficit financing and of the unpopularity of higher taxes, the Indian Government has had an interest in making PL 480 imports and sales as large as possible, to raise funds to finance its plans. Larger PL 480 sales exert a downward pressure on food prices, and thus may reduce incentives for cultivators. They also divert limited sources of credit away from agriculture. A difficult choice has therefore faced the Indian Government:

to acquire a non-inflationary source of finance for its plans, or to provide incentives for agriculture. The critics argue that the Government has favoured the former too much.

There are two ways for the Government to control the net availability of cereals directly. It can vary PL 480 imports, or it can vary the level of its cereal stocks. Table 25.10 shows increases over the

TABLE 25.10

Percentage Changes in Net Production
and Net Availability

	Net production	*Net availability*
1956–7	+4·7	+4·0
1957–8	– 6·3	– 4·7
1958–9	+16·1	+14·8
1959–60	– 0·9	– 0·3
1960–1	+6·7	+6·3
1961–2	+2·4	+2·8
1962–3	– 5·6	– 4·7
1963–4	+4·7	+9·1
1964–5	+8·3	+5·7

Source: Ministry of Finance, *Economic Survey of India 1965–6* (1966).

previous year of net production of cereals and of net availability, i.e. net production plus imports less additions to stocks. It will be seen that government imports and stocks policy has in most years had a stabilising effect on the supply of cereals. However, this stabilising effect has been very slight; in 1958–9, for example, the Government did very little to offset the large increase in the supply of cereals following the excellent harvest. In Table 25.11, column 4 shows the contribution to net availability of imports of cereals and changes in stocks. The trend of imports less additions to stocks has clearly been upwards. Only in two years since 1956 – when the first PL 480 agreement was made with the US – has this trend been halted: 1958–9 and 1960–1, both years of bumper harvests. But the fall in imports less stock additions in these two years has been very small. The pattern is now clear: in years when agricultural production has fallen or risen only slightly, imports less stock additions have increased; in years of good harvests, they have remained stable. In years of bad harvests, therefore, the Government has used imports and stocks to put downward pressure on cereal prices, but in good years it has not lowered imports and added to stocks to offset the downward pressure on prices exerted by domestic production, but has simply kept cereal imports less stock additions at their former levels.

TABLE 25.11

Production, Availability and other Indices of Cereals

	1 Net production of cereals (a)	2 Imports of cereals	3 Change in govt. stocks	4 Imports plus stock reductions	5 Net avail- ability of cereals	6 Index no. of cereals prices (b)	7 Cultivators' terms of trade
1956	50·34	1·04	− 0·60	1·64	52·34	96	91
1957	52·68	3·63	+0·86	2·77	55·45	101	93
1958	49·36	3·22	− 0·27	3·49	52·85	107	95
1959	57·30	3·86	+0·49	3·37	60·67	104	90
1960	56·77	5·13	+1·40	3·73	60·50	104	83
1961	60·65	3·49	− 0·17	3·66	64·31	102	82
1962	62·08	3·64	− 0·36	4·00	66·08	106	83
1963	58·63ᵃ	4·55ᵃ	− 0·02	4·57	63·20	116	86
1964	61·41ᵃ	6·26ᵃ	− 1·26	7·52	68·93	139	91
1965	66·52ᵃ	7·45ᵃ	+1·12	6·33	72·85	148	—

ᵃ Provisional.

Cols. 1 2 3 4 and 5 units: mill. tonnes.

(a) Refers to agricultural year July–June: 1956 figure refers to net production in 1955–6. Net production is 8·75 per cent of total production, 12·5 per cent being provided for feed, seed requirements and wastage.

(b) Refers to financial year March to February: 1956 figure for example refers to 1956–7. The base year of the Index is 1952–3 (= 100), as for col. 7.

Sources: *Economic Survey of India 1965–6.* Reserve Bank of India, *Report on Currency and Finance 1965–6* (1966) statements 12 and 13.

Turning now to the actual prices of cereals, it can be seen from Table 25.11 that cereal prices rose from 1956 to 1958. Also the cultivators' terms of trade, i.e. the ratio of the wholesale price index of cereals to the general wholesale price index, improved. But in 1959 production was 8 million tons higher, while imports and stock withdrawals were still at the same level as in 1958 – the net result was a fall in cereal prices from 107 to 104, and in the cultivators' terms of trade from 95 to 90.

In 1960 net availability of cereals was just below that of 1959, since the small fall in net production was offset by a large increase in imports, most of which was used to build up government stocks. The quantity of cereals available was not sufficient to push cereal prices down, but it was sufficient to prevent them from sharing in the general price rise; as a result the cultivators' terms of trade fell from 90 to 83. In 1961 net output increased by 6·7 per cent; imports and stock withdrawals fell only slightly; net availability increased by 6·3 per cent; cereal prices and cultivators' terms of trade again fell. There followed three years of stagnation in agriculture.

The evidence linking PL 480 imports and lower levels of cereal production is strong but circumstantial. There are a number of possible objections. Firstly, while PL 480 imports are mostly in the form of wheat, a high proportion of cereal consumption is in the form of rice. The two are not perfect substitutes. Secondly, the ratio of the wholesale price index of cereals to the general wholesale price index may be a poor indication of the actual terms of trade of agriculturalists.[1] Thirdly, though the agricultural stagnation of the early 1960s came after large imports of PL 480 cereals, the weather and shortages of agricultural inputs were probably more important contributing factors. Fourthly, change in area cultivated is possibly a more accurate indication of producers' decisions than output. The impact of PL 480 on crop areas is less clear – in 1964, for example, the area under cereals was slightly higher than in 1961, and the area under wheat, the commodity most affected by PL 480, was only slightly lower. However, a recent econometric study of PL 480 in India by J. S. Mann lends support to the view that PL 480 has had a depressing effect on cereal prices and production.[2] In this study Mann estimates that an increase in per capita imports of cereals under PL 480 of one pound (219,995 metric tons with the estimated 1962 population of 485 million) has resulted in a 0·54 per cent drop in wholesale cereal prices in the same year and a decline in output in the second year of about 0·5 pounds of cereals per capita (about 109,997 tons with the same population). Output tends to rise in later years so that the depressing impact on output is trimmed to about 0·3 pounds per capita in the long run. This study measures only the direct impact of PL 480 imports; the indirect impact via the effect of readily available food aid on planners' attitudes to agriculture is not estimated.

The conclusion is not that ending PL 480 imports is an urgent matter deserving a higher priority. Indeed, Mann uses his analysis to argue the opposite: that since PL 480 cereal imports are only partially offset by the decline in domestic supply, they can make a positive contribution to filling the food gap. The inescapable fact is that for the time being India simply cannot do without food from abroad. In the two years 1965–6 India will have received about 19 million tons of food aid, which is equal to the Draft Outline estimate for the whole Plan period. As late as 1975/6, minimum likely average import requirements for foodgrains will still be as high as 7 million metric tons per year.[3] This continuing need for foreign

[1] See in this connection V. G. Mutalik-Desai, 'Terms of Trade and Food Surplus', *Indian J. Agric. Econ.*, Jan–Mar 1966 (Bombay).

[2] J. S. Mann, 'The Impact of P.L. 480 Imports', *J. of Farm Economics*, Feb 1967, vol. 49, 1, pt. 1.

[3] US Dept of Agriculture, *Supply of and Demand for Selected Agricultural Products in India, Projections to 1975–6*, ERS For. 100.

food is reflected in the special Consortium arrangements for co-ordinating food aid to India; they amount in essence to a method which enables the US to share with other donors the task – one it considers far from finished – of feeding India. Given a still sizeable flow of food aid to India over the next decade, the important lesson from past experience is the need to control the amount reaching the consumer, in particular to limit it when domestic harvests are good. In years of good harvests PL 480 cereals should be stockpiled.

VIII. NEW INITIATIVES

UK policy and the Fourth Indian Five-Year Plan

Apart from trying to clear away the obstacles to the traditional methods of raising aid to India, it is worth exploring new methods. There are a number of ways in which modernisation in the UK could be geared to assist India. In these sketchy remarks no clear distinction will be drawn between aid and trade reforms.

Matching markets

The late John Strachey proposed a scheme by which Britain and India would agree to identify specific markets in each country to be supplied by the other. The intention was to treat such markets separately from aid arrangements through the Consortium. Britain would reduce barriers to specified Indian exports. Particular areas hit thereby, such as Lancashire or Dundee, would erect factories producing goods for which a ready, guaranteed market in India would be found. Thus the problem of raising Indian exports, of transferring workers from declining industries, and of finding new export markets would be solved simultaneously.

It may be asked whether the best location for these new factories would necessarily be the areas hit by the additional imports. Furthermore, there would be the question whether the new British export industries would supply the desired products at competitive prices to India. It is not, on the face of it, obvious that a bilateral arrangement is necessarily better than some more indirect way of substitution. But it is worth exploring methods of shifting resources in Britain so as to permit better access to Indian exports.

Aid from surplus capacity

The problem of aid from surplus capacity, additional to existing aid, is also worth exploring. There are three main objections:

(a) delays in getting orders so that the surplus capacity has disappeared by the time the process is completed; (b) uncompetitively high prices and undesired products; (c) the difficulty of avoiding underwriting malinvestment in the UK. The Indians are confident that they could give an answer to the question whether specific types of goods would be required within fifteen days. In any case, a glance at the list of Indian imports should make it fairly clear what types of goods are required. The problem of uncompetitive prices, which has been made a lot of in Britain, does not seem to worry the Indians. To the problem of preventing desirable adjustments in Britain, the answer is that aid from surplus capacity should be found for those sectors in which demand has *temporarily* receded, and resources are not intended to be redeployed. It is important that aid from surplus capacity would have to be additional to other aid.

Second-hand equipment

Since modernisation often involves the replacement of physically workable but technologically obsolete machinery, it would be worth looking into the question whether, subject to arrangements about transport costs, such second-hand machinery could be used by India. It may, however, be true that breakdowns may occur more frequently, that maintenance costs are higher and that for export industries only modern equipment can be used.

Long-term planning

Our own five-year and fifteen-year projections should accommodate not only increased trade with India, but also the flow and composition of aid. Debt servicing has to be reflected in admitting more Indian exports into the UK.

The value of aid to India could be greatly increased if the quantum, pattern and terms were pledged over five or ten years, and committed, not annually, but for several years ahead. Not only the Indian Perspective Planning Division, but also such commissions as the Energy Commission (with Prof. E. A. G. Robinson) aim at projections for 1975, and a longer-term view, which embraces at least two plans, would give a more rational and effective pattern of aid.

Joint enterprises

Another idea worth exploring is that of joint UK-Indian enterprises, whose aim it would be to promote exports to Europe and other developed countries. They would join UK private firms to either Indian private or public enterprises. What appears to be lacking in India is know-how of export promotion, and in particular of styling, design, etc., suited for selling light labour-intensive goods. An increase in export earnings must have a very high priority in Indian development. To provide not only export know-how but also easier entry into European markets would make it possible for Indian industry to earn foreign exchange. In addition to consumer goods such as dresses, shoes, ties, etc., there should be emphasis on light engineering goods.

Aid for population control

One area where the UK can take a major initiative is aid for population control. In the next five years India will add to its population a number of people roughly equal to the present population of Britain. It is this rapid rate of population growth rather than the modest though not unsatisfactory increase in incomes which makes the outlook for India disturbing. However, India is one of the few countries which has taken up family planning as a national programme – Rs 950 million are to be spent in this field between 1960 and 1970, while Britain is the major donor with few religious and other objections to giving aid for population control. But British policy has been to wait until asked for assistance. The result is that British aid for population control has been very small – £11,000 in 1965–6 and possibly £40,000 in 1966–7. Since there is a willingness on both sides, Britain should prompt India to ask for more assistance for population control. This should be in addition to the aid India is already receiving.

But all the initiatives discussed in this section are of comparatively minor importance. It is important to recognise that India is grossly under-aided by whatever criteria one may wish to apply, and to break through the crust of pessimism, cynicism and disenchantment which has weakened effective co-operation on both sides.

ABBREVIATIONS

AID	Agency for International Development (US Govt)
4DO	*Fourth Plan Draft Outline*
IBRD	International Bank for Reconstruction and Development (World Bank)
IDA	International Development Association (soft loan part of IBRD)
IMF	International Monetary Fund
MFB	*Material and Financial Balances*
PL 480, 665	Public Law 480, 665 of the USA

26 Aid to India: II

BY development aid we properly mean the transfer of resources –
physical, financial, human or know-how – from rich to poor countries,
which involves an economic sacrifice by the donor, for the purpose
of the social and economic development of the recipient. The fact
that, correctly defined, aid must be given on concessionary terms
means that it excludes private investment and possibly should exclude World Bank loans. Donor countries normally like to include
these in what they call 'development assistance' and World Bank
loans are always included in multilateral aid.

Aid is a new phenomenon in international relations. The Indian
Consortium came into existence in 1958. Technical assistance is
somewhat older than capital aid. Truman's Point Four goes back to
1948 and the Colombo Plan to 1950. But financial aid to India is
only fourteen years old. It is important to remember this in order to
gain historical perspective. Unwarranted expectations aroused by
Marshall Aid to Europe, combined with impatience with the development process, have bred disappointments, which would appear un-
grounded if allowance were made for the very short time-span of
experience.

In addition to the temporal perspective, we need a quantitative
perspective. Aid to India, utilised over the three Plans 1951–1966
totalled $9,400 million, including $2,800 million in food and fibre.
Total net official receipts (i.e., net of repayment of principal but not
net of interest payments) ran in 1967–1968 at an annual rate of over
$1,000 million.

According to how one presents this figure, it can be made to look
large or small. It is certainly by far the largest single amount of aid
transferred to any one country. In the period 1964 to 1967, it
amounted to 18 per cent of the total net (of repayments) flow of
resources under the Development Assistance Committee's bilateral
programmes (i.e. excluding Soviet donors), and from multilateral
agencies. Next came Pakistan with 7 per cent. Aid contributed in the
Third Plan one-fifth to Indian investment. But these ratios neglect
the fact that India is both very large and very poor. India contains
one-sixth of humanity. Yet, according to the 1964–1965 figure,
official aid per head was only $2·5 per year, while smaller countries

like Israel were receiving $50, Jordan $37, and Liberia $31, per head. Pakistan received $4·2. The average aid per head, throughout all recipient countries, has been $4·1. Aid has contributed 2·3 per cent of India's gross national product. India suffers the penalty of her size. The smaller the country, the larger tends to be the aid per head which it receives. While the aid received by India can therefore be made to look large, if the wrong measuring rod is used, it was in fact quite small.

To the aid total, the United States contributed 40 per cent and Great Britain 10 per cent. The volume of aid has grown over the period of the three Plans: the first, $224 million; the second, $1,617 million; and the third, $5,000 million (excluding debt service). There is, however, little prospect of the same rate of growth, or even the same level, being maintained for the current Plan.

Types of aid

Aid has many dimensions and the total volume tells us very little, until we know its composition and quality. Four aspects of the quality of aid are important: the question of political strings; the division between project and non-project aid; the terms of the loans; and the amount of debt relief.

In the early days, donors, especially the United States, had doubts about the emphasis put by the Indians on the public sector and on basic industries. They also disliked acceptance of aid from the Soviet Union. These feelings found expression in the conditions on which aid was then given. By the time of the Third Plan these overtones had disappeared and aid had become relatively free from these types of political pressures.

No doubt, it is in the nature of the bilateral aid relationship that aid is given on certain conditions, although the alignment of interests does not normally run along lines separating countries but may run across national boundaries, so that interest groups in donor countries support policies desired by interest groups in recipient countries. The shift in emphasis from industries producing capital goods to those producing consumer goods, greater reliance on private enterprise for industrial expansion, and a policy favourable to foreign capital have been attributed partly to the influence of aid donors, especially the United States. The devaluation of 1966 was also the result of outside pressures towards reduced direct controls and a more liberal policy in respect of imports.

The difficulty in identifying donor pressure is that it may take very different forms. First, conditions might be crudely laid down, e.g. the liberalisation of imports, without which aid would not be forthcoming. Secondly, it might be that no explicit conditions are laid down but that, nevertheless, recipients are made aware that only if they commit themselves to certain policies, like import liberalisation, will they receive aid. Thirdly, donors might wish that recipients pursue certain policies (e.g. import liberalisation) which require additional foreign exchange whilst declaring themselves ready to provide the means to carry out the new policies. The evidence in the three cases would be similar, yet in each case the pressure would be of a very different nature.

The second aspect of aid to be considered is its division between project and non-project aid. Non-project aid, which is a particularly useful form of aid for the Indians, had risen from 20 per cent in the Second Plan to 84 per cent in 1967–1968.

TABLE 26.1

Share of Non-Project Assistance as
Percentage of Total Aid

	Percentage of total authorisations (Agreements signed)	Percentage of total (Utilisations)
During		
1st Plan	—	—
2nd Plan	22	27
3rd Plan	41	42
1966–1967	49	46
1967–1968	84	63

(The above table excludes United States agricultural commodity assistance and grants.)

The terms became softer. In 1965 the average interest rate was 2·98 per cent; the grace period 7·4 years; the terms to maturity 30 years; and the grant element in aid, calculated at a notional 8 per cent commercial interest rate, was 70 per cent and, calculated at 10 per cent, 75 per cent. In 1966 the average interest rate had fallen to 1·78 per cent; the grace period had lengthened to 9·6 years; the period of maturity had grown to 36·5 years, and the grant element had increased, at 8 per cent to 78 per cent and, at 10 per cent, to 88·6 per cent. Whilst the grant element calculations suffer from a number of defects, the trend of the terms of aid has been in the right direction, whatever measure we adopt.

Assurance of relief of debts is particularly important because, without it, the Indians have to accumulate scarce convertible foreign exchange to service them. In 1968–1969 $100 million was assured for the following two years for relief of debts.

The impact of aid

Is it possible to say how much has been achieved by foreign aid? It is now recognised that growth rates of gross national product are a very inadequate measure of development performance. The number of children educated, the number of lives saved, the reduction in illness – these do not show up in growth rates but are real contributions to human welfare. In these terms, there can be no doubt that India has achieved a good deal. The annual growth rate of national product for 1960–1965 was 3·1 per cent; in 1966 2·2 per cent; and in 1967 9·2 per cent. The corresponding growth of product per head was 0·6 per cent; 0·2 per cent; and 6·5 per cent.

During the Third Plan India used $4·83 billion of foreign aid, or 21 per cent of net investment, excluding the cost of servicing the debts she had accumulated. If one were to link the growth rate of national product with investment, one-fifth of the growth rate would be attributed to foreign aid. All this was done with relatively few disagreeable arguments between donors and recipient, and with more good will than one would have expected from such a sensitive relationship.

The contribution of foreign aid does not consist merely in a supplementation of domestic resources. If properly deployed, aid contributes to the elimination of bottlenecks. This means that its value to the recipient is a multiple of its nominal value, because it enables the Indians to make fuller use of their own, otherwise under-utilised, domestic resources. The particular bottlenecks, to whose obliteration aid may have contributed, are the availability of foreign exchange with which to purchase goods which could not be produced in India, or could be produced only at prohibitive costs; technical know-how; and particular types of skill.

A number of criticisms can be levelled against aid to India. Too much of it is bilateral; the pledging procedure is cumbersome; hard terms in the past have led to a heavy burden of debt servicing in the present and future; service payments on external official debts have increased from 9·8 per cent of export earnings from goods and services in 1963 to 15·2 per cent in 1964 to 16·3 per cent in 1966; the share of loans to grants has increased; far too much of the aid is still tied, while debt service payments have to be rendered in convertible currency; and there is an absence of forward commitments which increases uncertainty and reduces the value of aid to India. Tying loans, while demanding payments in untied form, and insisting on Indian planning while frustrating this planning by refusing to gear aid into the Plan, provide examples of inconsistency in the behaviour of donors and reflect a double standard, about which the Indians complain with justification.

The incidence of aid on the Indian economy is, unfortunately, largely unknown. We do not know whether aid improves or worsens the Indian terms of trade; we do not know what its effects are on domestic saving or on income distribution, or on the distribution of income between urban and rural populations; nor do we know its effects on the will to carry out desirable though painful domestic reforms.

Some research has been done on the impact of aid on agriculture. Only 10 per cent of the aid goes to a sector employing 70 per cent of the working population. Estimates have suggested that for every £1 worth of food aid, seven shillings worth of domestic food production is discouraged. We know hardly anything about how much gets absorbed by corrupt officials or the black market, or how much aid really benefits the foreign investor or the foreign exporter at the expense of the Indians.

In spite of these uncertainties and difficulties about aid, it is almost certain that there is far too little of it. For whatever the detrimental effects of aid on domestic efforts may be, it is certain that they amount to no more than a small fraction of the aid. By whatever criteria we judge the allocation of aid to India, she ought to get substantially more than she does – 30 per cent or 40 per cent instead of the present 15 per cent of total aid.[1] Whether the criterion is poverty; absorptive capacity; development potential; cold war borders; historical links and obligations; or constitutional democracy and shared values, India should top the list: in fact she is very low down.

Motives for aid giving

There has been a certain disenchantment with Indian development efforts. The reasons for this must be sought largely in the psychology or the psychopathology of donors, rather than in any failure on the part of India. The reasons stem from the origins of aid in the height of the 'cold war' when there were hopes that aid might be a weapon; they stem from the mistaken hope to win friends, votes and markets, which were bound to be disappointed. Aid had been oversold and overbought. The illusion was nurtured that aid would come to a speedy end when India achieved 'take-off'. False parallels drawn from Marshall Aid, combined with doctrines of imminent 'take-off', aroused false expectations. Having been disappointed and disillusioned, donors have adopted a hard line and blamed India. As hypocrisy is the tribute vice is said to pay to virtue, so the currently fashionable insistence on hard-headed national self-interest is the

[1] See P. Streeten and M. Lipton (eds.), *The Crisis of Indian Planning* (1968) p. 332; p. 428 in this volume.

tribute virtue pays to vice. Our actions have sometimes been better than our words, and governments, in this field, better than voters. I believe that, in spite of all its many faults, aid to India has been more disinterested than the professions of politicians occasionally suggest. Mr J. Freeman in his Rabindranath Tagore Memorial Lecture in 1968 said: 'We believe that we benefit from trying to bridge the gap between haves and have-nots, from investing in and later trading with newly independent countries, to our mutual advantage. This element is not dishonourable and should be acknowledged frankly.'

If we were to spend the money devoted to aid in such a way as to maximise the returns from sales promotion and peace promotion, we would spend different amounts and spend them very differently. Whether what Mr Freeman says is honourable or dishonourable, the question is: is it true? The facts are that there is no chance of reducing the gap between haves and have-nots for a long time; that there is no evidence that aid increases security, peace, political freedom or trade; and that more aid can make recipients more powerful enemies and trade rivals as well as more powerful friends and partners. If aid did contribute to any of these goals a geographical distribution guided by these goals would be different from what it is. It is a political error to hold out hopes which are likely to be disappointed, as the early, differently motivated hopes in aid were. The proper basis for an effective aid programme is that the needs of the poor are greater than ours, and that we can meet them. Like self-interest, moral motivation is not dishonourable.

India's performance

To return to India's domestic performance. India has been involved in two wars – with China in 1962 and with Pakistan in 1965 – with the consequential doubling of the proportion of expenditure devoted to defence. She has also suffered two exceptionally bad harvests – in 1965–1966 and 1966–67 – and the loss of two great leaders – Nehru in 1964 and Shastri in 1966. These misfortunes coincided with a period when the United States laid greater emphasis on 'performance', combined, as we have seen, with a very low amount of aid per head.

We have already shown how India suffers from being large. India is not just one country; it is a subcontinent. Hence large sums of aid amount to a very small share for each person. The way in which the United Nations is organised so that every country, however small, has a vote, and the administrative overheads of aid administration reinforce the so-called 'small country effect'. There are other disadvantages in size. Whether it is true or not that no news is good news, it certainly is true for large countries that good news is no news. The performance of regions in Madras, Punjab, or Gujarat has been as good as, and better than, that of many successful much smaller countries. While South Korea, Taiwan or Israel are often cited as success stories, the regional Indian successes are swamped in the morass of less successful regions. If we drowned the success of Venezuela in Latin America or that of Israel in the Middle East, development stories would be told very differently.

There are, furthermore, compromises with efficiency imposed by political federation. Rational central planning must, for the sake of political unity, compromise with the claims of the States. One way of looking at this is to say that there are other objectives besides high growth rates, which may compete with these. Political unity is one. But, less certainly, political unity may also, in the longer run, promote accelerated development, so that the sacrifice becomes one in the service of long-term growth.

Future prospects

What then are the prospects for the future? The 1969 Consortium in Paris saw the United States, for the first time in the history of the Consortium, unable to pledge itself firmly to any commitments. The lowest aid budget at $2·2 billion made it impossible for the United States officials to promise what Congress might not be able to deliver.

Great Britain pledged £35 million for 1968–1969 and £1 million mixed project loan counted towards the previous year's pledge, bringing the total up to £36 million. The components of this pledge were as follows:

	£ million
Debt refinancing	7·5
General purpose	10·0
Non-project (including Kipping aid)	7·0
Total non-project aid	24·5
Industrial Credit and Investment Corporation of India Ltd.	1·0
National Small Industries Corporation	0·5
Capital goods: public	3·0
private	5·0
Mixed project	2·0
Total project aid	11·5
Total pledge	36·0

The 1969–1970 pledge was raised to £38 million. The composition has not yet been decided but the project proportion will again be about one third, i.e. £12 million and of the non-project aid £7·5 million are earmarked for debt relief. The British terms of the loan are interest-free, repayable over twenty-five years with a grace period of seven years before repayment begins. India also receives £2·7 million under the Rome Food Convention.

The uncertainty arising from the lack of firm American commitment happens at a time when India is on the verge of a substantial recovery and a breakthrough in agriculture. The Consortium recommended for this year $700 million non-project aid, $100 million debt relief and $400 million project aid.

The Indian Government has now published the draft of a new Fourth Five-Year Plan for the period 1969–1970 to 1973–1974. Its motto is 'Self-reliant Growth with Stability'.

The Indians have, in the past, consistently underestimated the time within which dependence on foreign aid will cease. Once again, self-reliance is postulated for the end of the Fifth Plan in 1978–1979 when it is envisaged that aid will be eliminated. Over the Fourth Plan, net aid is to be reduced to about half in 1973–1974. It is understandable that the growing debt burden and the uncertainties and costs of aid should create a desire to have done with it. But while aid has its costs, it also bestows benefits and while it is accompanied by uncertainties, doing without aid also creates new uncertainties. It would have been more rational to map out different development strategies and development paths, based on different aid assumptions. This would have the incidental advantage of spelling out to donors what development their aid 'buys'. Nor is it clear whether self-reliance, as defined by the Plan, is a political objective in its own right, or whether it is dictated by the uncertainties and costs of expected aid or whether it conceals the political pressures of vested interests behind trade protection. In other words, we do not know whether 'self-reliance' is an objective, a constraint, a sop, or a realistic political assessment. It could, of course, simply be a gambit in the game of aid negotiations, based on the assumption that if you ask for little you are likely to get more.

The Draft Plan sets up a target of 4·5 to 5 per cent per year agricultural growth, 9 per cent industrial growth and 5·5 per cent growth of national income. A quarter of these, what many would regard as optimistic, additions to income, would have to be saved to hit the savings target. The Plan thus contains rather high projections in terms of income, combined with high requirements in terms of marginal savings. Much of this relies on an heroic strengthening of fiscal policy. From our point of view, it is interesting to note that these high expectations of growth, combined with the high investment ratios and greatly increased tax collections to maintain financial stability, are accompanied by reduced reliance on foreign aid. According to the Plan, net foreign aid requirements for the next five years would be about $2,300 million, or about 8 per cent of total planned investment.

While exports are expected to grow at 7 per cent per year, imports are assumed to grow only very modestly. There is a substantial reduction in the planned ratio of imports to industrial production. Trade is thus envisaged to replace aid. These policies are understandable in the light of past uncertainties, restrictions and limitations of aid. But the planned aid requirements seem much too low. The Indians may well be realistic in lowering so drastically their demand for aid, although the investment and growth targets, as well as the attainment of financial stability, seem very ambitious in the light of this. One can make out a strong case for a modest plan, with heavy emphasis on agriculture, where relatively high returns can be reaped from small outlays of foreign exchange and where expenditure gives rise to low demands on foreign exchange. There could be a second, enlarged plan, which could be activated if more aid became available: an optimistic contingency plan. The Indian Draft Fourth Plan seems, however, to combine highly optimistic expectations and ambitious investment targets with a small contribution from aid.

The need to raise the volume, ease the terms, and reduce the tying by procurement, project and commodity is undiminished either by the low Indian estimates or by the low aid utilisation in 1968–1969. Receipts of aid fell from over $1 billion in 1967–1968 to only about $600 million in 1968–1969. This drastic fall was the result of a recession and very slow revival of investment. The low level of aid is reflected in a low level of investment and development and the slowing down of development accounts for the low aid utilisation. If, therefore, one assumes acceleration of investment and economic growth, a substantially larger sum of aid than that put forward by the Indians could be used productively. A more realistic figure than the Indian $400 million net aid per year would be the restoration of the recently achieved $1 billion net per year.

The servicing of debts is estimated at $548 million in 1969–1970 and $560 million in 1970–1971. If new aid is given on very soft terms, debt service may rise to $610–650 million by 1973–1974, depending on the level of new aid. If new aid were to be stabilised at around $1 billion per year, gross aid disbursements would have to rise to an annual level of $1·6 billion within the next five years and this would have to be almost entirely non-food aid.

Aid in the form of food constituted about one-third of gross aid in recent years. On the assumption that production of foodgrains will grow, as planned, at 4·5 per cent per year, India's dependence on food imports will be first reduced and later eliminated. The decrease in aid in the form of food, which has been so readily absorbed while food was short, will present problems of adjustment in the balance of payments and in the transfer of the changed composition of aid. If the growth of non-food imports is to be absorbed, India has to generate a sufficiently large deficit in her balance of payments. This implies reducing protection and freeing imports. It may well be that political forces and vested interests would oppose this and make the transfer of the aid impossible. Equally, donors have to take certain actions to effect the transfer. A high proportion of non-project aid, an easing of terms and reduced tying would be important components of such a policy.

The danger of over-optimistic planning can be seen in the need for the imposition of controls of domestic finance to avoid foreign exchange crises. These take the form of restrictions on investment (which tend to have a higher import content than consumption) and on imports directly. These measures in turn reduce efficiency and prevent cost reductions and export growth. The vicious circle of controls, higher costs, reduced competitiveness, more controls, is thus perpetuated.

We may conclude that, in spite of many and serious obstacles to the transfer of a larger quantity of aid of a better quality than is envisaged in the Draft Fourth Plan, this is an essential condition for the ambitious targets of this plan. If the planners' pessimism or pride or submissiveness to pressure groups with regard to aid turns out to be justified, it is difficult to see how their optimism with regard to investment and growth can also be justified. It looks as if two disparate components of two contingency plans had been combined, to get the best of two incompatible worlds.

After a period of growing and improving aid from 1958 to 1965, and at a time when a new technology in agriculture looks promising, both donors and Indian planners seem to turn away from aid. This is a pity.

Perhaps it is permissible to end this brief survey on a personal note with a general lesson. Working on and thinking about aid to India has brought me together with Indians. Some of them have become my friends, amongst them my best friends. Many of us in Great Britain and elsewhere have identified ourselves with the cause of India (though not to the exclusion of, or in rivalry with, the causes of other countries, and in particular that of Pakistan). The identification has sometimes reached a point where we are critical of Indian actions in a way in which perhaps only Indians have a right to be critical. We may, of course, be wrong, both in what we justify and in what we criticise. The first duty of a scholar is to accurate analysis and correct reporting, without regard to tact, friendship or diplomacy. But it would be deficient to conclude an essay on aid without mentioning an important by-product of the aid relationship in the widest sense: at its best, it can create a sense of community which transcends national boundaries and which may hold out a hope for a better world community, with a stronger sense of world solidarity. In this way, a firmer foundation may be laid for the future of international co-operation. This casts a ray of hope on an otherwise gloomy picture.

TABLE 26.2

External Assistance

ᵃ By source

(Million dollars)

($1 = Rs. 7·50   Post-devaluation)

Source	*Authorisations up to end of March 1966*	*Utilisation up to end of March 1966*
United States Total of which	4,070	3,490
(a) Loans & Grants	1,935	1,680
(b) Commodity Assistance	2,135	1,810
International Bank for Reconstruction and Development (IBRD)	617	507
International Development Association (IDA)	372	269
Soviet Union	647	377
West Germany	599	463
Great Britain	488	391
Canada	254	210
Japan	231	150
Others	479	153
Total	7,757	6,010
Total excluding commodity assistance	5,622	4,200

ᵇ By utilisation

(classified by varieties of aid in million dollars)

($1 = Rs. 7·50)

Details of Assistance	*Utilisation up to end of First Plan*	*Utilisation during Second Plan*	*Balance available for utilisation as on March 31 1961*	*Aid authorisation for Third Plan*	*Aid utilisation during Third Plan*
A. Loans repayable in foreign currency	120	521	637	2,510	1,916
B. Loans repayable in Rupees	3	156	168	66	208
C. Grants	94	214	38	109	117
D. Total (A + B + C)	217	891	843	2,685	2,241
E. Assistance under US Public Laws	7	726	759	601	1,137
Total (D + E)	224	1,617	1,602	3,286	3,378

[1] I am indebted to Deepak Nayyar for help with the statistical annex.

TABLE 26.3
Consortium Aid to India for Third Plan
(Million dollars)

($1 = Rs. 7·50 post devaluation)

Service	Commitments				Authorisation in 1965–66	Utilisation in 1965–66
	1961–62 and 1962–63	1963–64	1964–65	1965–66		
Austria	3·2	4·5	0·6	3·2	3·2	2·9
Belgium	6·4	6·4	—	2·5	2·5	4·8
Canada	39·0	20·0	26·0	26·0	9·0	21·0
France	38·4	12·0	12·0	12·0	12·0	10·7
West Germany	231·0	63·0	60·5	53·5	53·5	61·2
Great Britain	168·0	53·4	53·4	53·4	44·0	57·0
Italy	33·6	38·5	22·8	22·8	22·8	3·2
Japan	66·6	40·0	38·2	38·2	38·2	40·5
Netherlands	6·7	6·7	6·7	6·7	6·7	8·7
United States	621·3	278·0	278·0	278·0	184·0	240·0
IBRD and IDA	286·0	154·7	154·7	154·7	149·0	143·0
Total	1500·2	667·2	652·9	651·0	524·9	593·0

TABLE 26.4

External Assistance, Authorisation and Utilisation

A Authorised
U Utilised
Composition Loans and Grants in $ million Pre-devaluation $1 = Rs. 4·75 * includes PL 480 and PL 665 imports

Sources	1949–56 Loans A	U	Grants A	U	1956–61 Loans A	U	Grants A	U	1961–66 Loans A	U	Grants A	U	Total 1949–66 Loans A	U	Grants A	U
United States*	221	203	217	104	746	339	2585	1366	1848	1751	1030	1932	2815	2293	3832	3402
Soviet Union	143				702	165	2	2	220	455	2	2	1065	720	2	2
Great Britain					271	269	2	2	533	374	2	4	804	643	4	4
Canada			71	44	35	35	126	132	69	26	121	112	104	61	318	288
West Germany					295	264	4	2	650	484		2	945	748	4	4
Japan					77	35			304	213			381	248		
Australia			24	11			4	16			4	4			32	31
New Zealand			4				4	7			2				10	7
Switzerland					16				40	13			56	13		
France									126	46			126	46		
Belgium									26	11			26	11		
Austria									20	11			20	11		
Czechoslovakia					51				88	29			139	29		
Yugoslavia					42				4	22			46	22		
Poland					31				60	24			91	24		
Norway			2	2			4	4			4	4			10	10
Italy									178	26			178	26		
Netherlands									49	22			49	22		
Denmark									4				4			
Sweden									4				4			
IBRD	126	75			574	489			318	271			1018	835		
IDA									614	442			614	442		
Ford Foundation			13	4			22	20			9	13			44	37
Total	490	278	331	165	2840	1596	2753	1551	5155	4220	1172	2069	8485	6194	4256	3785

TABLE 26.5

Inflow of Foreign Assistance – Gross and Net

(Million dollars)

Item	1961–62	1962–63	1963–64	1964–65	1965–66	Total Plan Period	
						Second Plan	Third Plan
1. Gross Aid Disbursement[a]	711	914	1235	1506	1621	3014	6049
2. Amortisation	121	101	113	145	177	115	656
3. Interest	70	81	96	110	139	135	496
4. Total Debt Service[b] (2 + 3)	191	182	209	255	316	251	1152
5. Net Aid Inflow (1 – 4)	520	732	1026	1251	1305	2765	4897

[a] Gross Aid includes loans repayable in foreign currency, loans repayable in Rupees, and P.L. 480 assistance.
[b] Debt Service Payments relate to those involving foreign exchange.

27 The Distribution of the Gains from Trade and Technical Progress

IT is now more than twenty years since Prebisch, Singer and Myrdal announced the thesis that the poverty of the poor countries is largely the result of bad and worsening terms of trade between their primary exports and their manufactured imports. The remedy recommended by these authors was liberation from dependence on primary exports through import-substituting industrialisation behind protective barriers. Whether it was the power of this idea that created the vested interests, or whether it was the vested interests of the budding industrialists that seized the idea as a convenient ideology, many countries have in fact adopted the recommended policies and now find it difficult to change course, in the direction of a strategy of encouraging agriculture and exports. The trade pessimism that underlay the import-substituting industrialisation policy has turned out to be a self-fulfilling prophecy: neglect of exports has led to poor export performance.

At the same time, the terms of trade pessimists exhorted the rich industrial nations to abandon protection and to grant in their markets free access to the primary exports of the poor countries. These recommendations were contradictory from the beginning. The pessimists complained that the poor countries were condemned to remain hewers of wood and drawers of water, and, in the same breath, asked that the rich should increase their demand for wood and water, thereby perpetuating the sorry state of the poor. If the pessimists thought that the long-term comparative advantage of the poor agricultural countries lay in industrialisation, they should have recommended agricultural protection in the rich industrial countries. This would have reduced the comparative advantage that the rich countries had in industry and would have helped to establish the superiority in manufacturing in the poor countries which had been the aim of policy.

It could be replied that, though this would have given the poor countries the *incentive* to industrialise, it would have deprived them of the *means* (whereas free access would have given them the *means* without the *incentive*). But the means could have been provided through aid, commercial loans or direct private foreign investment.

The Prebisch–Singer–Myrdal argument has been criticised both on theoretical and on empirical grounds. The disparity between the industrial centre, where productivity increases are reflected in higher money wages, and the agricultural periphery, where productivity growth lowers prices, was said to be one of the reasons for the tendency of the terms of trade to deteriorate. This kind of monetary mechanism requires a number of assumptions which were never clearly stated. If the demand and supply elasticities are such that the periphery suffers balance of payments deficits, the movement of the terms of trade will depend upon how these deficits are corrected or financed. If the trouble is simply the movement in relative prices, why can it not be remedied by more inflation or an appreciation of the exchange rate in the periphery? There may, of course, be asymmetrical responses. But if the demand curves or the supply curves are kinky, it is not the different mechanism by which productivity increases are passed on that accounts for the bad terms of trade. Nor is it clear, whatever the mechanism, why the periphery should suffer a worsening *trend* in the terms of trade; nor why the *commodity* terms of trade rather than the single or double *factoral* terms of trade are considered the appropriate index. Worsening terms of trade may, after all, give a country a competitive edge that enables it to reap larger gains from trade, whereas improving commodity terms of trade may simply be a symptom of rising costs and inefficiency.

The doctrine is vulnerable not only *a priori* but also *a posteriori*. There is no evidence of a secular deterioration of the terms of trade of primary products in relation to manufactured products, unless one chooses arbitrarily base years to prove the thesis. (For a brief discussion in the light of the evidence, see the Note at the end of this chapter.)

While many of these criticisms appear to be damaging to the doctrine, its core may well survive the onslaughts. The core of the doctrine is that in the world economy there are strong forces at work that make for a very uneven distribution of the gains from trade and economic progress generally, so that the lion's share goes to the lions, while the poor lambs are themselves swallowed up in the process.

Already in the late fifties, Kindleberger pointed out that, while it was not proven that the terms of trade of primary *products* deteriorated, it *was* then true that the terms of trade of underdeveloped *countries* tended to deteriorate, if the exceptionally good years 1950–

TABLE 27.1

Terms of Trade,[1] 1938, 1948, 1950–1969

(1950 = 100)

Year	Developed Countries	Developing Countries
1938	109	71
1948	103	85
1950	100	100
1951	96	105
1952	98	95
1953	102	94
1954	100	100
1955	100	98
1956	101	96
1957	100	93
1958	104	93
1959	105	94
1960	107	93
1961	108	89
1962	109	88
1963	109	89
1964	109	91
1965	109	89
1966	109	91
1967	110	90
1968	110	91
1969	111	93

[1] Terms of trade means unit value index of exports divided by unit value index of imports.

Sources: *United Nations Monthly Bulletin of Statistics, April issues.*

1951 are taken as the base. (See Table 27.1.) This led him to turn the doctrine upside down: it is not bad terms of trade that cause poverty, but poverty that causes bad terms of trade. It is their inflexibility and their lack of adaptability that prevent underdeveloped countries from seizing new trade opportunities, that condemn them to remaining stuck in dead ends. The sooner they drop the 'terms of trade hypochondria' (it was then argued) and get on with producing and marketing what the world wants, the sooner their terms of trade, and in any case and more relevantly, their gains from trade, will improve. Singer accepted the shift from commodity to country but emphasised, rightly, that the causal process can be both ways: poverty causing poor terms of trade, but poor terms of trade preventing the earnings that could lift the economy out of poverty.

Trade pessimism was given an additional knock by the successful export records of the developing countries in the sixties and the quite fantastic (by historical standards) rates of growth of exports of some of them. Exports of LDCs grew by 7 per cent annually in the sixties and in 1969 by 9 per cent. Some countries achieved 30 per cent and 40 per cent. It has been argued that the *share* of developing countries in world trade has shrunk (from 30 per cent in 1948 to 17·2 per cent in 1970) and that the exports of developed countries grew even faster. But this is surely beside the point. The mere fact that trade between industrialised countries grew even faster is irrelevant. More to the point is the argument that the import requirements of the developing countries, on average, have risen even faster than exports.

The search continued for the reason why the international system appeared to distribute the gains from trade and from foreign investment so unequally. There is one obvious reason for this. If there are cumulative processes – as there obviously are – *within* a country, so that certain growth poles enrich themselves at the expense of, or without spreading any benefits to, the regions left behind, powerful national economic policies will attempt to remedy the situation. Tax and subsidy policies, social services, regional policies and public works all contribute to compensating those who are losing out. But, internationally, there is no government to impose taxes, disburse subsidies, direct public works or provide social services for the victims of growth. This by itself goes a long way towards explaining the uneven international distribution of the gains from trade. But it is not the whole story.

Another line of argument was sketched out by Albert Hirschman:[1]

> . . . The opponents of free trade have often pointed out that for a variety of reasons it is imprudent and harmful for a country to become specialised along certain product lines in accordance with the dictates of comparative advantage. Whatever the merit of these critical arguments, they would certainly acquire overwhelming weight if the question arose whether a country should allow itself to become specialised not just along certain commodity lines, but along factor-of-production lines. Very few countries would ever consciously wish to specialise in unskilled labor, while foreigners with a comparative advantage in entrepreneurship, management, skilled labor, and capital took over these functions, replacing inferior 'local talent'. But this is precisely the direction in which events can move when international investment, proudly bringing in its bundle of factors, has unimpeded access to developing countries. . . .

[1] Albert O. Hirschman, 'How to Divest in Latin America and Why', *Essays in International Finance*, no. 76, Nov 1969.

And he goes on to quote the wittily perceptive formulation of Felipe Pazos: 'The main weakness of direct investment as a development agent is a consequence of the complete character of its contribution.'[1]

Something like this has been the result of some forms of foreign investment. The doctrine of the uneven distribution of the gains from trade and investment must therefore be reformulated in terms of the impact of modern technology and its carrier, the multinational corporation, not in terms of different commodity groups.[2] And the analysis must not be conducted in terms of countries, but of divergent interest groups within countries.

Modern technology is partly inadequately communicated to the poor countries and partly inappropriate to their factor endowments and their physical, social and cultural conditions. There is both a *Communications Gap* and a *Suitability Gap*. By Suitability Gap I mean that technologies that are capital saving, efficient, and physically and socially appropriate to underdeveloped countries often do not exist. They have to be invented. With a labour force growing three times as rapidly as that of advanced countries and with a ratio of savings per head of about one-twentieth, the appropriate amount of capital that would give jobs to all workers is one-sixtieth of what it is in advanced countries (and even this would provide equipment only for the *extra* hands offered annually, without removing unemployment of those already without work). Even the most ingenious adaptation is not always capable of bridging such a vast gap. But only a negligible proportion of the large volume of research and development expenditure is directed towards inventing more appropriate technologies.

By Communications Gap I mean the imperfections in communicating to potential users the technologies that already exist and might need only minor adaptations. Reducing the Communications Gap may conflict with reducing the Suitability Gap. Speedier and more effective communication may simply communicate the wrong technology – one that raises unemployment, underemployment, domestic inequality and capital requirements; and mobilising resources for an appropriate technology may be possible only by cutting off communications with the modern, sophisticated, capital-intensive, catering-for-the-rich type of process and product.

---

[1] Felipe Pazos, 'The Role of International Movements of Private Capital in Promoting Development' in John H. Adler, ed., *Capital Movements and Economic Development* (Macmillan, 1967), p. 196.

[2] This is done in a paper by Hans W. Singer, 'Distribution of Gains from Trade and Investment – Revisited', for a conference of the Institute of Development Studies.

The remedy then is seen to lie not in industrialisation *per se*. There is overwhelming evidence now that industrialisation is not a safe escape from poverty and dualism, but can follow along high-cost, inefficient lines that reinforce dualism, increase inequality, raise unemployment and worsen balance of payments crises, thereby aggravating the ills against which it was to be a remedy. More particularly, import-substituting industrialisation is no escape from deteriorating terms of trade. What is needed is the building up of an indigenous technical capability, combined with the human attitudes and social institutions and the national integration that can implement the benefits of such a capability. As long as these are absent, trade, private foreign investment and even capital aid and technical assistance may aggravate rather than soften international inequalities. Dependence results not from being hewers of wood and drawers of water: even those countries that produce manufactured products have remained dependent. Dependence derives from absence of an indigenous range of technological and organisational inputs: from not having the know-how and the management to respond to investment and trade opportunities. It is something like this that lies behind the idea of *technological dependence*.

UNCTAD, in its two conferences in 1964 and 1968 and in its committees and secretariat, has tended to emphasise the trade aspects rather than the features stressed here. Technology, the multinational corporation, the transfer of institutions and the brain drain appear, of course, on the agenda. But then almost everything does. To be effective, a few priority thrusts should be selected and scarce time and skills devoted to carrying these through. The very heavy emphasis on, indeed the obsession with, preferences for manufactured products and commodity agreements seems to be misplaced in the light of the preceding discussion. It reflects an intellectual lag from the forties.

Another fault of UNCTAD has been its uncritical acceptance of what might be regarded as a politically necessary evil: the nation state. Important interest groupings run across nation states and if UNCTAD had built upon interest alignment rather than appeals to national resolutions, these cross alignments could have been exploited in the cause of development. Here again, UNCTAD has accepted a nineteenth-century framework instead of using and building on the new institutions of the second half of the twentieth century. Consumers are not as well organised as producers and are therefore easy victims of the powerful protectionist claims of producers in rich countries. Appeals to governments are therefore not likely to succeed. But the retail chains that are independent of the large producers could be harnessed to side with the labour-intensive low-cost producers of the developing countries. The Atlantic and Pacific Stores in America have a commercial interest in lowering the cost of processed coffee and other food items; Sainsbury's and Waitrose's in Britain are interested in low-cost fruit and off-season vegetables. A department store interested in supplying low-cost clothes can contract out the making of these ('putting out' it was called in the eighteenth century) to small manufacturers or craftsmen in less developed countries. Marks and Spencer can do more for the poor of the world – the spinners, the weavers and the landless labourers – than Marx and Engels.

Problems of uneven distribution of gains arise from the transfer of not only technology but also institutions and standards. Thus the transfer of social services evolved in high income countries and, in particular, health services for the urban middle classes, of trade union legislation, of educational services especially higher education, has reinforced internal inequalities, raised unemployment and impeded national integration. By educating a small group beyond existing employment opportunities, education has contributed to the brain drain which deprives poor countries of its professional people and to the frustration of those who are not lucky enough to be drained. Here again, it is the impact of technology in a wider sense that has aggravated inequalities and distributed the gains from progress unevenly within and between countries.

The diagnosis is easier than the therapy. But the general direction in which a cure will have to be found emerges fairly clearly. There must be a shift from an emphasis on trade concessions, and in particular on preferences and commodity agreements, to the institutional conditions of productive science and technology, including public administration and private management. There must be a shift from emphasis on gaining concessions by rich nation states to using fully interest alignments cutting across national boundaries. In particular, there should be a much stronger emphasis on the common interest of developing countries. National self-interest will have to be sacrificed for greater solidarity if the developing countries wish to match the power and skills of the transnational corporations and to achieve a transfer of technology on acceptable terms. There are vast untapped sources of bargaining power in the concerted action of developing countries if they were willing to unite. The exhortation of the last sentence of the *Communist Manifesto* (slightly adapted)– still applies.

NOTE ON THE TERMS OF TRADE OF DEVELOPING
COUNTRIES[1]

Terms of Trade for Developing Countries

1. The major problems in estimating the terms of trade of developing countries include:

(*a*) Product innovation and quality improvements occur
mainly in industrial products. As a result, the benefits derived
from industrial products are understated and the rises in their
prices are overstated. What appears as a worsening of the
terms of trade reflects in many cases new and better industrial
products. This is, of course, a general problem and applies
also to measured rates of inflation in industrial countries.

(*b*) New industrial products subject to increasing returns
often have initially high prices and become cheaper as they
become more plentiful. To use the initial small quantities as
weights for the price reductions understates the fall in prices
in a price index of all manufactured products. (The use of
current period quantity weights would overstate the reductions.)

(c) Export price statistics for developing countries are often
based on commodity markets in London, New York, etc. Thus
lower freight costs and constant f.o.b. prices will apparently
give lower export prices by this method.

(d) The terms of trade for primary producers do not necessarily move identically with those for developing countries,
which may even be net importers, as a bloc, of some primary
products (e.g. wheat, butter, rice).

2. On any basis, it is clear that the terms of trade for most primary
producers, and most developing countries, were unusually
favourable in the early fifties; that they were worse before, and
have declined since. However, it is difficult to show any long-
term trend, e.g. late forties to the present. Also, the terms of
trade of developing countries did not deteriorate in the sixties
(except for the oil countries).

3. *Data from UN Monthly Bulletin of Statistics:*

Year	1953	54	55	56	57	58	59	60	61	
Series I						104	105	104	100	Base year: 1963
Series I		(excluding oil)				101	103	104	99	
Series II	103	109	108	104	100	100	99	99	97	Base year: 1958

[1] I am indebted to Michael Sharpston for help.

Year	1962	63	64	65	66	67	68	69	70	
Series I	98	100	101	99	101	100	102	103	102	Base year: 1963
Series I	96	100	103	102	105	103	104	108	109	
Series II	95	97	97							Base year: 1958

Series I: From July 1971 edition.
Series II: From 1965 and 1963 July editions.
(N.B. Separate series, different base year.)
Index = unit value index of exports over unit value index of imports.

For Series II, 1951 was 115, and a breakdown of Series II, for Latin America (excluding petroleum), gave 132 as the index for 1954 – because of the very high price of coffee.

4. *Data on (Santos 4 New York) coffee, and (Spot Accra New York) cocoa, deflated by the U.S. General Wholesale Price Index (1947–49) as base for U.S. price levels):*

Coffee	Deflated Price	
	28$/lb.	*37$/lb.*
1921–48	Above in only six years	Never a year above this
1949–70	Never a year below this	Above in eleven years

Cocoa	Deflated Price
	17$/lb.
1921–46	Above this in only three years
1947–70	Below this in only one year

5. *Primary agricultural product exports of developing countries, indices:*

	Tropical beverages	Non-food raw agricultural materials (1963 = 100)	Manufactured goods (Imports)
1960	105	105	98
1961	99	102	99
1962	96	97	99
1963	100	100	100
1964	121	102	101
1965	111	103	103
1966	113	104	106
1967	111	96	107
1968	111	96	106
1969	120	101	110

Source: FAO *Commodity Review and Outlook*, 1969–70, Table 3.

N.B. – With 1963 = 100, cereals (a major import of developing countries) rose from 1960 – 94 to 1967 – 106, then fell to 1969 – 102.

6. Rather than terms of trade *per se*, one could perhaps argue that developing countries are unfortunate in having slow-growing exports, though this does not settle the question whether slow growth is the result of supply or demand limitations or an interaction of the two.

(a) 1955–67, the value of world exports of agricultural products (excluding Eastern Bloc) grew at less than $4\frac{1}{2}$ per cent per annum, far less than overall growth of world trade.

(b) *Export growth (1955–67):*

	LDCs	DCs
	% p.a.	
Value agricultural exports	2·1	6·1
Value total exports	4·5	7·8
Per caput agricultural exports	–0·4	4·9
Per caput total exports	2·0	6·6

Source: FAO op. cit. – originally UNCTAD, Table 52.

A partial explanation of the differential growth rates of DC and LDC exports is that DCs specialise more in the growth of agricultural commodities (protein-rich food, animal food-stuffs). But to the extent that LDCs and DCs competed in the same agricultural product markets, LDCs often did less well: thus 1961–63 average to 1968, DC exports grew more/declined less for rice, fats and oils, oilcakes and meals, butter, beef and veal, wool, hides and skins. The reverse was true only for coarse grains, sugar, wheat, cotton (Table 1, FAO op. cit.). For rice, concessional sales by Japan affected market shares, but for fats and oils, and oilcakes and meals, shortfalls in supplies by LDCs were a major factor.

(c) Those LDCs whose agricultural exports grew fastest, 1955–67, were particularly likely to export products with fast-growing demand. On the other hand, these countries often included products with slow-growing demand among their major exports, and achieved well-above-average growth rates in exports of such commodities. Thus of 19 cases where countries with over $5\frac{1}{2}$ per cent annual growth of agricultural exports had major exports of commodities with world export growth of 0·3 per cent per annum or less, *they* achieved export growth rates above $4\frac{1}{2}$ per cent per annum in 9 cases, *for these commodities* (FAO op. cit., Chapter 3).

7. *Growth of exports 1953–65* (Index numbers of value in 1965, 1953 = 100):

	Primary products	Manufactures	Total exports
LDCs	165	283	174
World	168	291	220

Source: Little, Scitovsky, Scott, *Industry and Trade in Some Developing Countries*, Table 7:5.

I.e. LDC exports grew more slowly than those of DCs because of their higher primary product content, but also because of lower performance in each category.

8. *Access for LDC manufactures*

Despite discussion of preferences for LDC manufactures, DC protectionism seems to be growing:

Quotas extending from cotton textiles to all textiles.

New restrictions on flatware (certain cutlery) in US and UK.

UK now has tariffs *and* quotas on cotton textiles, not tariffs instead of quotas.

Index of Authors

Index of Subjects

References to tables and figures are given in brackets after the relevant page number(s), T indicating a table and F a figure.

Absorptive capacity, 194–5
  agricultural, 19
  limited, 188
  raised by aid, 195
Abundance, coexistence with poverty,
    3–11, 35, 335
Aden, British aid to, 274 (T 15.3), 276
Advertising, profitability of, 120
Africa, urban labour élite in, 163
Agency for International Develop-
    ment (AID), 262 n.
Aggregation
  in cost-benefit analysis, 373
  ideology of, 303–5
  isolation and, 58 (T 5.1)
  Keynesian, 70
  misplaced, 52, 55–7, 61, 73, 74–5,
    107, 146
Agricultural employees, skilled
  opportunities for, 18, 151
  pay scales, 151
Agriculture
  aid at expense of, 308
  aid unpopular with donors, 310
  balance of payments improved by,
    20
  betterment of, 149–52, 392–3
  breakthrough prerequisites, 17–18
  capital/output ratio in, 101
  diversification of, 405
  education in betterment of, 150–2
  Food and Agriculture Organisa-
    tion's technocratic approach to,
    168
  incentives for, 17–19
  investible surplus from, 19–20
  investment in, 19–20
  irrigation and land tenure, 118
  labour surplus unnecessary, 18
  manpower, in rich and poor
    countries, 133

Agriculture—(cont.)
  marketable surplus from, 19–20
  migration from, see Rural areas
  minimum wage standards in, 163
  reform of, 18–20, 152
  research in, 152, 398
  taxation of, 20
  technical aid for, 17
  tropical, 32, 392–3
  wages in, shadow, 362
  world board for surplus from, 256
Aid
  absorptive capacity as function of
    form of, 195
  balance of payments and, 240–1,
    243, 245, 264, 293, 310
  benefit to donor, 308–9
  bilateral, 261, 269 (T 15.2), 274
    (T 15.3), 275–6, 445
  special drawing rights and, 242–3
  breaking bottlenecks, 194, 430, 447
  British Labour Government and,
    258–79, 282–3
  British Labour Party and, 256–8,
    265, 267, 269, 275, 290–1
  budgetary, 299
  Cold War, 275, 283, 297, 307, 448
  complementary financing of multi-
    national corporations, 229, 231
  consultants on, 311
  co-ordination of, 205
  cost-benefit analysis and, 375–6
  cost of, to donor, 292–6, 307–8
  cost of, to recipient, 308–9
  crisis in, 301
  defence and, 298
  definition of, 444
  dependence on, reducing, 431–3
  debt servicing, 196–207
  development obstructed by, 10
  disbursement, 421